THE CHANGING ENVIRONMENT OF BUSINESS

Pennzoil Place, Houston, Texas; Johnson/Burgee Architects

Grover Starling

University of Houston at Clear Lake City

THE

CHANGING

ENVIRONMENT

OF BUSINESS

A Managerial Approach

Kent Publishing Company
Boston, Massachusetts

A Division of Wadsworth, Inc.

To my mother and dad

The Changing Environment of Business was prepared for publication by the following people at **Duxbury Press:**

Sponsoring Editor: **Patrick J. Fitzgerald**

Special Projects Editor: **Sylvia Dovner**

Copy Editor: **Kathleen J. Leahy**

Art Editor: **Joanna Prudden Snyder**

Line Art: **Phil Carver & Friends, Inc.**

Interior Design: **Duxbury Press staff**

Cover Designer: **Margaret Tsao**

Composition: **Publishers' Design**

Library of Congress Cataloging in Publication Data

Starling, Grover.
    The changing environment of business.

    Bibliography: p.
    Includes index.
    1. Industry—Social aspects.   2. Management.
I. Title.
HD60.S68   658.4   79–26814
ISBN 0–87872–251–3

Kent Publishing Company
A Division of Wadsworth, Inc.

Printed in the United States of America
2 3 4 5 6 7 8 9 — 84 83 82 81

Contents

Chapter Eight   Implementation   315

PART IV   Social Impact Management in Major Functional Areas   363

Chapter Nine   Production and Operations Decisions   365

Chapter Ten   Financial Decisions   409

Chapter Eleven   Marketing Decisions   438

Chapter Twelve   Human Resources Decisions   473

Preface

T his book builds on a single premise: Tomorrow's managers will have less time to adapt to changes in their environment and will have to pay greater penalties for their mistakes. It attempts to convey to students, whether undergraduates or graduates, my picture of the new expertise they will need to react quickly and effectively to change.

While the study of business and society relations has not become a science, it is no longer a mere clothesline of issues and opinions. In the past few years, it has acquired, along with many new facts, a set of organizing principles that have made business-society relations much easier to comprehend. At the same time, these principles should help managers alert their organizations to the opportunities and threats that impending changes carry. Thus, in a larger sense, the proper study of business and society offers a more powerful way of analyzing many important problems in business administration.

Every field of study—biochemistry, marketing, or whatever—at some time in its development undergoes a transition: Suddenly, what was once a collection of widely scattered facts and hypotheses crystallizes into a logical pattern, unified by a few basic concepts. I, along with many of my colleagues,* believe that the study of business-society relations has been undergoing such a transition, stimulated by new research findings in academia, insights from various observers of business, and especially practices within the corporate world itself. What are these new findings, insights, and practices? To name but a few: the recognition that what we call "society" is really a system that is composed of various interrelated components (the economy, technology, households, culture, government, and so forth); that change in each component tends to follow a general pattern; that today's turbulent environment increases the need for strategic planning; that virtually every major management decision has an ethical dimension; that techniques for managing the social impacts of a company do exist; and that Americans today are confronted by an awesome array of choices whose resolution will compel many fundamental changes in the institutional environment during the next decade or two. Among these choices, I would include big versus little government, big versus small business, control versus deregulation, capital-intensive technology versus appropriate technology, and continued growth versus no-growth. Not surprisingly, this "new knowledge" about the larger environment of business is transforming all of management.

Some authorities argue that the subject matter of business and society can best be taught together with traditional business courses such as marketing, organizational theory, and business policy. I cannot agree with them for a couple of reasons. First, if the subject is broken up and then distributed among other courses, the logical pattern, unified by a few basic concepts that I have tried to present here, will inevitably be lost. In short, the student will develop neither a clear, coherent mental "map" of what the environment of business is nor a general method for coping with change within it. My other reason for not agreeing with those who advocate integrating business-society concerns into existing courses is a simple and practical one—namely, these concerns would probably not get taught. The point is not that there is anything wrong with course integration in theory but rather that it is doomed to failure in practice.

This book is concerned primarily with business-society relations at the company level; it tries to maintain a balance between the concerns of big business and those of medium- and small-sized firms. Although the book is not without details, my aim has been to emphasize central concepts rather than to offer an encyclopedic treatment of all the issues. These central concepts pro-

---

* See, for example, Roger A. Buchholz's *Business Environment/Public Policy: A Study of Teaching and Research in Schools of Business and Management* (Washington, D.C.: American Assembly of Collegiate Schools of Business, 1979).

vide the basis for Parts II, III, and IV of the book: the macroenvironment of business, strategic planning and forecasting, and the management of social impacts. Each of the chapters in the three major parts is subdivided into a logical progression of topics, and each of the chapters, I believe, can be handled in one week during a regular semester course. A fourth central concept—what the future is likely to hold—is contained in the Epilogue. Finally, I have provided a few short-and-to-the-point exercises and case studies at the end of the book so that the student can apply the central concepts of the book to some realistic business situations. I have also written an accompanying instructor's manual and case notes for *The Changing Environment of Business* that is available on request to instructors from the publisher.

I now know what I had previously only guessed: It is very hard to write a comprehensive book on the environment of business. Nevertheless, I have been confirmed in my initial view that while difficult, it is not foolhardy, and I hope that those who use this book will agree. Certainly a one-person attempt is bound to contain certain faults, but without someone's taking big risks in areas in which he or she cannot pretend expertise, there can be no truly unifying vision of the subject. Fortunately, my publishers have made it possible for me to enlist the criticism and advice of a number of experts in the areas covered by the book. To the following reviewers, I give my most sincere thanks: James E. Post, Boston University; Dennis Callaghan, University of Rhode Island; David Vogel, University of California, Berkeley; Walter H. Klein, Boston College; Steven Holmberg, American University; and John Logan, University of South Carolina.

My thanks go to many corporations that were helpful in a variety of ways. Among these are General Electric, Coca-Cola, Xerox, PET, Boston Gas, Monsanto, Firestone, S.G. Johnson and Son, Uniroyal, Motorists Insurance, Kaiser Aluminum & Chemical, Gulf Oil, Lockheed, Bendix, AT&T, Volvo, Teledyne, and Union Carbide. I especially want to express my appreciation to Patrick D. Maines and National Distillers and Chemical Corporation who have been most generous in the support they have given this project. Without this support, it is unlikely that the book would ever have been written. I also want to express thanks to my students at the University of Houston at Clear Lake City and to Kenneth D. Carpenter and the group at U.S. Industrial Chemicals Co. These people bore a particularly heavy burden in hearing and discussing partially thought-out ideas and hypotheses. Unfortunately, I cannot even begin to mention by name all of the local executives who, by visiting my classes, have helped in the writing of this book.

I am also grateful to the officers and staff of Duxbury Press for their genuine interest in this project and their desire to produce an educationally useful book. Patrick J. Fitzgerald and Sylvia Dovner deserve particular thanks. Finally, to Lilia Carrera, I am indebted for invaluable help with typing and proofreading.

In conclusion, let me note that it is perhaps inevitable that some errors of fact, interpretation, or emphasis will be found in this book. The blame for these, of course, is entirely mine. I shall greatly appreciate receiving from students and instructors their comments, criticisms, notices of errors, and advice about improvements that can be made in later printings and editions. I hope that you will keep this in mind as you read and that you will write to me with your suggestions.

Grover Starling
School of Business and Public Administration
University of Houston at Clear Lake City
Houston, Texas 77058

Acknowledgments

The author gratefully acknowledges permission to reprint copyrighted textual material:

From Eli Ginzberg, "The Pluralistic Economy of the U.S.," *Scientific American* 235, no. 6 (December 1976):29. Reprinted with permission.

Reprinted by permission of the Harvard Business Review. Excerpt from "Myth of the Well-educated Manager" by J. Sterling Livingston (January –February 1971). Copyright © 1970 by the President and Fellows of Harvard College; all rights reserved.

Reprinted by permission of the Harvard Business Review. Excerpt from "Opportunity and Threat in Technological Change" by James R. Bright (November–December 1963). Copyright © 1963 by the President and Fellows of Harvard College; all rights reserved.

From Gene Bylinsky, "Industry's New Frontier in Space," *Fortune,* January 29, 1979, p. 77ff. Reprinted with permission.

From Mel Mandell, "A Natural Electronic Marriage of Information Tools," *New York Times,* July 9, 1978. © 1978 by The New York Times Company. Reprinted by permission.

From Herbert Stein, "Humphrey-Hawkins and the Nature of Unemployment," *The AEI Economist* (March 1978). Reprinted by permission of the American Enterprise Institute.

From Alfred L. Malabre, Jr., "More and More People Seek and Find Jobs," *Wall Street Journal,* January 18, 1978. Reprinted with permission.

From James Baughman, George Lodge, and Howard Pifer, *Instructor's Manual to Accompany Environmental Analysis for Management* (Homewood, Ill.: Richard D. Irwin, 1974), pp. 13–14. © 1974 by Richard D. Irwin, Inc. Reprinted with permission.

From Paul Craig Roberts, "The Breakdown of the Keynesian Model." Reprinted with permission of the author from *The Public Interest,* No. 52 (Summer 1978), pp. 21–22. © 1978 by National Affairs, Inc.

From Theodore Levitt, "Corporate Responsibility: Taking Care of Business," *The American Spectator* (November 1977):21. Reprinted with permission of the publisher and the author.

Reprinted by permission of the Harvard Business Review. Excerpt from "The Real Costs of Regulation" by Robert A. Leone (November–December 1977). Copyright © 1977 by the President and Fellows of Harvard College; all rights reserved.

From Ralph Nader, "A Citizen's Guide to the American Economy," *New York Review of Books,* September 2, 1971, p. 14. Reprinted with permission from *The New York Review of Books.* Copyright © 1971 Nyrev, Inc.

Excerpts from *The Kennedy Promise* by Henry Fairlie. Copyright © 1972, 1973 by Henry Fairlie. Reprinted by permission of Doubleday & Company, Inc.

From Yale Brozen, "Antitrust Witch Hunt," *National Review,* November 24, 1978, pp. 1470, 1476. Reprinted with permission.

From Editorial, *Wall Street Journal,* January 10, 1973. Reprinted by permission of *The Wall Street Journal,* © Dow Jones & Company, Inc. 1973. All rights reserved.

From Paul H. Weaver, "Regulation, Social Policy, and Class Conflict." Reprinted with permission of the author from *The Public Interest,* No. 50 (Winter 1958), p. 55. © 1978 by National Affairs, Inc.

Reprinted by permission of the Harvard Business Review. Excerpt from "Technology Transfer by Multinational Companies" by James Brian Quinn (November–December 1969). Copyright © 1969 by the President and Fellows of Harvard College; all rights reserved.

From P.T. Bauer and B.S. Yamey, "Against the New Economic Order." Reprinted from *Commentary,* April 1977, by permission; all rights reserved.

From Charles McCarry, *Citizen Nader* (New York: Saturday Review Press, 1972), pp. 75, 108. Reprinted by permission of the publisher, E.P. Dutton.

From Irving Kristol, "Corporate Capitalism in America." Reprinted with permission of the author from *The Public Interest,* No. 41 (Fall 1975), pp. 124–41. © 1975 by National Affairs, Inc.

From Theodore Levitt, "Marketing and Corporate Purpose," in John A. Czepiel and Jules Backman, eds., *Changing Marketing Strategies in a New Economy* (Bobbs-Merrill, 1977), pp. 29–30. Reprinted with permission.

Excerpt totalling approximately 83 words from *A World Split Apart* by Aleksandr I. Solzhenitsyn. Copyright © 1978 by Aleksandr I. Solzhenitsyn. English translation copyright © 1979 by Harper & Row, Publishers, Inc. Reprinted by permission of the publisher.

From Robert A. Newman, "Internal Decision Making," in *Selected Proceedings Workshops on Implementing Social Responsibility* (Washington, D.C.: Public Affairs Council, June 12–13, 1974). Reprinted with permission.

From William Bennet, "When Values Are Substituted for Truth," *The Wall Street Journal,* July 25, 1978. Reprinted with permission of the author.

From Michael Maccoby, "The Corporate Climber," *Fortune,* December 1976, p. 108. Reprinted with permission.

Reprinted by permission of the Harvard Business Review. Excerpt from "The Corporation and Its Obligations" by C. Peter McColough (May–June 1975). Copyright © 1969 by the President and Fellows of Harvard College; all rights reserved.

From "A Price Monitor Keeps the Dough Rising." Reprinted from the December 7, 1974 issue of *Business Week* by special permission, © 1974 by McGraw-Hill, Inc., New York, NY 10020. All rights reserved.

From Thomas Griffith, "Weyerhauser Gets Set for the 21st Century," *Fortune,* April 1977, p. 75ff. Reprinted with permission.

Reprinted by permission from Russell L. Ackoff, "Management Misinformation Systems," *Management Science,* Vol. 14, no. 4, December 1967. Copyright 1967 The Institute of Management Sciences.

Reprinted by permission of the Harvard Business Review. Excerpt from "Technology Transfers" by James Brian Quinn (March–April 1967). Copyright © 1967 by the President and Fellows of Harvard College; all rights reserved.

Rene Zentner, "The Shell Oil Company—Planning with Multiple Scenarios," *World Future Society Bulletin* (September–October 1976). Reprinted with permission of the World Future Society, 4916 St. Elmo Avenue, Washington, D.C. 20014.

Reprinted with permission from Karl E. Henion, *Ecological Marketing,* pp. 127, 152, 154–55. Grid Publishing, Inc. (Columbus, Ohio, 1976).

From David Novick, "Cost-Benefit Analysis and Social Responsibility," *Business Horizons,* February 1973. Copyright, 1973, by the Foundation for the School of Business at Indiana University. Reprinted by permission.

From Ramon J. Aldag and Donald W. Jackson, Jr., "A Managerial Framework for Social Decision Making," pp. 33–40, *MSU Business Topics,* Spring 1975. Reprinted by permission of the publisher, Division of Research, Graduate School of Business Administration, Michigan State University.

From Terry McAdam, "How to Put Corporate Responsibility into Practice." Reprinted by permission from the *Business & Society Review,* Summer 1973, Number 6, Warren, Gorham and Lamont Inc., 210 South Street, Boston, Mass. All rights reserved. Copyright © 1979.

Reprinted by permission of the Harvard Business Review. Excerpt from "How Companies Respond to Social Demands" by Robert W. Ackerman (July–August 1973). Copyright © 1973 by the President and Fellows of Harvard College; all rights reserved.

From Robert Green and Michael Mazis, "Implementing Social Responsibility," pp. 68–76, *MSU Business Topics,* Winter 1971. Reprinted by permission of the publisher, Division of Research, Graduate School of Business Administration, Michigan State University.

Reprinted by permission of the Harvard Business Review. Excerpt from "Can the Best Corporations Be Made Moral?" by Kenneth R. Andrews (May–June 1973). Copyright © 1973 by the President and Fellows of Harvard College; all rights reserved.

Excerpt from pp. 32–39 in *The Political Economy of the New Left* by Assar Lindbeck. Copyright © 1971 by Assar Lindbeck. Reprinted by permission of Harper & Row, Publishers, Inc.

From Amitai Etzioni, "Why We Chose to Have Stagflation." Reprinted from the February 27, 1978 issue of *BusinessWeek* by special permission, © 1978 by McGraw-Hill, Inc., New York, NY 10020. All rights reserved.

From *Anarchy, State and Utopia* by Robert Nozick, © 1974 by Basic Books, Inc., Publishers, New York. Reprinted with permission.

From Charles Wolf, Jr., "A Theory of Non-Market Failures." Reprinted with permission of the author from *The Public Interest,* No. 55 (Spring 1979), pp. 123, 129. © 1979 by National Affairs, Inc.

From Wassily Leontief, "The Trouble with Cuban Socialism," *New York Review of Books,* January 7, 1971, p. 19ff. Reprinted with permission from *The New York Review of Books.* Copyright © 1971 Nyrev, Inc.

From Deborah Baldwin, "Motherhood and the Liberated Woman," *Washington Monthly,* July–August 1978, pp. 50–56. Reprinted with permission from *The Washington Monthly.* Copyright 1978 by The Washington Monthly Co., 1611 Connecticut Ave., N.W., Washington, D.C. 20009.

Excerpts from Richard Sennett, "The Boss's New Clothes." *New York Review of Books,* February 22, 1979, p. 45. Reprinted with permission from *The New York Review of Books.* Copyright © 1979 Nyrev, Inc. Reprinted by permission of the Harvard Business Review. As abridged from "The Dynamics of Subordinacy" by Abraham Zaleznik (May–June 1965). Copyright © 1965 by the President and Fellows of Harvard College; all rights reserved.

From *Con Edison Annual Report,* 1978, pp. 2–3 and 5–7. Reprinted with permission.

From the Trend Analysis Program of the American Council of Life Insurance, Washington, D.C. Reprinted with permission.

Reprinted by permission of the Harvard Business Review. Excerpt from "Doing Away with Factory Blues" by Donald N. Scobel (November–December 1975). Copyright © 1975 by the President and Fellows of Harvard College; all rights reserved.

From Isaac Asimov, "Dreaming Is a Private Thing." © 1955 by Fantasy House. Reprinted with permission of the author.

INTRODUCTION

PART I

CHAPTER ONE

Perspectives on Business
and Society

"It is not the lofty sails but the unseen wind that moves the ship," W. MacNeile Dixon wrote. No observation better explains what is happening in the world of business. Management textbooks and training programs focus on the "sails" of management—that is, marketing, control, finance, and the rest. Important as these functions are, they are not the "unseen wind" that really moves business enterprises in fresh directions. If management today seems to be a multidimensional tightrope act, it is because virtually all of a manager's time is spent tending the sails and too little is devoted to considering shifts in the wind.

Our argument then is this: Turbulent change and increased complexity in the external environment of business have compounded enormously the manager's task. In fact, Peter Drucker argues that managing the impacts of a business on society in an ethical manner has become one of the three primary tasks of management. The other two are insuring economic performance and making work productive.

Drucker hardly overstates the importance of society to business. At all levels of an organization, managers face increased challenges from the external environment. Often these challenges come from technological change; sometimes they arise from economic uncertainty; and at other times, from subtle shifts in the people's values or (much less subtly) from citizen action groups. At still other times, challenges are posed by new government regulations and, with increasing frequency in virtually all sectors of the economy, by foreign competition. As if all these challenges were not enough, managers must still deal with the traditional tasks of economic performance and the problem of making work productive.

So, to repeat, management has become a multidimensional tightrope act. While this book provides no guaranteed safety nets, it does attempt to provide a systematic framework for understanding change in the external environment and for developing responses to the challenges these changes present to managers. Therefore, we shall take this introductory chapter to develop some perspective on how business and society interrelate. Specifically, we shall consider the relationship from three perspectives: conceptual, historical, and managerial.

If a book is well engineered, if its pistons are well oiled, if it runs fast and smooth on rubber tires, then it needs to provide a no-nonsense *conceptual* framework fairly early. Thus, the first section of the chapter provides a few clear-cut definitions and concepts to help us sort through the welter of events, facts, and opinions that constitute our subject.

Next, in order to better appreciate the nature of the challenges facing the American business system today, we need some rudimentary grasp of the *historical* interrelations of business and society. Indeed, it is precisely this lack of historical perspective that keeps today's senior corporate executives from appreciating the current hostility to the larger corporation. Most of these executives reached maturity during the postwar period through the 1960s. As it happens, this period was, with the possible exception of the 1920s, just about the only period in American history when public opinion was, on the whole, well disposed to the larger corporation. Irving Kristol (1975:126) explains: "After 15 years of depression and war, the American people wanted houses, consumer goods, and relative security of employment—all the things that the modern corporation is so good at supplying. The typical corporate executive of today, in his 50s or 60s, was led to think that such popular acceptance was "normal," and is therefore inclined to believe that there are novel and specific forces behind the upsurge of anti-corporate sentiment in the past decade."

In addition to helping us understand "today," a good historical perspective can help us make intelligent assessments about the future evolution of business-society relations. For these two important reasons, the second section of this chapter attempts to highlight some of the more important stages in the evolution of business in Western society.

While these two perspectives are useful in gaining a better understanding of business-society interrelations, it is the third perspective that is most important to our purposes. In the third section, we look at these relationships from the explicit viewpoint of the manager. This essentially *managerial* perspective is meant to serve as an introduction to the detailed discussions that lie ahead. ☐

THE CONCEPTUAL PERSPECTIVE: SOME BASIC DEFINITIONS

Forms of American Business Enterprise

Business enterprises customarily take one of three forms: individual proprietorships, partnerships, or corporations. In a *proprietorship,* a single person holds the entire firm as his or her personal property; in most instances, it is an enterprise that he or she manages on a day-to-day basis. Of the almost thirteen million business establishments conducted in the United States in 1972, more than ten million were proprietorships.

A *partnership* may have from two to fifty or more members, as in the case of large law firms, brokerage houses, accounting firms, and advertising agencies. The partners themselves own this form of business, although they may receive varying shares of the profits, depending on their investment or contribution.

In terms of its size, influence, and visibility, the *corporation* has become the dominant business form in the Western industrialized nations. While corporations may be large or small—ranging from enterprises having hundreds of thousands of employees to the neighborhood business of very modest proportions—public attention has increasingly focused on the several hundred giant companies that play a preponderant economic role in the United States, Canada, Japan, and Western Europe.* This focused attention is not without basis. Though accounting for only 14 percent of the total number of enterprises in the United States, corporations are responsible for nearly 86 percent of annual sales (see Exhibit 1–1). Even more significant, however, is the economic role of the five hundred largest industrial corporations, which comprise about two-thirds of all manufacturing companies. For example, Standard Oil of New Jersey's sales exceed the taxes collected by New York, Georgia, Indiana, Massachusetts, Minnesota, New Jersey, and Texas taken together. Another corpo-

---

* No account will be taken in this book of the so-called public corporations that have risen in recent decades in these nations. Such government bodies, in the United States, include the Tennessee Valley Authority and the Port of New York Authority.

**EXHIBIT 1–1   Who Does Business in the United States:
The Role of the Corporation**

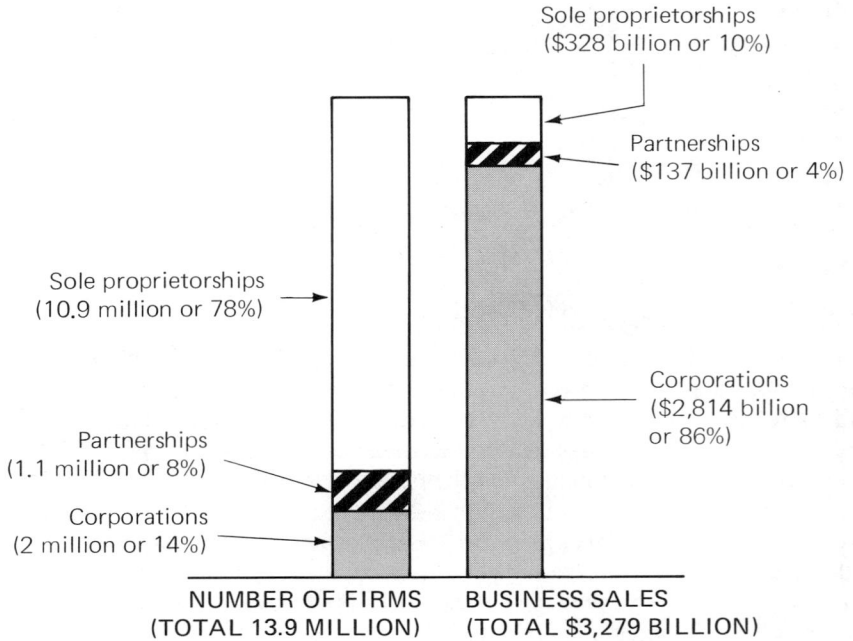

Sole proprietorships
($328 billion or 10%)

Partnerships
($137 billion or 4%)

Sole proprietorships
(10.9 million or 78%)

Corporations
($2,814 billion
or 86%)

Partnerships
(1.1 million or 8%)

Corporations
(2 million or 14%)

NUMBER OF FIRMS   BUSINESS SALES
(TOTAL 13.9 MILLION)   (TOTAL $3,279 BILLION)

Source: Data from U.S. Internal Revenue Service, 1977.

ration, American Telephone & Telegraph, has nearly as many employees as the state governments of California, Illinois, Michigan, Ohio, Pennsylvania, and Florida combined.

Given this magnitude, it is hardly surprising that corporate organizational arrangements tend to be more complex than those of the proprietorship and partnership. The pivotal group within the corporation are the managers. They steer the firm, assess its prospects, study alternatives, and decide what to do. The top ranks can take many forms, with considerable power being held by the president (the chief executive officer), chairman of the board, or some top management team.

We should not overestimate the influence of this top echelon of corporate management. As Galbraith (1977) points out, chief executive officers tend to be little known outside the company. Were they the vital factor in the enterprise, their heart conditions would be a source of the gravest concern; the

Dow-Jones wire tape would carry their electrocardiograms and latest lung X rays. So, to a larger and perhaps increasing extent, power is shared by top management with staffs of executive vice presidents, financial and marketing vice presidents, assistant vice presidents, controllers, and the head of the Washington office. It is also shared, by necessity, with those whose specialized knowledge contributes to decisions in the many operation divisions: engineers, scientists, sales managers, advertising specialists, dealer relations staff, designers, lawyers, accountants, economists, computer scientists, and the like.

In order to buy the capital equipment necessary for new or expanded operations, corporations have traditionally gone to the investing public for funds. The result has been that the legal ownership of corporations has become widely dispersed. At the beginning of 1971, for example, General Electric and International Business Machines (IBM) each had over 500,000 shareholders. General Motors had nearly 1,500,000, and the American Telephone & Telegraph Company's list exceeded 3,000,000. While large blocks of shares may be held by wealthy individuals or institutions, the total amount of stock in these companies is so large that even a very wealthy person is not likely to own more than a small fraction of it. The chief effect of this dispersion has been to give effective control of the companies to their salaried managers.

At the annual meetings, shareholders elect directors who, in turn, select and supervise the president and other officers of the corporation who will make up its top management. Such is the theory. In practice, directors are usually rather passive to management; they require good management in general rather than directing in detail. Only when the company gets into serious trouble do they intervene—often too late. Often more influential, though less visible, are the banking relationships of the corporation: Since senior banking officials decide the terms of loans, they often can shape top management in detail.

Business as a System

Thus far, we have been describing the *forms* business enterprises can take. Now we need to begin to think of these millions of entities as components in a *system*. Exhibit 1–2 attempts to provide a bird's-eye view of this system. The great virtue of this exhibit is that it helps us avoid falling into the trap of thinking of American business as being too homogeneous.

For example, one popular and long-running line of thought is that the giant corporations are gobbling up small- and medium-sized business. But this theory is refuted by Drucker (1974:648–49):

> Small business and big business are not alternatives. They are complements. The big business depends on small- and medium-sized businesses, who in turn depend on big business .... Typically, there is ... a big manufacturer, say, an automobile company such as General Motors, Volkswagen, or Toyota. But this company depends on a host of suppliers and subcontractors who are mostly

EXHIBIT 1–2   The American Business System: An Overview

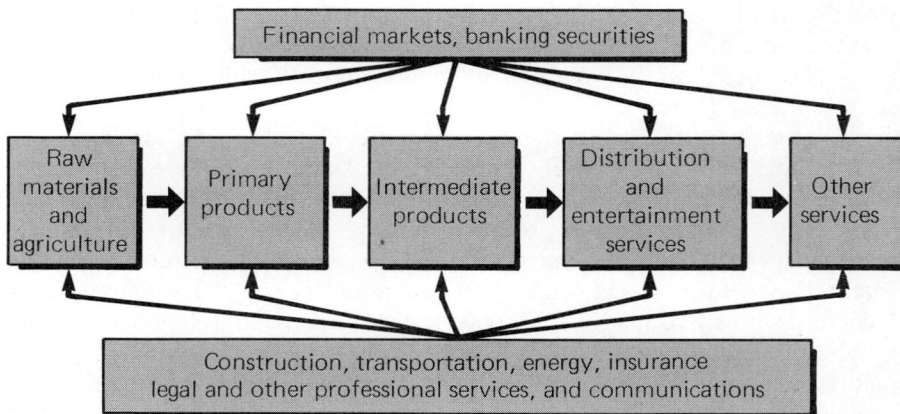

small- or fair-sized . . . . The large retailers such as Sears, Roebuck, Marks & Spencer, and the department store chains in Japan, depend on a host of small manufacturers, who in turn depend on the big stores for access to the market. There is no economic chain in a modern economy that is composed entirely of big businesses, but also no economic chain that is composed entirely of small businesses. Businesses of different sizes are interdependent.

Business as a Component of the Social System.   Thus far, we have been speaking rather loosely about business-society interrelations. The time has come, however, to make those interrelations more explicit and to give them a solid theoretical basis. The first step is to be clear on what *society* means.

Certainly, one way to clarify the term is to ask ourselves what functions must every society—American and Japanese, Peruvian and Polish, ancient and modern—perform in order to survive. Perhaps no one has struggled with that question more persistently and successfully than Talcott H. Parsons (1951), the American sociologist. Parsons sees four basic functions for society. First, in order to survive, a society must *adapt* itself to changing conditions in natural environment. The adaptive part of society is the economy, which is reinforced by the technology. Second, a society must *maintain* its own basic patterns so that the next day or the next year finds the social system still recognizable and in charge of its own actions. The main part of society responsible for this function in the United States is families and households. Not only do these units provide individual members of society food and shelter, they also provide mutual support and transmit the culture of society. Third, society must *integrate* its different tasks and functions. The integrative part consists mainly in culture, which includes education, religion, mass communications, philosophy, and art. And, fourth, society must move beyond mere maintenance, adaption, and integration to the *attainment* of goals. The goal-attaining part of society is, of course, the government and politics. In recent years the government has, with varying degrees of success, organized American society for a variety of goals: resolving race relations, combating unemployment, making higher education more widely available, conserving energy, and even exploring Mars.

For greater clarity, let us drop the terms "maintenance," "adaption," "integration," and "goal attainment" and use instead more concrete ideas: for adaption, *technology and the economy;* for maintenance, *households;* for integration, *culture;* and for goal attainment, *politics.* Two further modifications we can make on Parsons' formidable scheme are (a) to combine households and culture and call the resulting concept the *social environment,* and (b) to split technology and the economy into separate environments. Thus, we now have a generalized picture of society as consisting of four parts or environments: technological, economic, social, and political.

While the foregoing discussion might seem unnecessarily elaborate, even baroque, it is absolutely essential if we are to avoid the loose and woolly talk, the outright arbitrariness that so often surrounds the concept of society. Thanks to Parsons, we have a rigorously thought-out picture of just what makes up the environment of business. Now we are less likely to ignore some vital element, or to include some irrelevancy, in our analysis of the environment of business.

Exhibit 1–3, which is based on Parsons' theoretical work, shows the relationship of the American business system to society, or what we shall call its *macroenvironment.* It would be hard to overemphasize the importance of this exhibit; in a sense, one could view all that follows in this book as an elaboration of this one schematic. But what does it tell us? Envision every corporate manager as located in the middle of the figure. In the past, he or she has been primarily concerned with what we shall call the *immediate environment* of business, which consists of suppliers, customers, employees, creditors, shareholders, and competitors.

A moment's reflection will reveal that if the manager studied business in school, virtually all course work was probably directed toward learning to deal with this immediate environment. Unfortunately, he or she is now being told to take on a major new role: envoy from the corporation to the society at large, or macroenvironment. Although the average manager is neither trained nor selected for this role, in most companies it now occupies an ever greater share of his or her time and energy. "Just a few years ago the chief executive of a big company spent 10 percent of his time on external matters," says a managing partner of McKinsey & Company, a consulting firm. "Today the figure is generally 40 percent" (*Business Week,* May 4, 1974).

EXHIBIT 1–3   The Macroenvironment of Business

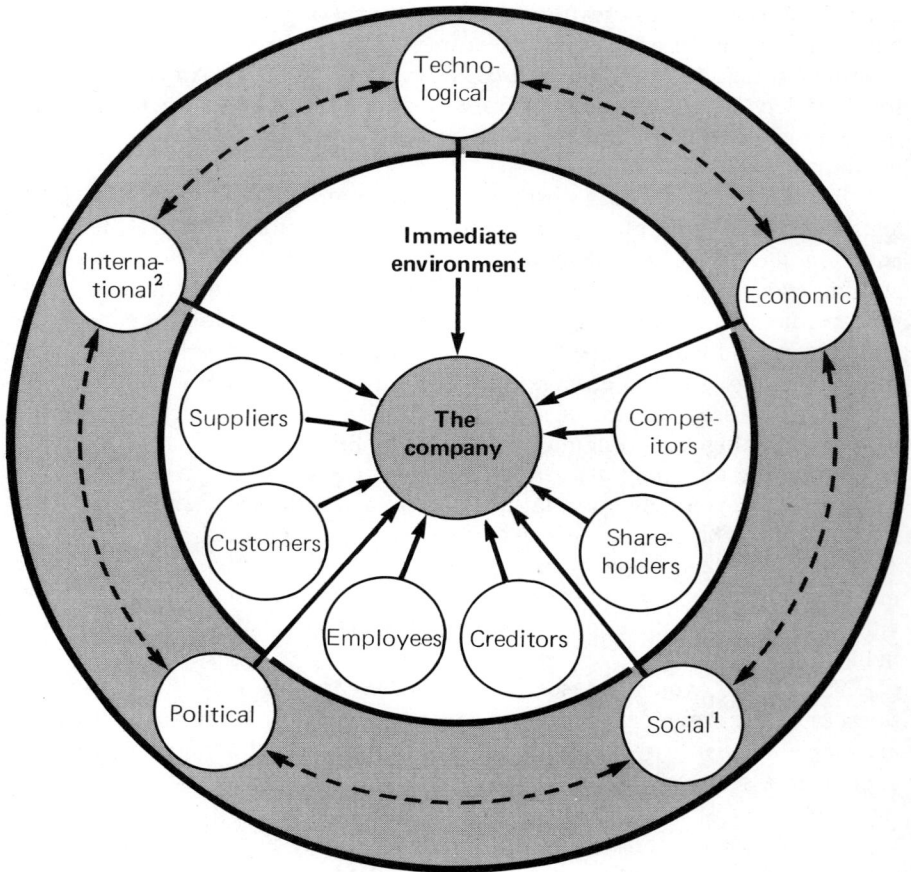

Techno-
logical

Immediate
environment

Interna-
tional[2]

Economic

Suppliers

The
company

Compet-
itors

Customers

Share-
holders

Employees Creditors

Political

Social[1]

[1] The social environment consists of households and culture.

[2] The international environment consists of worldwide (as opposed to domestic)
aspects of the other four environments that make up the macroenvironment.

Since this book analyzes in considerable detail the concept of the macroenvironment and explains how it affects the manager, we need not say everything all at once. But one point merits brief attention. Exhibit 1–3 is a system—that is, all the components are interrelated. Therefore, changes in the
technological environment (e.g., a new invention) can affect the economic en-

vironment; changes in the social environment (e.g., a decline in birth rate) can affect the immediate environment and, in turn, the company; changes in the political-legal environment (e.g., new pollution control laws) can affect directly the internal operation of the company; and so forth. The cross-impacts among the five environments that make up the macroenvironment are represented in Exhibit 1–3 by the dotted arrows.

Types of Economic Systems

Now we come to a final set of definitions that will help us understand the kind of economy in which U.S. business operates. Let us begin by noting two tasks that every economy must perform:

—Organizing a system for producing the goods and services it needs for its own perpetuation;
—Arranging for distribution of the fruits of production among its own members, so that more production can take place.

In any nation, the set-up that determines how these tasks (which look deceptively simple) are performed is the economic system. A *command* system is one in which the government makes economic decisions. A *market* system is one in which supply and demand among many companies and individuals, casting their "dollar votes" in the marketplace, determine the answers.

The terms *capitalism* and *socialism* are essentially synonymous with the market system and the command system. In a capitalist system, to be a little more exact, the means of production are privately owned, and production is guided and income distributed *through the operation of a market.** Socialism is a little more difficult to define. Even Friedrich Engels complained that the socialism of many Germans was "vague, undefined, and undefinable." Nevertheless, I think it safe to say that a true socialist economic system requires common (not private) ownership of the major means of production and some kind of common control over the way in which income is distributed (rather than dependence on the vagaries of the market).

But market (or capitalism) and command (or socialism) are pure, ideal types: Most of the economic systems found in the world are "mixed"—that is, they contain both command and market elements. This principle certainly holds for all advanced industrialized societies such as the Soviet Union and the United States (see Exhibit 1–4).

---

* Interestingly, the emotion-charged word *capitalism,* which conveys mindless accumulation of wealth by greed-driven individuals at the expense of the laboring population, was invented by European socialists about the middle of the nineteenth century. Seeing no good reason for permitting their enemies to appropriate the vocabulary of public discourse, antisocialists later invented another common expression, *free enterprise,* and thereby saved the day for Chambers of Commerce everywhere. With due respect to the creativity of both socialists and Jaycees, I prefer the term *market-based.*

EXHIBIT 1–4   Types of Economic Systems

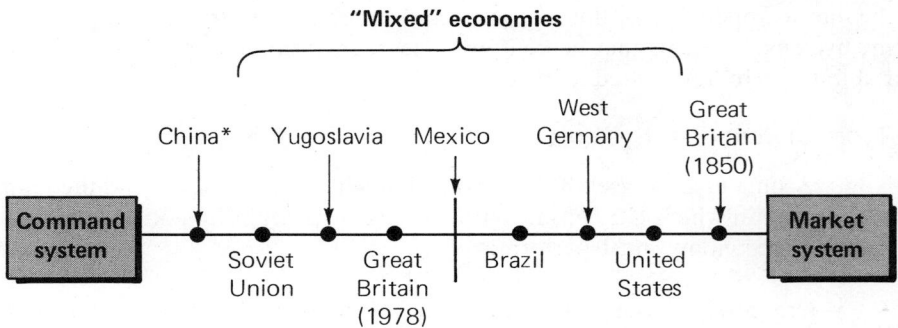

"Mixed" economies

China*   Yugoslavia   Mexico   West Germany   Great Britain (1850)

Command system ———●——●——●——●——|——●——●——●——●—— Market system

Soviet Union   Great Britain (1978)   Brazil   United States

*Charles E. Lindblom (1977:19) suggests that China, at least under Mao, might represent a third type of economic system: persuasion. More than relying on centralized authority to marshal and manipulate behavior (as in the command system), or on incentives of monetary reward and penalty (as in a market system), a persuasion system relies on the techniques of education, propaganda, and the deliberate inculcation of social values.

The U.S. Market System. Because the United States appears to have the market system par excellence, a few more features of this type of economic arrangement need to be understood. Its intellectual history begins with *The Wealth of Nations,* the great work of Adam Smith published in 1776. According to Smith, the great motivator of economic activity is self-interest, ". . . the uniform, constant, and uninterrupted effort of every man to improve his condition," and only this drive moves men to produce the goods that society needs: "It is not from the benevolence of the butcher, the brewer, or the baker, that we expect our dinner, but from their regard to their own interest."

Self-interest expresses itself as the drive for profit and produces the self-regulating market. Smith's message to his fellow economists was not to interfere, not to recommend policy to help the market: "You think you are helping the economic system by your well-meaning laws and interferences. You are not. Let be. The oil of self-interest will keep the gears working in almost miraculous fashion. No one need plan. No sovereign need rule. The market will answer all things." If consumers are free to spend their money any way they wish and business can compete uninhibitedly for their favor, then capital and labor will flow "naturally"—a favorite word of Smith's—into the uses where they are most needed. If consumers want more bread than is being produced, they will pay high prices and bakers will earn high profits, which will lure investors to build more bakeries. If bakers wind up turning out more bread than consumers want to buy, prices and profits will fall and capital will shift into making something that consumers need and desire more—shoes, perhaps. Thus business executives seeking only their own profit are "led by an invisible hand to promote an end which was no part of [their] intention"—that is, the common good.

Moreover, in Smith's view, the process has its own purification system: Competition keeps wiping out the inefficient business, rewarding those who can turn out the most goods at the lowest prices, and forcing even them to keep reinvesting their profits in new products or better operating methods if they want to stay ahead of the competition. As a result, production keeps rising, pulling up wages, and distributing to everyone more of "the necessaries, conveniences, and amusements of human life."

Smith never did prove any of these ideas, but he showed how government economic policies fail and provided a theoretical foundation for the general equilibrium of supply and demand. Although his ideas are dear to most of the business community, Smith's system was not designed for their welfare. Far from admiring merchants, Smith looked upon them as a greedy lot who were forever trying to bypass the market by conspiring to fix prices and hold down wages: "People of the same trade seldom meet together, even for merriment and diversion, but the conversation ends in a conspiracy against the public as in some contrivance to raise prices."

The United States as a "Mixed" Economy. How "mixed" is the American economy? Looking at statements by Presidents Johnson, Nixon, Ford, and Carter is of little help, for the tendency remains to say that "five out of six jobs" are based in the private sector. The problem with this bit of arithmetic is that it merely compares direct government employment to everything else that is called "private." But the important distinction is between the private, profit-seeking sector and the total not-for-profit sector.

Upon close examination, the private sector is not all that private, according to an analysis by Ginzberg (1976). For example, when the federal government buys missiles from Lockheed, workers employed in that company are classified as employees of the private enterprise sector. But are they? The wages those workers earn come from federal funds, and their output is absorbed exclusively by the federal government. Therefore, in seeking to draw realistic boundaries between the private and public sectors, all employment generated by government purchases of all kinds (not just defense) in the private sector should be counted as part of the public sector.

Using this approach, we can derive a more realistic estimate of the role played by the entire not-for-profit sector of the economy in terms of employment. We can also develop a complementary picture in terms of dollars by calculating the total output of goods and services accounted for by government and nonprofit institutions as a proportion of the gross national product. The total share of the not-for-profit sector is 31.9 percent of employment and 26.3 percent of GNP. Clearly, the American economy is much less private than either its defenders or its critics have assumed.

Finally, this analysis assumes a clear-cut differentiation between the private, profit-seeking sector and the not-for-profit one. A more sensitive delineation of the boundaries of the profit-seeking arena would need to include the fact that various government controls over the nation's largest industries constrict their freedom with respect to both prices and profits.

In this section, we have looked at a number of concepts and definitions that will prove invaluable to our understanding of the nature of contemporary business-society interrelations in the United States that begin to unfold in subsequent chapters. First, however, we must examine another perspective that can also prove quite useful.

THE HISTORICAL PERSPECTIVE

In studying business history, one confronts immediately the danger of trying to study all human history. In *The Wealth of Nations* Adam Smith perhaps unintentionally pointed to this danger when he wrote about "a certain propensity in human nature . . . to truck, barter, and exchange one thing for another." Indeed, there can be little doubt that exchange—buying and selling—lay at the heart of the societies he was describing.

How then did we get to modern capitalism from the Babylonians who invented such indispensable aids as bank checks, promissory notes, leases, contracts, and bills of sale; from the efforts in the seventh century B.C. to accumulate resources for future economic enterprises and to earn individual profits; from the partnerships of Athenian or Phoenician merchants pooling their savings to build trading vessels? Historians and readers of history who like sweeping vistas, who long to trace the majestic progress of humanity, delight in such questions. Such curiosity may seem innocent or even worthy, but the question of how earlier institutions gave way to capitalism is neither simple nor neutral. Given these difficulties we need to plot our course carefully. Basically, what we shall do in this section is consider three major stages in the economic transformation of Western society. These stages and their respective dates are shown in Exhibit 1–5.

Note that the story begins with the twilight of the period known as feudalism. Strictly speaking, feudalism refers to the network of relations between lords and vassals. Reciprocal loyalty required each to protect the other, with force of arms if need be. In order that a vassal should carry out his side of the bargain, the lord typically gave him a block of land known as a *fief* or *feudum*, from which the name *feudalism* was derived long afterward (see Fourquin, 1977). As can be seen from the illustration in Exhibit 1–5 representing this period, feudalism was preeminently agriculturally based.

The Commercial Society

The breakdown of feudalism did not at once make for the triumphant entry of capitalism. Rather, there was a gap of about two centuries, roughly from 1350 to 1550, during which neither feudalism nor capitalism prevailed; capitalism developed slowly throughout, and feudalism persisted well into the capitalist period. The forces driving this great transformation can be found by looking to the technological, economic, social, and political environments of the time.

Technological Forces. Recent research by historians of technology has forced us to discard the distinction commonly made between the medieval and the modern world. As they now see it, by the end of the fifteenth century Western Europe was already more advanced from a technological point of view than the Roman world would ever have been. Jean Gimpel (1977), in a valuable synthesis of the current state of knowledge on medieval technology, argues that the period from the tenth to the fourteenth centuries "was one of the great inventive eras of mankind." The astonishing degree of competence among engineers of this period was especially evident in the development of new agricultural techniques; in the improvements in the harnessing of horses; in the development of water and wind power; in the superb achievements—architectural and structural—of Gothic builders; in the emergence of mining, that most characteristic European branch of technology; and in the subtle evolution of the mechanical clock, whose role as "the key machine" is as intriguing as it is debatable. It is hard to see how a feudal society possessing such technology *could* fail to evolve.

Economic Forces. Equally important to the emergence of capitalism were the changes taking place in the economic life of society. For a market society to emerge, one thing is essential: People must have cash, for only with cash can one enter a market. But, if cash is to permeate society, people must earn money for their labors. In other words, for a market to exist, nearly every task must have a *monetary reward.* Robert L. Heilbroner (1962:58–59) describes this "monetization" of the economic environment well: "Whereas in the tenth century, cash and transactions were only peripheral to the solution of the economic problem, by the sixteenth and seventeenth centuries cash and transactions were already beginning to provide the very force of social cohesion."

As a consequence of monetization, the trading areas, or markets, began to widen. But craftsmen, organized in guilds, were not prepared to take advantage of this change. They lacked the money (or "capital") to tie up in stocks of unsold articles; they also lacked knowledge of what distant customers wanted and at what price. In this situation, a new type of man appeared: the "enterpriser" or *entrepreneur.*

In Rembrandt's *The Synics* (see Exhibit 1–5), we see a group of such men. Leaning forward, intent as judges, they typify the new class of entrepreneurs

EXHIBIT 1–5   Timetable of Capitalism's Development

1400	1500	1600

Feudalism

Comm

Brevarium Grimani, agricultural scene at the end of the 15th century.

Rembrandt, *The Synics: The Sampling Officials (W dens) of the Amsterdam Drapers Guild.*

'00	1800	1900	2000

ety

Industrial society

Information society

Employees at work expediting long-distance calls in a Bell System's Network Operations Center.

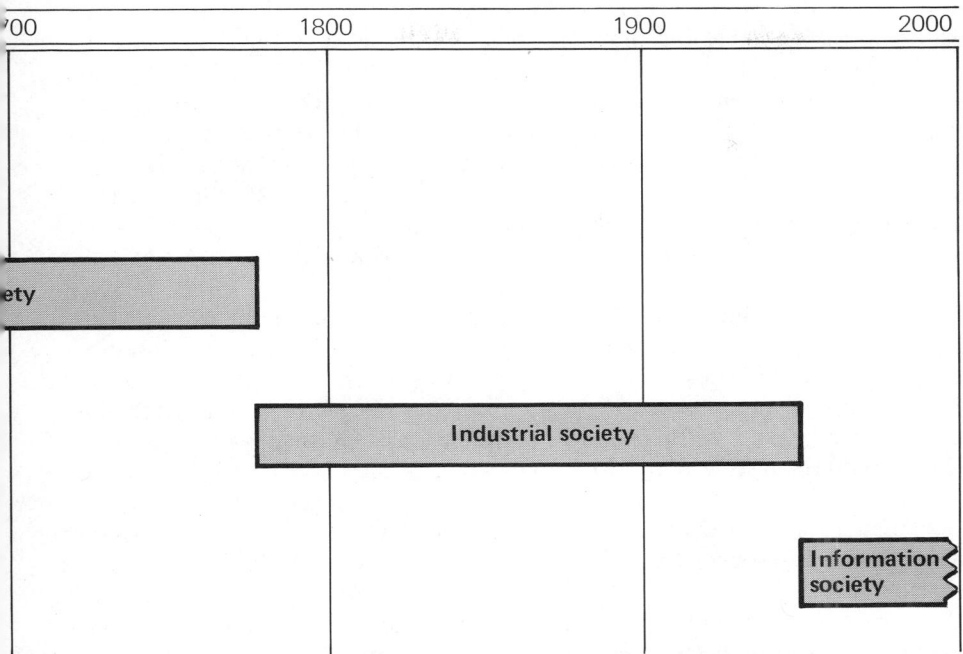

orkers operating a nineteenth-century power
om.

Source: Feudalism painting from The Bettmann Archive, Inc.; commercial society painting from Rijks Museum (Amsterdam); industrial society drawing from Yale University Art Gallery, The Mabel Brady Garvan Collection; information society photo reproduced with permission of AT&T Co.

who conducted the affairs of Holland, the first center of bourgeois capitalism. One cannot imagine a group like this being produced in medieval times or even in seventeenth-century Italy. At last, a group of individuals had come together to take corporate responsibility; they could afford to do so because they had had some leisure; and they had some leisure because they had money in the bank. This is the society represented in the portrait (Clarke, 1968:197).

The entrepreneur usually started out as a merchant and ended up as a banker. Typical of this pattern were the German Fuggers. The first entrepreneurs of this family began as cloth merchants, but gradually the family began to expand into other commodities, such as spices and silks. Profits were then reinvested in mining. Eventually, having become bankers, they were lending money to Renaissance popes and financing Portuguese trade.

Social Forces. Along with these sea changes in the technological and economic environments came changes in the social environment. For instance, historians and sociologists who have looked for the cultural motivations of sixteenth- and seventeenth-century capitalism have sometimes suggested that they may be found in Protestantism. In 1904 the German sociologist Max Weber put forward the proposition that capitalist merchants, such as the Fuggers and Rembrandt's "sampling officials," with their unprecedented desire for systematic work and saving, were the product of an anxiety neurosis—a "salvation panic"—induced by Calvinism.

Unqualified, Weber's proposition cannot be maintained. In the first place, the growth of capitalism in the early modern world received many stimuli unknown to Weber, including the growth of population. Toward the end of the fifteenth century a new population cycle began. Society was moving into an entirely new situation for reasons having little to do with the Protestant Reformation.

The Weber proposition also becomes suspect once the theology of Martin Luther and John Calvin is closely examined: their theology suggests more a medieval than a modern outlook. (Think, for example, of the Puritans in New England, inheritors of Calvinist thought, with their ideals of social stability, order, and discipline.) And, as Paul Johnson (1977:60) asks: "Why, if Calvinism was the key to capitalism, did not the Industrial Revolution take place in predominantly Calvinist Scotland rather than in Lancashire and the English Midlands?"

David S. Landes (1974) offers a more accurate assessment than Weber of the effect of cultural changes on the development of capitalism:

> Radical religions that emphasized the importance of character and conduct and that even preached socially egalitarian doctrines seemed to give purpose even to humble occupations. The doctrines of election and predestination had a special appeal to those who could believe that economic success based on thrift and sobriety was clear evidence of God's favor. It seems probable that in the casual,

easy-going society of the early modern world, men thus motivated toward steady and methodical work would inevitably tend to rise in the social scale. On this interpretation, while the initial attraction of the new religions to capitalists may have been exaggerated, the practice of their beliefs and social habits may have contributed to the rapid growth of a class of capitalists later on.

Political Forces. One final driving force of the transformation from feudalism to capitalism was a set of governmental policies that go historically under the name of *mercantilism*. These policies, which all major trading nations more or less followed from 1500 to 1800, were based on the premise that national wealth and power were best served by increasing exports over imports and collecting precious metals (especially gold) in return. Hence the state encouraged foreign trade above domestic trade and favored manufacturing, which provided the goods for foreign trade, over mining and agriculture.

Under mercantilist policies, nations sought a favorable balance of trade; by selling more than it bought, so the theory ran, the nation would build up its supply of precious metals. But mercantilism represented more than the pursuit of an abstract economic principle: These economic initiatives were considered the indispensable other arms of the military and the requisites for a strong, self-sufficient nation.

To carry out these policies, governments took a variety of actions: removal of import duties to encourage the maximum influx of raw materials for industry; imposition of export duties on local raw materials for industry; encouragement of local manufactures by imposition of protective tariffs against foreign competition; granting of subsidies to assist local manufactures; introduction of new crafts and manufactures; and the discouragement of idleness ("set the poor on work," as they said in England).

Particularly important in carrying out mercantilist policies was the chartering of companies. Since merchants trading in remote parts of the globe required a good deal of capital, they often had to obtain special privileges and support from the state. So it was that merchants and their respective governments came together to found official, state-approved companies. Each of the companies, forerunners of the modern large corporation, was a monopoly since only merchants that belonged to the company could legally engage in the trade for which the company had a charter. Thus, the first joint-stock companies, though financed with private capital, were created by public charters that set down in detail the activities in which the enterprise might operate.

The Industrial Society

Curiously absent from commercial society was any real interest in the actual process of production. The "commercial capitalist" person who knew where the article could be sold prevailed over the "industrial capitalist," the person who knew how to make the article. Amusing, as well as instructive, is the prescription for the best ways of getting rich enumerated by a fifteenth-century commentator (cited in Heilbroner, 1962:73). They are: (1) wholesale trade; (2) seeking a treasure; (3) ingratiating oneself with a rich man to become his heir; (4) making loans; and (5) renting land, horses, and the like. A seventeenth-century commentator brings the list up to date by adding royal service, soldiering, and alchemy. Manufacturing is conspicuously absent from both lists.

To be accurate, there was one capitalist enterprise employing intensive industrial equipment in the centuries before the Industrial Revolution: the great breweries of London and of the large cities of Holland and Germany. But this was the exception to the rule. The typical pattern was for the merchants to put the work out to weavers, hatters, metal workers, gunsmiths, glass workers, and so forth, who were often located in the countryside rather than the city. These workers would then work to fill the orders.

Beginnings of the Industrial Revolution in England. The Industrial Revolution, which appeared first in England toward the end of the eighteenth century, changed the entire economic structure. First, work activities, rather than being "put out," were now organized into large, centrally powered units such as factories and mills that made possible the immediate supervision of the production process and a more efficient division of labor. In a famous passage in *The Wealth of Nations,* Adam Smith described the division of labor in the manufacture of pins:

> One man draws out the wire, another straights it, a third cuts it, a fourth points it, a fifth grinds it at the top for receiving the head; to make the head requires two or three distinct operations; to put it on is a peculiar business, to whiten the pins is another; it is even a trade by itself to put them into the paper . . .

Ten men so dividing the labor, Smith calculated, could make forty-eight thousand pins a day, or forty-eight hundred apiece. One man doing all the operations would make maybe one pin, maybe twenty. It is arguable that with this reorganization of the production process, management as a field of study began.

Second, the Industrial Revolution brought the rapid substitution of inanimate sources of power, particularly steam power–fueled coal, for animal sources of power. Third, and closely related to the second change, the Industrial Revolution brought the substitution of machines for human skills. The picture of the power loom in Exhibit 1–5 epitomizes this switch.

As a consequence of these three changes in the production process, output soared. In the space of a century, for example, cloth production grew 3,000 percent. In the small amount of time the world production of pig iron rose from 10 million tons to 357 million tons. The statistics are much the same for every area the new technology penetrated.

But these changes had other, less easily quantified, consequences. The poet William Blake, a contemporary of Adam Smith, was perhaps the first to notice the social consequences: "Dark Satanic mills" were wiping out the cottage industry and jamming workers into ugly new factory towns. Though the purchasing power of the factory workers began to rise slowly, a father's earnings were often insufficient to support a family. Although working conditions varied widely, weaker, less efficient firms cut corners to compete. One of the worst features of the new mode of production was extensive reliance on women and children. The picture of the woman tending the power loom in Exhibit 1–5 is again indicative of the period. Although the drawing fails to capture the more egregious aspects of the arrangement, the following passage, appearing in Chapter 10 of Marx's *Capital* (1867) and taken from an official British government report of 1860, does:

> In the beginning of June, 1836, information reached the magistrates of Dewsbury (Yorkshire) that the owners of 8 large mills in the neighbourhood of Batley had violated the Factory Acts. Some of these gentlemen were accused of having kept at work 5 boys between 12 and 15 years of age, from 6 A.M. on Friday to 4 P.M. on the following Saturday, not allowing them any respite except for meals and one hour for sleep at midnight. And these children had to do this ceaseless labour of 30 hours in the "shoddy-hole," as the hole is called in which the woolen rags are pulled to pieces, and where a dense atmosphere of dust, shreds, etc., forces even the adult workman to cover his mouth continually with handkerchiefs for the protection of his lungs! The accused gentlemen affirm in lieu of taking an oath—as Quakers they were too scrupulously religious to take an oath—that they had, in their great compassion for the unhappy children, allowed them four hours for sleep, but the obstinate children absolutely would not go to bed. The Quaker gentlemen were fined £20.

It is not too gross a generalization to say that Marx was able to base an entire system of philosophy on such early nineteenth-century excesses.

However, the early excesses of industrialization were gradually alleviated during the course of the nineteenth century. Johnson (1977:72) writes:

> . . . As capitalist industrialization spread . . . the positive benefits were acquired more easily and more rapidly, and the incidental miseries gradually eliminated. No other country had to go through Britain's sufferings, in part at least because Britain was able to supply the industrial matrix she had forged for herself—capital, patents, capital goods, skilled labour and management. The United States and Germany were thus able to industrialize on a scale and at a speed which would have dazzled the British pioneers of the 1780's; and feudal empires like Japan and Russia were able to telescope a development process which in Britain had stretched over centuries into a mere generation or two. Yet, curiously enough, the attention of analysts and ideologues remained almost exclusively fixed on the original British experience; and conclusions were drawn from it long after it had ceased to be relevant to the actual world.

Moreover, the social consequences of the Industrial Revolution were not so uniformly bad as they have been made out—though, to be sure, they were far worse than they had to be. The cruder social consequences struck many people at the time as unacceptable for two reasons. First, the Industrial Revolution's beginning coincided with a new phase of human sensibility, which expressed itself not least in the art of realism. Compare the romanticized view of work in feudal society that appears in Exhibit 1–5 with that disturbing symbol of hard work, *The Man with a Hoe* (Exhibit 1–6). The painter, Jean-François Millet, was a socialist, and he saw chiefly the brutalities of society.

The second, and related, reason for people's opposition to the social consequences of industrialization was that industrialization made the more horrific aspects of life more visible, as Johnson (1977:70) shows:

> The world of the eighteenth century was still hideously poor. . . . The great majority of human kind, even in relatively prosperous western Europe, spent most of their incomes on basic foodstuffs, which did not include fresh meat as a rule. But poverty and degradation were concealed and scattered in the countryside. Industrialization, by concentrating the poor in factories and city housing, brought the perennial sufferings of the working class to the attention of the new humanitarians. In fact, in strict material terms, the poor were better off in the factories. . . . Preindustrial rural poverty was something the new urban philanthropists could not comprehend, for they had never seen it. Hence they tended to categorize the urban poverty they could see, and smell, as something new and unprecedented.

Why the Industrial Revolution should occur first in England is not hard to see. First, England was the scene of the most complete transformation from feudal to commercial society: The joint-stock company was established; insurance, securities, and commodity markets were organized; and the banking system expanded. Within a framework of parliamentary law, the notion of personal property was fully developed, and the concept of private ownership was guaranteed by the courts and was safe from the crown. Further, the victory of Parliament in the mid-seventeenth century ensured a comparatively low level of taxation. Thus the capitalist could be reasonably assured that the law was clear, stable, and objective. Second, England was relatively wealthy, and riches had accrued not merely to a few nobles but to a large commercial upper–middle class as well. Third, England was the center of a new enthusiasm for science and engineering.

Spread of the Industrial Revolution to the United States. The three conditions that made it possible for the Industrial Revolution to begin in England were, to a high degree, also present in the United States. As might be expected, it was not long before the Industrial Revolution spread across the Atlantic. From 1839 to 1899, the value added in the American industrial sector rose over twenty-five times, or 5.3 percent per year. The United States passed Britain in steel output in 1890, in coal in 1898, and in raw cotton consumption at the turn of the century. It had become the greatest industrial power in the world

EXHIBIT 1–6   Realism in Nineteenth-Century Social Attitudes

Jean-Francois Millet, *The Man with a Hoe.*

Source: The Bettman Archive, Inc.

and was pioneering the passage to new technologies that would give impetus to further growth. Some have called this array of new technologies (such as electrical power, internal-combustion engines, petroleum fuel, automobiles and science-based chemical manufacture) a second Industrial Revolution.

Industrial society in the United States, however, was no Xerox copy of Britain's. Perhaps the most striking difference was in the role of government vis-à-vis the business system.

In 1925 Calvin Coolidge uttered a sentence that has proved, apparently, a source of endless amusement for the critics of business: "The business of America is business." Yet, the historical fact is that much of North America's settlement was initially underwritten as a business venture.

It is also a historical fact that the American Revolution was, in large measure, a rejection of this essentially British, and quite mercantilist, idea. Indeed, one result of the Revolution was to establish the idea that a corporation did not have to show, as did the British companies that helped in the founding of North America, that its activities would advance specific public policies. Hacker (1974:182) cites Alexander Hamilton, the first secretary of the treasury and an admirer of Adam Smith, who took the view that businessmen should be encouraged to explore their own avenues to enterprise: "To cherish and stimulate the activity of the human mind, by multiplying the objects of enterprise, is not among the least considerable of the expedients by which the wealth of a nation may be promoted," he wrote in 1791.

But this theory of a totally free and unhampered market, commonly referred to as *laissez-faire*, was not really put into practice until the last quarter of the nineteenth century. Soon after the Revolution, it was apparent that the interrelations between private enterprise and public policy would remain vital. The reasons are not hard to see. After all, public authority in a territory with a vast amount of rich land being steadily opened up and a frontier constantly threatening to get out of control had an obvious part to play. As an upshot of the geographic imperative, the role of government during the first half of the nineteenth century became that of entrepreneur on a large scale—operating either independently or, more commonly, in partnership with private business. Railways, turnpikes, canals, docks, waterworks, banks, and insurance companies were all treated as proper spheres for government intervention. For example, according to Louis Hartz (1948:290–91), a total of over 150 "mixed corporations"—in which the state government of Pennsylvania and private enterprise were partners—appear in the official records of the year 1844.

But coexisting with these cooperative arrangements were traces of laissez-faire. By 1811, in fact, New York had adopted a general act of incorporation that set the precedent that business had only to provide a summary description of its intentions for permission to launch an enterprise. By the 1840s and 1850s, the rest of the states had followed suit.

It is commonly recognized in American historical folklore that the presidency of Andrew Jackson (1829–1837) marked a new phase in the expansion of freedom for business. No doubt much of the basis of this view is Jackson's decisive rejection of the United States Bank in 1832—an action that delayed the establishment of a central banking system in the United States until 1914. Was this a blow for business independence? Perhaps. But we must also note that during this period there was little evidence of opposition to the use of public power in the economic system. Moreover, state and municipal governments certainly remained free to expand; for example, states systematically regulated the standards of all exported goods.

Thus it was not until the last quarter of the nineteenth century (ironically, about the time Britain was turning away from some of the excesses of laissez-faire) that private enterprise really became private and the theories of Hamilton became standard practice. Andrew Shronfield (1965:302) explains in both political and economic terms how this reversal in the balance of public and private initiatives came about:

> Part of the explanation is possibly the shift in the alignment of the political parties during and after the Civil War, with the earlier exponents of active interventionist government, in the northern states, absorbed into a Republican Party which was now dominated by the big business interests. But there were, in addition, two economic factors which helped to sharpen the reaction against all forms of public enterprise at this stage. The first was simply that there was no longer any lack of private risk capital on a sufficient scale to finance large enterprises, particularly in the field of public transport. Private investors were now eager to engage in this lucrative business. Secondly, and probably more important in terms of national politics, the management of too many public enterprises had been thoroughly inefficient.

This was the era of the *trust*—that is, a combination under a central management of several firms competing in the same industry. Better but costlier production equipment raised the price of entry into the trust and offered new *economies of scale*—that is, the savings generated by large-scale production of a product. (In other words, cost per unit produced tends to be less for large-scale operations than for small.) Meanwhile, improvements in communications made centralized management a possibility. The defense of these arrangements was waged on pragmatic grounds. "Trusts are natural, inevitable growths out of our social and economic conditions," argued James B. Dill, an articulate corporation lawyer of the era. While none of this is startlingly new, it has never been assembled in such complete detail or demonstrated with such clear economic logic as in Alfred D. Chandler's *The Visible Hand.* At the same time, Chandler has interwoven the story of how managers, as a distinct economic and social group, came to be recognized in the business world. Chandler's major themes are summarized in the Commentary section, "The Managerial Revolution in American Business."

Unfortunately, the trend toward bigness sometimes helped to stabilize profits and minimize competition, either by absorption or elimination. President Theodore Roosevelt recognized the problem and urged in 1901 that government regulate trusts ". . . if they are found to exercise a license working to the public injury. It should be as much the aim of those who seek for social betterment to rid the business world of crimes of cunning as to rid the entire body politic of crimes of violence." During Roosevelt's administration (1901–1909), the government pressed indictments against no less than forty-two trusts. The number of prosecutions was even larger during the Taft administration (1909–1913), and President Woodrow Wilson continued the attack. The "trustbusting" crusade was only partially successful since the government was not always able to obtain convictions. Eventually the corporations simply reorganized, stopped calling themselves trusts, and continued to operate pretty

COMMENTARY: The Managerial Revolution in American Business

While most business historians are more attracted to the robber barons than the institutions these men created, Alfred D. Chandler, Jr. (1977) corrects the bias. In a major contribution to "business history," he provides numerous powerful insights into the ways in which certain imperatives of capitalism shaped the growth of the giant companies in some industries but not in others. He documents carefully how, between 1840 and 1920, the "visible hand" of management replaced what Adam Smith called the "invisible hand" of market forces in coordinating the activities of the economy and allocating its resources.

Essentially, two conditions were necessary for the rise of giant firms. The first was the appearance of a technology capable of significantly lowering production costs and thereby opening the way for an industrial pioneer to steal an irretrievable advantage over competitors. These technological advances came mainly in those industries in which the velocity of "through-put" could be raised by machinery and energy. Steel, petroleum, or sugar are obvious examples. Similar advantages did not accrue in industries with discontinuous processes such as apparel, leather, woodworking, and the like.

The second prerequisite for the rise of giant firms was the development of a marketing apparatus capable of disposing of vast quantities of output, first by creating a network of wholesale and retail outlets, later by mobilizing "latent" demand by advertising.

A significant event occurred on 5 October 1841: two passenger trains of the Western Railroad collided head-on. It was not the first serious accident in the nascent railroad industry, but it was one of the worst. The head-on collision made it painfully clear that one boss could not keep his eye on everything and that a well-defined organizational structure was needed. Specifically, the Western was broken into three operating divisions that reported to a newly formed headquarters at Springfield, Massachusetts. Standard operating procedures and strict timetables were drawn up, regular operating reports filed, responsibilities defined, and a hierarchy held accountable.

It was, in brief, the dawning of modern management. Chandler describes the Western as "the first American business enterprise to operate through a formal administrative structure manned by full-time salaried managers." Prior to 1840 the biggest industrial enterprise in the nation had been the Springfield armory, with 250 employees. By 1891 the Pennsylvania Railroad employed over 110,000 people; its capitalization of $842 million was only slightly smaller than the national debt of $997 million. Prior to 1840 the traditional American firm was a single-unit enterprise with an owner-manager. Little more than sixty years later, the multiunit enterprise administered by a set of salaried and top managers had become dominant. "Rarely in the history of the world has an institution grown to be so important and so pervasive in so short a period of time," Chandler observes.

Organized enterprise, then, arose originally in the railroad industry and spread laterally to other forms of transportation. We find the new pattern of organization in industries where flow processes and national marketing possibilities converged: food and tobacco, oil and rubber, chemicals and metals, and, later, automobiles and consumer durables.

The 1880s was the watershed decade. The completion of the railroad and telegraph systems provided not only the vital infrastructure of communications, but the administrative models for the modern mass marketer who purchased directly from growers and manufacturers and sold directly to retailers and final consumers. The new concept of low margins and high volumes was enshrined in the famous department stores and mail-order houses: Marshall Field; Macy's; Bloomingdale's; Sears, Roebuck; and the redoubtable Woolworth chain stores, which opened in 1880.

In each case the visible hand of management, rationalizing production within the enclave of an integrated industry or allocating it across the national marketplace, replaced the coordinating mechanism of the invisible hand; management, in effect, now performed the task that buying and selling did before businesses grew "vertically" or "horizontally." And meanwhile, among the emerging industrial giants, the visible hand appeared in the form of pools, trusts, mergers, and holding companies, as the new managers sought to regulate production among themselves as they had already regulated it within each of their companies.

By 1890 new organizational imperatives resulted from the integration of continuous-process production with mass distribution and the emergence of branded-goods marketing. Companies like American Tobacco, Singer, Remington, National Cash Register, and Armour developed the first true middle management structures. But top management still had to learn how to delegate day-to-day operations. And it was not until 1918, at Standard Oil, General Electric, and DuPont de Nemours, that the modern organizational hierarchy finally emerged, with middle management handling production and distribution and top management planning and allocating total resources. By 1920, managers were recognizable as a distinct economic and social group.

As business firms expand, we see them struggle to find methods of supervising functions and processes that are now hopelessly beyond the scope of a single-person enterprise, or even a group of close-working partners. Thus branches arise, then departments with complicated tables of organization. Each department, each production or merchandizing element, requires its own directing personnel that is at once subordinate to a higher authority and yet in command of its own demarcated area. Thus a "managerial" function appears, first, in the middle ranks of the growing firm and then moves upward until "management" takes over every task, including entrepreneurship itself, and gradually but decisively displaces in authority the tycoons who started the business and held its stock.

---

much as before. Still, when the government did have its occasional victories, the effect on the public morale was great.

Until some scholar does the definitive psychobiography of Coolidge, we shall never know exactly what the laconic president really meant when he said,

"The business of America is business." But, if he meant simply that the shapers of public policy in the United States have been constantly concerned with how to treat private enterprise, he surely was not far off the mark. If he had only added, "But regarding the correct policy toward it (business), we are uncertain," he would have had a bull's-eye.

The Information Society

Thus far, we have traced the development of Western society from feudalism to commercial capitalism to industrial capitalism, European and American style. Some observers would argue that after World War II the United States entered a new stage. While there is no consensus on what to call this third stage of capitalism, the terms *information society* and *postindustrial society* are most frequently heard.

What are the characteristics of this new society? The first and simplest characteristic is that the majority of the labor force is engaged, not in farming (as was the case in feudalism and even in commercial society), not in manufacturing (as was the case in industrial society), but in providing services and especially information. As shown in Exhibit 1–7, these occupational shifts have been major ones.

Stating precisely who is an information worker and who is not is a risky proposition. While every human endeavor involves some measure of information processing and cognition, some occupations do seem *primarily* engaged in the production, processing, and distribution of information. Marc Uri Porat (1977) has developed a conceptual scheme for classifying information workers in the United States (see Exhibit 1–8).

The people in the final illustration of Exhibit 1–5 make excellent examples of information workers. They are employed in the Bell System's Network Operations Center to expedite long-distance calls. In round numbers, the center helps manage nearly forty million calls on a normal day. A bank might also serve as an example of an information industry (see Exhibit 1–9).

The Lessons of History

Historical surveys such as the foregoing can give us added insight into the nature of business-society relations in the United States today. The historical perspective shows that cozy relations between government and business, like those that seemed to prevail in the last quarter of the nineteenth century and the years immediately following World War II, were really the exception rather than the norm. During the first three-quarters of the nineteenth century, government seldom hesitated to use law to shape priorities in a developing economy. And even before the close of the century, trustbusting was a frequent and popular pursuit among government officials. Nor should we overlook the Depression of the 1930s, which enormously strengthened the

**EXHIBIT 1–7   Four-Sector Aggregation of the U.S. Work Force
by Percent, 1860–1980**

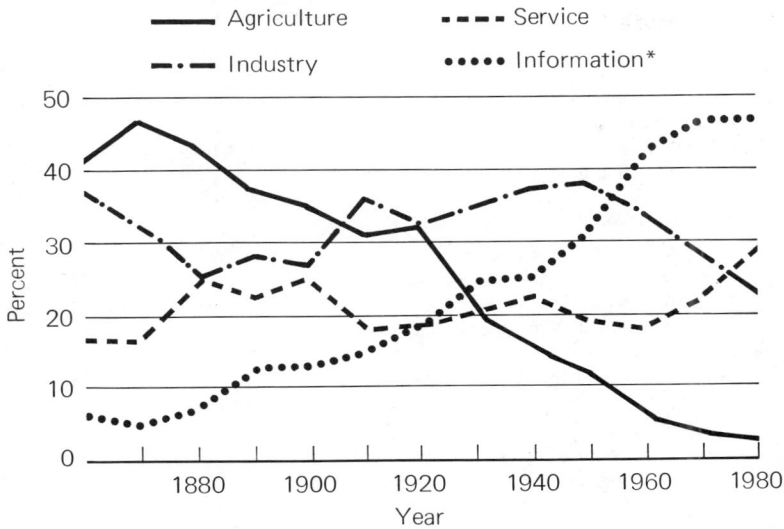

*Median estimates of information workers.

Source: Marc Uri Porat, "The Information Economy," Office of Telecommunications, U.S. Department of
Commerce, *Special Publication 77–12* (Washington, D.C.: U.S. Government Printing Office, 1977), p. 121.

hand of government in its relationship to private enterprise. The point, then, is
this: History teaches us unequivocally that current government "attacks" on
business, with the public on the sidelines applauding, are really nothing new.

History also teaches us that when governments intervene in the private
sector, the results can be quite mixed. Stated differently, neither a consistently
activist government policy (such as mercantilism) nor a consistently passive
government policy (such as laissez-faire) serves the long-term public interest
very well; intervention seems to depend on the situation.

For example, Colbert, finance minister to Louis XIV, struggled to encourage the rising bourgeoisie and to promote the interests of manufacture and
commerce in general. But, being a mercantilist, he proceeded in a curiously
self-defeating way: He cast a web of regulations, tariffs, and ordinances that
suffocated the entrepreneurial impulse at the same time that it sought to
strengthen it. And on top of these regulations was a harsh and corrupt feudal
system of taxation. David S. Landes (1974) offers this general assessment of

EXHIBIT 1–8   Typology of Information Workers in the United States

		Employee compensation [a] (Millions)
Knowledge producers		$ 46,964
Scientific & technical workers	18,777	
Private information services	28,187	
Knowledge distributors		$ 28,265
Educators	23,680	
Public information disseminators	1,264	
Communication workers	3,321	
Market search & coordination specialists		$ 93,370
Information gatherers	6,132	
Search & coordination specialists	28,252	
Planning and control workers	58,986	
Information processors		$ 61,340
Nonelectronic based	34,317	
Electronic based	27,023	
Information machine workers		$ 13,167
Nonelectronic machine operators	4,219	
Electronic machine operators	3,660	
Telecommunication workers	5,288	
Total information		$243,106
Total employee compensation		$454,259 [b]
Information as % of total		53.52%

[a] Includes wages and salaries and supplements (1967).
[b] Excludes military workers.

Source: Marc Uri Porat, "The Information Economy," Office of Telecommunications, U.S. Department of Commerce, *Special Publication* 77–12 (Washington, D.C.: U.S. Government Printing Office, 1977), p. 107.

the efficacy of government sponsorship of manufactures in eighteenth-century Europe:

> Much of this development from above was misdirected. Technical knowledge and managerial talent were in short supply, and the effort to force progress inevitably led to misallocation of resources and the manufacture of goods of poor quality at high cost. Subsidies only encouraged waste and inefficiency, while monopoly privileges eliminated the competition that might have compelled better performance. The difficulty was compounded by the preference of most rulers and their officials for large, centralized establishments—visible symbols of industrial achievement. The "manufactories," so called to distinguish them from

true factories, were not centrally powered and were ordinarily equipped with the same devices used in convention workshops. They had, therefore, no technical advantage over dispersed cottage manufacture yet were burdened with higher capital costs and were far less attractive to workers, who resented supervision and discipline—hence the need to assign labour, which was invariably sullen and unproductive. Most of these hothouse enterprises collapsed as soon as the state withdrew its support and the setback was proportional to the amount of support.

Still, there were instances where state intervention was called for. It was a stable legal and financial framework that made the industrialization of Britain a reality, but it was also *political* passivity that made industrialization needlessly costly in human terms.

The special virtue of American reformers has been their refusal to accept the simple dichotomy between mercantilism on the one hand and laissez-faire on the other. Shonfield (1965:308) says that the New Dealers saw the future as "a mixture of public and private initiatives, with the public side very much reinforced but still operating in the framework of a predominantly capitalist system." Schlesinger (1959) has also delineated the emergence of these two distinct lines of thought. One may be broadly described as the corporatist view of an entirely new relationship between government and business collaborating actively with one another in the pursuit of agreed economic objectives. The other line emphasized supervision or regulation of the activities of private enterprise. Its purpose was to ensure that certain rules were obeyed, not to exact any help from business in the objectives of public policy. The basis of this fusion of the public (not-for-profit) and private sectors, in the view of Eli Ginzberg (1976:29), is the principle of complementarity:

> The prosperity of the automotive industry has long depended on an expanding national highway system. Similarly, the argument can be made, the research-based and science-based industries and advanced services that continue to provide the frontiers of the economy—from more powerful computers to strengthened capital markets—depend on the trained manpower produced in the colleges and universities based in the not-for-profit sector. To discuss the not-for-profit sector as a profligate spender of scarce resources without reference to its critical contribution to enlarging the wealth and welfare of the American economy and society may arouse enthusiasm among certain components of the body politic, but it is not likely to win much favor or have much influence on public policy, even among a people that considers its tax burden onerous.

The last lesson we shall note is surely the easiest: capitalism is a constantly evolving arrangement. The great danger in analyzing it is to become swept up in the headlines of the day and lose sight of the system's enormous capacity for change.

EXHIBIT 1–9   The Bank as an Information Industry

It is clear that Bell Telephone, libraries, and palm readers sell information; and it is equally clear that truckers, restaurants, and plumbers sell noninformation services. But, alas, a variety of industries have output that is less clearly classified. I shall briefly introduce one industry, finance, as an example of how we view 'information.''

The financial industries are fundamentally organized around *intermediation*— that is, the brokerage of money and financial assets. Money itself is nothing more than a symbolic store of value, carrying information as the holder's claim on assets. When money is deposited in a saving or checking account, it completely loses its sense of being a ''commodity'' and instead assumes the form of pure information: it is converted into information and stored in computer-driven data banks. Money in this form is exchanged between banks over a telecommunications network, where only information flows between the vendors of financial services. An electronic funds transfer system is a pure information medium for carrying out financial transactions.

The business of finance provides many informational services: some earn an explicit income, and others are not explicitly charged. For example, a bank may provide the following, explicitly charged services:

    Transactions charges on demand deposit,
    Transactions charges on money orders,
    Transactions charges on trust accounts,
    Transactions charges on travelers' checks,
    Transactions charges on funds transfers.

In addition, there are a variety of informational services that are not explicitly charged, but rather are paid out of the net interest income; for example:

    Analysis of borrowers' risk,
    Analysis of investment portfolio,
    Analysis of foreign exchange rates,
    Analysis of macroeconomic development,
    Internal management and bookkeeping,
    Legal, political, and promotional activities,
    Transactions with the Federal Reserve.

The banking industry's output is defined as the sum of net interest plus service charges. The entire output just equals the expenses of producing, processing, and transmitting financial information. About 80 percent of the industry's costs are used in providing information services, and 19 percent represents the cost of capital. Therefore, a bank can be thought of as a system for transforming inputs, which are predominantly informational, into outputs that are all informational (see diagram). For example, when a consumer pays for commodities by check, the clerk is secure in the knowledge that a transfer of funds from one account to another will eventually take place. The consumer pays not only for the purchased good but also for some transmittal of information. This information exchange is costly to produce and banks often levy explicit service charges to perform the information services.

INPUTS = COSTS

(80%)

OUTPUTS = NET
INTEREST AND
SERVICE CHARGES

Information

Managers
Tellers
Clerks
Accountants

Computers
Calculators
Telephones

File cabinets
Office buildings

(1%)

Noninformation

Janitors
Guards
Carpets
Overstuffed
couches

(19%)

Capital
account

Transform

Checking
account activity

Savings
account activity

Mortgage loans
Management risk

Business loans
Management risk

Trust
accounts

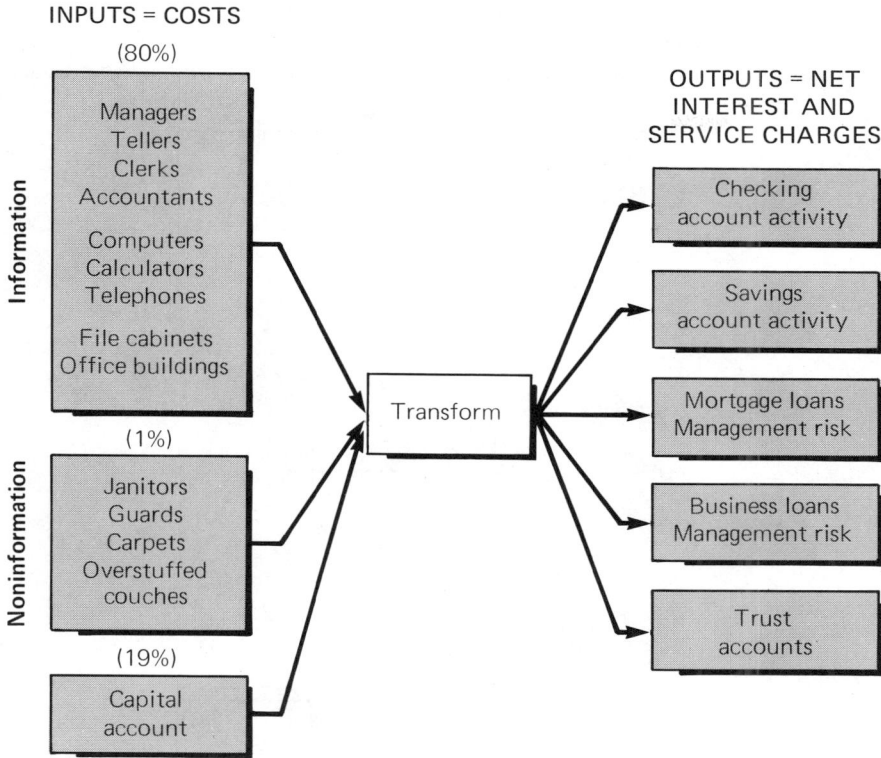

Source: Marc Uri Porat, "The Information Economy," Office of Telecommunications, U.S. Department of
Commerce, *Special Publication* 77–12 (Washington, D.C.: U.S. Government Printing Office, 1977),
pp. 29–30.

THE MANAGERIAL PERSPECTIVE

The Problem of Accelerating Obsolescence

Now we must return from our time warp and reenter the present by considering business-society relations from the perspective of the contemporary manager. To set the stage, let me offer an intentionally provocative thesis: The rate
at which a manager becomes obsolete is accelerating (see Exhibit 1–10). Why?
Because of increasing turbulence and complexity in the technological, economic, social, political, and economic environments.

The thesis suggests several things. For example, some of the things
learned by a student of business administration in 1960 are not applicable today; some of the things being learned today will not be applicable tomorrow;

**EXHIBIT 1–10   Potential Obsolescence
among Business Administration Majors**

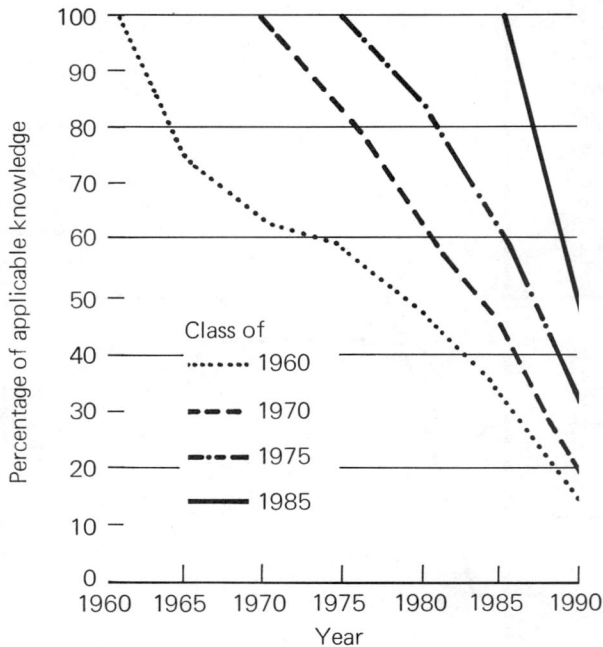

and, perhaps most disturbing of all, some of the things tomorrow's manager will need to know are *not* being taught today.

These three propositions cannot, of course, be proven, at least in the sense that one can prove the Pythagorean theorem. Nonetheless, there is evidence that tends to support all three inferences and, at the very least, puts the burden of proof on anyone who denies their validity.

Exhibit 1–11 attempts to give a synoptic view of how a typical student of business administration, who was graduated in 1970, might have experienced obsolescence. The exhibit also attempts to suggest some ways in which the student today might have a similar experience. I should like to stress rather strongly that the exhibit does not purport to give a 100 percent accurate or complete picture of obsolescence. If only a handful of the items listed in the two columns seems reasonable, then the exhibit has served its purpose. (It would be awkward to try to fully explain here each of the items that appears in the exhibit; however, the majority will be touched on in later chapters.)

Proposals for Combating Obsolescence

The preceding line of inquiry leads us to the rather obvious question of what can be done about obsolescence. Although a completely satisfactory answer is yet to be found, the battle against creeping obsolescence of managers need not end in ignominious defeat. Counterattacks are possible and, like all combat strategies, range from the obvious to the creative, from the straightforward to the sophisticated. Let us consider a few of these strategies.

Individuals can avail themselves of the educational opportunities provided by professional associations: publications, meetings, workshops, and seminars. For instance, the push to get accountants to do more auditing of management fraud prompted Peat, Marwick, Mitchell & Company, the largest CPA firm in the United States, to arrange a two-day session with several dozen representatives from such other professional disciplines as sociology, psychology, and criminology; their task was to uncover new tools that auditors might use to detect management fraud. Or, perhaps with the sponsorship of organizations and associations, managers can participate in university programs. This participation might be no more than an evening refresher course in cost accounting, or it could be thirteen weeks at the Harvard Advancement Management Program or some similar program.

But organizations can do more than periodically send their managers off to school: Adjustments in the work environment can also help to reduce the bite of obsolescence. Jobs can be made challenging: Young managers can be allowed to put their skills to work solving problems, and individuals can be rotated through a variety of assignments. In fact, companies can motivate their personnel at almost no cost simply by improving the organizational climate. This requires a top management commitment to excellence and professional growth, group problem solving, training opportunities, and communication on company goals.

Because of managerial obsolescence, the role of the individual manager in encouraging professional development takes on new importance. Recent surveys find that most managers are noncommital about the value of professional development of their employees. In a sense, this position could mean that the manager fears change and new ideas as rivalry from younger professionals. "The characteristic of the obsolescent manager," says Professor Dubin (in Fowler, 1977), "is that he hires people in his own role model. He is afraid to bring in anyone with more knowledge or competence." But even good managers cannot do it all alone: To effectively spur their subordinates, they need from top management a written policy that outlines the need for updating skills and that rewards staff members who take additional training.

How much time does it take managers to keep updated? According to a study by Dubin, about 20 percent of a person's working day *ought* to be spent keeping up to date. This equivalent of a day's work each week should be spent not only on learning new ideas but also on reviewing significant old ones that have been forgotten.

EXHIBIT 1–11   The Anatomy of Obsolescence in Business Knowledge: A Partial Listing

What was often omitted in 1970	What is being (possibly) omitted today
Economics	
Macroeconomic policies focusing on the augmentation of supplies	Subjective factors in the model of Economic Man
The relationship among energy, ecology, and economics	Effect of consumer and worker expectations on the economy
Stagflation	Increasing technological competition from Japan and Western Europe
Wage and price controls	The New International Economic Order
The no-growth debate	Forecasting inflation
Finance	
Implications of a rapidly changing, uncertain, and inflation-ridden environment for operating leverage	Debt aversion and greater use of internally generated funds
Tax investment credit	Growth of a supernational banking system (stateless money)
Financing R&D	Implications of various tax reform proposals (e.g., Proposition 13) for corporate taxes
Financial instrument figures	
International cash management	Indexation of the whole U.S. economy
Commercial paper market	Interest rate futures
Eurodollars	National Market System (NMS) and International Trading System (ITS)
Accounting	
Inflation accounting (replacement cost accounting)	Consequences of electronic funds transfers ("cashless society")
Government regulation (e.g., ERISA) and disclosure requirement	Expanded scope of auditing
Management	
The representing (or external relations) function	Industrialization of services
Ethics and administrative responsibility	Behavior modeling
Human resources management	Management in different cultural settings; management of "knowledge workers"
Statistics	
Bayesian and other subjective approaches	Determination of factors for computer decision making
Law	
Administrative law; procedures of administrative agencies	Commercial arbitration as a large and growing alternative system of justice
EEO, EPA, OSHA, and many other new laws—and penalties	Concept of "shared monopolies"
Marketing	
Marketing of services	Marketing strategies for penetration of new foreign markets (e.g., Japan)
Caveat Venditor philosophy	Need to pass through costs rapidly; quarterly rather than annual price boosts
Flexible pricing	
Reverse distribution (product recalls)	Stalking overseas markets
Computer Use	
Generally not required	Computers commanded by voice (rather than, say, COBOL)
	Computers based on magnetic bubbles and laser holographic technology
	Satellite Business System (SBS)
	Decision Support Systems (DSS)

These are a few of the things that individuals and companies can do to combat obsolescence. But what can be done in existing programs for business management? The easy answer is to teach students what tomorrow's executive will need to know. To be sure, this is teaching of a high order—but, amazingly, it is not enough. Even if a faculty could know the future, and thus what to teach, there remains the problem of *which* future to teach. Does one prepare for the 1980s or the 1990s or the twenty-first century, when many of today's students will enter their prime?

A Sense of the Future

One answer to managerial obsolescence is to teach a "sense of the future." Although this term lacks precision and is difficult to define, it is recognizable. For example, according to Lewis B. Ward (cited in Livingston, 1971), all but a few Harvard Business School graduates find that their salaries level off fifteen years after graduation; the few who find their salaries continuing to rise dramatically had, in all likelihood, a sense of the future. Better yet, consider the executives profiled in Exhibit 1–12; they were indeed "ahead of their times." As Nelson Rockefeller said in his eulogy to one of them: "In David Sarnoff, the word 'visionary' meant a capacity to see into tomorrow and make it work."

On the other hand, if there are executives ahead of their times, charged with a sense of the future, there must be an opposite group, the "dodo birds" (the label is *Forbes'* not mine). "Because its eyes are in the back of its head, the mythical dodo bird, as opposed to the real one, knows only where it has been but not where it is going. The dodo bird never graces the skies, but many of them grace the boardroom." Executives of this type are like generals prepared to fight yesterday's battles but not today's, or as *Forbes'* description continues:

> This type remembers everything and learns nothing. In the military it insists that the tank will never replace cavalry. In business it insists that the airplane will never replace the pullman car . . . that the tiny TV screen will never replace the glamour of giant movie palaces, that Volkswagen beetles will never sell in the U.S.

This group, in short, has no sense of the future.

EXHIBIT 1–12   Executive Profiles

• **William Blackie** grasped the overseas potential for Caterpillar Tractor in the aftermath of World War II and made the company as multinational in earthmoving as General Motors in cars or International Business Machines in data processing.

• **David Sarnoff** first achieved fame as young telegraph operator by receiving SOS from sinking *Titanic.* Sarnoff became president of Radio Corporation of America in 1930; and when GE spun off RCA shortly thereafter, he turned it into a pioneering home entertainment company, both in broadcasting and manufacturing, both in radio and television.

• **Ralph T. Reed** became president of American Express in 1944, when international trade and travel had been decimated by World War II. Foreseeing an unparalleled boom in both, he expanded fast. The American Express he took over had 50 offices; when he retired in 1960, it had 278 offices and had passed the once far larger Thomas Cook. He introduced the American Express credit card—whose negative float could be neatly balanced by the positive float from travelers' checks.

• **Bernard Kilgore** launched his editorship of the *Wall Street Journal* in 1941 when circulation was a mere 33,000. First as managing editor, later as Dow-Jones Co. president, he turned the *Journal* into a brightly written paper that defined business news as just about anything that happened anywhere. Still bearing the stamp of his genius, the *Journal* today has a literate, affluent circulation of 1.6 million.

• **Owen Cheatham** once said: "Debts get paid off by the harvest, but carefully maintained timberland goes on forever." That principal built Georgia-Pacific Corporation from a small plywood wholesaler into a giant forest-products company.

• When Donald Douglas Sr. hesitated, Boeing's **William M. Allen** acted. His military aircraft company gambled on the 707, beating Douglas into the jet age and wresting from it leadership in commercial aviation.

Source: Adapted from *Forbes,* February 15, 1977.

During the drastic changes of the last several decades, the person who did sense change and knew how to take advantage of it had the edge over alert competitors. Such people not only anticipated change, they helped make it happen. For example, cosmetics are as old as history, but Charles Revson had a way of thinking about his business that put him far ahead of his time—so far ahead that he probably knew what women would respond to before they knew themselves. Revson was fairly unusual in his management style—certainly not a friendly team-leader type. But he was not unique in his ability to anticipate the business future; like a handful of other business leaders, he had, I think, a sense of the future.

Today's management theory still incorporates the belief that large and complex organizations, honeycombed with formal procedures and committees, cannot make important decisions. This is refuted by the record of Standard Oil of New Jersey (now Exxon) and the career of Monroe Jackson Rathbone. When Rathbone started his five-year stint as the company's chief executive in 1960, the industry's and the company's skies were relatively unclouded. Rathbone, however, saw trouble ahead. He believed that the demand for oil, rising faster than new discovery, would convert a glut to scarcity, and that the Middle East oil-producing countries would be able to impose much tougher terms on oil users. Patiently, Rathbone led Jersey's top management to accept his premises and drew from them a logical, though costly, policy conclusion: Jersey should embark on an immense search for oil outside the Middle East. The program cost $700 million, but Exxon now has 19.3 billion barrels of proven reserves outside the Middle East—far more than any other major company. J.K. Jamieson, Exxon's present chief, gratefully says Rathbone's policy was perhaps the most important decision in the company's history (*Fortune*, January 1975).

When we study closely the record of the few individuals who did manage to stay ahead of their time, does any pattern emerge? Without discounting too heavily the element of sheer intuition, I think it can be said that they each had an extraordinary understanding of the macroenvironment of business. They were problem solvers, yes; *but they were also problem finders*. The distinction is crucial.

Problem finding, as J. Sterling Livingston (1971) points out, is more important than problem solving and involves cognitive processes that are very different from problem solving and much more complex. Problem solving and decision making in the classroom require what psychologists call "respondent behavior." It is this type of behavior that enables a person to solve problems that already have been discovered and to make decisions based on facts generated by someone else. But successfully finding problems and opportunities demands a different kind of behavior; psychologists have labeled this second type "operative behavior."

Instruction in problem solving has its shortcomings, but they are not as significant as the failure to teach problem finding. Livingston (1971) writes:

> The importance of a manager's ability to find problems that need to be solved before it is too late is illustrated by the unexpected decline in profits of a number of multimarket companies in 1968 and 1969. The sharp drop in the earnings of one of these companies—Litton Industries—was caused, its chief executive explained, by earlier management deficiencies arising from the failure of those responsible to foresee problems that arose from changes in products, prices, and methods of doing business.

**EXHIBIT 1–13   The Changing Environment of Business:
A Conceptual Framework**

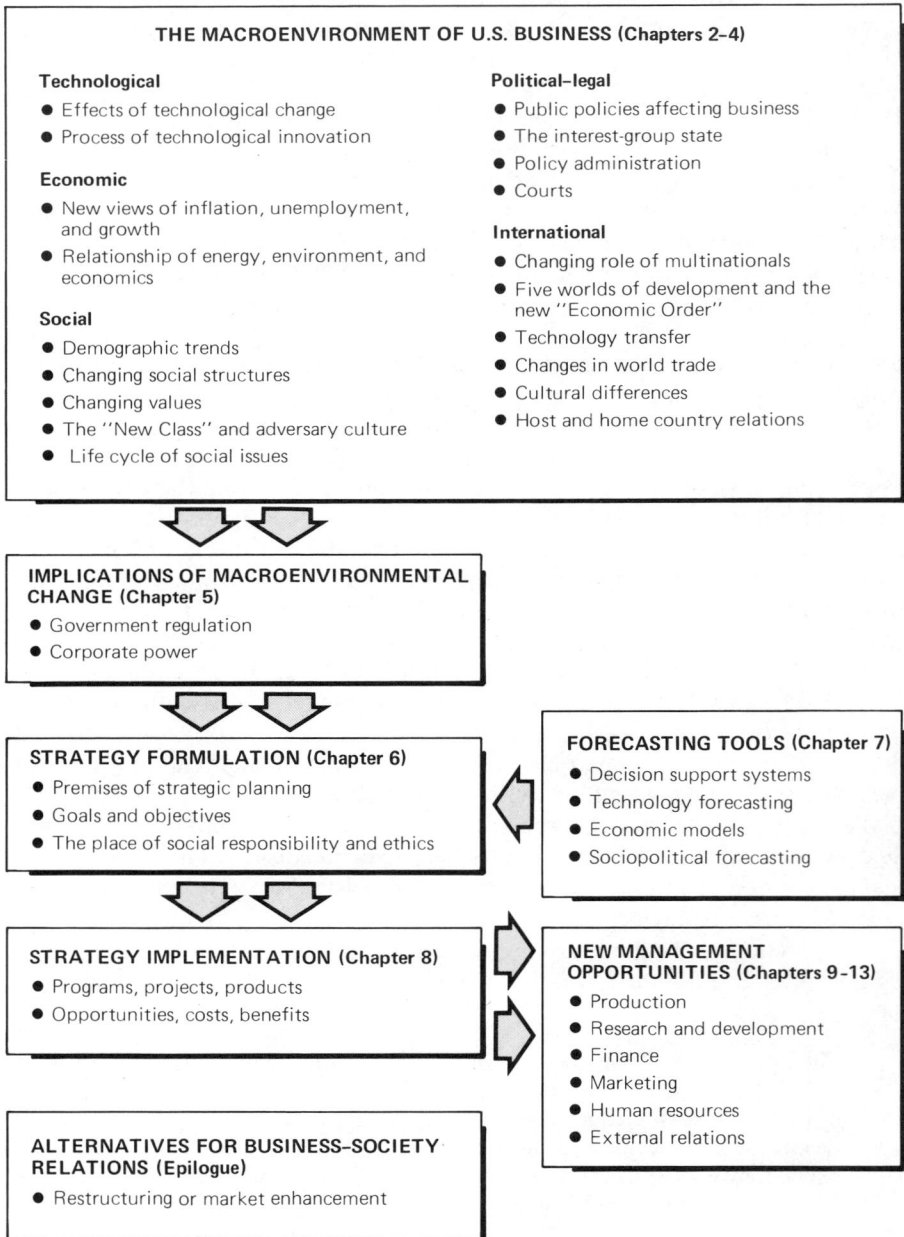

THE MACROENVIRONMENT OF U.S. BUSINESS (Chapters 2–4)

Technological
- Effects of technological change
- Process of technological innovation

Economic
- New views of inflation, unemployment, and growth
- Relationship of energy, environment, and economics

Social
- Demographic trends
- Changing social structures
- Changing values
- The "New Class" and adversary culture
- Life cycle of social issues

Political–legal
- Public policies affecting business
- The interest-group state
- Policy administration
- Courts

International
- Changing role of multinationals
- Five worlds of development and the new "Economic Order"
- Technology transfer
- Changes in world trade
- Cultural differences
- Host and home country relations

IMPLICATIONS OF MACROENVIRONMENTAL CHANGE (Chapter 5)
- Government regulation
- Corporate power

STRATEGY FORMULATION (Chapter 6)
- Premises of strategic planning
- Goals and objectives
- The place of social responsibility and ethics

FORECASTING TOOLS (Chapter 7)
- Decision support systems
- Technology forecasting
- Economic models
- Sociopolitical forecasting

STRATEGY IMPLEMENTATION (Chapter 8)
- Programs, projects, products
- Opportunities, costs, benefits

NEW MANAGEMENT OPPORTUNITIES (Chapters 9–13)
- Production
- Research and development
- Finance
- Marketing
- Human resources
- External relations

ALTERNATIVES FOR BUSINESS-SOCIETY RELATIONS (Epilogue)
- Restructuring or market enhancement

Managers need to be able not only to analyze data in financial statements and written reports, but also to scan the business environment for less concrete clues that a problem exists. They must be able to "read" meaning into changes in method of doing business and into the actions of customers and competitors which may not show up in operating statements for months or even years.

But the skill they need cannot be developed merely by analyzing problems discovered by someone else; rather, it must be acquired by observing firsthand what is taking place in business. While the analytical skills needed for problem solving are important, more crucial to managerial success are the perceptual skills needed to identify problems long before evidence of them can be found by even the most advanced management information system. Since these perceptual skills are extremely difficult to develop in the classroom, they are now largely left to be developed on the job.

LOOKING AHEAD: A CONCEPTUAL FRAMEWORK

If we assume that the foregoing analysis is roughly correct, then a keen understanding of the macroenvironment of business—especially how it changes and how one should cope with that change—becomes an important task of management indeed. The remainder of this book flows directly from the assumptions we have touched upon in this chapter. Exhibit 1–13 provides an overview of how the discussion of the macroenvironment of business will proceed.

We begin in Part II by surveying the five environments external to a private company. Chapter 5 brings this survey to a close by examining two questions: The first concerns government regulation; the second, business power.

In Part III we consider the sometimes awesome problem of how a manager can respond strategically to the challenge of a turbulent environment. In Part IV we take up a wide variety of more specific concerns suggested by the external environment—pollution control, product safety, equal opportunity, and political action committees, to name but a few. These concerns will be approached, not as a laundry list of specific issues, but as a set of problems associated with the traditional functions of most businesses: production and operations, finance, marketing, human resources management, and external relations. In Part V we consider two strikingly different futures for the external environment of business in the United States. Each of these futures has the profoundest of implications for management; our aim will be to make these implications explicit. Part VI, which is not shown in Exhibit 1–13, provides a set of exercises to provide practice in finding and handling the problems of a changing business environment.

THE MACROENVIRONMENT OF U.S. BUSINESS (Chapters 2–4)

Technological
- Effects of technological change
- Process of technological innovation

Economic
- New views of inflation, unemployment, and growth
- Relationship of energy, environment, and economics

Social
- Demographic trends
- Changing social structures
- Changing values
- The "New Class" and adversary culture
- Life cycle of social issues

Political–legal
- Public policies affecting business
- The interest-group state
- Policy administration
- Courts

International
- Changing role of multinationals
- Five worlds of development and the new "Economic Order"
- Technology transfer
- Changes in world trade
- Cultural differences
- Host and home country relations

IMPLICATIONS OF MACROENVIRONMENTAL CHANGE (Chapter 5)
- Government regulation
- Corporate power

STRATEGY FORMULATION (Chapter 6)
- Premises of strategic planning
- Goals and objectives
- The place of social responsibility and ethics

FORECASTING TOOLS (Chapter 7)
- Decision support systems
- Technology forecasting
- Economic models
- Sociopolitical forecasting

STRATEGY IMPLEMENTATION (Chapter 8)
- Programs, projects, products
- Opportunities, costs, benefits

NEW MANAGEMENT OPPORTUNITIES (Chapters 9–13)
- Production
- Research and development
- Finance
- Marketing
- Human resources
- External relations

ALTERNATIVES FOR BUSINESS–SOCIETY RELATIONS (Epilogue)
- Restructuring or market enhancement

ENVIRONMENTAL ANALYSIS FOR MANAGEMENT

PART **II**

CHAPTER TWO

Understanding Change in the Technological, Economic, and Social Environments

"Results are obtained," Peter Drucker (1974) writes, "by exploiting opportunities, not by solving problems. All one can hope to get by solving a problem is to restore normalcy." But, to exploit opportunity, managers must first appreciate what is happening outside their organizations—not only in the immediate environment of customers and competitors but also in the macroenvironment.

Consider for a moment how crucial changes in the macroenvironment can be to the future of an organization: New technologies arise out of completely correlated industries, raw material supplies dry up or become prohibitively expensive, interest rates go up, people change their buying or living habits, laws are passed, regulations are promulgated, foreign trade patterns shift. The list goes on.

Although these kinds of changes are evolutionary and seldom come quickly, most managers tend to see them rather late, when response times are short. This need not be. By understanding better the ways in which change occurs in the macroenvironment, managers should be able to discern impending changes earlier. Therefore, the aim of this chapter and the two that follow is to explore the dynamics of change in each of the five environments of Exhibit 1–3. Later, in Chapter 7, we shall be interested in exploring analytical techniques for forecasting change, but here our discussion is limited to the goal of gaining a better understanding of what the five environments consist of, how they change, and what it all means to the manager.

The first environment we take up in this chapter is the technological one. We consider several examples of how technological change presents opportunities as well as threats to management. Examples are both general and specific, and they are drawn from the future as well as the past. The section concludes with a model of how technological changes occur. This model consists of eight stages that run from the basic scientific breakthrough in the laboratory to the widespread adoption of a technical device in society and its application to other uses.

Next, we consider the economic environment and how it affects the profits and decisions of business decisionmakers. The discussion is action oriented and builds around three topics: the meaning of inflation, productivity, unemployment, and growth; the analysis of economic policy debates; and the building of economic models.

Finally, we explore social change in terms of aggregate attributes (e.g., population), social structures (e.g., the family), and cultural patterns (e.g., values). For each, we shall try to see how they are measured, how they change, and what it all means for the manager. Then, as with the technological and economic environments, we consider a model that helps us understand the dynamics of how changes occur in this environment. This model, the "Life Cycle of Social Issues," will prove to be one of the most important and useful concepts introduced in this book. Mark it well. ☐

THE TECHNOLOGICAL ENVIRONMENT

Changes in the technological environment are probably not only the fastest unfolding, but also the most far-reaching in extending or contracting opportunity for a company. Today few industries have a truly stable technological base protecting them from change; traditional products, materials, skills, and production facilities become obsolete in a few years or, in some cases, a few months. The massive efforts of Continental Can to keep its technology competitive is a case in point. Not without reason, this corporation changed its name in 1976 to the Continental Group.

Moreover, technological change increases cross-industry pressure. Thus, the steel industry must be concerned with technological development in the plastics and aluminum industries as well as in the steel-making process itself. Increasingly, a large part of any one company's sales growth will come out of another company's market share, rather than from any automatic expansion of the total market. This means, according to Philip Kotler, that there will be less emphasis on imitative, "me-too" products and more on products that are really new and preemptive in technology. Technological change determines more than what next year's product line will be; it can also radically reorder the internal management processes of a company.

Thousands of businesses are going to rise or fall on the ability of their managers to respond effectively to technological change; in many businesses, such as aerospace and electronics, technological change will be the most important force. How can managements understand this environment and cope with it wisely? While no one has yet found a certain way to success and security in this technological ferment, the beginning of wisdom for managers is probably a keen awareness of, and receptivity to, technological change as a major environmental force that they can employ and *must* respond to.

Effects of Technological Change

The following list (adapted from Bright, 1963) provides a good indication of just how multifarious are the ways in which changes in the technological environment can potentially affect a company:

1. Effects of increased transportation capability: Mastery of greater distances in less time or cost; movement and operations in space, under seas, and in the arctic regions.
2. Effects of growing mechanization of physical activity: Cheaper production costs; wider distribution; more rapid movement of paper and mail; recording and assembly of data; advances in recovery of fossil fuels.
3. Effects of increased mastery of energy: Availability of greater magnitudes and intensity of power; availability of minute quantities of energy, controlled with increased precision; generation and distribution of power from new sources and by new devices; advances in storage of energy; new techniques for large-scale transportation of fuels and electric power.
4. Effects of increased ability to alter characteristics of materials: New properties for old materials; synthetic materials; combinations of materials to provide new and unique characteristics.
5. Effects of increased ability to extend, control, and alter life: Longer life for living things and perishable foods; new products from gene transplants.

6. Effects of extension of human sensory capabilities: Advances in vision, via electronics; in hearing, via amplification techniques; in touch, via power controls; in power of discrimination, via instrumentation to detect minute quantities and dimensions; in memory, via recording and duplication.
7. Effects of growing mechanization of intellectual processes: Direction of intricate and extended machine processes; information processing; problem solving.

If this summary seems too general, then consider the effects of technological change on two specific fields: space manufacturing and telecommunications.

Space Manufacturing. In near-earth space, where a satellite can be placed in stationary orbit rotating in unison with the earth, NASA sees the possibility of an industrial bonanza. Operating in this pure and gravity-free environment, spacelabs can manufacture novel materials worth as much as thirty thousand dollars a pound on earth. Some enthusiasts, especially those in West Germany and Japan, call space manufacturing the key to opening up the next industrial revolution.

How could business benefit? Because of the adverse effects of gravity, material manufacturers have never been able to achieve the strength and other mechanical properties for metals that theory predicts. Steels, for instance, could be anywhere from 100 to 1,000 times stronger than they are today. Parts of jet engines now fall apart at temperatures where the efficiency of engine operations would be higher. The wires in heart pacemakers and the pins of bone prosthetics fail much sooner than they should. In the weightlessness of outer space, most of these problems in the processing of materials disappear. Gene Bylinsky (1979) reports on still other possibilities:

> In certain compositional ranges, metals such as copper and lead, or aluminum and lead, would display self-lubricating properties, possibly leading to automobile engines that could last 500,000 miles and more. BMW, the West German automaker, has shown an interest in financing some experiments with aluminum-lead combinations.
>
> The most immediately promising field for materials processing in space is the culture of crystals, which have become the sum and substance of modern electronics and electro-optics. Crystal culture here on earth is generally not a science but an art. Impurities (called dopants) which impart the desired electronic properties to a semiconductor crystal, are difficult to distribute evenly on earth because of convection currents induced by gravity. Consequently, the yield of usable chips from a crystal is low. What can be accomplished in space was shown dramatically aboard Skylab, and on the Apollo-Soyuz flight, where experiments produced remarkably smooth samples of crystals.
>
> Space holds vast possibilities for biology and medicine. Microgravity should greatly improve man's ability to separate specific cell types, cell compo-

nents, cell products, and proteins. Vaccines may attain a purity not possible on earth.

Telecommunications. Much closer to home, rapid developments in telecommunications are changing the way the American business office operates; where there was once a secretary armed only with typewriter, paper, and eraser, now there is word processing. Consider the following office scenario for the 1990s from a recent advertisement for word processing (Mandell, 1978):

> All executives have multifunction terminals. The ultimate dictation system— computer-based voice recognition—allows draft documents to be output directly from spoken words. The words first appear on the terminal's display for editing and revision by the author; then they are run through a dictionary and a grammar/syntax validator before the final draft is ready to be sent (via electronic mail) anywhere in the world—with a duplicate automatically filed in a micrographics storage system. As a matter of course, no paper is used.

As computers become smaller and telephone systems more advanced, experts believe people will need to spend less time in the office. By 1990 mobile phone service will be able to accommodate more than a million customers and meet the growing demand of people whose business takes them away from their desks. Portable computer terminals are also being used by an increasing number of companies for employees on the go. In the years ahead, observers believe many more executives and staff members will be working away from offices, using portable terminals, and thus saving commuting time and gasoline.

Three basic technologies are involved in the telecommunications revolution. First is the *computer,* which each year grows cheaper, smaller, and more reliable. It is estimated that since the early 1950s, the physical size of computers has diminished by a factor of about 1,000, the costs have dropped a hundredfold, and the capacity has grown by a factor of 1,500. Ruth Davis (1977) has described the results of these changes. In 1950 the federal government ordered its first two big computers; today there are 220,000 computers in the United States (40 percent of them medium to large size) manned by 2.5 million computer professionals.

The second key technical development is the *high-altitude communication satellite,* which can transmit directly to rooftop antennas. In a world where large numbers of nations in Africa, South America, and Asia are unable to afford conventional television broadcast stations, the social and educational possibilities are enormous. In another application, Satellite Business Systems, Inc., a company established by IBM and Aetna Insurance, has won permission from the Federal Communication Commission* to launch a satellite that

---

* See Appendix A for a brief description of major federal laws and regulatory agencies.

would permit corporations to transmit data between offices and factories all over the United States without employees ever having to pick up a telephone or go near a post office. Local TV stations might be bypassed by beaming TV signals directly into homes, as Japan and Canada already are doing experimentally.

The third, and possibly most significant, new technology is the use of *glass fibers* to carry voice, data, and video signals. This technology is now being pursued by American Telephone & Telegraph, the International Telephone & Telegraph Corporation, Siemans A.G. of Germany, Nippon Electric, and Corning Glass. According to virtually all experts, fiber optics is expected to cost less than coaxial cable, to be far smaller and lighter, and to be capable of transmitting far more information.

What is fiber optics? *Fiber optics* deals with the transmission of light and images, around bends and curves, through a flexible bundle of plastic optical fibers. Assuming the resolution of the remaining technical problems, such as how to achieve simple splices, many experts believe that within a few years AT&T can begin a program to replace the copper telephone wire running into almost every building with fiber optics, which would be able to carry two-way television, a variety of two-way teletype services, dozens of conventional television channels, and telephone messages.

The combined impact of these new technologies on business operations will be enormous, most experts agree. For example, the threat these technological changes present to the Xerox Corporation is awesome. What Xerox must do is make a transition from the office of today to the office of tomorrow, where the mountains of paper work it helped to create will have melted into an uncluttered world where files are stored electronically and mail zips from desk to desk via computers and television screens. The risk in moving into this potentially lucrative "automated office" is that Xerox must deemphasize the field of copying, in which it dominates, and venture into one already dominated by a tiger four times its size, IBM.

Forecasting changes such as these may seem extremely difficult—even naive. Nonetheless, managers must somehow try to anticipate technological progress. Forecasting efforts, however, can be greatly enhanced if we are clear on the process through which technology emerges into social use. This process is called *technological innovation.*

The Process of Technological Innovation

Technological innovation embraces all those activities by which technical knowledge is translated into physical reality and becomes used on a scale having a substantial effect on society (see Exhibit 2–1). Several things need to be noted about this definition. First, it includes more than just the act of invention. Technological innovation also includes the initiation of the technical idea, the acquisition of the necessary knowledge, its transformation into usable

EXHIBIT 2–1   Stages in the Process of Technological Innovation

	Stage	Identified by	Comment
Research, Basic	1	Scientific suggestion, discovery, recognition of need or opportunity	The latter source seems to be the origin of the majority of contemporary innovations.
	2	Proposal of theory or design concept	The crystallization of the theory or design concept that is ultimately successful is usually the culmination of much trial and error.
Research, Applied	3	Laboratory verification of theory or design concept	The existence or the operational validity of the concept suggested in the previous stage is verified. The concept may be difficult for the forecaster to assess, since the thing demonstrated usually is a phenomenon rather than an application.
	4	Laboratory demonstration of application	The principle is embodied in a laboratory "breadboard" model of the device (or sample material or its process equivalent), which shows the theory of stage 2 applied to perform a desired function or purpose.
Development	5	Full-scale or field trial	The concept moves from the laboratory bench into its first trial on a large scale. A succession of prototypes follows, leading eventually to a salable model.
	6	Commercial introduction or first operational use	The first sale of an operational system may be deliberate or unconscious premature application of the previous stage and thus be replete with debugging problems.
Production and Marketing	7	Widespread adoption as indicated by substantial profits, common usage, significant impact	This stage is not sharply defined. An individual firm might choose to classify this as recovering its R&D investment through profits on the sale of the innovation or simply the achievement of profitability.
	8	Proliferation	The technical device is applied to other uses (e.g., the adapting of radar to police highway patrol work), or the principle is adapted to different purposes (e.g., radar microwave technology is adapted to cooking ovens).

Source: James R. Bright, *A Guide to Practical Technological Forecasting* (Englewood Cliffs, N.J.: Prentice-Hall, 1973), pp. 3–12. Reprinted by permission of the author.

hardware or procedure, and its introduction into society (Bright, 1973). This definition is not restricted to physical things, but includes intellectual concepts such as operations research, decision theory, flexible work weeks, and no-fault automobile insurance.

Second, the full process takes time measured in years—even decades. Some authorities agree that the process may be getting shorter, but generally speaking, stages 1 through 3 still involve many years. Moving from stage 6 to 7 is almost certain to take up to five years. For example, xerography took about eighteen years to move from stage 1 to 7, and another five to achieve the goal of producing an office copier. Integrated circuits, however, took only twelve years to move from stage 1 through 7, and the laser reached stage 6 in about five years.

Third, external events and other environments influence the innovation process decisively. For example, the political-legal environment certainly shaped the future of the SST, high-speed passenger trains, DDT, and cyclamates. Likewise, cultural values of Americans doomed to failure Ford's efforts in 1957 to emphasize safety in their automobiles (see Exhibit 2–2 for some illustrations of technological innovation).

EXHIBIT 2–2   Illustrating the Process of Technological Innovation

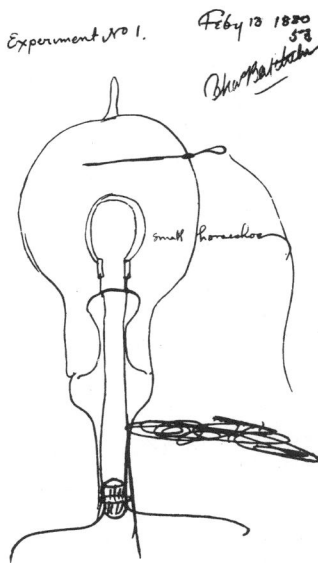

Stage 2: Proposal of Theory

Stage 3: Laboratory Verification

Stage 4: Laboratory Demonstration

Stage 5: Full-Scale Trial

Stage 2 shows an early sketch of an incandescent lamp, which appeared in Edison's notebook dated 13 February 1880. It is probably the first illustration of the bulb that eventually became the electron tube. Stage 3 is a replica of Edison's experimental lamp of 1883. It was demonstrated in 1884 at an electrical exhibition in Philadelphia. The patent for this lamp, which was granted to Edison in the same year, was the first patent in electronics. Stage 4 shows an experimental model of the type used in outdoor tests of preliminary VTOL (Vertical Takeoff and Landing) designs. Crude as this flying framework may seem, it told the designers what they needed to know. Stage 5 is a multiple-exposure photograph of the VTOL taking off; it shows the transition from vertical to horizontal flight. Thus, we can see what the experimental VTOL to the left looked like when it was sold to the U.S. Army.

Source: Stage 2 and 3 photos courtesy of Edison National Historic Site, West Orange, New Jersey; stage 4 photo, NASA, courtesy of Lockheed-California Company, Burbank; stage 5 photo © Ryan Aeronautical, a division of Teledyne, Inc.

Two things to note about the process of technological innovation as depicted in Exhibit 2–1 are, first, the process does not always unfold in a smooth, linear manner. There can often be great delays between the stages. For example, the U.S. Patent Office in 1902 issued a patent for a process to manufacture plate glass by floating a continuous ribbon of glass, as it moves out of the melting furnace, along the surface of a bath of molten tin. But it was clear that the inventor had not produced an operative process; he was stuck at stage 3. It was not until fifty-two years later that Alastair Pilkington was able to conduct a successful laboratory verification of the process and thus complete stage 4. In other cases, researchers find it necessary to retrace their steps—that is, to move back from stage 5 to stage 4, or even to stage 2. In still other cases, the idea might be abandoned altogether. In fact, abandonment of a technological proposal is more likely than not.

The second thing to note about the process of technological innovation is that it does not unfold in a vacuum. Developments in different technologies often affect one another. The classic example here is the effect that transistors have had on the development of computers. Also, lasers have already enhanced development in fusion-energy research. And microprocessors have even managed to have an impact on the stodgy technology of the American automobile industry.

This complex and incompletely understood process in which developments in one area of technology affect those in another area is an instance of *technology transfer*. Generally defined, technology transfer involves any communication in which the message contains technological elements. (Chapter 4 considers international transfers of technological information.)

Surely, a great deal more ought to be said about technology. The preceding discussion is by no means the last word on the subject, but it suffices for what we said were the modest aims of this chapter. See the last section of Chapter 10 for a further treatment of the technological issue.

THE ECONOMIC ENVIRONMENT

Broad economic developments, like technological ones, pose both problems and opportunities for managers. An expanding economy, of course, has a direct effect on the demand for a company's product; it also facilitates the establishment of new companies. As growth continues, however, the mix of consumer demand shifts from food and shelter to consumer durables and to the second automobile and the electric carving knife. But even this kind of consumption can taper off as people begin to spend for leisure activities and shop for items that offer convenience, beauty, and ego satisfaction as well as performance.

A major slowdown or cessation in growth, on the other hand, can bring failure, as was common in the late 1960s and early 1970s, though companies offering lower-priced goods can do very well during slow periods. Indeed, during the recession of 1969–70, retailers such as Kresge, Penney, and Woolworth had sales gains, as did sellers of used cars, copying equipment, wedding gown rental services, and fabrics for making one's own clothes.

Negative economic development can influence more than the demand for a company's goods and services. For example, a planned stock issue may have to be curtailed; a planned borrowing, perhaps for expansion, may prove too expensive (because of the higher interest rates); or plans for a new plant may need to be scaled down (because of inflationary spirals in the construction industry).

Sometimes the effects of negative economic developments affect the company later rather than immediately. Obviously, these delayed effects make managerial decision making more difficult. What steps should be taken *now*? Should a firm curtail production, cut back on inventories, or cut research and development? McCarthy, Minichiello, and Curran (1975:189) write:

> These steps can have major implications if unwisely taken, or similarly if they are not taken .... Thus in assessing economic factors, management must be careful not only to consider those that influence the firm's longer run ability to satisfy that demand. For example, increases in the costs of a firm's capital resulting from a change in general economic conditions such as occurred in 1974 can interfere with plans to construct a new plant, thus limiting the firm's ability to satisfy expected future demand. Increases in financial costs might also cause a cutback in expenditures for research and development, the consequences of which might take several years to become significant.

The case for surveillance of general economic conditions is, therefore, a solid one.

The remainder of this section is devoted to topics necessary for understanding the economic environment. First, we discuss the meaning of basic concepts—inflation, productivity, unemployment, and growth—since effective understanding requires that words should convey the meaning intended. The analysis of economic policy debates, our second topic for discussion, provides the principles of logical thinking essential to understanding changing economic conditions. Third, understanding economic problems requires discussion of the tools of the economist, especially model building (see Robinson, Morton, and Calderwood, 1967).

Understanding Basic Concepts

Inflation. In economics a great deal of confusion arises because terms mean different things to different people. Let us begin by examining the concept of *inflation*. The battles against Enemy No. 1 have been muddled by a good deal of ignorance on all sides. If we start with the question of who has been hurt, a good case can be made that, thus far, no important group has been seriously hurt. Real income per person, after taxes, has gone up every bit as much in the high-inflation period of 1973–1978 as in the preceding six years.*

Moreover, the years of inflation have apparently done relatively little to alter the income shares going to the rich, the poor, and the middle class. According to Lester Thurow (*Forbes,* January 8, 1979), consumer income numbers from the Commerce Department ". . . show essentially no change in the distribution of money incomes between rich and poor. The top 40 percent of the population had 69.5 percent of the total income in 1972 and 69.6 percent in 1977. The bottom 40 percent of the population had 13.7 percent in 1972 and 13.8 percent in 1977." Looked at in another way, however, inflation has hurt one group—the corporations. Thurow finds that since 1972 the corporations' net share of GNP has fallen from 7.6 percent to 7.1 percent, primarily because of larger interest payments (a direct consequence of higher inflation).

The fact that the distribution of income has not changed means that the entire economy, not just parts of it, is in effect *indexed to inflation.* So, the good news is that inflation is easier to bear and less of a distortion than most people believe. And the bad news is this: Inflation is extraordinarily hard to stop. As Thurow puts it: "If the economy is indexed, an 8 percent rate of inflation today leads to 8 percent wage and price hikes tomorrow. But as a result, inflation is 8 percent tomorrow."

On balance, therefore, the news is bad. The cold fact is that inflation contributes to *uncertainty,* which makes business reluctant to invest. Moreover, when the U.S. inflation rate runs higher than the rate in Japan or Germany, the dollar suffers. Finally, unless the United States fights inflation, the problem will get worse: Each shock pushes inflation up a notch, and the index nature of the economy keeps it there. Clearly, a level of inflation similar to that in some Latin American countries would be dangerous to American society. Hence, we have a paradox: The United States can live with inflation, but it ought not accept it.

Productivity. Most economists agree that inflation is gravely worsened by Enemy No. 2: sagging *productivity.* During most of the 1960s, the U.S. economy grew rapidly, with low unemployment and low inflation. But in the 1970s the economy grew much less rapidly, with high unemployment and high inflation. Why the difference between the decades? One trend seems especially important in explaining the difference: The growth of productivity—that is, the output per hour worked—has slowed sharply in the 1970s. Exhibit 2–3 shows how productivity growth has fallen significantly in many industries over the past several years. Indeed, since 1976, it has almost stopped. For example, in

---

* Disposable income per capita (expressed in constant 1972 dollars) rose by $563, to $3,837, from 1966 to 1972. Since then, it has gone up another $571, to an estimated $4,408 in 1978. Of course, the rate of increase slowed from 17.2 percent over six years to 14.9 percent. But the gain, absolutely, was just as big.

EXHIBIT 2–3   Productivity Growth by Industry, 1950–1977

Industry	1977 output share (percent)*	Percent change per year		
		1950 to 1965	1965 to 1973	1973 to 1977
Agriculture	2.9	4.9	3.6	3.0
Mining	1.5	4.3	1.9	−6.1
Construction	4.3	3.4	−2.1	0.3
Manufacturing				
Nondurable	9.9	3.2	3.3	2.2
Durable	14.4	2.5	2.2	1.2
Transportation	3.9	3.0	2.9	1.0
Communication	3.2	5.3	4.6	6.7
Utilities	2.3	6.1	3.5	0.2
Trade				
Wholesale	7.3	2.6	3.4	−0.8
Retail	10.0	2.3	2.1	0.8
Finance, insurance, and real estate	15.4	1.6	0.2	2.3
Services	12.0	1.2	1.7	−0.3
Government	12.5	0.4	0.5	0.1

Note: Growth data relate to output per hour worked for all persons.
* May not add to 100 percent because of rounding.

Source: U.S. Department of Commerce, Bureau of Economic Analysis; and Council of Economic Advisers, *Economic Report of the President* (Washington, D.C.: U.S. Government Printing Office, 1979), p. 71.

1978 productivity grew only .4 percent, whereas in the 1960s it rose on the average about 3 percent a year.

The annual report of the President's Council of Economic Advisers (CEA) submitted to Congress in 1979 pessimistically suggests that the U.S. economy may be entering a new era in which productivity growth for many years will average no more than 1.5 percent. The implications of this prediction for American business are cause for no small concern. When each worker produces more, then total output will grow rapidly and employers can raise wages without also raising prices; the rise in output per employee will offset the higher costs. If productivity is flat, almost every dollar of wage gains is translated into price boosts.

In the short run, low productivity can create jobs as more workers are needed to supply rising demand, but in the long run low productivity hurts employment too. In the 1960s it was thought that the economy could grow 4 percent each year without setting off inflation. Mostly because of the collapse in productivity, the CEA's 1979 *Economic Report* considers a safe growth ceiling to be 3 percent. An economy growing that slowly cannot create enough jobs for all the people who are looking for work.

Why has productivity grown so sluggishly? The CEA (1979:67–72) suggests at least four reasons: excessive regulation, reduced R&D expenditures, a changing work force, and inadequate investment. Companies have had to pour more and more money into costly antipollution equipment and devote increasing attention to complying with health and safety rules, rather than buy productive machinery and establish more efficient operating methods. Although lives undoubtedly have been saved and the air and water cleansed, the CEA estimates that regulation may be cutting annual nonfarm productivity growth by four-tenths of a percentage point.

In 1964 research and development spending accounted for 3 percent of the gross national product; in 1978 the share was down to 2.2 percent. The toll on productivity is hard to calculate, since it would have to be measured in inventions not made and labor-saving processes not developed, but it surely has been high.

Since the mid-1960s women and youths born during the postwar baby boom have flooded the job market. Many lacked the training and experience to become highly productive workers in their first few years. By the CEA's estimate, industry's reliance on them to fill jobs has lowered productivity more than a third of a point per year. Also, as noted in Chapter 1, the work force contains a higher proportion of service and information workers. It seems harder for doctors, credit counselors, teachers, and the like to raise, or even measure, their productivity than for, say, steelworkers to do so.

Between 1948 and 1973, business spending on new plant and equipment added 3 percent a year to the capital investment supporting each hour of work. Since then this capital-labor ratio has increased only 1.75 percent annually. Economists argue fiercely whether the chief reason has been tax policies that favor consumption over investment or the business fear that recession and inflation will wipe out the profit on new investment. In either case, the result has been to slow the introduction of cost-cutting, labor-saving machinery and, according to CEA, to slash the growth of productivity by half a percentage point each year.

Unemployment. Like inflation, the concept of *unemployment* means different things to different people. The amount of hardship associated with unemployment varies greatly from individual to individual. As Herbert Stein (1978) reminds us, the concept and measurement of unemployment used in the United States was initiated in 1939, when Franklin Roosevelt was president. Roosevelt himself was amazed to learn what was included in the new unemployment statistics his government was publishing:

> "Do you mean to say," he asked a member of his staff, "that if my neighbor on Park Avenue has a daughter who graduates from Vassar and looks for a job as

senior editor of *Vogue,* which she is unable to get, that she is counted as unemployed?"

Roosevelt could hardly believe that the answer was yes. He had fought against unemployment for years, as a political campaigner and as a President. His thinking, language, and policy had been premised on a certain picture of what unemployment was like. The idea that the Vassar graduate was one of the unemployed was a threat to that picture.

Roosevelt's concept of unemployment, and the concept of many who lived through the 1930s, was of a head-of-household, probably male, who had lost his job, who had been out of work for a long time, whose family was very poor, and who was willing and eager to take any kind of work for any wage.

Today the fact that there are systematic biases in official unemployment statistics is slowly gaining recognition. While widespread agreement on the need for full employment continues, there is less agreement on just what full employment is, how unemployment should be defined, and what specific data should be used in judging the performance of the economy. There is even disagreement on whether the focus should be on *unemployment* or *employment* statistics. The media and the professional literature have focused mostly on unemployment. This focus has led analysts who believe the emphasis should be placed on employment to entitle the debate "the doughnut or the hole?"

Unemployment figures are used by many persons for different purposes. Many use them to assess current conditions and short-term prospects—that is, as a cyclical indicator (see Chapter 7). Others use the data as a measure of how well the economy relieves the economic and psychological hardships experienced by job seekers. But judgments as to what constitutes hardship arising from unemployment vary greatly among different groups. Some view economic hardship in terms of the three basic elements of food, clothing, and shelter. Others consider it in terms of relative standing in the income distribution and classify all people who fall in, say, the lowest one-fifth of the range as experiencing economic hardship. Still others consider unemployed people with adequate income from sources other than employment to be experiencing psychological hardship if they cannot find a job and are therefore denied an opportunity for a fuller life in some sense. Further, many believe long spells of unemployment for teenagers to be especially damaging to young people's development as responsible members of society.

Thus, no single way of measuring unemployment can satisfy all analytical or ideological interests. To meet the multiple needs of data users, the Bureau of Labor Statistics regularly publishes a wide variety of unemployment rates. It also publishes separate data on people involuntarily working less than full time and on discouraged workers, which can be added to the figures on the unemployed by those who wish to do so. Exhibit 2–4 presents a grouping of unemployment indicators, or categories of the unemployed, identified by the symbols U–1 through U–7.

Employment statistics also provide information for analysis and have numerous advantages over unemployment figures. In December 1977 the U.S.

EXHIBIT 2–4   Range of Unemployment Indicators Reflecting Value Judgments about Significance of Unemployment, 1974–1975

| | | Annual averages | |
	Indicator	1974	1975
U–1	Persons unemployed 15 weeks or longer as a percent of total civilian labor force	1.0	2.7
U–2	Job losers as a percent of civilian labor force	2.4	4.7
U–3	Unemployed household heads as a percent of the household head labor force	3.3	5.8
U–4	Unemployed full-time job seekers as a percent of the full-time labor force (including those employed part time for economic reasons)	5.1	8.1
U–5	Total unemployed as a percent of civilian labor force (official measure)	5.6	8.5
U–6	Total full-time job seekers plus half part-time job seekers plus half total on part time for economic reasons as a percent of civilian labor force less half part-time labor force	6.9	10.3
U–7	Total full-time job seekers plus half part-time job seekers plus half total on part time for economic reasons plus discouraged workers as a percent of civilian labor force plus discouraged workers less half of part-time labor force	7.7	11.5

Note: Reflects recent revisions of basic data, including seasonal experience through December 1975.

Source: Julius Shisken, "Employment and Unemployment: The Doughnut or the Hole?" U.S. Labor Department, *Monthly Labor Review* 99, no. 2 (February 1976):3–10.

economy managed to generate jobs for a larger portion of the country's working-age population than at any previous time on record. This figure—known among economists as the country's *employment ratio*—had reached 58 percent; in other words, 58 percent of the age-sixteen-and-over citizenry held at least one job. Yet, in the same month, unemployment amounted to 6.4 percent of the labor force—high enough to sound more like a recession rate than a rate prevailing after nearly three years of economic expansion.

The explanation for this apparent contradiction is the enormous flow of women into the labor force. Today about half of the country's population of adult females work or are seeking work, while only about one-third were in the labor force in the early years after World War II (Malabre, 1978).

A glance at some data from abroad also indicates the U.S. economy's extraordinary ability to generate jobs. Exhibit 2–5 is based on data compiled by the U.S. Labor Department. The figures are adjusted so that definitional distinctions are eliminated. They represent an average for a recent twelve-month

EXHIBIT 2–5   Employment Population Ratios and Unemployment Rates in the United States and Selected European Countries, 1975

Country	Employment ratio	Unemployment rate
United States	57%	7.7%
France	54%	4.6%
West Germany	51%	3.6%
Italy	46%	3.6%

Source: Data published by U.S. Labor Department, Bureau of Labor Statistics, in *Employment and Earnings,* on a quarterly basis.

period. The first column shows employment ratios for the various countries, and the second shows unemployment rates.

Such comparisons cause Malabre (1978) to raise an interesting question:

> It is often assumed that an economy with a jobless rate of, say, 3 percent is healthier than one with, say, over six percent joblessness. But is this necessarily so? In early 1953, U.S. unemployment stood at only 2.5 percent of the labor force, and yet the employment ratio, at about 55 percent, was lower than now. If all working-age Americans not currently at work or seeking employment were to rush out today in search of jobs, the country's unemployment rate, quite obviously, would soar to depression levels. But would the economy really be less healthy?

Growth. In the preceding discussion of inflation, productivity, unemployment, and employment, we made several references to one popular measure of *economic growth,* the gross national product. What does it mean? Let us give the standard definition and then consider the limitations of the concept.

In computing GNP, economists count only the production of final goods and services. As can be seen in Exhibit 2–6, there are four major components of GNP: consumer spending, business outlays on investment, government spending, and net exports (i.e., the difference between exports and imports). We can also see from the exhibit that since 1929 when GNP was first measured, consumer spending has ballooned. (This category of GNP includes all consumer spending financed by government transfers—for example, welfare, Social Security, and unemployment insurance.) Direct purchases by government have also grown briskly. Meanwhile, business investment has shrunk as a proportion of total spending. As was noted earlier, this shrinkage is one of the factors in the productivity decline, and as will become apparent in subsequent chapters, it is not the only adverse effect of the decline in business in-

EXHIBIT 2–6   How the GNP Has Grown

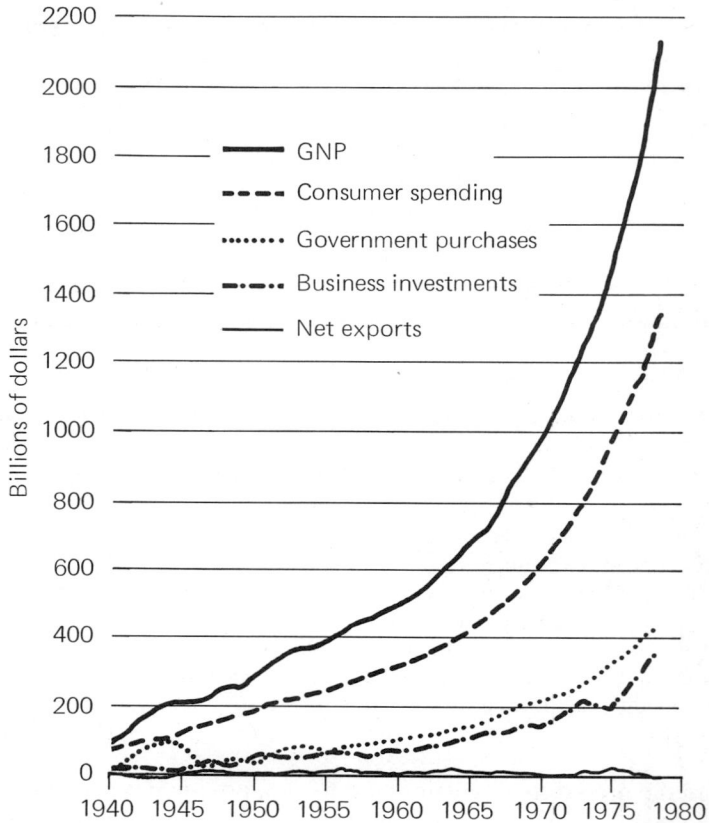

Source: Data from Council of Economic Advisers, *Economic Report of the President* (Washington, D.C.: U.S. Government Printing Office, 1979), p. 183.

vestment. Exhibit 2–7 might also prove helpful in understanding what the GNP really is and, especially, in seeing its relationship to other macroeconomic measures.

As an aid in helping us understand growth, GNP is not without limitations. Since the number must be pieced together from incomplete data, it is riddled with error: The GNP, in fact, must constantly be revised. In fact, the Department of Commerce calculates that by the time its preliminary estimate of the real GNP growth rate in any given quarter goes through its first annual revision, the figure might fall by as much as 1.9 percentage points or rise by up to 2 percentage points. For example, suppose the first estimate shows a healthy

EXHIBIT 2–7   The Flow of Spending

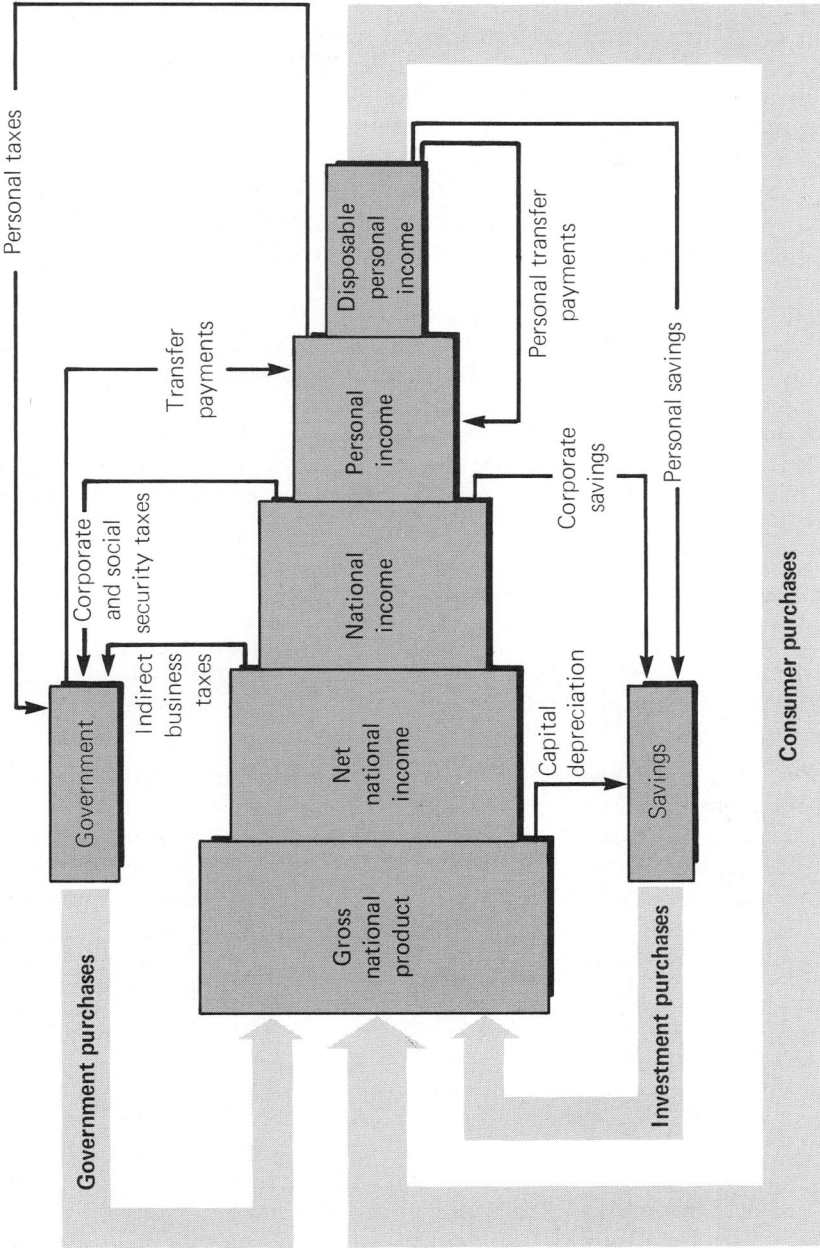

growth rate of 4 percent. By the time of the first annual revision, that 4 percent
may transform itself into an anemic 2.1 percent or a robust 6 percent (Meadows, 1978:100). Revisions are an inescapable fact of life at the Commerce Department's Bureau of Economic Analysis, where the statistics for gross national product are produced. The bewildering truth is that no GNP figure is
ever final, for there are six routine revisions of each original estimate, and major revisions of the whole series every few years.

Even if the GNP was error free, what would it tell us about social well-
being? Not much, say William Nordhaus and James Tobin (1972). Accordingly, these two innovating economists present their view of what the GNP
would look like if it accounted for social well-being. They call it "measure of
economic welfare," or net economic welfare. It is computed by modifying
GNP in three ways: (1) subtracting certain costs, or "bads," such as pollution;
(2) excluding "regrettable necessities," such as police services; and (3) adding
activities that are not included in GNP, such as household services, home repairs, and leisure.

Exhibit 2–8 shows net economic welfare compared with GNP. The results
of this comparison are interesting: The net economic welfare has been growing—but at a considerably lower rate (1.1 percent per year) than per capita income (1.7 percent per year).

Analyzing Economic Policy Debates

The understanding of economic change requires adherence to principles of
logical thinking. Here we consider five types of errors that frequently creep
into debates on economic policy.

The *Post Hoc, Ergo Propter Hoc* Fallacy. First is the fallacy that if one thing
precedes another (or always precedes it), the first is the cause of the second. In
logic, this is called *post hoc, ergo propter hoc* (after this, therefore necessarily
because of this). The error is clearly illustrated in the following sequence:
great property damage follows from a great number of fire trucks' being present at a fire (while less damage follows situations in which the number of
trucks is relatively small). It is easy to smile at this simple example, for we all
know that prior to the apparent causal relationship between fire trucks and
damage is a third variable: size of the fire. But things are not quite so simple
when we try to understand economic phenomena, which are far less concrete
than fires.

Consider, for example, the apparent linkage between inflation and price
increases. A common interpretation is that corporations cause inflation by exploiting their market power and continually raising prices. I would argue that
this answer is wrong, an example of fallacious thinking. Corporations and
unions are "carriers" of inflation; neither is its cause. As with the fire damage

EXHIBIT 2–8 Growth in Net Economic Welfare Compared to Growth in Gross National Product

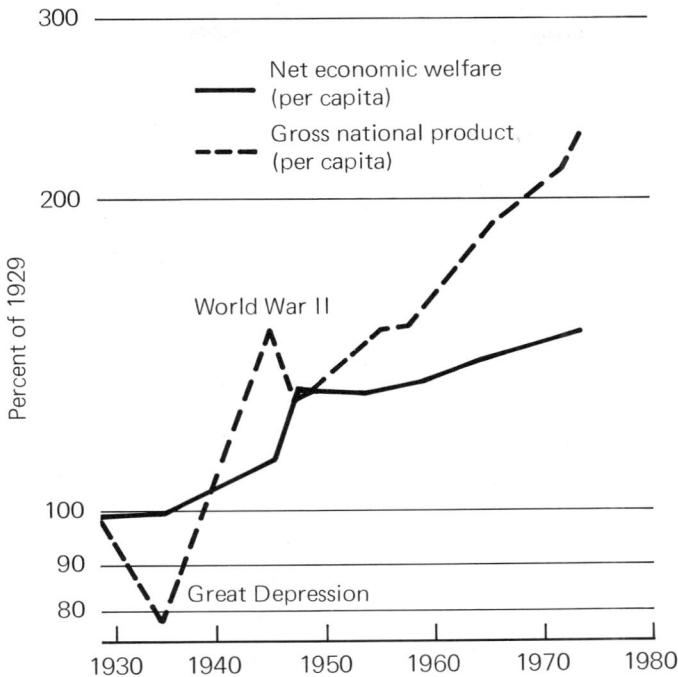

Source: William Nordhaus and James Tobin, "Is Growth Absolute?" *Fiftieth Anniversary Colloquium V,* National Bureau of Economic Research (New York: Columbia University Press, 1972). Reprinted by permission of the National Bureau of Economic Research.

example, there is a third variable: excessive monetary expansion. Robert L. Crouch (1978:187) explains:

> Without an increase in the money supply, any corporate temptation to raise prices would soon be suppressed, since the increase in prices would diminish the community's stock of real purchasing power. To rebuild real purchasing power, persons and corporations would be motivated to decrease their demand for other assets, current output, and factors of production. These deflationary forces would soon curb corporations' alleged tendency to unilaterally increase prices. Excessive monetary expansion has been permitted by the Federal Reserve System, which in turn has been seduced into such expansion by the importunate deficit spending and debt-increasing activities of the federal government.

How does this explanation square with facts? Exhibit 2–9 presents some relevant evidence. The change in money supply per unit of real GNP is plotted along the horizontal axis. The annual average of this statistic is calculated for forty countries for the period 1952–1969. The average annual change in prices for each of the forty countries over the same period is also calculated and is plotted on the vertical axis. Thus, the dot in the upper right-hand corner (representing Brazil) indicates that the 30 percent average annual increase in money per unit of real gross national product from 1952 to 1969 was approximately matched by a 30 percent average annual increase in prices over the same period. Each dot in the figure reflects the experience of a different country. (The dot for the United States is included in the group in the lower left-hand corner.) The positive relationship between the two variables is obvious by inspection.*

The Single-Factor Fallacy. A second error common to discussions about economic problems is the single-factor fallacy. Though a combination of factors may be responsible for a given result, many people fall into the trap of thinking that a single factor is the cause. Recall how, in explaining decline in productivity, CEA avoided this fallacy by focusing on four factors. Similarly, the *New York Times* (June 6, 1978) reported that in a survey of 1,100 American business leaders conducted by the Chamber of Commerce, 99 percent of the respondents cited the federal budget deficit as a "very important" or "important" cause of inflation. But nine other factors were also mentioned. In order of importance, these were: wage increases (92 percent); Social Security increases (80 percent); federal government pay increases (78 percent); federally mandated minimum-wage increases (75 percent); farm price support increases (72 percent); the dollar decline abroad (70 percent); nonunion wage increases (68 percent); increases in unemployment insurance (55 percent); interest rate increases (50 percent); workmen's compensation increases (49 percent); and business profit margins (10 percent).

The Fallacy of Composition. Third is the fallacy of composition—that is, of supposing the whole to be like the parts with which one is familiar. In economic policy debates, a good warning to keep in mind, Samuelson (1976:14) tells us, is that things are often not what at first they seem, and he offers the following true statements as examples:

1. If all farmers work hard and nature cooperates in producing a bumper crop, total farm income may *fall,* and probably will.
2. *One* man may solve his own unemployment problem by great ingenuity in hunting a job or by a willingness to work for less; but *all* cannot necessarily solve their job problems in this way.

---

* The coefficient of correlation is .97.

**EXHIBIT 2–9   Rate of Change of Prices Compared to Rate of Change
of per Unit of Output in Forty Countries**

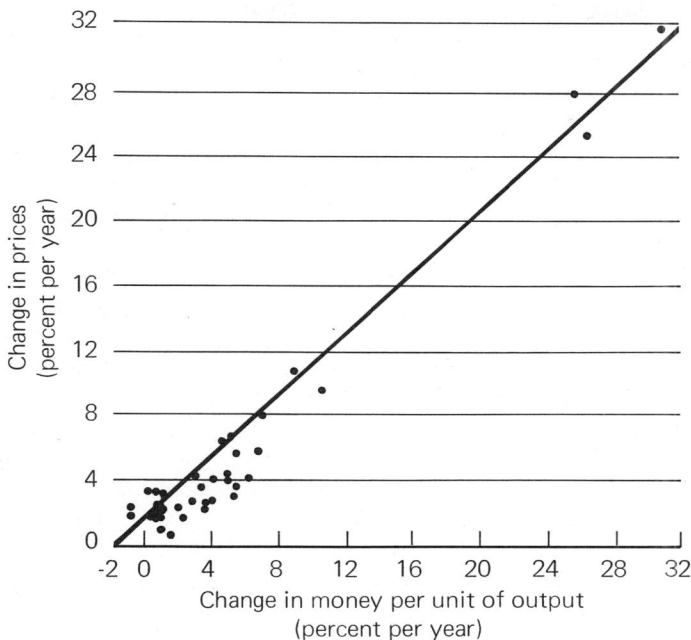

Source: Anna J. Schwartz, "Secular Price Change in Historical Perspective," *Journal of Money, Credit &
Banking,* February 5, 1973. Reprinted by permission of Ohio State University Press.

3. Higher prices *for one industry* may benefit its firms; but if the prices of *every-thing* bought and sold increased in the same proportion, *no one* would be better off.
4. It may pay the United States to *reduce* tariffs charged on goods imported, even if *other* countries refuse to lower their tariff barriers.
5. It may pay a firm to take on some business at much *less than full costs.*
6. *Attempts* of individuals to save more in depression *may lessen the total* of the community's savings.
7. What is prudent behavior for an *individual* may at times be folly for a *nation.*

The Fallacy that History Repeats Itself. Fourth is the fallacy that if things happened in a given sequence in the past, they will happen that way again. In the late 1970s this notion led a number of national political figures to support the biggest tax cut proposal in history—namely, the Kemp-Roth bill.

According to proponents of this bill, lower taxes, presumably, would send employment and investment soaring to the point where tax revenues would actually rise, despite the lower rates. Some economists have argued that a large tax cut would generate an economic boom of such proportions that in a few years the government would recoup all the initial revenue loss and then some. The reason: the huge tax cut should spark incentive to work and invest and thus increase the tax base. Why did proponents of the Kemp-Roth bill believe this would occur? They pointed to the Kennedy tax cuts of 1962 and 1964 as indications of how sharp reductions in tax rates can generate sustained economic growth.

This line of reasoning was attacked as fallacious by none other than Walter W. Heller, CEA chairman under Kennedy and Johnson. Heller fought hard for the Kennedy tax cuts, and he would certainly like to take credit for engineering the above-average economic growth that took place between 1962 and 1967. The beneficial effects of those cuts—about $12 billion, or $36 billion in today's prices—were on the demand side, not on the supply side according to Heller. The key difference between the early 1960s and the late 1970s is that the latter inflation rate neared the double-digit level, compared with about 1.5 percent in the sixties. A tax cut—even one of only $36 billion—would carry with it the danger of fueling an inflation from which the nation would take years to recover.

The Fallacy of Wishful Thinking. The final fallacy commonly present in discussions of economic policy is the error of wishful thinking—that is, seeing what one wants to see or believing what one wants to believe. For example, as Uyterhoven, Ackerman, and Rosenblum (1977:23–24) have noted, preparing for downturn during economic boom is not easy, psychologically. Booms bring shortages and the typical management response is plant expansion—let tomorrow worry about tomorrow. But what happens when conditions change, as they surely will? The firm, along with its competitors, finds itself with excess capacity and high fixed costs. So, everyone starts cutting prices to avoid loss of volume sales. Thus, the firm, by taking logical but shortsighted action during good economic conditions, has actually aggravated its problems in the future. Economic booms also tend to cover up weaknesses in product characteristics and distribution strategies. How many managers want to bother probing for such weaknesses as long as demand is high? Yet, when the downturn eventually occurs, those weaknesses are brutally uncovered and management finds it often too late and too costly to adequately respond.

Building and Using Economic Models

Simple Econometric Diagrams. Model building allows us to simplify the analysis of complicated situations. Rather than attempt to consider all factors at once, the analyst may set up a hypothetical model that enables him or her to consider various possibilities, one at a time. To take a simple model, let us consider a page of "Nixonomics."

In an August 1971 address to the nation, President Nixon announced that the time had come for a "new economic policy" for the United States. Its targets would be unemployment, inflation, and international speculation. In the passage that follows, he explains how he planned to attack them:

> ... I shall ask the Congress, when it reconvenes after its summer recess, to consider as its first priority the enactment of the Job Development Act of 1971.
>
> I will propose to provide the strongest short-term incentive in our history to invest in new machinery and equipment that will create new jobs for Americans: A 10 percent Job Development Credit for one year, effective as of today, with a 5 percent credit after August 15, 1972. This tax credit for investment in new equipment will not only generate new jobs; it will raise productivity and it will make our goods more competitive in the years ahead.

What are the models behind President Nixon's proposals? What are the assumptions made in his analysis? To begin to answer these questions, it is useful to construct simple econometric diagrams.* Essentially, what we want to do is translate Nixon's words into the more precise language of economics and thus make explicit his assumptions about how the economy works.[†]

For the investment tax credit, the model for what Nixon says will happen is as follows:

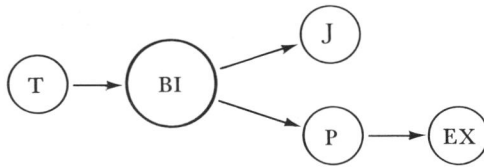

where: T = taxes, specifically a tax credit for investment,
         BI = business investment,
          J = jobs,
          P = productivity,
         EX = net exports.

In other words, by reducing taxes, the government can encourage increased investment; this, in turn, will both increase the number of jobs and the productivity of the work force. The latter will increase the net exports of the United States.

---

* To see how these simple econometric diagrams can be applied to "Carter Economics," the reader might wish to turn ahead to Exhibit 4–6.

[†] I am indebted to Baughman, Lodge, and Pifer (1974:13–15) for the simple, yet pedagogically powerful, exercises in econometric modeling contained in this section.

The model raises questions about economic behavior. First, although Nixon can make taxes a function of investment, it is not clear that this will make investment a function of the tax level—that is, will an investment tax credit actually increase investment? Nixon is assuming that government fiscal policy can, in fact, affect the propensity of business to invest in new plants and equipment.

A second question raised by the model concerns the possibility of a contradiction between the statement that this investment would produce more jobs and at the same time increase productivity. Nixon could, of course, be referring to new jobs that will make the new plants and equipment or to new jobs that will result from the multiplier effect of the investment. The diagrammatic relationship between BI and J would be:

or

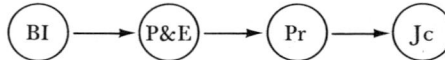

or

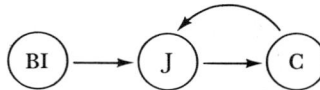

where: P&E = new plant and equipment,
          Jp&e = jobs to build new plant and equipment,
          Pr = production,
          Jc = jobs for production of new consumption,
          C = consumption.

The first diagram indicates that increased investment increases production of new plants and equipment, for which new workers are required. The second diagram indicates that increased investment increases production of new equipment, which, once installed, increases production, which requires more jobs. The final diagram indicates that increased business investment will create more jobs, which will increase consumption, which will in turn increase jobs via the multiplier effect.

A third question concerns how the tax credit for investment in new equipment will generate new jobs. If the new equipment is labor-saving equipment—that is, equipment that increases productivity—it should reduce the number of jobs. If the new equipment is merely more equipment, like previous equipment, it will create more jobs but probably will not significantly increase productivity or "make our goods more competitive." Only if the new equipment is based on new technology, available but not in use, and if the factor previously preventing its use was lack of money, will the investment tax credit increase both jobs and productivity.

More Complex Models. More intricate forms of model building depend, of course, on many more assumptions.* These assumptions are chosen either to approximate the conditions actually expected in a given problem or to see what the consequences might be in a special situation. For example, Otto Eckstein, when president of Data Resources, Inc. (DRI), ran the earlier mentioned Kemp-Roth tax cut proposal through DRI's huge computer-forecasting model. Assuming that the proposal took effect and that there were no compensatory spending cuts, the DRI model showed that the deficit would grow progressively worse. In just a few years, the red ink in the budget, including additional interest payments, would increase to a mind-numbing $100 billion. So, rather than recouping the entire tax cut, as the massive tax cut proponents argue, the treasury would recoup only about $25 billion according to the DRI model.

Today in the United States much economic modeling, and more importantly, policymaking, enshrines the Keynesian assumption that GNP and employment are determined only by the level of aggregate demand, or total spending, in the economy. Unemployment and low rates of economic growth are seen as evidence of insufficient spending. The remedy is for government to increase total spending by incurring a deficit in its budget. In Keynesian theory, GNP will then rise by some multiple of the increase in spending. Keynesian economics focuses on estimating the "spending gap" and the "multiplier" so that the necessary deficit can be calculated (see Exhibit 2–10).

The model in Exhibit 2–10 raises several important questions. First, how relevant is it to the economic conditions of today? The model's original purpose was to explain the problem of unemployment to government decision-makers in the Great Depression. The explanation then was plausible: A great many people who wanted to work were unemployed because aggregate demand (the C + I + G curve in Exhibit 2–10) was insufficient to absorb the output of the available labor force. And the proposed solution was marvelously simple: By spending more than it received in taxes, government could increase demand enough (specifically, to C + I + G') to create a condition of full employment (E'). Although Keynes did not stress the point until later, his theory also implied a remedy for inflation: The government could eliminate "excess demand" by taking in more money than it spent—that is, by running a budget surplus.

Few economists would deny that modern inflation is different from that of the past. Specifically, prices and wages begin to rise before full employment, before tight labor markets, and before full-capacity utilization. Under modern

---

* To see what these more complex econometric models look like, the reader may wish to turn ahead to Chapter 7.

**EXHIBIT 2–10   The Keynesian Model of Effect of
                 More Government Spending**

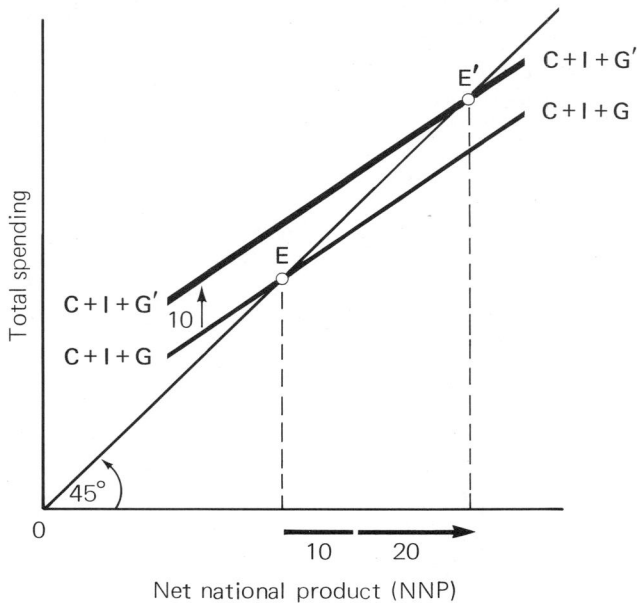

Net national product (NNP)

In this figure, NNP represents net national product; C represents consumption spending; I represents investment spending; G represents governmental spending; E represents equilibrium point of national income. An increase in governmental expenditures on goods and services will shift C + I + G up to C + I + G', raising national income from E to E'.

Source: Paul Samuelson, *Economics*, 10th ed. (New York: McGraw-Hill, 1976), p. 243. Reprinted by permission.

cost-push, or "sellers' inflation," * the United States economy can experience *stagflation*—that is, stagnation of growth and employment at the same time that prices are rising. As Samuelson (1976) puts it, no sophisticated wielding of the tools of C + I + G is going to cure this new disease. If government applies the fiscal brakes, inflation may come down, but the economy also slams into recession and even higher unemployment.

* A.P. Lerner (1946) defines "sellers' inflation" this way: If all sellers, whether of labor or of property services or of goods, negotiate and determine their prices to try to get among them all more than 100 percent of the total national product, then the result cannot help but be a frustrating upward push of the price level—a case of sellers' inflation.

A closely related question about the Keynesian model is this: What happens to production as tax rates rise to pay for the increased government spending? Paul Craig Roberts (1978:21–22) writes:

> This question confronts economic policy with the incentive effects it has disregarded. It should be obvious even to Keynesians that when marginal tax rates are high, people will prefer additional leisure to additional current income, and additional current consumption to additional future income. As work effort and investment decline, production will fall, regardless of how great an increase there might be in aggregate demand. Such a recognition of disincentives implies a recognition of incentives. Once one recognizes that people produce and invest for income, and that income depends on tax rates, one has reached the realization that fiscal policy causes changes not just in demand but also in supply.

Perhaps the central difficulty of the Keynesian model lies as much in the realm of politics as it does in that of economics. As Joan Robinson, the Cambridge economist, pointed out many years ago, full employment and price stability may be inherently incompatible in a democracy. Robinson's prediction seems to have proven true: With governments committed to the management of aggregate demand, the traditional business cycle would be replaced by a "political business cycle" generated by the public's alternation of concern, first with the problem of unemployment, then with the problem of inflation.

The message of this section on the economic environment can be summed up quickly. The ability to apply the rules for clear thinking and the ability to use meaningful information and relevant tools are basic requirements for better decisions. Only if a manager masters the use of simplified assumptions and learns to follow economic changes through to their many possible consequences can he or she arrive at useful conclusions for the conduct of business affairs.

THE SOCIAL ENVIRONMENT

While technological changes may tend to be the most visible forces impinging on business operations and economic changes the most pervasive, a no less important force involves people: who they are; where and how they live; and, above all, what they think.

Technology and economics, in other words, are not the final arbiters of what will be. Consider the following interactions:

—Ralph Nader and consumerism on product standards and automobile safety;

—Environmentalism and DDT, phosphate detergents, strip mining, and offshore drilling;

—The antitechnology atmosphere and nuclear power plant opposition (see Exhibit 2–11).

EXHIBIT 2–11   The Relationship Between Social Attitudes and Technology: Nuclear Opposition Reduces Sales by U.S. Nuclear Suppliers

Sign-carrying demonstrators invading nuclear plant sites (see photo) can translate into a sharp slump in business for U.S. nuclear suppliers (see graph).

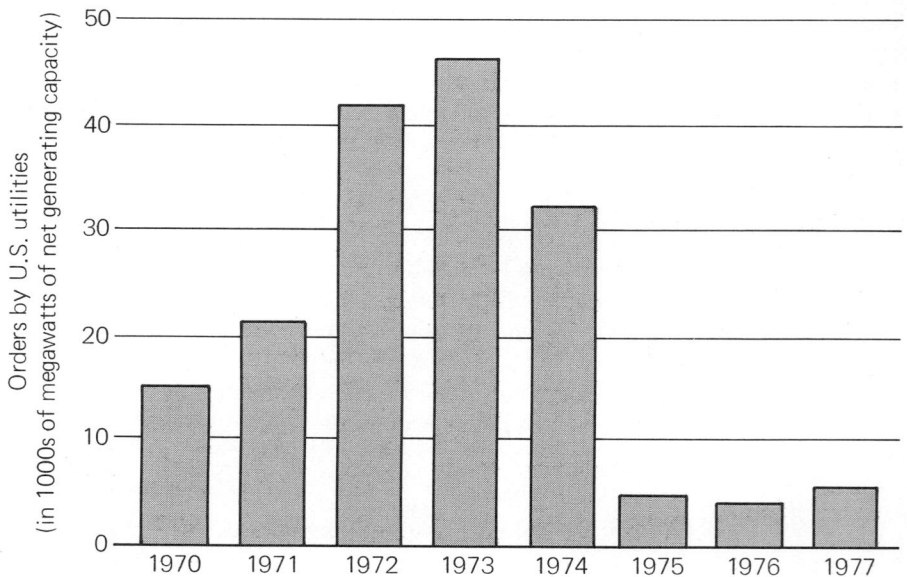

Source: Data from Atomic Industrial Forum; photo © Johan Elbers, New York. All rights reserved.

A manager should not view the social environment as primarily a source of threats. It is worth recalling the observation by Peter F. Drucker with which we opened this chapter: "Results are obtained by exploiting opportunities, not by solving problems." This section will provide numerous examples of how social change generates business opportunities.

In this section we shall examine three broad classes of social change: changes in aggregate attributes (e.g., population or demographic trends); changes in social structures (e.g., the family); and changes in cultural patterns (e.g., values).

Changes in Aggregate Attributes: Population

To a large measure the people who compose a society determine the structure of its economy, the economic problems it faces, and the solutions it devises for those problems. Everyone who will be a mature worker, pensioner, or executive in the United States in the next twenty years is already born. By looking closely at who these people are, what they will want, and what they can do, business and government can tell a lot about what sort of country the United States will be in the next two decades and what opportunities and risks it will face.

Nevertheless, even economists consider *demographics*—that is, the study of population—a rather unexciting and unrewarding subject. Business managers, distracted by inflation, shifting markets, technological threats, and increasing government regulations, have little time to listen to the demographers. But the fact is that the United States is going through a fundamental demographic transition that managers will have to take into account. These shifts have already begun to affect the economy, and further effects are still to come. "Demographic statistics make dull reading," says Michael L. Wachter, a University of Pennsylvania economist (*Business Week*, February 20, 1978), "but they helped lay the groundwork for our current economic problems."

Indeed, over the next two decades, probably nothing that the federal government can do by way of fiscal or monetary policy is likely to affect U.S. business as much as the huge shifts that will occur in the nation's population pattern. Assuming that the fertility of young women continues without substantial change, there will be a gradual "aging" of the new population, with a growing proportion of people aged forty-five to sixty-five and over and a reduced proportion of people under fifteen years of age. To be more specific, in just the next ten years the percentage of teenagers will decline 17 percent; the percentage of young people of middle age (thirty-five to forty-nine) will increase 31 percent.

Not surprisingly, demand for all sorts of goods and services will shift during the decade ahead, as the age groups change their relative size. While the full brunt of these trends will not be felt for years, harbingers abound (adapted from Reinhold, 1977):

● Levi Strauss, the jeans maker whose ads with psychedelic and sexual overtones were the commercial embodiment of the youthful culture of the 1960s, has made subtle changes in its pitch. The company now promotes sportswear with a fuller cut, for that 1965 college boy who can no longer squeeze into his size 30 Levis.

● Faced with declining sales of baby food, the Gerber Products Company has diversified and now makes such products as vaporizers and shampoo. It is also testing adult foods such as ketchup and peanut spreads, as well as single-serving foods for the elderly. As it is, company officials privately estimate that as much as 10 percent of its baby food is actually consumed by the elderly.

● The FM rock radio stations that emerged in the 1960s are still thriving, but the sponsors are selling condominium apartments and suburban homes as well as phonograph records and acne remedies.

Obviously, the consequences of population shifts are difficult to predict because taste, innovation, and other unpredictable factors also affect modes of living. Still, it seems safe to assume that a country dominated by the old will need less baby food, toys, teachers, and maternity wards. Conversely, demand should rise for retirement homes, medical care, recreational facilities, and entertainment that suits the taste of the elderly. Exhibit 2–12 summarizes, industry by industry, what the changes will mean to markets over the next ten years.

Changes in Social Structures: The Family

A second way of measuring social change is to focus on the patterns of interaction among individuals. The family structure is one example of such a "pattern of interaction." To the sociologist, the term *family structure* has a precise meaning: The same people—an adult male, an adult female, and several young persons—regularly sleep under the same roof, share economic goods, and otherwise interact in repetitive ways. Thus, looking at the social structures is a quite different thing from looking at the aggregate attributes (e.g., population) of a society or the behavior (e.g., crime rates) of a society's individual members. The difference is this: When speaking of social structures, we are assuming that the relations among the members are not merely statistical, but involve two types of social forces—namely, *sanctions* (such as rewards and deprivations) and *norms,* or standards of conduct.

Today, as American men and women attempt to shape new relationships, the family is in transition as never before. Experts intensely debate the social implications of this transition; some envision the dawn of an enlightened, creative society, while others are deeply disturbed by what they see as burgeoning instability. Regardless of what interpretations are drawn, the statistics of basic change within the family show a clearly dynamic trend:

EXHIBIT 2–12   Projected Effects on Industry of Population Shifts in the United States during the 1980s

Market	Predicted change
Autos	Slower rise in demand
Houses	Substantial increase
Apartments	Moderate growth
Furniture	Increase in demand
Travel	Up sharply
Entertainment	Substantial increase
Appliances	Rising demand
Teenage clothing	Down somewhat
Baby food, clothing, toys	Expanding market
Adult clothing	Up substantially
School construction	Sharply cut back
Alcoholic beverages	Continued increase
Medical services	Up sharply
Adult education	Continued growth
Fuel	Slow increase in demand
Metals	Steady increase, except for autos

Source: Reprinted from *U.S. News & World Report,* May 30, 1977. Copyright 1977 U.S. News & World Report, Inc.

—The divorce rate has doubled in the last ten years.

—It is estimated that two out of every five children born in this decade will live in single-parent homes for at least part of their youth.

—The number of households headed by women has increased by more than a third in this decade and has more than doubled in one generation.

—More than half of all mothers with school-age children now work outside the home, as do more than a third of mothers with children under the age of three.

—Day care of irregular quality is replacing the parental role in many working families. Similarly, there has been extraordinary growth in the classification that sociologists call "latchkey children"—children unsupervised for portions of the day, usually in the period between the end of school and a working parent's return home.

—A trend particularly relevant to business, as we shall see presently, appears in Exhibit 2–13. From the limited data available, it is evident that the single-person household as a percent of all households is on the rise, not only in the United States but also in countries such as Sweden and West Germany.

EXHIBIT 2–13   Single-Person Households as a Percent of All Households in Selected Countries, 1955–1975

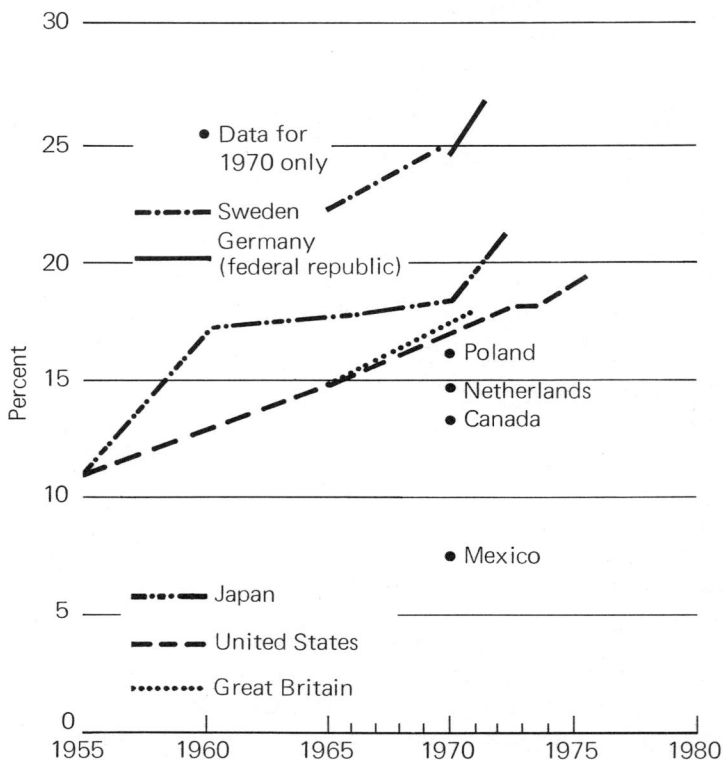

Source: Data from U.S. Department of Commerce, *Social Indicators 1976* (Washington, D.C.: U.S. Government Printing Office, 1977), p. 60.

Explaining such trends is not easy. Christopher Lasch (1977) has gone considerably beyond popular perceptions of the decline of the family. Lasch argues that ". . . the family has been slowly coming apart for more than a hundred years. The divorce crisis, feminism, and the revolt of youth originated in the nineteenth century. . . ." In fact, as he concludes his book *Haven In A Heartless World,* the erosion of the family has been in progress ever since bourgeois society conceived of it as a refuge ". . . where the woman ministered to her exhausted husband, repaired the spiritual damage inflicted by the market, and sheltered her children from its corrupting influence." *

According to Lasch, though the capitalist system needed the family, it paradoxically helped weaken the family. In the course of development, advanced industrial society, as we saw in Chapter 1, shifted from the production of goods to the provision of "human services"—for example, schooling or selling or surgery. In such an economy, Lasch argues, personality becomes a crucial commodity, and "interpersonal skills" emerge as survival skills. The family, in order to fit into this new order, must smooth out its inner stresses so that it can help all its members succeed in the new "personality market." In short, family life becomes more pleasant and agreeable without really becoming more human at its core.

We must leave off speculating on the causes of social trends and return to the more germane question of how these trends, such as more people living alone, affect business. How people live is important to business, because it tends to determine how they spend their money (people who live alone earned $115 billion in 1976, an average of $7,400 each). A person living alone spends more money on companionship-related activities like travel and entertainment than a family does. People who live alone have more or less the same fixed costs that a working couple has, but they have less income, so they save less. Since there is no specialization of labor in the one-person household—no such thing, for example, as a husband's trimming the hedge while his wife rakes the leaves—singles tend to buy more services, from car repair to lawn care. These new patterns of behavior especially affect the housing, automobile, and appliance industries (adapted from Kronholz, 1977):

- The housing industry probably more than any other has felt the impact of single living. Singles bought about 15 percent of the homes sold in 1977. Since enactment of the Equal Credit Opportunity Act in 1976, single women have become the fastest-growing segment of the home-buying market and could account for one of every ten sales within three years. Builders even have an abbreviation for their new single, separated, widowed, and divorced buyers—SSWDs.
- Singles, widows, and divorcees have other distinct spending habits. They buy 26 percent of all passenger cars, but half of the Ford Mustangs and other small specialty cars. Bigger cars are less popular among them: only 8 percent of the Ford LTDs go to singles. Accordingly, Ford plans to emphasize

---

* As recently as 1955 Adlai E. Stevenson told the graduating women at Smith College (of all places) that their role in life was to "influence us, man and boy" and their task to "restore valid, meaningful purpose to life in your home," and to keep their husbands "truly purposeful." A couple of decades later those graduates—"you girls," Stevenson called them—were living in a different world.

the specialty cars as the singles market increases.

   • But while singles tend to spend more on luxury durables like cars, they spend less on other expensive items. Since so many of them live in apartments, the National Association of Appliance Manufacturers says, people who live alone buy refrigerators at only half the rate of the population in general and washers and dryers at about one-quarter the rate. So appliance manufacturers are scratching their heads for new products that appeal to the single-person household. So far the industry has come up with appliances that grill one sandwich, slow-cook one serving of stew and fry one plate of french fries; and other small appliances are on the way. Analysts also are enthusiastic about the future of food-processing concerns that play to the singles market: Campbell Soup Co.'s Soup-for-One and Green Giant Co.'s single-serving casseroles are already fixtures on supermarket shelves.

   But changes in the structure of the family are not the only kinds of change to be found: Every bit as important to business are trends in social mobility and social participation. Both help explain the consumer and environmental movements. For example, it seems reasonable to expect that the rising educational attainments of adults in American society, an important indicator of social mobility, might be associated with a greater sensitivity to consumer and environmental issues.

   Comparing the results by the Department of Commerce surveys of March 1962 and March 1973, we find that the oldest group covered in either survey (the birth cohorts of 1897–1901) attained, on average, 9 years of formal schooling, or 2 years more than their parents before them. Those who were born twenty-five years later (the birth cohorts of 1922–1926) attained, on average, 11.3 years of schooling—an increase of about 3.5 years over that of their fathers and the largest intergenerational gain of any of the cohorts included in these surveys. Since then, the younger cohorts have enjoyed smaller gains relative to their fathers. The youngest cohorts shown (born 1947–1951) reported an average attainment of 12.8 years, but this was only 2.1 years above that of their fathers.

   Improved levels of education only indicate, at best, a potential for upward social mobility; they do not indicate that such mobility has in fact occurred. A better indicator of actual social mobility is provided by information relating to the occupational distribution of sons relative to that of their fathers. The data collected in both the March 1962 and March 1973 surveys indicate the prevalence of a substantial amount of social mobility in our society—both upward and downward. Among all males, for example, about 20 percent of the sons whose fathers held lower manual occupations had themselves achieved upper white-collar positions. Conversely, about 16 percent of the sons whose fathers held upper white-collar jobs were themselves engaged in lower manual jobs. Another important feature of these findings is the improvement between 1962 and 1973 in the upward mobility of black males. In 1962 only 8 percent of the sons of black fathers who held lower manual jobs had moved into upper white-collar occupations. By 1973 the corresponding figure had risen to 12 percent.

Changes between 1965 and 1974 in the proportions of the population engaged in various kinds of volunteer work offer another instance of changes in social structure important to business. From 1968 to 1973 the number of national organizations involved with public affairs grew from 446 to 792. Many of these 792 have a strong interest in consumer and environmental issues.

Changes in Cultural Patterns: Values

Cultural patterns—including, for example, values, world views, and ideologies—supply systems of meaning and legitimacy to daily life. When understood in their broadest sense, cultural patterns are a way of organizing a particular, coherent view of society; they enable people to orient themselves to a complicated and confusing world.

Changing cultural patterns affect the business system in three important ways. First, they generate new consumer demands and cause other demands to shrink. To pick a quite obvious example, in the late 1950s the consumer taste in automobiles tended, on the whole, towards larger, more garish models equipped with tailfins and lots of chrome. By the late 1970s, however, taste had shifted (again, on the whole) toward safer, more economical (in fuel consumption, not list price), more comfortable models. What had happened? In general, the consumers' world view had shifted somewhat from "conspicuous consumption in a world of plenty" to "stylish adaptation" to "a world of finite resources" (see the Commentary section, "Monitoring America").

COMMENTARY: Monitoring America

Take a simple thing like breakfast. Not many years ago, millions of mothers felt duty-bound to cook a nourishing hot breakfast for their children. Today, they ask, "Why suffer?" Increasingly, they find it morally acceptable to feed their children quickie breakfasts, or even let them fend for themselves.

This may be ghastly news to America's nutritionists, but it is dandy news for companies that make instant breakfasts.

Tracking such social changes that affect business demand keeps a staff of researchers busy at Yankelovich, Skelly & White Inc., the Madison Avenue public opinion and market research concern. Working for 96 sponsoring companies, including General Electric and Procter & Gamble, Yankelovich puts numbers on seemingly nebulous trends ranging from "tolerance for chaos and disorder" to "social pluralism," "living for today" and "focus on self."

The theory is that managers know a great deal about their own industries but lack hard data on broad social trends and changes in values that affect demand for their products . . . .

Therefore, Yankelovich's "Monitor" project each year asks 2,500 people nationwide about, say, how important they think it is to plan in advance and how much they enjoy doing things at the spur of the moment . . . .

Monitor studies point up a pervasive trend: We really are becoming a more self-centered people. As accepted values, sacrifice for children and general self-denial are declining, and the pursuit of individual pleasure and interests is rising. It's not for nothing that the new magazine from the publishers of Vogue will be a fitness book called "Self." As Florence Skelly, executive vice president of Yankelovich, puts it, "We're now a country of 'what about me?' "

Arthur Shapiro, a Yankelovich senior vice president, says the trend in general means consumers are "willing to spend on the 'me' items (from perfume to entertainment) but they look closer at the price-value relationship for the 'we' items (like family room furniture)."

Consumers are also increasingly willing to pay for new experiences, Monitor finds. This is because the quest for "fulfillment" of the 1960s is giving way to a "thirst for excitement" in American society, Mrs. Skelly says. In the 1960s, she notes, millions looked for personal fulfillment through their work, their avocations and even social service. "People were looking for the hidden Mozart straining to break free, but our research shows a declining percentage now thinks this kind of fulfillment is really possible," she adds.

Fewer than one-quarter of Monitor's sample now look to work as a source of fulfillment, compared with nearly half in 1970. To fill the gap, the public increasingly looks for experience and escape, Monitor finds. "You have to make sure that nothing in life passes you by. You have to go to Europe, play backgammon, go on a survival weekend, try every new restaurant and every new drink," Mrs. Skelly says. This is exactly the kind of thinking that sells airline tickets, backpacks and bottles of amaretto. To get the detailed data on such trends, with some individual consulting tossed in, Monitor sponsors each pay $13,800 a year.

Changing cultural patterns affect business in nonmarket areas, too. Another service provided by Yankelovich (see Commentary section, "Monitoring America") is called "corporate priorities." This service examines how much the public and a cross-section of the leadership community really care about controlling air pollution, regulating business, and responding to other such demands. One obvious value of the service is to show its thirty sponsoring corporations which issues they must seriously address—and which they can safely ignore. The sponsors are mostly big, visible companies like General Motors, Exxon, DuPont and Union Carbide, all of which have felt their share of public wrath over the years. As government regulation expands, demand for information on public attitudes toward issues has grown.

Finally, cultural patterns help determine the attitudes of employees toward their work and toward authority. Obviously, such attitudes are decisively important to business management.

COMMENTARY: Cultural Adversaries of American Business

American executives who began their careers in the 1950s and 1960s are frequently puzzled by steady criticism leveled at them by writers and the media in our society. As John Leonard (1977), the chief cultural correspondent of the *New York Times,* put it, "On the whole, the Mafia gets a better press."

Criticism of American business—if not total indifference toward it—is nothing new in American cultural history. In 1922, for example, Sinclair Lewis published *Babbit,* a study of the complacent American businessman whose individuality has been sucked out of him by Rotary Clubs, business deals, and general conformity. (About this time satirist H.L. Mencken was to remark that "the first Rotarian was the first man to call John the Baptist 'Jack'.") To Babbit, the world, in all its beauty and multiplicity, was just one big business office. E.E. Cummings put the case with unparalleled bitterness and conciseness: "A salesman is an it that stinks to please." And Arthur Miller was hardly less savage and bitter when, in one of the most celebrated plays of modern times, *Death of a Salesman,* he created Willy Loman, a character pathetically victimized by his own false values and the values of conformity, aggressiveness, and profit that characterized the business world in which he tried to succeed. Yet Miller wrote sympathetically, too, of Willy's plight. "Nobody don't blame this man," he had another character say after Willy's death:

> You don't understand: Willy was a salesman. And for a salesman, there is no rock bottom to the life. He don't put a bolt to the nut, he don't tell you the law or give you medicine. He's a man way out there in the blue, riding on a smile and a shoestring. And when they start not smiling back—there's an earthquake. And then you get a couple of spots on your hat, and you're finished. Nobody dast blame this man. A salesman is got to dream, boy. It comes with the territory.

Actually, after Fitzgerald, money pretty much disappeared as a serious subject in mainstream American fiction. Norman Mailer, Saul Bellow, John Cheever, William Styron, Kurt Vonnegut, and other contemporary novelists do not know anything about money, Leonard maintains, ". . . except when it comes to the subsidiary rights on their books." He adds: "As our writers all end up in artists' colonies and the English departments of our universities, they know less and less about anything, period."

Motion pictures (not precluding masterpieces), when they do deal with business, are negative with lunar regularity. For example, Orson Welles's great film *Citi-*

zen Kane raised some sharp questions about the values of American business by focusing on the life of a business tycoon. The key moral question is what happened to Charles Foster Kane? What destroyed his youthful hopes and excitement? Gerald Mast (1976:312) writes:

> The answer is a dark, sickly spot at the heart of Kane's values and, by implication, at the heart of the values of American life. The three abstract themes that constantly flow through *Citizen Kane* are wealth, power, and love. The questions that the film raises are whether the first two exclude the third, and whether a life that excludes the third is worth living at all. Kane obviously has wealth; his wealth bought him newspapers and his newspapers brought him power. But Kane thinks that money and power can buy him the affection of men. Kane is a man of quantities.

More recently, we have seen award-winning films like *Network,* in which the business executives associated with a communications conglomerate are minor-league fascists who sell out to the Arabs.

The picture television gives is little different: to be in business is, in Leonard's terms, "to ride a monorail of avarice to disaster." Except for Colonel Sanders and commercials, a *happy* businessman is seldom seen on television.

The Life Cycle of Social Issues

As we have seen, companies must interact with a dynamic social environment that places demands on them over time. In responding to environmental changes, managers must make tough decisions. But, before the nature of decision making can be discussed, it will be helpful to have a simple way of thinking about how social change occurs.

The first step toward simplification is to begin to think in terms of social issues like equal opportunity, air pollution, and product safety. In a sense, social issues are no more than concrete manifestations of the various shifts in technological, economic, and social environments. The second step is to look for a pattern in the development of social issues that will apply over a wide range of issues. The following six-stage process, presented here in brief, accomplishes these goals.

- *Stage 1.* Structural changes occur in society. These changes may include such things as the appearance of new technologies, the rise of inflation, the decline in birth rate, and the adaptation to equality.
- *Stage 2.* Problem is recognized. Discussions of a specific societal problem begin to appear in the media.
- *Stage 3.* Formal organizations are established. To promote these discussions and advocate public action toward resolving the problem, interest

groups of various types begin to appear. Older groups begin to expand their goals to include consideration of the new problem.

● *Stage 4.* Issue is placed on policy agenda. Wide discussion of an issue is no guarantee that public action will follow. The issue must come under consideration by those who *can* shape public policy. Congressional hearings on the issue are an indication that it has arrived at this stage.

● *Stage 5.* Solution is formalized. Finally, either a public law is passed (e.g., Clean Air Act of 1970) or a social action is widely adopted (e.g., collective bargaining).

● *Stage 6.* Social control becomes routine. Public interest in the problem tends to level off at a point somewhat below that of stage 5, as the administration of the law becomes the daily task of some governmental agency, but the rate of decline of public interest may vary greatly, depending on the issue.

Because of the way in which the public's interest in the social issue varies through the six stages, it is useful to think of the process as following a kind of a life cycle—not unlike the life cycle of a product (see Exhibit 2–14).

EXHIBIT 2–14   Life Cycle of Social Issues

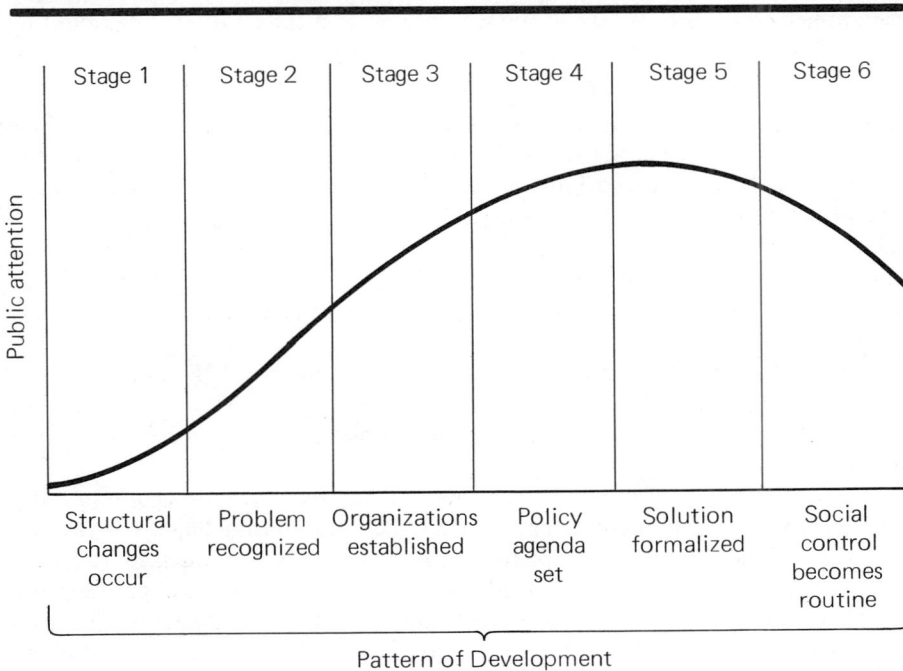

| Stage 1 | Stage 2 | Stage 3 | Stage 4 | Stage 5 | Stage 6 |

Public attention

| Structural changes occur | Problem recognized | Organizations established | Policy agenda set | Solution formalized | Social control becomes routine |

Pattern of Development

Knowledge of this general pattern of development is important to managers charged with making decisions in areas of public concern, *which are constantly changing.* The reason is not hard to see: Such knowledge helps provide insight into things to come. To the blind, all things seem sudden. They can also be quite costly. Crash programs—in response, say, to "sudden" government mandates for higher product performance and safety standards—are notoriously expensive. Research by Edwin Mansfield et al. (1971:136–56) suggests a time-cost trade-off function like that shown in Exhibit 2–15. When available time (or "lead time," as it is called by project managers) is cut from t_2 to t_1, cost jumps from C_2 to C_1.

Knowledge of the pattern of social issues can also provide a company with a competitive edge. For example, by carefully following public concern over aerosol spray cans, a company might be able to replace their product line almost immediately with pump sprays when legislation bans aerosols. Meanwhile, the competition not only loses sales but also must launch a costly crash program.

The Life Cycle of Social Issues Model

We now turn to a more detailed discussion of the six stages in the life cycle of social issues. The specific examples in each stage illustrate how this model can be applied to a wide variety of social concerns and thus aid in understanding the dynamics of change in the social environment.

Stage 1: Structural Changes. Most social issues affecting business have their roots in rather basic changes that have occurred in society. The connection between such changes and social issues is often subtle, barely perceptible to even the most astute observer. In other cases, the connection is quite obvious. A case in point is the connection between pollution and the environmental movement, since long before the notion that pollution was a problem gained popularity, certain structural changes were taking place that made the emergence of such a belief possible.

First, the U.S. population was increasing—from only 131 million in 1940 to more than 210 million in 1975. Such an increase obviously puts an increased strain on the environment; more people, it is not hard to see, mean more air, water, and solid waste pollution.

Second, modes of living were changing. Americans were becoming more affluent, as per capita income rose from $2,620 to more than $6,000 (measured in 1972 dollars). Since more affluent people tend to occupy much more space, consume more natural resources, disturb the ecology more, and create more land, air, water, thermal, and radioactive pollution than poor people, the environmental effects of affluence are not hard to see: Vast increases in rubbish disposal disfigure the landscape; increased numbers of air conditioners and private swimming pools create water shortages in many cities; and automobile exhaust and power plant discharges fill the atmosphere.

EXHIBIT 2–15   Time-Cost Tradeoff Resulting from Crash Programs to Meet New Government Standards

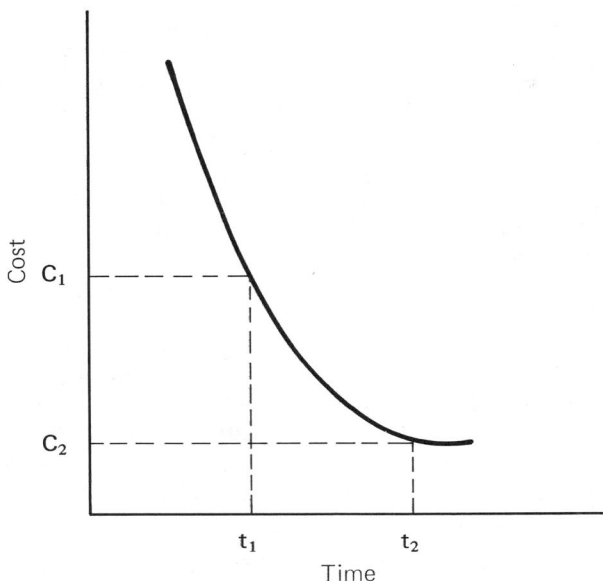

Barry Commoner (1972) suggests a third even more important structural change at the root of our environmental problems. Commoner argues persuasively that the increases in population and affluence are much too small to account for the 200 to 2,000 percent rise in certain kinds of pollution since World War II. According to Commoner, it is not so much the *volume* of industrial production but the change in its *composition.* Commoner finds especially disturbing the growth in environmentally harmful synthetic products and the relative decline in natural products.

In addition to changes in population, affluence, and technology, a fourth structural change ought to be noted, for it affects the emergence of not only the pollution issue but also virtually every other social issue. Following Neil T. Smelser (1963), let us call this change "conductiveness." In other words, as educational levels rise, as telecommunications advances, and as political participation levels increase, the rapidity and relative ease with which citizens become aware of issues inevitably increases as well.

In thinking about structural changes, we should not overlook more subtle varieties, such as changes in values. William Tucker (1977), for instance, suggests that to the extent affluence brings new cultural values, as well as increased consumption, it was doubly helpful in the emergence of the environmental movement:

> The great appeal environmental solutions offer is that they can be worn like a badge of success. To say that one is an "environmentalist," or that one favors "no-growth," is to say that one has achieved enough well-being from the present system and that one is now content to let it remain as it is or even retrogress a little—because one's material comfort under the present system has been more or less assured.

Although Tucker's intriguing analysis lacks much in the way of empirical support, it does serve at least to point out possible ways in which shifting cultural patterns prepare the way of the emergence of social issues.

Stage 2: Problem Recognition. Social issues do not arrive with labels; they first must be recognized and defined. Traditionally, this function has been fulfilled in society by intellectual elites who analyze and articulate social problems and tend to emerge around an issue. Although less capable of articulating their plight, the victimized emote their feelings and often become powerful propaganda symbols for change. Graham T.T. Molitor (1975), director of governmental relations for General Mills, thinks that usually less than twelve people who are innately innovators can be pinpointed on any issue. But, by monitoring these early vanguards whose ideas ultimately are diffused widely through society, early indications of emerging social issues are possible.

One classic example of such an innovator is Vance Packard. In *The Hidden Persuaders* (1957) Packard attacked the use of motivation research and what he called "manipulation" of consumers by advertising; in *The Waste Makers* (1960) he attacked planned obsolescence. Another example is Rachel Carson, who in 1962 published *Silent Spring*, a devastating account of how our products are polluting our environment. Other innovators include Jessica Mitford, whose best-selling criticism of the undertaking industry was published in 1963 under the title *The American Way of Death;* Ralph Nader, whose *Unsafe At Any Speed* came in 1965; and John Galbraith, whose *The New Industrial State* (1967) among other things popularized the notion of the large company as a monster that held the consumer completely in its grip.

During this stage other authorities and advocates begin to join the dialogue. Molitor (1975) suggests the following rough sequence:

—Innate innovators,
—Leading experts,
—Public-spirited crusaders,
—Disciples spawned by crusaders,
—Research institutes (the "think tanks"),

—Government-sponsored research,
—Academia,
—Informal study networks ("invisible colleges"),
—Public policy research centers (e.g., Brookings),
—General intelligentsia,
—Idea synthesizers (who distill the research),
—Opinion molders,
—Issue popularizers (book reviewers, cabbies, barbers).

Stage 3: Establishment of Organizations. The third stage in the development of an issue involves the establishment of organizations, especially interest groups, to press forward demands that "something be done," that some social action be taken with respect to the issue. Advocates and authorities who emerged in the preceding stage are now trying to attract adherents who build up into formal followings and usually become institutionalized. Obviously, there is considerable overlap between this stage and the previous one. "Growth of institutional backing for a cause—whether measured by numbers of organizations, persons involved, or resources committed—follows exponential increases which tend to force serious consideration of the issue by public policymakers" (Maddox, 1972:209).

Stage 4: Policy Agenda. Wide discussion of an issue does not lead automatically into a public policy for several reasons. First, the distribution of influence and access in any political system has inherent biases. Consequently, the system operates to the favor of some and the disadvantage of others. Second, the range of issues that will be considered by a political system is restricted. In other words, the range and types of issues and alternatives considered represent the interests and most salient concerns of existing political powers. Third, the political system's inertia makes it extremely difficult to change the prevailing bias that determines which issues are viewed as legitimate concerns. From these three points flows a fourth: What happens in Congress and the White House may be less important than the prepolitical, or at least predecisional, processes.

To better understand these realities—to see the ways in which groups articulate needs and transform them into viable issues that require some type of ameliorative response by government—political scientists Cobb and Elder (1971) suggest greater attention to the notion of policy agenda. A *policy agenda* is that set of items explicitly up for active and serious consideration by authoritative decisionmakers. Cobb and Elder make a distinction, however, between serious and "pseudo-agenda items" to account for those issues that get only vocal attention from decisionmakers. The precise identification of the agenda is no simple matter, since one must establish criteria for determining what constitutes "active and serious consideration." But surely we can include here such formal expressions of agenda items as the president's State of the

Union Message, specific policy messages by the president, counterassessments by congressional leaders, and major bills introduced into Congress.

It is useful to think of the problem confronting any newly formed interest group of stage 3 as one of penetrating a screen of bias. For example, almost irrespective of the particular issue, there is a bias against groups whose members lack status and community standing. "In other words, people without resources (e.g., lower-income groups) will have more difficulty attaining legitimacy than their higher-status counterparts" (Cobb and Elder, 1971:909–10). If one puts this statement alongside the analysis of the environmental movement by Tucker (1977), an interesting conjecture becomes possible: To the extent that most groups opposing business activities today are made up of higher-status members of society, they will have less difficulty in penetrating the screen of bias.

Cobb and Elder also note cultural constraints on the range of issues that are considered legitimate topics for government action. For this reason, federal aid to elementary and secondary education was long considered by many to be an inappropriate area for federal action. Many other biases in the policy agenda might be noted: giving priority to older items, the selective attention of the political decisionmakers, unequal access to key officials, the existence of prior political debt to the interest group, resources of the group, and so forth. But the decisiveness of such biases must not be overstated. Likewise, the role of the media and of innate innovators who seize upon issues must not be underestimated.

Stage 5: Formalizing a Solution. Once a major social issue reaches the policy agenda, the process of formulating a specific plan of action can begin. The end is usually a public law—that is, assuming the issue does not evaporate or its resolution reach a stalemate. But the passage of a public law does not bring the cycle to an end: now the issue enters a stage in which the formalized solution is put into practice.

Stage 6: Social Control. Success here depends on (a) the degree to which the relevant administrative agencies (e.g., the Environmental Protection Agency) choose to enforce the new law, and (b) the degree to which affected businesses choose to resist it. In any event, over time, public attention with regard to the issue tends to decline and then level off, much like the sales of a product. But not in every case: False starts can occur when the initial "solution" proves ineffective. Public policy to deal with smog in Los Angeles, for example, began by seriously underestimating the contribution of automobile emissions to the problem. In addition to false starts, another phenomenon can occur in this final stage: *backlash*. In other words, many laws passed in a euphoric atmosphere of "solving a problem" begin in time to appear more costly and more troublesome than most had imagined when the solution was being formalized.

Already there is some indication that the environmental issue is experiencing some backlash.

After a decade of impressive gains in cleaning up the nation's air and water, the environmental movement by 1977 appeared to have entered a period of hard times. Jobs and energy seemed more important than pristine surroundings. Moreover, the mounting costs of antipollution equipment were outstripping original estimates. The upshot of all this was that, for the first time since they surged to popularity, environmentalists appeared to be losing more battles than they were winning.

Before concluding our discussion of the stages in the life cycle of a social issue, we should note the role that *precipitating events* can sometimes play in propelling an issue onto the next stage. For example, by exposing what he believed to be the lethal design of the Corvair, Ralph Nader hoped to flush the corporate managers from their cover and make them more accountable. He succeeded—thanks in no small degree to the fortuitous discovery that General Motors had instituted a spying campaign against him. This revelation seemed to validate Nader's argument that the corporation cared more about image and profit than about safety. "When a chagrined GM President James M. Roche offered Nader a public apology before a Senate committee, the Nader legend was born. An aroused citizen had waged a successful guerilla campaign against the world's most powerful corporation" (Ignatius, 1976). Similarly, precipitous events such as the Santa Barbara blowouts and Three Mile Island nuclear reactor breakdown have helped propel the issues of oil-pollution control and nuclear energy investment forward towards a solution.

It should be fairly apparent from this discussion that once an issue in the social environment has entered the last two stages in the life cycle model, it has entered the environment of politics and government as well. Because this arena is so important to the American business system, we need to consider it carefully. In this chapter we have explored the technological, economic, and social environments of business, but because the political environment is so poorly understood, we consider it separately in greater detail in the following chapter.

CHAPTER THREE

Understanding Change
in the Political
Environment

This chapter continues the tour of the macroenvironment of business we began in the last chapter. Of the five components making up the macroenvironment, the political one has perhaps the most visible impact on the daily operations of a company. As Theodore Levitt (1977a:21) writes:

> A listener these days to the sounds that fill the air where businessmen gather would think that instead of getting customers, he who builds a better mousetrap only runs into design difficulties, material shortages, patent-infringement suits, unauthorized work stoppages, collusive bidding, discount discrimination, confiscatory taxes, the Department of Justice, OSHA, EPA, the Equal Employment Opportunity Act, the Toxic Substances Act, HEW, exchange controls, currency fluctuations, environmentalists, the women's movement, and consumerists.

Furthermore, it is the political environment that seems to have increased the most in relative importance. Levitt continues:

> Compared to businesses today, business in the 1950s operated more confidently and securely, except for occasional audits by the Internal Revenue Service and gentle inquiries by the Federal Trade Commission. Presumably, business controlled its internal affairs pretty much without governmental intrusion. To be sure, there were a few officially regulated industries . . . but the regulators were widely advertised, not entirely without justification, as being in the hip pockets of the regulatees. The antitrust division of the Department of Justice and the Federal Trade Commission were, if not quiescent, docile. Occasional ritual sniffs at concentration in the steel industry and at the advertising artistry of hemorrhoid-remedy manufacturers confirmed their somnambulism . . . . Ralph Nader was a good little schoolboy from Winstead, Connecticut, sent off later for purification and acculturation in the melting pot of Princeton University. The NAACP had a proper regard for the rules of civility in representing its people, environmentalists (not yet so baptized officially) hiked the Appalachian Trail far, far away; judges (men of property to the core) were strictly strict constructionists; and Congressmen did their duty evenhandedly for local veterans' organizations and local industry . . . .

Because of this increased importance of the political environment to business, it might be wise to begin this chapter by discussing in a little more detail the implications of what some observers call the "second managerial revolution." We can then turn to some real nuts-and-bolts issues.

Specifically, in this chapter we develop a comprehensive framework for viewing at a glance the vast array of relationships that exist in the United States between government and business. For convenience, these relationships are grouped into two broad classes: supports and controls. Supports, in turn, are subdivided into at least four categories of government action: subsidies, promotion, contracts, and research. Similarly, controls are subdivided into investigation, antitrust, price control, and direct regulation.

Thus, we have eight major categories of interrelations between government and business. Once each of these has been defined and illustrated, our inquiry turns to the question of how specific supports and controls come into existence. (Here the life cycle of social issues model, discussed at the end of Chapter 2, should prove to be a fairly powerful explanatory theory.) Our search for the origins of government supports and controls then leads us into a discussion of interest group politics—who its participants are and how they interact with existing government institutions to help formulate public policy affecting business.

We see that public policy is the result of a complex interplay among interest groups, industry, the White House, Congress, the courts, and the government agencies. Particular emphasis is placed on the role of the courts, who review congressional legislation as well as agency actions, and also the agencies, who make rules and adjudicate in ways that profoundly affect business. The chapter concludes with a brief review of the increasing importance of the political environment at the state and local levels of government. ☐

A SECOND MANAGERIAL REVOLUTION?

Recall the thesis of Alfred D. Chandler, Jr., from Chapter 1: The real story of the late nineteenth century was the rise of the manager. While the Rockefellers, Carnegies, and Morgans did make fortunes, the important historical fact was the increasing distance between the owners and the managers who actually ran the companies and allocated the resources.

According to James Burnham (1941), technological progress and the growth of large-scale economic organizations deprived the old capitalist class of control of the means of production. Effective control within business enterprises had passed to the professional managers; formal ownership of the modern corporation had been separated from actual management. Although he was not the first to note this phenomenon,* Burnham did offer a snappy title for it: "the managerial revolution."

Today, in response to a number of changes in society, the U.S. government is becoming increasingly active in supervising the regulation of business activity. Some observers have, perhaps prematurely, viewed this activity as the dawn of a second managerial revolution—one in which the locus of real control over the corporation shifts from private executives to public officials within government agencies. Clearly, every major function of the company's operation is subject to governmental influence, if not outright control.

One way to see the pervasiveness of government regulation is to take the case of a specific industry such as steel. Robert A. Leone (1977) gives a thumbnail sketch of government's influence over that industry's inputs, processes, output, and general environment:

> Its *inputs* are strictly regulated: labor costs are controlled by state and federal Occupational Safety and Health Administration (OSHA) agencies, the Employee Retirement Income Security Act (ERISA), and the Department of Health, Education, and Welfare (HEW); the cost and availability of raw materials are regulated by the Bureau of Mines, the new Department of Energy, and the federal power authorities; and returns on capital are effectively regulated by the policies and practices of the Internal Revenue Service.
>
> The industry's *processes* are also heavily regulated: not only must U.S. Steel reduce water pollution, but it must do so using the best available technology.

---

* Almost a decade earlier Berle and Means (1932) observed that in the modern corporation, "ownership" had become a mere symbol. Power and responsibility, which had been an integral part of ownership in the past, were now lodged in the hands of a separate group, the managers.

Safety hazards cannot be eliminated by strict discipline and organizational control; they must be "engineered out."

Outputs are even more closely controlled. The size of the market available
to domestic producers of steel is regulated by foreign trade policies; price levels
are controlled—albeit implicitly—by jawboning. Even product characteristics
are effectively dictated by the purchasing criteria of the nation's biggest consumer—the federal government.

As if these controls were not enough, the government also regulates the
general business environment in which the steel industry operates through its
antitrust powers, enforcement of corporate law, and other activities that directly
limit the scope of private decision making. In short, the government controls the
steel industry's inputs, processes, and outputs as well as its overall business
environment.

Obviously, steel is a regulated industry. But so is virtually every other industry
in the United States.

One might think that since government bureaucrats have manfully shoul-
dered an increasing share of private sector decisions, business managers now
can become a more leisured class. However, nothing like that has happened.
What has happened is that piggy-backed onto the traditional tasks and responsibilities facing a manager are new ones, all pretty much generated by this
new wave of government regulation. Executive desk calendars reflect the
change; for example, Wednesday's production meeting is slashed from two
hours to thirty minutes in order to allow time for catching a 1:00 P.M. flight to
Washington to meet the EPA officials, or Friday's lunch with the company's
number-one customer is postponed in order to allow time for a talk to a local
consumer group. In short, the complexity of managing has increased.

Yet, aside from the costs in time and money and perhaps an uneasy feeling that the boundaries of managerial discretion are eroding, most business
managers today have very little idea where this mass of regulation has come
from or what it is really doing to the businesses they operate. They do not, in
short, understand the nature of the transition American business is in. Thus,
uncertainty compounds the complexity. This is the essence of the second managerial revolution.

The message of the foregoing discussion should be clear: The direct and
indirect influence of government action on business changes the kinds and mix
of skills that one needs to succeed as a manager. Among these new skills, the
ability to understand and work with government is surely at a premium today.
Indicative of these new realities was the selection of Irving S. Shapiro in 1974
as chief executive of DuPont. In the view of that company's board at least,
new conditions in the United States required a new kind of leadership—one
that understood government and the political conditions in the country and
that could address itself to some of those issues. Shapiro, luckily, had spent
eight years with the Department of Justice before joining DuPont.

Government and Business:
A Framework for Analysis

The number and variety of government programs affecting business is huge, although many are not necessarily designed with that goal in mind. On the contrary, they are directed toward goals as disparate as economic growth, job security, and environmental quality. It is useful and necessary for our purposes to establish a framework for organizing government actions into a number of self-contained program areas that reflect the major themes of current government policy. Such a framework can (a) provide a convenient analytical diagram for viewing the programs, (b) illustrate the program's relationship to business operations, and (c) furnish a common structure within which proponents of different viewpoints can make a case for reorientation of national policy regarding business. The framework developed for these purposes is shown in Exhibit 3–1.

PUBLIC POLICIES AFFECTING BUSINESS: SUPPORTS

Direct and Indirect Subsidies

Subsidy is a sensitive word around Washington. It rarely appears in announcements by public officials; nor does it appear in the index of the *Catalog of Federal Assistance,* which runs to nearly 1,000 pages.

Subsidy once took the form of directing the flow of resources to preferred users. Thus, land was granted in large amounts to stimulate the construction of railways so that agriculture, industry, and commerce could expand. Today it takes the form of directing the flow of money income to politically determined purposes. To chart the scope of subsidies to private enterprise, the Associated Press (see Shaw, 1973) examined the details of federal programs administered by sixty-one agencies. Among its findings were these:

- No breakdown is available in the number and value of government loans to profit-making concerns, but in fiscal year 1971 the total of outstanding loans—direct, guaranteed, and insured—had reached $250 billion, six times the outstanding installment credit advanced by all commercial banks.
- Transportation still ranks among the biggest recipients: millions a year are provided to keep the maritime industry afloat, to keep local-service airlines flying, and to help commuter railroads buy 875 new passenger cars.
- Defense contractors have custody of over $14 billion worth of taxpayer-owned property and can use government equipment for commercial work at least 25 percent of the available time.

Probably the loans in 1971 to Lockheed and in 1979 to Chrysler Corporation and the loan activities of the Small Business Administration (SBA) offer

EXHIBIT 3–1   Governmental Support and Control of Business

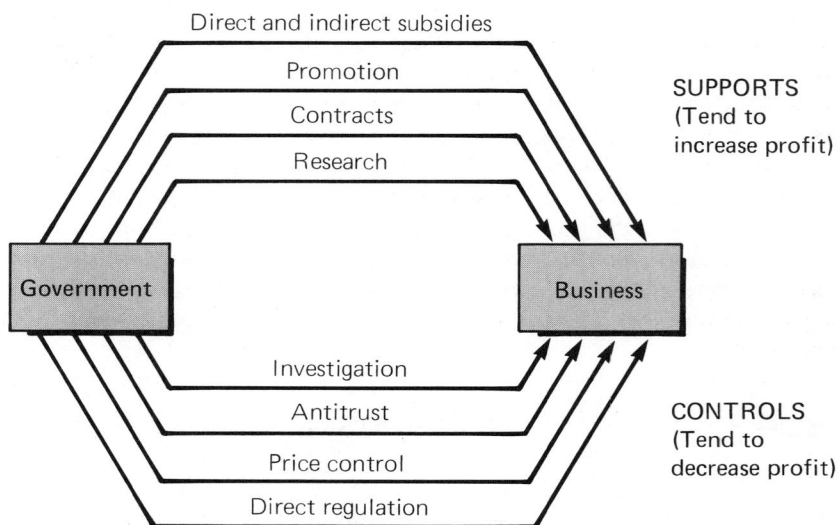

```
                    Direct and indirect subsidies
                         Promotion                            SUPPORTS
                         Contracts                            (Tend to
                                                              increase profit)
                         Research

        ┌──────────────┐                      ┌──────────────┐
        │  Government  │                      │   Business   │
        └──────────────┘                      └──────────────┘

                         Investigation
                         Antitrust                            CONTROLS
                                                              (Tend to
                         Price control                        decrease profit)
                         Direct regulation
```

the best-known examples of loan programs aimed directly at business. Guaranteed loans, such as Lockheed's or Chrysler's are private loans on which the federal government guarantees to pay all or part of the principal amount of the borrower's defaults. Actually, many individual loans make money for the government because of fees charged for the guarantees. The Lockheed loan, for example, netted the government $31 million.

A more direct form of subsidy involves *tax exemptions,* or *tax expenditures,* as they are increasingly called. (Business executives have their own preferred term—*incentives*—as the Doonesbury cartoon shows.) The most notorious tax benefit for a particular industry is probably the depletion allowance for the oil and mineral industries. Thanks to the oil-depletion allowance, among other tax benefits, the Atlantic Richfield Company, to take an extreme example, had a net income of $797 million and paid no federal tax from 1962 until 1968, when it paid at the rate of 1.2 percent. Nader (1971:16) provides us with a bouquet of other notorious examples:

> A survey by University of Texas Law School students shows that underassessment of the value of oil and gas properties belonging to Texaco, Shell, and Atlantic Richfield in one part of west Texas caused county taxes for homeowners and small businessmen to be 33 percent higher than they should have been. Over a period of seven years, a country school board in the region lost $7 million in taxes that it should have collected. Another inquiry by law students showed

that in Houston, Texas, industrial and commercial properties are assessed at about 13 percent of fair market value, while residential property is assessed at 31.94 percent.

In Gary, Indiana, the mayor, in an attempt to meet the city's financial crisis, ordered all city agencies to cut their budgets, including the budget for education. The big company in Gary is U.S. Steel. Between 1961 and 1971 its property assessment only rose from $107 million to $117 million, although during that period the company installed $1.2 billion worth of capital improvements. U.S. Steel refuses to allow the city authorities to examine its books and it refuses to apply for building permits, as required by city law, because this would reveal the size of its taxable investment.

Doonesbury

Doonesbury cartoon Copyright 1979 G.B. Trudeau/distributed by Universal Press Syndicate. Reprinted by permission.

Focusing exclusively on such examples, however, can be misleading. As Emmette S. Redford (1965:367) has pointed out, tax favoritism is also a form of budgeting of national income to purposes that have obtained a preferred position in the political arena. In other words, tax expenditures are in general due more to political decisions than to corporate conspiracies. Thus, to help reverse the deterioration of cities, President Carter proposed $1.7 billion in tax breaks in March 1978 to stimulate private investment in needy areas.

One final point on tax policy. It is arguable whether tax expenditures are really supports; in a sense, the tax collector also controls business activities. We can see this possibility most clearly in examples like the following: A plant, in order to qualify for rapid tax amortization of pollution control devices, must first be certified by both the state involved and the regional office of the Environmental Protection Agency. Similarly, for company contributions to a pension program to qualify as a tax deduction, the program must meet detailed requirements spelled out in the Employment Retirement Income Security Act of 1974.

Excise taxes are a less subtle way in which government can use taxes to control behavior. These taxes—imposed on the manufacturer, the retailer, or both—ultimately affect the consumer. The tax on cigarettes, for example, illustrates quite clearly how a tax can be used to curtail a potentially harmful practice (according to health officials, someone in the United States dies every 1½ minutes as a result of smoking) as well as to raise money. Indeed, the tax on cigarettes is now based on the individual brand's potential health hazard. In sum, taxes can be carrots spurring business to public goals, or they can be sticks nudging business away from activities that conflict with the public good.

Promotion

Government can also support businesses in ways that do not directly or indirectly involve payments of money. For example, the federal government, as we saw in the last chapter, attempts to manage the economy—that is, to smooth out the business cycle and to provide a reasonably certain environment with steady growth but without runaway inflation and bank failures. Stabilization policy benefits business enormously; without it, long-range planning would be futile.

Another very important example of promotion is the galaxy of efforts in which government engages to protect home industries from foreign competition. These efforts, among which tariffs on imports are perhaps the best known, will be dealt with in the next chapter.

The only major agency devoted almost exclusively to promotion is the Small Business Administration (SBA). In 1953 this agency started out with the simple duty of promoting "free competitive enterprise" by making credit, government contracts, and management advice available to small businesses. Since then, lobbyists for a bewildering array of special interests have persuaded the SBA to give priority to, among others, mass transit, job creation, energy conservation, antipollution investment, "urban neighborhood revitalization," and medical services. The agency also has special programs to secure government contracts and provide finance for small businesses set up by veterans and minorities.

The SBA's most useful service is unglamorous and, so far, underpublicized: The guarantee of up to 90 percent of the amount loaned by a bank to a small business. Direct loans, at an interest rate of only $6\frac{5}{8}$ percent, are made to those businesses that cannot raise credit from banks, even under the guarantees. (The scheme is compromised, however, by the "buddy system." The SBA knows, but cannot usually prove, that friendly but dishonest bankers give creditworthy businessmen letters saying that they are uncreditworthy.)

The SBA also has a program to make equity capital and long-term funds available to small businesses. The money is funneled through small-business investment companies (SBICs) that are owned by private-sector investors (often by banks) and licensed by the SBA.

Contracts

A third type of support is the government contract for construction, production, service, or analysis. The immediate objective may be the stimulation and support of industry, as when public works are expanded in recession or public expenditures are directed towards industrial revival in depressed areas. But the supportive objective is usually secondary to another objective of contracts: the furtherance of public goals such as national defense or education. Still, the benefits to business may be substantial.

Contracting itself is not new. All levels of government have hired contractors to construct public office buildings, dams, airports, sewers, schools, barracks, government-owned utilities, and similar projects. But, as Exhibit 3–2 shows, in recent years the scope of public sector contracts has moved far beyond capital projects.

Contracting explains the melancholy paradox of how the federal budget could increase from $70 billion a year to nearly $370 billion in twenty years without any significant increase in the number of full-time federal civil servants (see Starling, 1977:442–45). In 1946 the civil service payroll constituted 30 percent of the federal administrative budget; by 1966 only 22 percent was spent on full-time government employees, while 34 percent went to contractors. Since 1966 the government employee–private contractor breach has widened considerably. Today it takes nearly sixty-thousand full-time government employees merely to administer the almost $70 billion we spend annually on such contractors and the more than $50 billion we spend each year in grants to state and local governments, nonprofit organizations, and universities.

In an effort to bring order from the chaos of government purchasing policies and practices generated by an undertaking of this size, the federal govern-

EXHIBIT 3–2   The Expanding Scope of Governmental Contracts

Subject	Governmental customer	Corporate contractor
Auto safety	New York State	Fairchild-Hiller
Classroom scheduling	St. Louis junior colleges	McDonnell-Douglas
Desalinization plant design	U.S. Department of Interior	Lockheed
Education information system	City of Philadelphia	Philco-Ford
High speed ground transportation	U.S. Department of Transportation	Hughes Aircraft
Information system	State of Massachusetts	Lockheed
International development	Agency for International Development	Lockheed
Medical information system	State of Vermont	TRW, Inc.
Parcel sorter	U.S. Post Office	Aerojet-General
Power management system	U.S. Department of Interior	North American Rockwell
Regional development	Department of Commerce	Litton
Satellite communications	Comsat Corporation	Northrop
Supersonic transport aircraft	U.S. Department of Transportation	Boeing
Systems analysis of poverty	State of Colorado	Philco-Ford
Traffic-control system	New York City	Sperry-Rand
Waste management	State of California	Aerojet-General

Source: Abridged from *The Modern Public Sector,* by Murray Wiedenbaum, © 1970 by Basic Books, Inc., Publishers, New York. Reprinted by permission.

ment in August 1976 established the Office of Federal Procurement Policy (OFPC) as a semiautonomous wing of the Office of Management and Budget (OMB). As the first administrator of the new office, Hugh E. Witt, put it, "We are the interface between the executive branch and industry."

The contract should not be confused with public-private partnerships and governmental corporations. The former are businesslike corporations that are permitted to make a profit while performing some specific function desired by government. The Federal National Mortgage Associations and the Communications Satellite Corporation are cases in point. Such organizations operate in close cooperation with the government.

A government corporation, on the other hand, is a totally different corporate form designed to accomplish assigned public purposes. Such corporations are totally owned by the government, operated on a not-for-profit basis, and staffed by civil service employees. They have been in operation for as long as forty years, whereas public-private corporations have become significant only within the last dozen years. The TVA and the Port Authority of New York and New Jersey are examples of governmental corporations.

Contracts, like tax provisions, can have a dual effect—that is, government can use them either to support or to control business. And the latter effect should not be underestimated. Government procurement contracts, for instance, spell out not only what goods and services the contractors must provide but also how they should go about producing them. These requirements can range from hiring and training minority groups to adopting federally set wage and hour standards to favoring depressed areas and small business firms in subcontracting. Furthermore, a number of laws require federal contracting agencies to prefer domestic to foreign products (Buy American Act), to ship all military and at least one-half of foreign aid goods in U.S. vessels (Cargo Preference Act), to purchase all brooms and similar items from nonprofit agencies for the blind (Blind-Made Goods Act), to purchase only U.S.-made buses (1969 Defense Authorization Act), and to purchase meat only from suppliers who conform to humane standards (Humane Slaughter Act).

Research

In a gritty industrial area of Chicago stands a surrealistic gasworks: Banks of parallel pipes wind through a fourteen-story tower, flanked by spindly turrets seen amid spooky plumes of steam. The plant converts sulphurous Illinois coal into 1.5 million cubic feet of methane a day. Since methane is the chief component of natural gas, this plant's output could be sold as a cleanly burning fuel. But the owner, Bill Bair, does no such thing. After heating the coal ("kind of like cooking meat," he says), adding hydrogen, and carefully analyzing the resulting methane, he simply burns the gas in the air.

Mr. Bair is just practicing, and the federal government is watching closely to see what he learns. So far, the U.S. Energy Department and its predecessor agencies have sunk $44.5 million into work on this particular method of extracting gas from coal, with the gas industry contributing $15.4 million more. The scaled-down pilot plant here is supposed to test whether the process is good enough to enable a private company to build a commercial-sized plant someday and make money from it. The project just described (cited in Large, 1978) is just one example of federally financed energy research and development in recent years. In the name of the energy crisis, the federal government is trying to foster creation of whole new industries. As a crutch for future energy sellers and their customers, perhaps there has been nothing like this kind of government-sponsored research since the nineteenth-century gift of federal land for railroad rights-of-way in the West.

The federal government supports nearly one-fourth of all industrial scientists and engineers and, even more importantly, provides over half of all the money spent annually for research and development (see Exhibit 3–3). What makes the latter fact so important is that much of this research can be of po-

EXHIBIT 3–3   Research and Development: Who Puts Up the Money and Who Does the Work

Sector	As source of R&D funds (billions spent)	As R&D performer (billions spent)
Federal government	$25.8	$ 7.0
Industry	23.4	35.9
Universities	1.1	6.6
Other nonprofit institutions	.8	1.6
Total	$51.1	$51.1

Note: 1979 estimates; data converted to 1972 constant dollars.

Source: Adapted from Willis H. Shapley, *Research and Development in the Federal Budget: FY 1977* (Washington, D.C.: American Association for the Advancement of Science, 1978), pp. 91–92.

tential use to the business system. Of course, there is more behind the government's support of research and development than a desire to see big corporations make higher profits. The future health of the nation's security and economy (the two are not unrelated) depends on adequate support for research. The connection between national security and research expenditures should be apparent enough; not surprisingly, more than one-quarter of the $51 billion shown in Exhibit 3–3 is defense related.

To see the connection between the economy and research, however, requires that we recall a concept introduced in the preceding chapter: productivity—that is, output per man-hours. To measure it for a given country, we divide total output by labor-hours employed. Since 1967, the growth of productivity in the United States has been poor relative to other nations. For example, in the 1967–1976 period, U.S. output per man-hour grew 23.6 percent, while West Germany's grew 62.4 percent. To explain such a difference, we might say that the Germans just decided to work longer and harder. But that notion takes us almost nowhere, and it surely cannot explain such a wide difference.

A much stronger reason for the difference was that other nations were investing more in research on new technology. Clearly, technology plays a key role in boosting productivity. One need only consider how much farm machines and fertilizers have increased the productivity of farmers, or electric typewriters and copiers the productivity of office workers. Seen in this context, the following account from the British weekly *The Economist* (February 4, 1978) takes on special significance:

Continental Europe's capabilities in product and process innovation have, by and large, been growing relative to those of the United States (and Britain). There has been a striking decline in the proportion of America's GNP spent on research and development since the mid 1960s, while expenditures in continental Europe (especially in West Germany) grew rapidly. German and Swiss research and development as a percent of GNP surpassed the American level in 1973; and West German, Swiss, Dutch (and Japanese) privately funded research and development, as a percent of GNP, have come to surpass that of the United States.*

PUBLIC POLICIES AFFECTING BUSINESS: CONTROLS

Investigation and Publicity

Turning now to the four types of control that government can exercise over business, we begin with probably the least effective, namely, investigation and publicity. By means of hearings, reports, and news conferences, the government attempts to apply pressure on the behavior of business leaders. But the results are often no more than meaningless controversy, cascades of empty words.

Like all generalizations, this one has its exceptions. One of the most notorious occurred in April 1962 when Roger Blough, chairman of the U.S. Steel Corporation, handed President Kennedy a mimeographed copy of an announcement his company was making to the press at that moment: It was increasing the price of steel by six dollars a ton. The rights and wrongs of the increase need not concern us here; it is enough to say that all major steel companies followed the lead of U.S. Steel, and the president regarded the industry's action as a challenge to his policies. He immediately called a "crisis council" to resolve this issue. The publicity surrounding the following events was indeed effective and the offending corporations ultimately surrendered (based on Fairlie, 1973:162–66).

- The president denounced the steel companies, in a televised press conference at 3:30 P.M. on April 11, as selfish and unpatriotic, reminding his audience that "... we are confronted with grave crises in Berlin and Southeast Asia." He concluded: "I asked each American to ask what he would do for his country and I asked the steel companies ... we have had their answer."

---

* *The Economist* surveyed 64 large continental companies with extensive foreign manufacturing. The 38 that provided data for 1970 indicated they were spending an average of 3.2 percent of sales revenue for research and development; 90 American multinationals supplying similar data for 1967 averaged 2.4 percent of sales, and 114 American companies supplying data for 1974 averaged 2.6 percent. The proportion of U.S. patents issued to foreign individuals and firms has also risen markedly, from 21 percent in 1966 to 38 percent in 1973.

• Agents of the Federal Bureau of Investigation, ordered to assist in the inquiries of the Department of Justice, telephoned a reporter of the Associated Press at 3:00 A.M. on 12 April, and two of them arrived at his home at 4:00 A.M. to question him. Another reporter, John Lawrence of the *Wall Street Journal,* was awakened at 5:00 A.M., and at 6:30 A.M., when James L. Parks, Jr., of the *Wilmington Evening Journal,* arrived at his office to commence his day's work, two agents were waiting for him.

• The Federal Trade Commission began its own investigation of the commercial practices of the steel companies, with an implied threat of action.

• The Department of Justice announced that a grand jury had been convened.

• Committees of both the Senate and the House of Representatives were encouraged to commence their own investigations.

• The Department of Defense announced that it would deny contracts to the offending steel corporations, and awarded a $5-million contract for armor plate to Lukens Steel Company, one of the smaller corporations that had not raised prices.

• An intensive telephone campaign was waged to keep the smaller companies from raising prices.

• Throughout the few days of the crisis, there was an intensive process of leaking to the press vague threats of intended actions that the administration was considering—for example, to break up U.S. Steel into smaller units.

• A group from the Bureau of Labor Statistics prepared a study showing that the price increases were unjustified.

The real masters of the art of investigation are found in Congress, and by the mid-1970s, with the public looking for a scapegoat for high energy prices, many prominent business executives were getting used to appearing before congressional committees. On June 16, 1977, for example, it was the executives from Gulf who were scheduled to catch it. Before an overflow audience and color television cameras, Jerry McAfee, Gulf Oil chairman and chief executive officer, and S.A. Zagnoli, executive vice-president of Gulf Mineral Resources Company, faced a half-dozen congressional representatives (see Exhibit 3–4).

As chairman of Oversight and Investigations, a House subcommittee of the Committee on Interstate and Foreign Commerce, Representative John E. Moss was to investigate the effect that the now-disbanded international uranium producers' cartel had on the mineral's 600 percent rise in price. Moss set the testimony against a sinister backdrop: "Our hearings . . . will detail secret agreements between nations and companies to control the price of uranium." Representative Douglas Walgren told the crowd the cartel's documents "read almost like a Watergate transcript." Representative Albert Gore topped that by dubbing Gulf "a corporate Patty Hearst" and suggesting that a jury would find Gulf guilty "in about thirty seconds."

Late in the questioning, Zagnoli fell into an interrogator's trap. Yes, he said, it was hypothetically possible that if a cartel had not existed, uranium

EXHIBIT 3–4   One Type of Government Control: Investigation and the Ensuing Publicity

In June 1977, a congressional subcommittee investigated Gulf Oil Company in regard to high energy prices. As a part of the investigation, the subcommittee interrogated Gulf Chairman McAfee beneath four banks of blazing Klieg lights for four hours.

Source: Photo from Wide World Photos, Inc.

prices paid by American utilities might have been lower. The representatives closed for the kill:

> REP. SANTINI: You have just conceded on the record before this committee that [the cartel] did have an impact.
>
> MR. ZAGNOLI: I would say the impact was insignificant . . . .
>
> REP. MOSS (gaveling): Don't ever presume to do that [i.e., try to set the record straight] in this committee. You will let the congressman ask the question. When he has one for you, he will address it to you. Don't interrupt.

To summarize, as a means of controlling business, investigation and publicity may lack the force of law. Nevertheless, to the extent that these tools allow a president or a Congress to influence public opinion about an industry, investigation and publicity in the long run can be very important indeed.

Antitrust

Unlike investigation and publicity, the second type of control is rooted in law. A nationally prominent attorney, who later became an associate justice of the Supreme Court, once told a meeting of the American Bar Association that there was no sense worrying too much about the complexity of the antitrust laws. Antitrust, the attorney said, is in the good old American tradition of the frontier sheriff; he didn't sift evidence, distinguish between suspects, and solve crimes, but merely walked the main street and every so often pistol-whipped a few people. (Robert H. Bork tells that anecdote in the opening pages of his *Antitrust Paradox: A Policy at War With Itself.*)

Before we see why some observers consider this story an apt description of the state of the antitrust laws these days, we need to outline the three main federal antitrust statutes. First is the Sherman Act of 1890, which aims at restraints of trade and monopolies. The key passages are these:

> *Section 1:* Every contact, combination in the form of trust or otherwise, or conspiracy, in restraint of trade or commerce among the several States, or with foreign nations, is hereby declared to be illegal.

> *Section 2:* Every person who shall monopolize, or attempt to monopolize, or combine or conspire with any other person or persons, to monopolize any part of the trade or commerce among the several States, or with foreign nations, shall be deemed guilty of a misdemeanor.

Second is the Clayton Act, originally enacted in 1917, which expands the Sherman Act and regulates mergers (see Exhibit 3–5 for an illustration of the different types of mergers). The key passage is this:

> *Section 7:* [Corporations cannot hold stock in another company]...where in any line of commerce in any section of the country, the effect of such acquisition may be substantially to lessen competition, or to tend to create a monopoly.

Third is the Federal Trade Commission Act, also enacted in 1914, which is directed toward unfair and deceptive trade practices. The key passage is this:

> *Section 5:* Unfair methods of competition in commerce, and unfair or deceptive acts or practices in commerce are declared unlawful.

The philosophic essence of the U.S. antitrust laws is the belief in free and open competition fairly conducted and in the idea that business is better conducted by a large number of smaller entities competing against one another than by one or a few large entities. In this sense, big is bad. Thus, over the years antitrust enforcement in the United States seems to have had two essential purposes: to maintain and foster competition and to ensure fairness and prevent competitive excess.

EXHIBIT 3–5   Types of Mergers

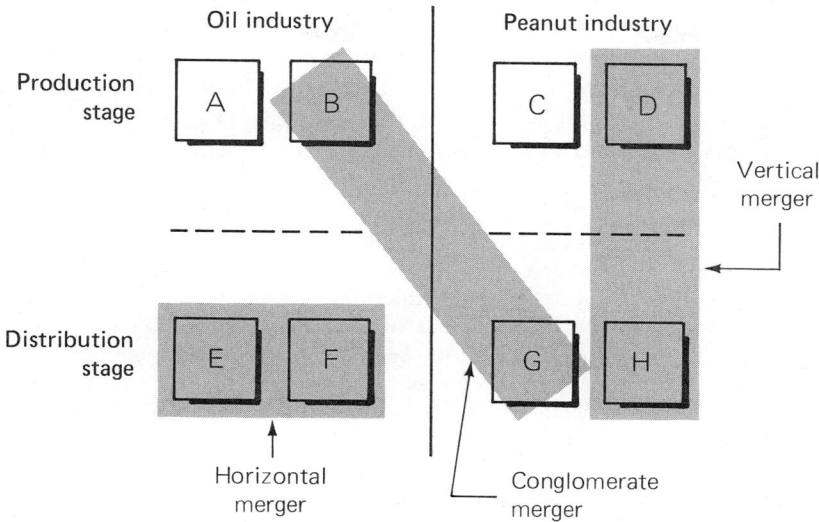

If Company E, which distributes petroleum products, takes over Company F, which is also involved in distribution of petroleum products, a horizontal merger has occurred. If Company D, which produces peanuts, takes over Company H, which is involved not in the production but in the distribution of peanuts, a vertical merger has occurred. Conglomerate mergers, however, involve acquisitions across industry lines—for example, the takeover of Company G by Company B.

Source: Adapted from Clair Wilcox and William G. Shephard, *Public Policies Toward Business* (Homewood, III.: Irwin, 1975).

Government Efforts to Promote Competition. Antitrust authorities attempt to create and maintain competition in various industries and markets and to ensure that it is not eliminated by cartels or other restrictive agreements that set mutually acceptable prices among industries. The authorities are particularly concerned with the structure of markets and industries. The objective is to procure the right conditions and ensure enough participants for viable competition to exist.

The classic examples of the concern with market structure were the 1911 cases breaking up the Standard Oil and tobacco trusts. We see the same purposes at work in more recent times in the Justice Department's attempt to break up IBM, AT&T, and Xerox. At this level there is little concern with evil intent on the part of companies or individuals; the aim is primarily to increase competition as such.

The rationale for stopping mergers by large companies is that this action stops the trend towards bigness—that is, the concentration of more and more business activity in fewer and fewer hands. Setting aside the question of whether such a trend even exists, let us look at the logic of the argument.

The problem with bigness, so the argument goes, is that it leads to "obscene" profits because of market domination. Sam Peltzman (quoted in Brozen, 1978:1470), however, is skeptical:

> No field in the industrial organization literature has been as well plowed as the relationship between concentration and profitability. . . . Despite its bulk, the literature fails to inform us how to interpret its main findings . . . . If concentration and profitability are indeed related, what market process produces the relationship? The traditional answer has been that high concentration facilitates collusion . . . . Unfortunately, this answer does not logically follow from the usual evidence, so its acceptance by economists and practitioners of antitrust policy is little more than an act of faith.*

So much for the logic behind efforts to stop mergers by large firms. Let us now take up the question of whether there is any discernible trend toward bigness. Is there a "creeping giantism" in the U.S. economy?

Exhibit 3–6 allows us a few simple conclusions. Between 1954 and 1976, the percent of sales accounted for by the largest one hundred industrial companies declined from 67.1 percent to 65.4 percent. Yet these figures tell us little about concentration in specific industries, such as automobiles, chemicals, textiles, and so on. (*Concentration* is the degree to which a relatively small number of firms account for a significant proportion of output, employment, and so on in an industry. An industry is highly concentrated, for example, if 80 percent of output is in the four largest firms.)

As J. Fred Weston (1972) shows us, most concentration in manufacturing is confined to six industries of very high capital intensity, in which enterprises of large scale are essential to realize economies of scale. No less than fifty-three of the largest one hundred American corporations are in petroleum refining, motor vehicles, steel, industrial chemicals, nonferrous metals, and aircraft. These are also the industries of highest concentration in other industrialized nations—an indication that common causal factors are at work.

Government Efforts to Prevent Competitive Excess. Antitrust officials also attempt to regulate competition in order to ensure that it is not excessive or cutthroat. The idea is to promote competition, but not "too much" or "too raw" a

---

* "From 1967 to 1973, prices in our most concentrated industries rose less than half as rapidly as prices in all manufacturing. From 1958 to 1965, prices in our most concentrated manufacturing industries actually fell while prices in other manufacturing industries rose" (Brozen, 1978:1476).

EXHIBIT 3–6   Percentage of Sales Accounted for by the Largest Industrial Corporations, 1955–1976

Industrial corporations	Percent distribution					
	1955	1960	1965	1970	1975	1976
First 500 largest	100.0	100.0	100.0	100.0	100.0	100.0
Lowest hundred	3.9	4.1	4.2	4.3	4.0	3.9
Second hundred	5.3	5.7	5.9	6.2	5.7	5.6
Third hundred	8.5	9.0	9.3	9.4	9.1	9.1
Fourth hundred	15.2	15.9	15.8	17.8	16.4	16.0
Highest hundred	67.1	65.2	64.7	62.3	64.9	65.4

Source: Adapted from Fortune Publishers, *The Fortune Directory,* New York, 1976, May, June, and July issues. Copyright by Time, Inc. Reprinted by permission.

type. The attack is on unfair trade practices such as price discrimination, refusal to sell, and boycotting. This aspect of U.S. policy is more concerned with how people behave than with larger questions of market structure. The focus is on predatory activities in the marketplace. Concomitantly, there is great concern at this level with the degree of wrongful intent of those accused of violations.

COMMENTARY: Antitrust's "Naughty" Words

These comments are among what Chicago attorney John Loughlin terms the "naughty" words of antitrust. They are the kinds of statements by aggressive corporate managers and salespeople that can trigger costly antitrust suits for employers: "We'll cut prices so low our competitors will be cut off at the knees."—"To you, Larry, and to you alone, the price we charge will be below cost."—"We'll scurry to become the industry leaders with the ultimate goal of grabbing at least 40 percent of all business."

Source: Reprinted by permission of *Wall Street Journal* (May 8, 1978), © Dow Jones & Company, Inc. (1978). All rights reserved.

Antitrust and Contemporary Business. Some people are arguing today that laws designed to meet the problems of the United States at the beginning of the twentieth century are not suitable to the economic conditions and political realities of the 1980s. According to this argument, business has grown too complex to be forced into the Adam Smith model of many small companies competing in local markets.

Robert H. Bork (1978), former solicitor general and now professor of law at Yale, believes that the Sherman Act was passed for a necessary and coherent public purpose: to maximize the economic welfare of American consumers. But over the years, he asserts, the courts—as well as the enforcement authorities and even defense lawyers who depend on the courts' judgments—have interpreted the antitrust laws to sanction a much vaguer, broader set of prohibitions against various business practices. It is not simply that the courts have made the antitrust laws "stricter" than the framers intended them to be; rather, the interpreters have actually succeeded in bringing about the exact opposite of what Congress had in mind. Senator John Sherman clearly wanted to enhance the efficiency of economic arrangements by putting an end to the artificial restriction of output that occurs when monopolists urge rivals to hurt each other. If the competition is promoting efficiency—that is, working well for the population as a whole—it may indeed destroy rivals who are relatively inefficient. By protecting the inefficient competitor, antitrust judges have done harm to competition. Perhaps most importantly, the law has had a pernicious effect with respect to the issue of mergers and levels of concentration. Bork thinks that current merger policy often bars the increased efficiency a merger might bring, even when the market shares involved could not possibly pose a real threat to the existence of significant competition in any line of commerce.

Bork does not wish to do away with antitrust law; instead, he wants to reform the standards by which it is applied and to direct it against those sorts of actions—for example, price fixing, horizontal mergers that create very large market shares, or deliberately predatory behavior—that make little or no redeeming contribution to efficiency. In all other cases, Bork would have us follow the imperatives of competition.

Price Control

In an effort to stop cost-push inflation (see Chapter 2), government may intervene in the private determination of wages and prices in a variety of ways. The mildest intervention is a general appeal to business and labor to exercise restraint in increasing wages and prices. We refer to this practice—this use of moral persuasion—as *jawboning*. But government can take more specific steps, such as setting voluntary standards, or *guidelines* considered to be in the public interest, for wages and price changes. Intervention can also involve pressure or even coercion, ranging from public chastisement of individual businesses and labor unions to threats to cancel government contracts or other benefits (like the threats used in the Kennedy–U.S. Steel controversy). Finally, government can either limit increases in wages and prices or absolutely freeze wages and prices for a fixed period of time.

The government's rationale for mandatory wage and price controls, at least in the case of large corporations, is the same one used for antitrust actions. High inflation, it is argued, is caused by the ability of relatively strong organizations in the economy to advance their income or to put up their prices. For example, large corporations contribute about half of all private production, and most are linked in a sort of mating dance with equally powerful unions. Enterprises with unorganized or fewer than a thousand workers do not need to be controlled because where there is no power to raise prices, no controls are needed.

In a speech before the Americans for Democratic Action, John Kenneth Galbraith (quoted in the *New York Times,* July 4, 1978) put the case for controls this way:

> Controls in their useful sphere do not interfere with operation of the market. They are made necessary by the very fact that organized power has displaced the market . . . with control over prices. The government is fixing prices that, in effect, are already fixed. It is private price fixing that makes necessary the public price restraint.

Politically, an argument like Galbraith's is attractive stuff. Yet, almost all economists say that compulsory wage and price controls are not the answer to inflation. Opposition to wage and price controls is found not only among conservative economists who generally oppose any government meddling in the economy, but also among liberals who generally favor government activism. Why?

In the first place, controls distort the normal allocation of resources. It is instructive to consider some of the thousands of practical difficulties that were involved in the efforts to control prices in the complex U.S. economy in the years 1971–1973 (following examples from Guzzardi, 1975, and Shultz and Dam, 1977).

● One source of frustration to the controllers arose from the undeniable but inconvenient truth that many products—cars and cabbages, to mention two—sell at different prices at different times of the year. The need for an adjustment for "seasonality" was easy to perceive, but hard to fill. Could resort hotels charge more over Labor Day than they charged over the Fourth of July? Was Halloween candy a seasonal product?

● From the start, agriculture presented a problem: too many farms growing and selling too many different products on too many markets. Consequently, raw farm products were exempt. The result was administrative chaos. Was honey a "raw" food, or was it processed by the busy bees? What if the honey were strained or drained? What about fish and other seafood when "shelled, shucked, skinned or sealed"? Cucumbers went up, but pickles were controlled; popped corn was controlled, raw corn was not. Since broilers were cut up and packaged before being sold, they were considered processed food, and their price was frozen. Thus, when the price of feed went up, the farmer simply discontinued production; the nation was shocked at pictures of thousands of chicks being drowned.

• Controls carried a number of hidden costs—for example, the amount of time that management spent to find ways to defeat them. In the lumber industry, some companies cut one-eighth of an inch off plywood sheets, described the cut as a "service," and then increased the price. Since domestic lumber was controlled but imported lumber was uncontrolled, lumber was "exported" and then "imported"—sometimes in fact and sometimes merely on paper, while the lumber sat in the yards. Corporate ingenuity also found other outlets. For example, General Motors made some standard equipment into optional equipment on some models. Some companies introduced "superior" products at higher prices than the ones being replaced. Cheaper products were phased out and only the more expensive left available. Alternatively, many companies that kept their full line on the market achieved savings by allowing quality to deteriorate.

A second reason why the experts tend to oppose controls is that controls affect only domestic prices. If prices are held below the world market value, then U.S. producers will be encouraged to export more. This leads to shortages at home and thus to more inflation. When prices were controlled in the years 1971–1973, fertilizer prices abroad climbed about three or four times their domestic levels. The result was a sharp increase in fertilizer exports and demands for export quotas.

Another example might be useful. Farmers use bailing wire to bundle crops. Before controls, much of the wire was imported from Japan. After controls, the Japanese producers withdrew from the U.S. market, since prices were going up elsewhere. Meanwhile, U.S. Steel found that the last price at which it sold bailing wire, which was the controlled price, would bring a loss to the company of about $100 for every ton of bailing wire it shipped. Under conditions so discouraging to production, the wire remained in short supply.

A third reason for the opposition to controls is that they are inherently unfair. They tend to freeze price and wage relationships as they exist at one moment in time and to prevent adjustments that are necessary as circumstances change. Consider the implications of attempting to control prices of only the larger firms as Galbraith proposes. The attempt breaks down when the commodity in question becomes scarce. Control of large firms' prices would result in a flow of the commodity to smaller firms that could buy it and subsequently sell it at the higher price. "Over a long enough period, we would have large firms with low prices and nothing to sell," George P. Shultz (1977:77) writes. Or consider what wage and price controls could do to high technology industries that believe they have earned a right to pay their employees at rates above some across-the-board ceiling. Since the only way employees could get a realistic raise would be to take a new job, a tight lid on wages would result in employees' quitting and going to work for the competition—a wasteful game of musical chairs.

Fourth, controls only delay inflation. Some economists argue that controls helped hold prices down in late 1971 and in 1972. But as controls were lifted, prices shot up 8.8 percent in 1973 and 12.2 percent in 1974. Some experts even say the inflation in those years was worse than it would otherwise have been because controls led to shortages. Furthermore, they discouraged investment. In the market, the reasonable expectation of an adequate return is what attracts new capital. That capital is used for new and more efficient facilities that increase supply, meet growing demand, and provide an elemental anti-inflationary force. To constrain prices discourages such investment. A study by a leading New York bank shows that the gap between planned and actual capital spending was larger during the control years than at any other time since 1953. The European experience with controls has been no better. All the nations of Western Europe have tried controls repeatedly in their efforts to contain inflation. All have failed.

Finally, controls deal only with the symptoms, not the causes, of inflation. Inflation basically results from an increase in the supply of money that exceeds the supply of goods and services. So long as this condition persists, inflationary pressures will increase and eventually explode in higher prices and wages.

What happens when more money is being created at the same time that some prices are being controlled? As a *Wall Street Journal* editorial (January 10, 1973) explained during the Nixon controls:

> If consumers have $10 and sellers offer five widgets and five gidgets, the widgets and gidgets can go for $1 each. If suddenly consumers have $12 and the stores still have the same five widgets and five gidgets, the price is likely to go up to $1.20.
>
> So along comes some Hammurabi and says we will stone to death anyone who buys or sells a widget for more than $1. So consumers can only spend $5 for the five widgets. But this leaves them $7 to spend on the five gidgets. Hammurabi is shocked to find that the price of gidgets soars to the unheard-of height of $1.40.

In short, uncontrolled prices will be bid up with whatever funds are available; an average 11 percent money growth will mean something like 11 percent inflation, with commensurate wage-insurance payments.

Direct Regulation

Broadly defined, our fourth type of control, *regulation*, refers to the prescription of standards of conduct, operation, or service. In this sense, it certainly applies to the two preceding types of control: antitrust and price control. The term *direct regulation* specifically highlights regulations that are designed to do one of the following: (1) protect health, morals, and safety; (2) protect the interests of customers and employers from business exploitation; (3) protect the interests of inventors and competitors from business exploitation; or (4) control the entry into certain markets like transportation or broadcasting. Because the first two kinds of regulation have generated so much controversy in recent years, they will be dealt with in depth in Chapter 5. Our discussion here focuses chiefly on the last two varieties.

Protecting Inventors and Competitors. A special kind of governmental control is the body of law governing copyrights, trademarks, and patents. Although commonly regarded as regulation, these laws might be considered a form of protectionism.

Copyrights protect the originators of literary, dramatic, musical, artistic, and other intellectual works. Any printed, filmed, or otherwise recorded material can be copyrighted. The owner of a copyright has the exclusive right to reproduce (hence "copy"), sell, or adapt the work. The registrar of copyrights in the Library of Congress issues copyrights upon an application from the creator or from someone deriving his or her right directly from the creator. (For a book, the applicant would be either the author or the publisher.) Since January 1978, under new copyright law, the duration of copyright protection is the life of the author or creator plus fifty years.

A *trademark* relates to any work, name, symbol, or device that is used in trade with goods to indicate the source or origin of the goods and to distinguish them from the goods of others. Trademark rights may be used to prevent others from using a confusingly similar mark, but not to prevent others from making the same goods or from selling them under a nonconfusing mark. Similar rights, called *service marks,* may be acquired for marks used in the sale or advertising of services. Trademarks and service marks used in interstate or foreign commerce may be registered in the U.S. Patent and Trademark Office.

U.S. exporters generally regard adequate trademark protection abroad for their goods and services as essential to development of foreign markets. A trademark provides important identification for a firm's products and services in foreign markets, just as it does in the United States, and also serves as the focal point around which that firm can develop its advertising and sales promotion campaigns. The mark also symbolizes to the buying public the goodwill, quality standards, and reputation inherent in the firm's products and services.

As with copyrights and trademarks, how one views the third form of protectionism, *patents,* depends upon where one sits. For the inventor of a new product or process, a patent means that the government has granted him or her the privilege to exclude others from making the invention. In the United States any process or device may be patented if it is novel and useful and if plans and a working model are supplied to the U.S. Patent Office. The patent is valid for seventeen years. This period, presumably, is sufficient time for the inventor, or his or her company, to secure an adequate return on the investment but does not deprive the public and other companies the free use of the invention for an unreasonable length of time.

Controlling Entry into Certain Markets. The essence of *licensing,* one of the most persistent forms of government control, is that government consent must be obtained before action is taken. Ernest Freund (1928: Ch. 7), therefore, called it the "enabling power" of government; Anshen and Wormuth (1954: 136) refer to it as "governmental preconditions to business action." Licensing was widely used in the states in the early part of our history (see Redford, 1965:9). It was the core of the first national act for regulation of a major industry—an act of 1863 that required chartering for national bank status.

The most common usage of the word *licensing* is in expressions such as "license to teach," "license to practice medicine (or law)," "license to sell," and "license to broadcast." But, given the broad meaning of the word, which covers all types of requirements for government approval before action is taken, it is not hard to see how it can also apply to other commercial activities. Thus, entry into regulated transportation for, say, a household utility service generally requires a *certificate of public convenience and necessity.* Cities require a *franchise* for municipal utility service. States require *articles of incorporation* to organize in the corporate form.

Permit is yet another kind of license. During the 1970s many companies began to find that to obtain a permit required considerable skill and endurance in bureaucratic maze running. And not all companies reached the cheese. For example, in early 1975 Dow Chemical proposed a $500 million petrochemical facility in the San Francisco Bay Area. The project faced a host of overlapping and intertwined regulations, and local pollution control authorities denied Dow a permit to construct the first phase, despite their admission that it was the cleanest facility they had ever seen. Rejection came on the basis of a restrictive regulation that related to local and federal ambient air standards. The Air Pollution Control officer told Dow that under present regulations there was no way he could grant a permit, even if the company were to meet all emission standards. His only suggestion was that Dow persuade the U.S. Congress to change the Clean Air Act. Consequently, after two years of intensive effort—after spending $4 million in costs and $6 million for the property—Dow was able to obtain only four minor permits of the required sixty-five. Paul E. Oreffice, Dow's president, commented: "Sadly, we were not turned down on most of these permits—only one out of the 65. We were simply unable to hack through the regulatory morass and get straight answers. Early this year, therefore, we took our sole remaining option: We cancelled the California project" (*Wall Street Journal,* July 26, 1977).

More successful than Dow, however, was a consortium of ten oil companies that sought to drill an exploratory oil well off the New Jersey coast. In early 1978 they finally received the needed permits from the Department of

Interior Geological Survey and from the Environmental Protection Agency, as well as approval from the Army Corps of Engineers.

ORIGIN OF SUPPORTS AND CONTROLS: INTEREST-GROUP POLITICS

In light of this vast tangle of controls and supports, one might be inclined to take a step or two backward and ask how the U.S. government got to this point. An answer is not hard to find: Just recall the life cycle of a social issue model. Structural changes—technological, economic, demographic, and cultural—begin to occur in a society. Then the belief grows that something is wrong, that a problem does exist. Soon organizations, either new or established, begin to pick up this belief and articulate it. If these groups are successful, then the issue enters what was called in the last chapter the policy agenda—that is, important decisionmakers in society begin to take note of the problem. In time, various plans of action are propounded. If any plan gathers sufficient political support, it becomes law or public policy, which is the same thing. The last step is social control, which simply means that some part of the bureaucratic machinery of government has been assigned responsibility for obtaining the goals of the new policy. In a sense, the last step in the cycle has no terminal point for implementation of public policy is generally a continuous process.

While the foregoing summary does answer the question of where public policies affecting business come from, it is really too superficial to be of any use to a business manager. Managers need to know three things. First, in order to anticipate future public policy initiatives, they need to know something about the organizations that press the political system with demands. In order to be in a better position to influence the formulation of public policy, they need to know something about how policy is hammered out. And, then, in order to cope with various government agencies assigned to implement public policies, managers need to understand policy administration.

Functions of the Interest Group

In the United States the interest group performs two basic political functions in the making of public policy. The first, as we have seen, is to aggregate, compromise, and define the interests (and therefore the policy positions) of a certain sector of the population with respect to a social issue. As Redford (1968:61) has pointed out:

> This is an important intermediary step in policymaking. If performed successfully it will reveal to the ultimate policymakers the basic clusters of interests that exist. If performed openly, it may reveal also the disunities within interest-group communities. Let me illustrate from my studies of the Air Transport Association. Its members are certificated commercial air carriers. These member com-

panies have a common interest: a favorable regulatory climate that prevents entry of new companies, safeguards profits, provides safety, and in general promotes air transportation. They also have conflicting interests—for example, between trunk lines and local service carriers, and between carriers in each category seeking expansion of their routes. The association will aggregate and define the common interest but leave to the individual companies the representation of their separate interests.

The second function of interest groups is to provide access to government for the common interests of the group. This means bringing to the attention of public officials information about what the interests are, the number of people affected, and the intensity of feeling about an issue. Thus, interest groups participate in the bargaining through which an accommodation of interests is achieved. We shall consider this second function more closely in Chapter 13; in this section, however, we want to see which groups represent the interests of business and which groups challenge those interests.

Types of Interest Groups

It is useful to classify these many groups by their objectives. If a group's objectives are quite broad, we can simply call it a *big-interest group*. (Examples of such groups include the Chamber of Commerce, U.S.A. and the AFL-CIO.) Such groups sometimes attempt to integrate so many diverse interests that we might think of them as "umbrella" organizations. If a group's objectives are more narrowly defined—and here we must make a subjective judgment—then we can call it a *special-interest group*. A special-interest group tends to be based on a particular industrial sector, trade, or occupation. (Examples are the American Bankers' Association and the United Mineworkers.*)

In the last decade it has become necessary to give recognition to a third type of interest group, the *public-interest group*. Jeffrey M. Berry (1977:7) gives this definition: "A public-interest group is one that seeks a collective good, the achievement of which will not selectively and materially benefit the membership or activities of the organization." The term *collective good* refers to any public policy whose benefits may be shared equally by all people, independent of their membership or support of a given group. This component of Berry's definition distinguishes public-interest groups from the other two types. Common Cause and Zero Population Growth, Inc., are examples of public-interest groups.

---

* Almost every line of industrial and commercial activity has its own association. The enumeration of a few organizations will suggest their variety: the American Petroleum Institute, the National Coal Association, the Associated General Contractors of America, the National Canners' Association, the Distilled Spirits Institute, the American Cotton Manufacturers' Association, the National Lumber Manufacturers' Association, the American Iron and Steel Institute, the American Newspaper Publishers' Association, the National Fertilizer Association, the Automobile Manufacturers' Association, the Pin Manufacturers' Institute, the National Retail Dry Goods Association, and the American Federation of Retail Kosher Butchers.

Big-Interest Groups. It is important to recognize from the start the diversity of political and economic objectives among business groups. "The intricacies of political and economic relations create endless clusters of companies, each with its own common concern and common enemies. Business is crisscrossed by divisions that set this category of enterprises off against that" (Key, 1964:84–85).

Economist Edward J. Mitchell (1974) has provided an excellent illustration of this kind of complexity of interests in an energy policy situation (see Exhibit 3–7). Mitchell introduced the chart in Exhibit 3–7 as follows:

> Perhaps the most crucial energy issue to come before the Congress is the president's bill to deregulate the wellhead price of new-contract natural gas to be sold in interstate commerce. It is assumed here that the natural gas–producing industry is competitive and that the principal initial impact of deregulation would be to raise the price of new gas .... I will attempt here to indicate some of the winners and losers if such a bill were to pass, but it must be recognized that this is only a rough speculation.

EXHIBIT 3–7   Gainers and Losers from Deregulation of Natural Gas Prices

Gainers	Losers
Owners of natural gas resources	Natural gas consumers with assured supplies of domestic gas for many years
Oil and coal consumers	
Owners of resources complementary to gas in consuming states	Intrastate pipelines
Suppliers of drilling equipment	Owners of resources complementary to gas in the producing states
Suppliers of oil in regions where gas would no longer be competitive with oil (New England, for example)	Shipyards building LNG ships (and their employees)
Natural gas consumers who would otherwise be cut off	Oil producers (highly correlated with gas producers)
Interstate pipelines	Coal producers
Consumers of imported items (due to higher exchange value of the dollar)	Builders of synthetic gas plants
U.S. importers (other than oil and gas)	Suppliers of oil in regions where gas has been short (e.g., Middle Atlantic states)
	Propane suppliers
	Natural gas consumers in producing states
	Oil-exporting nations
	U.S. exporters

Source: Adapted from Edward J. Mitchell, "Research on Energy Policy-Making," in Landsberg et al., Energy and the Social Sciences (Washington, D.C.: Resources for the Future, 1974), p. 587. Reprinted by permission.

Obviously, without a clear-cut notion of where business interests lie, the job of the spokesperson for the entire business community is not easy, and probably impossible. The most conspicuous candidate for the job, however, is the Chamber of Commerce of the United States. It is a federation of over three thousand other business organizations, such as state and local chambers of commerce, trade associations, and so on.

Unlike trade associations, which may only incidentally be concerned with public policy, the major function of the Chamber is to speak for American business on issues of public policy. Given the previously noted types of conflicts of interest on particular issues among the diverse membership, the Chamber cannot take a stand on all issues of concern to all types of business. Still, it does speak—often with considerable forthrightness—on those issues on which business as a whole has a common interest and a common view.

Although the Chamber of Commerce is the most conspicuous organ for the promulgation of the business viewpoint, other organizations articulate shades of opinion within the business community. One of the more important of these is the Committee for Economic Development. Incorporated in 1942 the CED represented a sharp departure from the past for the business community: A group of business leaders had come to the conclusion that both big business and big government were here to stay, that the policy of obstruction that had characterized the more vocal organs of business was self-defeating, and that business had a responsibility to propose rather than merely oppose. Thus, the CED has undertaken to develop through "objective research and discussion" recommendations that will contribute to maintenance of employment, increased productivity and living standards, and greater economic stability. The CED attempts to bring about public understanding of its recommendations for achieving these ends, but it leaves the lobbying to others.

Another articulate organ of business is the National Association of Manufacturers, formed in 1895 to promote the cause of trade and commerce by aiding in the passage of legislation and by other means. Like the Chamber of Commerce, this association has a heterogeneous membership and must concentrate its efforts on those matters in which its membership has common cause. Yet, since the NAM has a much less varied membership than the Chamber, it is "a more zealous and hard-hitting organization." Or, at least, that was the estimation of political scientist V.O. Keys, writing in 1958.

Of all these broad-based organizations, the newest, and perhaps most influential, is the Business Roundtable, an organization of the chief executive officers of the largest and most prestigious corporations. The Roundtable was founded in 1972, when business was doing badly in politics and Nader was winning victory after victory. The Roundtable has its own staff and activities, although it works with the older and larger groups and uses the services of the traditional Washington lobbyist-lawyers. Its aim is to analyze issues (energy, taxes, the environment, and so on), take positions, and get members of top management personally involved in presenting views to the Congress and to senior officials in the executive branch. In short, Roundtable's objective is political clout.

Wiedenbaum (1977) thinks that the trend toward the formation of business "umbrella" organizations in Washington is likely to continue because federal regulations—those from the EPA, for example—extend to nationwide activities and cut across industrial boundaries. In the past, federal regulations—those from the Interstate Commerce Commission, for example—affected primarily only one industry, transportation.

Special-Interest Groups. Trade associations also stand between government and business. Besides holding membership in the Chamber of Commerce or NAM, almost every company belongs to an industry association. There are big ones like the American Bankers' Association, small ones like the National Association of Women's and Children's Apparel Salesmen, odd ones like the American Horse Council. Government affects all businesses; ergo, all businesses organize.

The operations of the American Iron and Steel Institute (AISI) illustrate how trade associations can help industries win friends and influence. After facing sometimes hostile presidents (as in the case of the Kennedy–U.S. Steel controversy), an indifferent public, and a suspicious Congress, the steel industry since 1977 has gained a modicum of favor. In explaining this fundamental change in the way the steel industry is regarded in the nation, one must consider more closely the institute and its chairman, Edgar B. Speer.

Originally headquartered in New York, with largely a research and statistical role, the AISI moved to Washington in 1971 to cope with the increasing pressure of federal regulations in the environmental and safety fields. It began to bring greater coordination and sophistication to the industry's lobbying efforts by preparing position papers for public relations campaigns and to develop common strategies for industry lobbyists through its Government Relations Committee. In the past, the industry's top executives tended to stick to running their companies and letting their lobbyists do the infighting in Washington. Mr. Speer called the prevailing attitude one of "We fight our battles and you fight yours."

Appointed chief executive officer of U.S. Steel in 1972, Mr. Speer made it evident that, unlike his predecessor, he intended to make himself accessible to the press. Within months, he went on television's "Face the Nation" to present the industry's case in a struggle with the Nixon administration over a price increase. The *New York Times* (January 15, 1978) noted that his "craggy, lean face, sometimes topped by a white safety helmet, on a plant tour peered from the covers and front pages of the nation's publications." In 1976, when Mr. Speer was elected chairman of the AISI two of the most powerful positions in the industry were held by one man, and, in this case, it was a man who had long been convinced that the industry as a whole must assert itself more forcefully in Washington. The results? The public became interested, even sympathetic—though, to be sure, mill closings and cutbacks in mid-1977 also helped raise the level of public concern. Congress, spurred by dozens of its members organized into steel caucuses, also offered support, and the president developed a wide-ranging assistance program.

It seems fairly clear that this pattern will be repeated more often. As federal agencies establish newer forms of controls over business, member companies will look increasingly to their associations to (a) explain the rules to them and (b) take public stands that companies may not want to take individually. Indeed, federal agencies often foster the relationship between associations and member companies, since rather than meet with the companies individually, they encourage many companies in a given industry to present their views through a single association. For example, the secretary of the treasury meets four times a year with two industry-association committees that advise the department on the quarterly financing of the public debt (see Wiedenbaum, 1977:264).

Public-Interest and Consumer Groups. In contrast to the special-interest groups, public-interest organizations claim to speak for the public—that is, consumer—interests. They also follow different strategies. The special-interest lobbies, on the one hand, reward friendly legislators with campaign contributions—still important despite the trend toward public financing of elections—and rely on business and union leaders in the legislator's district to apply pressure. Public-interest lobbies, on the other hand, concentrate on the press and television; their weapons are the news conference and streams of studies and reports.

An example of the effectiveness of public-interest groups is the defeat in 1977 of the cargo-preference bill that would have required 9.5 percent of imported oil be carried on U.S. ships. Three years earlier, a tougher version, requiring 30 percent of imported oil to be brought in on American ships, breezed through Congress, though it was vetoed by President Ford. Why had this cargo-preference legislation failed to breeze through Congress in 1977? One answer—probably the main one—was that Common Cause, a broad-based public-interest group, had attacked it. Common Cause published a list of 215 House members who had received a total of $449,410 from maritime unions in their 1976 campaigns. Common Cause called the bill "a political payoff," one that would also increase the cost of oil to the consumer.

The defeat of the cargo-preference bill, which had White House and labor support, illustrates both the growing influence of public-interest groups and the way concern for procedures of accountability have affected legislation. It was Common Cause, for example, that led the successful fight for disclosures of campaign contributions, and it was those same disclosures that the lobbying group used effectively to kill the cargo-preference bill. "It's self-perpetuating,"

COMMENTARY: A Contradiction in Terms for at Least One Public-Interest Group

"The oddest thing about Nader is that despite what he believes and despite the way he conducts his life, he has become very much like the corporations he sees as his enemies. His organization has become so large and diffuse and bureaucratic that it resembles the divisions of General Motors or some interlocking directorate . . . . He so dominates the consumer movement and consumer journalism that it is hard to conceive what it would be like without him. He's a kind of monopoly."

The Nader Network

Source: Drawing by Randy Jones, © 1978 by The New York Times Company. Reprinted by permission.
Text from David Sanford, *Me and Ralph* (Washington, D.C.: New Republic Book Company, 1976).

one member of the House said. "They support measures that provide for more information and spotlights, and then the information produces more reforms" (*New York Times,* November 20, 1977).

In contrast to the broad-based organizations—such as Common Cause, the Consumer Federation of America, and the various Ralph Nader groups— are the public-interest groups with a single purpose. These single-purpose groups include such organizations as Energy Action, Friends of the Earth, Bread for the World, and the National Clean Air Coalition. Sometimes, however, these groups conflict with each other: The Committee for Handgun Control, for example, opposes the Citizens' Committee for the Right to Bear Arms while the National Abortion Rights League works against the National Committee for a Human Life Amendment.

Overall, what kind of results have public-interest groups had? In general, they have been fairly effective. In addition to the successes already mentioned, they also played an important role in 1977 in the passage of ethics codes in both the House and the Senate, the Clean Air Act, a strip mining bill; a water pollution control act, and legislation to create a Legal Services Corporation and a consumer cooperative bank. They did, however, lose the consumer-protection bill and a battle for public financing of congressional elections, legislation on which was postponed. They were also defeated on a bill to provide managerial reforms in the House and to give consumers standing in various lawsuits.

From Jefferson to Jarvis:
How the Interest State Grew

The number and influence of interest groups pressing their special demands on government seem to be reshaping the character of the American political environment. The success of Common Cause, consumer activists, the women's movement, environmentalists, and other groups on the political Left has brought a reaction on the Right. Disturbed by what they see as excessive or unfair government regulation, more and more corporations and trade or professional associations have set up political action committees through which their employees or members may contribute to campaigns (see Chapter 13).

Today, therefore, many more activists are sounding off on more issues. Consumerism is broader and deeper than it ever was, even among unaffiliated people. It dwarfs the labor movement of the 1930s, according to pollster Louis Harris. Even if he did not count those who see themselves first as business people, farmers, or union or minority-group members, he says, more than seven out of ten American adults are potential consumerists. For example, in 1976 "citizens coalitions" managed to place bread-and-butter economic proposals of vital concern to many businesses on state ballots. In fact, of the twenty-three states that permitted such petitioning for citizen-sponsored ballot proposition, fourteen had such initiatives on the ballot (see Exhibit 3–8).

EXHIBIT 3–8   The Business Issues on State Ballots

Proposition	State
Nuclear power	
Tighten safety requirements for nuclear power plants or nuclear waste disposal systems	Colorado, Montana, Ohio, Oregon, Washington
Utility rates	
Reform utility rate-setting procedures	Ohio, Massachusetts
Increase consumer representation before state utility commissions	Colorado, Ohio
Prohibit including the cost of power plants under construction in rate bases	Missouri
Taxes	
Replace sales tax on food with severance tax on oil and minerals and higher cor, orate taxes	Colorado
Remove sales tax on food and drugs and impose a special sales tax for conservation projects	Missouri
Remove sales tax from electricity, reduce sales tax on most other items	North Dakota
Spending	
Limit state spending to 8.3% of total personal income	Michigan
Replace flat rates with graduated income tax	Massachusetts, Michigan
Freeze state spending at present level for next five years and phase out federal aid to state	Utah
Ethics	
Tighten conflict-of-interest rules and other ethics requirements for legislators and other state employees	Florida, Illinois
Create office of state prosecutor to probe official corruption	Maryland
Environment	
Require mandatory deposits on throwaway beverage bottles and cans or ban their use	Colorado, Michigan, Massachusetts, Maine
Repeal mandatory state auto-emission testing	Arizona

Source: Data from Council of State Governments.

Consumers, it seems, are creating a multifaceted revolt against what they perceive as wasteful government spending that only adds to the inflationary spiral. The so-called tax revolt is a central issue; it began in June 1978 with the passage of California's Proposition 13, by which voters severely restricted the state's ability to assess property taxes. The antitax campaign in California was spearheaded by retired businessman Howard Jarvis, aged seventy-five. The tax revolt quickly spread and, by 1979, an effort to amend the Constitution to restrict government spending was well under way.

As Ester Peterson, President Carter's special assistant for consumer affairs, says, "People are simply not afraid to complain anymore." Ms. Peterson is happy—but should she be? Not a few political officials and experts see the trend toward more and stronger interest groups weakening the two national political parties. *Issue politics,* as it is called, has gained ground at the expense of party politics. Briefly described, the sequence of events is as follows:

1. An immense shift of institutional power from the executive branch to the legislative has followed the excesses of the so-called imperial presidency.
2. Within this more independent Congress, individual members also are more independent, to the point where party or presidential programs—even in vital areas such as energy—have become all but impossible to sustain.
3. Since the highly charged 1960s, virtually everything has been politicized, organized, and computerized, all of which enhances the proliferation of single-interest lobbying, conducted with effective new mailing and research techniques and largely directed at preventing action on issues a group considers important.

These developments, as some see them, are tending to bring the American political system to a halt—a view apparently not shared by Ms. Peterson. In 1975, a small group of political scientists became so concerned that they decided to stage a small demonstration in Washington. Gathering at the foot of the Jefferson Memorial, they distributed a statement that began:

> We meet today, at the shrine of American democracy, to deplore the disintegration of a basic American institution. Our political party system, first inspired by Thomas Jefferson, is in serious danger of destruction. Without parties, there can be no organized and coherent politics. When politics lacks coherence, there can be no accountable democracy.

POLICY FORMULATION: A CONCEPTUAL OVERVIEW

The question before us now is this: How do these various interest groups interact with major governmental institutions to develop new, or modify existing, public policy? Since we are interested primarily in policies that affect business operations, the question is of some import. However, no general description of policy formulation can ever adequately answer this question; such a description would have to be valid over a staggering range of public policies and multiplicity of bureaucratic agencies and commissions. (The list of laws and agencies in Appendix A only hints at the scope of the problem.)

Nevertheless, there is much to be gained if we have a conceptual view of how public policy is formulated. Building on the work of Easton (1965) and Krasnow and Longley (1978), Exhibit 3–9 identifies six recurring participants in the formulation of public policy. In addition to the regulated industries and citizen groups are four key political institutions: Congress, the White House, the courts, and the bureaucracy. The last-named institution may be either an agency within an executive department or an independent regulatory agency. Generally, presidential control of the agency is much weaker in the latter case, since it is limited largely to appointment power and persuasion, but many agencies within an executive department enjoy considerable autonomy due to their strong ties with Congress, industry, and citizen groups.

Exhibit 3–9 plots these and other channels of influence among the participants in policy formulation. The roles of the White House, the courts, and citi-

EXHIBIT 3–9   The Policy Formulation System

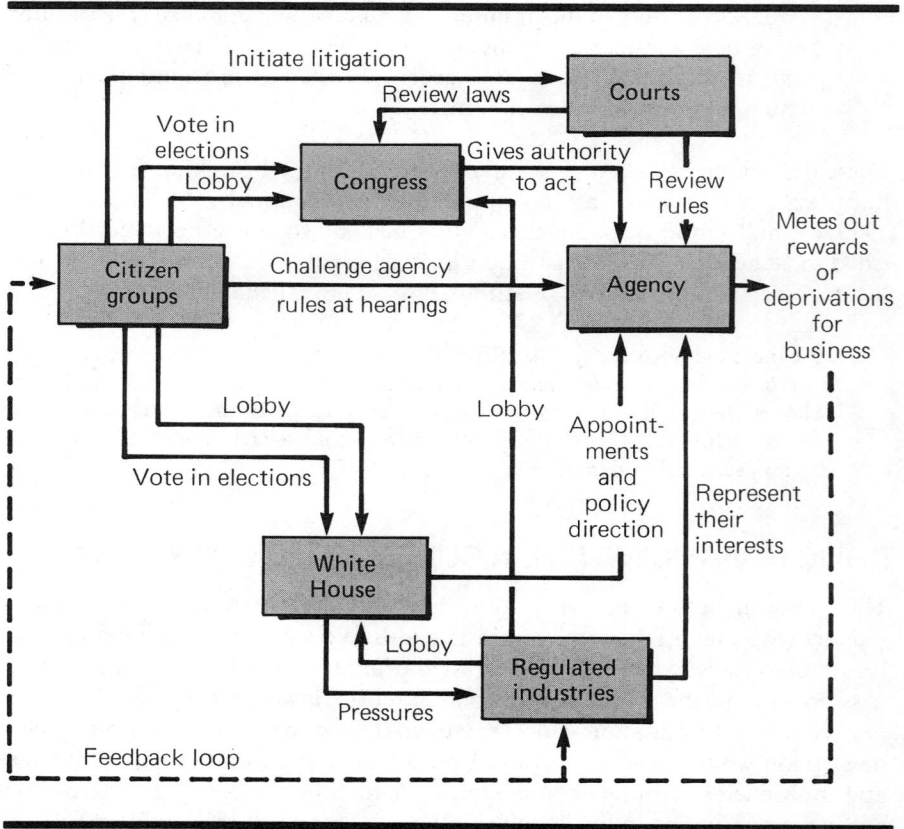

zen groups are usually less crucial than those of the agency, Congress (especially the relevant subcommittees), and the regulated industries.

Because the agency performs the vital task of converting all the demands of the other five participants into outputs, it is the linchpin of the entire system. The outputs of the agency are rules and adjudicated decisions that bestow rewards or impose deprivation upon the various participants and, more often than not, the general public. Reactions to these agency outputs reverberate through the system—as indicated by the feedback loop—and become new input demands for future policies.

This conversion process does not operate in a vacuum but occurs in a macroenvironment, identified in Chapter 1 as consisting of the technological, economic, social, and international environments. These four other environments together not only constitute constraints upon the policy formulation process but also help determine the substance of demands.

The Role of the Courts

The courts' relationship to the making of public policy cannot be overstressed. In many instances, the very meaning of the policy flows from judicial interpretation of rules or statutes. For example, judicial interpretation and implementation of the Sherman Act has substantially shaped antitrust policy. Furthermore, much of the recent legislation setting up new agencies specifically allows individuals and groups to file private suits to collect damages. In fact, it is possible for citizens to file suit against a pollution control agency for not enforcing a law, as well as against a company for not obeying it. And it is in the courts that business managers battle an agency they think has gone too far. As Richard Goodwin, general counsel for the National Association of Manufacturers puts it, "The courts are increasingly where the action is." He asserts that "... given the dollar, employment, and interference-with-business impact of the regulatory actions, businessmen realize more and more that in order to get relief they have to go to the courts" (*Wall Street Journal,* September 30, 1977).

The Administrative Procedures Act of 1946 provides for broad judicial review of administrative decision. The courts have always had the power to overturn the agency's judgments on points of law—for example, in cases where an agency had exceeded its authority, misinterpreted the law, or simply been unfair. But under the 1946 act, the courts acquired more authority to examine questions of fact—that is, to go over the mass of technical evidence examined by the agency.

The basic rule during a trial is this: no surprises, only reasoned arguments and facts. Both sides fire lengthy lists of pretrial questions (interrogatories) at each other, both to get facts and often to confuse or delay. This pretrial activity often takes even more time than the usual three-year delay on most federal court calendars. Either side can demand a trial by jury rather than by the judge alone. Complex cases usually are tried and decided by judges, but in damage cases—for example, claims of unfair competition or monopoly damages—one side usually prefers appealing to a jury. Trial may be lengthy and may involve masses of documentation and ranks of expert witnesses on both sides. In major cases, a decision by the judge often takes several months.

Either side may appeal the district court decision. The appellate court hears only a brief restatement by both sides; the original trial record (often running to thousands of pages) contains the facts. Further appeal to the Supreme Court is also possible. The delay is often a year before each appeal hearing, and half a year more before the decision is given out. The upper courts can declare for either side, revise the issues, and/or send the case back down to the district court for (1) retrial on some or all points or (2) a practical remedy (see the examples in Exhibit 3–10). The whole sequence can take ten or fifteen years in complex cases, as each side exhausts its chances to win or delay. At any point, a compromise may be reached or relief obtained from some other quarter—for example, by getting Congress or the city council to change the law directly.

The Role of Governmental Agencies

We cannot end our discussion of the political environment of business without a little further probing of what we have referred to somewhat abstractly as agency "outputs"—or, more darkly, "rewards" and "deprivations." Agencies must administer or implement public policy on a day-to-day basis—that is, someone, somewhere, sometime must take specific actions if the goals of a public policy are to be attained.

Congress affects implementation in a number of ways. In some cases the Congress passes detailed legislation that severely limits the amount of discretion agency administrators have available to them. The literature on government regulation of business, however, does not always reflect this kind of congressional action, which is occurring with increasing frequency. The conventional view is that regulation is based on terse statutes that confer extremely broad powers on the agencies and provide little specific policy guidance except to enjoin the regulators to act in the public interest.

As a result, according to the literature, regulatory agencies have legislative as well as administrative functions. While this statement might apply to older agencies such as the Interstate Commerce Commission, the Federal Communications Commission, and the Civil Aeronautics Board, we cannot accurately apply it to most of the newer ones. Typically, the laws establishing these newer agencies are extraordinarily lengthy and specific. Weaver (1978:51) observes:

> The Employee Retirement Income Security Act, under which the IRS and Labor Department jointly regulate private pension plans, runs to more than 200 pages and spells out in excruciating detail what kinds of information are to be collected, and even how often they are to repeat the process. The Environmental

EXHIBIT 3–10 Business and the Supreme Court

In a three-month period in 1978, the Supreme Court made the following unanimous decisions that were of more than passing concern to business:

Listerine Case (April 3)
Left standing (no vote) a Federal Trade Commission order requiring the Warner-Lambert Company to spend $10 million on a corrective advertising campaign.

Vermont Yankee Nuclear Case (April 3)
Ordered lower federal courts to stop interfering illegally in awarding construction and operating permits for nuclear power plants.

SEC v. Sloan (May 15)
Barred the Securities and Exchange Commission from indefinitely suspending trading in a stock by imposing a string of ten-day stock trading suspensions.

OSHA Case (May 23)
Required Occupational Safety and Health Administration inspectors to have search warrants in order to inspect premises.

TransAlaska Pipeline Cases (June 6)
Denied eight oil companies the right to charge pipeline users higher rates until the Interstate Commerce Commission sets final rates.

Class Action Case (June 19)
Strengthened ability of corporations to defend themselves in class action lawsuits.

Zenith Case (June 21)
Ruled that the Treasury Department is not required to impose a countervailing duty on electronics equipment imported from Japan.

Duke Power Nuclear Case (June 26)
Upheld the constitutionality of a ceiling on power company liability in case of nuclear plant accident.

Protection Agency administers statutes that fill hundreds of pages in the Federal Code. The Clean Air Act is so specific that it spells out precise pollution-reduction targets and timetables and leaves the EPA virtually no discretion whatsoever. And these detailed specifications have teeth in them. For the laws establishing the new regulation typically give nearly everyone an all but unlimited standing to sue the agency in question for any seeming failure to do precisely what the law tells it to do. Citizen groups and other organizations have made liberal use of this opportunity, and the courts have not been notably latitudinarian in their reading of the statutes.

Depending on statutory requirements and circumstances, administrative agencies, old and new, use a variety of means in implementing policy. As a practical matter, any would-be business manager should know something about these means. Given the growing inclination of Americans to utter the words "There ought to be a law" and for their legislative representatives to oblige them, the life of even the lower-level manager can become complicated by the actions of administrative agencies.

The procedures used by agencies to accomplish their objectives do not readily lend themselves to neat classification and simple explication. This body of information—*administrative law,* as it is called—often bewilders even the experts. Nevertheless, we may say that agencies proceed on two major fronts: rule making and adjudication.

Rule Making. Rule making refers to an agency's interpretation of a public policy that will apply in the future to all people engaged in the regulated activity. For the regulated industries, having influence over this procedure can be as important as having influence earlier, when the legislation is still being debated in Congress—perhaps *more* important. As one lobbyist put it, "I don't care who writes the law, as long as I can help the agency write the administrative rules to carry it out." Exhibit 3–11 illustrates how the process works for one agency, the Federal Trade Commission. It should be borne sharply in mind, however, that there is really no typical agency or process of rule making.

In recent years, two important and closely related changes in the rule-making process have occurred. First, public participation has taken on even greater importance since March 12, 1977 when the Sunshine Act went into effect. This act says that as a general rule the public must be allowed to sit in on all meetings of some fifty different federal agencies, ranging from the Indian Claims Commission to such regulatory heavyweights as the Securities and Exchange Commission and the Federal Trade Commission. Access to meetings is not limited to formal sessions at which votes are taken; the public is entitled to listen any time a majority of an agency's board members holds important discussions about official business.

This new public access has both pluses and minuses for business. It seems sure to mean fewer surprises because companies will find it easier to know just when a regulatory decision is coming and what is the drift of decisionmakers' thinking. But the act also increases the chances that private corporate information, given to a regulator in confidence to support a particular position, will become public. Also, the act seems sure to lead to increased legal expenses, simply because Washington lawyers will be spending more time at the agencies watching out for the interests of their corporate clients.

The second development in the rule-making process was the affirmation in 1978 of the right of federal agencies to subsidize public participation in their rule-making proceedings, even when no specific statutory authority exists for such funding. This decision was viewed as a major victory for public-inter-

EXHIBIT 3–11   FTC Trade Regulation Rule Flow

An FTC Trade Regulation Rule is a statement of general or particular applicability which defines unfair or deceptive acts or practices within the meaning of Section 5 of the Federal Trade Commission Act. FTC Trade Regulation Rule proceedings are commenced by the Commission either upon its own initiative or in response to a written petition by any interested person stating reasonable grounds.

An investigation takes place prior to the formal commencement of the proceeding to determine whether such action is warranted. Once a determination to propose a rule has been made, a presiding officer is appointed to conduct the public proceedings.

Formal commencement begins with publication in the *Federal Register* of an initial notice of proposed rulemaking.* This notice includes the substance of the proposed rule or a description of the issues involved, the legal authority for the proposed rule, the particular reason for it, and an invitation to interested persons to propose specific issues and to comment on the proposed rule.

After sufficient time for receiving comments and proposed issues from interested persons, the presiding officer publishes a final notice in the *Federal Register.* This indicates the designated issues upon which limited cross-examination may be permitted, the time and place of informal hearings, and instructions for those wishing to appear at the hearings.

Informal hearings are then held to receive the views of interested persons. After the hearings have been completed, the presiding officer prepares a summary of the record and initial findings and conclusions with regard to those issues designated by the presiding officer and such other findings and conclusions as he sees fit. The FTC staff then prepares a report containing its recommendations based upon the rulemaking record, taking into account the presiding officer's findings. Both of these reports are placed on the public record for sixty days for public comment.

Next, the Commission reviews the rulemaking record, including the reports of the presiding officer and the staff. The Commission may issue, modify, or decline to issue the proposed rule. If it determines to issue a rule, it must adopt a Statement of Basis and Purpose to accompany the rule. The final rule is published in the *Federal Register.* Once a rule is promulgated, any interested person has sixty days to petition the appropriate U.S. Court of Appeals for judicial review of the rule.

* See Appendix B.

Source: Federal Trade Commission, "Your FTC—What It Is and What It Does," Washington, D.C., n.d.

est and consumer advocates, who maintained that because of the high costs of research and legal work, they were often unable to participate in agency decision making. As a result, they claimed agencies were able to consider only the opinions of affected industry groups that could afford to lobby for their views.

Intervenor funding, as such financing is known, is a central concern of public-interest activists, both because of the great increase in government regulations and a decline in private foundation support for public-interest litigation and representation.

Adjudication. The other broad avenue that agencies can follow in implementing public policy is to proceed on a case-by-case basis. This approach is called *adjudication,* and the easiest way to understand it is to consider the example of a single agency, the FTC, described in Exhibit 3–12.

STATE AND LOCAL GOVERNMENTS: NEW ADVERSARIES FOR BUSINESS

This chapter has focused almost exclusively on federal laws and agencies affecting business. In light of the scope and power of federal authority, this emphasis is easily justified, but we must not let it cast a shadow over some significant trends at the state and local levels of government. Clearly, the scope of consumerist activities and the authority of the typical agency at these levels are growing.

Perhaps most apparent to big national companies is the power of state legislatures. One estimate says that some 350 companies had full-time staff members watching state legislatures in 1978, and that the number is growing by 50 a year. But many of these companies have failed to notice action in other parts of state and local government. For example, after decades of being little more than in-house legal advisers to the governor and other state officials, state attorneys general have begun dusting off old statutes, working up new legal theories, and aggressively prosecuting business. While antitrust is probably the area of greatest interest, environmental cases, securities fraud, and consumer protection have also been popular areas of investigation.

Even if state attorneys general were not so aggressive, companies would still have to contend with various consumer protection departments. Connecticut, for example, has one of the most vigorous. Created in 1959, the department has grown from a licensing and regulatory agency for the food industry to an omnibus agency for many consumer interests—drug control, pharmacies, weights and measures, consumer fraud, consumer education, athletics, industry fraud, and so on.

Meanwhile, at the local level, business faces city and county consumer advocates whose accomplishments include the following (*Business Week*, September 26, 1977, p. 143):

> —In Florida, the Dade County consumer advocate put together a $700 million class action suit against Ford on behalf of 3,000 Dade motorists disgruntled over the extent of rusting in their automobiles.

EXHIBIT 3–12   FTC Case Flow

How does a case start at the Federal Trade Commission? What happens to it along the way? Where does it end?

Formal FTC complaints develop from Commission investigations. The investigations may be initiated by the Commission or they may arise from letters sent to the FTC by businessmen or consumers citing alleged illegal practices. These letters are called "applications for complaints" to distinguish them from formal complaints brought by the Commission.

Applications for complaints also come from members of Congress, other federal, state, and local government agencies, and trade associations.

Each application is reviewed to determine whether the practice questioned involves interstate commerce, or may affect interstate commerce, the public interest, and violation of a law administered by the FTC.

If it does, an investigation is begun. This may start with correspondence from the Commission requiring the business concerned to file a special report, or with a request of a subpoena for information by the staff of a bureau or regional office.

From the information obtained during the investigation, the decision is made (1) to close the case (for lack of public interest, or failure to find that a violation has occurred), or (2) to issue a complaint, along with a proposed cease and desist order . . . .

Cases can also be settled by consent order, a formal document signed by the businessman or company involved certifying that the challenged practices will be corrected or discontinued. The public has the opportunity to comment on a proposed consent order and the Commission takes these comments into consideration before the order is finally issued. Violations of consent orders can result in assessment of civil penalties.*

Cases which are not settled are litigated before an FTC Administrative Law Judge. Following hearings, either the respondent or the Commission's complaint counsel can appeal the judge's initial decision to the five Commissioners.

The Commission hears the argument and announces its decision: to issue a cease and desist order or to dismiss some or all of the charges.

If the Administrative Law Judge's initial decision is not appealed, it may be adopted—with or without modifications—by the Commission. FTC staff cannot appeal an adverse decision by the Commission.

If a cease and desist order is issued, the respondent has sixty days to appeal the Commission's decision to a U.S. Court of Appeals. Either side may ultimately appeal to the United States Supreme Court.

* See Exhibit 3–10.

Source: Federal Trade Commission, "Your FTC—What It Is and What It Does," Washington, D.C., n.d.

—In Atlanta, Georgia, a state consumer affairs officials' crackdown on deceptive car-repair practices closed fifteen service stations representing all the major oil companies. [The officials] investigated forty to fifty alleged fraud cases in the used-car industry.

The reasons for this new toughness at the state and local levels are not hard to find. First, key positions are now being filled by young men and women nurtured in the activism of the 1960s; they are not content to sit and wait for problems to be presented to them, but seek out problems on their own. The second reason is economic: corporations have the ability to pay big fines and thus return to state coffers some enforcement expenditures. For example, Bethlehem Steel paid Maryland $500,000 in an antipollution case. Third, the federal government has made money available to the states to move into new fields. And, finally, consumer protection cases can have a direct and immediate payoff for voters. *Business Week* (May 15, 1978, p. 56) cites the following example: In early 1978, Maryland for the first time held it a deceptive trade practice to put into an apartment lease provisions that landlords know cannot be enforced in court. Five tenants of one complex got refunds, with interest, of security deposits that had been kept by the owners when the tenants moved out, even though the vacant apartments had been rented quickly.

In sum, the deluge of state and local action compounds business's already considerable task of complying with expanding federal regulation. Dealing with the political environment, as we have seen in this chapter, has become a job in itself for the business manager. In the chapter that follows we consider the international environment—the fifth and final component of the macroenvironment of business—which is becoming equally complex and challenging.

CHAPTER FOUR

Understanding Change

in the International

Environment

With this chapter we come to the last stage on our tour of the macroenvironment of business. In this chapter we begin by briefly putting into perspective the importance and uniqueness of the international environment of business. The point of the first section is simple: As the United States moves toward the year 2000, continued prosperity will increasingly depend on the ability of American business to compete in the world arena. In the second section, we take a look at some of the major institutions and issues with which an international manager should be familiar. Among these are the multinational corporation, and political and trading arrangements such as the New International Economic Order and the General Agreement on Tariffs and Trade (GATT).

The remainder of the chapter is devoted to looking at the three problem areas that form the foundation, but not necessarily the entire edifice, of management in the international environment. For convenience, we can label these three areas as follows: (1) international finance and trade, (2) cross-national differences in culture, and (3) relationships with the governments of host and home countries.

   1. Just as Chapter 2 discussed the importance of the national economy to business decisionmakers, this chapter considers the ways in which the international economic framework affects decision making. Managers must be able to deal with many different currencies and foreign exchange risks. They must be able to take advantage of the fact that at any given time interest rates and capital markets in other countries can differ decisively from what they are in the United States. From this discussion, we can thus see that the major challenge the international economic framework presents to management is how to optimize on a systemwide basis.
   2. Cross-national differences within the international environment make it unique and are therefore important for us to consider in this chapter. Specifically, we examine (a) the conflicts that arise because of different national and cultural identities of owners, customers, employees, and suppliers; and (b) the problems that arise from attempts to apply American marketing approaches in different cultures.
   3. The discussion of Chapter 3 centered on the basic notion that the effective manager today must be familiar with the complex array of controls and supports that U.S. government has developed for the business system. In this chapter, we examine the set of controls and supports developed by governments to deal not only with foreign companies operating within their borders but also with their own companies operating in the international arena. While these controls and supports may not be any more complex than the set discussed in Chapter 3, we can argue that they can pose greater risks for managers who choose not to familiarize themselves with them. These risks range from a variety of lesser harassments to outright takeovers by the host government. But expropriation is not the only lethal blow the host can strike; just consider the long-term dangers facing oil companies (so large, so visible) in the international political environment. □

THE IMPORTANCE OF THE WORLD ARENA

A skeptic might ask, "Why a separate chapter on the international environment? Don't exports make up only 7 percent of the U.S. gross national product, compared to West Germany's 27 percent and Japan's 14 percent?" Before getting to the sinew of this chapter, we had better take a moment to answer these questions by putting the international arena into perspective.
   Let us begin with a few statistics. Countries have come to depend so much on each other that from a relatively piddling total of $76.7 billion in world-

wide imports back in 1951, worldwide imports reached a record $1.15 trillion in 1977. This figure is in the same mind-boggling mathematical league as the U.S. gross national product ($1.89 trillion for the same year). While it is true that exports constitute a mere 7 percent of the U.S. GNP, we are still talking about a sizable amount of money—for example, $121 billion for 1977.

Furthermore, most forecasters expect the role of foreign trade within the U.S. economic picture to continue to expand. Economist Otto Eckstein has said that "the health of the world economy will be of increasing importance to the United States" in the years just ahead. He anticipates that U.S. exports will constitute a larger and larger share of the country's expanding GNP. By 1990, Eckstein estimates, exports will amount to about 16 percent of the GNP. (This forecast, however, needs to be considered in light of the possibility of rising protectionist sentiments, a possibility to be treated later in this chapter.)

In 1977 the following internationally minded companies had over $1 billion worth of exports: General Electric, Caterpillar, Boeing, McDonnell Douglas, Lockheed, and DuPont. But we should not infer that international trade is the exclusive domain of these industrial behemoths. Many small and medium-sized firms have competed quite successfully in the world arena. Just one quick example: BRK Electronics of Aurora, Illinois, won a substantial share of world sales of smoke detectors by sensibly marketing a competitive product. First, the company's president went to the Department of Commerce to learn whom he should see in Europe. Then he and his sales manager traveled to Italy, France, England, and other countries to line up local distributors. In addition, BRK exhibited its goods at trade shows in Paris and Stockholm. By 1978 the company was selling to forty-six countries, and its exports had climbed from $124,000 in 1973 to about $4 million.

Moreover, for companies of all sizes, exporting is becoming a necessity. The "we-don't-export-it's-too-much-trouble" attitude prevails less and less. The reasons are not hard to find: American executives today realize that the richest market on earth is not necessarily the domestic one; and even if it were, the fact remains that foreign companies have been aggressively capturing significant chunks of it. Japan's superior economic performance, for example, derives in large part from one of the most elementary concepts taught in Economics 101: the importance of market share in achieving economies of scale. In other words, by expanding sales through overseas markets, a firm is able to reduce its prices. While some American managers may have trouble grasping this economic concept, the Japanese clearly do not—as illustrated by the fact, for just one example, that almost all motorcycles in the United States are made in Japan.

At the same time foreign companies are expanding their sales, they have also stepped up their investments in the United States. In 1978 most estimates put direct foreign investment in U.S. businesses at more than $33 billion. Total foreign assets in the United States are today well over $300 billion. Some of this investment is perhaps surprising. For example, to not a few architectural experts, Houston's thirty-six–story Pennzoil Place, a picture of which appears at the front of this book, is an important work of art. Its twin trapezoidal sky-scrapers seem to shift into infinite varieties of complex, subtle new forms as one's viewpoint shifts. The illusion is one of movement, of action. That makes it an altogether fitting expression of a city that takes pride in a charge-ahead spirit of free enterprise that is both very Texan and very American. But Pennz-oil Place today is in the hands of neither Texans nor any other Americans. West Germans own it now.

According to the Conference Board, the number of announced foreign in-vestments in the United States in 1977 was a record 274, up from 254 in 1976, and 161 in 1975. West Germany accounted for 53 of the foreign investments; Canada, a close second, accounted for 49 new investments, while Britain and Japan accounted for 37 and 36, respectively. Most of these investments in-volved acquisition of existing firms and plants.

So much for the statistics of the game of world trade; let us now take a look at the players.

INTERNATIONAL INSTITUTIONS AND ISSUES

The Multinational Corporations (MNCs)

Roughly speaking, MNCs are large companies that have significant operations in more than one country. Beyond this general statement, there is little agree-ment on what precisely constitutes a MNC.

- Some authorities define a multinational corporation as a company whose foreign sales have reached a ratio of, say, 25 percent (or some other share) of total sales. Others find the definition in organization—for example, a company that has global product divisions rather than an international divi-sion is defined as multinational. Still others look to the distribution of own-ership or to the nationality mix of managers or directors as the determining characteristics.

- In cases where a company does not merely sell a product in several countries but actually integrates factors of production across national bound-aries to make a single product, a few authorities prefer the term *transnational corporation* to MNC. Whatever term is used, production sharing is a growing trend as illustrated by the familiar hand-held calculator. The semiconductors that do the calculating are "made in America" and then assembled in a devel-oping country. The final product is marketed in the developed countries. The Ford Pinto is yet another example: the engine comes from Ford's German company, its transmission from Ford's British company, and much of its elec-trical equipment from Ford's Canadian company. Like the production and marketing functions, financial activities can also take on a "transnational" quality. General Electric Company, the biggest U.S. exporter, illustrates this financial meshing. GE's International Sales Group, a headquarters team, operates as an in-house trading company with the objective of promoting exports from any GE manufacturing affiliate around the world, not just the U.S. plants. Most GE operating units pay a basic fee to support the ISG, which has offices in seventy-odd cities in the United States and abroad, and the ISG also gets a commission from the operating units on sales that it negotiates.

• Professor Raymond Vernon (1977) of Harvard University, an outstanding authority on the multinational corporation, regards it as a company that attempts to carry out its activities on an international scale, as though there were no national boundaries, on the basis of a common strategy directed from a corporate center. According to Vernon, affiliates are locked together in an integrated process and their policies are determined by the corporate center in terms of decisions relating to production, plant location, product mix, marketing, financing, and so on.

• Jacques Maisonrouge, president of IBM World Trade Corporation, characterizes the multinational corporation as one that (a) operates in many countries; (b) carries out research, development, and manufacturing in those countries; (c) has multinational management; and (d) has multinational stock ownership (cited in U.S. Department of Commerce, 1972b:7).

• Neil H. Jacoby (1970) seems to suggest "degrees of multinationalization" when he notes that a typical company goes through the following six stages:

1. Exports its products to foreign countries,
2. Establishes sales organizations abroad,
3. Licenses use of its patents and know-how to foreign firms that make and sell its products,
4. Establishes foreign manufacturing facilities,
5. Multinationalizes management from top to bottom,
6. Multinationalizes ownership of corporate stock.

Because these definitions are imprecise, it is impossible to say how many companies qualify as multinational corporations. For purposes of regulation, the Office of Foreign Direct Investment lists over 3,000 U.S. companies, although not all would satisfy the criteria cited above. The International Chamber of Commerce estimates that 150 companies, about half of them U.S. companies, fall into the category of international companies. *Fortune*'s lists of the 500 largest U.S. and the 200 largest foreign corporations include the most important multinational corporations. Because European corporations are less forthcoming in making data available, the picture of their activities is less complete. From what is available, however, the projection of the European multinational corporation abroad is just as pervasive a phenomenon as American corporate expansion.

Why have MNCs grown so rapidly in this century? Drucker (1974) seems to suggest that their growth is the result of worldwide demand for the same products (such as Singer sewing machines) and services (such as Sears catalogs). Not everyone agrees; as we shall see in the Epilogue, for example, Marxists surely have a different perspective. But, whatever the ultimate cause of the growth of MNCs, there are certain savings involved in handling foreign sales through foreign operations. Transportation costs, labor costs, and taxes may be lower for goods made locally than for goods imported from the United States (though these savings are probably substantially less than they used to be), and operating locally may permit an American to take advantage of local expertise.

The New International Economic Order

From the end of World War II until 1974, one international political arrangement prevailed: The United States led the First World, opposed the Second World (the communist countries), and attempted to help the Third World (less-developed countries—LDCs). Then the Organization of Petroleum Exporting Countries (OPEC) quadrupled the price of oil. This action not only greatly aggravated the problems of the LDCs that were not oil producers but ended the fiction that the so-called Third World was a homogeneous group. George W. Ball (1976:283) writes:

> The members of OPEC assumed a special position as the true Third World countries. A second group that had already achieved a considerable growth momentum, such as Taiwan, South Korea, Brazil, Israel, and Singapore, could properly be called the Fourth World countries, while at the bottom of the list was a Fifth World, consisting of nations such as Bangladesh, whose prospects for even holding their own are exceedingly dim.

The OPEC action also affected the powers and influence of the United States. Exhibit 4–1 provides a simplified but useful indication of what occurred. Since 1950, the U.S. share of world product declined slowly, from about one-third in 1950 to one-fourth in 1974. Western Europe's share stayed remarkably steady. Meanwhile, there were sizable increases in the shares of postwar Japan and the rapidly developing ˙countries of the Third World (mostly OPEC) and a small increase in that of the USSR. Living standards in Western Europe and Japan became much closer to those in the United States than they were a generation previous, and their shares in world trade grew.

The OPEC action on oil prices, however, was not the only event significant to American business that occurred in 1974. At the sixth special session of the General Assembly, the declaration on the establishment of a New International Economic Order (NIEO) was adopted. The following year, the General Assembly reaffirmed the "fundamental purpose" of the declaration, in particular "the imperative need of redressing the economic imbalance between developed and developing countries." The declaration really went beyond the usual agenda of remedies such as trade references, commodity schemes, international monetary reforms, and better cooperation among LDCs. It stated an

EXHIBIT 4–1   Distribution of World GNP, Selected Years, 1950–1974

Country or group	1950	1955	1960	1965	1970	1974
Industrial countries						
United States	34.2%	33.3%	29.7%	29.4%	26.5%	25.1%
Western Europe	24.4	24.9	25.2	25.0	25.3	24.8
West Germany	5.2	6.5	7.1	7.1	6.9	6.5
France	4.8	4.7	4.7	4.9	5.0	5.1
United Kingdom	5.5	5.0	4.6	4.2	3.6	3.3
Other	8.9	8.7	8.8	8.8	9.8	9.9
Japan	2.8	3.5	4.3	5.5	7.3	7.7
Other OECD countries	3.8	3.8	3.7	3.8	3.8	3.8
USSR	11.4	12.1	13.0	13.1	13.1	12.8
Eastern Europe	4.7	4.8	5.1	4.8	4.6	4.9
Developing countries						
Noncommunist	12.3	12.5	12.5	13.0	13.1	14.6
OPEC	n.a.	n.a.	n.a.	n.a.	n.a.	2.8
India	2.7	2.6	2.5	2.3	2.2	2.1
Brazil	1.0	1.1	1.2	1.2	1.3	1.7
Other	n.a.	n.a.	n.a.	n.a.	n.a.	8.0
China	3.1	3.6	3.9	3.7	3.7	3.7
Residual	3.3	1.5	2.6	1.7	2.6	2.6

Source: Data from U.S. Department of State, *The Planetary Product in 1974,* Publication 8838 (Washington, D.C.: U.S. Government Printing Office, 1975), p. 14.

explicit link between the alleged responsibility of the West for the poverty of the LDCs and the *duty* of the West to "correct inequalities and redress existing injustices."

A 1975 address by President Julius K. Nyerere of Tanzania, one of the African leaders most respected in the West, epitomizes this idea (Bauer, 1977:27):

> I am saying it is not right that the vast majority of the world's people should be forced into the position of beggars, without dignity. In one world, as in one state, when I am rich because you are poor, and I am poor because you are rich, the transfer of wealth from the rich to the poor is a matter of right; it is not an appropriate matter of charity . . . . If the rich nations go on getting richer and richer at the expense of the poor, the poor of the world must demand a change, in the same way as the proletariat in the rich countries in the past.

But George W. Ball (1976:289) finds little logic in Nyerere's contention that LDCs are entitled to receive a large share of the world's wealth as compensation for their exploitation under colonialism. Can any country conclusively demonstrate that it is economically worse off as a result of its colonial experience? Would India have fared any better, for example, if the British had stayed home?

The major premise of the entire argument for redistribution of wealth derives from a statement in the preamble to the NIEO declaration: ". . . the gap between the developed and the developing countries continues to widen." A number of analysts, however, have taken issue with this popular idea.

First, Bauer and Yamey (1977) believe it is inappropriate to lump together and average the incomes, living standards, and rates of growth of the so-called Third World in order to make comparisons with the developed nations. It is better to think of this huge and diverse aggregate, from millions of aborigines to many millions of inhabitants of huge cities, in terms of the Third, Fourth, and Fifth worlds.

Second, the idea of the gap is static; it ignores history (Bauer and Yamey, 1977:26):

> Countries have at times been promoted from the less-developed to the developed category (for example, Japan and Italy). Such reclassifications affect the size of the gap and preclude valid comparisons through time.

A third argument, according to Bauer and Yamey, is that ". . . the gap often widens when economic conditions in poor countries improve, and even as a result of such improvement. This is because economic improvement results in longer life expectancy, which in turn widens conventionally measured income differences between rich and poor countries, since relatively more poor people then survive." Also, national-income statistics are seldom adjusted for differences in age composition. The proportion of children is much larger in the Third World than in the West. Since both the incomes and the requirements of children are usually much lower than those of adults, comparisons that do not take age composition into account confuse differences in income with differences in age.

Setting aside these arguments, let us accept for a moment the recommendations of the NIEO declaration. Can it be demonstrated that the outright aid the developed countries might provide LDCs would be distributed among their own people with any semblance of justice? Would the benefits outweigh the transfer? Clearly, there is little reason for taxing the poorer groups in the United States, Scandinavia, and Switzerland if the answer to both questions is not affirmative.

The record is not encouraging. Bauer argues that many aid-recipient Third World governments have pursued economic policies "ranging from wasteful to the inhuman, and damaging to the well-being and material progress of their people." Among these policies he notes the following:

—Enforced collectivization of farming; the expulsion of productive minorities or the imposition of economic restrictions on them;

—The establishment of state export monopolies which pay farmers a small fraction of the market value of their produce and deny them access to other marketing opportunities and to Western economic contacts;

—The proliferation of costly state trading, transport, banking, and industrial enterprises and monopolies;

—The suppression of private commercial activities in favor of state enterprises, including officially sponsored "cooperatives";

—The widespread restrictive licensing of economic activity;

—The prohibition or restriction of private foreign capital (when shortage of capital is adduced in pleas for official aid); and

—Wasteful policies of import-substitution and exchange controls, which usually raise the prices of consumer goods.

This analysis does not mean that transfers of wealth never benefit the population of Third World countries at large. It simply means that aid does not automatically lead to benefit.

Later in this book we shall look at the problems of LDCs from a micro-perspective and consider what can the multinational corporation do in LDCs to benefit development and the population at large. MNCs can in fact do quite a lot—for example, help LDCs acquire technology (Exhibit 4–2), equipment, capital, and markets that will enable them effectively to utilize their resources, both human and material, to improve their standard of living.

International Trade Agreements

The large numbers of organizations and the complexity of the many trading arrangements suggest a high degree of disarray in world trade today. In one sense, this is true. MNCs must keep informed about, and participate in, numerous trade negotiations around the world. But in another sense, the picture is really quite simple. All we have to do is think of three participants, each with its own set of objectives. First are the developed nations of the West, led by the United States, that favor free trade. (Exhibit 4–3 shows the leading trade partners of the United States.) Second are the LDCs that want, as we have seen, certain trade restrictions and a *new* international economic order. Finally are the communist countries that seek to expand their trading relations with the other two groups but desire a minimum of change in internal economic structures.

Roback, Simmonds, and Zwick (1977:144) explain that the multinational trade agreements "game" is one in which each of the participating groups, and each country within a group, tries to move a few more steps toward its goals:

The game cannot stop because of the growing interdependency of the three worlds. Also there are usually enough mutual benefits involved to warrant the

EXHIBIT 4-2   MNC Transfer of Technology and Management Skills

American MNCs transfer technology and management skills in a variety of ways. In Nigeria, the policy of Nigerianizing top jobs is taken very seriously by government and by Gulf Oil Company. This photo shows a Nigerian oil worker in the control room of Gulf's storage facility near Escravos, Nigeria. In 1978 Gulf named its fourth Nigerian manager, Joseph Adedapo, to take over its financial administration department. Mr. Adedapo replaced an American executive with whom he had worked.

Source: Photo courtesy of Gulf Oil Corporation.

continuing search for new trade arrangements. The results of the negotiations depend, of course, on the respective bargaining power of the participants. The bargaining power keeps changing and involves geopolitical factors as well as economic considerations, such as growing world scarcities of certain natural resources.

This model of a three-group game is a useful one, and we should keep it in mind as we pick our way through the framework of international trade today.

Restrictions on International Trade. In theory and to a lesser degree in practice, the developed countries favor free trade. But what is *free trade*? Simply

EXHIBIT 4–3   Leading U.S. Trade Partners, 1977

20 Top buyers of American products	Total purchases (billions)	20 Top sellers to Americans	Total sales (billions)
Canada	$25.5	Canada	$28.7
Japan	$10.4	Japan	$18.2
West Germany	$ 6.0	West Germany	$ 7.0
Britain	$ 5.5	Saudi Arabia	$ 6.6
Netherlands	$ 4.8	Nigeria	$ 6.3
Mexico	$ 4.6	Britain	$ 5.2
France	$ 3.5	Mexico	$ 4.6
Saudi Arabia	$ 3.5	Venezuela	$ 4.3
Belgium–Luxembourg	$ 3.2	Libya	$ 3.7
Venezuela	$ 3.1	Indonesia	$ 3.7
Italy	$ 2.8	Taiwan	$ 3.6
Iran	$ 2.7	Italy	$ 3.1
Brazil	$ 2.6	Algeria	$ 3.0
South Korea	$ 2.4	France	$ 3.0
Australia	$ 2.3	Iran	$ 2.9
Taiwan	$ 1.9	South Korea	$ 2.9
Spain	$ 1.9	Hong Kong	$ 2.9
USSR	$ 1.7	Brazil	$ 2.3
Israel	$ 1.5	Trinidad and Tobago	$ 1.7
Switzerland	$ 1.3	United Arab Emirates	$ 1.6

Note: The 1977 annual rate is based on January–September trade.

Source: U.S. Department of Commerce, U.S. Bureau of the Census, *Foreign Commerce and Navigation of the United States; Highlights of U.S. Export and Import Trade*, FT990, monthly.

put, it is trade without such restrictions as tariffs, quotas, embargoes, and non-tariff barriers.

Tariffs, also called *customs duties,* are taxes placed on imported goods. *Quotas* are absolute limits placed on the quantity of foreign goods (say, textiles) that can be imported into a country. A tariff allows consumers to buy as much of a foreign good as they wish, but only at a higher price; a quota restricts the quantity available at any price.

While tariffs and quotas have traditionally been the main barriers to the free transfer of goods, restrictions on exports have been increasing in recent years. Under the Export Administration Act of 1969, as amended in 1974, the U.S. Department of Commerce has established general licenses that permit most goods to be exported without specific approval to all except *embargoed* destinations—for example, Cuba, Vietnam, North Korea, and Zimbabwe-Rhodesia. Specific licenses are required, however, for three kinds of products:

those with a high-technology content that have military potential, nuclear weapons and crime-control technology, and petroleum. Embargoes also have been placed on a variety of drugs and agricultural products coming *into* the country.

Finally, we should note restrictions on trade in the form of *nontariff barriers* (NTBs). Although not as visible as tariffs, NTBs can be extremely effective and important. The principal categories of NTBs are as follows.

- *Customs and entry procedures.* Examples are valuation, classification, documentation, and health and safety regulations.
- *Standards.* Examples are product standards, packaging, and labeling and marking.
- *Import charges.* Examples are prior import deposits, credit restrictions for imports, special duties, and variable levies.
- *Trigger pricing.* Under this elaborate system, steel from all nations is pegged to the costs of Japanese production and shipping, on the assumption that the Japanese make the lowest-cost steel. If steel is sold in the United States below these levels, the government can impose stiff penalties after holding a speeded-up investigation.
- *"Buy American" campaigns* (or *comprate Italiano* and *achetez francais* campaigns). By the end of the 1970s, an increasing number of U.S. states and cities, as well as foreign countries, were clamoring for curbs on imports of automobiles, buses, typewriters, steel, electrical equipment, lumber, and other products produced by hard-hit domestic firms. For example, steel industry officials in Pennsylvania figure that one out of every four tons of steel used in building highways, and one in five tons used in government buildings, is imported and thus contributes to layoffs of thousands of steelworkers. As a result, the Pennsylvania legislature passed, and the governor signed, a bill requiring that all steel used in state-funded construction be American made.

Protectionist measures such as these generally favor one group in a country and have a negative impact on other sectors of the economy. Therefore, governments have to evaluate the tradeoffs involved in protectionist policies and determine the net benefits or cost to the country (see Exhibit 4–4). Protection policies have been justified on several grounds. The most important include the protection of infant industries, the protection of public health, and the desirability of diversifying the domestic economy to improve stability and stimulate growth.

Other justifications for protectionist measures are less persuasive, but are nevertheless heard in the United States. The fact is that the United States, despite its avowal of free trade principles, has instituted a number of tariffs and quotas. As we saw in Chapter 3, the realities of interest-group politics give a decided advantage to special-interest groups that stand to make big gains from public policies, provided the net loss to the rest of society is fairly evenly dis-

EXHIBIT 4–4   Tradeoffs in International Trade

When the police in Greensboro, North Carolina, bought a pair of Volkswagen Rabbit subcompacts in an experimental program, Lt. W.L. Henderson said, "We've been called everything from 'hareway patrol' to 'freeway bunnies'." The director of Georgia's Purchasing Department, Jim Roberts, has raised a related point: "We've got a lot of foreign countries buying our goods, too. Common sense tells you that you can't take a position against government agencies' buying foreign goods when Georgia is looking for foreign manufacturers to locate in the state."

Source: Text adapted from *U.S. News & World Report,* July 3, 1978; photo courtesy of Volkswagen of America.

tributed and not too great. If the American steel industry, for example, is given protection against foreign steel imports and domestic prices remain higher than they might otherwise be, the steel companies and the workers in the industry may directly benefit. The first-round effects may result in foreign exchange savings to the United States. On the cost side, however, other U.S. industries that use steel to produce machinery for export are certain to become less competitive in foreign markets. Their profits, their workers, and their foreign exchange earnings for the country are likely to suffer. Domestic consumers of steel products will have to pay higher prices and, in effect, subsidize the protected industry. Furthermore, foreign countries are likely to retaliate with their own protectionist measures, which could reduce exports, profits, and employment in other U.S. industries. Both the positive and negative effects will have different weights, depending upon the economic situation of the country. Even where the net economic impact is negative, however, a nation may be willing to pay this price to satisfy long-run or noneconomic goals.

In addition to restricting imports, developed nations deviate from the path of free trade by adopting programs for promoting exports. For instance, government itself can sponsor market research on foreign sales opportunities and establish trade promotion offices in foreign countries. Further, government can offer tax incentives if goods are exported, as well as insurance programs under which government assumes varying degrees of political and commercial risk. For example, the U.S. Export-Import Bank promotes exports by providing medium and long-term financing to foreign buyers. Also, in 1972 Congress created a new corporate category for tax purposes called the Domestic International Sales Corporation (DISC). DISC members are entitled to defer taxes on 50 percent of their export income until this income is distributed to stockholders.

The General Agreement on Tariffs and Trade (GATT). Since 1948, the chief institutional mechanism for shaping trade arrangements between the developed countries has been the General Agreement on Tariffs and Trade (GATT). The goal of GATT is to achieve a broad, multilateral, and relatively free system of trading through the gradual reduction in tariffs, adoption of the principle of nondiscrimination (i.e., equal treatment with respect to customs duties and procedures), and the provision of an organization for settlement of trade disputes. In spite of the provisions regarding nondiscrimination, members may form customs unions or free trade areas, provided there is no net overall increase in barriers to outsiders.* A wide range of other exceptions is also allowed, under which restrictive policies could continue, or be adopted temporarily, in a country with aggravated trade or financial problems. In working toward its goal of reducing tariffs, GATT sponsored six major bar-

---

* The most important free trade area has been the European Community. Other significant regional arrangements have been the European Free Trade Association (EFTA) and the Council of Mutual Economic Cooperation (COMECON). (The latter appears to be primarily a device for implementing and integrating central development plans among member countries—unlike the European Common Market, which was planned to facilitate the unrestricted movement of goods and productive inputs. Exchanges among COMECON countries do not appear to be directed by the considerations of price and quality that govern trade in the Western world; at any rate, the patterns of COMECON trade are often difficult for an outsider to interpret.) In addition, numerous regional trading organizations have been established by the developing countries. For example, the Andean Group and the Central American Common Market are regional groupings that involve cooperation in many development areas as well as in trade liberalization. The six participating countries in the Andean Group (Bolivia, Chile, Colombia, Ecuador, Peru, and Venezuela) are aiming at a full-fledged economic community in which free trade will be achieved and in which common development aspirations will be pursued through a concerted effort at regionwide industrial planning.

gaining sessions from 1947 to 1967 that resulted in substantial tariff cuts. The last of these was the so-called Kennedy Round (1963–1967), which resulted in an average tariff reduction of 35 percent.

In 1973 a new round of negotiations was launched in Tokyo. Five-and-a-half years later, representatives of the industrialized nations endorsed a complicated set of trade agreements aimed at further liberalizing global commerce. This agreement, the Tokyo Round, called for the industrialized nations to cut tariffs on thousands of imports by an average of 33 percent from 1980 through 1988.

Other major points were a series of international codes aimed at the worst of nontariff barriers and a prohibition on *export subsidies* (government-sponsored subsidies designed to give a country's domestic companies an advantage in the international market). The new code forbids subsidies on exports of industrial goods and prohibits any agricultural subsidies that would "materially undercut" another country's domestic products.

Our purpose in this section, it will be recalled, was to gain an understanding of the uniqueness of the international environment of business. Having examined the characteristics of the phenomenon known as the multinational corporation, drawn distinctions about the relative development of countries, and briefly reviewed the tangle of international trade agreements, we can now turn our attention to the major areas of concern to management.

INTERNATIONAL FINANCE AND TRADE

The complexity of international finance and trade theory bewilders, even overpowers, the nonexpert. Yet these topics cannot be ignored. For example, because currencies fluctuate in value, cash flow management for the MNC becomes a mixture of business acumen and sheer wizardry. The theoretical explanations for international trade are important simply because a belief in theory underlies much government action. Thus at least a working knowledge of why governments find advantages in international trade is required.

Balance of Trade and Payments

Why do governments impose tariffs, quotas, and other trade barriers? One answer, a political one, has already been provided: Such barriers to free trade are the result of much diligent effort by special interests seeking protection. But governments themselves also desire a *favorable balance of trade*—that is, governments seek to maintain a situation in which the goods and services exported from their countries exceed those imported. In 1970, for example, the United States exported about $42.5 billion worth of goods and services and imported about $39.9 billion. Thus, its favorable balance of trade was about $2.6 billion. In 1976, largely due to massive oil imports, the story was quite dif-

"Don't be childish, man! Kicking Toyotas is no answer to our balance-of-trade gap."

Drawing by Donald Reilly. © 1971 The New Yorker Magazine, Inc.

ferent: Imports totaled $124 billion; exports, $114.7, and the balance of trade was −$9.3 billion.

The desire of governments for a favorable balance of trade is not new; as we saw in Chapter 1, the mercantilists of the sixteenth and seventeenth centuries sought favorable balances for their countries with a vengeance. They held the belief that such a balance would bring money, which they confused with wealth, into the country. The classical theory of the adjustment mechanism is that a country whose exports fall short of its imports must export part of its stock of gold, thereby affecting its prices and its ability to compete in world trade.

But exporting and importing are not the only transactions between nations. Other transactions include long-term investments made abroad by business, tourist outlays, weapons exports, loans and other gifts the government makes to foreign nations, and the money that foreign individuals deposit or withdraw on a short-term basis from a country's financial institutions. The net result of the balance of trade in merchandise and all these other transactions is the *balance of payments*—that is, the difference between a nation's *total* payments to foreign countries and its *total* receipts from foreign countries.

The Complexities of Currency Exchange
in the World Market

With virtually every nation having its own monetary system and, to varying degrees, placing restrictions on the flow of funds across its borders, business transaction becomes more complicated in the world market than in the fifty states. When a company wishes to buy goods from another country, the manager must obtain sufficient foreign currency to pay the exporter. The exchange of U.S. dollars by the American importer for the foreign currency is usually done through the importer's bank in the foreign exchange market. The units that one U.S. dollar will purchase in a foreign currency are expressed by the *foreign exchange rate*—that is, the price of one currency in terms of the other. In dealing with foreign currencies, the American manager should consult a bank's foreign exchange department to minimize the risk of loss through fluctuating currency prices. Exhibit 4–5 shows far better than words why such a call might be the prudent thing to do.

The U.S. Dollar and the International Money Market. What causes the dollar's international value—that is, its price in terms of other currencies—to fluctuate so wildly? Answer: its value today moves up or down largely in response to unchanging forces of supply and demand. The dollar tends to appreciate in terms of other currencies when demand for it is on the rise; it tends to decline in terms of other currencies when foreign demand for it lags. In effect, the dollar's international value tends to "float" in relation to other currencies. The following account of how we arrived at this floating arrangement in 1971 is based on Malabre (1976:183–86).

After World War II, the international value of the U.S. dollar was arbitrarily fixed, under international agreement, at a level of thirty-five dollars per ounce of gold. This so-called fixed-rate system was set up at an international monetary conference held at Bretton Woods, New Hampshire, in 1944. In theory, all currencies were fixed in terms of one another. The United States, with a huge supply of gold at the end of World War II, stood ready to buy or sell it in transactions with other governments at a rate of thirty-five dollars per ounce. At the same time, other governments stood ready to buy or sell dollars in such a way as to maintain the agreed-upon fixed relationships between their currencies and the dollar. Thus a commercial bank in Country X would, under the fixed-rate system, turn in dollars to Country X's central bank and, in return, receive Country X currency, at whatever happened to be the fixed rate of exchange between the dollar and that currency.

As things developed, this fixed-rate arrangement served to allow the United States to transmit inflationary pressures abroad. Exactly how this transmission occurred can best be illustrated, perhaps, by retelling the events in West Germany in 1971, the year in which the Bretton Woods system of fixed rates fell apart.

In May of that year, West Germany's central bank stopped buying dollars for marks and in effect let the dollar float downward in relation to the mark. Why had they abandoned the Bretton Woods procedure? Because it would have obliged them to have bought more than $2 billion at the fixed dollar-mark rate of exchange. German officials complained bitterly and correctly that

**EXHIBIT 4–5   Percentage Change in U.S. Dollar against
Selected Foreign Currencies in One-Year Period**

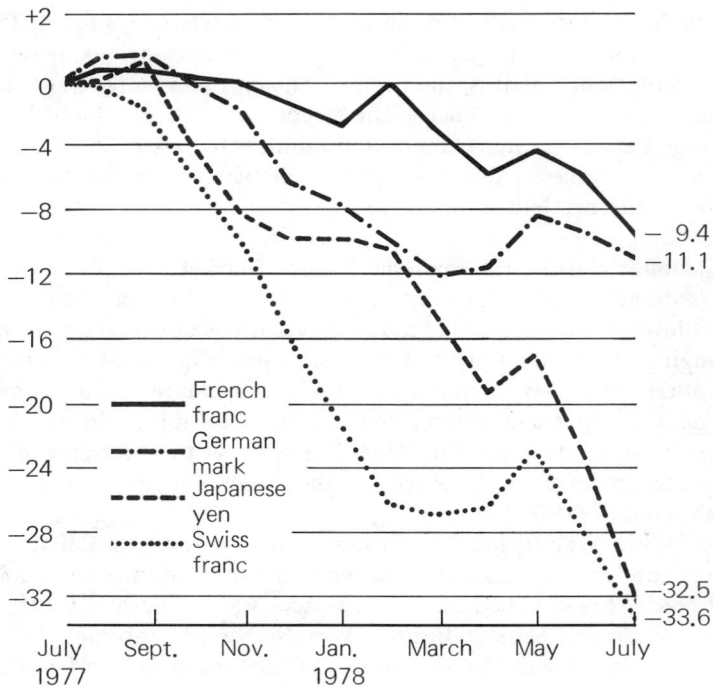

Source: Data from Council of Economic Advisers, *Economic Report of the President* (Washington, D.C.: U.S. Government Printing Office, 1977).

such forced buying of dollars for marks was exacerbating inflation in their own country by causing the German money supply to rise at about twice the desired rate.

To be sure, under Bretton Woods procedure, West German officials could have asked the U.S. government for gold, at the thirty-five–dollar price, for the unwanted dollars at their central bank. But as a practical matter West Germany—as well as other foreign countries similarly inundated with dollars—was hesitant to make such a request because it had become increasingly clear that America's dwindling gold supply could no longer meet the potential demands of dollar holders abroad.

The West German decision to stop buying dollars for marks was followed by similar decisions elsewhere. By the end of 1971, the United States did the inevitable: It abandoned its long-standing pledge to buy or sell gold at thirty-five dollars an ounce.

Today, no government is obliged to swallow American dollars at a fixed rate of exchange if dollars pile up. Now, when the Federal Reserve's monetary policy becomes overly expansionary, much of the resulting inflationary pressure must stay home; no longer may it be readily exported, as before, to such places as West Germany. Accordingly, excessive dollars now will more quickly generate domestic inflation. Under today's circumstances, the dollar's value in international currency markets is more likely to drop if Federal Reserve Board policy is overly expansionary. And any such drop would likely intensify inflationary pressures at home, since it would make imported goods costlier for Americans and spur demand for American-made products abroad.

The preceding discussion really suggests two explanations for the dollar's dramatic decline. The first, much preferred by Carter administration economists in the late 1970s, is this: The dollar problem stems directly from large balance-of-payments deficits. These deficits reflect both huge U.S. oil imports (which have run as high as $45 billion a year), and economic growth that encourages other imports. As a result, foreigners and multinational corporations hold more dollars than they want or need. This oversupply has caused them to sell a lot of dollars and thus to drive down the dollar's value compared with the German mark, the Swiss franc, the Japanese yen, and the French franc. The first diagram in Exhibit 4–6 attempts to portray this explanation schematically. Notice that the exhibit contains one other factor that also tends to fuel the balance-of-payments deficit: government regulations. By adding to the price of U.S. exports, regulations (environmental, safety, and so on) tend to make these products less competitive in world markets; thus, less are sold.

The second explanation, held by many private analysts, runs like this: The dollar problem is principally caused by the country's $60 billion-a-year budget deficits, which have forced the Federal Reserve System to create more dollars and thus add to domestic inflation. These analysts note that Germany's mark and Japan's yen are among the world's strongest currencies. These nations also repeatedly have budget surpluses, even though, like the United States, they import large amounts of foreign oil. The second diagram in Exhibit 4–6 provides a schematic explanation of this theory.

The iron logic of these two explanations fails to allow for powerful psychological elements that also underlie the dollar's decline. The dollar problem, in other words, is not wholly economic; it is partly a result of a lack of confidence in foreign currency markets in the will and ability of the U.S. government to significantly cut the payments deficit or curb inflation. These fears lead to a vicious cycle. As the dollar's value fails abroad, imported goods sold in the United States rise in price and allow competing domestic companies to raise prices too. It has been estimated that the dollar's decline added at least half of one percentage point to the U.S. inflation rate between September 1977 and April 1978. This added price push only increases foreign worries and drives the dollar down more, as holders rush to sell.

**EXHIBIT 4–6   Two Views on the Decline of the Dollar on
                 the International Money Market**

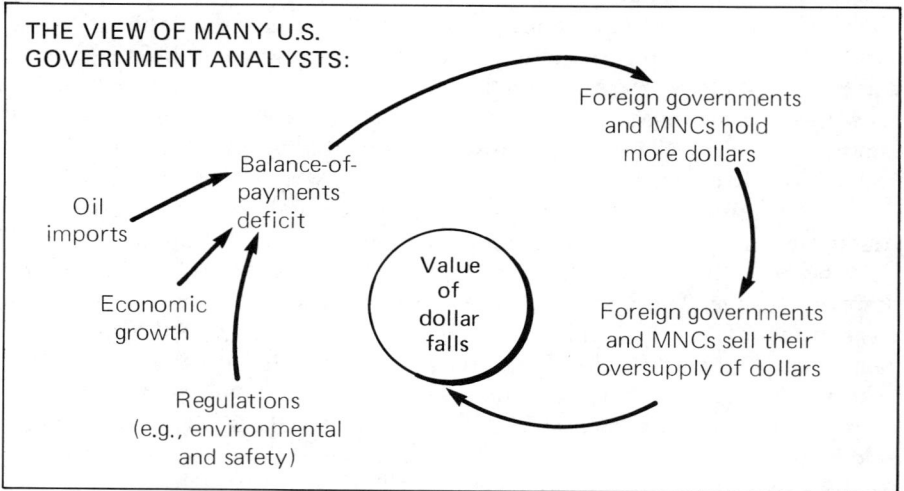

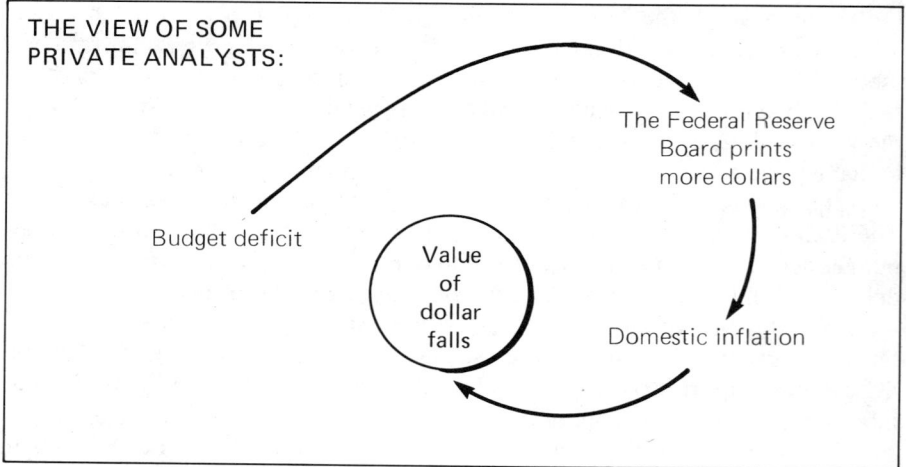

THE VIEW OF MANY U.S.
GOVERNMENT ANALYSTS:

Oil
imports

Balance-of-
payments
deficit

Economic
growth

Regulations
(e.g., environmental
and safety)

Value
of
dollar
falls

Foreign governments
and MNCs hold
more dollars

Foreign governments
and MNCs sell their
oversupply of dollars

THE VIEW OF SOME
PRIVATE ANALYSTS:

Budget deficit

Value
of
dollar
falls

The Federal Reserve
Board prints
more dollars

Domestic inflation

Effects of Floating Exchange Rates. The transition to floating exchange rates
has affected management in several ways. Obviously, great care must now be
devoted to the type of currency held since it can change rapidly in relative
value. Leslie C. Peacock (1978) discerns a more subtle problem for the interna-

tional manager: Floating exchange rates have introduced new and powerful barriers to the adequacy of private investment on a worldwide basis. In the industrialized nations, for example, nonresidential fixed investments as a percentage of real gross national product has continued to decline. Policymakers are correct to worry about this trend; its continuation will interfere seriously with satisfactory growth rates in the future. As Peacock writes, "... when exchange rates are changing quickly ... and with no assurance that differential rates of inflation will be accurately reflected in the changes, the entire basis for investment ... becomes riddled with dangers and uncertainties that were not there before." Imagine the perils envisioned by Japanese or German manufacturers who, knowing that they compete in American markets or in other markets with American producers, read the newspaper and find the American dollar depreciating out of all proportion to relative changes in costs of production! Far from being enthusiastic about the contemplation of new investment, these managers are much more likely to develop anxiety about the preservation of profit margins that make the existing investment viable.

Eurocurrencies and Their Markets. Another problem that the contemporary monetary system presents international managers is the rise of Eurodollars, Euromarks, and other "stateless" currencies.

Eurodollars are dollars held by individuals outside the United States. Through the 1950s and 1960s, because of the U.S. balance-of-payments deficit and the greater investment returns in Europe, dollars piled up in European banks. Today, huge amounts of these dollars and other Eurocurrencies have leaked across national boundaries and out of government hands, despite increasingly tough exchange controls.* This money market is run by a few dozen giant banks that now operate in virtually every part of the world. The Eurocurrency pool at their disposal by 1978 amounted to at least $400 billion, which is ten times more than it was in 1972. But, as Martin Mayer (1974) points out, exactly how much of that $400 billion is real, nobody knows.

The biggest supporters of this mind-boggling, though incredibly flexible, system are the MNCs. Today the huge pool of stateless money provides an enormous and free alternative capital market to all U.S. and foreign multinationals. This pool is an alternative not only to the mammoth U.S. domestic market, but also to the German, Belgian, French, Japanese, and other capital markets. MNCs, especially those in the United States, can use one or another subsidiary abroad to borrow in the Eurocurrency markets at rates far below anything available in their domestic markets.

---

* Controlling this outflow of currencies is a dubious venture for governments. Even under the Nazis, Mayer (1974:476) reports, a "system of controls backed by the death penalty" proved ineffective. Mayer tells the story from the 1930s about a man who had given up smuggling money out of Germany; it was too easy. He preferred the more stimulating and equally rewarding game of smuggling out people.

MNCs also use the Eurocurrency markets to play what is perhaps the most popular corporate game in international business: financing their subsidiaries' operations in the lowest-cost currency at hand. For example, Olin Corporation recently got its French subsidiary to bill its Italian subsidiary for goods in Belgian francs. Italian short-term interest rates were 18 percent, while Euro-Belgian franc rates were only 7 percent. Olin financed its operation by going into a third currency and by borrowing it in the Eurocurrency markets. And Olin is no rare exception. All foreign corporations today use the Eurocurrency markets as alternatives to their domestic markets. Dow Chemical Company uses the Eurocurrency markets to avail itself of the lowest possible interest rates around the world. In Brazil, for example, cruzeiros can be borrowed at an effective interest rate of 11 percent (the 46 percent interest rate charged on a loan, minus Brazil's 35 percent inflation rate). Dollars can sometimes be

COMMENTARY: Speculation Made Easy

Even an amateur can speculate against the dollar. For $26.75, almost anyone can buy an American Express traveler's check denominated in German marks and Japanese yen. The buyer can hold it as long as he or she likes and then cash it in at the exchange rate prevailing that day.

One big currency dealer reports that its sale of foreign-currency traveler's checks doubled between 1977 and 1978 and estimates that 25 percent of the purchases are not for travel but for speculation. If I had bought $100 worth of Swiss franc checks early in the summer of 1978, I would have made a return of 23 percent by October—better than the return on California real estate.

borrowed in Eurocurrency markets for only 9 percent. "Our treasurer in Brazil is trying to decide things like this all the time," explains Wilson A. Gay, treasurer of Dow (*Business Week,* August 21, 1978).

Advantages of International Trade

Given these balance-of-payment and currency exchange difficulties, there is a strong impulse to draw the wagons into a circle and to forget international trade. Yet Americans, like other people in the world, have become accustomed to finding West German automobiles in the United States, American jetliners in Japan, British machinery in Brazil, and French wines in Denmark. That free trade brings prosperity, efficiency, and wider consumer choice is agreed upon by nearly every economist and political leader. It is also the core idea of international trade theory—despite the fact that the United States sets price floors on Japanese steel, Europe accuses the United States of undercutting its papermakers, the Japanese complain about cheap textiles from South Korea, French farmers smash truckloads of Italian wine, and AFL-CIO President George Meany (to the consternation of exporters worldwide) calls free trade a "joke."

Notwithstanding Mr. Meany's opinion, free trade does offer advantages. Where unfettered trade among nations exists, each nation has the opportunity to specialize in producing those goods for which it is particularly suited. Such specialization leads to greater efficiency; if each nation specializes in goods it can produce most cheaply and trades them for goods that others can produce most cheaply, more goods are available at lower costs for everybody involved.

Early in the nineteenth century, the English economist David Ricardo offered a theoretical explanation of why specialization results in more goods at lower cost: the *comparative advantage principle*. Roger Leroy Miller (1973:359) demonstrates the concept with this example: William Howard Taft was perhaps the best stenographer in the world before he became president—that is, he had an *absolute advantage* in stenography. When he became president, by definition he also had an absolute advantage in being president. As president he did not specialize in stenography, even though he was the best. The advantage to him and to the nation of devoting all his time to being president was much greater than the loss of his stenographic output. His *comparative advantage* lay in presiding over the nation, not in taking dictation at 220 words per minute. In general, people discover their own area of comparative advantage by contrasting the return from doing one job with the return from doing another job.

Like the resources of an individual, resources of a nation are fixed at any moment in time. Individuals have only so much time in a day; nations, only so many people and machines per square mile. An individual, a company, and a nation must, therefore, decide how to allocate available but limited resources at a given moment. Even if a nation is absolutely better—that is, even if it has an absolute advantage at doing everything—it will still have to specialize in those tasks in which it has a comparative advantage. Through specialization, a nation maximizes the return for the use of its time and resources (just as did President Taft).

For example, the United States may have an absolute advantage in producing computers and skateboards—that is, the United States may produce both goods in fewer hours than any other nation. Nevertheless, the United States should let other nations produce the skateboards, because its comparative advantage is in producing sophisticated, high-speed computers. Moreover, the United States gains from trading the computers it produces for the skateboards produced by other countries. This brief example, however, does not do justice to the elegantly logical and mathematical structure of the concept of comparative advantage. As Paul Samuelson (1976:680) notes, "If theories could win beauty contests, comparative advantage would certainly rate high."

The theory is nevertheless a highly—some would say overly—simplified one that has a number of limitations. In the first place, the theory assumes that full employment prevails in all countries at all times; there are no problems of unemployment or recession. Second, within each country, resources are assumed to be "occupationally mobile"—that is, in terms of our simplified example, the labor, capital, and land needed for computer production can move to skateboard production, or vice versa, if so required by competitive pressures. Third, the theory of comparative advantage gives no consideration to exchange problems such as balance-of-payment surpluses and deficits and the maintenance of a particular currency exchange rate.

Fourth, as Robinson (1974:555) observes, the theory neglects the fact that "... the composition and development of a nation's stock of productive resources may be changed by international trade. Comparative advantage theory treats the resource stock as *given*. In point of fact, as a country becomes deeply involved in international trade, its resource stock (the size and nature of its capital stock, the training of its labour force) grows and changes in order to meet the particular demands of that trade."

Fifth, and quite understandably, the classical model of comparative advantage fails to account for the influence of MNCs. More specifically, an increasing share of U.S. exports—anywhere from 25 to 50 percent—is made up of intracompany shipments of materials, components, and finished products by parent companies of U.S. multinational concerns to thousands of their own affiliates abroad. The multinationals' huge financial stake in overseas production, as well as foreign government pressure against worker layoffs, inhibits any moves to cut back foreign output and replace it with stepped-up exports from the United States, *even if they are cheaper*.

Despite these five limitations, the comparative advantage concept does help shape governmental policy making, especially in the United States. To quote Samuelson (1976) once more: "A nation that neglects comparative advantage may pay a heavy price in terms of living standards and potential growth."

CROSS-NATIONAL CULTURAL DIFFERENCES

A Japanese executive sucks in air through his teeth and exclaims, "Ha! That will be *very* difficult!" He really means just plain "no," but among the Japanese, an absolute no is considered offensive; hence the euphemism. The American sitting across the negotiating table from our Japanese executive knows none of this and presses ahead to resolve the "difficulty." The Japanese executive finds this strange persistence abnormally pushy. The atmosphere deteriorates. The deal falls through.

As American business involvement abroad has expanded, avoiding the pitfalls of being a stranger in a strange land has become an important management problem. "Dozens of times every day, as airplanes touch down in Kuala Lumpur, Buenos Aires, and Dar es Salaam, nervous American executives wonder," Roger Ricklefs (1978) writes, "How on earth do I get things done in this place?" Companies should wonder and worry, too. Managers assigned to help run operations abroad sometimes do their work woefully, despite splendid records at home. Such failures are costly. It takes between $75,000 and $100,000 to transfer a manager overseas. If he or she cannot perform well at the new post, then the company's mission probably is not accomplished; moreover, poor performance in the new culture by one of the company's top managers can damage the company's public relations there.

Sending "the best person" is not necessarily an adequate insurance against such failures. Frederica Hoge Dunn (1978), who has done consulting in international personnel, writes: "Years ago, the people who were shipped overseas were usually a company's culls. Now that international business has become so important, however, the strategy has reversed: Send the best man who can be found." But who is best? If a certain executive has done a great job, doggedly and forcefully tackling tough problems in the Los Angeles sales office, he or she should be an ideal choice to tackle the company's tough problems in Tokyo. Right? Wrong. Some companies have watched their best and brightest fail miserably because no one in the home office recognized that the rugged skills that made their candidate a success in America would only antagonize people in Japan.

It is not enough to select a person solely on the basis of American criteria. Obviously, the person chosen must be technically qualified. But in interviewing people for an overseas post, extra weight should be given to the candidate's ability to adapt to an alien culture. A person who ranks third or fourth by domestic standards may be the best bet. Thus we come to an idea that a growing number of business schools and multinational companies are putting forward with verve: provide better cultural orientation before assignment. To avoid the pitfalls of attempting to apply American marketing and management approaches in foreign cultures, the following four types of cultural differences are particularly important in such orientation and training programs.

- *Differences in lifestyles of consumers.* Advertisements that somehow fail to reflect the local lifestyles can wind up a wasted effort. When General Mills made its attempt to capture the English market, for example, its breakfast cereal package showed a freckled, red-haired, crew-cut, grinning kid saying, "See kids, it's great!"—a promotional package that could not be more typically American. General Mills failed to recognize that the British family is not as child centered as the American family; the stereotyped American boy and his nearly banal expression had no appeal to the more formal and aristocratic ideal of the child upheld by the English. As a result, the cereal package repelled the British housewife and wound up almost untouched on retail shelves.
- *Differences in behavior and values of employees.* These differences can have a major impact on the effectiveness of management policies. The African

factory worker, for example, may find paternalism on the part of managers a desirable practice because it helps replace security feelings that are lost when the worker leaves the tribal group; the American factory worker, on the other hand, tends to feel that paternalistic management is outdated because it restricts a current need to express individuality. It is just not possible to say which management style along the authoritative-democratic continuum works best cross-culturally; it all depends. In Japan and West Germany, more authoritative methods work successfully, but in the United States and Yugoslavia, democratic methods prove equally successful in terms of efficiency.

• *Differences in patterns of managerial decision making.* In the United States, culture tends to dictate that decisions should be based on "objective analysis of the facts," which leads to large collections of data. Still, the ultimate decision is generally made in a hierarchical fashion—that is, the top management has the final say as to which course of action will be selected. In Japan, many more members of an organization are likely to be involved in the actual decision making. To avoid "loss of face," alternatives are put forward only indirectly. In still other cultures, decision making on a factual, rational basis is not the norm. Indeed, a request that a senior executive explain the rationale for a decision would be interpreted as a lack of confidence. Further, for senior executives to consult subordinates may be judged inappropriate in some cultures.

• *Different concepts of time.* A common frustration many American managers feel overseas involves dealing with the strikingly different concepts of time. What will take a week in the United States can take a month in some other countries. In many Third World countries, especially, anywhere from 50 to 80 percent of the time spent talking with local managers will be spent discussing anything but business. But while the American often views this personal chitchat as a waste of time, it can be crucial to business. American managers may want to separate professional life from personal life, but in many countries business is almost an indirect outcome of the personal relationship; you do business with your friends.

An Approach to Cultural Assessment

The Germans have a special expression for the ability that a business manager needs in any new environment. The word is *fingerspitzengefühl*—that is, sensitivity in the tips of the fingers. Since the extent of the effect of cultural differences on international business has been discussed, I trust the need for *fingerspitzengefühl* requires no elaboration.

Unfortunately, there is no approved method for developing it, no *Fingerspitzengefühl Made Easy* for sale. But the manager should, at a minimum, recognize that (a) what passes as ordinary, acceptable American behavior is often interpreted in such a way by foreigners that one's true intentions or sentiments can be distorted; and (b) a familiarity with one or two ways in which an overall culture can be conceptualized will provide a mental checklist that may prove important in the making of a particular decision.

One of the best checklists for cultural assessment has been developed by Edward T. Hall (1973). For many years this anthropologist has been concerned with the selection and training of Americans to work in foreign countries for both government and business. In addition to formal training in the language, history, government, and customs of another nation, Americans must also understand nonverbal language. Most Americans are only dimly aware of this "silent language" even though they use it every day. Hall (1973:XIV–XV) writes:

> They are not conscious of the elaborate patterning of behavior which prescribes our handling of time, and spatial relationships, our attitudes toward work, play, and learning. In addition to what we say with our verbal language, we are constantly communicating our real feelings in our silent language—the language of behavior. Sometimes this is correctly interpreted by other nationalists, but more often it is not.

To help overcome this problem, Hall developed a two-dimensional map of culture composed of ten separate kinds of human activity, which he labels primary message systems (PMS). Only the first of these involves language. All the others are nonlinguistic forms of communication. The ten primary message systems and how each gears into the overall network of culture are listed below (adapted from Hall, 1973:38–59):

1. *Interaction:* The ordering of people's interactions with others through language, touch, noise, gesture, and so forth;
2. *Association:* The organization (grouping) and structuring of society and its components;
3. *Subsistence:* The ordering of human activities in feeding, working, and making a living;
4. *Bisexuality:* The differentiation of roles, activities, and function along sex lines;
5. *Territoriality:* The possession, use, and defense of space and territory;
6. *Temporality:* The use, allocation, and division of time;
7. *Learning:* The adaptive process of learning and instruction;
8. *Play:* Relaxation, humor, recreation, and enjoyment;
9. *Defense:* Protection against the environment, including medicine, warfare, and law;
10. *Exploitation:* Turning the environment to human use through technology, construction, and extraction of materials.

By intersecting each of these ten primary message systems with all of the others, one can achieve useful categories of interrelationships within a culture.

For a direct application of Hall's cultural map to international business, Robock, Simmonds, and Zwick (1977:355) give the example of a large manufacturer of toys and games assessing opportunities in a new culture. The intersection of play (#8) with interaction (#1), would lead to questions about interaction in play and about the reciprocal category, play in interaction, in the new culture. The second intersection would ask about play and associations—that is, organizations involved in play, and games involving associations, and so on. Certainly, the cultural patterns of the new market will differ from those the firm is currently dealing with, and Hall's cultural map helps raise a number of critical questions about play patterns in the new culture. The map does not magically produce the right answers, or even the right questions; it is simply one structured approach to investigating how a new culture may differ. If one rejects a structured approach, one should be sure that his or her own ad hoc alternative does develop an adequate sensitivity to the important cultural differences we have discussed in this section.

RELATIONSHIPS WITH HOST AND HOME GOVERNMENTS

In addition to international economics and cultural differences, there is a third issue that concerns international managers. Its existence, however, should cause little surprise. As both industrialized nations and LDCs have become increasingly aware of the growing importance of MNCs, their governments have developed new policies to deal with these corporations. Although the timing and substance of policies may vary, depending on economic conditions, cultural attitudes, and national goals, the fundamental concern in all places is pretty much the same: The MNC is seen as a threat to national sovereignty.

In the industrialized countries, the purpose of the MNC—which, as we said, is to optimize resources on a global basis—often runs counter to the laws designed to stabilize the national economy and promote its general welfare. As George Ball (1967:26) has put it, "How can a national government make an economic plan with any confidence if a board of directors meeting 5,000 miles away can, by altering its patterns of purchasing and production, affect in a major way the country's economic life?"

In the developing countries, big and highly visible MNCs serve unwittingly and unwillingly as lightning rods for all sorts of discontent. As Vernon (1977:145–46) writes, "Their presence has drawn hostility of those eager to develop a strong national identity free of outside influence, those repelled by the costs of industrialization, those at war with capitalism as a system, and those distrustful of the politics of the rich industrialized states, especially the United States." And even the less big among corporations can raise discontent of sorts: Need there be a Kentucky Fried Chicken outlet on Kenyatta Boulevard in Nairobi?

"I pledge allegiance to the flag of the country that gives me the best deal..."

Drawing by Conrad. Copyright © 1975, Los Angeles Times.

This section deals separately with host-country and home-country relations. With each, our approach will be similar to that used in Chapter 3 when we analyzed government-business relations in the United States—first by considering various governmental supports and, second, various governmental controls (see Exhibit 4–7).

Host-Country Relations

LDCs and less-developed regions within industrialized countries (e.g., Italy's southern region) are obviously the most eager to support the establishment and expansion of foreign businesses—especially in those early, desperate stages of development.

EXHIBIT 4–7   Governmental Support and Control of International Business

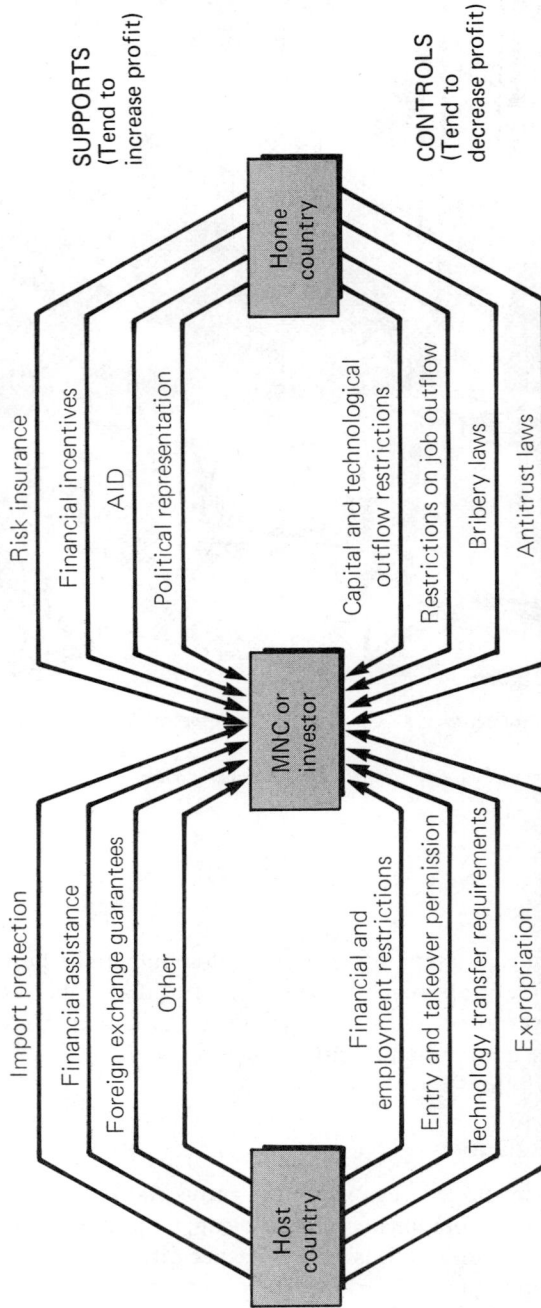

SUPPORTS (Tend to increase profit)

CONTROLS (Tend to decrease profit)

Home country

MNC or investor

Host country

Risk insurance

Financial incentives

AID

Political representation

Capital and technological outflow restrictions

Restrictions on job outflow

Bribery laws

Antitrust laws

Import protection

Financial assistance

Foreign exchange guarantees

Other

Financial and employment restrictions

Entry and takeover permission

Technology transfer requirements

Expropriation

Supports. A variety of supports are available to such governments. First, by imposing special high tariffs or import controls, these governments can protect the early growth of the foreign industry within their borders. Second, the host government can provide financial assistance in the form of low interest loans. Third, they can offer tax reductions, deferrals, or even ten-year tax holidays. Finally, the government can assist in building roads, acquiring facilities, and training personnel that the company might require.

Controls. Since a company planning on doing business in a foreign country is far more likely to face host government controls than supports, we need to consider controls in a little more detail. To begin at the beginning, we see that the first type of control involves *entry permission.* A firm wanting to invest in Dahomey must first apply to the Ministry of Finance, the Foreign Investment Board, or some such body. Thus the firm from the start is required to detail its operational, financial, and expansion plans and how these will contribute to the welfare of Dahomey. While conditions vary widely from country to country, this process of controlling the entry of foreign projects may be ripe with bribery and corruption.

A second type of control involves *finance and employment restrictions.* Many governments today require that foreign investments be financed with foreign capital. Other financial controls set limits on remission of profits, repatriation of capital, and royalty payments to the home office of the MNC. Also, because MNCs are subject to taxation in their home countries for profits earned abroad and generally receive credit for foreign taxes, many countries have raised thin tax rates to a level comparable to the principal home country of MNCs, the United States.

Another way host governments increase local benefits is through employment policies. The labor law of Mexico, for example, provides that at least 90 percent of a foreign company's employees must be Mexican citizens. Executives are generally excluded in calculating this percentage. The immigration of foreigners for managerial and other positions is permitted only if qualified Mexicans are not available.

The third type of control, *technology transfer requirements,* is often overlooked by host countries in their scramble to place financial and employment restrictions on the MNC. James Brian Quinn (1969:156) explains:

> Frequently, there will be little inquiry into what technologies the company is introducing to the country and how these may be diffused. Rarely is there specific discussion of the company's personnel training practices, decentralization of management decisions, participation in national research and educational activities, supplier development policies, customer-service activities, future development of product lines, or methods of transferring technology to overseas divisions.
>
> ... these factors are often much more important to the country's future growth than the short-term fiscal contributions the company makes.

The ultimate control is the fourth control, *expropriation.* Strictly speaking, the term refers to governmental action to dispossess someone of property but to provide compensation; dispossession without compensation is *confiscation,* as occurred in 1960 with the takeover of foreign investment in Cuba. Another term we need to disentangle from expropriation is *nationalization.* While expropriation refers to the takeover of a single property, nationalization refers to the takeover of an entire field of activities, as occurred in 1946 with the takeover of the steel industry in Great Britain. Thus, nationalization can involve a number of expropriations.

Is the expropriation of foreign property legal? Investor countries such as the United States maintain that international law mandates that the takeover be for a public purpose and accompanied by payment of "prompt, adequate, and effective" compensation. But, if these conditions are met, then the host country has little to gain. Not surprisingly, LDCs have chosen to overlook this "Catch-22" of international law; the number of expropriations and nationalizations since World War II has been large. (From 1968 to 1971, LDCs expropriated $1.2 billion in assets of American MNCs; by 1974, U.S. investments valued at $3.5 billion had been expropriated.) And today, as Middle East states elbow the U.S. oil companies out, they are merely following an example set in 1938 by Mexico's President Lázaro Cárdenas (see Exhibit 4–8). Mira Wilkins (1974) writes:

> More than any other event in history—much more than the Russian revolution—the Mexican expropriation taught the executives of the oil companies that foreign governments did have the power to confiscate, that talk could be translated into action, and that they must shape the policies of their enterprise in a fashion to mitigate the threat of nationalization.

Two further points need be considered before we turn to the relationship between home governments and MNCs. First, the leaders and advisers in some LDCs have in recent years become more knowledgeable about how MNCs operate and make decisions. They are coming to the realization that expropriation, aside from its symbolic purposes, is irrelevant. Ownership, in other words, means nothing. As they see it, money in the bank is ultimately what matters.

The second point is an ironic one. Recall that foreign investment in the United States is up and increasing. The surplus petrodollars that came out of the quadrupling of crude-oil prices in 1973 have been quietly invested in the United States. According to Toufic Mizrahi, editor of the *Mid-East Report* (quoted in the *Houston Post,* May 7, 1978), the Middle East investment is very large, running into the billions. According to recent estimates, investments in U.S. Treasury bonds and notes, as well as stocks, total about $7 billion. The extent of private investment, of course, is more difficult to determine. Point in question: What if Saudi Arabia, Iran, and Kuwait, the main investors, decided to manipulate their investments to attain political goals? Mizrahi considers

**EXHIBIT 4–8   Expropriation: The Ultimate in Host
Country Control of MNCs**

Lázaro Cárdenas, President of Mexico, set the expropriation example in 1938.

Source: Photo from Bettmann Archive.

such action possible but unlikely: "They can dump their stocks on the market, causing a chain reaction, but they have been pretty conservative economically." In any case, Mizrahi adds, the United States has an effective counterweapon: "Don't forget, the Arabs fear that the United States might impound—nationalize, if you will—their investment or seize their property."

Home-Country Relations

Supports. For obvious reasons, government likes to see home industries (exceptions allowed) be vigorous exporters. As with host-country supports, we can group home-country supports designed to foster exports into four types.

The first, *risk insurance,* includes all those programs designed to cover major foreign investment risks. These risks include not only expropriation, but also losses in war and inability to transfer profits. For example, the Overseas Investment Corporation, established in 1970 as a government corporation, insures foreign investments of U.S. corporations against expropriation.

Financial incentives, such as loans to foreign customers, also help support home-based exporters. When made by foreign governments, such loans make some U.S. companies turn to Washington for corrective action or similar assistance. The chief mechanism in the United States for such loans is the Export-Import Bank, which finances aircraft, nuclear plants, and other big-ticket items.

Financial incentives can sometimes take the form of tax deferrals and credits rather than loans. *Deferrals* provide that taxes will not be levied by the home country until profits are repatriated. *Tax credits* allow companies to get credit at home for taxes paid abroad. Some people argue that the latter should be treated simply as a business expense, as state and local income taxes in the United States are treated for federal tax purposes. Others, meanwhile, energetically defend the tax credits by saying that modern-day isolationists are trying to tax the foreign subsidiaries of U.S. corporations out of existence. In the United States, the Domestic International Sales Corporation helps to offset the tax advantages that other countries give to their export industries.

A third type of governmental support that warrants our attention is *development assistance* or, as it is more popularly known, *foreign aid.* The United States, chiefly through the Agency for International Development, attempts to contribute to the economic growth and welfare in the LDCs through grants and loans. In 1961 Congress authorized the AID to consolidate and administer most of the various foreign assistance activities and agencies. Funds for AID are authorized and appropriated by Congress. (AID does not administer military assistance programs, which are the responsibility of the Department of Defense.) In addition to AID's programs, the United States provides economic assistance through Food for Peace, the Peace Corps, and contributions to international financial institutions. Such measures, presumably, advance U.S. economic interests. Fried and Trezise (1976) summarize the assumption upon which development aid rests: "To be able to avoid a situation in which poverty and population pressure create intolerable moral, political, and economic tension, global material well-being must improve; this requires larger flows of capital to poor countries than market forces alone will provide."

With only .26 percent of its GNP going to development assistance, the United States ranks only twelfth among the noncommunist developed countries in providing aid to LDCs. Nevertheless, in recent years, public commitment to development aid has declined considerably, and the purpose and soundness of the program have come under criticism. It is likely that the program will be shifted gradually into the private sector and to multilateral institutions like the World Bank, which could regularize a lending program for the poorest countries through periodic world-aid budgets.

Government also provides business with *political representation,* a fourth type of support. A home country can use its political influence to persuade host countries to ease their controls, and even serve as a kind of middleman in a variety of global transactions. For example, the United States presses the

Japanese government to liberalize its tough restrictions on foreign investment. In wheat deals with the Soviet Union, the U.S. government intervenes in the market. While a few years ago it let oil companies negotiate with foreign governments about oil, now the U.S. government itself does much of that negotiating.

Controls. In contrast to the four types of supports we have just considered, the four types of controls the governments of home countries can apply are even more hotly debated subjects. For example, some people argue that unrestricted capital outflow can fatally compromise national security and lead to the end of Western civilization as we know it. Others maintain that allowing American MNCs to open plants overseas that should have been opened here evidences a cruel callousness towards Americans who need jobs to support their families. Still others believe that when American executives engage in bribery overseas, they sink to unfathomable depths of turpitude and sully the very ideals upon which this Republic was founded, while their opponents argue that U.S. antitrust laws fetter the hands and feet of American managers as they struggle in an increasingly competitive world arena. These are some of the points raised by home-country controls; in the paragraphs that follow, we shall try to sort out fact from fiction.

About the first control—*restrictions on capital and technological outflow*—we can be quite brief. As we have already seen in this chapter, most home countries—and the United States is certainly no exception—are concerned about the balance of payments; this concern, more than any other, is what inspires controls over capital outflow. Additionally, the United States has, from time to time, imposed restrictions on the outflow of technology (i.e., technology transfer), especially to communist countries (see Commentary section, "The Transfer of Technology").

COMMENTARY: The East-West Transfer of Technology

The transfer of technology occurs in several ways: through the travel or immigration of scientists and engineers or through their attendance at technical conferences; in the form of goods or services sold domestically or exported; and through foreign direct investment and licensing, which usually combines portions of both of the other two. MNCs are unquestionably the dominant institutions transferring industrial technologies across national borders. Controversy exists within the United States over how much technology it is desirable to transfer, what impact such transfer is likely to have on the U.S. economic and strategic position, and what additional controls, if any, should be instituted.

During the summer of 1976, the American press began to discover the immensity of the Soviet dependency on Western technology. On 26 July Arnaud de Borchgrave wrote in *Newsweek:*

> In recent years, the Soviets have imported vast quantities of Western technology, consumer goods and food . . . . The communist appetite for Western technology is staggering. The Russians have purchased nearly 1,000 "turn-key" plants—ready-to-go enterprises complete with a trained technical staff. Some of the current deals are even bigger. The Russians are buying several chemical plants, a new steel mill, oil drilling equipment and a complete shipyard from Britain. France is putting up a timber complex in Siberia and chemical refineries in central Russia.

But these events were really "business as usual." The fact is, technology transfer between East and West—or, more accurately, *from* West to East—goes back several decades ("from West to East" is more accurate simply because throughout this century the pattern of Soviet trade has remained essentially unchanged: ceaselessly importing technology, while exporting almost entirely nonmanufactured materials).

In 1921, four years after the revolution, Lenin created his New Economic Policy (NEP), which he called "industrial cohabitation with the capitalists." Lenin offered Western companies generous concessions in exchange for the rapid industrialization of Russia. During World War II, lend-lease replaced concessions as the vehicle for transfer. Lend-lease, which provided material equal to more than a third of the prewar level of Soviet production, included machinery, tools, complete industrial plants, spare parts, trucks, tanks, and aircraft.

After World War II, the Soviet Union engaged in its own version of technology transfer. From Germany alone the Soviets "transferred" iron and steelworks, chemical plants, shipyards, motorcar factories, electric power stations, railway networks, armaments factories, and the huge underground V-2 works. According to Vernon Keller (1962), 41 percent of Germany's industrial equipment was dismantled, packed, and transported to Russia.

Should the United States trade technology with the Soviet Union? Like most political questions, this one has two sides. Former Treasury Secretary William E. Simon (1978:30) expresses one view:

> Clearly, the Western nations, above all the United States, have been desperately unwise in providing the USSR with that continuous economic fix. We have supplied the Soviets with vast amounts of technology and know-how but have demanded almost nothing in return . . . . I am a strong advocate of economic cooperation and free trade, but I have come to believe that it is imperative for Western governments to stop financing Soviet industrial expansion . . . . Certainly there is no moral or economic justification for taxing American citizens in order to finance the industrialization of nations that seek to destroy them.

Fried and Trezise (1976:207) offer another view. They argue that the least productive of communist industries is agriculture, followed closely by consumer goods.

> Industries producing technically more advanced items, though lagging behind the best Western practice, seem to do better; and the production of military hardware

requiring a high level of technology is believed by observers of the Soviet economy to be the most efficient of all. To maximize its gains from trade, Moscow should be importing grain and trousers, where the Soviet system works badly.

In recent years the category of technology export that concerns U.S. companies the most seems to be that involving companies in Western Europe, Japan, and other advanced countries. The reason for the concern is that foreign products incorporating American technology are faring better and better in markets around the world— and even in U.S. markets. The growing feeling among the managers of U.S. companies is that they are harvesting too little return from the dollars they spend on these technological innovations.

J. Fred Bucy, president of Texas Instruments, argues: "Today our toughest competition is coming from foreign companies whose ability to compete with us rests in part on their acquisition of U.S. technology . . . . The time has come to stop selling our latest technologies, which are the most valuable things we've got." Horace G. McDonell, an executive vice-president of Perkin-Elmer Corporation, sums it up more piquantly: "We want to sell more milk and fewer cows" (both quoted in Meyer, 1978:106).

Regarding the second type of control, *job outflow restrictions,* we need to ask two simple questions: What are the issues? What are the facts? The American labor movement maintains that MNCs establish "runaway operations" or "export platforms" that allow them to use less costly labor from other countries to manufacture products that are then exported to the United States. According to Louis Turner (1973:177), by 1969, over 70 percent of Mexican exports to the United States consisted of products made entirely of U.S. parts.

What are the facts? The AFL-CIO notes that (cited in Turner, 1973) from 1966 to 1969 alone, over 500,000 American jobs were lost due to MNCs' switching production to more profitable foreign subsidiaries. Raymond Vernon (1977:116), who draws on the substantial body of research on MNCs that has been conducted at the Harvard Business School for fifteen years, offers a less clear answer:

> Whatever the direct and immediate effects of the multinational structure may be upon employment totals in the United States, the aggregates produced by such statistical exercises are small. The estimates range from a few hundred thousand jobs added to the U.S. economy to a few hundred jobs lost; and the estimates at the extremes are, on the whole, less plausible than the estimates in the middle. On the present evidence, therefore, the question of aggregate employment effects in the United States is a secondary issue.

More certain than the change in the total number of U.S. jobs is the change in the mix; the number of jobs available for the unskilled has been reduced, while the number available for the skilled has been increased. In social terms, that shift is hard to evaluate, for it may burden the present generation while offering new promise to the next.

Concern over the object of the third type of control, bribery laws, is a relatively new phenomenon. History does not record any burst of international outrage when Charles M. Schwab, an American businessman, presented a $200,000 diamond and pearl necklace to the mistress of Czar Alexander's nephew, although, in return for that consideration, Bethlehem Steel won the contract to supply the rails for the trans-Siberian railroad. But today, inducements (i.e., bribes) are quickly and universally denounced when used by U.S. companies doing business abroad. We are now living in what many observers call a post-Watergate age of morality, characterized by investigation, discovery, condemnation, and legislation.

Out of this context came the Foreign Corrupt Practices Act, which President Carter signed into law in 1977. For the first time in U.S. history, it is a crime for corporations to bribe an official of a foreign government or political party in order to obtain, or retain, business in another country. More specifically, the law requires publicly held companies to institute internal accounting controls to ensure that all transactions are made in accordance with management's specific authorization and are fairly recorded. In addition, the law makes it a crime for a corporation or any of its employees to "corruptly" influence officials of a foreign government or political party, or to make payments to any persons when the company has reason to believe that part of the money will go to a foreign official. If convicted, companies are liable for fines of up to $1 million, and individuals face maximum fines of $10,000, five years in jail, or both.

Designed to still the furor that erupted from revelations that more than four hundred U.S. corporations have made millions of dollars' worth of such payments, the law instead has succeeded mainly in raising questions about its meaning and applicability. These are, however, technical questions that quite possibly will be resolved in time. Meanwhile, in West Germany, Britain, and France, payments of bribes abroad remain not only legal but tax deductible.

Antitrust laws, which we discussed in Chapter 3, can and have served, as the basis for a fourth type of control over MNCs. Companies, in other words, cannot insulate themselves from the reach of antitrust laws by going outside the United States to make restraints of trade that affect the U.S. market.

What kinds of overseas deals are unlawful? The following situations would all be subject to prosecution under antitrust law. If American *and foreign competitors* set prices of uranium, phosphate, and ocean shipping rates, they are subject to prosecution by the Department of Justice. If MNCs make licensing agreements that contain certain price and territorial provisions that prevent overseas producers from selling in the United States, they are subject to prosecution. If Pan American World Airways, Trans World Airlines, and Lufthansa German Airlines conspire to fix prices of excursion flights for military personnel and their families between Germany and the United States, they are subject to prosecution. These examples are, of course, only illustrative of the kinds of activities that raise eyebrows in the antitrust division's foreign commerce section. According to Joel Davidow, who served as chief of that section in 1977, the highest priority in enforcement should go to "problems of market allocation"—that is, the situation of saying, "You stay out of my market and I'll stay out of yours" (cited in *Business Week,* March 14, 1977).

In 1977 a new law went into effect that said the federal government no longer need show any deference to the *commercial* activities of foreign governments. According to the law, a government like Germany, which owns Lufthansa, could be attacked for lawbreaking, just as any commercial venture could be prosecuted. The problem now is how to draw a line between political activity, which is immune from U.S. prosecution, and commercial activity.

In this discussion of host- and home-country relations, as well as in earlier sections of this chapter, we have touched on a number of the critical and complex issues that abound in the international environment of business. What does it all mean? Not long ago, Henry Kissinger (1977) said it very well:

> We have come a long way, and very rapidly, to the axiomatic proposition that international business depends decisively on international politics .... We have come a long way from the nineteenth century when the United States accounted for very little in the scale of world economics .... The future of American business will require the highest degree of sensitivity to the political framework in which it functions and to the great coming changes in the world political process.

CHAPTER FIVE

Central Problems
of Business - Society
Interrelations

Running just beneath the surface of the discussion in the preceding chapters were two problems profoundly important to our inquiry. The first concerns the relationship of government to business; the second, the relationship of business to society.

Each problem can be posed as a series of questions. The first raises these questions: What is the justification for government's attempting to control business activity through regulation? In other words, why not merely leave things to the mysterious, though often quite effective, workings of the market? What are the costs and the benefits of government interference? And what are the alternatives to regulation?

The second problem stands the discussion of the three preceding chapters on its head. Thus far we have been looking almost entirely at how the technological, economic, social, political, and international environments *affect business.* But surely the reverse is also true: The American business system affects these environments. While it will not be possible to detail how business affects each of these environments, we can at least raise these questions: What are the sources of business's political power? What are the checks on this power? And, does business have too much political power in American society?

We begin by considering four justifications for government's entering a market system to control business. These four justifications are (a) that certain businesses are "natural monopolies"; (b) that consumers and workers have inadequate information; (c) that some business costs are fobbed onto society (*externalities* is the economic term for such costs); and (d) that a market system, no matter how free, tends to underproduce certain goods that are important to the public good. Next, we attempt to assess both the benefits and costs associated with government intrusion into the marketplace. Our discussion of governmental control then concludes by considering a few alternatives to regulation, which in recent decades has been one of the government's chief methods for controlling business.

Turning to the problem of business's political power, we first note the principal sources of business power: the strength of its organization, its access to political decisionmakers, the dependency of other groups in society on business, and business's ability to "capture" certain government agencies. Next, we weigh these sources of power in the balance against certain limitations on business power. To do this, we need to introduce the concepts of "countervailing power," "pluralism," and "convertibility" (i.e., the difficulty of translating economic power into political power). We then finish our treatment of business power in pretty much the same way we did our earlier discussion of government control—that is, by looking at reforms. Among the more popular and thoughtful recommendations are these: require federal charters, revitalize the board of directors, and "rehabilitate" the corporation. ☐

Government Control

REASONS FOR GOVERNMENT CONTROL

The basic justification for government involvement in private economy—especially through regulation—can be stated in two words: market failure. To understand this justification, we need to recall from the first chapter Adam Smith's model of a freely competitive market. Under specified assumptions, the competitive market yields the "best" answers to the questions of what should be produced and how it should be produced—that is, the competitive market ensures that society's resources are used efficiently to make products that consumers want. The model of a free market tells us nothing about the desirability of the income distribution that results. Smith's competitive model of economic behavior has great appeal in a democratic society, because it does not require that economic activities be directed by a central authority. Individuals acting in their own self-interest maximize society's economic well-being. But the unfettered market does not always work ideally. In other words, certain failures within the market prevent the maximization of society's well-being. These failures have to do with natural monopolies, a lack of adequate information, externalities, and the attainment of social objectives.

Natural Monopoly

When the production of a commodity is characterized by increasing returns to scale (i.e., per-unit production costs decrease as the firm becomes larger), a *natural monopoly* exists. Consequently, the largest firm in the industry is also the most efficient—that is, it has the lowest cost per unit of output. Such a firm has the ability to underprice competing firms and drive them out of business. The surviving firm then becomes a *monopolist*, or sole producer of a product. And, in order to maximize profits, it pursues price and output objectives that are not considered desirable for society's economic well-being.

When compared to firms in a competitive system, unregulated monopolists usually produce too little output and charge prices that are too high, engage in discriminatory pricing behavior, and reap monopoly profits. This situation is usually remedied with classic public utility regulation in which a public utility commission determines what the monopolist may charge for output, what the minimum quality of the service must be, and what profit the monopolist is entitled to earn.

The primary attribute of a natural monopoly is that one firm can supply the entire market for a good or service more cheaply than any combination of smaller firms. Local telephone service is an excellent example of a natural monopoly. The value of telephone service is a function of the number of people with whom a subscriber can talk. A single firm can interconnect large numbers of local subscribers at a lower cost than competition would produce because the presence of more than one firm would require wasteful duplication of facilities.

Neither the natural monopoly aspects of an industry nor the resulting justification for regulation are fixed over time. Changes in the extent of the market or changes in technology can eliminate the natural monopoly status of an industry. Such changes would make continued regulation unnecessary and injurious because the costs of the regulation would not be offset by any benefits. For example, railroads were natural monopolies in the nineteenth century. The industry's economies of scale followed from the costs of assembling the rights-of-way and laying the track. Consequently, although some large cities were served by several railroad companies, the railroad monopoly was secure because there was no competition from trucks or planes. But the situation changed markedly over the next years; the development of trucks and the construction of a national highway system meant strong competition for the railroads. Today railroads would be incapable of exercising substantial monopoly power even if there were no government regulation. A price equal to the cost of shipping freight by truck would be the maximum amount an unregulated railroad could charge.

Inadequate Information

Government intervention in the areas of consumer product attributes and occupational safety can be justified on the basis of inadequate information in the marketplace. Private markets do not function well when adequate information is lacking. Consumers need to know the attributes and prices of a wide range of products in order to make the best use of their money. Workers need to know about, and be able to evaluate, occupational hazards in order to determine whether they are appropriately compensated. While in many instances markets are reasonably efficient providers of information, the existence of a serious deficiency in the provision or processing of information can justify government regulation.

In the area of consumer product attributes, the consequence of inadequate information is that consumers are unable to maximize their welfare or well-being. Consumers feel they have been overcharged for a product if its quality is less than is claimed. Also, if the risk of injury is greater than believed when the product was purchased, the consumer is subject to a higher-than-expected risk of injury.

The problem of insufficient product information can be remedied in two different ways. The first alternative is to increase the flow of information to consumers so they can make efficient decisions. The following examples of this kind of activity relate to both product safety and quality:

—Labeling requirements ("The Surgeon General of the United States has determined . . .");
—Grading standards ("All of our steaks are USDA 'Choice' or 'Prime' ");
—The policing of correct weight and size information ("This product is sold by weight, not volume; any settling . . .");
—Truth-in-advertising enforcement (". . . however, nothing can prevent colds").

The second alternative is for the government to set minimum acceptable safety standards that must be met if products are to gain entry to the marketplace. Under this system, products that are too dangerous are banned. Two different arguments support these bans on excessively risky products. The first is that the costs associated with banning such products are less than the costs of a "wrong" decision or, alternatively, less than the cost of producing and diffusing the information necessary to eliminate wrong decisions. The second argument is that consumers are unable to evaluate complex statistical information involving risk of bodily harm.

Government intervention in occupational or job safety may be justified by both insufficient information in the labor market and related cost and price distortions. A worker subjected to a job-related danger to physical well-being bears a cost of production—that is, the worker bears the cost of expected loss resulting from work-related sickness and injury. If workers were able to accurately estimate the actuarial value of a risk, and if they were fully compensated for it, the need for government intervention would probably be absent. Work-related risks would be removed to the extent that it was less expensive for firms to reduce the risks than to compensate the employees. But due to information problems or differences in bargaining power, some workers probably do not receive full compensation for their risks. The news media frequently carry examples of this situation. The reports of Kepone poisoning of workers in Virginia and lead poisoning of workers in Indiana are cases in point. Both producers and consumers share the benefits derived from this worker-borne production cost: Producers capture extra profits, and consumers receive lower prices.

It may be useful to distinguish between risk of accidental injury and risk of work-related illness. Predictable accidents are more readily adjusted for by the market. There has been some preliminary work indicating that workers in jobs with high risk of accidental injury receive compensating wage differentials. The decision of a worker to knowingly accept such a job is, in certain respects, not conceptually different from virtually all daily decisions people make. A driver who speeds trades the increased risk of an accident for the time saved; the individual who smokes in bed trades a sharply increased risk of a fatal fire for the pleasure of the cigarette. In comparison to accidental injuries, health hazards are less clearly understood and involve cause-to-effect time periods stretching into decades. The complexity of health hazards, coupled with a full range of informational problems, suggests that larger benefits may be associated with government intervention in this aspect of occupational safety (see Smith, 1976).

Externalities

Much recently instituted government intervention in the marketplace is the result of externalities or spillover costs and benefits. Regulation is warranted because the presence of externalities gives rise to questions concerning the use of resources and the shift of costs and benefits to third parties. *Negative externalities*—the type most pertinent to a discussion of regulation—are costs of production or consumption that fall on society but not on the person who causes them. For example, the automobile pollutes the air and impairs general health. The driver pays for the car and gasoline used but not for the consequences of the degraded air quality. Thus inefficient overconsumption follows because the driver pays less than the full cost of the resources consumed. Federal intervention to correct negative externalities includes environmental protection and some aspects of the regulation of nuclear power generation, health and safety, and financial intermediaries.

Environmental pollution is a clear-cut example of a negative externality. In the absence of government intervention, firms that cause pollution use the environment as a free input in the production process; consequently, the operating costs of the firm do not include the costs of the pollution. The firm's output is therefore underpriced from a social point of view. The free market yields an inefficient solution because the consumer of the goods produced pays less than the full cost of production, and some costs are borne by others who do not derive benefits from the product (see Exhibit 5–1).

The justification for nuclear power regulation rests on similar grounds; it differs only in the categorization of the external costs. Many of the costs of air and water pollution are readily apparent—even if it is difficult or, in some cases, impossible to measure them. For example, a river or beach that is lost to recreation is visible; respiratory difficulty during an air pollution alert can be felt; and studies have shown that excessive noise levels can cause hearing loss and personality changes. The external costs of nuclear power generation—as distinct from the nuclear waste problem—are not as easily observable. Nevertheless there is the possibility of a nuclear mishap, which imposes an external cost. That cost is the expected value of the damage produced by a nuclear accident—that is, the probability of a mishap times the injury that would be inflicted. Well-designed government standards would reduce the hazard and, in the process, internalize to the firm some of the external cost. Under such circumstances, the price of nuclear-generated electricity would rise to reflect the otherwise external cost of an accident.

Some health and safety regulations can also be justified by the presence of *positive externalities,* or spillover social benefits (see Exhibit 5–2). Automobile standards that specify tire, brake, and other handling requirements reduce the risk of injury not only to drivers, but to third parties as well. Construction standards reduce the risk of collapsing buildings and spreading fires. Health standards reduce the spread of disease from the careless to the more prudent.

The regulation of financial intermediaries is justified because of the vulnerability of the banking system to panic runs and the subsequent impact of bank failures on the rest of the economy. The insolvency of financial intermediaries contributes to real economic difficulties for nonbank firms and employees.

Social Objectives

The federal government may also intervene in the market to help insure the attainment of certain social objectives. Government can achieve a particular

EXHIBIT 5–1   Uncompensated Social Costs

Many types of economic activity, whether originating in the public or the private sector, generate uncompensated benefits or costs, which are often referred to as *externalities*. For instance, producing outputs in a factory in the private sector may result in smoke pollution or the dumping of wastes in rivers. The social costs of correcting this pollution—the real costs of alternatives or opportunities forgone and any reduction in incomes and benefits as a result of the clean-up process—will not be covered in the private costs of producing this output, that is, the actual production costs within the factory. As a result, the selling price of the outputs will fail to reflect the full social costs of producing this output.

The consequences of uncompensated social costs are illustrated in [the accompanying figure]. Given the demand (D), if only the private costs of producing the output (supply), S_p, are included, quantity Q_p will be sold at P_p. But if the costs of the pollution clean-up, represented by the vertical distance between the two supply curves are included, less will be supplied, S_s, and less will be taken, Q_s, at a higher price, P_s.

From a social point of view, *less* output of goods that do not cover their full social costs of production would be desirable. Government might attempt to reduce these outputs by levying a tax on them. For instance, in [the accompanying figure], a tax equal to the costs of pollution clean-up might be levied on the outputs. This would cause the supply curve, S_p, to shift to the left and result in only Q_s being produced and sold.

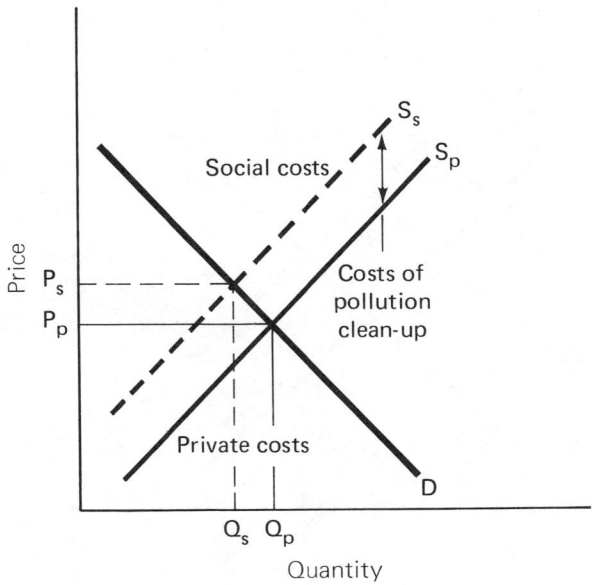

Source: Robert Persons, Sue Atkinson, and Robert Rouse, *Economics for the Citizen* (No. Scituate, Mass.: Duxbury Press, 1978), p. 192.

EXHIBIT 5–2   Uncompensated Social Benefits

The production of some goods and services . . . results in uncompensated social benefits, with the private benefits individuals, households, and firms are willing to pay for providing an added bonus, or spillover, in terms of social benefits. For instance, many individuals are willing to pay out of their own pockets for the additional training or education that will provide them with skills that will increase their earning power on labor markets, a clear private benefit. At the same time, these private expenditures result in gains by those who *did not make these expenditures* through a more enlightened and productive electorate and work force, a clear social benefit and one for which society as a whole did not have to pay—an uncompensated benefit.

   The consequences of uncompensated social benefits are illustrated in [the accompanying figure]. Given the supply (S), if only the private benefits are taken into account, then D_p will be demanded, with Q_p taken at P_p. But if the social benefits are added to the private benefits—the vertical distance between the two demand curves—then D_s will be demanded, with a larger quantity, Q_s, taken even at the higher price, P_s.

   By contrast, goods whose social benefits exceed their private benefits should be encouraged. This might be accomplished by government through a subsidy. For instance, in [the accompanying figure], those willing to pay for additional training and education might demand more of this training and education if they were given a subsidy equal to the added social benefits from this activity, resulting in a shift of the demand curve from D_p to D_s, with an increased amount produced and sold.

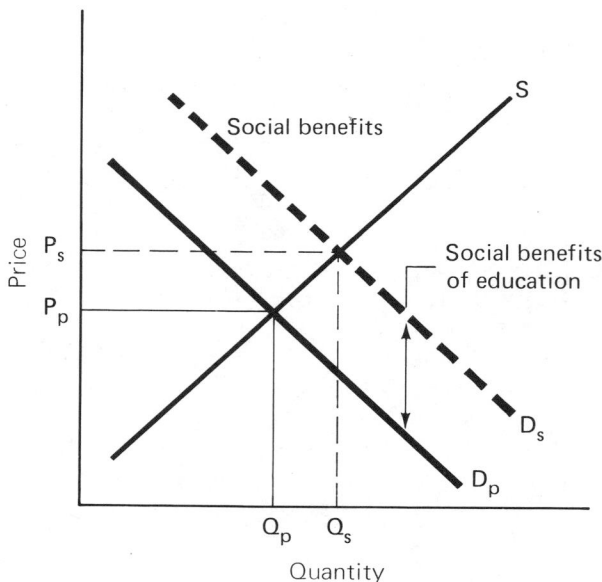

Source: Robert Persons, Sue Atkinson, and Robert Rouse, *Economics for the Citizen* (No. Scituate, Mass.: Duxbury Press, 1978), pp. 192–93.

objective in several different ways. The Congress can change the tax laws, vote to spend public funds, pass laws to encourage specific behavior, or decide to regulate a particular activity or industry. For example, providing air service to small communities might be desirable even though it is uneconomical. This service could be provided in any number of ways. Subsidies might be given by the federal government to the private airlines that provide the desired service. The subsidies might come out of the federal government's general tax revenues or be generated by a special tax. A quasi-public corporation might be set up to provide the service. Alternatively, the industry might be regulated. The regulation could limit entry into the industry and require that each airline allowed to operate serve a combination of profitable and unprofitable routes. The extra profits from the best routes could be used to subsidize service that otherwise would not be provided.

The decision to use regulation instead of the taxing and spending powers of the federal government to achieve social policy objectives is a political matter. Such a decision is subject to the judgments of policymakers; it cannot be made on the basis of arguments concerning inefficiencies in the marketplace. Regulation can thus be a difficult, if not unwieldy, policy instrument. Several examples of the difficulties and questionable effectiveness of using regulation follow.

• Some regulation may not produce the desired results. For example, one objective of FCC regulation is the promotion of local television broadcasting, the advantage of which is the supposed responsiveness to local interests. The FCC allocates licenses to provide as many communities as possible with local outlets (see Noll, Peck, and McGowan, 1973), and the number of compatible stations is increased by restricting the broadcast power and areas served of all stations. The consequences are a reduction in the potential number of stations each community can receive and a restriction of the number of viable commercial networks to three. But the cost of original television programming is so high that few local stations can afford to engage in it. New programs are mainly offered by the networks, which capture programming economies of scale. Locally originated programming, therefore, except for local news programs, has been dominated by reruns of old network series and movies. Thus there is an apparent conflict between the objectives of this regulation and the end result.

• Regulation that may have been effective at some time in the past may be continued even though it is no longer needed. According to some economists, for example, one of the original objectives of railroad regulation was to promote the development of the West (see Friedlaender, 1969). To that end, the Interstate Commerce Commission supported "value-of-service" pricing— that is, the low-value bulk products of the frontier, such as grains and other raw materials, were shipped at unprofitable rates, which enabled the frontier to compete with other regions. At the same time, the East's high-value industrial goods were shipped at tariffs sufficiently high to raise the railroads' total revenues to profitable levels. This practice of price discrimination worked successfully because industrial shippers in the nineteenth century had no alternative to using the railroads. But when the higher quality, more flexible motor truck appeared, shippers began to switch to trucks since the high railroad rates for industrial goods remained unchanged under ICC pricing policies. As a result, railroads continued to ship low-value bulk products, while trucks captured the high-value industrial trade, and this circumstance, not surprisingly, contributed to the decline of the railroads.

• Regulatory goals simply may not be adequately specified. The regulation of natural gas, for example, seeks to secure "just and reasonable" prices for that fuel. The phrase *just and reasonable* implies a price that is uniquely and correctly determined by regulation. But concern for price without an equal concern for quantity creates problems; price and availability of fuel cannot be independently determined. It is generally agreed that in recent years the Federal Power Commission (FPC) has kept the price of natural gas too low and thereby may have caused a serious shortage of that fuel.

The benefits of regulation appear when it successfully furthers certain social objectives: strengthening national defense; preserving equal opportunity; altering the maldistribution of income; providing services to small communities (e.g., surface freight transport, aviation, and telephones); supporting price stability and full employment; and so forth. But use of regulation to achieve any of these objectives merits prompt careful evaluation, even if the potential benefits are substantial.

THE ECONOMICS OF REGULATION

Assessing the economic effects of regulatory activities boils down to answering two fundamental questions: What benefits follow from the regulation? And, what costs are imposed by the regulation? Comparing the answers to these questions gives an indication of whether a regulatory agency is, on balance, beneficial. Unfortunately, the benefits and costs of regulation do not conveniently appear in a ledger or an annual report. Estimation of the amounts of money involved often requires sophisticated models and complex statistical techniques, and dollar figures for some costs and benefits cannot be estimated at all. The following discussion builds on this unhappy reality, and the best we can do is attempt to classify benefits and costs in a way that at least sheds a little light on the issue, even if all the benefits and costs are not quantifiable.

Benefits

The benefits of regulation can be quite large, but the difficulties in evaluating them are pervasive. Measurement problems are substantial, and in many cases no reliable estimates of benefits can be computed given the current state of the art. In cases where benefit evaluation is technically feasible, it is not always useful in determining the correctness of a regulatory decision. This is especially true in certain regulatory areas—nuclear power, product safety, the environment—in which all the possible consequences of a decision are not known and a wrong decision can have catastrophic results. Evaluating the benefits of regulation under such circumstances may thus be reduced to simply identifying the desired ones. Finally, even evaluating the fulfillment of objectives of some regulation is complicated because much enabling legislation specifies objectives that are vague or even contradictory.

In assessing the benefits of government intervention in business, we first need to consider whether a condition of market failure exists; lack of conditions requiring regulation precludes the derivation of benefits. If intervention is justified, we can assess the benefits of regulation in our first three areas of justification simply on the basis of whether the regulation functions to correct a failure in the market:

—Regulation of a natural monopoly should capture the efficiency of scale economies without the undesirable and costly practices of an unregulated monopoly.
—Regulation in the presence of inadequate information should improve the efficiency of private markets.
—Regulation in the presence of externalities should promote a more efficient use of society's resources and an equitable shouldering of costs.

In the case of regulations aimed at the achievement of social objectives, the evaluation should consider the following questions:

—What objectives are specified?
—Are the objectives in concert with the current conception of the public purpose?
—Does the regulation achieve the objectives?
—What are the unintended consequences?
—What are the total costs of using the regulation to achieve these objectives?
—Who bears the cost of the regulation?
—What alternative mechanisms can achieve the objectives?
—Are any of these alternatives less costly (i.e., more efficient) ways of reaching the objectives?

Costs

Costs can be divided into five categories: (1) administrative and compliance costs, (2) static efficiency costs, (3) dynamic costs, (4) shifted costs, and (5) uncertainty costs. With no illusions that we can measure these costs scientifically, let us take a look at what the categories mean.

Administrative and Compliance Costs. The most directly observable costs of government regulation are administrative and compliance costs. The administrative costs are incurred by both the government and the private sector. The costs to the government consist of the budgeted regulatory activities of the independent commissions, agencies, and executive departments. They cover such diverse activities as visits of Occupational Safety and Health Administration (OSHA) inspectors, rate-setting deliberations of the Interstate Commerce Commission, automobile safety standards set by the National Highway Traffic Safety Administration, nuclear plant inspections by the Nuclear Regulatory Commission, investigations by the Federal Trade Commission, and energy allocation by the Federal Energy Administration. A recent study by the Joint Congressional Economic Committee concluded that in fiscal year 1979, a budgetary expenditure of $4.8 billion was devoted to such administrative activities. But the federal government's out-of-pocket expenditures represent only a small fraction of the cost of regulation to the economy. The balance— the cost of compliance—must be paid by business and, eventually, by consumers. In fiscal 1979, the bill came to nearly $100 billion (see Exhibit 5–3).

The administrative costs to the private sector are the staff-hours spent filling out the application and reporting forms required to implement the regulations. The compliance costs are the billions of dollars in visible expenditures required to meet the regulatory standards. These include, for example, the increased costs of stack scrubbers and other equipment to cleanse factory effluents, the costs of factory safety equipment, and the costs of drug testing programs. Consider the following estimates of compliance costs.

- The *New York Times* (June 21, 1976) reports that Eli Lilly and Company, a major research firm, spends more man-hours filling out government reports than it does in research for cancer and heart disease combined. For example, one application by the firm to the Food and Drug Administration for permission to market an arthritis drug consisted of 120,000 pages, not including the duplicate and triplicate copies. Lilly's total cost for gathering information, analyzing data, and filling out government reports is more than $15 million annually. If these costs are applied to the company's U.S. pharmaceutical business, they theoretically add about fifty cents to the price of every prescription for a Lilly medicine.
- According to *Fortune* (November 1976), Kaiser Aluminum & Chemical Corporation has also made a thorough study of its paperwork burden. The vice president for planning and control found that Kaiser was making at least 231 separate filings of a strictly financial nature, not including tax returns or statistical reports for the Department of Labor, at a cost of $168,000 a year in manpower alone (see Exhibit 5–4). Amazed, he went on to make a rough survey of the company's total reporting burden. What he found was that, including tax returns, Kaiser submits at least 10,000 reports a year to all levels of government. The vice president's estimate, a conservative one, was that this

**EXHIBIT 5–3   The Multiplier Effect: The Cost of Compliance with
Federal Regulation in Fiscal 1979**

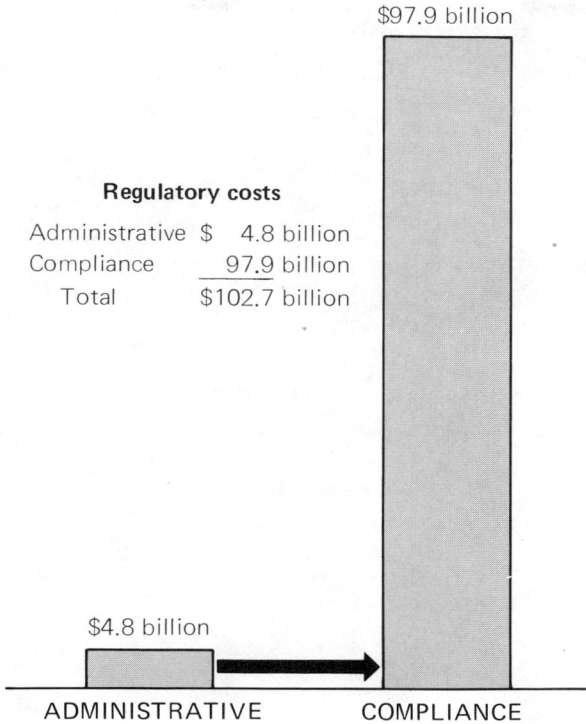

$97.9 billion

Regulatory costs

Administrative	$	4.8 billion
Compliance		97.9 billion
Total		$102.7 billion

$4.8 billion

ADMINISTRATIVE   COMPLIANCE

Source: Data from U.S. Congress, Joint Economic Committee, 1978.

paperwork soaks up $5 million a year in labor and overhead costs—not a negligible amount for a company that netted $95 million after taxes in 1975.

Static Efficiency Costs. The result of regulation in some industries is *static efficiency costs.* For example, many older regulatory commissions, such as the Civil Aeronautics Board (CAB) and ICC, regulate industries that would otherwise have a large number of competing firms. The agencies restrict competition by regulating entry, rates of return, and prices. Although the unregulated market is not perfectly competitive in a theoretical sense, the substitution of these three types of regulation for workable market forces can result in inefficiencies.

**EXHIBIT 5–4   An Example of Industry Compliance with
Government Regulation**

It takes some 240 file boxes to hold all the reports that the federal government required of Kaiser Aluminum & Chemical Corporation in 1975. These eighty people,
photographed on the grounds of Kaiser's headquarters in Oakland, California, represent the eighty man-years of employee time absorbed by all that paperwork.

Source: Photo from Woodfin Camp & Associates, © John Marmaras.

First, regulating the number of firms within an industry actually fosters collusion by conferring on firms, such as trucking and shipping companies, an exemption from antitrust prosecution, which can result in their forming rate bureaus. Restriction on entry, such as occurs in civil aviation and trucking, can also eliminate an important market mechanism: the guarantee that inefficient firms will either reduce their production costs or be replaced by new, more efficient firms.

Second, rate-of-return regulation can impose another source of inefficiency—that is, overcapitalization in pursuit of an enlarged rate base. Rate-of-return regulation operates by setting prices that generate sufficient revenue for a regulated firm to pay all its costs and earn a normal rate of return on its capital stock. Under this kind of regulation, one way to increase total firm profits is to increase the amount of the firm's capital and earn the allowed profit rate on a larger stock of capital. But inefficiencies result if the capital stock is increased beyond its most efficient level. While this problem was first discussed in the academic literature in the early 1960s, current research has identified other forces that tend to call rate-of-return regulation into question.

Third, the Federal Power Commission's regulation of the wellhead price of natural gas is a case in which price regulation resulted in too little capacity. FPC regulation kept the wellhead price of gas below the market price. When sharp increases in the prices of other fuels left natural gas greatly underpriced relative to its substitutes, the lower price encouraged gas customers to use it inefficiently in place of the more expensive fuels. Further, the pollution-free characteristic of natural gas added to its relative advantage over other fuels because firms using natural gas did not have to invest in expensive pollution-control equipment. Hence underpricing and overconsumption of gas, the superior fuel, resulted in shortage. The impact of regulation on the supply side of the market may also have contributed to the shortage, since the low price of interstate gas discouraged the shift of resources into the exploration and development of new gas fields.

Dynamic Costs. As we saw in Chapter 2, the gains in productivity resulting from technological change and entrepreneurial creativity have been important elements in the growth of the U.S. economy. Although some regulated industries have innovated rapidly, others, however, have been very slow to change, and it appears, on balance, ". . . that the performance of regulated industries falls far short of the ideal and even of a reasonable target" (Capron and Noll, 1971:221). In short, regulation can entail dynamic costs.

Many aspects of the regulatory process—for example, regulation of prices, rates of return, and entry—can discourage research and development and retard the rate of technological change. The potential to earn supranormal profits, for example, has long been recognized as a powerful incentive for promoting technological change. Excess profits are compensation for the risks associated with innovation, but are a temporary phenomenon because they are eventually shared with the competition. Therefore, regulatory control of profits, to the extent that it eliminates the ability of an innovating firm to capture substantial excess profits, removes one incentive to innovation.

But how does a regulating agency determine the "permissible profits" of a firm? An agency does so by multiplying the allowed rate of return times the value of the firm's capital stock. The upshot of this procedure is that regulated firms may tend to reject the most efficient innovations if they are of a low-capital variety and choose less efficient, high-capital alternatives that expand their capital stock—which is, of course, their rate base. Two examples from the telecommunications industry help illustrate how this works:

• In the early 1960s the Bell System was faced with a choice of two alternative communication satellite technologies. One involved a random-orbit system of fifty satellites coupled with expensive and complex ground stations. The second used a small number of high-altitude synchronous-orbit satellites and less complex ground stations. The random-orbit system was more costly and much more capital intensive, but some observers have suggested that the Bell System initially supported it because of its greater potential for expanding Bell's rate base.

• In 1968 the Bell System strongly advocated FCC approval of TAT-5, a new trans-Atlantic cable, even though satellite technology was, by that time, well developed, reliable, and less costly. One reason for Bell's preference for the cable was that it would represent a significant increase in the company's rate base and, hence, in allowable profits. The use of satellites would have required the Bell System to lease channels from the Communications Satellite Corporation (COMSAT), for which the company would only be compensated on a dollar-for-dollar basis (see Shepard, 1971).

Other types of regulation can also reduce the level of research and development and the associated introduction of new products. The 1962 Kefauver-Harris amendments to the Food, Drug, and Cosmetics Act added the requirements that firms provide documented scientific evidence that new drugs are effective as well as safe; that the Food and Drug Administration be given discretionary power over the clinical research process; and that controls be imposed on the advertising and promotion of prescription drugs. Recent studies of the drug industry have concluded that these amendments have reduced research and development efforts, induced multinational firms to divert research efforts abroad, sharply increased the time and cost of meeting all requirements for FDA approval of a new entity (see Commentary section, "The Price of Delay"), and reduced the number of prescription drugs currently being introduced.* According to Sam Peltzman (1973), the delay in the introduction of

---

* According to the Food and Drug Administration, in 1977 the average number of new chemical entities approved by the agency dropped from nearly sixty in the 1957–1961 period to less than fifteen during the 1972–1975 period.

new drugs and the reduction in their number as a result of stringent FDA regulation is far more costly to the nation's health than the possible cost of an inefficacious drug that might be marketed under less stringent legislation. Some authorities believe that if aspirin were discovered today, it would never get from laboratory to the market shelf.

COMMENTARY: The Price of Delay

It took Armour Pharmaceutical well over a year to get FDA approval for Calcimar, a drug developed by Armour Pharmaceutical, which is effective in controlling Paget's disease and other bone afflictions. And it is effective. I picked out an unsolicited letter—we have many—from a lady in Wyoming who was bedridden and, to quote her, "so sick and in so much pain I didn't want to live." She had Paget's disease in both legs, hips, pelvis, and up the spine. She says that "thanks to Calcimar I am able to walk again. I can travel and I have no pain. It's like being reborn." The letter itself is much more impressive than my hurried description, but the pathetic point is that this lady was deprived of Calcimar for months and months while the FDA pursued its weary regulatory process. In contrast, the drug was promptly approved in Europe, was written up most favorably in prestigious European medical journals, and was available there to sufferers of Paget's disease a very long time before it was available in the United States. Unfortunately again, the delay or the denial of the availability of an effective drug is not an uncommon occurrence here.

Source: Gerald H. Trautman in *Congressional Record,* January 26, 1977, p. S1477.

Shifted Costs. As noted earlier, many managers have voiced concern over the substantial costs involved in complying with regulatory requirements. But many of these costs are not new; they only appear new because they have gained visibility as a consequence of regulation. For example, compliance with OSHA regulations involves the *shift of a cost* of production from the worker (the expected loss from injury or illness) to the firm (the cost of removing the hazard). Similarly, compliance with EPA standards involves the shift of a cost of production from society (the loss due to environmental degradation) to the firm (the cost of pollution control equipment). Much of the cost shifting that takes place is beneficial, at least in the sense of promoting economic efficiency, because the prices of products are increased to reflect the full cost of production. Consequently, overall efficiency improves.

There is little argument about the inflationary impact of federal intervention as another type of shifting cost. Government economists estimated that regulation accounted for as much as three-quarters of a percentage point in the rate of inflation in 1978. In 1976 Richard Posner of the University of Chicago estimated that federal milk regulation added an extra 10 percent to the cost of milk. According to a study by Washington University in St. Louis, federally mandated safety and environmental features increased the price of the average passenger car by $666 in 1978, and, moreover, weight added to the cars by the new equipment increased fuel consumption by $3 billion annually. The price of a new home also went up by $1,500 to $2,500 because of federal, state, and local requirements as wider roads, special permits and licenses, and more detailed environmental impact studies imposed on developers. In sum, the average American family of four spent over $1,200 to meet the costs of federal regulation in 1976.

Uncertainty Costs. The last cost of regulation is perhaps the most difficult to measure: the cost to business of the uncertainty and delay that regulation generates. Examples are easy enough to find.

   • The Federal Meat Inspection Service ordered an Armour meat-packing plant to create an aperture in a sausage conveyor line so that inspectors could take out samples for testing. The company created the aperture. Then along came the OSHA to demand that the aperture be closed as a safety hazard. Each federal agency threatened to shut down the plant if it did not comply instantly with the agency's order.

   • Two different federal agencies have assumed jurisdiction over toilets. First, OSHA ruled that employers must provide special lounge facilities as part of their women's rest rooms. Then the employers found themselves in violation of an Equal Employment Opportunity Commission ruling that if special lounges are provided for women, they must also be provided for men.

Another kind of uncertainty cost is the "announcement effect" of federal regulation. Weidenbaum (1977:71–72) explains how it works:

> For many years economists have identified what is termed an "announcement effect" of government spending or taxation. That is, potential government contractors may start preparing to bid on a project before Congress has appropriated funds for it. Similarly, consumers may increase their expenditures as soon as a tax cut is voted on or even while it is being considered.
>
> It now seems that governmental regulatory programs may have somewhat similar effects. In Illinois, the very rumor of more stringent standards for migrant worker housing by the Occupational Safety and Health Administration caused strawberry farmers to reduce their production. Lester Pitchford, the largest grower in the central area, was quoted as saying, "We don't know if OSHA is coming or not, but when it was even rumored, it put [strawberry production] out."

The proceduralism of regulation can make a debacle of the best-laid corporate plans. The Seabrook Nuclear Power Station is a $2 billion facility intended to supply 80 percent of the electrical power in New Hampshire in the

1980s. After 110 days of public hearings before various bodies, the EPA regional administrator approved the plant's seawater cooling system, which would raise the temperature of a quarter-mile of the ocean by five degrees. The Nuclear Regulatory Commission issued the necessary permit, and the company started building. Then the regional administrator reversed himself and withdrew his approval. But the *national* EPA administrator reviewed this decision and, deciding that there were no unacceptable environmental effects, reversed the regional administrator's change of mind and gave the green light for resuming construction. The Seacoast Antipollution League then took the Environmental Protection Agency to court, claiming that in reaching his decision, the national EPA administrator had violated the Administrative Procedures Act. The court agreed and reversed the reversal because, it said, the agency had used faulty procedures in reaching its judgment—*not* because its judgment was faulty. Although the Seabrook saga did not quite end here, we have followed it far enough to make the point: Such confusion means costs to a company.

EXPLORING REGULATORY REFORM

Opposition to regulation centers on industry-specific regulation that offers little or no social benefit in return for the cost. Yet even the most ardent opponents agree that some industry-specific regulation is necessary. Suppose, for instance, that electric utilities, which are natural monopolies, were deregulated. The effect would be either freedom for the power companies to set prices as they pleased or a wasteful overlapping of facilities as companies tried to compete.

There is more disagreement, however, over functional regulation—that is, regulation of a particular function, such as pollution control, that usually involves only industrial sectors. While conservative economists concede that some kinds of functional regulation may be needed, they still argue—along with many liberal economists—that controls could be applied more effectively. In this section, we explore how.

Benefit-Cost Analysis

One proposed device for broadening the horizons of government policymakers and administrators is the economic impact statement (see Joint Economic Committee, 1978:22–26). In the fashion of the environmental impact statements, Congress could require each regulatory agency to assess the impact of its proposed actions on the society as a whole and particularly on the economy. Much, however, would depend on the teeth put into the requirement. Merely legislating the performance of some economic analysis by an unsympathetic regulator would serve little purpose beyond delaying the regulatory process and making it more costly; limiting government regulation to those in-

COMMENTARY: Is Regulation Here to Stay?

The reason we got into regulation was watered milk, rotten meat, and sloppy restaurants—the kinds of things that were inflicting all kinds of pain and agony on people. This kind of regulation will remain.

But as regulation has spread to other areas, disillusionment has set in at both ends of the political spectrum because the conservative, market-oriented people say that regulation makes it impossible for the system to function efficiently, while the critics on the Left say the special interests have captured the very agencies regulating them. The end result has to be something in the middle between total regulation and total free enterprise, and we're going to have to put up with red tape. No one is going to be completely satisfied with the degree of regulation we have, so the ideal is a degree that most people can live with.

Source: Herbert Kaufman of The Brookings Institution in *New York Times*, January 22, 1978. © 1978 by The New York Times Company. Reprinted by permission.

stances where the total benefits to society exceed the costs would be a major departure from current practice.

In the view of economists, government regulation should be carried to the point where the incremental costs equal the incremental benefits, and no further. Indeed, this balance is the basic criterion generally used to screen government investments in physical resources. Overregulation—that is, regulation in which the costs exceed the benefits—would thus be avoided under the benefit-cost analysis approach.

Further, many of the proposals to reform existing regulation involve the *sunset mechanism*—that is, the compulsory periodic review of each major regulatory program to determine whether it is worth continuing in the light of changing circumstances. A benefit-cost analysis would provide a quantitative mechanism as an aid in making these value judgments. Significantly, this is the direction in which President Jimmy Carter's administration was trying to move in the late 1970s. In addition to proposals to lessen industry-specific regulation, such as that applying to airlines, Carter established a Regulatory Analysis Review Group to evaluate the economic efficiency of between ten and twenty regulations a year. The emphasis was on cost-benefit ratios and on the need to write regulations that tell companies how much pollution can be tolerated, or how much occupational health is needed, but not how to achieve specific goals.

Changing Attitudes toward Regulation

Improving the effectiveness of government regulation of private activities requires a basic change in the approach to regulation. Experience with the job safety program provides a cogent example. Although the government's safety rules have resulted in billions of dollars in public and private outlays, the basic goal of a safer work environment has not been achieved. If the objective of public policy is to reduce accidents, then public policy should focus directly on the reduction of accidents. Rather than the emphasis being placed on issuing citations to employers who fail to fill forms out correctly or who do not post the required notices, it should be placed on the regulation of those employers with high, and rising, accident rates. Perhaps fines should be levied on those establishments with the worst safety records. As the accident rates decline toward some sensible average standard, the fines could be reduced or eliminated.

Government regulation need not always be concerned with the specific way an organization achieves a safer working environment. Some companies may find it more efficient to change work rules, others to buy new equipment, and still others to retrain workers. The making of this choice is precisely the kind of operational decision making that government should avoid, but that now dominates many regulatory programs. Without diminishing the responsibility of the employers, the sanctions under the federal occupational safety and health law should be extended to employees, especially those whose negligence endangers other employees. The purpose here is not to be harsh, but to set up effective incentives to achieve society's objectives and to provide an alternative to government's specifying the details of what it considers to be "acceptable" private action.

Consider the case of proposed job safety standards for exposure to lead in the workplace. OSHA could require smelters, battery manufacturers, and other firms to install engineering controls that reduce by one half the maximum exposure level. But the Council on Wage and Price Stability estimates that meeting that standard would cost the affected industries, and ultimately the consumers, over $300 million a year. Fortunately, there is an alternative: OSHA could allow each company to use the most efficient way of achieving the new standard, whether efficiency requires costly engineering controls or some other method, such as intensive employee training.

Alternatives to Regulation

Government promulgation of rules and regulations restricting or prescribing private activity is, of course, not the only means of accomplishing public objectives. Codes of behavior adhered to on a voluntary basis may also be effective. For example, trade associations have occasionally served to upgrade the level of business performance. Through its taxing authority, the government itself can also provide strong incentives for voluntary action. Rather than promulgating detailed regulations governing allowable discharges into the nation's waterways, for example, the government could levy substantial taxes on those discharges. Such sumptuary taxation could be "progressive" to the extent that the tax rates would rise faster than the amount of pollution emitted by an individual polluter. Thus firms would have an incentive to concentrate on removing or at least reducing the more serious instances of pollution.

The use of taxation would be meant neither to punish polluters nor to give them a "license" to pollute. Rather, it would be use of the price system to encourage producers and consumers to shift to less polluting ways of producing and consuming goods and services. For each organization, the cost of the removal of pollution, compared to the size of the tax, would determine the level of environmental cleanup that it pursued. Those that could control pollution cheaply would do so and thus pay less tax; those with high control costs would opt to pay more tax. This approach would attempt to achieve a given level of environmental quality with minimum resource use by equalizing the marginal cost of pollution control.

In the case of the traditional, one-industry type of government regulation—for example, in airlines, trucking, and railroads—a greater role should be given to the competitive process and to market forces. The older forms of regulation, as we have seen, are often mainly barriers to entry into a given industry; they serve to protect existing firms from competition by potential new entrants. While deregulation in this limited area is thus a viable option, the elimination of regulation in the areas of safety, ecology, and related fields does not appear to be a realistic alternative in view of the nation's long-term social concerns.

In sum, any realistic appraisal of government regulation must acknowledge that important and positive benefits—less pollution, fewer product hazards, reduced job discrimination, and other socially desirable goals—have resulted from the many regulatory activities we have considered here. Our examination of the various costs generated by federal regulation, however, raises questions about government's attempting to regulate every facet of private behavior. As Henry Owen and Charles L. Schultze (1976:10) have pointed out, a reasonable approach to the issue of regulation would thus seem to require sorting out the problems and hazards that require regulation from the lesser ones that can best be dealt with by "the normal prudence of consumers, workers, and business firms."

Corporate Power

THE SCOPE OF CORPORATE POWER

Large corporations affect the technological, economic, social, and political environments in the United States. Despite the billions that the federal government spends on research and development, business has a sizable influence over the direction, rate, characteristics, and consequences of technological innovation. This influence over the technological environment reveals itself probably at its worst in the automobile industry; in three decades and after the production of millions of automobiles, the only innovation of any significance has been the automatic transmission. Also, it was probably corporate management decisions, more than consumer preference expressed in government policy, that led to the distinctively American tendency to produce products that were energy inefficient. Consequently, when the energy squeeze of the early 1970s began, a wide variety of U.S. products were at a severe competitive disadvantage in overseas and, to a lesser extent, domestic markets. Further, because so many companies choose to externalize their production costs onto society in the form of increased air and water pollution, environmental problems have worsened.

Even more apparent than the technological and environmental effects of big business are the economic ones. Corporations can influence and often determine the price, production, distribution, and quality of goods and services. McCarry (1972:75) cites the following incident, which points with particular directness to the power once held by the automobile industry:

> President Johnson signed the Traffic and Motor Vehicle Safety Act of 1966, in the presence of Senator Ribicoff, Ralph Nader, William Haddon, and others, on September 9, 1966. At the White House gates, after the ceremony, Ribicoff turned to Jerome Sonosky and said, "Jerry, do you think we've saved any lives?" Sonosky replied that he did not know, but that that was not the issue. "The issue," as he explained later, "was, Who decides what's safe? Who decides whether these lives should be saved?"
>
> With the president's signature, the issue was resolved: the automobile industry had lost its power to decide how safe its products should be. From that point onward, the federal government would set the standards for safe vehicle design.

Moreover, corporations can affect the economic environment—which parts of the country will prosper and which will decline—by choosing where to locate their plants and other installations.

Corporate decisions also influence the social environment. Measuring the exact degree of influence can take us into some complicated behavioral research. But we need not risk statistical overload to recognize a pretty uncomplicated bit of truth: The hundreds of advertisements that bombard us daily must have some influence on cultural values, mores, customs, habits, and modern living. Vance Packard, in *The Hidden Persuaders,* was among the first to explore the extensive efforts made by large corporations to channel consumers' unthinking habits, purchasing decisions, and thought processes by the use of insights gleaned from psychiatry and the social sciences. As Packard (1957:4–5) explained in his opening chapter:

What the probers are looking for, of course, are the whys of our behavior, so that they can more effectively manipulate our habits and choices in their favor. This has led them to probe why we are afraid of banks; why we love those big fat cars; why we really buy homes; why men smoke cigars; why the kind of car we drive reveals the brand of gasoline we will buy; why housewives typically fall into a hypnoidal trance when they get into a supermarket; why men are drawn into auto showrooms by convertibles but end up buying sedans; why junior loves cereal that pops, snaps, and crackles . . . .

Certain of the probers, for example, are systematically feeling out our hidden weaknesses and frailties in the hope that they can more efficiently influence our behavior. At one of the largest advertising agencies in America psychologists on the staff are probing sample humans in an attempt to find how to identify, and beam messages to, people of high anxiety, body consciousness, hostility, passiveness, and so on. A Chicago advertising agency has been studying the housewife's menstrual cycle and its psychological concomitants in order to find the appeals that will be more effective in selling her certain food products.

We can see an even more clear-cut instance of how corporations affect the cultural and demographic environment if we consider the millions of people who have direct relationships with the corporation—for example, employees, stockholders, suppliers, and community members. One further point not to be overlooked: To the extent that large companies provide employment, their personnel requirements help shape the curricula of schools and colleges. For all these reasons, individuals' personalities are likely to reflect to some degree aspirations and dissatisfactions that have been shaped by corporations.

Finally, that large corporations wield power (see Exhibit 5–5) that can affect the political environment none would deny. That this political power is cause for concern few could deny. Clearly, then, the influence of business on politics merits our closest attention. In this section, therefore, we first consider the sources of corporate political power: the strength of corporate organizations, corporate access to political decisionmakers, the dependency of other groups in society on big business, and corporate ability to "capture" certain government agencies. Then we examine the various limitations on corporate power.

Principal Sources of Corporate Power

Organization. In trying to influence the political-legal environment, corporations draw upon and coordinate a wide variety of talents. In Chapter 11 we shall consider some of the more relevant corporate departments; governmental relations or public affairs, public relations, legal counsel, Washington office, and government contracting are obvious examples of corporate units devoting some or all of their time to tasks relevant to the political concerns of the company. Large corporations also possess the latest communications, transportation, and computers, which are of invaluable assistance to these diverse corporate units concerned with political matters.

EXHIBIT 5–5 Most Powerful U.S. Institutions and Executives

The most powerful institutions	The most powerful industrial executives
White House	Irving S. Shapiro, chairman, DuPont Company
Large business	
Supreme Court	Reginald H. Jones, chairman, General Electric Company
Television	
Labor unions	Thomas A. Murphy, chairman, General Motors Corporation
U.S. Senate	
U.S. House	John D. deButts, chairman, American Telephone & Telegraph Company
Federal bureaucracy	
Banks	Henry Ford II, chairman, Ford Motor Company
Lobby and pressure groups	

Source: Adapted from *U.S. News & World Report,* April 17, 1978, p. 38.

Organization is an important asset in another respect: Large corporations have branches in many geographical locations, both national and international. Despite the extent of company decentralization and the degree of policy initiative exercised by subunits, basic corporate policies are formulated and coordinated at a focal point within the organization and then implemented by subsidiary divisions. Corporations, therefore, can pursue political objectives over broad geographical areas and at the same time coordinate their activities from a central location. Further, having subunits located in many states and many congressional districts increases the number of members of Congress who are likely to have a keen and not unfavorable interest in the corporation.

Before leaving this discussion of organization as a corporate power source, three more subtle points warrant mention. First is John Kenneth Galbraith's (1967;1973) thesis that corporations have already killed Adam Smith's self-regulating market. In this view, the larger a corporation grows, the more it can escape from the workings of the market to become a law unto itself and thus paralyze Adam Smith's "invisible hand." According to Galbraith, large companies can set prices more or less independently of demand; produce what they rather than consumers want; and in effect ram the products down consumers' throats by the power of advertising. Or, if corporations cannot defy the market, they can sometimes resist it for a long time when it refuses to conform to their plans. A classic example is Detroit's stubborn insistence on building big, costly, gas-thirsty cars long after consumers had signaled a change in tastes by buying swarms of Volkswagens and Toyotas.

The second point to note about organization as a source of power is the maldistribution of incentives for political action. As numerous democratic theorists have noted, political involvement is, like any other investment, contingent upon the expectation of a reasonable rate of return on invested resources. Since each individual consumer-taxpayer typically bears only a small portion of the costs and enjoys only a small share of the benefits from public programs, he or she rarely has the incentive to spend the energy, time, and resources needed to influence the policy. But for other political actors, such as large corporations, the potential benefits and costs of government action are sizable and concentrated enough to make political involvement a rational investment. The consequence is a gross disparity in the incentives for political involvement—a disparity that works to induce the citizen-taxpayer toward passivity, while stimulating the large corporation toward political activism.

The third important point is that the power often stems from the size and complexity of the organizational structure of many modern corporations (see Exhibit 5–6). Raymond Vernon (1977:34) offers a classic example of how size and complexity translate into real power:

> When the oil crisis of the 1970s emerged full-blown, the limited capacity of governments to deal with the provisioning of vital materials became immediately evident. No government possessed the kind of data an operating agency would need for overseeing the day-to-day conduct of the international oil industry. The problem was not so much a lack of facts as it was the sheer complexity of the business. That complexity made informed discussion and reliable interpretation of the oil situation especially difficult, except among a few experts.

Access. The chances that a large corporation will get a hearing and an opportunity to make its case to government range from very good to excellent. Close connections between governmental decisionmakers and corporations result from a number of factors. In an interdependent economy in which business organizations are charged with the task of performing important public functions, corporate managers are thrown into continual contact with governmental officials and are perforce involved in the formulation of public policy.

In adopting new policies and implementing existing ones, wherever possible governmental officials seek to achieve the acquiescence, if not the active support, of influential business leaders. Such efforts take place on the commission and departmental levels, where top governmental officers speak to leading corporate executives to "get readings" on the acceptability of particular governmental actions.

At the highest level of our government, American presidents have, in recent years, frequently sought to bolster their positions on critical matters by obtaining the support of the Business Council, an organization founded in 1933, when President Roosevelt asked to have organized a group of top-echelon business leaders with whom the New Deal administrators could exchange views. Its prestige has grown through the years, and today it includes the heads of the most important corporations. The council has several meetings a year, at which its members receive briefings from top government officials and

EXHIBIT 5–6   How Big Are Multinational Corporations?

To put into perspective the size of the biggest U.S. multinational corporations, we can compare the gross national product of the leading nations of the Organization for Economic Cooperation and Development (OECD) with the annual sales of the MNCs. Both GNP and sales (in billions of dollars) are indicated in parenthesis in the following list of the "top 36" for 1976.

1. United States (1,962)	19. FORD (29)
2. Japan (550)	20. Finland (28)
3. West Germany (462)	21. TEXACO (26)
4. France (346)	22. MOBIL (26)
5. Britain (217)	23. Greece (23)
6. Italy (163)	24. STANDARD OIL (19)
7. Canada (188)	25. GULF (16)
8. Spain (102)	26. IBM (16)
9. Netherlands (87)	27. Portugal (16)
10. Australia (92)	28. GENERAL ELECTRIC (16)
11. Belgium (68)	29. CHRYSLER (16)
12. Switzerland (60)	30. ITT (12)
13. EXXON (49)	31. New Zealand (11)
14. GENERAL MOTORS (47)	32. SHELL OIL (9)
15. Turkey (41)	33. U.S. STEEL (9)
16. Austria (40)	34. ATLANTIC RICHFIELD (8)
17. Denmark (37)	35. DUPONT (8)
18. Norway (30)	36. Ireland (8)

Source: U.S. Department of Commerce, *Statistical Abstract of the United States 1977,* Table 1513, and *Fortune,* May 1977, p. 366.

enjoy the company and the attention of presidents who are anxious to build business confidence in economic policies. In addition to the meetings, the council maintains liaison committees, which work with individual government departments concerned with the economy: Labor, Treasury, Commerce, the Council of Economic Advisers, and the Office of Management and Budget. These committees give unofficial advice to the departments.

The size, importance, and reputations of corporations contribute to the relatively easy political access they enjoy. For example, a high-level representative of General Electric, DuPont, General Motors, IBM, or Alcoa can readily get to see an important government official; busy politicians and bureaucrats will juggle their appointments books largely on the basis of a representative's organizational affiliation (see Exhibit 5–7).

Corporate heads also serve at the top levels of presidential cabinets and on top-level presidential public service commissions. On less lofty planes, busi-

EXHIBIT 5–7   Business and Politics in the Capitol

Irving Shapiro, chairman of DuPont, meets with Thomas P. (Tip) O'Neill, Speaker of the House.

Source: Photo from Woodfin Camp & Associates, © John Marmaras 1978.

ness leaders serve in various capacities with administrative agencies and executive departments. Business leaders also participate in government without compensation—that is, as WOCs—or as paid consultants on myriad advisory panels, boards, councils, and commissions concerned both with broad policy decisions and with the minutiae of policy implementation affecting their industries. Furthermore, most of these officials return to business careers after their tours of government service.

One final aspect of business access to government, which we shall consider in greater depth in Chapter 13, concerns political contributions. Public officials, obviously, do not wish to offend past contributors. While contributions by no means guarantee favorable results, they do assure corporations of a forum in which to present their case. In the words of Senator John L. McClellan of Arkansas (quoted in Epstein, 1969), "I don't think anybody that gave me a contribution ever felt he was buying my vote or anything like that, but he certainly felt he had an entree to me to discuss things with me and I was under obligation at least to give him an audience when he desired it to hear his views."

Dependency. The concept of dependency, as used here, refers to the dependency of other social groups upon the activities of the corporation. Epstein (1969) writes:

> This dependency manifests itself in numerous ways. Employees are dependent upon the firm for their livelihoods. Job mobility is often possible and, to the extent that it is, lessens worker dependency; but lower-level employees whose skills are widely available in the labor market are largely denied the advantages of mobility. Moreover, in certain locations, companies possess a geographical monopoly as a source of employment. Dependency, therefore, is a function of the existence of practical employment alternatives. A firm is provided with leverage over its workers by the potency of a possible threat to close a plant in a particular area unless certain conditions considered by management to be undesirable are changed. While in times of rising unemployment such threats may be particularly forceful, even under normal conditions workers are dependent upon job incomes to enable them to meet the financial obligations that they have assumed.

Corporate patronage also assumes another form: A patron-client relationship may develop with governmental units such as states and cities because of the overriding importance of the corporation to the area in which it is located. A classic model at the state level would be the relationship between DuPont and Delaware. (In their study of American business and public policy, Bauer, Pool, and Dexter, 1972, have a chapter entitled "Delaware: Where the Elephant Takes Care Not to Dance among the Chickens.") A classic model at the local level would be the relationship between Caterpillar Tractor Company and Peoria, Illinois, where one of every three people employed in Peoria owes his or her job directly or indirectly to Caterpillar and its payroll. In 1978, two out of nine city council members were Caterpillar employees, as was the mayor of East Peoria and the state legislator. While the degree of influence undoubtedly varies depending on the time and the issue, it is probably true that over the long run public policy in such areas will seldom directly conflict with the fundamental interests of the great corporate enterprises.

What if it does conflict? Then business begins to view the jurisdiction as "inhospitable" and starts moving out or, at least, stops moving in. This pattern has been evident in New York City since the late 1960s and more recently in California. Not surprisingly, by the late 1970s both jurisdictions were waging vigorous campaigns to convince business that this inhospitable atmosphere no longer existed.

Capture. Certain administrative agencies have been primary areas of past corporate political success; consequently, in certain industries, *client control* has been a prime characteristic of the regulatory process. Thus, according to the critics, one reason why the Federal Communications Commission delays actions and fails to impose rules with teeth is that the agency has a cozy relationship with the communications industry. The Brookings Institution reports that during a twenty-five–year period ending in 1970, twenty-one of the twenty-three FCC commissioners left for jobs with interests regulated by the agency. The House Subcommittee on Oversight and Investigations reports that between 1971 and 1976 FCC commissioners and staff spent $89,206 attending industry conventions. The commissioners took 781 trips to industry conferences and went to only 7 consumer meetings. Barry Cole (1977), a special consultant to the FCC for five years, writes that the agency often delayed actions favorable to broadcasting until just before conventions so that decisions could be announced to applause. In 1976 the National Association of Broadcasters' convention had so many such announcements ("NAB specials") that *Broadcasting* magazine reported that a "grab bag of FCC favors greets NAB in Chicago" (Cole, 1977).

Examples of other governmental agencies that have been characterized in the past by client control are the Departments of Commerce and the Interior, the Food and Drug Administration, the Interstate Commerce Commission, and the Civil Aeronautics Board. Indeed, the last two mentioned agencies had their geneses in legislative designs to protect the regulated industry and—particularly in the case of the CAB—to promote it.

Of all the many aspects of corporate political activity, this tendency for some industries to "capture" administrative agencies has caused the greatest concern. For example, Grant McConnell (1966:254) has expressed the view that "in this capture of public authority in particular areas lies the most important problem," since the consequence of such a capture is "the formulation of separate narrow constituencies for particular parts of government." But other observers draw a distinction between the old regulatory agencies and the new (see Exhibit 5–8). "The new regulatory agencies," Paul H. Weaver (1978) writes:

> . . . were deliberately organized along functional lines, and their jurisdictions therefore cut across industry boundaries. The EPA, for example, deals with pollution problems created by all industries, and OSHA regulates safety and health conditions for workers in all industries. The Consumer Product Safety Commission controls the safety of virtually every consumer product on the market and so involves itself in the design and marketing of everything from rag dolls to power lawn mowers. . . . The new regulatory agencies are accordingly resistant to cooptation by any single industry. If they are vulnerable to cooptation at all (and they are), it is cooptation by safety or environment-oriented groups, not by business organizations.

Limits to Corporate Power

In addition to regulatory restrictions discussed in the first part of this chapter, what other limits can be put on the scale against the corporations' sources of

EXHIBIT 5–8   The Old and the New Regulation

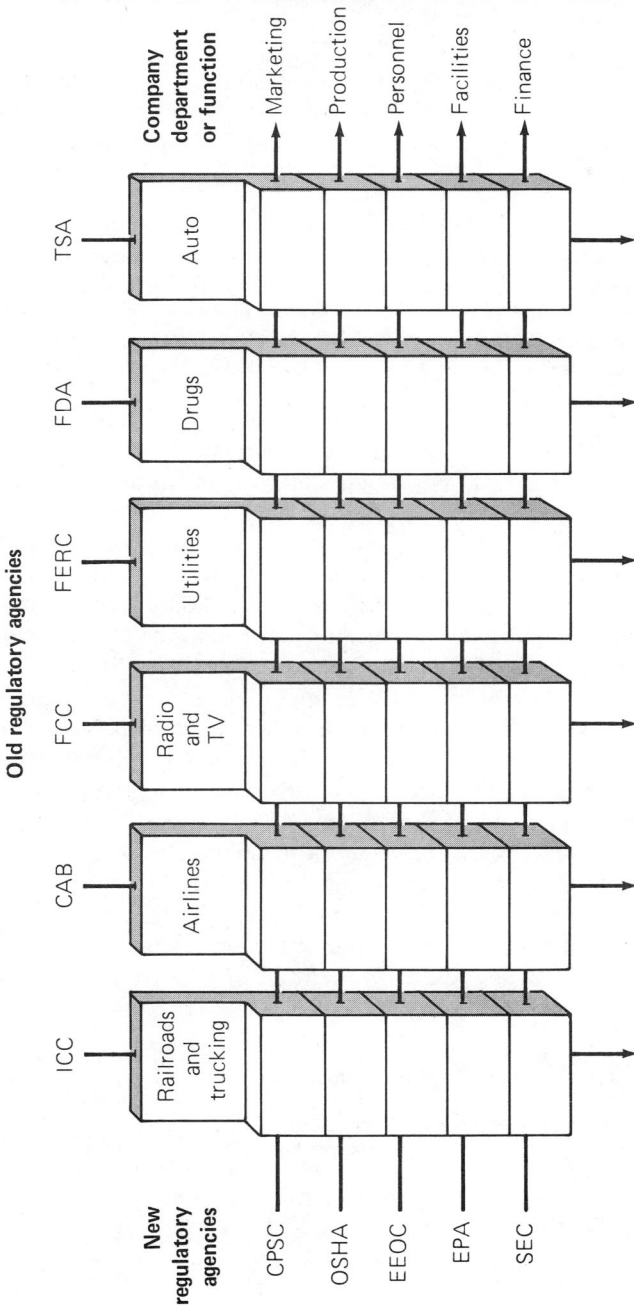

Note: Although the FDA and TSA regulate single industries, they do not maintain the cozy relations that the ICC, CAB, FCC, and FERC do with their respective industries.

Source: Data from U.S. Congress, Joint Economic Committee, 1978.

power? Among the more significant limitations are countervailing power, pluralism, and the convertibility problem—that is, the difficulty of translating economic power into political power.

Countervailing Power. To identify the first limit on corporate power, we can return to an early work of that mordant critic of U.S. business, John Kenneth Galbraith. Corporate power is checked by what Galbraith described as the *countervailing power* (1962:111):

> Private economic power is held in check by the countervailing power of those who are subject to it. The first begets the second. The long trend toward concentration of industrial enterprise in the hands of a relatively few firms has brought into existence not only strong sellers, as economists supposed, but also strong buyers, as they have failed to see. The two develop together, not in precise step but in such manner that there can be no doubt that the one is in response to the other.

Corporate power is thus checked not only by the new regulatory agencies, but also by unions, news media, customers, minority groups, and the "new class." *

Another countervailing force against corporate power is the activity of rival corporations. Corporations use their political power against each other at least as frequently as against other groups in society. To understand this point, we need only consider the issue of trucking deregulation. Despite trucking's arguments to the contrary, Sears, Roebuck & Company, for example, has pushed trucking deregulation for years, manufacturing companies are uniting to lobby for it, and the National Association of Manufacturers has endorsed it. The International Brotherhood of Teamsters regards deregulation as a threat to jobs, but the Independent Truckers' Association, which represents independent owner-operators, supports it strongly.

In addition to the activities of rival corporations, intracorporate conflict also limits corporate political power. Intracorporate conflict refers to competition within large, diversified organizations regarding both company goals and the allocation of organizational resources. For example, since various divisions within DuPont stood to benefit quite differently from the passage of reciprocal

---

* The term *new class* is Irving Kristol's (1978) way of describing "some millions of people whom liberal capitalism had sent to college in order to help manage its affluent, highly technological, mildly paternalistic, 'postindustrial' society" and who are now allegedly fighting and undermining capitalism in their own class struggle for power. The new class, he says, consists of "scientists, lawyers, city planners, social workers, educators, criminologists, sociologists, public health doctors, and so on," as well as the economists with whom he doesn't agree. Many of these people, he says, "find their careers in the expanding public sector rather than the private." Although they still speak the language of "progressive reform," he says that "in actuality they are acting upon a hidden agenda: to propel the nation from that modified version of capitalism we call 'the welfare state' toward an economic system so stringently regulated in detail as to fulfill many of the traditional anticapitalist aspirations of the Left."

trade legislation, the company never took a unified stance on the issue. Consequently, DuPont's political effectiveness with regard to the tariff fight was reduced (see Bauer, Pool, and Dexter, 1972:270–71). Even "monolithic" IBM seems to be following the General Motors' model of restructuring along divisional lines with head-to-head interdivisional rivalry. For example, IBM's mainframe operation (its big-computer operation) unveiled a small computer at about the same time its small-computer division entered a new product in the big-computer arena.

Besides intracorporate conflict, the absence of any demonstrable desire on the part of corporate leaders to achieve political control over either other groups or the formal institutions tends to limit corporate domination of the political order. Corporate managers appear happy to work solely for the parochial interests of their firms; in this context, narrowness of perspective—even outright selfishness—becomes a virtue. It is worth remembering here that delightful quote from John Maynard Keynes (1936):

> There are valuable human activities which require the motive of money-making and the environment of private wealth-ownership for their full fruition. Moreover, dangerous human proclivities can be canalised into comparatively harmless channels by the existence of opportunities for money-making and private wealth, which, if they cannot be satisfied in this way, may find their outlet in cruelty, the reckless pursuit of personal power and authority, and other forms of self-aggrandisement. *It is better that a man should tyrannise over his bank-balance than over his fellow citizens* . . . . [italics added]

Countervailing power, it can be argued, prevails even in highly concentrated industries. Alcoa, Reynolds Metals, and Kaiser, for example, share the aluminum market; but a customer can still choose among them, and they must vie with one another for that customer's business. General Electric, Westinghouse, and Sylvania make 90 percent of the country's light bulbs; Goodyear, Firestone, and Uniroyal, almost that proportion of tires. While many observers believe that the pricing patterns among the leading firms in such industries show a lack of competitiveness, it can be argued that competition in quality and service may be as important as in price, and that consumers often have the option to shift to the products of another industry—for example, from steel to aluminum or from glass to plastics.

Neil H. Jacoby (1977:24) thinks that when we take into account the expanding size of markets, as a result of growing interindustry and international competition, concentration is much lower than is usually perceived and is diminishing through time. He believes that interindustry competition for consumers' *discretionary income*—income not required for the purchase of conventional "necessities"—is becoming more intense as the relative amount of such income rises. Thus, the critical decision for a consumer often is not which brand of auto to purchase, but whether to buy an auto, a vacation, a boat, a summer cottage, or a high-fidelity music system. Such interproduct competition puts pressure upon firms in many industries to keep prices down and to offer new or improved products in order to gain the favor of fickle and fancy-free consumers. In an affluent society, product substitution may be the most severe and devastating form of competition.

International competition has risen as scores of foreign corporations have penetrated American markets since World War II. Twenty years ago the American auto, steel, electrical, and electronic manufacturers had the domestic market to themselves. Today the behavior of General Motors is disciplined by Volkswagen, Toyota, Datsun, Volvo, and Fiat, as well as by Ford and Chrysler. The prices of U.S. Steel are tempered by those of Nippon Steel and Thyssen, as well as by those of Bethlehem and Youngstown. General Electric bids on turbines are held down by the actions of Siemens, English Electric, and Brown-Boveri, as well as by those of Westinghouse. Indeed, when markets are international, the true *concentration ratios*—that is, the total share of the largest four firms in each industry—are about half as large as the ratios measuring the American market only.

Today many observers of American business argue that corporations—rather than face countervailing power—are able to dominate, manipulate, and control their markets. There may be grains of truth in this analysis, Scott (1973) concedes, but it suffers from being modeled on very large, production-oriented, industrial companies, such as Lockheed and Raytheon, or even on the ailing coal or railroad companies.

The argument assumes a model of American business that fits what Scott terms Stage II of historical, organizational development. In that stage, the corporation has a single product line and an integrated structure. Performance is measured by technical or cost criteria. In Scott's Stage III, however, the corporation is *diversified*. Its research and development are directed toward new products, and the performance of its decentralized divisions is measured by market criteria, such as return on investment and market share. It is increasingly sensitive to competitive market pressures. Indeed, as the postwar movement toward corporate diversification has gained momentum, an increasing number of large companies, having both the motive and the necessary resources, stand ready to enter any market where profit opportunities appear bright. An established firm in any industry cannot prudently ignore the probability that firms from many other industries will enter its market if they stand to achieve high prices and high profits.

According to Scott's figures, only half of the *Fortune* 500 companies (e.g., General Motors, IBM, Texaco, U.S. Steel, Xerox, and Scott Paper) conform to Galbraith's description, and they are the declining half. The half that is growing in importance—the half that Scott accuses Galbraith of ignoring—is composed of companies that have either diversified into related areas (e.g., Du-Pont, Eastman Kodak, General Electric, and General Goods) or into unrelated business (e.g., Litton, Olin, and Textron).

Pluralism. Closely related to the notion of countervailing power is a second limitation on corporate power: the widespread public commitment to a pluralistic political order. Since American society is made up of heterogenous institutions and organizations that have diversified religious, ethnic, economic, and cultural interests, political power must be shared. Even if there are political elites, they tend to be fragmented, and their variety reduces their influence.

While there are some political observers,* of course, who disagree with this pluralist view of American politics and allege that there is a homogenous ruling elite that we have missed seeing, they have all failed to document convincingly the existence of any model of political power other than what has been described as the pluralist view.

Perhaps the best summary of the hypothesis underlying the pluralist view is Nelson W. Polsby's (1963:123–24):

> One of the most common patterns of behavior to be observed in American community life is that participation in the making of decisions is concentrated in the hands of a few. But this does not mean that American communities are ruled by a single all-purpose elite . . . . First, different small groups normally making decisions on different community problems, and likewise, the personnel of decision-making groups often change, even over the short run. Secondly, the decisions made by small groups are almost always considered routine or otherwise insignificant by most other members of the community. Thirdly, when small groups undertake innovation or decision making in cases salient or likely to become salient to others in the community, they must achieve special kinds of legitimacy or risk the likelihood of failure.

Accordingly, efforts by the corporate community to exert power to the extent that it is inconsistent with democratic processes or is threatening to the pluralistic character of the American political order would engender opposition. While business as an occupation enjoys some status in American society—just below athletes and artists and just above entertainers and journalists according to a Louis Harris survey (October 1977)—the legitimacy of business and its values are not accepted in all areas of community life or by all people. Since the legitimacy of corporate political activity has traditionally been viewed with suspicion, any deviation from widely accepted political practices would almost certainly arouse certain segments of the public. And, given an increasingly politically active and educated American society, continued public vigilance over the business community seems more likely than ever. Indeed, fears of an antagonistic public have been important in restraining corporate political activity. For example, Bauer, Pool, and Dexter (1972:258) report:

---

* For example, see C.W. Mills, *The Power Elite* (1956) and G. William Domhoff, *Who Rules America?* (1967).

GM's reluctance to speak up for its views on foreign trade was at least in part a reflection of the marked sensitivity which certain giant corporations in America have developed over their public image. Large firms which have been the object of antitrust action or have been generally viewed as throwing their weight around may, indeed, sometimes use their economic strength to influence public policy or to take advantage of their business competitors. But, if they sometimes do so in fact, such industrial giants must take all the more pains to avoid the appearance of so doing. And, as many of them have learned by harsh experience, the best way to maintain the image of probity is to maintain its practice, too.

Such fears are not altogether misplaced, since we have seen numerous consumer boycotts for "inappropriate" political positions. (Witness, for example, the boycotts against Coors Beer for that company's support of Equal Rights Amendment foes.)

Moreover, it is not always possible to determine what the "business interest" is since at any given time, the corporate community is split on most national issues. As Epstein (1969:227) points out: ". . . conflict among business organizations constitutes much of the substance of corporate political activity. The net result is a degree of *political pluralism within* the corporate community that has prevented the emergence of a monolithic business political force" (italics added). Thus, domestic petroleum companies have opposed liberal oil import quotas, while petrochemical companies have favored them in order to obtain less expensive feedstocks. Steel companies have sought quotas upon imports of foreign steel, while auto companies and other large steel users have fought them.

Finally, the power of business can be restrained by the pluralism that appears among policymakers and even within the regulatory bureaucracy. Vernon (1977:188–89) writes:

> The diffuse structure of public power in the United States has been accentuated by the nature of the country's political parties. No strong ideological cement ties the politicians of any party together; from an ideological viewpoint, many leaders of the Democratic party could as easily be Republicans and vice versa. The party that occupies the White House or dominates the Congress is generally led by regional politicians, comparative strangers who happen to be sharing national power. . . . That, however, leaves plenty of room for the regulation and restraint of business . . . : New England's interest in cheap crops and cheap power, for instance, versus the South's interest in high-priced crops and high-cost power. . . .
>
> The heterogeneous quality of the U.S. political parties is matched by the diffusion and variety of the American bureaucrats . . . . high-level U.S. public administrators may be expected to come from almost anywhere, with almost any kind of training and background. . . . Their ideologies are diverse and their loyalties diffuse.

The Problem of Convertibility. Economic power and in a larger sense all the political resources of corporate power noted earlier are not synonymous with actual political power. Regarding economic power, for example, one need only think of the less than decisive political influence of a Howard Hughes or H.L. Hunt (in comparison, say, to a relatively impecunious Coretta King or Henry Kissinger). Or take the efforts of big business to influence the outcome of the battle over whether deposits should be required on beverage bottles and cans. In Michigan the so-called Committee against Forced Deposits poured $1.3 million—83 percent of it contributed by big national companies—into the most expensive campaign on a public issue in Michigan history. Environmentalists raised only a tenth of the opponents' total funds but launched a well-organized drive, and the measure passed with 68 percent of the vote. In Maine, industry spending also backfired. "It was overkill," said Maine Audubon official William B. Ginn. "They spent $500,000 to our $40,000. People got fed up with this immense show of muscle" (quoted in the *Houston Post,* March 1, 1979).

Regarding political resources, one simple point needs to be kept clearly and constantly in mind: Resources constitute merely the ingredients (inputs) of power and must be used (converted) efficaciously before they become power. And capability for this conversion varies substantially from corporation to corporation, from executive to executive. As David Riesman (1961:219) points out, psychological factors may affect the effectiveness of a company in converting its resources: "Power . . . is founded in large measure on interpersonal expectations and attitudes. If businessmen feel weak and dependent, they do in actuality become weaker and more dependent, no matter what material resources may be ascribed to them."

In fact, there may be a kind of tradeoff between the resources of a corporation and its reluctance to use political power. The paradox is seen quite clearly in the case of the small Idaho company that went to court to stop federal safety inspectors from conducting plant searches without a warrant. Why did not General Motors do that? Do big corporations tend to become timid about rocking the boat and more inclined to go along with government regulation? The whole subject is a fascinating area for research.

EXPLORING CORPORATE REFORMS

Federal Chartering

Ever since James Madison first proposed it, business has fought the idea that the federal government should have exclusive power to charter corporations. But critics of state regulation have long pushed the idea because, they argue, states can be very arbitrary and can ignore the national interest.

In 1938, the critics of state-level regulation only barely failed to get a federal chartering bill through Congress and, in 1976, the Senate Commerce Committee held hearings on a bill that would require federal charters for large corporations. Ralph Nader, Mark Green, and Joel Seligman's *Taming the*

Giant Corporation (1976) is perhaps the best known case for the proposal. But an article by William L. Cary (1974), former SEC chairman, is perhaps the most scathing analysis of the way in which states bid against each other and use relaxed chartering standards to woo corporations.

According to Cary, the problem with existing corporation law is, in a word, Delaware. "Delaware," he writes, "has a laissez-faire attitude toward the fiduciary role and responsibility of management to its shareholders." The legislatures of many states have engaged in a competitive "race for the bottom" by recklessly outbidding each other in their efforts to "provide management with maximum freedom from restrictions." Most states have followed Delaware's lead in a nationwide "trend towards permissiveness" and have created a Gresham's law effect (bad corporation law drives out good). It is no surprise that more than half of the top 500 industrial corporations have chosen Delaware as their state of incorporation. The victims of this legislative competition, Cary continues, are the stockholders. Delaware has "watered the rights of shareholders vis-à-vis management down to a thin gruel." Its motive is financial: "The raison d'être behind the whole system [is] revenue for the state of Delaware."

However, Cary's analysis does not form the main current in the drive to give the federal government a major new role in corporation law. That current has less to do with neglect by management of stockholders' interest than it does with the accountability of the powerful corporation to society. More specifically, advocates of federal chartering see the giant corporations engaging in a host of socially damaging activities—for example, pollution, strip mining, production of hazardous products, monopolistic practices, price fixing, employment discrimination, and persecution or discharge of employees who "blow the whistle" on corporate misconduct. Corporations failing to meet federal standards on such social issues could have their charters withheld, suspended, or revoked.

Federal chartering could mean an expansion of the decision-making apparatus of the corporation to include communities affected by corporate decisions. Communities would be given the opportunity to veto certain corporate decisions by referendum. For example, the members of a community in which a manufacturing plant was located could decide how to require the corporation to stop emitting pollutants. Federal chartering could also require publicizing of many matters not now required to be compiled or released under the federal securities laws, including data bearing on pollution by the corporation, the health and safety of corporate work places, employment and hiring policies, truth in advertising, lobbying, and profits and losses on specific products. Such disclosure would ostensibly enhance the decision-making abilities of voters, investors, consumers, competitors, employees, and the general public. Finally, federal chartering could mean deconcentration of industries whose companies have "excessive" market power, as well as prevention of future concentration through mergers.

Critics of federal chartering argue that additional controls over business are not needed. Business, we have seen, is already strapped with hundreds of federal, state, and local controls designed to achieve many of the objectives of federal chartering—for example, issues concerning the economic and civil rights of the workers. Critics also find astonishing the charge that corporations operate "in secrecy," since U.S. business discloses more than business in any other country in the world.

Still, federal chartering could establish a uniform national pattern of corporate governance. It could put a stop to the progressive permissiveness, or "charter mongering," that has marked state chartering for many years. It could also require that corporate boards have a majority of outside directors and audit committees dominated by outsiders. Many observers, in fact, view revitalizing the board as a reform so important that it merits our separate consideration, whether or not federal chartering is adopted.

Revitalizing the Corporate Board of Directors

The proposals to revitalize corporate boards come in three forms. The first plan is to increase the responsibility of the board's audit committee for monitoring sensitive disclosure issues, such as questionable payments. Indeed, one of the most striking developments over the past decade has been the emergence of board committees, not only for auditing, but also for public policy, compensation, and nominating. Since 1978, the New York Stock Exchange has required that all listed companies have audit committees composed of outside directors.

The second plan is to raise the level of federal and state standards for corporate behavior in relation to investors and the public. This might spell increased liability of board members for corporate misbehavior.

The third plan is to make sure that the directors are independent—that is, not under management domination. Harold Marvin Williams, whom President Carter appointed chairman of the SEC in 1977, has argued that in most cases corporate directors are little more than puppets of the management: "One of my former colleagues used to suggest that the way to handle boards is to treat them like mushrooms. Keep them in the dark, water them well, and cover them with horse manure" (*New York Times,* April 3, 1977).

Independence of corporate directors can be achieved in a variety of ways. A number of commentators and scholars have advocated the mandatory appointment of public directors to boards to represent the interests of the community at large. In 1971, for example, Robert Townsend advocated that boards of large corporations each have one public director whose job was to protect the investing public and to represent the community at large. Townsend proposed giving such public directors an annual operating budget of $1 million. Others, believing that too many boards are dominated by insiders, advocate boards with "a truly independent character" to monitor management.

Finally, some observers propose the appointment of individuals who would reflect or represent specific segments of the public, such as blacks, women consumers, or environmentalists. Even Nader rejects these proposals for "special-interest" directors (elected by employees, consumers, or other groups) or "public-interest" directors (appointed by a federal agency) on grounds of impracticality. Still, selection of the board of directors could be made "more democratic" by permitting shareholder groups to nominate directors, by prohibiting any person from serving on the board of more than one federally chartered company, by requiring cumulative voting, and by forbidding staggered terms for directors.

Managing with Management

Christopher D. Stone (1975) has provided still another approach toward corporate reform: a model code for "corporate rehabilitation." Under this plan, conviction of a criminal offense or loss of a civil verdict involving payment of over $250,000 would subject any company to the requirement that it investigate and report to a court how it became involved in the wrongful act and how it plans to avoid doing so in the future. Among the model code's provisions is the requirement that the company designate particular officers responsible for implementing the "rehabilitation agenda."

Let us see how this idea might be put into practice. Say that a large oil company is found guilty of spilling oil into a ship channel. The typical response of the company would probably be, "Just send us the bill." After all, what is a $5,000 fine to a billion-dollar company? Recognizing these economic realities, the government's attorneys propose something else: that the court suspend sentence and place the company on probation, and that the company begin a program to handle the oil spillage.

Although there is little previous law to support such a proposal, there is an imaginative analogy to consider. When a guardian interferes with the probation and rehabilitation of a minor, a judge can remove the minor from that guardian's custody. If the company's management interferes with the company's "rehabilitation"—that is, if the program to handle the oil spillage stalls—then why not put the company under a "probation officer" with powers of trustee under supervision of the court? This officer could go into the plant to make sure the company was doing what was necessary. The practical advantages to zeroing in on a problem this way are not hard to see.

In sum, we have dealt in the second part of this chapter with the power of corporations. We have considered the scope and sources of this power, as well as the limitations on it both within society and within the business system itself. In the first part of the chapter we also considered the constraints imposed on business in the form of government regulations. As a consequence of all these constraints and limitations, and despite an impressive array of political assets, we have seen that corporate political power is hardly absolute. But neither are corporations exactly political eunuchs. If it were somehow possible to measure corporate power and then to measure the limitations on it, we might just find that the former exceeded the latter by some finite amount (X). Since this idea is quite abstract, let us look at it schematically:

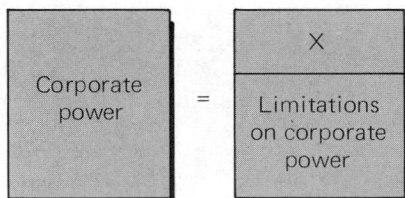

$$\text{Corporate power} = \frac{X}{\text{Limitations on corporate power}}$$

Now we come to the central point of our concern with business-society interrelations—namely, society expects all power to be balanced by responsibility. Our discussion has shown that *power* means the ability to effect something, to get one's way; and responsibility, the condition of being subject to external authority. Nothing is intrinsically wrong with power, but society becomes concerned when the power of an institution begins to outstrip the responsibility of that institution. That, after all, was the great message that went out from the Constitutional Convention of 1787. The Founding Fathers were keenly aware of the tyrannical potential of unlimited governmental power. In rejecting the arbitrary abuses and almost unlimited power of George III, the colonists made sure that governmental power would be dispersed among different institutions; political officials would be chosen electorally (and hence personally accountable for their actions); delegations of power would be limited to those specified in written law; and so forth.

If the Constitution did not mention the corporation, it was not because the principle of balancing power and responsibility did not apply, but rather because the scale of business enterprise (read: power) was relatively small two hundred years ago. Things have changed, however: Corporate power has grown, as have the limitations on it. Still, all things considered, there is, as our equation shows, an imbalance between power and limitations. Unfortunately, no calculus exists to tell a society exactly what balance between power and responsibility ought to be. Irving Kristol (1975:125), who could hardly be described as a critic of business, expresses well the sense of imbalance when he writes that the Founding Fathers and Adam Smith would be perplexed by the kind of capitalism we have today. To Kristol, the domination of economic activity by giant corporations does not represent the working of a "system of natural liberty." Rather than entrepreneurial capitalism, we seem to have a group of big businesses committed not to any particular line of business, but only to achieving immortality.

It would be foolish—perhaps even perilous—for the leaders of U.S. business to ignore the quantity X, for our equation *must* be balanced. Davis and

Bloomstrom (1975:50) have very neatly summed up the reason in their Iron Law of Responsibility: "In the long run, those who do not use power in a manner which society considers responsible will tend to lose it." As the law applies to business, it says that to the extent business leaders do not accept social obligations as they arise, other groups eventually will step in to assume those responsibilities. This prediction of diluted social power is not a normative statement of what *should happen*. Rather, it is a prediction of what *will tend to happen* whenever business managers do not keep their political power in balance with some sense of social responsibility. The shape and scope of social responsibility are a major theme of the chapters that follow in Part III.

THE MACROENVIRONMENT OF U.S. BUSINESS (Chapters 2-4)

Technological
- Effects of technological change
- Process of technological innovation

Economic
- New views of inflation, unemployment, and growth
- Relationship of energy, environment, and economics

Social
- Demographic trends
- Changing social structures
- Changing values
- The "New Class" and adversary culture
- Life cycle of social issues

Political–legal
- Public policies affecting business
- The interest-group state
- Policy administration
- Courts

International
- Changing role of multinationals
- Five worlds of development and the new "Economic Order"
- Technology transfer
- Changes in world trade
- Cultural differences
- Host and home country relations

IMPLICATIONS OF MACROENVIRONMENTAL CHANGE (Chapter 5)
- Government regulation
- Corporate power

STRATEGY FORMULATION (Chapter 6)
- Premises of strategic planning
- Goals and objectives
- The place of social responsibility and ethics

FORECASTING TOOLS (Chapter 7)
- Decision support systems
- Technology forecasting
- Economic models
- Sociopolitical forecasting

STRATEGY IMPLEMENTATION (Chapter 8)
- Programs, projects, products
- Opportunities, costs, benefits

NEW MANAGEMENT OPPORTUNITIES (Chapters 9-13)
- Production
- Research and development
- Finance
- Marketing
- Human resources
- External relations

ALTERNATIVES FOR BUSINESS–SOCIETY RELATIONS (Epilogue)
- Restructuring or market enhancement

STRATEGIC PLANNING IN A TURBULENT ENVIRONMENT

PART **III**

CHAPTER SIX

Strategic Planning, Social Responsibility, and Applied Ethics

Having examined the macroenvironment of business as well as the important issue of business-society relations within an environment of change, we are now in a position to begin considering the implications for management. In this chapter and the next two, our attention centers on general approaches that managers adopt in responding to the rapidly changing environment. The need for this focus cannot be emphasized enough. The great temptation in inquiries such as ours is to charge pell-mell into a consideration of specific issues—pollution, financial disclosure, discrimination, safety, and the like. While the need for grappling hand-to-hand with such specific issues cannot be denied (witness Chapters 9 through 13), we also need to recognize that lineups change. If this book were written in 1972, for example, the word *energy* would probably not appear. Accordingly, who can know what words soon to be on the lips of every manager are being overlooked today?

Thus the real need is for a general approach to coping with the challenge of change.

Obviously, management can respond in a number of ways to the challenges presented in Chapters 2 through 4. The first section of this chapter reviews some of the popular but not always effective responses. Some firms, for example, appear to be engaged in a never-ending *reaction to* events. These firms are following what we can call the fire-fighting approach to challenges in the macroenvironment. Other firms try to deal with such challenges as environmentalism and consumerism as if these issues were essentially problems in public relations. Then we have a third group of companies that adopts an ad hoc approach—that is, they view challenges much more seriously but, unfortunately, treat each problem in isolation. Finally, we come to the fourth response firms can make—dealing with challenges in the macroenvironment in the context of strategic planning. But what is strategic planning? Answering that question will be the aim of the second section of this chapter. For now, let us simply say that strategic planning is a process whereby a company sets goals for itself and then systematically thinks through the steps necessary for the attainment of those goals.

As we shall see, a company can have many goals. In the third section of this chapter we return to the issues raised in Chapter 5 and zero in on one possible goal: meeting the challenge of social responsibility. Since a great deal of ink has been spilt in recent years over this concept, we need to examine it very carefully and note what both the advocates and critics have to say about it. The section concludes by presenting one particular interpretation of what social responsibility might mean—namely, social impact management.

The last two sections of the chapter are devoted to the role of values in the strategic planning process. We begin by considering why values are actually an important ingredient in management decision making and why the study of values, or ethics, is a subject that managers ignore at their own peril. The final section, by way of illustration only, will sketch one possible approach to business ethics that seems demonstrably workable, though the theory itself is several centuries old. ☐

RESPONSES TO THE CHANGING ENVIRONMENT

Given the turbulence in the macroenvironment of business, what can a manager do? What options, what general responses, are available? In this section we consider four.

Fire Fighting

This response to change in the macroenvironment, though not very effective, is surprisingly popular. Although companies usually do not explicitly adopt this approach to changes in the macroenvironment, many do so unconsciously. The essence of the fire-fighting approach is to sit back and let things happen, and then attempt—often with a great surge of activity—to meet the resulting challenge. The problem is that too often the challenge has grown so great that the struggle becomes uphill and costly. Companies that do not innovate in the technological environment, for example, are always playing a game of catchup with the industrial leaders. This situation has certain advantages; for one thing, less money needs to be spent on research and development. But the liabilities are more easily cited. First, by always being a little late into the market with a new product, a company can allow market penetration by the competition to become enormous and in some cases fatal. A tempting remedy then is to try a crash program. Unfortunately, the company that relies on crash programs too much will learn about what Edwin Mansfield (1971:136–56) calls the time-cost tradeoff function—that is, the more quickly a product is brought to market, the steeper the cost gets (recall Exhibit 2–15).

Such observations about fire fighting in the technological environment are equally valid for the other four environments, especially the political-legal. Consider, for example, the benefits of early reaction to government dissatisfaction with business performance. If an industry acts promptly, it can set its own standards and thereby possibly preclude government action altogether. At worst, the industry can have a hand in shaping the law that it must subsequently follow. The alternative, ignoring government dissatisfaction, can result in laws written and administered largely by individuals with little appreciation of the problems of managers. With the laws on the books and the regulators swinging into action, then top management must respond with that most hoary of all fire-fighting methods: seeking help from a law firm. Needless to say, good legal advice does not come cheaply: In 1975, for example, the Singer Company paid the Winthrop, Stimson firm of New York City $1.98 million; Pennzoil paid $1.5 million to Baker & Botts of Houston; CBS, $1.5 million to Cravath, Swaine, & Moore in New York City; and American Electric Power, $1.46 million to Simpson, Thacher, & Bartlett of New York City.

As a means of responding to forces in the environment, fire fighting appears just as frequently in the public sector as in private sector. In an illuminating discussion of the leadership of John Kennedy, Henry Fairlie (1973: 209–10) argues that Kennedy's tenure in office was marked by a series of reactions to communist initiatives; his foreign policy was "more in the nature of a fire-fighting exercise than a careful and long-range campaign for fire prevention." In the area of domestic policy, Fairlie offers the same criticism: Instead of trying to improve the machinery for the arbitration of labor disputes, Kennedy relied on the willingness and ability of his secretary of labor "to spend more time putting out fires than running the Labor Department." And, in the issue of civil rights, Kennedy waited for an occasion to which he could react, an occasion that he could seize by a dramatic exhibit of his personal leadership. "It was by this method that the American people were, for three years, kept in a state of anxious expectation of the perils which beset them, on the one hand, and of stupefied admiration of the brilliance of the administration which rescued them, on the other: always at the edge of danger, always in time brought back from it."

Public Relations Blitzes

Management's second option for responding to changes in the macroenvironment is the public relations blitz. Although public relations has a useful role to play in the operations of any company, it is wanting as a means of responding to challenges in the macroenvironment. Public relations really does nothing about demands for safer working conditions and equal employment; it simply tries to paste over poor performance with a cannonade of slick advertising and gimmickry.

The response of Firestone Tire & Rubber Company to its widely publicized radial-tire crisis may well become a classic in the annals of public relations. In 1978 the government accused Firestone of selling a line of defective tires. According to the federal authorities, the 500 series of steel-belted radials were prone to blowouts, tread separations, and other dangerous deformities and were the target of thousands of consumer complaints. Records supplied to congressional investigators by Firestone and other sources indicated that the 500-series radials were involved in hundreds of accidents and that these accidents caused at least thirty-four deaths. In its attempts to ward off disagreeable consequences and defend its honor, Firestone began a public relations blitz spearheaded by none other than Jimmy Stewart. This response, coupled with attempts to thwart investigations of its tire and impugn the motives of the investigators, only provoked prolonged public suspicion, since people expected a company convinced of its rectitude to cooperate fully with the investigation (see Louis, 1978).

Quite clearly, the public has grown increasingly skeptical of claims made by business for business. Such skepticism was beautifully captured in a recent cartoon, based no doubt on an element of truth. One executive, standing by a flip chart, is shown announcing to his colleagues, "OK, it's agreed: We'll spend $1 million on our new environmental clean-up program and $10 million on announcing it." Public skepticism leads us to a second deficiency of the public relations blitz: Unless corporations evoke more credibility than they presently possess, many advertising dollars will be wasted.

Ad Hoc Responses

Recognizing perhaps the shortcomings of the first two responses, corporations more frequently react to challenges in the macroenvironment, particularly the social environment, in a manner that can be classified as an ad hoc response. The distinguishing feature of ad hoc responses is that they focus on narrow and specific problems and do not become integrated as a regular and pervasive feature of the organization's activity.

In order to see the limitations of the ad hoc response, we need turn to only one example: Standard Oil of Indiana's program for development of minority vendors (see Drotning). For at least a decade, the company had been attempting to implement a minority purchasing program. But efforts had been focused in the general office purchasing department, with no sharing of responsibility by the operating departments. Despite the designation of staff people to seek out minority suppliers, and even the use of an outside black consultant for this purpose, buyers insisted that they could not find qualified minority suppliers. The program was not working. Obviously, the narrow focus of the approach—an ad hoc response to the problem—was not the solution. A new executive, however, was able to turn things around, in his own words, "by applying the same principles that made for effective programs in equal employment opportunity." Among those principles, the executive noted this one: The minority purchasing effort must not be perceived as a kind of extracurricular social venture; it must be integrated into normal corporate operations.

A Fourth Response

While thinking about ways business can meet the challenges of the macroenvironment, we should not forget one old reality: Business still must provide goods and services in a competitive market. The two tasks—formulating responses to external challenges and producing goods and services—are not necessarily unrelated. An obvious illustration of this close connection is product design: Consumerism places a certain set of demands on the design of a company's products; but a company's competitors, production facilities, and marketing network place another set of demands or restraints on product design. In the long run, the more successful companies will be those that can balance the two sets of demands. And the best way to achieve this integration is through the strategic planning process. What is strategic planning? We need to answer this question in a separate section since it is a response to meeting challenges that merits our careful consideration.

STRATEGIC PLANNING: A CONCEPTUAL FRAMEWORK FOR MEETING CHALLENGES

Strategic planning is a big subject, and the intent here is not to cover it in any detail.* Instead, we want to see how it can provide managers with a conceptual framework for thinking about meeting the challenges of environmental change and social responsibility. Simply put, strategic planning is a management process that involves the determination of the basic long-term goals of an enterprise and adoption of specific actions for attaining those goals. Strate-

---

* For more on the concept of strategic planning, the following sources are highly recommended: Andrews (1971), Ackoff (1970), Chandler (1962), Ewing (1958), Steiner (1969), and Larange and Vancil (1977). For strategic planning in service industries, see Thomas (1978).

gic planning involves at least four interrelated elements: (1) analyzing the environment of the enterprise to determine threats and opportunities; (2) establishing goals, consistent with environmental conditions and the enterprise's resources, for where the enterprise wants to be at a certain time; (3) selecting a number of programs, projects, and products to successfully attain the goals that were established; and (4) implementing actions necessary to create organizational structure and motivations for program operations.

Exhibit 6–1 shows these four elements and their relationship. The exhibit also shows how management values impinge on the planning process throughout. In a sense, the values that the members of an organization hold determine the upper and lower limits of what can be planned. If economic values clearly dominate a manager's other values, he or she will be more inclined to emphasize opportunities for growth and profitability and to make strategic decisions that call for stretching or adding to present resources to attain these goals. But, if a manager has strong political values or dominant social values, he or she will tend to choose strategies that maximize the opportunity to achieve goals related to the particular value. The best way to see how this works is to consider a few examples (McCarthy et al., 1975:242):

> Hugh Hefner, president and founder of HMH Publishing Company, publisher of *Playboy,* worked for several magazines prior to striking out on his own. Having dominant economic and aesthetic values, he found the jobs with other magazines wanting in opportunity to achieve personal satisfaction. Accordingly, he started his own company to publish a magazine which represented his aesthetic point of view. Fortunately for him, his particular form of aesthetic value was shared by many others and a market existed for *Playboy.* As a result, Hefner not

EXHIBIT 6–1   The Strategic Planning Process

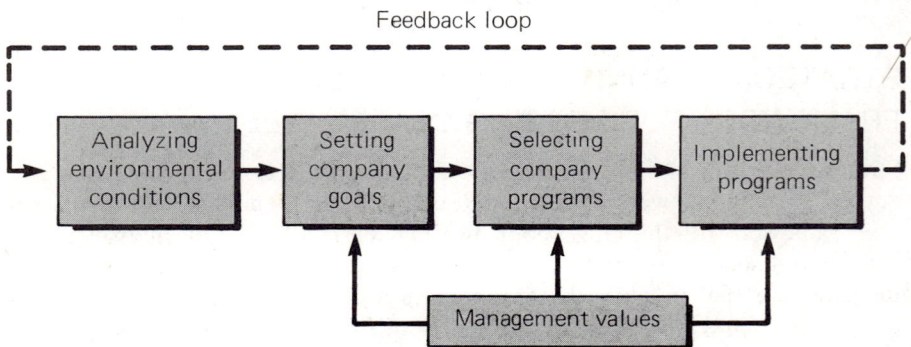

only works each day on something consistent with his concept of what a magazine should be, but his labors also make him increasingly wealthy, bringing economic satisfaction as well.

The executives and staff of the *New York Times,* according to all published sources of information, appear to have a highly dominant theoretical and social value orientation. Their product—yesterday's news reported intelligently, accurately, and without bias or sensationalism—is apparently valued more for its own sake than as a means to economic ends. This high level of personal commitment to the product has been a defense against increasing pressures to modify the *New York Times* in the interest of economy and expanded circulation. The present production and the pattern of operations supporting it yield at best only moderate growth and return on investment.

Exhibit 6–1 also shows that strategic planning is a cybernetic process—that is, goals are not chiseled into granite blocks. Rather, they are only guides to action and always subject to change, which is the meaning of the feedback loop shown in the exhibit. As programs are implemented, either successfully or unsuccessfully, environmental conditions are changed. Accordingly, the goals of the enterprise should be periodically reviewed and revised as necessary.

COMMENTARY: A Case for Strategic Planning

In the last ten years or so, one of the pioneers in the use of strategic planning has been General Electric. It is, therefore, illuminating to compare the performance of GE with one of its closest competitors, Westinghouse Electric Corporation. What makes this comparison especially useful is that, until only recently, the two companies have had remarkably dissimilar management and operating philosophies.

Pervading Westinghouse during most of the 1960s and well into the 1970s was the fuzzy philosophy of achieving rapid growth by entering whatever field appeared promising at the moment and gaining volume without regard to risk. This approach led the corporation into a series of money-losing ventures in fields unfamiliar to its managers. For example, Westinghouse thought it had found a way of making money by doing good, by being "socially responsive." Thus, it leaped into building low-cost, multifamily housing on government contracts. It set up its Urban Systems Development Corporation and granted it greater borrowing power than other divisions. Urban Systems' managers were given freewheeling authority to achieve the fastest possible growth. At one time, Urban Systems was committed to nearly seventy housing projects that ultimately produced $61.5 million in pretax losses in 1974 and 1975. Before the project was shut down, Westinghouse also had to repay $85 million in short-term debts. Other debacles included Westinghouse's ventures into the mail-order and record-club businesses (which cost $64 million in losses and write-offs), into water treatment operations, and into the car rental business. By 1974, gross income from continued operations dropped 28 percent, to $139 million, and net income dropped 80 percent, to $28.1 million. Instead of strategic plans, Westinghouse fostered a laissez-faire attitude. As the vice chairman put it, "We were able to say to our people—and mean it—that if they had a good business proposition, we could finance it" (*Business Week,* January 31, 1977, p. 61). In short, top management provided neither guidance on what a good proposition was nor any analysis of whether the company should enter the field in the first place.

An altogether different philosophy permeates GE's management. To begin with, GE is acknowledged to have a sophisticated management training program that brings executives up through succeeding levels of responsibility while acclimating them to corporate methods and goals. Although operations are decentralized, managers are under strong corporate controls, with limits to the directions they may take and the amounts they may spend or commit. GE's corporate plans, to be sure, are not always successful, but they begin at the top with a team of economic, financial, technological, and marketing experts that assists corporate chiefs in determining areas of growth. Middle, or line, managers are charged with implementing top management's plans and providing feedback. And continual monitoring makes certain that projects live up to expectations within a specified time; otherwise, they are sloughed off. The most important function of the GE planners is to determine what growth areas the company should explore. A new service-center acquisition, for example, may be selected first by the corporate planning group as an area where the company should grow. The executive within the country in question will then be charged with spotting potential candidates, justifying them to the planning group, and making the deal. If it costs over $2 million, the group executive needs what Charles E. Reed, senior vice-president for corporate strategic planning, calls "GE's appropriation routine—complete documentation of markets, costs, expenses, financial projections, and market projections." These are reviewed, says Reed, "by a large number of corporate accounting and finance people, our internal consulting service—engineering, manufacturing, and marketing people—and the strategic planners. Those plans really have to run the gauntlet" (*Business Week,* January 31, 1977, p. 64).

By the late 1970s Westinghouse, not too surprisingly, had begun to adopt many of GE's planning methods. Ironically, while Westinghouse still views GE as its major competitor, GE no longer sees Westinghouse that way. According to one top GE executive, West Germany's Siemans is now his company's major competitor.

Establishing Goals

For a profit-making enterprise, a statement of goals will almost certainly include sales, earnings, and profitability. Strategic planning helps protect the enterprise from overemphasizing one goal to the detriment of the others.

Why is balancing goals so important? Say that the sales goal is to increase worldwide sales by 15 percent. If a company merely set a sales-volume goal, management would be simple. Almost anyone can increase sales by buying sales—that is, by cutting prices, increasing quality, using excessive advertising, or providing extraordinary customer services. To put some limit on the price it is willing to pay for sales, however, a company must consider a second goal: total dollar earnings after tax. But a sales goal and an earnings goal still do not define the success of a business. By pouring enough assets indiscriminately into the company, a manager can pump up both sales and earnings. Clearly, for a company to be well managed, it must also insure that its resources are being used effectively. The third goal, therefore, is profitability—that is, a determination of how much net income is being produced by each dollar of resources at the management's disposal. Setting aside some valid theoretical objections, the simplest number to use in calculating profitability is return on total assets (ROA). The third goal, therefore, looks like this:

$$\text{ROA} = \frac{\text{Net Income after Taxes}}{\text{Book Value of Total Assets}}$$

Having set these three goals, a company has still not insured the long-term vitality of the enterprise or minimized its vulnerability to unsettling events in the macroenvironment. Managers throughout the organization must now begin to concentrate on short-range operating figures. Therefore, the statement of goals must include goals aimed specifically at future development of the company. What might these be? Here are five candidates worth considering.

Goals Involving Market Rank and Share. Today some executives and analysts call *market rank* (the company's standing first, second, or eighteenth in an industry) and *market share* (the company's percentage of the industry's sales) the most important indicators of future prospects. This view is based on the idea that the company with the largest share in any industry has the best opportunity for profit. The market leader can achieve lower unit-production costs and can spread product development, marketing, and advertising expense over a larger sales volume; as a result, the leader can do a better job in all these areas and still have a better profit left after overhead costs are paid. Second-ranked companies can do fairly well if they have a decent market share, according to the theory; third-largest companies can survive but won't be very profitable. Those further down the ladder won't have the sales volume to compete effectively, so they are doomed to stagger along, making inadequate profits and falling further and further behind. This view of market rank is based on the assumption that each step down the ladder means a far smaller market share.

The basic concept of market position is not particularly new. What is new is the emphasis being placed on it. One reason for this attention is management concern about the cost of capital; managers are eager to improve return on invested capital and want to avoid tying up money in businesses that do not appear promising.

Slow economic growth is another reason for the new emphasis on market share. Many markets have expanded little in recent years, and imports are grabbing up much of what growth has occurred. That leaves scant opportunity to improve profits by increasing sales, except by the very expensive route of taking markets from other producers. In this less fluid situation, present market share becomes more important.

Not surprisingly, market-position goals lead companies to weed out more businesses and to drop products with small market shares. The goal also leads companies to look at segments of industries as separate markets, instead of trying to compete industrywide. Thus, TRW, Inc., in expanding its position in computer-based electronic communications, steers away from products that would compete directly with IBM.

Goals Involving Research and Development. For high-technology firms, or for those with a high rate of product obsolescence, a goal for research and development is highly desirable. The goal should not read, "Spend x percent of sales income on R&D programs"; this is only a statement of action and says nothing about results. Preferable would be statements that declare an intention to lead the field in some performance characteristic or frequency of new product introduction. For example, this was Dow Corning's new product goal in 1973: "Products less than five years old should contribute a minimum of x percent of total sales."

General Motors, until only recently, tended to follow essentially financial goals that had, after all, earned it dominance of the highly profitable big-car market. Accordingly, they opted not to develop the less profitable small cars. For a while, events seemed to justify this reasoning; sales continued to rise. But GM was slow to realize that in addition to efficiency, features such as agility and a certain sporty functionalism were increasingly appealing to a broader public. There were executives at GM in 1970 who actually thought that, as one explained to a reporter, "There's something wrong with people who like small cars." GM's domestic and foreign competitors, knowing better, brought out new models and captured a lot of the growth, while GM's chosen territory was contracting.

Goals Involving Growth and Cutbacks. In a turbulent environment, companies might be concerned about overdependence on a single customer or market and justifiably so. In such circumstances, top management might set a goal for growth in other areas.

For example, in the late 1970s many steel and oil companies set ambitious goals of diversification aimed at reducing their investment in steel and petroleum operations from, say, 75 to 50 percent. Thus, Armco Steel became simply Armco, while Sun Oil became the Sun Company.

One of the most painful, yet necessary, goals for some companies is to eliminate over a period of time all products or divisions that do not meet some performance criterion. In short, companies need to shuck their losers. The Boston Consulting Group has suggested a simple way for companies to rethink their investments (see Exhibit 6–2).

Goals Involving Social Responsibility. Goals related to the social responsibilities of a company are perhaps the most difficult to fulfill. Much of this difficulty stems from confusion over what the fundamental purpose of business really is.

Not a few business managers—and not a few business students—when pressed as to what the fundamental purpose of business is, reply, "To make money." Making money becomes, to use that voguish expression, the bottom line.* In Theodore Levitt's opinion (1977b:7–8), to say that the fundamental purpose of business is to make money is "as vacuous as to say that the purpose of life is to eat." He goes on:

> Eating is a requisite, not a purpose of life. Without eating, life stops. Profits are a requisite of business. Without profits, business stops. Like food for the body, profit for the business must be defined as the excess of what goes in over what comes out. In business, it's called positive cash flow. It has to be positive because the process of sustaining life is a process of destroying life. To sustain life, a business must produce goods and services that people will, in sufficient numbers, want to buy at adequate prices. Since production wears out the machinery that produces and the people who run and manage the machines, to keep the business going there's got to be enough left over to replace what's being worn out. That "enough" is profit, no matter what the accountants [or] the IRS . . . call it. That's why profit is a requisite, not a purpose, of business.
>
> Besides all that, to say that profit is a purpose of business is, simply, morally shallow. Who with an audible heartbeat and moderate sensibilities will go to the mat for the right of somebody to earn a profit for its own sake? If no greater purpose can be discerned or justified, business cannot, morally, justify its existence. It's a repugnant idea, an idea whose time has gone.
>
> Finally, it's an empty idea. Profits can be made in lots of devious and transient ways. For people of affairs, a statement of purpose should provide gui-

---

* What is the bottom line? Everybody knows what corporate profits are, right? Wrong, the rule-making body of the accounting profession, the Financial Accounting Standards Board, says. The reason is that there are two equally respectable accounting definitions of profit. One concept is that profit is what is left over after a company's expenses are subtracted from revenue over a period of time. The other concept involves the change in the net economic resources of a company that is calculated by subtracting liabilities from assets at year's end to see if the figure has grown since the previous year.

Many present accounting conventions are questionable or conflicting because they reflect differences in underlying concepts. The most basic difference involves profit. For example, the view that profit is the difference between revenue and expenses leads to a concern for matching particular costs with related sales during a period of time. This, in turn, leads to such controversial practices as deferring certain kinds of charges. An example is paying out cash for research and development of a product one year, but reporting expenses on the earnings statement only in later years as the new product is sold.

EXHIBIT 6–2   Eliminating Losing Investments

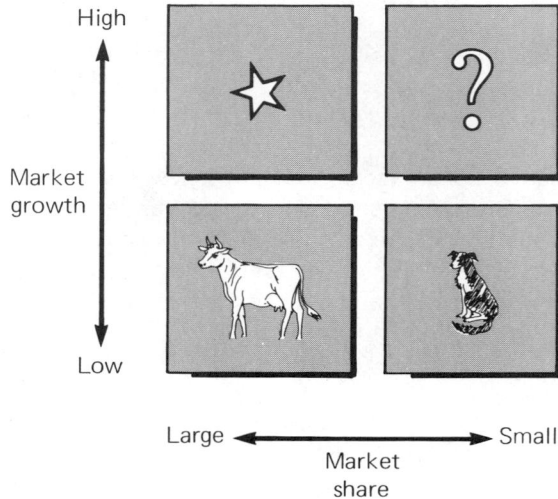

Recommended strategy:
For a "star," inject new money and fight for an even bigger market share.
For a "question mark," consider fighting for more of a market share, but avoid letting it become a "cash trap."
For a "cow," remove money from it ("milk it") and reinvest in a "star."
For a "dog," get rid of it!

Source: Adapted from the concept developed by the Boston Consulting Group, Boston, Mass.

dance to the management of their affairs. To say that they should attract and hold customers forces facing the necessity of figuring out what free people really want and value, and then catering to those wants and values. It provides specific guidance, and has moral merit.

What then might be a more meaningful purpose than making money? It is arguable that the fundamental purpose of business is (a) to create and keep a customer and (b) to survive over the long haul. Once this is recognized, it becomes apparent that providing a reasonable return on investment must be pursued within a framework of, and in harmony with, certain guiding principles: respect for all employees, respect for the customer's opinion, fairness to suppliers and business-venture partners, and good corporate citizenship. These principles are, of course, just another way of referring to what we have been calling social responsibility.

Implementing Goals

Setting goals—for sales, earnings, profit, market share, R&D, diversification, and social responsibility—does not mark the end point in the process of strategic planning. These general goals must now serve to help management decide on new programs, projects, and products. Strategic planning, in effect, ties together goals with programs and programs with actions.

Thus—and this is a core idea in the strategic planning concept—the chances of piecemeal decisions fade. Look again at Exhibit 6–1. The block labeled "Setting Company Goals" shapes the decisions made in the block labeled "Selecting Company Programs." In other words, during a year a company is confronted repeatedly with decisions regarding new products, new markets, plant and equipment acquisition, mergers and diversification, human resources and organizational change, and research and development. A company that practices strategic planning will try to make these decisions in light of previously established goals. The emphasis is on "in light of" here because goals are not blueprints. To repeat: [Plans are only guides to making decisions and implementing actions; they should contain an element of flexibility.

In sum, we have seen in the first two sections of this chapter that in coping with the challenges of a turbulent environment, management has available a variety of responses. Among these responses, the case for strategic planning seems strongest. When challenges are viewed strategically, top management has a chance to respond to them earlier and with a greater degree of freedom. There is what Ackerman and Bauer (1976) call a "zone of discretion." As we saw in Chapters 2 and 3, technological innovation, social issues, and legislative innovations all pass through stages. It is during these periods of change that the management of a company has the most options available for responding. Once these changes enter their final stage, however, management options die off rapidly, as if struck by the plague.

In Chapter 5 we saw that many of the challenges facing American business are, at the deepest level, manifestations of the working out of the Iron Law of Responsibility. The consumer movement, for example, is nothing if not an early warning sign that unless business begins to act more responsibly in the marketplace—with regard to product safety, pricing, and so forth—it will, in the long run, lose much of its power. To whom? Probably to new, and still larger, regulatory agencies. And even more Draconian measures are visible through the haze of the future. It follows then that business will ignore the demands of society at its own peril. Including social responsibility in the strategic planning of a company makes such indifference less possible.

Strategic planning helps to insure that something will be done. One of the bedrock ideas upon which strategic planning builds is the notion that setting objectives (e.g., the achievement of a more racially balanced work force) must be linked with specific actions (e.g., Work Center A hires three new black workers). Strategy, in short, provides a measure of organizational cohesion and common understanding and is essential for the implementation of society-oriented programs. Moreover, if social responsibility is rooted in the strategic plan it is less likely that in times of economic downturns society-oriented programs will always be the first to go. Further, by considering social responsibility as a part of the strategic planning process, top management insures that society-oriented activities will always be compared against other, more traditional organizational activities and needs.

The great danger in the foregoing analysis is oversimplification. Take the notion that management ought to respond to challenges earlier. Who could disagree? What could be more eminently sensible? The catch is how managers,

COMMENTARY: On the Relationship Between a Corporation's Strategy and Its Response to Social Demands

Managers and business critics alike seldom give specific attention to this relationship, at least not until the economic consequences of the social forces have become manifest. This lapse is both surprising and unfortunate. The manager frequently concludes at the outset that acquiescing to demands imposed by government regulators or suggested by social advocates requires unproductive investments or activities which divert resources from the core functions of the business. Moreover, they are viewed as constraints to the exercise of management prerogatives; yielding to them may limit the manager's future alternatives as well as his control over the day-to-day direction of the enterprise. Resistance is the knee-jerk response to social initiatives from an organization in which these perceptions predominate.

In some respects that resistance is entirely appropriate. Indeed, the advocacy system which underlies the formation of public policy in the United States depends on the effective presentation of both sides of an issue. Thus, without a clear understanding of the implications of consumer protection legislation obtained through industry's rebuttal, it is less likely that balanced and useful regulation will result. But automatic and unrelenting opposition seriously misses the mark for the competent business strategist. So too does the support of social programs for philanthropic reasons alone. Charity, of course, has value, and we do not wish to denigrate it. However, programs rooted in this soil frequently do not survive the heat of economic adversity. The commitment is often insufficient to provide them with sustenance during such times at the expense of the remainder of the business.

The development of an effective social posture, therefore, begins with the consideration of social demands in the context of the corporation's strategy.

Source: Robert W. Ackerman and Raymond A. Bauer, *Corporate Social Responsiveness*, 1976. Reprinted with permission of Reston Publishing Company, Inc., a Prentice-Hall Company, 11480 Sunset Hills Road, Reston, Va 22090.

already flooded with information, are going to cultivate the ability and then find the time to scan the environment for changes. (The solution, imperfect though it is, awaits us in Chapter 7.)

Or take the notion of including social responsibility in a corporate plan. What exactly do we mean by social responsibility? Yes we defined it earlier, but that was the easy part. The hard part is translating that definition into a statement that can guide the operations of an enterprise in a useful way. Unless these matters are thought through carefully, a company will in the end wind up with policy statements such as, "One of our goals is to be a good corporate citizen" or "We shall always act in a socially responsible manner." Such fuzziness will open the sluice gates for a flood of public relations, but for very little in the way of really responsible behavior.

The purpose of the next section is to analyze the ideal of social responsibility more fully. The remainder of the chapter then enlarges upon a second ideal: business ethics. One need not live on Baker Street to suspect that these two ideals are related.

THE MEANING OF SOCIAL RESPONSIBILITY

Contrary to what many might assume, the ideal of social responsibility was not some recent invention by business critics, but came from the very depths of the American business system. Despite this long and close affiliation with American business, the term remains less than sharply defined. Nevertheless, we might safely say that social responsibility is a term like *hot* or *cold* in that it refers to degrees rather than to an absolute.

Accordingly, we might want to think of it as the continuum shown in Exhibit 6–3. Each point on the horizontal line represents a social responsibility. At the right end, we have a philosophy that dictates to managers that the overriding question in all their decisions is "What will benefit society the most?" Managers at the opposite end, meanwhile, ask "What is in it for our company?"

Position A on the continuum represents a "fight all the way" philosophy. For example, when Theodore Roosevelt accused J.P. Morgan of forming a transportation monopoly, the financier became one of the first businessmen to contend with federal regulatory clout. He didn't like it. "Mr. President," he said, "I'll get my lawyer, and you get yours." Both did. Roosevelt's lawyer won. And managers taking position A when faced with government regulation have been growing in number and tenacity ever since. Today one of the key issues upon which managers adopt position A concerns equal employment opportunity. For instance, the government in 1978 ordered John Hancock Mutual Life Insurance Company to turn over its personnel records for examination of possible job discrimination. The company flatly refused. The National Bank of Commerce of San Antonio went to court rather than furnish an affirmative action plan. And Harris Trust & Savings Bank of Chicago, among

EXHIBIT 6–3   The Social Responsibility Continuum

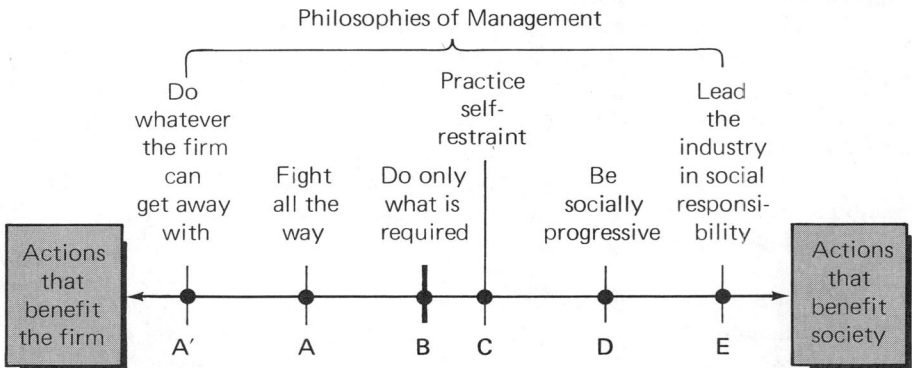

Philosophies of Management

| Do whatever the firm can get away with | Fight all the way | Practice self-restraint
Do only what is required | Be socially progressive | Lead the industry in social responsi-bility |

Actions that benefit the firm ← A′   A   B   C   D   E → Actions that benefit society

other companies, risked legal battles after the collapse of negotiations with the government over discrimination charges (cases cited in *Wall Street Journal,* February 17, 1978).

Some writers on business responsibility see the level of effort required at position A as no action other than defensive reaction to likely criticism and investigations (see, for example, McAdam, 1971). Managers at point A may indeed "hang tough" when social demands mount and legal action looms, but this position should not necessarily be viewed every time as unmitigated Neanderthalism. Many laws and rules *are* subsequently modified or even overruled by higher courts.

As the continuum shows, further distinctions can be made here. There are positions to the left of A, such as A′, where the outlook is much colder. At A′, no time is lost wrestling over the real merits of the law or, as Harris Trust chose to do, hiring an outside consultant to study the company's operation and report on whether discrimination exists. The central question at A′ becomes simply "Can we get away with it?"

The premiere example of a firm adopting the position is provided by Velsicol Chemical Corporation. In 1973, Velsicol somehow substituted an undetermined amount of a poisonous flame retardant commonly called PBB for an animal-feed supplement in a shipment from one of its plants and thereby touched off one of the worst agricultural disasters in U.S. history. The company has consistently fought back against its accusers, both inside and outside of court. In 1976, for example, it refused to cooperate with a federally requested recall of two chemicals—making it the only manufacturer to ever take this tack. As a spokesperson for the Environmental Protection Agency puts it:

"Velsicol's record of compliance with environmental statutes is one of the worst of any company." As might be expected an official of the Environmental Defense Fund puts it even more strongly: The company is a "corporate renegade that seems to be totally lacking in public responsibility" (both officials cited in *Wall Street Journal,* February 13, 1978).

At point B, management does only what is required by law, and no more. It will make a careful investigation of all existing legal requirements and try to anticipate likely new ones. Like Garry Trudeau's Duke, this management takes pride in "working within the system" (see cartoon). Unfortunately, neat and convenient dividing lines between where business should be allowed to prevail and where government restrictions are appropriate and helpful do not exist. In the absence of a clear dividing line, it is essential to a free society that managers have philosophies that *allow for evolving standards.*

Law alone does not provide the solution; its role is to articulate preestablished norms of a society. Today many businesses have acquired considerable skill in manipulating the law to their own advantage. Position C recognizes the limitations in the letter of the law; it is, therefore, a philosophy of mild self-restraint. No one is likely to express the nuances between positions B and C better than did Alexander Solzhenitsyn (1978) in his momentous Harvard address:

> I have spent all of my life under a communist regime, and I will tell you that a society without any objective legal scale is a terrible one indeed. But, a society with no other scale but the legal one is not quite worthy of man either . . . . Wherever the tissue of life is woven of legalistic relations, there is an atmosphere of moral mediocrity, paralyzing man's noblest impulses . . . . Life organized legalistically has shown its inability to defend itself against the corrosion of evil.

At point D on our continuum of social responsibility management is progressive. The effort here, in McAdam's (1971) words, is to grapple with a full range of issues; some breaking of new ground is likely. Finally, at point E, management attempts to lead the industry in social responsibility. It is not afraid to experiment with programs and projects in new, socially relevant areas, and it recognizes that some failure is inevitable when breaking new ground.

Thus, we can think of social responsibility as the degree to which a company considers and responds to issues beyond the narrow economic and legal requirements for growth and survival. Given this definition, the really interesting question is just how socially responsible a company should be.

Arguments for Social Responsibility

Here we consider three arguments in favor of greater social responsibility on the part of business. The first essentially reiterates the Iron Law of Responsibility: If business fails to evince a higher degree of social responsibility today,

Doonesbury

Doonesbury cartoon Copyright 1979 G.B. Trudeau/distributed by Universal Press
Syndicate. Reprinted by permission.

it will have much less freedom tomorrow. In the long run, social responsibility
is in the self-interest of business. Business should be concerned about the quality of life; when that declines, so too do profits. Detroit-based companies provide perhaps a microcosm of what happens to business when the quality of life
around it is diminished.

Second, social responsibility is preferable to government regulation, as
the discussion of regulation in the first part of Chapter 5 has already indicated.
To see the advantages of greater social responsibility on the part of corporations over more government regulation, consider the following case (taken
from Stone, 1975:117–18). The National Institute of Mental Health has estimated that American pharmaceutical companies are manufacturing between 8

and 10 *billion* amphetamine pills each year—a number vastly in excess of the amount required for legitimate medical use. Much of the excess—destined for consumption by illegal drug users—is shipped to Mexico and then smuggled back into the United States via an elaborate underground. One Chicago company, for example, in a period of a few years had shipped 15 million amphetamines to the post office box of an alleged drugstore in Tijuana, which a congressional committee later discovered was not only fictitious in name, but located, according to the address given, on or about the eleventh hole of the Tijuana Country Club golf course.

Even though it may be difficult to make pharmaceutical companies legally responsible for how its products are ultimately used, there can be little doubt that a socially responsible corporation would undertake some systematic efforts to determine the ultimate destination of its shipments. All the companies are aware that illegal drug traffic goes on and must be aware that, statistically, some of their own products are probably involved. But it is one thing to know in principle what is happening and quite another actually to track one's particular shipments. The latter action involves not only an expense, but the introduction of systematic changes in the company's information net— changes that involve finding out information it might rather not know. However, without this kind of responsible action on the part of companies, the government can set industrywide production quotas and gross shipments to foreign countries can be curtailed. "In other words," Stone points out, "when costs and benefits are considered, responsible self-policing—in which the company, as a first step, designs its own information network appropriately to find out where its products are going—may be part of a solution that is preferable to across-the-board, and possibly futile or even self-defeating, legal measures."

The third and final argument for social responsibility is that it is profitable. In Chapter 8 we shall consider several examples of how companies, through pioneering new products and services, have been able to turn the ecology and consumer movements into profits. We shall also see the subtle ways in which practices such as fair employment can make good economic sense.

Arguments against Social Responsibility

The arguments *against* greater social responsibility also can be summarized under three points. First, social responsibility is too expensive. In the 1970s, for example, hundreds of plants had to close because of environmental regulation. (Ironically, we might note, most of the companies involved would cluster at points B or C if placed on our social responsibility continuum.) Some proponents of the too-expensive argument have also pointed out that the higher environmental standards, as well as product quality control, have hurt the competitive position of many U.S. products in international markets.

Second, social responsibility can be viewed as illegal. Rather than say business has responsibility to society, those who hold this view say that business's only responsibility is to make a profit for the stockholders. For management to spend some of a corporation's money the way they wish to spend it borders on theft. The money should be returned to the stockholders, who may then spend it on philanthropic causes or anything else they wish. Milton Friedman (1971:13–14) writes:

> In a free enterprise, private property system, a corporate executive is an employee of the owners of the business. He has direct responsibility to his employers. That responsibility is to conduct the business in accordance with their desires, which generally will be to make as much money as possible while conforming to the basic rules of the society, both those embodied in law and those embodied in ethical custom .... Insofar as his actions in accord with his "social responsibility" reduce returns to stockholders, he is spending their money. Insofar as his actions raise the price to customers, he is spending the customers' money. Insofar as his actions lower the wages of some employees, he is spending their money.

Friedman's critics come back strong with the argument that the authentic shareholder of yesterday is a vanishing breed. Most stock today is purchased by people and institutions whose sole intention is to hold it for a relatively brief period and then sell it at a profit. They do not "invest" in a company, but are rather in the business of trading in its securities. These are the people to whom corporate managements are, in the end, responsible.* In their annual reports and in their advertising, corporations still like to sustain the legend that their legal owners are "shareholders"—people who have invested their capital in the company and, over a lifetime, share in the company's fortunes for better or worse. In reality, the fate of corporate management is ultimately decided by a group of speculators, and just about the sole criterion of successful management is whether or not a firm has managed to establish a relatively fancy price for its securities in the stock market. Moreover, management could in many instances argue that some of its efforts in pouring part of the profits into socially responsible causes are essential to "long-run survival." In this view, social responsibility is a normal operating expense and hence is actually in the best interest of the stockholder.

Notwithstanding arguments to the contrary, the charge that extreme social responsibility is illegal has merit. But we need to shift from the muddle about stockholders' rights to this question: What gives these small groups of top management the right to spend, and the expertise to know how to spend,

---

* Here is a simple, telling fact: In 1970, 31 million people owned stocks; now only about 25 million do. And many individuals who have not dropped out now allow financial intermediaries to do their investing for them. In 1949, institutions owned 14.5 percent by value of all common stocks listed on the New York Stock Exchange. Now institutional holdings are over 33 percent. Last year financial institutions accounted for 54.7 percent of the value of all shares traded on the Exchange. Individuals were responsible for only 23.1 percent.

COMMENTARY: Robin Hood in Reverse?

The corporation acts as Robin Hood, with the significant difference that while Robin Hood robbed only the rich to distribute to the poor, the corporate Robin Hood robs rich and poor indiscriminately. Moreover, corporate programs often tax the poor to pay the affluent.

Consider the case of the corporations that provide grants to the public broadcasting network to produce "superior" television drama. These programs are not commercially feasible, precisely because public demand for them is insufficient to pay their costs. While these programs reduce the excess profits of the companies, they are paid for, in the form of higher prices, by consumers, including some who are on the edge of poverty. The viewers, on the other hand, tend to be relatively affluent, well educated, and ethnically advantaged. Thus, real income is transferred from poor to rich by this exercise in corporate "social responsibility."

Some corporate programs impose especially heavy costs on the relatively poor. For example, a bank's program to subsidize mortgage interest rates for those who do not qualify at market rates, while increasing the real incomes of the target beneficiaries, will reduce incomes of potential borrowers in the income class just marginally above the beneficiaries, who will either be rationed out of the mortgage market or forced to pay higher rates. Not only will they contribute to the taxation that makes this program possible, but also they will be especially taxed as a consequence of its implementation.

Source: "Companies as Heroes? . . ." by Dean Carson, *New York Times,* December 25, 1977. © 1977 by The New York Times Company. Reprinted by permission.

profits in areas not *directly* related to business operations? Given a typical set of social issues—say, controlling air and water pollution, rebuilding our cities, enabling people to use their creative talents fully, giving a college education to all qualified people, eliminating religious prejudice, controlling crime, raising moral standards, reducing the threat of war, and eliminating racial discrimination—on which of these issues should a chief executive have spent corporate time and money in 1968? in 1975? in 1985? Are not these problems political issues and as such best thrashed out among elected officials?

The third and final argument against social responsibility is that it is inefficient. One great strength in most organizations, public and private, is clear-cut, well-focused goals. If business enterprises begin to concern themselves with ministering to the whole person and molding people and society (perhaps into a corporate image of what is good), business loses much of its indisputable efficiency in the delivery of a finite number of specific goods and services.

Social Responsibility as Social
Impact Management

From the foregoing analysis of the arguments that surround social responsibility, two broad conclusions are possible. First, managers cannot afford to be insensitive or indifferent to social responsibility. To put the argument in terms of Exhibit 6–3, there are cogent reasons for a company to generally avoid positioning itself to the left of point C.

But it is one thing to be a decent and good citizen, to behave with civility and restraint, and to be responsive to social demands; it is quite another to strive for unattainable goodness, an elimination of all conflicts of interest, and in the process to destroy the ideals of American pluralism as business melds into government. The advocates of the extreme social responsibility position want a kind of utopian perfection without fully understanding the difficulties or considering the price. So our second conclusion is this: Business managers cannot afford to adopt the more extreme social responsibility position. I would say, in terms of Exhibit 6–3, that managers should avoid being too far to the right of point E.

Admittedly, these two conclusions provide little guidance for a manager; we need to make the conclusions operational. Thus, a rough-and-ready rule: A company's management should consider itself responsible for all the direct effects that the company has on its environment.* Following Peter Drucker (1974), we can call this view of social responsibility *social impact management.* The purpose of this section is to make its meaning and practical implications clear.

We can begin by considering a research undertaking in the early 1970s by Daniel Yankelovich of New York and the Government Research Corporation in Washington on behalf of twenty-nine major corporations. The purpose was to study the major demands, in order of priority, that the public was making on the corporation, and the findings were summed up by Robert A. Newman (1974), vice president of community affairs for TRW, Inc.:

> ... what the vast majority of the public expect from corporations in terms of social performance relates largely to our internal affairs or business practices—not especially to our external affairs or community activities. I run into many people who seem to feel that corporate responsibility means being more active in community problems and issues and giving larger and larger amounts of contributions to an ever expanding variety of social causes. I'm suggesting, based on research and our own judgment, that this is not what responsibility is all about, although it should be considered part of the definition. As David Burke, vice president of Dreyfus Third Century Fund, told us: "Who cares if a corporation gets into helping low-income housing groups? That's a dodge. Look, we have oil

---

* The medical profession has stated the rule even more succinctly in the aphorism *primum non nacere:* first of all, do no harm, that is, take care not to knowingly do harm.

companies that come to us and say, 'We gave $500,000 to Bedford-Stuyvesant and we sponsor Sesame Street.' So what? Who cares (about that) if a black man can't get a job as plant foreman in Houston?"

Social impact management includes, therefore, every aspect of traditional business activity: quality of products and services, fair hiring and promotion practices, pollution control, and so on. These are the concerns that upset the public, and these are the concerns that industry must respond to in an aggressive, voluntary way.

Newman has also provided some of TRW's own findings with respect to setting priorities for managers who are concerned about social impact management:

1. Consider periodic research to find out what the public—particularly your most important constituents—expects of your company; set targets for improvement where indicated; measure progress against benchmarks.
2. Get top management involvement and commitment in your program and communicate that fact throughout the organization.
3. Concentrate your efforts on the internal, so-called "mainstream," issues of corporate responsibility.
4. Once you have a successful track record, do not fail to fully communicate this to your constituents, but do so with taste, accuracy, and understatement.

Regarding external or community activities, Newman makes these thoughtful points:

1. Concentrate in those locations where your company has a presence as an employer.
2. Get involved in activities where your special expertise can be utilized; in other words, carefully match company resources against community needs.
3. Remember that giving time and talent is more important than giving money; and when you give money, follow it to see what the "return on investment" turns out to be.
4. Look for involvement in those community issues where there is some payoff for the company (example: if you are going to get involved in drug-abuse prevention or day-care centers, then link it with serving your employees, achieving less absenteeism and turnover, and greater productivity and morale).

In short, social impact management means that a company has a responsibility, not to that amorphous entity called society, but to those groups in society that are affected either directly or indirectly by what the company does. Obviously, management cannot satisfy every group, any more than a big-city mayor can satisfy all his or her constituents. The best that can be hoped for is an effort on the part of management to balance public demands with company interests and to remain sensitive to the effects the organization has on the lives of many people.

Thus, social impact management asserts that management's political role takes precedence over its economic function, rather than vice versa. This does not mean that management must be socially responsible in the sense of righting all racial wrongs (here and abroad), creating a pristine environment, underwriting community activities, and the like. But it does mean that companies must convince their numerous publics that *within the powers companies exercise,* they have not ignored public interests. As Neil W. Chamberlain (1973: 204) observes, more and more business is "forced to seek legitimacy by demonstrating its responsiveness to its publics like a political officeholder."

One final, very practical point needs to be made. Managers, particularly the middle-level ones who implement company policy, must have a *commitment* to whatever philosophy of social responsibility top management has chosen. And the notion of social impact management seems to fit nicely with what research indicates are the areas of responsibility considered most important by managers (see Exhibit 6–4).

In sum, the importance of accepting some doctrine of social responsibility for private business requires management to look for ways to reconcile the conflict that occurs when the older notion of profit and the newer notion of social contribution appear on the same company's planning agenda. Kenneth B. Andrews (1971:119) writes:

> The creativity required to effect this reconciliation, that is, to make a company competitively successful by way of a corporate strategy that meets demands for responsibility from its members, its owners, and its customers, may well appear to us at last as the essence of the professionalization which is presently contributing both competence and conscience to the practice of management.

MANAGEMENT VALUES: A DECISION THEORY PERSPECTIVE

Why Study Ethics?

In discussing social responsibility, there is a widespread tendency to take for granted that more of it is a good thing, at least among those who spend time discussing it. In some situations, of course, responsibility means helping someone and offending no one. Issues like the following ones are not likely to cause deep moral dilemmas, for what is "right" is clear enough:

—Flammable children's pajamas without warning labels,
—Clandestine dumping of garbage or toxic substances,
—Resetting odometers on secondhand cars,
—Bribery and kickbacks,
—Tax evasion,
—Fraud,
—Discrimination against blacks seeking housing mortgages.

EXHIBIT 6–4   The Top Eight Areas of Business Responsibility as Viewed by Managers

Areas of business responsibility as viewed by managers	Degree*
Being an efficient user of energy and natural resources	4.00
Assessing the potential environmental effects flowing from the company's technological advances	3.96
Maximizing long-run profits	3.78
Using every means possible to maximize job content and satisfaction for the hourly worker	3.35
Having your company's subsidiary in another country use the same occupational safety standards as your company does in the United States	3.05
Acquiescing to State Department requests that the company not establish operations in a certain country	3.01
Making implementation of corporate affirmative action plans a significant determinant of line officer promotion and salary improvement	2.91
Instituting a program for hiring the hard-core unemployed	2.28

* The ranking is calculated on a scale of 1 (absolutely voluntary) to 5 (absolutely obligatory).

Source: Reprinted by permission of the Harvard Business Review. Table from "Is the Ethics of Business Changing?" by Steven N. Brenner and Earl A. Molander (January–February 1977). Copyright © 1977 by the President and Fellows of Harvard College; all rights reserved.

But as we have seen, social responsibility is not always so clear-cut. Often it becomes a matter of choice among alternative values. In matters of social responsibility, Thomas G. Schelling (1974:89–90) writes, there are always conflicts of interest:

> Higher-cost low-sulphur fuels clean the air for the people who live downwind from the smokestacks; [but] use of these same fuels may add to the cost of electric power and other commodities, with an incidence that falls disproportionately on the poor. Pity the "responsible" refuse company that has to decide in which community to locate its dumping ground.

Schelling notes that being responsible for a business firm is similar to being responsible as a senator or as a university president. "Often the question is not, Do I want to do the right thing? It arises in the form, What is the right thing to want to do?" The choice is not always between some selfish temptation and some obviously responsible course. It is a matter of choice among values:

> What should a business do about drug addiction among its employees? What should it do about admitting men to jobs that have been traditionally

women's—secretaries, receptionists, or file clerks? Or smoking on the job? Or eliminating some hazard in the product by producing it more expensively and selling it at a higher price? Or letting a black organization dictate policy toward blacks, letting a woman's organization negotiate on behalf of women? Consider the business that is under pressure to discontinue operations in South Africa, throwing people out of work there. What is the right thing to do? To whom should the company defer in deciding the right thing to do? Is there a "right thing" in this case or just a choice between equally unsatisfactory options?

Of course, not all decisions involve dilemmas of conscience. Nor do they involve major policy decisions for a company. They may concern matters of how to deal with employees on a one-to-one basis or of how far to go in bluffing during a sale or job interview. Often the right choice is clear enough, yet managers still do the wrong thing. One thing seems sure: On the issues confronting managers today, reliable guidance is often absent.

Why then have not more students of business begun to study ethics, which is the branch of philosophy dealing with values? While a number of reasons might be offered, one or two seem especially important. First, the typical American view of ethics is, as Michael Walzer (1978) has so accurately noted, that values are deeply personal and private—not really a thing to be discussed "among men, or among *real* men":

> The American hero is masculine and reticent, strong and silent. (In his urban embodiment, a stream of wisecracks conceals the deeper reticence.) Hence, there cannot be any serious moral dialogue or criticism, though there can be a kind of inarticulate contempt or disgust for unforgivable behavior. In public, we can only hold a man to his own standards: honor, sincerity, grace under pressure. These can be talked about, but not virtue or goodness. Moral judgment focused on questions of virtue or goodness is moralizing, the sure sign of self-righteousness, priggishness, and hypocrisy.

Second, William J. Bennett (1978) tells this story about one of his colleagues who teaches ethics. Inevitably, at the beginning of this teacher's classes, student skepticism surfaces:

> STUDENT: Mr. Jones, I don't think you can teach ethics because there really aren't any in any real sense. Each person's values are as good as anybody else's. Values are subjective.
>
> TEACHER: No, that's not true. Some people's values are better than others.
>
> STUDENT: No, they're subjective. No one can impose his values on somebody else.
>
> TEACHER: That's not true.
>
> STUDENT: Yes, it is.
>
> TEACHER: No, it isn't.
>
> STUDENT: Well, that's your opinion and I have mine and it's just like I'm saying: We disagree, and you can't impose your viewpoint on me.

TEACHER: Well, I'm the teacher here and I say values are not subjective.

STUDENT: So what? I'm a student and I say they are.

TEACHER: Well, what do you think of this? I say values are not subjective, and if you don't agree with me then I'll flunk you.

STUDENT (gasp): What? What? You can't do that! Are you crazy?

TEACHER: No. I can do that. Why not?

STUDENT (sputtering): Because it's not fair.

TEACHER: "Fair," "fair," what do you mean "fair"? Don't impose your values and sense of right and wrong on me.

STUDENT (pause, and eventually): I see your point.

The point of the story is neatly made: It is ridiculous to hold all values equally valid because they are "personal." Further, it is a quite extraordinary conception, for one could hardly be moral, or immoral, without other people. Ethics is a thoroughly public—not a private—matter.

Studying ethics is no guarantee of effectiveness in making moral choices. But it may help a manager to talk about moral questions with others or to con-

COMMENTARY: On Moral Education

The strong silent hero remains attractive, I suppose. One would not want Humphrey Bogart to stop in the middle of *Casablanca,* say, and deliver a lecture on just and unjust wars. But it is important to understand that his gut feelings and his instinct for the good are parasitic on other people's lectures, on a whole tradition of moral discourse. It is also important to understand that his silence is at least in part inauthentic and historically false. For in war, men and women face hard choices, and have to think about them. And since those choices are not only personal but also collective, they have to think out loud, to argue, to criticize, to persuade. On these occasions it is not all that helpful to be heroic but inarticulate.

When men and women can't talk about moral questions—when they imagine all such talk to be unscientific, a sign of weakness and sentimentality—then they simply live off the accumulated stock of older decisions and understandings. Or they function without controls of tradition and common discourse, and fall prey to the crudest kinds of moral extremism. They become fanatics of the cause ready to do anything for their party or country. Or, as easily, they become fanatics of the self, ready to do anything to advance their own careers. Against this sort of thing, moral education should aim not at moderation, which is not always appropriate, but at publicity, argument, and discipline.

Source: Michael Walzer, "Teaching Morality," *The New Republic,* July 10, 1978. Reprinted by permission of *The New Republic,* © 1978 The New Republic, Inc.

template them by himself or herself. The study of ethics may help managers make more reflective judgments—ones that can be defended in public. As Hannah Arendt (1978) has argued, wickedness, however defined, is "*not* a necessary condition for evildoing." Instead, our "faculty for telling right from wrong" is connected with our "faculty of thought." Arendt follows Plato in viewing the thought process as a "soundless dialogue" that each person carries on with himself or herself—a private activity demanding withdrawal from the world. The distinguishing mark of this inner conversation, she maintains, is consistency. A criminal, like Adolf Eichmann, who is unfamiliar with this silent intercourse (in which we examine what we say and what we do) does not mind contradicting himself, "nor will he mind committing any crime, since he can count on its being forgotten the next moment." Although Eichmann's deeds were monstrous, he was quite ordinary. Arendt believes that it was not any kind of willfulness, but a profound *thoughtlessness*—an utter unreflectiveness—that made the proper operation of his conscience impossible.

The study of ethics may also help us see moral issues hidden in legal jargon and technicality. For example, not long ago a group of thirty Cornell law students viewed a film about a man who had been burned and blinded in an automobile accident and wanted to hire a lawyer in order to get out of the hospital—a move that would almost certainly mean his death. In the ensuing discussion, virtually all the students began by taking the position that they would accede to the client's wishes. Unfortunately, they were not perceiving the moral dimensions of the case; they didn't sense the indecision and the guilt in the man's voice until it was pointed out to them (Fiske, 1978).

Finally, studying ethics may expedite business decision making. Managers without a fairly well thought-out set of values are relatively poor decisionmakers; when confronted with decisions with ethical implications, they tend to dither. In other words, they take longer to arrive at a decision because they are so unsure of how to handle it. In contrast, the manager who has given some prior thought to ethics moves swiftly to a decision and thereby saves time, avoids worry, and shows subordinates firm consistency.

Understanding Value-Driven Decision Systems

How do managers make decisions? The answer seems obvious, the steps simple. First, they consider some alternative courses of action (bribe, do not bribe; pad expense accounts, do not pad; comply with EPA rules and install new, expensive pollution-control equipment, or take the matter to court, or shut the plant down). Next, managers try to predict the consequences of each alternative. Finally, they assess the "desirability" of the consequences and try to select the most desirable alternative. A fundamental problem with this simple process is often overlooked: How does one decide which consequences are most desirable? George Edgin Pugh (1977) observes that "the question may seem academic or theoretical. We all 'know' what is desirable. Why waste time asking how we know?"

"Miss Dugan, will you send someone in here who can distinguish right from wrong?"

Drawing by Dana Fradon. © 1975 The New Yorker Magazine, Inc.

But Pugh found that the problem is not easily avoided when one is designing a decision system. In the early 1960s Pugh was working for the Defense Department on the attempt to develop automatic planning of bomber flight plans. Some experienced military officers had already assembled a list of about forty rules to be followed—for example, "Aircraft will normally fly in a straight line between targets"; "Angles of turn from one target on the route to the next should not exceed forty-five degrees"; and so on. Unfortunately, exceptions to the rules kept coming up, and that meant writing still more rules.

As the list of rules became more and more cumbersome, Pugh suggested giving the computer a set of values. The computer could then generate alternative flight plans and select those that came closest to satisfying the chosen set of values. Alternatives could be scored in terms of their contribution to two objectives: (a) estimated probability of successful recovery of aircraft and crew and (b) value of targets attacked. The computer, in short, would make value-driven decisions.

Based on this experience, Pugh began to consider the role of decision criteria in life. It is easy to see how the concept of value-driven decisions could have simplified evolution's problems in the design of biological decision systems. If we wanted to design such a system we would have to start with a basic question: What might be the ultimate source of basic human values? Throughout history, philosophers and religious leaders have held that certain fundamental and enduring values are intrinsic to human nature. But today, behavioral comparisons among different species are revealing that many of the behavioral characteristics of a species are genetically inherited; somehow, each individual of a species is endowed with certain specific behavioral "tendencies" that cause it to behave in a way that is characteristic of its own species (see Wilson, 1978).

Although the existing work on comparative behavior helps clarify our understanding of sources of human values, it leaves a number of very important questions unanswered. What are the enduring "human values" that are an essential part of evolution's basic "design concept" for a biological "decision system"? Abraham Maslow provided one fairly well known list—although, to be sure, he referred to it as his "hierarchy of needs" rather than as a built-in value system. Maslow's five basic human needs or motives are as follows: physiological needs, safety needs, social needs, esteem needs, and self-actualization.

Pugh has provided his own list of instinctive human motives. Since any such list is sure to be controversial and research in this area is still in its infancy, he stresses that the list is purely illustrative and certainly incomplete. Moreover, it probably includes some "motives" that may later prove to be *learned* rather than *innate*. Pugh's list is as follows:

1. Desire for dominance (rivalry),
2. Desire for approval,
3. Desire for social acceptance,
4. Gregariousness,
5. Enjoyment of conversation,
6. Desire to exercise body and exploit one's physical skills (activity motive),
7. Enjoyment of humor in conversation and play,
8. Social preferences,
9. Desire to work with others for common goals (team motive),
10. Desire to make or build something (constructive motive),
11. Desire to contribute or do something meaningful for society (contribution motive).

Thus the decisions that govern human behavior appear to be the result of the interaction of criteria within a value system.

A Model for Ethical Behavior

In order to understand how ethics can be applied in society, we need to consider the interactions between different value criteria. Take the problem faced by an individual who must make a decision involving a moral judgment, for example. Presumably, the alternative decisions will be evaluated in terms of that individual's value system. Just as no two individuals have exactly the same face, no two individuals have quite the same value system. In terms of Pugh's list of motives, an individual may place more emphasis on the personal values, such as "desire for dominance" and "activity motives," or may tend to stress the social values, such as "desire for approval" and "contribution motives."

The model of ethics shown in Exhibit 6–5 provides an idealized representation of the relationships among values. The vertical axis represents the rela-

EXHIBIT 6–5   A Model of Ethical Behavior

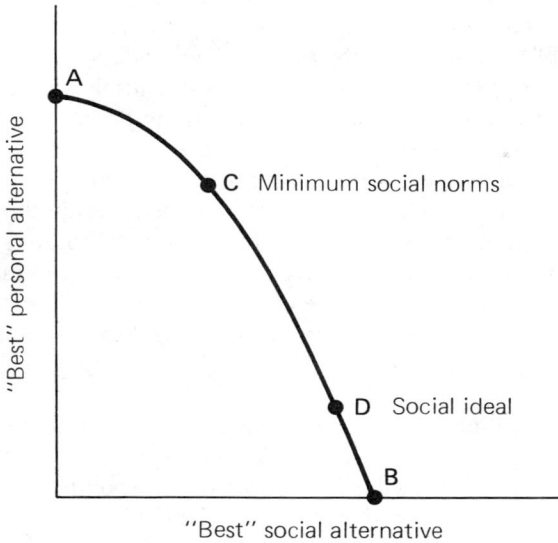

A is maximum selfish decision.
B is maximum altruistic decision.
C is minimum socially beneficial decision.
D is ideal socially beneficial decision.

tive importance or utility of a decision's consequences for an individual. The horizontal axis represents the relative importance or utility of those consequences for society. A completely selfish decisionmaker would always choose the alternative closest to A, while a completely altruistic decisionmaker would always choose the alternative closest to B. Because of some innate desire for approval, an individual will probably wish to select a balanced alternative—somewhere between A and B—that will be "good" in terms of *both* valuative criteria.

Society has an interest in encouraging individuals to make their decisions as close to B as possible, but it is obviously unrealistic to expect individuals to ignore their own personal preferences. To assist individuals in making decisions (and to encourage them to make socially beneficial decisions), society defines certain minimally acceptable social norms. The moral boundary defined by these norms is located at point C in Exhibit 6–5. Any decision to the left of these norms will be definitely disapproved; thus, individuals have a strong incentive to at least stay to the right of this boundary of disapproval. But society would like to obtain even more favorable decisions from individuals. It therefore tries to define a kind of ideal behavior that is represented by point D. This ideal offers decisionmakers a model of behavior that will get a much higher "approval" score. Individuals who are highly motivated by the "approval" factor will try to model their behavior to correspond closely with this social ideal. In deciding what to do, individuals must weigh the benefits of social approval against other conflicting benefits in their own *innate* value systems.

The exhibit helps clarify the commonsense language of morality. The point marked "minimum social norms" is, in effect, the dividing line between behavior we call right and wrong. Right behavior is that falling on the arc *below* the minimum social norms; wrong behavior, that falling on the arc *above* point C. In addition to clarifying the commonsense language of morality, the exhibit helps to clarify the wide diversity of approaches that philosophers have used to deal with the subject of ethics.

Approaches to Traditional Ethics. A number of approaches to ethics, or moral philosophy, are represented on our model of ethics as shown in Exhibit 6–6, *Utilitarian ethics,* the horizontal axis (which corresponds to point B in our original model), was developed in the late 1700s by Jeremy Bentham in his *Principles of Morals and Legislation.* In brief, Bentham asserted that "it is the greatest happiness of the greatest number that is the measure of right and wrong." While, with few exceptions, utilitarianism never caught on among business managers, it has attained some degree of popularity among public administrators, who refer to it as the *social benefit function.*

To clarify utilitarianism as the social benefit function, it is helpful to define a formal mathematical value function that could be used within a decision science analysis. We shall define the total social value, V, of an alternative to be equal to the summation of the expected valuative satisfaction, V_i, that the consequences of the alternative should yield for each individual, i. If we are not sure that all individuals should be treated equally, we can use a weighting coefficient, α_i, to allow us to assign greater importance to some individuals (e.g., Leonard Bernstein and Jimmy Carter) than others (e.g., Farrah Fawcett-Majors and Billy Carter). The criterion might then be written mathematically as follows:

$$V = \Sigma_i \, \alpha_i \, V_i$$

In this form, the equation states that the total social value, V, of any alternative is equal to the summation of the value V_i for all individuals i, weighted (or multiplied) by a factor α_i that reflects the "importance" of each individual.

Not without reason, Walzer (1978) refers to utilitarianism as body-count morality:

> When decisions are unavoidable, they must be hard-headed, tough-minded, unsentimental, worked out in terms of the actual or supposed preferences of dis-

EXHIBIT 6–6   A Model of Some Ethical Theories

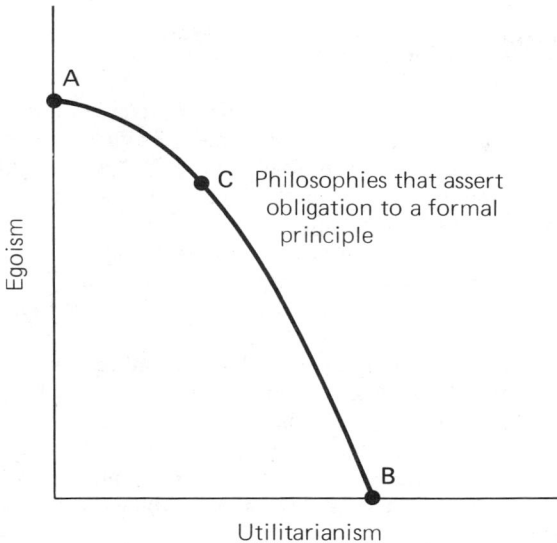

crete individuals. The standards must be clear—utiles of pleasure, dollars, lives—qualities that can be turned into quantities, so that the ultimate decision is as indisputable as addition and subtraction and so that there is, once again, no room for moralizing.

Such economic models of life hardly serve to enhance our moral understanding. Other difficulties are also apparent. From the perspective of innate values discussed earlier, the utilitarian approach to personal ethics seems unrealistic; there appears no rational explanation for why an individual should use an altruistic criterion for making personal decisions. "Even as a basis for a social ideal, the principle seems naive, since, to be most effective, even the social ideal should give reasonable consideration of personal preferences" (Pugh, 1977:393). Another difficulty involves issues of equity. For example, how does the utilitarian criterion provide for the interests of future generations? Should the weighting of α_i depend in any way on the age of an individual?

Point A in Exhibit 6–6 represents quite a different approach to moral issues. *Egoist theory* holds that the duty of all people is to maximize the good of only one person—himself or herself. One of the earliest recorded exponents of this moral philosophy was Epicurus (341–270 BC). To Epicurus, pleasure was the means by which nature gives us the word—that is, tells us what is right—therefore, pleasure must be the chief good.

However, other egoist theories have led in radically different directions. A notable case in point is Friedrich Nietzsche (1885), who, as the following excerpt shows, hardly preached pleasure, comfort, and high living as the good:

> A great man—a man whom nature has constructed and invented in the grand style—what is he?
>
> First: There is a long logic in all of his activity, hard to survey because of its length, and consequently misleading; he has the ability to extend his will across great stretches of his life and to despise and reject everything petty about him, including even the fairest, "divinest" things in the world.
>
> Secondly: He is colder, harder, less hesitating, and without fear of "opinion"; he lacks the virtues that accompany respect and "respectability," and altogether everything that is part of the "virtue of the herd." If he cannot lead, he goes alone; then it can happen that he may snarl at some things he meets on his way.
>
> Third: He wants no "sympathetic" heart, but servants, tools; in his intercourse with men he is always intent on *making* something out of them. He knows he is incommunicable; he finds it tasteless to be familiar; and when one thinks he is, he usually is not. When not speaking to himself, he wears a mask. He rather lies than tells the truth: it requires more spirit and *will*. There is a solitude within him that is inaccessible to praise or blame, his own justice that is beyond appeal.

Point C on Exhibit 6–6 represents philosophies that assert *obligation to a formal principle.** The main difference between these philosophies and those of the utilitarians and egoists centers on the question of how to judge an action as right or wrong. While utilitarians and egoists look to the *consequences* of a decision, philosophers in this third group hold that the rightness or wrongness of an action is to be judged by how closely it conforms to some formal principle or principles.

Perhaps the greatest moral philosopher of the third group was Immanuel Kant (1724–1804). Kant found that ultimately all moral decisions should be based on a single principle: Act as if the maxim of your action were to become a general law binding on everyone. Because the principle does not admit to proof, but is justified from principles of pure, practical reason, Kant calls his principle the *categorical imperative.* Kant was an absolutist about lying; he could find no justification for any lie whatsoever. In his words, "a lie is an abandonment or, as it were, annihilation of the dignity of man." Principles like Kant's should toll regularly, like cathedral bells, and call us back to the sources of morality. But perhaps Kant was too much an absolutist—he would have forbade those Christians who sheltered Jews during World War II from turning away the Gestapo at their door.

Kant's categorical imperative is not the only formal principle that we can associate with point C. Predating it by nearly 2,500 years was the principle of

---

* In the technical language of philosophy, this group is called deontologists, from the Greek *deontos* ("of the obligatory").

COMMENTARY: On Corporate Codes of Conduct

When corporate codes of conduct become too general, they tend to contain contradictions and omissions. But, when they become too detailed, codes tend to be too cumbersome to provide much practical guidance, and still they cannot anticipate every possible ethical decision in advance. And, finally, rigorous applications of detailed codes can sometimes lead to decisions that conflict with common sense.

An Example Code

—TO PROVIDE our employees a stimulating work environment that will attract and challenge effective people and provide rewarding employment opportunities.
—TO DETERMINE consumer wants or needs and to fulfill these with quality products or services.
—TO IDENTIFY with appropriate local issues and to contribute to the economic and social development of the community involved.
—TO HOLD a single standard of integrity everywhere.
—TO INSURE the highest level of objectivity in our procurement practices.
—TO REQUIRE that our employees refrain from actions that constitute a conflict of interest.

. . .

According to a 1977 survey of 497 top corporations by the University of Virginia's Graduate School of Business Administration, 90 percent of the companies responding had formal standards of conduct for their executives. These written codes of conduct—or creeds—attempt to establish the general value system of the company. Large, geographically spread-out companies hope that such codes will help to establish a more uniform ethical climate and provide guidelines for more consistent decision making. About two-thirds of the reporting companies, the survey disclosed, had fired one or more managers for unethical conduct within the 1975–76 period.

How effective are such codes—long or short, general or specific? In a survey by Brenner and Molander (1977:68), the responses suggested the following assessment:

Codes can be most helpful in those areas where there is general agreement that certain unethical practices are widespread and undesirable. Ethical codes do not, however, offer executives much hope for either controlling outside influences on business ethics or resolving fundamental ethical dilemmas. This is not to minimize the potential for codes to have an impact in narrow areas of concern. It is to emphasize that regardless of form they are no panacea for unethical business conduct.

Not surprisingly, 89 percent of the survey respondents felt that a code would *not* be easy to enforce.

primum non nocere ("above all, not knowingly to do harm"), the first responsibility of a professional as spelled out in the Hippocratic oath. Nor should we overlook the Golden Rule. And Arthur Furer, chief executive of Nestle, likes to describe the proper role of the entrepreneur in terms of *libertas oboedientiae*, the "freedom within duty" of the medieval Christian knight.

In regard to the issue of lying, Sissela Bok (1978) offers three practical principles for assessing a situation in which lying may be acceptable:

1. Role taking: View the situation from the perspective of the person being lied to. Would that person accept your reasons for lying?
2. Self-analysis: To what degree is your justification for lying a rationalization in favor of your self-interest?
3. Publicity: Would your justification for lying convince members of society at large, rather than just a small circle of friends who may share your biases?

In contrast to Kant's categorical imperative, which sets forth a single, uniform principle as the criterion of rightness, other ethical theories that can be associated with point C are more pluralistic. That is, they put forward *several* rules or principles that should be obeyed: Keep one's promises, repay benefits, show consideration of other's feelings, and so forth. A major problem with the pluralistic theories should be apparent. If fairly limited in number, like the rules embodied in many corporate codes of conduct, they can be replete with contradictions and loopholes.

One approach to ethical decisions that does not fit well into Exhibit 6–6 is called the *naturalistic* approach. The label is appropriate, since this theory of ethics is consistent with the notion that there are natural values, the evolutionary inheritance of the human decision system. We consider this theory in the section that follows.

A NATURAL THEORY OF BUSINESS ETHICS

Spinoza's Ethics

Benedict Spinoza (1632–1677) recognized the importance of an ethical system's being consistent with human nature (see Exhibit 6–7). In the opening chapter of his *Tractatus Politicus,* Spinoza wrote:

> Philosophers regard the emotions by which we are torn as vices into which men fall by their own fault; they therefore laugh at them, weep over them, sneer at them, or (if they wish to appear more pious than others) denounce them. So they think they are doing something wonderful and preeminently scientific when they praise a human nature which exists nowhere and attack human nature as it really is. They conceive men, not as they are, but as they would wish them to be. The result is that they write satires instead of ethics, and that they have never produced a political theory which is of any use, but something which could be regarded as a Chimera, or put in practice in Utopia or in the Golden Age the

poets talk about, where, to be sure, it was not needed. The result is that theory is held to be discrepant from practice in all the studies intended to be of use . . . .

But it is Spinoza's *Ethics* that is the most relevant to our purposes. The chapter titles are revealing: "Of human bondage, or the strength of emotions" and "Of the power of the understanding, or of human freedom." We are in bondage, Spinoza thinks, insofar as what happens to us is determined by outside causes, and we are free insofar as we are self-determined. Spinoza believes that all wrong action is due to intellectual error: The person who understands his or her circumstances—that is, who thinks things through—will act wisely and will even be happy in the face of what, to another, would be misfortune.

Spinoza makes no appeal to unselfishness, as the utilitarians do. He holds that self-seeking—and, more particularly, self-preservation—in some sense governs all human behavior. "No virtue can be conceived as prior to this endeavor to preserve one's own being." But—and the "but" is crucial—Spinoza's conception of what the wise person will choose as the goal of self-seeking is, in effect, different from that of the ordinary egoist: Spinoza views the mind's highest good as obedience to reason. Consequently, the wise person's course of action will not depend on any superficial consideration of what he or she would like to do, or what might give immediate gratification. Rather, the decision will be based on a concentrated effort to see everything in its totality. To restate all this rather plainly, Spinoza seems to be saying that many unethical decisions are the result, not of self-seeking, but of failing to see clearly one's true self-interests. "Joy can never be evil which is controlled by a *true* consideration for our own profit."

The ethics of Spinoza reveals a deep sensitivity to the welfare of others, though its justification is not to be found in the shifting sands of altruism. To Spinoza, a true consideration of one's own long-term profit dictates such sensitivity. So far as people are guided by reason, they necessarily agree in their natures. There is nothing in the nature of things more serviceable to people than their fellow human beings, so long as all are controlled by reason; and the more each person seeks his or her own good, the more all forward one another's true interests. The shallow misanthropy of the pessimists, the empty ridicule of the satirists, and the otherworldliness of the priests are all refuted by the facts. A sane judgment of life bears irrefutable witness to the need of people for one another, and to the value of human society for the realization of the ideal.

Spinoza's reasoning is strikingly close to contemporary research in animal behavior. As Edward O. Wilson (1978:197) has written:

> The individual is an evanescent combination of genes drawn from this pool, one whose hereditary material will soon be dissolved back into it. Because natural selection has acted on the behavior of individuals who benefit themselves and

their immediate relatives, human nature bends us to the imperatives of self-ishness and tribalism. But a more detached view of the long-range course of evolution should allow us to see beyond the blind decison-making process of natural selection and to envision the history and future of our own genes against the background of the entire human species. A word already in use intuitively defines this view: nobility. Had dinosaurs grasped the concept they might have survived. They might have been us.

Spinoza's reasoning is equally close to a great deal of contemporary research in the social sciences. Roland N. McKean (1974:121–22) writes:

> In the aggregate, the impact of a society's ethical and behavioral principles is great. Much of the impact is desirable. Many rules, such as "Don't cheat on un-written contracts" or "Don't bribe government officials," may impose short-run sacrifices on many businessmen but, if nearly all adhere to the rule, yield net long-run benefits to most. Habits of trust, friendliness, neatness, fairness, generosity, and nonviolence are to some extent public goods that are produced by the observance of behavioral traditions. Some of these are extremely important to the functioning of a private enterprise economy. Social contracts about honesty can save extra burglar alarms, time clocks, monitoring devices, legal actions, hours spent checking up on each other's statements, time wasted when appointments and promises are broken, energy and good humor squandered on bitterness and reprisal, and gains from trades that would otherwise not take place. Business and households find it advantageous to save contracting costs by relying heavily on trust and on tacit, rather than written, understandings . . . . Lack of basic moral codes and mutual trust aggravates material as well as spiritual poverty.

EXHIBIT 6–7   A Spinoza Sampler

In his general social philosophy Spinoza combines a fundamental egoism with a benevolent altruism. He has faith in the principle that "when each man seeks most that which is profitable to himself, then are men most profitable to one another. It is most useful for each individual to have others agree with him in nature, since a thing which agrees with our nature is necessarily good. Through social union and mutual assistance, men further their common aim of self-preservation and perfection of life."

"Clearly, therefore, if we are to live the rational life, we must endeavour to win the friendship of our fellow men by every means in our power. Above all, we must try to lead them to live the rational life themselves, in order that we may be strengthened by common pursuit of our true good."

"Each person's life is an end in itself and must not be used as a means for the life of others. In the last analysis, since self-preservation is the foundation of all virtue; the good of each person is prior to that of others. Justice demands that each

Spinoza, oil painting by an unknown artist, c. 1665.

person seek the good and perfection of others as much as his own but not more so. The justification of altruism is egoism.''

"The free man realizes his place in the scheme of things, and his mind is filled with the peace that comes of this understanding. Fully conscious of the supreme value of this peace of mind and of the intelligence which it implies, he endeavours, without passion and without prejudice, to fulfil it in himself and in all men. His life is an unswerving effort towards this end: he does not adopt inconsistent means—however plausible they may seem—to attain it. He is not misled by the pleasure or pain of the moment to underestimate or overvalue a future 'good' or 'evil.' For his whole activity is the expression of clear knowledge; and for clear knowledge or science what is true once is true always. Hence he sees things as they are—in their eternal necessity, their intrinsic value—not as they illusorily appear in the shifting lights of temporal contrast. And inasmuch as his whole being is filled with the joy of realization, the consciousness of doing his utmost for an ideal which he knows to be the true one, he is untouched by remorse, or by shame. He neither frets nor fears, but is at peace.''

"The 'free man', of course, respects the law from intelligent motives; that is, because he realizes that the order, which the state maintains, is the indispensable basis of the ideal life.''

'' 'To know' means to apprehend things in their eternal or timeless necessity. If, therefore, we form a clear idea of an emotion of pleasure, we cannot refer it to a series of temporal and local conditions: still less can we regard a single object, pictured in isolation as merely 'there,' as its cause. We must take the passion in our thought out of the imaginative series, and conceive it in its necessary and timeless determination.''

Source: Text from David Bidney, *The Psychology and Ethics of Spinoza* (New Haven: Yale University Press, 1940): Harold H. Joachim, *A Study of the Ethics of Spinoza* (New York: Russell & Russell, 1964). Photo from The Bettman Archive, Inc.

Natural Theory in the Modern Key:
Enlightened Self-Interest

In 1976 a social and clinical psychologist Michael Maccoby published a book, *The Gamesman,* that put forward the thesis that a new type of person is taking over the leadership of the most technically advanced large corporations in the United States. According to Maccoby, corporate personalities divide roughly into four categories: the craftsman, the company man, the jungle fighter (both fox and lion), and, finally, the gamesman.

The goal of persons in the *craftsman* category is the perfection of the work at hand. Careful and painstaking, these people identify only with their own jobs. Because they ignore the broader ramifications of corporate goals, they often feel put upon when other priorities are superimposed on their work. The narrowness of their view often limits them to middle management.

People in the category of the *company man,* on the other hand, identify only with corporate goals. In a literal sense, the company is their life, and their ideal is to fit their desires perfectly to those of the company. They question little and follow blindly. Their loyalty is invaluable, but their vision is limited, and they often end up as second in command.

The term *jungle fighter* is self-explanatory. Lions, because of their great strength and ability, lead naturally but ruthlessly. Foxes scheme and manipulate. While a lion might lead when a disaster strikes, a fox will rarely reach the top.

Lastly, people in the category of the *gamesman* see business life in general, and their careers in particular, in terms of options and possibilities, as if they were playing a game. They like to take calculated risks and are fascinated by techniques and new methods. The contest hypes them up, and like the quarterback on a football team, they communicate their enthusiasm to their peers and subordinates. Unlike the jungle fighter, the gamesman competes not to build an empire or to pile up riches, but to gain fame, glory, and the exhilaration of victory. The main goal is to be known as a winner; the deepest fear, to be labeled as a loser.

In a chapter titled "The Head and the Heart," Maccoby shows how "careerism"—the goal of gaining the top—becomes perverted. Through years of struggle, it becomes an end in itself instead of a means to total fulfillment.

Maccoby follows the inexorable path of the careerist: "To compete and win, he detaches himself from feelings of empathy and compassion. To devote himself to success at work, he detaches himself from family feelings. Ultimately, to gain his goals, he is detached from social responsiveness."

This ambivalence shapes and shades the gamesman's portrait throughout Maccoby's work. Gamesmen often have a kind of adolescent macho; they are not afraid of taking risks, but they lack courage, which demands commitment to goals beyond self-interest. They will gamble to win a "victory" with, say, a better product or systems approach, but will never oppose a socially harmful company policy. Few are greedy or hungry for power; rather, they seek control to escape bureaucratic pressures (some deliberately set up their own small empires within the corporate domain for that very reason). They are interested in money mainly because it is the accepted way of keeping score. Maccoby describes the gamesman as follows:

> The gamesman will not initiate social programs that leave his company in an unfavorable competitive position. Nor will he pass up a chance for a big win in the market. He will trade anywhere he can, whether or not he approves of the regimes . . . .
>
> The gamesman will pollute the environment, even when he privately supports environmentalists, unless the law is such that each corporation must clean up its mess and none is penalized for being cleaner than the others. He will produce and advertise anything he can sell unless food and drug laws or other legislation stops him.
>
> Even when he believes that the government spends too much on weapons, he will make them. Even though he values privacy and is outraged by illegal intrusion of the state in the individual's affairs, he will build the technology that makes this possible. (A gamesman told me that his corporation had tried to build a new automated retail store system without hidden TV cameras to check employees as well as customers. Despite his distaste, his corporation had to build in the spying technology to remain competitive.)

Maccoby concludes that, "given our socioeconomic system, with its stimulation of greed, its orientation to control and predictability, its valuation of power and prestige above justice and creative human development, these fairminded gamesmen may be as good as we can expect from corporate leaders."

What makes this conclusion so disturbing yet pertinent is a second thesis Maccoby puts forward: The direction of the corporation flows from its leaders. In other words, the nature of the leader determines the form and content of social responsibility within the corporation. (More recent empirical research by Brenner and Molander, 1977, supports this thesis.) In an interview, Maccoby (1976b:108) expresses his concern this way:

> The emotional and spiritual underdevelopment of corporate executives is a problem not only for the individual careerist, but also for society as a whole.

Acting through the market, managers serve society's material needs out of their own greedy self-interest. If they meet those needs successfully, they will in turn be rewarded. The system has given us what we asked from it: unprecedented wealth and material comfort.

In the process, executives must use their heads—to analyze demand, to design products, to fashion effective advertising, and so on. And at this, they are extremely adept. The trouble is that, in rising to the top, they sacrifice the capacity to develop values that go beyond winning the game. And the larger society, of which business is but a subsystem, depends for its greatness not only on the head but on the heart—the qualities of courage, compassion, generosity, idealism. If the most dynamic sector of society continues to select out these qualities, where will we find future leaders who possess the moral strength to know right from wrong and the courage to act on those convictions?

Obviously, gamesmen do not sleep with well-thumbed copies of Spinoza's *Ethics* under their pillows. But the triumph of the gamesman need not be inevitable. Indeed, the numbers of successful executives of another sort point to the possibility that what we have called a natural theory of personal ethics *can* work in the real world of American business. When these executives make decisions, they calculate self-interest—but in a much broader context than the gamesman. That is to say, they are concerned with the total, long-term ramifications of their decisions.

Listen, for example, to Irving S. Shapiro (1978:101), chairman of DuPont, explain why he feels that his company has certain social obligations:

> I think we're a means to an end, and while producing goods and providing jobs is our primary function, we can't live successfully in a society if the hearts of its cities are decaying and its people can't support their families. We've got to help make the whole system work, and that involves more than just having a safe workplace and providing jobs for the number of people we can hire. It means that, just as you want libraries, and you want schools, and you want fire departments and police departments, you also want businesses to help do something about unsolved social problems.

Or listen to C. Peter McColough (1975:127–28), president of Xerox, put his responsibility to produce a good return for shareholders in perspective:

> Unless you look after customers and unless you have a good product at the proper price, you're not going to benefit the shareholders. Or to take another argument, unless you have the right employees, properly motivated, and unless you look after them, you're not going to have any wealth in the long run to give to the shareholders. *They all go together.* So I find it difficult to set any priorities among groups—be they shareholders, employees, communities, or countries. [italics added]

What does McColough mean by "community" and by "country"?

... when you operate in an area, you have a responsibility in that area. You have to have an awareness of the needs of the particular area, and your responsibility is to meet those needs, whether they're employment, trade, or trade balances. To broaden the focus to the country, unless you really try to meet the needs of a particular country, you're not likely to be in business very long, or at least very successfully, in that country.

It is not too great a simplification—nor too crass a summation of Spinoza—to call this kind of ethics *enlightened self-interest.* As McColough adds:

I'm not saying the shareholders should be last; that doesn't work, either. If they are disregarded or neglected, you won't be able to raise the capital you may need in the future. Also, they deserve a good return for putting the equity or risk capital into the business. *If the expenditure doesn't give any benefit to the company long-term, it probably shouldn't be pursued.* Now, a lot of expenditures a company makes may, at least in the short run, cost the shareholders money. But if an expenditure is for the purpose of training employees or getting better employees, or motivating them through various benefit programs, or doing work in our society that will make it a better society and therefore a better market, you justify it on that basis. [italics added]

But let us consider specifics. Xerox has a social-service leave program that many shareholders no doubt feel is extraneous to the business of the company. But not necessarily, as McColough points out:

My answers to a shareholder who objected to the program would be several. The first thing I would say is that Xerox has attracted and held, I think, a superior type of employee who has evidenced some interest in the social welfare of this country and other countries where we operate. Our philosophy here has been very important in attracting and retaining such employees. Secondly, there are a lot of problems in our society and other societies, and to the extent that we can remove those problems, we have a better climate and a better economy long-term for business. The third argument is that there is a direct benefit to the employee. When he goes into the voluntary sector, working for the drive for the United Way or a ghetto program, he can only lead through his own persuasiveness, his selling ability, ideas, and so forth—which is really the heart of good management. If we can develop those skills partly outside the company, we have a better employee.

Enlightened self-interest would also seem to suggest that a company develop trust among its employees through job security, equitable pay, excellent working conditions, and participation (in decisions directly affecting them). The reason is clear once we begin to recognize that up to half of labor costs can be attributed to *distrust.* In a more recent article, Maccoby (1978) has written:

The obvious costs of distrust are spontaneous walkouts, strikes and the inevitable slowdowns of the precontract bargaining period. There are also the costs of policing, auditing, work-performance measures and elaborate control systems.

Distrust also contributes to misunderstanding, absenteeism, turnover and sabotage (both intentional and unintentional), all of which are costly, and one might also add costs that could be saved if workers trusted management enough to contribute their ideas and cooperate in solving problems.

What light might an ethics of enlightened self-interest shed on the problem of dealing with bribery? We are told—by hard-nosed gamesmen, I presume—that in most foreign countries corruption is a way of life that U.S. corporations should not even *try* to change (lest they be accused of "exporting morality") and that petty extortion and bribery have become entrenched over time, because these countries and their people have decided they want it that way. *Want* it that way? For the most part, those payments are not really bribes but rather extortion payments made by companies helpless to resist. And the most casual reading of newspapers in developing countries, in which press freedom survives, suggests that the people hardly want such a system. Neil H. Jacoby (1977) quotes a leading Nigerian paper to good effect: "Of all the ills that have so long befallen this country, lack of fair play, godfatherism, unequal opportunities, barefaced cheating in high places remain the most malignant."

The biggest problem by far in developing countries is the inefficiency of their institutions. Corruption is both a cause and a consequence of inefficiency. "Grease" has the effect, not of oil, but of sand in the machinery of an already inefficient bureaucracy. Self-interest would seem to dictate that the multinational corporation try to combat this malaise and thereby improve the extremely difficult operating environment that massive corruption creates and nurtures, rather than try to seek short-term gains from adapting to it. Moreover, the size of the typical multinational, its opportunities for diversifying risks, its frequently unique products or services, and its superior efficiency confer many advantages that can be used for swimming against the tides of local corruption.

Finally, consider the case of bribery within the United States. Silk and Vogel (1976:225–26), in their interviews with executives of leading U.S. corporations, found many who felt that the only way to deal with the problem of stopping dishonest or illegal corporate behavior was for top management itself to adopt high standards, make these crystal clear to everyone below them, and then lay down the line in unmistakable terms. As one businessman put it:

The highest code is something like that expressed by Irwin Miller of Cummins Engine, who called his top management together, after the American Airlines' illegal political contribution was disclosed, to reiterate his policy of "100 percent adherence to 100 percent honesty, even if we lose by it." . . . Miller's way may not only be shorter but better. When it comes to immoral behavior that may benefit the corporation, such as payoffs, the record of opposition is considerably less than 100 percent, although, moral standards aside, there is a lot of truth in the street wisdom that once you start to pay all you can do is pay more. Gulf made payoffs of close to $500,000 to the president of Bolivia to prevent expropriation by a successful regime. Now that the bribe has been disclosed, the new regime has said it will withhold over $50 million still due Gulf in indemnity.

The same businessman reiterated that top management support was crucial to honest behavior within the firm. He cited his own experience:

> With top management support, almost all pressures, including societal, can be resisted, but without it you are in need of deliverance. I once had to obtain a building permit to build a cement silo in greater Chicago. In three communities—one after another—I was asked for a $5,000 payoff by either the mayor or the building inspector. A major Chicago law firm to which I turned for legal help said there was no recourse except the payoff, which they of course would not handle, but they would give me the name of a lawyer who would, billing it as a service. Our sales department gave me to understand they wanted the silo now, not tomorrow, and whatever had to be done to get the permit should be done. I was fortunate on two counts. The president was an Irwin Miller type, and before too long I obtained the permit legally in a community where a citizen-reform ticket had just thrown the syndicate out of power. Business morality, as so many of you have pointed out, is rarely higher than that made visible by top management.

In sum, the purpose of this section has not been to suggest that corporations begin sending out copies of Spinoza's *Ethics* with next year's W-2 forms. Nor has the purpose been to suggest any particular ethical system. Rather, the purpose of the entire chapter has been to stimulate thinking about how ethics and values impinge on managerial decisions throughout the process of strategic planning as well as in many day-to-day decisions. The need for more effective decisions, the climate of public opinion, and the emergence of the amoral gamesman justify the effort.

CHAPTER SEVEN

Decision Support Systems

C hapter 6 introduced the idea of strategic planning or, more exactly, the idea of strategic planning as a response to the turbulent environment in which American business finds itself today. The quality of decisions taken during the planning process is very much predicated on the appropriateness, timeliness, and accuracy of the information available to management. This chapter is about that information.

Of course, not just any information will do. What is needed is a system by which raw data can be converted into information that management can actually use. The term *decision support system* (DSS) describes a "... wide variety of systems which have the direct objective of supporting managerial decision making. Thus, a *management information system* (MIS) is a DSS if, and only if, it is designed with the primary objective of managerial decision support. A computerized data processing system is *not* a DSS—despite the fact that it may, as a byproduct, produce aggregated operating data that are useful to management in making decisions. Only those systems that have the direct and primary objective of supporting managerial decision making are considered DSSs" (King, 1978).

Despite the close relationship between the DSS concept and the MIS concept, according to King (1978), other systems also qualify as DSSs. For example, a strategic planning system that incorporates organizational planning activities such as forecasting and econometric models may also be a DSS. So too may a simulation model that has the purpose of permitting managers to ask "What if?" questions concerning alternative strategies and courses of action they wish to evaluate. In sum, there are many varieties of DSSs, but they are all coupled through their common objective—namely, management decision support.

This chapter is in five sections. The first section expands on the importance of information to contemporary business operations. We shall see how specific companies have been able to make the DSS and MIS concepts work. But we must not paint too rosy a picture, for these companies tend to be the exceptions to the rule. What then is the problem with the way information is used in the modern corporation? Why has not the full potential of the computer been realized? Three reasons are suggested. First, business managers, until only recently, simply did not understand how computers worked. Second, computer technology—again, until only recently—has remained rather primitive. Third, and most important, we lack good computer models of how the external environment operates.

The next three sections of the chapter focus on the operation of the external environment. In the second section we shall look at a variety of approaches to forecasting technological change: trend analysis, expert opinion, monitoring, substitution theory, scenario writing, and cross-impact analysis. While it might sound as if the section were taken from the notebook of a tenth-century wizard, it really is nothing but applied common sense.

The third section considers forecasting in the economic environment. After briefly examining what is meant by the term *business fluctuations* (or business cycles), we consider several types of economic forecasts, including deterministic forecasts, cyclic indicators, and econometric models. But technological and economic forecasting are not enough; strategic planning must also rely on sociopolitical forecasts. The next section of the chapter is thus devoted to how sociopolitical forecasting aids strategic planning. The final section of this chapter summarizes the status of corporate forecasting programs and lists some of the keys for implementing successful ones. ☐

THE IMPORTANCE OF INFORMATION

The idea that information is powerful is not new. "A wise man is strong, yea, a man of knowledge increaseth strength," Solomon said. In 1597 Francis Bacon wrote with even greater concision, "Knowledge is power." In the 1920s Alfred P. Sloan rose to the top of General Motors and proceeded to overthrow Henry Ford's dominance of the auto industry (see Exhibit 7–1). Sloan was soon at the top because he demonstrated an ability to marshal information around points of decision. The ideas of these three men are no less true today. Indeed, because we are now living in an Information Society, they may in fact be truer than ever.

Information and Control

As we saw in Chapter 6, one way in which managers can respond to rapid environmental change is to apply the concept of strategic planning. But to do this effectively, managers must link their plans to change. Because information provides feedback, it is the medium of control.

Consider the case of Campbell Taggart in coping with the 1973–74 inflation. During this period, rapid price increases in key industries hit the baking industry hard. Compared with 1971, prices paid in 1974 were up over 400 percent for sugar, 40 percent for flour, and 300 percent for lard. Most of the baking companies found it difficult to make profits in this inflationary environment. But Campbell Taggart was the exception to the general decline in the profits of the large bakers. How was Campbell Taggart actually able to increase profits? "The key ingredient of these increased profits," *Business Week* reported (December 7, 1974), "is a control system that monitors costs and pricing so precisely that Campbell Taggart can instantaneously pass on cost increases to its consumers—something that its competitors often cannot do." The control system at Campbell Taggart is linked to specific management procedures. If a bad profit trend develops over two or three weeks at a plant, the manager can expect a visit from a team of specialists who analyze sales figures, inspect production facilities, and search for inefficiencies. Key efficiency indicators also revealed by the computer (such as the number of product pounds sold per sales route and the amount of bread returned to the plant stale) can alert the inspection team to problem areas even before they arrive.

Other companies are also learning to use management information to gain a modicum of control over a rapidly changing environment. For example, one of the largest manufacturing companies in the country has used it to develop an equal employment compliance program. The control system compares company employment by category of workers (women, blacks, people with Spanish surnames, and so on) with the population in each of two hundred plant locations. The system maintains a record of affirmative action efforts by category of worker for a number of activities, such as job-applicant interviews, job offers, promotions, and training. Each company location has equal employment objectives, and actual performance compared with objectives is monitored in this management information system. The corporate employee relations group gives seminars for management in order to create an understanding of the compliance standards of the Equal Employment Opportunity

EXHIBIT 7–1   Alfred P. Sloan and the Power of Information

Alfred P. Sloan, Jr., reconstituted General Motors in the 1920s so successfully that most large U.S. corporations, including Ford, have come to run on principles that Sloan developed. He had previously built the Hyatt Roller Bearing Company to the point where William C. Durant, the brilliant assembler of GM, was glad to pay $13.5 million for Hyatt. Sloan liked and respected Durant, whose own operating style was intuitive. But too many decisions crowded in haphazard fashion on Durant's desk with its ten busy telephones. In 1920 Sloan produced a memo on how the management should be restructured; he recognized that in so large an enterprise a high degree of operating authority must be left in the divisions, but he built a strong central staff and a system of forecasts against which performance was measured. Sloan, in short, dealt effectively with one of the fundamental problems of modern life: how to handle information within an orderly framework of policymaking. He rose to the top because he demonstrated an ability to marshal information around the points of decision.

Source: Photo courtesy of MIT Historical Collections, Cambridge, Massachusetts.

Commission. This company has been hit with a relatively small number of EEOC suits and has not suffered serious penalties from litigation with the government.

This research-based equal employment compliance program provides a typical example of the kinds of information control systems that will be standard practice in future management responses to the large number of government regulations initiated in the last decade. As we saw in Chapter 3, the government has created a regulatory environment in which firms with a strong management information capability will have a definite edge.

In sum, the most significant function of information control systems is to make sure that an implemented plan is living up to expectations. Once a project is being carried out by a company, the need for control arises because the future cannot be predicted with certainty and because the conditions leading to the original project change *on account of* the project.

Information and Business Challengers

Good, reliable data can do more than help managers implement plans and keep those plans up to date; it can also help a company deal more effectively with its challengers. An excellent case in point is Weyerhaeuser, a forest products company (see Griffith, 1978). The company prefers to get on top of an issue before the issue gets into the papers, to "surface concerns," and to participate in any legislation it sees coming. For example, though small forest owners in Washington State were not very keen about forest-practices legislation, Weyerhaeuser saw it coming and was in on the writing of it. The detailed forest-practices law that was finally enacted illustrates Weyerhaeuser's effectiveness in getting in early on issues and using a process that might be called "seizing the data base." For instance, environmentalists had wanted clear-cutting strips to be no wider than a quarter of a mile, the presumed limit of open space that deer and elk would cross after dark to feed; Weyerhaeuser, however, came up with meticulous counts to show that animal droppings were just as numerous in the center of a wide patch as on the edge.

Thus rather than respond to challengers with negative resistance after the fact, the company makes every effort, in the words of George Weyerhaeuser, the president, "to be ahead of criticism—to be our own advance critics." Weyerhaeuser's most effective gambit, as illustrated by the forest-practices legislation, is to supply accurate data to congressional staffs. "We're acting in our self-interest, but you can believe us," Weyerhaeuser says. "We don't lie to 'em." The art, he believes, is to provide solid data and sound criteria "before guidelines drawn by attorneys in response to the loudest activist voices are imposed upon industry." The company fights to keep unwanted restrictions from being frozen into law; it urges instead that they be written into regulations. And what is written into regulations the company often seeks to have reduced to guidelines. In advance operations, Bernard L. Orell, a veteran forester who heads the company's lobbying and public affairs, has shrewdly made it a practice to tell legislators dispassionately what he thinks are the soundest arguments they will hear from the other side; as he says, "We don't want a friend to take a Weyerhaeuser, or an industry, position and get blind-sided."

Weyerhaeuser is not the only company that has learned to put information to use in coping with challenges. For example, L.H. Berul (1977) of the

Aspen Systems Corporation reports on a system that can be used against product liability. Product liability costs have become a threat to the very existence of a growing number of companies. Since 1967, increasingly strict interpretations by the courts, which have fixed responsibility on the manufacturer for any product defects that cause injury, have had a compound effect on escalating claims and insurance premium rates. Most products eventually spawn some form of liability action. What can a corporation do to protect itself? One answer is to create an ongoing "defense data base" that contains and gives instant access to all information on product-related activities from design to marketplace. Such a data base, Berul writes, is "a strong prophylactic for keeping the company out of trouble." It is quite possible that insurers will establish a "preferred risk" category for firms having the comprehensive information capability to minimize liability exposure and provide documentation for administrative hearings and lawsuits.

The Crisis in Business Information

So far we have been talking about how business can use information. And, unfortunately, we have been looking at exceptions rather than typical firms. The fact is that most companies do not do a very good job at tapping the power in their information systems. But what exactly are the information needs of modern managers? A Financial Executives Institute (1970:52–53) survey found that 95 percent of the respondents agreed with the following statements: A management information system should be designed to provide selected, decision-oriented information needed by management to plan, control, and evaluate the activities of the corporation within a framework that emphasizes profit planning, performance planning, and control at all levels. It should involve a systematic approach toward providing information that is timely, meaningful, and readily accessible. It should allow for consideration of the current and future management information needs of the administrative, financial, marketing, production, operating, and research functions. And, finally, a successful management information system should have the capacity to provide the environmental, competitive, or regulatory information required for evaluating corporate objectives, long-range planning (strategy), and short-range planning (tactics).

As business faces environmental pressures, more rapid change, and a better-educated and more articulate labor force, information requirements for business decision making have indeed increased. The reality of the situation, however, is that business managers today receive more information than they know what to do with. Reports, letters, memos, telephone calls, summaries of meetings, journals, and books flood in. And—thanks to Xerox, computers, and college English courses—very little information gets condensed. In short, many managers are faced with data overload. As William H. Gruber and John S. Niles (1976:131–32) have correctly observed:

It is difficult to find a coordinating force responsible for the management information system in many companies. As one goes from firm to firm searching for a central link that coordinates the system, all one finds are frustrated managers. These managers appear to recognize that there is critical information easily available to them, but they do not understand how to find it or even how to find the time to look for it. . . . In sum, *the information needs of management and the capabilities of computers have not been matched up* [italics added].

Problems in the Use of Computers. One possible reason for the failure to link computer capabilities with management needs is that until recently managers have not been effectively educated to use the computer. Moreover, the professional computer staffs in most companies have not been qualified to program computers for management needs. Not surprisingly, until only recently most managers took a dim view of the computer's usefulness—or, more accurately, a dim view of the more sophisticated uses of the computer. As F.G. Withington (1974:100) points out in his analysis of the history of computer utilization, computers were used and accepted in the early years by managers in the somewhat limited, though still important, role of "paper pushers." From 1952 to 1966, Withington says, computers "were highly practical and oriented to tasks that were well understood. They were designed to support batch processing methods, which were satisfactory to most users because they knew no better way to handle large volumes of transactions; hence these machines were put to a wide variety of uses, appearing everywhere that large quantities of information were to be processed in a routine manner."

A second reason why computers have not really been used as aids to management decision making involves not the education of managers but the technology of the computer itself. Many operations that involve the restructuring of large files of data, telecommunications, and interactive time-share processing were not feasible ten years ago because computer technology was either too expensive or unavailable. Fortunately, the technology of computers is constantly evolving—from vacuum tubes to transistors to large integrated circuits and on to satellite computers and magnetic bubble memories. And each of these technological changes spells faster, cheaper data processing. For example, in 1955 a mix of about seventeen hundred computer operations (including payroll, discount computation, file maintenance, and report preparation) required 375 seconds and cost $14.54. In 1975 the same mix could be done in 5 seconds for $.20.

A third reason why computers have not fulfilled the information needs of management stems from the lack of good models for establishing a useful data base. A prerequisite to utilization of information is a clear understanding—a theory or model, if you will—of the phenomenon in which the manager is interested. The model, in short, is the key to the data. Because scientists have more and better theories of the physical world, we hear less about their drowning in information; when scientists seek data, they are likely to know—better than business managers do—what they are after. Russell L. Ackoff (1967:149) has provided some insight into the business managers' situation:

> For a manager to know what information he needs he must be aware of each type of decision he should make (as well as does) and he must have an adequate model of each. These conditions are seldom satisfied. Most managers have some conception of at least some of the types of decisions they must make. Their conceptions, however, are likely to be deficient in a very critical way, a way that follows from an important principle of scientific economy: the less we understand a phenomenon, the more variables we require to explain it. Hence, the manager who does not understand the phenomenon he controls plays it "safe" and, with respect to information, wants "everything." The MIS designer, who has even less understanding of the relevant phenomenon than the manager, tries to provide even more than everything. He therefore increases what is already an overload of irrelevant information.

To help crystallize the point, we can consider the example of a good model of the macroenvironment used in the aircraft industry. As Boeing knows, the mere growth of air traffic is not the key to selling aircraft. More important is selecting a plane that most efficiently serves each route. Therefore, Boeing is highly attuned to the ever-shifting traffic patterns of the airlines. In fact, seventy airlines feed Boeing's computers data on the number of people that fly between each city every day, the frequency of service, and just about every other available fact. As a result, Boeing can forecast with some accuracy the combination of plane sizes that airlines will need to make the best return on their investments. Boeing's data base also indicates that because of the hundreds of aging (and thus inefficient) aircraft in the fleets, airlines will have no choice except to buy planes in the years ahead. Moreover, Boeing factors into its data base significant political issues and events—for example, the strict enforcement of federal noise standards, which could force retirement of older planes. Boeing researchers also factor in social trends—for example, the shrinking size (and presumably comfort) of automobiles, which could cause fewer people to want to drive more than a few hundred miles.

But, again, we are looking at an exception. Most companies have much more simplistic notions about their environment than Boeing. In 1967 Frank J. Aguilar examined the ways in which executives in the chemical industry looked for or obtained information about events and relationships outside their companies that would assist them in charting their companies' courses of action. Few firms, he found, attempted any systematic means for gathering strategic information.

A decade later the Green Giant Company attempted a similar survey. Based on a random sample of sixty-nine corporations from the *Fortune* 500 list, the results were as follows: Thirty-five companies indicated they had no formalized way of scanning their environment for social and political future trends. Twenty companies reported only limited future trends analyses, with input mainly from secondary sources or studies or occasionally from senior executives. Ten firms stated that they had formalized such activities in some fashion, but that these were divided among several departments and had limited significance for overall corporate planning. Only four of the sixty-nine firms surveyed indicated that they had any means of systematically scanning the environment for future social, political, technological, and economic trends.

In sum, the moral of this section is obvious: The process of gathering strategic information for coping with the changing environment of business is far from being systematic or complete (see Exhibit 7–2). The complexity of a company's macroenvironment, the rate at which change is taking place, and the in-

EXHIBIT 7–2   Modes of Scanning the Environment

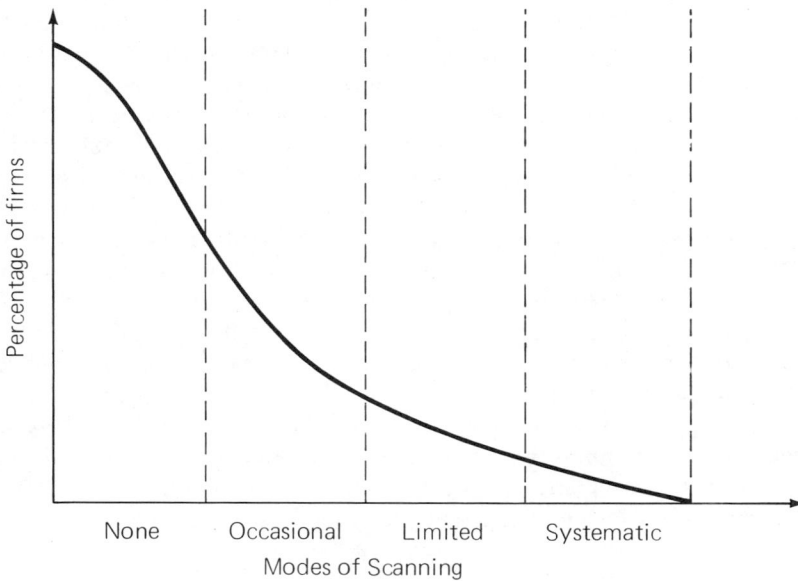

How do executives obtain information about events outside their companies that would help them in strategic planning? All indications suggest a pattern somewhat like that shown in the figure above. Most firms have no formal means at all for scanning their environments; some engage in occasional or limited analysis; and only a small minority have a systematic, continuing means of scanning their environment for significant change.

completeness of conceptual apparatus for defining the relevant characteristics of the environment, however, certainly do not constitute a good excuse for ignoring the importance of information. The assessment of a company's informational needs can be completed only when its strategy is known or the strategic alternatives being considered have been identified; information must be gathered and understood in relation to the company's goals, policies, and plans. As we have seen from the examples in this section, it is possible to organize the gathering and integrating of environmental data essential for successful strategic planning. In the following sections we look at a variety of approaches for gaining useful information in the technological, economic, and political environments.

TECHNOLOGY FORECASTING

Technology forecasting (TF) uses logical, reproducible methods to forecast, in explicit terms, the character and rate of technological advance. What separates it from crystal ball gazing is the reproducible and quantifiable nature of technology forecasting. Different investigators, applying the same forecasting technique to the same data base, should obtain the same results. The technology forecaster should not hide behind vagueness, like the astrologer, but should make definitive statements. The statement that "some day urban mass transit will be able to pick up passengers without decreasing speed" is not a technology forecast. The statement that "by 1985 at least 75 percent of all passenger trains between cities of more than 1 million people will have the capability of picking up passengers at intermediate stations without reducing speed" is.

When done properly, technology forecasting can provide managers with information about the probable directions and rate of technical progress. More specifically, technology forecasting can be used to help identify areas where product improvements or replacement will be needed and to provide an early warning of possible ecological, social, and political consequences of technical progress. In this section we will discuss the nature of technology forecasting, some of the important techniques, a number of the nontechnical factors affecting forecasts, and, most important, how a company can use TF to assist in the performance of management functions.

The Basis of Technology Forecasting

How is it possible to predict scientific breakthroughs, fortuitous accidents, and strokes of genius? The answer is that it is not possible to make such predictions and that technology forecasting is not based on the hypothesis that such predictions are possible. Rather, the theoretical viability of TF is based on the supposition that, in a reasonably free society, expressed and implied societal needs, business and government efforts to meet those needs, and the technical activities resulting from those efforts will combine to produce inexorable forces for technical progress. As John H. Vanston (1975) has observed, although a great number of individual decisions, each based on differing incentives and circumstances, will be involved, the total result of these decisions will form a pattern that can be reasonably well forecasted and analyzed. Just as the demographer cannot predict the eventual size of a given family but can predict the trend of the total population; as the economist cannot predict the effect of a financial policy on a given business but can predict the effect on the economy as a whole; as the sales manager cannot predict the effect of a sales campaign on the buying habits of a particular customer but can predict the increase in overall sales—so the technology forecaster cannot predict the success of an individual research project but can predict the rate and direction of progress in a given technical area. The basis for this type of forecasting is the seven stages of technological innovation discussed in Chapter 2. In other words, we *know* technology follows a general pattern in its development; the process has a certain logic.

Methods of Technology Forecasting

Although there are many particular applications of general techniques, and different names for similar techniques, in a general sense all technology forecasting methods are based on one or more of the following basic principles: (1) trend analysis, (2) the appraisal of expert opinion, (3) the monitoring of various sources for indications of potential changes, (4) substitution theory, and (5) alternative scenarios. In practice, most specific techniques rely on some combination of these principles. Finally, most of these techniques can also be applied to forecasting in nontechnological areas; in this sense, their appearance here is an arbitrary decision.

Trend Analysis. Among other things, this method of forecasting involves comparison of related trends. Through trend analysis, technical advances in one area can serve as precursors for advances in different areas. A classic example of matched trends can be taken from the aircraft industry: For many years transport aircraft speeds lagged approximately nine to eleven years behind combat aircraft speeds. If one wished to forecast the speed of transport aircraft, therefore, one could simply look at the speed of combat aircraft about ten years earlier.

Trend analysis can also involve the process of extrapolation, which can be illustrated with another example from the aviation industry. In 1952 Dr. H.V. Noble and his colleagues at the Avionics Laboratory at Wright Air Force Base studied the number of component electronic circuits involved in mainline Air Force bombers since World War II. The trends based on this information allowed them to extrapolate the number of components that would be necessary for the next major aircraft then being planned—namely, the B-58 bomber, as shown in Exhibit 7–3.

**EXHIBIT 7–3   Trend Analysis in Technology Forecasting: Number of
Components Needed for the B-58 Aircraft**

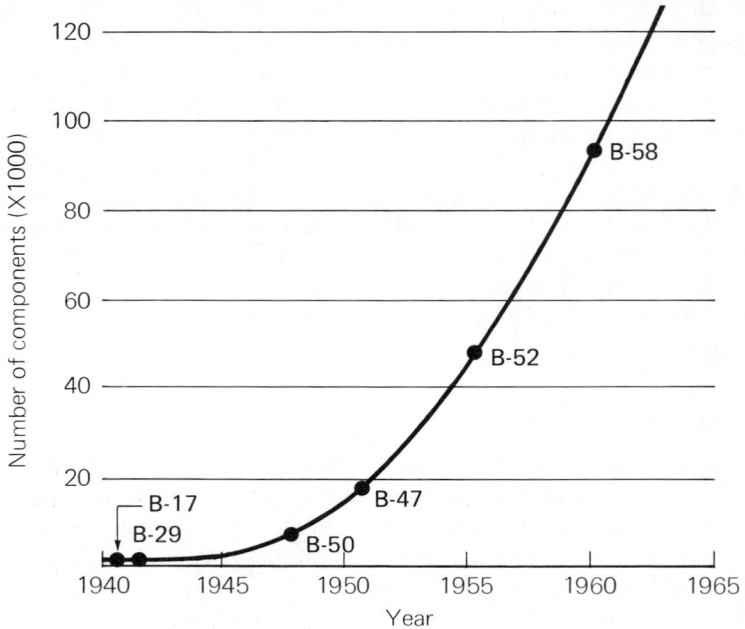

Source: Data from H.V. Nobel, "Microelectronic Progress," *Ordinance* (May–June 1975).

To understand the usefulness of trend analysis in technology forecasting, let us consider Bright's (1968:361–63) example of an airplane manufacturer in 1940. According to Bright, the manufacturer first plots the maximum speeds of aircraft and gets the curve indicated in Exhibit 7–4 by the solid line; then he extrapolates or extends the curve (indicated by projection A), which leads him to think something must be wrong. The projected speeds violate the speed of sound (what his technical people claim is the theoretical limit of air speed), and the only way the projections could come about, it would seem, is for aircraft to begin to employ some new technology. He investigates (or better yet has a young engineer investigate for him) and learns that development of the jet engine is indeed well under way. In England a jet engine company has already been formed and an engine actually tested; in fact, by 1939 the British government had become so impressed that it had agreed to finance all future work by the company.

EXHIBIT 7–4   Trend Analysis in Technology Forecasting: 1940 Projections of Aircraft Speeds

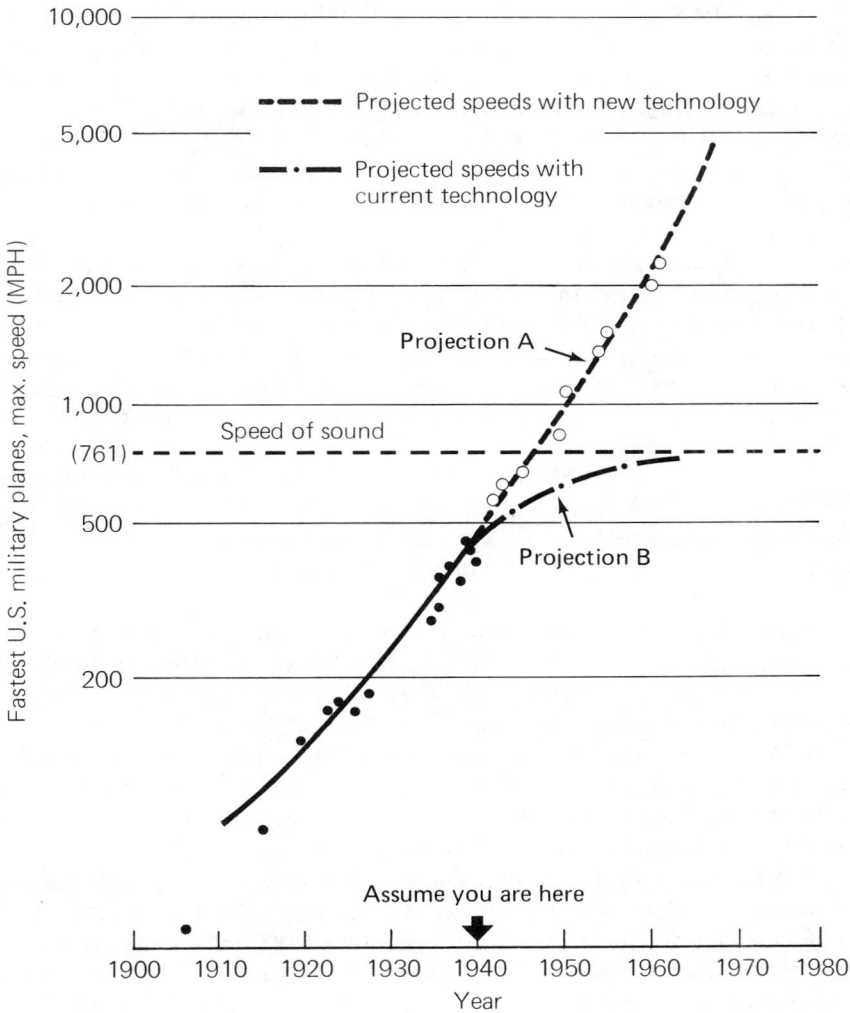

Source: *Technology Forecasting for Industry and Government: Methods and Application,* James R. Bright, Ed., © 1968, p. 362. Adapted by permission of Prentice-Hall, Inc., Englewood Cliffs, New Jersey.

This information forces several management decisions on our hypothetical American manufacturer. First, the most obvious: Will the company want to move with this new technology (projection A) or, as did so many U.S. plane manufacturers in 1940, continue to turn out prop-driven aircraft and drain the last bit of performance out of that technology (projection B)? But the information leads to even more subtle decisions. According to the manufacturer's projections, supersonic speeds are just a few years away, and at such speeds current aircraft frames are unlikely to work. Should the company begin aerodynamic research on new aircraft designs? Also, at such speeds the pilots of military aircraft will have greater difficulty firing their weapons. Should the company begin research and development on new fire-control systems?

Expert Opinion. Probably the most common method of forecasting is intuition. It seems quite logical to ask the most qualified person in the appropriate field his or her opinion of the future. Although the prediction may turn out to be accurate, it may also turn out to be quite wrong. Despite their qualifications, experts, like laymen, are subject to their own biases, prejudices, and idiosyncrasies, as the following examples (adapted from Clarke, 1962) illustrate.

- When Thomas Edison announced that he was working on an incandescent lamp, the British Parliament set up a committee of experts to investigate. The committee reported that Edison's ideas were "good enough for our trans-Atlantic friends . . . but unworthy of the attention of practical and scientific men."
- The airplane, the telephone, the space rocket, the atomic bomb, the computer, and radio and television broadcasting all met derision shortly before becoming practical realities. The derision usually came from leading scientists or engineers, and often from committees of them.
- In 1956, the British astronomer royal, Dr. Woolley, announced to the press that "Space travel is utter bilge." This remark was made after President Eisenhower had announced the United States' satellite program. The very next year the Russians launched *Sputnik I.*
- Although several thousand German V-2 rockets had blitzed London and Belgium in World War II and caused great loss of life, Dr. Vannevar Bush advised the U.S. Senate in December 1945 that a 3,000-mile–range, bomb-carrying rocket was "impossible." He added: "I say, technically, I don't think anyone in the world knows how to do such a thing . . . . I think we can leave it out of our thinking. I wish the American public would leave it out of their thinking."

It is difficult for even the most energetic investigators to keep fully abreast of all research going on in their fields. Even if experts are completely informed in their own fields, it is quite conceivable that they would be unaware of advances in supporting fields. Yet advances in one technology may lead to the dramatic advances in others. To some extent, the disadvantages of basing forecasts on the opinion of a single expert can be alleviated by gathering together a committee of experts. But, unfortunately, any committee has inherent shortcomings: the reluctance of some members to express their opinions, the domination by certain individuals, a possible bandwagon psychology, and a tendency to accept compromise positions.

Because of these shortcomings involved in forecasting through expert opinion, a research group at RAND Corporation devised the *Delphi technique* (named for Apollo's oracle at Delphi), a set of procedures for eliciting the opinion of a group of people, usually experts, in such a way as to reduce the undesirable aspects of group interaction. In its traditional form, Delphi forecasting calls for:

—A prediction of important events in the area in question, from each expert in a group, in the form of a brief statement;

—A clarification of these statements by the investigator;

—The successive, individual requestioning of each of the experts, combined with feedback supplied from the other experts via the investigator.

The process of requestioning is designed to eliminate misinterpretation of the questions and the feedback and to bring to light knowledge available to one or a few members of the group but not to all of them.

An example from the field of molecular biology (adapted from North and Pyke, 1969) will make clear how this set of procedures works to generate a consensus of opinion. In the first round of questioning, the experts are asked to list developments that they think will occur in their fields within, say, the next century. One expert, for instance, might predict that people will be able to control heredity to a large extent within the next 100 years. The investigators then edit all experts' predictions and prepare a questionnaire for the second round. In the second round, the experts are given questionnaires that ask them to estimate certain numerical quantities—say, the date by which we shall have chemical control over hereditary defects through molecular engineering. By asking for such simple numerical estimates, the investigators can easily summarize the responses in statistical fashion.

In the third round, the digested information from the second round of questioning is fed back to each of the experts; they are then asked to scrutinize their first responses. In addition, if an expert's first response falls outside the middle (interquartile) range of responses, it is customary to ask his or her reasons for the "extreme" opinion. The questionnaire for the third round of a study of the future of molecular biology might look like that shown in Exhibit 7–5. Experience has shown that obtaining reasons from respondents whose opinions fall outside the interquartile range achieves two things: It permits the investigator to refine the original question and to state the minority opinions,

EXHIBIT 7–5   Forecasting with the Delphi Technique: Requestioning Experts

DESCRIPTION OF POTENTIAL OCCURRENCE:	CONSENSUS OR DISCORDANCE TO DATE:	IN YOUR OPINION, BY WHAT-YEAR DOES THE PROBABILITY OF OCCURRENCE REACH		IF YOUR 50% ESTIMATE FALLS WITHIN EITHER THE EARLIER OR THE LATER PERIOD INDICATED BELOW, BRIEFLY STATE YOUR REASON FOR THIS OPINION.
FEASIBILITY OF CHEMICAL CONTROL OVER HEREDITARY DEFECTS THROUGH MOLECULAR ENGINEERING	CONSENSUS IS THAT IT WILL OCCUR; THERE IS DISAGREEMENT AS TO WHEN.	50%?	90%?	WHY BEFORE 1982? _____ _____ _____ OR, WHY AFTER 2033? _____ _____ _____ _____

Third-Round Questionnaire

DESCRIPTION OF POTENTIAL OCCURRENCE:	MAJORITY CONSENSUS TO DATE:	MINORITY OPINION	RECORD YOUR ESTIMATE
FEASIBILITY (THOUGH NOT NECESSARILY ACCEPTANCE) OF CHEMICAL CONTROL OVER SOME HEREDITARY DEFECTS BY MODIFICATION OF GENES THROUGH MOLECULAR ENGINEERING	BY 2000 A.D.	WILL TAKE LONGER, OR NEVER EVEN OCCUR, BECAUSE IT WOULD NECESSITATE INTERVENTION DURING EMBRYONIC DEVELOPMENT, WHEN THE FETUS IS INACCESSIBLE, AND HENCE WOULD REQUIRE PRIOR DEVELOPMENT OF TECHNIQUES OF GESTATION IN VITRO.	50%-YEAR _____ _____ _____ 90%-YEAR _____ _____ _____ _____

Fourth-Round Questionnaire

and then to feed this information back to the whole group on a fourth round of questioning. Almost invariably, a number of the experts change their estimates after rethinking the question, and the consensus narrows as a result. In the fourth round, once the investigator has digested the new estimates and calculated the new consensus on the year of achievement, he or she can approach the experts with another questionnaire. The fourth-round questionnaire in Exhibit 7–5 shows how the description of the occurrence under study has been refined. If it seems desirable, the questioner can manipulate the results of this version and go on to a fifth, or even sixth, round.

In sum, the Delphi method achieves a true consensus without the sacrifice of important opinion and background information and avoids the difficulties and impracticalities of group discussion. The investigator helps the experts toward a consensus by rewording the questions, and the experts help themselves toward a consensus by rethinking the problem in the light of divergent estimates. The method has worked quite successfully. In 1973, for example, four big companies—DuPont, Scott Paper, Lever Brothers, and Monsanto—were getting a peek at the 1980s. The four were backers of Project Aware, an attempt to predict long-range changes in the social, economic, and technological environment that the companies will face in the next decade. As the sample findings shown in Exhibit 7–6 suggest, if such forecasts do nothing else, they at least highlight trends that businesses need to be aware of.

Monitoring. In 1799 Coleridge provided a beautifully succinct rationale for monitoring as a forecasting technique: "Often do the spirits of great events stride before the events/And in today already walks tomorrow." That coming events do indeed cast their shadows before is generally recognized by all competent managers. The manager who failed to keep abreast of activities related to his or her company or division would probably have a very short tenure in that position. But how many have a very carefully planned and managed sys-

**EXHIBIT 7–6   The Delphi Technique: An Application in
                the Chemical Industry**

Event	Percent probability
Many chemical pesticides phased out	95
National health insurance enacted	90
Spending on environmental quality exceeds 6% of GNP	90
Insect hormones widely used as pesticides	80
Community review of factory locations	80
Substantial understanding of baldness and skin wrinkling	40
A modest (3%) value-added tax passed	40
Wide use of computers in elementary schools	25
Development of cold vaccines	20
Autos banned in central areas of at least seven cities	20
Breeder reactors banned for safety reasons	20

Source: Data from *Project Aware* (Menlo Park, Calif.: Institute for the Future, 1973). Reprinted by permission.

tem for monitoring selected data? Because it is impossible to adequately monitor all information sources for all material that might be relevant to the company, the need for a system to monitor selected data seems clear. A formal monitoring system would include at least four elements:

1. Searching the environment for signals that may be forerunners of significant changes;
2. Identifying possible alternative consequences if these signals are not spurious and if the trends that they suggest continue;
3. Choosing those parameters, policies, events, and decisions that should be followed in order to verify the true speed and direction of the issue and the effects it could have for the company;
4. Presenting the data from the foregoing steps in a timely and appropriate manner for management's use in decisions about the organization's reaction.

James R. Bright (1972:8) writes:

> Monitoring includes much more than simply "scanning." It also includes much more than collection of traditional library reference lists. The essence is evaluation and continuous review. Monitoring, philosophically speaking, is the acceptance of uncertainty as to meaning and rate of change of developments. The forecaster "runs scared"—he tries to stay ahead of developments and their implications—and presents his conclusion relatively late. His contribution lies in providing early warning and in remaining open-minded about possible significance. Monitoring includes search, consideration of alternative possibilities and their effects, selection of critical parameters for observation, and a conclusion based on synthesis of progress and implications.

Properly applied monitoring techniques can be very useful forecasting methods. For example, a study conducted by the British intelligence service after World War II revealed that the most accurate predictions of German military intentions were those based on a study of German newspapers. In an open society in peacetime, a tremendous amount of useful information about current and projected research is presented at professional conferences, in technical papers, in contracting notices, in requests for proposals, and in other sources, such as patent applications, which provide an excellent indication of the nature of advanced research efforts.

A number of companies conduct structured monitoring programs. One of the most successful is supervised by Richard Davis at the Whirlpool Corporation. For several years Davis has used and improved monitoring systems to give his company advantages in the consumer market. Perhaps his most important forecast to date was the emergence of prepressed fibers, a prediction that not only prevented the company from building a large clothes-iron plant, but also permitted it to be the first on the market with a dryer designed especially for the new fabrics. Over the years, Mr. Davis has developed a computer-based WIN (Whirlpool Information Network) system that involves all of the key company people in information-gathering activities (see Exhibit 7–7) and provides periodic and spot forecasts in all fields of interest to the company (see Exhibit 7–8).

Substitution Theory. Although it is important to be able to predict when a new technology will become available, a company manager is also quite interested in the rate at which the new technology will replace the old. Based on a combination of theory and observation, Fisher and Pry (1971) have developed a formula for making such predictions. Application of this formula to historical examples has indicated that forecasts based on a 20 to 25 percent rate of displacement per year are quite accurate. Even predictions based on a 5 to 10 percent displacement rate are of value. One example of the use of the technique is illustrated in Exhibit 7–9, in which a forecast of the displacement of sailing ships by steam-driven ships is compared with actual displacement observations. The 1860 forecast based on an 18 percent rate of displacement proved quite accurate.

Clearly, if one understands the dynamics of displacement, one has a better idea of whether to enter a new technological field. Looking ahead, it will be interesting to see if the rate at which videotape recorder–equipped televisions (such as Sony's Betamax) replace color televisions is the same rate at which color televisions replaced black and white sets.

Alternative Scenarios. Forecasting by means of alternative scenarios can help managers not only to accommodate the uncertainty of future events, but also to profit by it. In essence, this method involves the development of a series of possible sequences of future events—or, in the idiom of the futurist, *scenarios*—that might affect company prospects, profits, and programs. Once these scenarios have been produced, a plan is developed for each of the projected futures. These separate plans are then evaluated to determine similarities and differences. After evaluating the probability that each scenario will approximate future events, management evolves an overall plan that effectively accommodates as broad a range of scenarios as possible, while giving consideration to the relative probabilities of each plan's actually occurring. Until the mid-1970s, multiple plans had little use in most companies. But today, because it is increasingly clear that no planner or forecaster will ever bat 1.000, alternative scenarios are rapidly becoming standard operating procedure.

The Shell Oil Company serves as an example of a major company that has used alternative scenarios in their planning. According to Zentner (1975), prior to 1972 the company had developed an energy forecast for planning purposes that was a ten-year analysis of energy supply and demand. Although it used the best economic, demographic and political premises available, this forecast approach came under question as predictability began to decay in the

**EXHIBIT 7–7   Monitoring as a Forecasting Technique: WIN
Information-Gathering Form**

WIN	WHIRLPOOL INFORMATION NETWORK	SUMMARY

1. TITLE (OR CITATION):	3. *Class category:
	4. *WIN summary no.:
	5. Division:
	6. Department:
2. AUTHOR(S) (OR SUBMITTOR):	7. Report date:
	8. Report file no.:
	9. No. of pages:

10. SUMMARY:

Columbia Gas will import \$1.4 billion in LNG from Sonstrack, Algeria Oil Agency. Will buy from El Paso. Price \$0.50/10^6BTU. Gas runs 1030–1200, BTU/ft^3, ergo priced 52.5¢–60¢/1000 ft^3. Pipeline gas Pittsburg--today--38.64¢/1000 ft^3--Boston--69.21¢/1000 ft^3.

11. SUPPLEMENTARY NOTES:

13. KEY WORDS: (Suggested by Author)

14. *WIN INDEX TERMS:

12. DISTRIBUTION:

PROPRIETARY INFORMATION. This information is CONFIDENTIAL to the extent it is original, and is intended for the exclusive use of authorized personnel of Whirlpool Corporation and its subsidiaries, Warwick Electronics, Inc. and Heil-Quaker Corporation.

S8W001020

*NOTE: ITEMS 3, 4 AND 14 WILL BE COMPLETED BY INFORMATION CENTER.

Source: Reproduced courtesy of Whirlpool Corporation, Benton Harbor, Michigan.

EXHIBIT 7—8   WIN System Information Distribution Form

Whirlpool
CORPORATION

PAGE NO.
PROJECT NO.

TEXTILE TOPICS

I.   Cotton

1.   The Cotton Producers Institute has allocated more than one million dollars in research funds to try to develop Permanent Press cotton. Some of the best known organizations (Stanford Research, Gillette, Battelle, Gagliardi and Southern Research) have been brought into the picture with grants ranging from $7,500 to $120,000.

2.   U.S. needs of cotton from the 1969 crop will be down by 700,000 bales from last years usage of 8.9 million.

3.   The three big U.S. shirt manufacturers have begun production of a line of pure finish cotton shirts. Prices for these garments will range from $8 to $20 per garment.

WHAT THESE MEAN TO WHIRLPOOL: A part of the cotton industry realizes that their market has shrunk and is trying to do something about it. Unfortunately, the projects they are funding are the same projects which have not been successful in the past. The projected usage of 700,000 fewer bales in 1969 reflects the textile industry's attitude toward cotton. The entry of high priced cotton shirts should not be construed as a change in philosophy. There will be few of them made from those people who have been slow in shifting to synthetic/cotton blends.

4,   Cotton is witnessing a big intrafamily feud these days. It seems that growers expected high 1967 prices to carry into 1968, so they planted low bearing, high quality varieties. Prices fell and their incomes tumbled. Now they blame textile mills, ginners, Cotton Council, and just about everyone for their troubles. They say they will revert to high yield, lower quality varieties in 1969.

WHAT THIS MEANS TO WHIRLPOOL: Just more fuel on the fire that is burning out cotton and promoting synthetics. It seems cotton will remain controlled by individualists and will never become an industry.

II.   Synthetics

1.   Monsanto announced recently that they will start production soon on a new polyester fiber differing in chemistry from any now on the market. The fiber will be expensive and is not expected to gain mass usage for a number of years. It is a specialty.

Source: Reproduced courtesy of Whirlpool Corporation, Benton Harbor, Michigan.

EXHIBIT 7–9   Forecasting with Substitution Theory: Displacement of Sailing Ships by Steam-Driven Ships

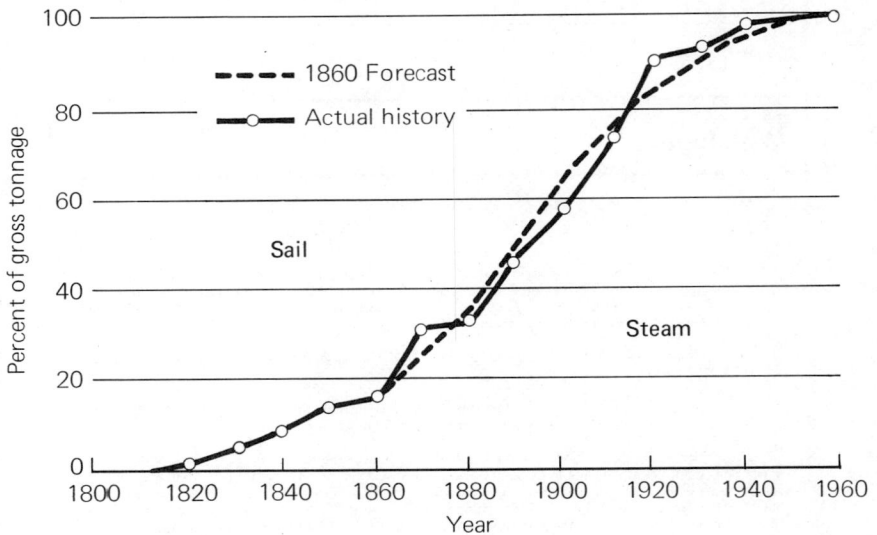

Source: James R. Bright, *A Guide to Practical Technological Forecasting* (Englewood Cliffs, N.J.: Prentice-Hall, 1973). Reprinted by permission of the author.

early 1970s. Accordingly, Shell introduced scenarios in addition to the energy forecast in their 1972 planning cycle. In the first three years in which multiple scenarios were the future-oriented component of the planning process. Shell learned some lessons that are useful to other practitioners. Six of these lessons are discussed by Zentner:

> *Number of Scenarios:* Shell settled on three scenarios after considering six and trying four. They found that when planners were given too many scenarios some were just ignored. They reasoned that using just two scenarios would be too much of an either-or orientation.
>
> *Use of Themes:* Themes provide a focus for the number of factors included in any one scenario and in turn relate to how many scenarios are appropriate. An example of a theme for a 1975–1990 extrapolative scenario: "The future evolves through a series of *ad hoc* compromises between conflicting public demand for protection of the environment, fuel, energy and economic growth."
>
> *Time Span and Degree of Detail:* The time span covered by a scenario depends on the nature of the planning being done. At Shell, short-term planners had a two-year horizon, whereas long-term planners had needs from ten to

twenty-five years out. The degree of detail is greatest for the two-year future, somewhat less so for the ten-year need and modest in the twenty-five–year term.

Packaging the Scenarios: Shell has steered away from overwhelming their planners with too much detail. By eliminating the references employed and assumptions used, they have been able to present a scenario in twenty-five pages. They have also found it necessary that all scenarios have the same length and degree of detail.

Composition of the Scenario Writing Group: Shell's strategy was to bring together a small group with a mix of skills and personalities. Disciplines included economics, engineering, economics, law, and sociology. Some of these skills were available within the company. Others had to be recruited outside.

Linkage with the Planning Process: At Shell multiple scenarios are a component of the formal planning system. As part of the scenario development process, planners within the company review and comment on the drafts prior to presentation to senior management. Following approval or revision, the scenarios are distributed and presented to the planners, who then incorporate them in their planning effort. Each scenario requires a different corporate strategy to deal with it. The planners develop a variety of plans to cope with the several scenarios.

The major benefit of scenario writing is that it forces managers to think about what they would do in an "unpleasant" future. Mark it well; a manager, like any other person, tends to view the future optimistically. We all resist thinking about dire events; we prefer to think of the future as, at the very worst, an extension of the present. Although history repeatedly proves this assumption false, the mind set remains. Scenario writing has other benefits as well. It encourages the development of structured systems for monitoring trends of importance to the company. It serves as a tool for communication between different parts of the company and encourages cross-fertilization of ideas. It helps develop a forward-looking attitude among company personnel and makes them more aware of the myriad of influences that affect company plans, policies, and operations. And, most obviously, it identifies important management decisions that will have to be made in the future and, therefore, allows time for adequate consideration and data gathering.

Cross-Impacts. Over the last few years it has become increasingly obvious that attempting to make technology forecasts based on technological facts alone—or even on technological and economic factors together—is risky. As pointed out earlier, the nature of technological advance is greatly influenced by the needs and desires of a society; as the needs and desires of that society change, the incentives for technological advances also change. Recall, for instance, the earlier example of the aircraft manufacturer in 1940. He would have had even stronger reason to assume the high-speed projections indicated on his graph if he had asked the simple question: How is the political situation going to affect the progress of airplane power? The conclusion was not hard to see: The 1940 war was bound to accelerate aircraft-engine performance. The point is crucial: No forecast should be considered in isolation. This is, among other things, what Exhibit 1–13 is all about—everything relates to everything else.

Think of the corporate planning department in 1960 that used only economic data, marketing statistics, and a smattering of demographic information to estimate the profit potential of new products; the department would have looked at birth rates without considering the impact of birth control pills.

Consider these other cross-impacts:

—The population's growing older leads to new public policies, such as an increase in mandatory retirement age.
—State pollution laws lead to industrial relocations that, in turn, lead to population shifts.
—Federal public policies, such as interstate highways and home mortgages, encourage migration from the nation's cities.
—Economic change leads to increased affluence that, in turn, brings about a change in certain values.
—Changes in telecommunications lead to changes in the organizational structure of corporations.
—Events in international politics lead to economic change that, in turn, changes modes of living in the United States (see the OPEC cartoon, for example).
—Revolutions in transportation as a consequence of technology create new economic interdependencies and new social interactions (consider the example of the automobile).

Thus a meaningful technology forecast will, of necessity, embody forecasts of relevant trends in other influencing environments—namely, economic, political, social, and ecological environments. Proper consideration of these factors is necessary for both the formulation and utilization of a technology forecast. Conversely, to forecast economic, social, and political events, one need consider technological change.

ECONOMIC FORECASTING

The importance of economic forecasting can scarcely be exaggerated: Correct forecasts can spell profits and growth; wrong forecasts can cause serious financial losses or failure. Growing awareness of the critical importance of forecasting to business and to the economy in general has led economists to concentrate on the task of improving forecasting techniques. American corporations are increasingly drawing upon economic and statistical techniques of forecasting as a means of strengthening the basis for business decisions.

Drawing by Don Wright; © 1976 NYT Special Features.

Management decisions in the areas of production, purchasing, finance, personnel, marketing, inventories, and capital spending depend upon the answers to questions such as these (Silk, 1963):

—What will the general state of business be? What will be the demand for our products?

—Will we be able to get the number and kinds of employees we will need? Or will we be laying off people? What is going to happen to wage rates?

—What will be the effect on our sales if we change our prices? What are our competitors likely to do?

—Where will the growing markets for our products be? What new industrial or regional developments are likely to create new opportunities for us?

—What types of new products ought we to be developing?

—Have we enough production capacity to meet probable future demand?

—What outside financing will we require? What is it likely to cost us? Is this a good time to seek it, or should we wait?

—Should we be working down our inventories? Or are we likely to get caught short?

Although seldom addressed in introductory economics courses, questions such as these cut to the very heart of business management. The answers to all such questions must begin with a forecast of general economic activity. Since a number of marketing and managerial economics texts do deal with how to build forecasts for industries and companies, the focus of this section will be chiefly on forecasting the overall business climate.

Business Fluctuations

When we speak of the "overall business climate," we refer to such economywide variables as employment and unemployment, income, output, and prices. In fact, two of the most important aspects of the overall business climate are changes in unemployment and changes in prices. In Chapter 2, it will be recalled, we examined unemployment and inflation. In the paragraphs below, we shall take a brief look at how the business climate changes.

Sometimes the climate is buoyant: Few workers are unemployed, many companies are growing, and few companies are going broke. The economy is in a period of expansion. At other times, however, the climate is not so good: Many people are unemployed, companies are cutting back their production, and not a few are going out of business. The economy is in a period of recession. These ups and downs we call *business fluctuations*.

Economists used to refer to the recurrent fluctuations in business and economic activity that took place over a period of years as *business cycles.* Because the severity of these fluctuations has been somewhat tamed, the term is less in vogue. Nevertheless, the worldwide business cycle of 1973–1975, while no Great Depression of the 1930s, was the most serious downturn of the whole period since World War II.

What, then, might be said scientifically about the outlook for business fluctuations? Most economists would pretty much agree with Samuelson (1976:266):

> Although nothing is impossible in an inexact science like economics, the probability of a great depression—a prolonged, cumulative, and chronic slump like that of the 1930s, the 1890s, or the 1870s—has been reduced to a negligible figure. No one should pay any appreciable insurance premium to be protected against the risk of a total breakdown in our banking system and of massive unemployment in which 25 percent of the workers can find no jobs.

If depressions are virtually a thing of the past, it does not necessarily follow that we must have perpetual prosperity or that depressions have been replaced with "pauses." Samuelson (1976:266–67) advises caution:

> A mixed economy still is subject to occasional *recessions:* investment fluctuations can still occur; changes in government spending can have initially destabilizing effects upon general business activity; attempts to bring inflation under control sometimes result in downturns and slowdowns; foreign events like the OPEC oil boycott and price rise can adversely affect American economic activity.
>
> Nevertheless, now that the tools of income analysis are understood and their use is politically mandatory, the probability of recession in any one year is

less in the mixed economy than it used to be. Expansion periods tend to be frequent and longer. Now we must redefine the cycle so that stagnant growth below the trend-potential of growth is to be called recession, even though absolute growth has not vanished.

As Exhibit 7–10 shows, the long-term trend of the U.S. economy— whether measured in output, income, or employment—is upward. The exhibit also reveals the fluctuations within this long-term trend. In other words, we have periods when business activity temporarily pulls us below our upward growth pattern and other periods when business activity moves with or in excess of our normal growth path.

EXHIBIT 7–10   Phases of the Business Cycle

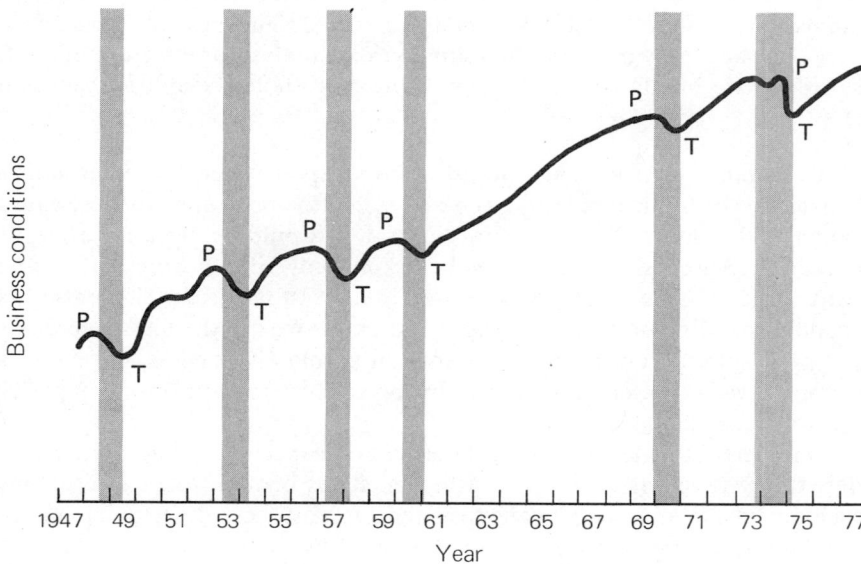

This graph shows the successive phases of the business cycle. From any *trough phase* (T) to the next *peak phase* (P) is an *expansion phase;* from any peak to the next trough is a *recession phase*. Each of these four phases of the cycle is characterized by different business conditions. For example, during expansion, employment, production, prices, money, wages, interest rates, and profits are usually rising; during a recession, the reverse is true. Note that despite the six recession phases shown in the figure above, the long-term trend of the U.S. economy is upward.

Methods of Economic Forecasting

To forecast economic fluctuations, managers have several approaches available. The most straightforward—namely, trend analysis—is a carryover from our discussion of technology forecasting. For example, management could obtain a concise and useful overview of the economy by extrapolating past trends in the following areas.

—GNP real growth	—Balance of payments
—Population	—Balance of trade
—Per capita income	—Public debt
—Minimum wage	—Government reserves
—Inflation	—Price and availability of specific
—Money supply	raw materials
	—Futures market

Then, too, managers can turn to the experts for not only technological forecasts but also for economic forecasts. One such expert forecast appears in the Commentary section, "Galbraith on the Future." The best corporate forecasters, however, rely on more than simple trend analysis or expert opinion. In this section we briefly consider a few of the more noteworthy approaches in use.

The Deterministic Approach. The assumption upon which the deterministic approach to economic forecasting is based is that the present has a close causal relation to the future. The deterministic strategy would be used, for example, to predict construction expenditures by a knowledge of construction contract awards already made. It may also be used to forecast particular elements, such as capital spending or consumer expenditures. As we use the term *deterministic,* however, we do not mean it to imply an absolutely fixed and irreversible relation between present and future. In the real economic world, completely fixed relationships do not exist.

One deterministic technique, the so-called expectational approach, considers the *determining role* that consumers' states of mind play in economic developments. While many economists tend to pay short shrift to changes in attitudes, expectations, beliefs, and values held by the public, economic forecasting, both for short-term and long-term purposes, can in fact be greatly enhanced by measuring and analyzing people's expectations, for those expectations play a significant role in shaping subsequent economic behavior. For example, several years ago George Katona constructed an Index of Consumer Sentiment in order to measure the willingness of consumers to buy goods and services. The index is a summary measure derived from quarterly surveys of consumer attitudes and expectations about personal finances, business trends, and buying conditions. Over the past quarter-century, it has been found that the index has a definite forecasting value—that willingness to buy *does* influ-

COMMENTARY: Galbraith on the Future

I have reached the age where I comment on this with confidence, for I will not be around to hear about it if I am wrong. What will be the major anxieties ten years hence? Some kind of rapport will have been established on incomes and prices and the regulation of public and private expenditure so that inflation will not be the primary problem. In Europe there will be much concern over regularizing the role of the mass of foreign workers. No one should imagine that they can be kept forever as a special subproletariat. All the older countries will be reconciled to the departure of the simple, tedious industries to the more competent countries of the Third World. Steel, heavy chemicals, tires, ordinary textiles, shipbuilding, will be gone. (Steel is already in deep trouble in the United States, France, Britain, and the old districts of Belgium.) The older industrial countries will still have computers, aircraft, missiles, and other advanced weapons of mass destruction. And, if they survive their excellence in the latter, they will have anything else requiring good or original design.

ence discretionary expenditures by consumers. Furthermore, in an economy where two out of every three dollars are spent by consumers, those expenditures can lead and influence the entire economy in recession as well as in recovery. Exhibit 7–11 shows movements of the Index of Consumer Sentiment as used by the Survey Research Center from 1969 through 1977. The index during those years twice showed sharp declines in consumer confidence during periods of otherwise relatively stable economic activity—that is, in 1969 and again from late 1972 through late 1973. On both occasions the fall in consumer optimism was followed by a recession.

Overall, the advantage of the deterministic approach is its simplicity. It is useful, for example, in a period of defense buildup, such as occurred during World War II, when the use of vast and complex analyses to predict the government's steel or copper requirements would have been in vain. Because of its emphasis upon the necessity of full, fast, and accurate reporting as part of the forecasting operation and because under many circumstances it is the surest forecasting technique, the deterministic approach will never be made obsolete by more "sophisticated" methods. Nevertheless, the accuracy of forecasts produced by the deterministic method varies greatly—and it varies inversely with the length of time to be covered by the forecast. For any extremely complicated forecasting problem, such as the course of the American economy for a year or more ahead, there can obviously be no deterministic solution.

EXHIBIT 7–11   Index of Consumer Sentiment

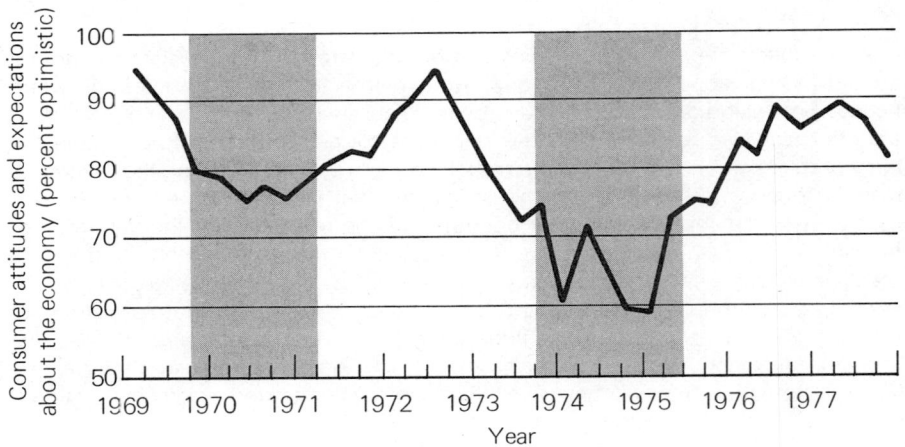

Note: February 1966 = 100; shaded portions indicate recessions.

Source: Data from the Survey Research Center, University of Michigan.

The Cyclical Indicators Approach. The assumption upon which the second approach to economic forecasting is based is that present signs show how the future is developing; such signs, or "straws in the wind," do not "determine" the future, but they do reveal the process of change that is already taking place. This strategy calls for the spotting of *leading indicators*—that is, specific measures of economic activity (e.g., housing starts) whose movements foreshadow rises or declines in *general* business activity. Andrew Carnegie, for example, used to count the number of factory chimneys belching smoke to tell whether business would rise or decline.

For many years, business analysts have been searching for a single indicator or set of indicators that would always lead general business developments. A brief description of some of the single indicators follows.

● Research has established that a close, regular, and predictable relationship exists among the supply of money, national income, and prices. Milton Friedman (1953) argues that control of the nation's supply of money, rather than fiscal policy, brings about orderly economic growth; severe and sustained contractions in the rate of money-supply growth have invariably preceded recessions. Conversely, Friedman contends, a rapid increase in the supply of money lowers interest rates and stimulates investment, but such heightened activity, in turn, raises income and eventually increases the transaction demand for money. This trend produces generally rising prices, including the price of credit, and leads to spiraling inflation in a chain of action and reaction (see Exhibit 7–12).

• Retail sales, which generate the impetus for most business recoveries, are another leading indicator. Sustained increases in expenditures for such items as autos and appliances lead, of course, to major increases in manufacturers' capital investment. Retail sales figures are issued weekly and monthly by the Commerce Department. The monthly figures give a rough clue to consumer attitudes. A long slowdown in spending leads to cutbacks in output.

• Housing starts are worth watching as an indicator of possible trouble ahead. Recent recessions have been preceded by a period of tightening credit and rising interest rates, which tends to suck money out of the mortgage market and thus depress home building before the rest of the economy turns down. That is one reason why the Labor Department's monthly figures on building permits are a leading indicator. Monthly figures on contracts placed for new construction also tend to foreshadow work in a major industry.

• Of all the leading indicators of general economic activity, stock prices are the only barometer where virtually no lag exists in compiling the statistics. To be significant, a general rise in stock prices must coincide with comparable, underlying improvement elsewhere in the economy. In the last four expansion periods since 1949, Standard & Poor's index of 500 common stocks has always increased significantly in the first year of expansion.

• Other indicators that move in advance of the business cycle are: the average work week in manufacturing, job placements in industry, net business formations, industrial material prices, corporate profits after taxes, ratio of prices to unit labor costs in manufacturing, and changes in consumer installment debt.

When the index of leading indicators is up, economists say there is a good chance that business will move up. But one can be sure of this only when the movement of the leading indicators has been confirmed by both coincident and lagging indicators. All of these indicators are logged in a U.S. government publication called *Business Conditions Digest* (see Appendix B).

Econometric Models Approach. The third approach to economic forecasting, the construction of econometric models, is based on the assumption that, though changes in the real world may seem chaotic, careful analysis can reveal certain underlying regularities.* The way to find these regularities is to black out much of the reality and hold only to the abstractions that make up an economic system. There are several ways in which a forecaster can apply this

---

* The term *econometric* refers to analytical techniques that combine economic theory with mathematics and statistics.

EXHIBIT 7–12   Money Growth as a Leading Indicator

As money goes, so goes inflation. One of the simplest rules of thumb for predicting price changes in any year is to average the growth rate of money in the previous three years. The margin of error is usually less than 1 percent.

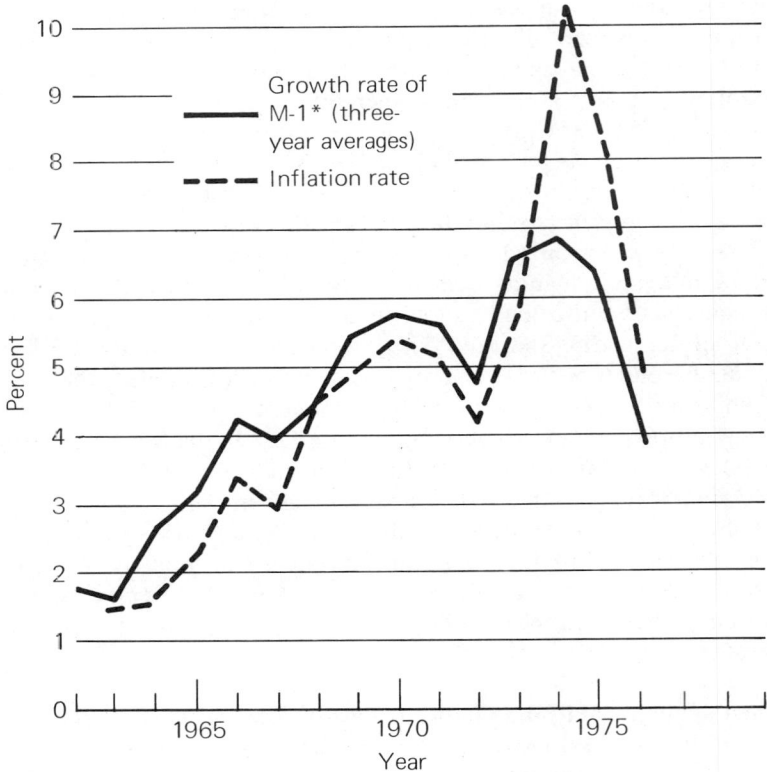

* Economists refer to the money supply in two ways: M-1 (currency plus demand deposits held by the public) and M-2 (M-1 plus commercial bank savings and time deposits other than large certificates of deposit).

Source: Courtesy *Fortune* Art Department / Paris Studios, © 1977.

systematic approach. Some are judgmental; others complex and highly quantitative.

For example, in this age of computer forecasting we have dozens of econometric models of the GNP. Since Lawrence Klein of the Wharton School has produced one of the better known, we might consider it as fairly representative of how these models operate. The Wharton model, like every econometric, is based upon a set of theories about what will determine business activity. But these theories must be translated into mathematical equations, such as

$$G = C + I + E,$$

where G stands for gross national product; C, for consumption; I, for investment; and E, for government expenditures. Klein contends that the best predictions will be made from the best structural models. To achieve this goal, national models must be large enough to accommodate the basic transactions in an economy. Consequently, an entire set of simultaneous equations must be used.

The U.S. Office of Business Economics (OBE) employs a simplified version (Exhibit 7–13) of the model used by Wharton to make short-term projections. Each box shown in Exhibit 7–13 represents a major component in the equations upon which the model is based. A line from one box to another indicates that the value of the first element has a direct effect on the value of the second. Most of the boxes have lines going in and out, which means that they are both predicted by, and are themselves used to predict, other components. The column of boxes on the far left (e.g., "Population") represents *exogenous variables*. These must be either predicted independently or ignored. Other exogenous factors (not shown) include technological change, tax laws, tastes, and monetary trade.

All econometric models reflect the circularity of economic relations; everything influences everything else. The circularity in the OBE model is highlighted in the exhibit by the heavy arrows. Personal consumption is a major component of the gross national product; therefore, an arrow leads directly from it to the GNP. The GNP, in turn, has a direct effect on nonlabor income (profits). Profits minus taxes affect disposable personal income, and disposable personal income affects personal consumption. Thus, the circle is completed.

The Wharton and OBE models are actually only two of several models whose findings are available to business for a fee. The two principal other models are by Data Resources, Inc. (DRI), headed until recently by Otto Eckstein of Harvard who was a member of the Council of Economic Advisers from 1964 to 1966; and Chase Econometric Associates, started by Michael Evans, a former colleague of Klein's at Wharton. Although their marketing approaches differ, the Wharton, DRI, and Chase models are similar and usually weigh in with similar forecasts. All three models are capable of forecasting the major components of the GNP, as well as unemployment, inflation, and interest rates. All their proprietors have incorporated into these models a major notion of Keynesian economics—namely, that changes in the level of government spending and taxation have a multiplier effect on spending and income. And all three models have relatively large financial sectors that link changes in monetary policy to output and prices.

**EXHIBIT 7–13   Condensed Flow Diagram of the Econometric Model
Used at the U.S. Office of Business Economics**

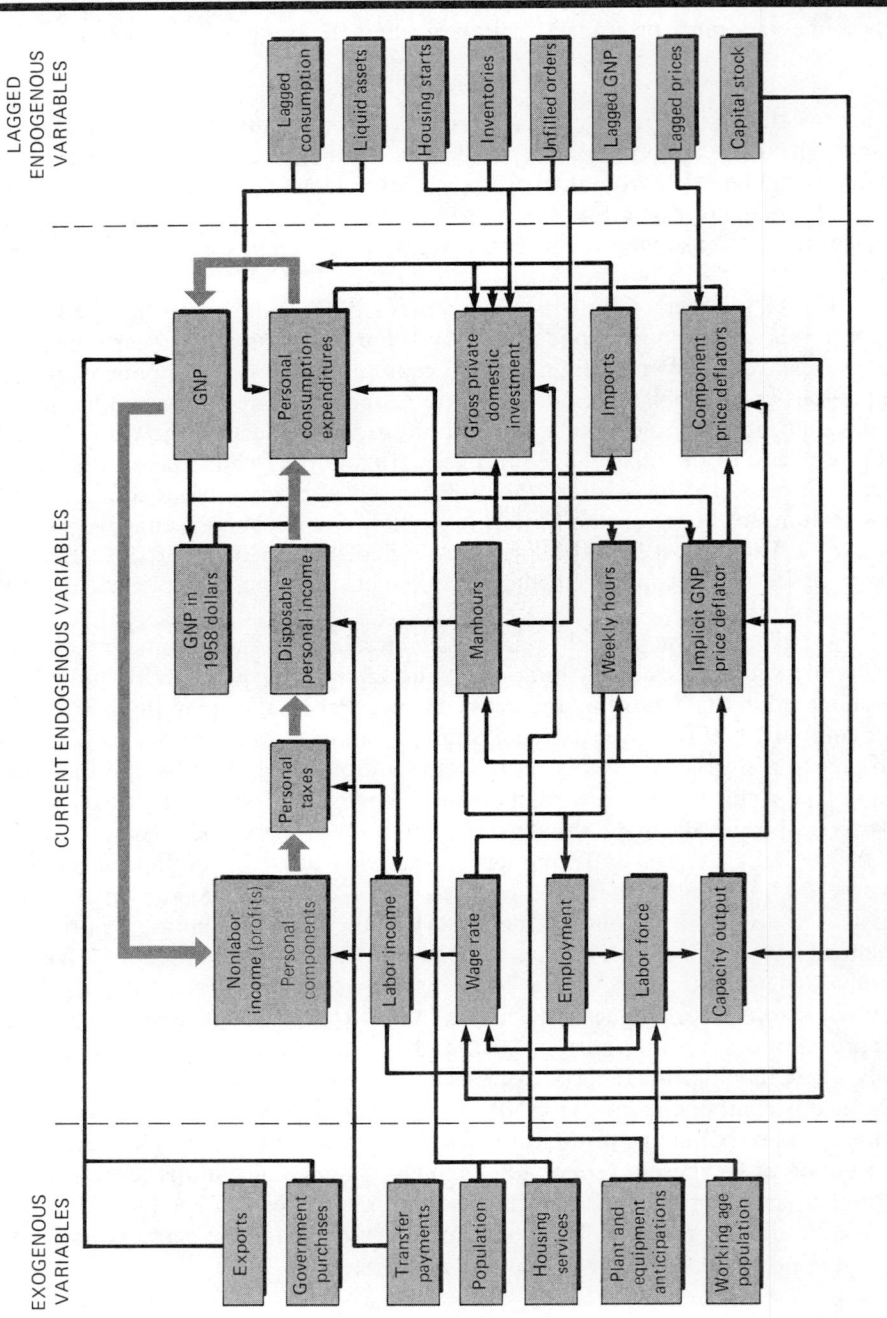

Economic forecasters like to joke about outsiders who ask to see their models, as if they expected some mechanical contraption. Actually, an econometric model is no more than a complex cluster of equations that define in numerical terms the ways in which sectors of the economy seem to interact with one another. In the model shown above, can you find the simple equation $G = C + I + E$ as "gross national product equals consumption plus investment plus government expenditures"? Such formulas are fed into a computer for analysis of what happens to different variables—symbolizing everything from employment to prices—when certain assumptions are made.

Source: U.S. Department of Commerce, Office of Business Economics, *Survey of Current Business*, vol. 46 (Washington, D.C.: U.S. Government Printing Office, 1966), p. 19.

The advantage of econometric models is that they can serve business in various ways: They provide a superior way of organizing the economy's complicated materials; of systematizing the whole forecasting process; of providing straightforward, less subjective conclusions; and, afterward, of discovering what may have gone wrong in a forecast and thereby allowing forecasters to profit from past mistakes. How successful are econometric models? Econometric models failed to predict the recession of 1973–1975, though, as we saw, analysis of consumer expectation did lead to such a prediction.

Since 1968 the American Statistical Association and the National Bureau of Economic Research have been jointly collecting forecasts from a panel of business economists—some who used econometrics and some who did not. In 1975 Vincent and Josephine Su, two National Bureau economists, presented an evaluation of these forecasts in the bureau's publication, *Explorations in Economic Research*. The conclusions did not offer any comfort to anybody. "No method predicts consistently better or worse than other methods, and no method predicts consistently better in levels or in changes," the researchers said. They also compared all the forecasts with those produced by the Wharton econometric model. The conclusion: There is not any clear evidence that other methods are any better—or any worse—than the Wharton model. Nevertheless, for the best practitioners of computer forecasting with econometric models, the expectation is not to have incontrovertibly accurate forecasts, but to increasingly reduce the importance of judgment in comparison with the elements of science in computer forecasting. Perhaps the only sure-fire forecast is that there will always be economic forecasts, but whatever method or approach is used, they must take into account the critical interrelationships that exist among the other components of the macroenvironment.

SOCIOPOLITICAL FORECASTING

As we have repeatedly seen throughout this book, over the last decade the notion that the key strategic issues for a business are almost exclusively technological and economic has become increasingly difficult to maintain. Consider these interactions: the Arab-Israeli conflict and the eventual effect on energy research; the decline in consumers in the 13–24 age group and the effect on the soft-drink industry; the antitechnology mood and nuclear power plant needs; environmentalism and the bans on phosphate detergents and delays in offshore oil drilling; the 1978 Carter administration proposal to change virtually every aspect of the regulation of prescription and over-the-counter drugs and the possible changes in the way pharmaceutical companies do business. The crucial, inescapable point is that these kinds of interactions are, and will continue to be, central to a company's planning and operations. Accordingly, sociopolitical issues deserve the same attention that management gives to the development of technology and the state of the economy.

Ian H. Wilson, a consultant in business environment studies at General Electric, helps us visualize this new dimension in strategic planning with two models. The planning parameters of the past (and present) can be conceptually represented by the two models in Exhibit 7–14. Certainly the technological and economic inputs have been, and will continue to be, vital to the planning process, but Wilson's studies at GE suggest that these inputs will no longer suffice, since they leave "exposed flanks," as the model shows. The planning model for the future, therefore, will be more like the four-sided framework in the exhibit. In fact, as early as 1970, an approximation of this model was incorporated in the revamping of GE's strategic planning system.

Methods of Sociopolitical Forecasting

How does one go about forecasting changes in the cultural-demographic and political environments? What methods are available? The easy way to answer this pair of questions is to go back to the technology forecasting techniques discussed earlier in the chapter. Among those techniques that can be applied to sociopolitical phenomena, expert opinion is the most obvious and is always in plentiful supply, perhaps because the qualifications one needs to be an "expert" on social and political events are far more ambiguous than those required in technological and economic matters. We all feel eminently qualified to speak on changing sexual mores and coming presidential elections but prefer reticence on changing magnetohydrodynamics technology and a coming European monetary system. However, all of the other technology forecasting techniques—expert opinion, trend analysis, monitoring, substitution theory, and scenarios—are equally applicable to forecasting sociopolitical phenomena. In this section, we consider how only two of these techniques—trend analysis and monitoring—can be applied. We also take a look at an essentially new technique: age structure analysis.

Trend Analysis. As we have seen, trend analysis can be a useful tool for forecasting technological change. In sociopolitical forecasting, it is helpful in predicting population growth, but the possibilities do not end here. Dwight E.

EXHIBIT 7–14   Models for Strategic Planning

"Exposed Flank" Model

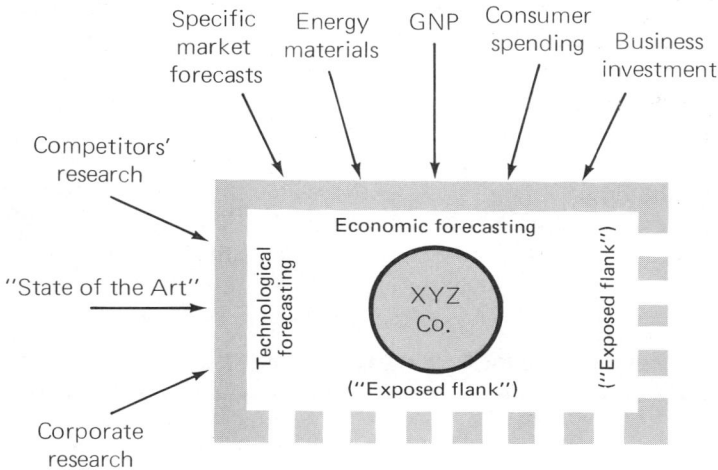

Specific market forecasts   Energy materials   GNP   Consumer spending   Business investment

Competitors' research

Economic forecasting

Technological forecasting

XYZ Co.

("Exposed flank")

("Exposed flank")

"State of the Art"

Corporate research

Four-Sided Planning Model for the Future

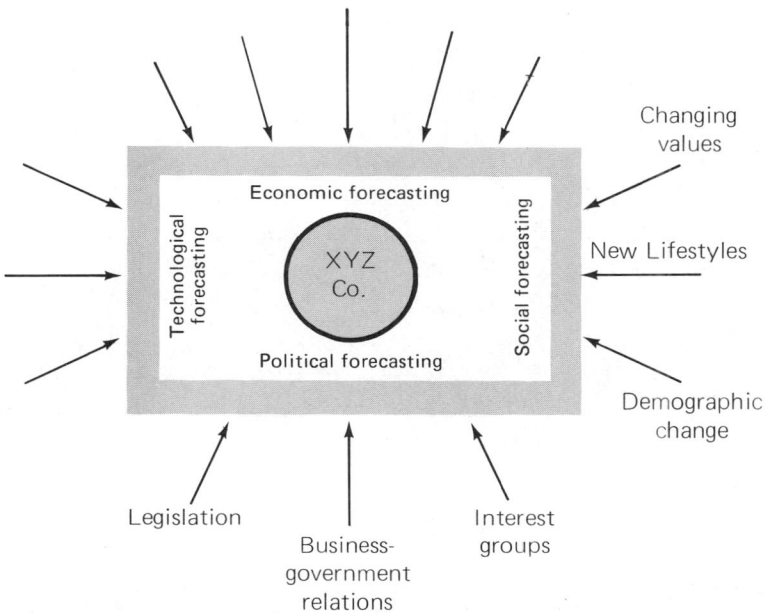

Changing values

Economic forecasting

Technological forecasting

XYZ Co.

Social forecasting

New Lifestyles

Political forecasting

Demographic change

Legislation   Business-government relations   Interest groups

Source: Adapted from Ian H. Wilson, "Socio-Political Forecasting: A New Dimension to Strategic Planning," *Michigan Business Review* (July 1974). Reprinted by permission.

Robinson (1975) suggests, for example, that analysis of social trends can help forecasters anticipate changes in consumer tastes that can affect product planning decisions. By seeing the patterns of matched trends and knowing where the current product is in a cycle, both short- and long-range planners can make decisions that fit the anticipated change. Exhibit 7–15 shows how such trend analysis might be used in the fashion industry to study changes in style.

Monitoring in the Sociopolitical Environment. Graham T.T. Molitor, who is director of governmental relations for General Motors, suggests that by monitoring the sociopolitical environment, the forecaster can develop clear ideas on what to expect in the future. The premise of the monitoring method is this: Issues of public policy are almost always the result of unusual events that give rise to abuse or excess so extreme that public action eventually is required. We

EXHIBIT 7–15   Trend Analysis: An Example from the Fashion Industry

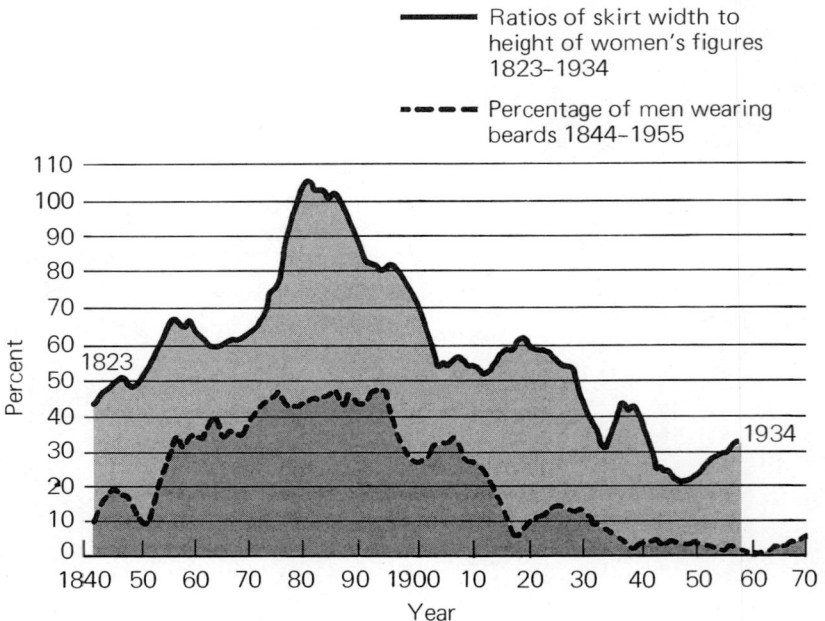

Note: The curves are based on five-year moving averages.

know that intellectual elites, who analyze and articulate social problems, tend to emerge around issues. Similarly, the victimized express their feelings and thus become powerful symbols for change. "By monitoring these ... vanguards, whose ideas ultimately are diffused widely, early indications of change can be forecasted" (Molitor, 1975:206).

Between the occurrence of the first, isolated event and the creation of public policy, Molitor thinks a fairly consistent pattern of behavior unfolds.* The analyst's job, then, is one of monitoring the unfolding of this pattern. The sequence, which might extend over 100 years, could go as follows: At first, the early warnings about emerging problems appear in the more visionary classes of literature (for example, it would appear that the poet Blake was one of the first to recognize the arrival of the Industrial Revolution and its social implications). Then the idea is rendered into specifics in monographs and speeches in specialized journals. Next, we have these phases: corroboration of details; institutional responses through journals for the cause; consideration in the mass media; politicization of the issue in governmental reports; and a diffusion of the idea among opinion leaders. Molitor has provided the following descriptive chronology of these phases through which an issue passes:

- —Artistic, poetic works;
- —Science fiction;
- —Fringe media, underground press;
- —Unpublished notes and speeches;
- —Monographs, treatises;
- —Scientific, technical, professional journals;
- —Highly specialized, narrow-viewpoint publications;
- —Statistical documents (social indicators, statistical services);
- —Abstracting journals, services (National Technical Information Service);
- —Data search composites (Predicast, Scout*);
- —Egghead journals (*Science, Scientific American*);
- —Insider "dopesheets" ("Product Safety Letter");
- —Popular intellectual magazines (*Harper's, Atlantic*);
- —Network communications (bulletins, newsletters, slipsheets);
- —Journals for the cause (*Consumer Reports*);
- —General-interest publications (*Time, Newsweek*);
- —Condensations of general literature (*Readers' Digest*);
- —Poll data, public opinion, behavioral and voter attitudes;
- —Legislative/governmental services, reports;
- —Books (fiction provides social analysis of times; nonfiction pulls together discordant parts into easily understood whole);
- —Newspapers (the *New York Times* and the *Washington Post* are examples of early commentators; Southern rural papers, of late commentators);

* This premise is the same one upon which the life cycle theory of social issues (discussed in Chapter 2) builds. The life cycle theory itself is a kind of forecasting tool.

* See Appendix B.

—Radio/TV (networks comment earlier than local stations);

—Education journals;

—Historical analysis (doctoral theses).

For a social issue to really affect business, however, it must do more than be talked about in *Rolling Stone* or the *New York Times;* the behavior of significant groups of people must be somehow changed by it. Thus the forecaster needs to monitor *bellwether jurisdictions*—that is, geographic locations that traditionally adopt new fashions or public policies before others. These early innovators show the way; after the idea is proven, other jurisdictions emulate the bellwether areas. As Exhibits 7–16, 7–17, and 7–18 indicate, certain jurisdictions invariably are the first to innovate social trends and public policies. For example, it should not have been surprising—nor insignificant—that California in 1978 passed Proposition 13; nor should it have been surprising to watch the idea of mandatory fiscal restraints spread to the rest of the country.

To see the benefits of monitoring the sociopolitical environment, we can turn to the example of Johnson Wax. In June 1975 the chairman of the Council of Environmental Quality called a press conference in order to release the results of a preliminary report, prepared by a federal scientific task force, that warned of the dangers aerosols presented to the earth's ozone belt. A few days after the press conference, Johnson Wax responded by placing in ninety-nine newspapers in forty-eight states the advertisement that is displayed in Exhibit 7–19. Its message to the public, in the form of a letter from the company's board chairman, was clear: Our aerosol-packaged products can be used with

EXHIBIT 7–16   Bellwether Jurisdictions of Sociopolitical Changes

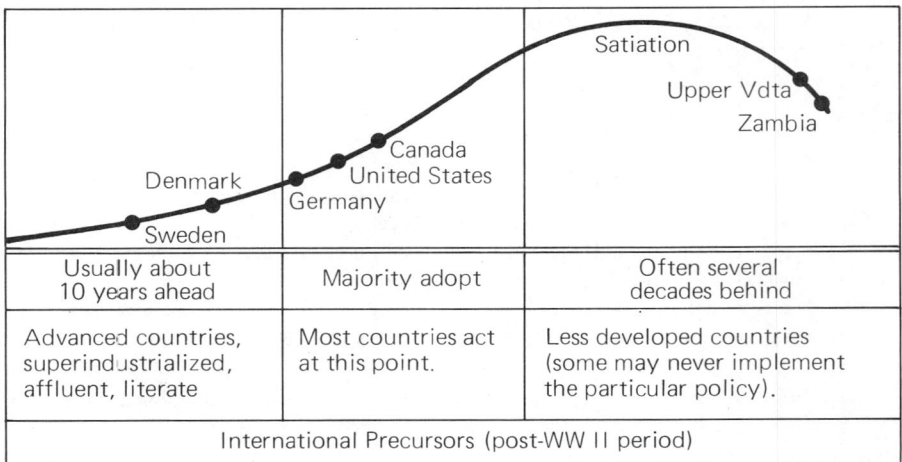

Usually about 10 years ahead	Majority adopt	Often several decades behind
Advanced countries, superindustrialized, affluent, literate	Most countries act at this point.	Less developed countries (some may never implement the particular policy).
International Precursors (post-WW II period)		

Graph labels: Satiation; Upper Vdta; Zambia; Canada; United States; Germany; Denmark; Sweden

New York Dade County, Fla. NYC Boston, Mass. California Illinois Massachusetts			Deep South (Miss., La., Ala., etc.) Rural areas (Wyo., etc.)
Usually about 4 years ahead	Majority adopt		Often 2–6 years behind
Early innovators	Early adopters	Early majority	Late majority	Laggards
Highly urban, densely populated, superaffluent, highly educated, youthful, progressive	Most states, cities, and counties act at this point.		Rural, tradition-bound, nonaffluent, etc.
Domestic (state and local) Precursors (post-WW II period)			

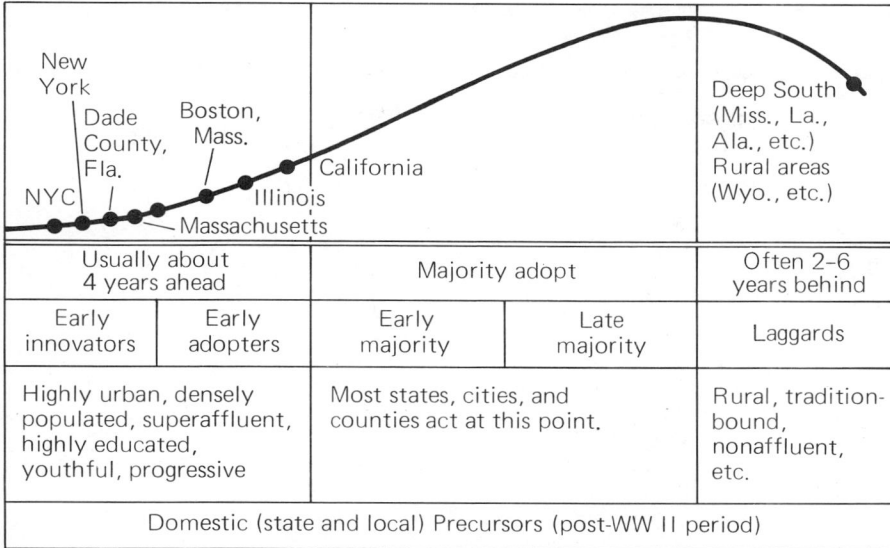

Source: From "Schema for Forecasting Public Policy Change" by Graham T.T. Molitor from *The Next 25 Years*, published in 1975 by the World Future Society, 4916 St. Elmo Avenue, Washington, D.C. 20014.

confidence because they contain no fluorocarbon propellants. As indicated in the advertisement, "use with confidence" labels were also placed on all of their aerosol cans. How had Johnson Wax been able to react so swiftly to the task force report? Henion writes (1976:152):

> Johnson Wax had been monitoring [the situation] for many months. Its opinion survey in December of 1974 showed that 44 percent of the public was aware of and concerned over the possible harmful effects of fluorocarbons in the ozone. The company's marketing response, spearheaded by its newspaper advertisement, was a remarkable demonstration of how a company effectively turned to its advantage a situation that could have caused a serious erosion in the market position of its aerosol-packaged products.

Age Structure Analysis as a Forecasting Technique. According to Richard C. Easterlin (1978), the real engine of social and economic change in the United States since World War II has been age structure. The crucial unit of this kind of analysis is the *cohort*—that is, all of the men and women born in the same calendar year. According to Easterlin, the size of the cohort exerts powerful societal leverage; it affects the cohort members' job opportunities and their desire to have families. When cohorts are large, young people glut the labor market. As competition for jobs increases, so too does a subjective feeling that

**EXHIBIT 7–17   Innovative Jurisdictions: Establishment of
State Consumer Offices**

Year	States
1957	New York
1958	
1959	
1960	New Jersey
1961	Illinois, Washington
1962	
1963	Massachusetts
1964	
1965	California, Connecticut, Delaware, Iowa
1966	Michigan, Rhode Island
1967	Arizona, Maryland, Missouri, New Mexico, Texas, Vermont, West Virginia
1968	Kansas, Kentucky, Pennsylvania, Puerto Rico
1969	Colorado, Florida, Hawaii, Minnesota, North Carolina, Utah, Wisconsin
1970	Alaska, Maine, New Hampshire, Virginia
1971	Arkansas, Georgia, Idaho, Indiana, Louisiana, Oregon, South Carolina, Virgin Islands
1972	Alabama, North Dakota, Ohio, Utah
1973	Montana, Nevada, Wyoming, Tennessee, Washington, D.C.
1974	Mississippi, South Dakota

Source: Data from Graham T.T. Molitor, "How to Anticipate Law-Making Action." Paper delivered to Public Affairs Council Conference, Mayflower Hotel, Washington, D.C., June 23, 1977, p. 19.

times are tough. This attitude, in turn, inhibits the whole family formation process; young people are less willing to marry and have children. But the converse is also true: When cohorts are small, feelings are optimistic. Families are formed, and the birth rate goes up. If correct, this age structure analysis suggests a cycle. Every two decades or so, a substantial shift should occur in the relative supply of young versus older workers.

Easterlin sees a rising birth rate in the 1980s, as children of the small cohorts of the baby-bust era discover that job competition is not so fierce and start to form families. From his projections, Easterlin draws a number of interesting, though not universally accepted, conclusions about the 1980s. First, the divorce rate should begin to go down, because studies show that children of small cohorts tend to keep marriages together. Second, the inflation rate should also begin to go down because the lower unemployment and higher average income will eliminate the need for government to stimulate demand. (We know that actions that stimulate demand—for example, deficit spending—promote inflation.) And finally, crime rates and worker alienation should decline.

EXHIBIT 7–18   Innovative Jurisdictions: Establishment of State Unfair and Deceptive Trade Practice Laws

Year	States
1957	New York
1958	
1959	
1960	New Jersey
1961	Illinois, Washington
1962	
1963	
1964	
1965	Hawaii, Iowa, California, Connecticut, Delaware
1966	Michigan
1967	Arizona, Guam, Maryland, Massachusetts, Missouri, New Mexico, Vermont
1968	Kansas, Kentucky, Pennsylvania, Puerto Rico, Rhode Island
1969	Colorado, Florida, Minnesota, North Carolina, Wisconsin
1970	Alaska, Maine, New Hampshire, Virginia
1971	Arkansas, Idaho, Indiana, South Carolina, South Dakota
1972	Louisiana, North Dakota, Ohio, Oklahoma, Utah
1973	Montana, Nevada, Texas, Virgin Islands, Wyoming
1974	Mississippi, Nebraska, West Virginia

Note: Three states have no apparent act: Alabama, Georgia, and Tennessee.

Source: Data from Graham T.T. Molitor, "How to Anticipate Law-Making Action." Paper delivered to Public Affairs Council Conference, Mayflower Hotel, Washington, D.C., June 23, 1977, p. 20.

Easterlin's analysis is elegant, but it leaves out a number of outside variables. Birth rates do not fluctuate in isolation. It would seem that wars, climate, and the supply of energy—to name a few outside variables that help to shape the rate—need to be factored in.

In sum, this section has attempted to do no more than suggest how a couple of technology forecasting techniques may be applied, with profit, to forecast sociopolitical change. But, as the preceding discussion of age structure analysis should have also suggested, forecasters of sociopolitical change need not always rely on hand-me-down techniques. Indeed, as we traverse the 1980s, efforts to develop additional techniques for anticipating *political risks*—such as adverse actions by foreign governments or American regulatory agencies—will surely intensify.*

To the blind, all things seem sudden. That is probably the best and most concise way to express the importance of trying to pierce the fog of the future.

* For a brief introduction to political risks, see Robock et al, (1977, Chapter 14); for an example of how MNCs analyze political risks, see Rummel and Heenan (1978).

**EXHIBIT 7–19   The Advantages of Monitoring: Johnson Wax's
Response to the Aerosol-Spray Controversy**

An Open Letter To Consumers About Aerosols

From Samuel C. Johnson, Chairman, Johnson Wax, Racine, Wis.

Dear Customer:

For 89 years my family and our company have endeavored to develop new, modern, efficient quality products.

Our company still is a family venture; I am the fourth-generation member to head it. We have four children who, I hope, will want to carry on the tradition.

Aerosols Today

About 25 years ago, modern technology brought to the American homemaker a familiar symbol of the age of ease and convenience. This was the aerosol can.

As you are no doubt aware, a lot of confusion, misunderstanding and anxiety has developed over the last few months about aerosols. Since we have been closely involved in their development over the past couple of decades and because we know a great deal about aerosols, I want to try to clear up some of the misapprehensions you may have about them.

Fluorocarbons and Ozone

The most important problem right now is that some aerosol cans release a certain kind of propellant gas that some scientists feel may be damaging the upper atmosphere ozone layer around the earth.

Although this was a totally unforeseen concern, scientific investigation is constantly providing a vital public service by calling to our attention things about our environment that may present serious problems.

The particular aerosol propellant under question is a fluorocarbon. It has several trade names, (e.g., Freon, Genetron, Ucon, Isotron). Some scientists feel that the possible impairment of the ozone layer in the upper atmosphere would permit greater penetration of the sun's ultra-violet rays with unforeseen effects on our health. Obviously this is a very serious concern; our own company scientists confirm that as a scientific hypothesis it may be possible, but conclusive evidence is not available one way or another, at this time.

We concur that the pressing need is for reliable scientific investigation; this is being carried on by the Inter-Agency Task Force on the Inadvertent Modification of the Stratosphere which has

concluded that there may be a legitimate cause for concern. In addition, the National Academy of Sciences has stratospheric investigations underway which are expected to be completed early next year. Additional investigations are being sponsored by aerosol manufacturers and suppliers.

Not All Aerosols Contain Fluorocarbons

In the meantime, it is important to note that not all aerosol products sold in this country contain fluorocarbon propellants. As a matter of fact, approximately half of all aerosols use other kinds of propellants, including hydrocarbons and carbon dioxide.

About 15 years ago, Johnson Wax invented what is known as the "water-base" aerosol system that permitted the use of propellants other than fluorocarbons in many household products.

As a result, we have been reducing our use of fluorocarbon propellants over a long period for a variety of different reasons, including the fact that our unique water-base formulations using other propellants are less expensive.

During the past three years, fluorocarbons have made up less than five per cent of the total propellants we use. And because we share the concern of our customers and others and since we are technically equipped to do so in our products, we have made a policy decision.

What Johnson Wax Is Doing

Effective today, our company has removed all fluorocarbon propellants from our production lines in the U.S., and we are aggressively reformulating our product ingredients worldwide to achieve the same goal.

We at Johnson Wax are taking this action in the interest of our customers and the public in general during a period of uncertainty and scientific inquiry. We are taking this newspaper advertisement and other available means to tell our customers so that they may use our aerosol products with greater confidence.

In addition, we plan to inform the consumer by having information avail-

able within the next 30 days in stores where our products are sold and by changing as soon as possible the labels of our containers to carry the following statement:

Use With Confidence

Contains no Freon or other Fluorocarbons claimed to harm the ozone layer*

Millions of Americans have learned that in order to have the advantages of aerosol cans, they have to exercise common sense, because the aerosol — like the automobile, or even a simple stepladder — can be dangerous if improperly used.

For example, the aerosol can does contain propellant gases under pressure. It could explode if carelessly placed down on a hot kitchen stove. Fortunately, these dangers are so well known that it almost never happens.

What We Believe

We believe that aerosols are good and useful, or we wouldn't manufacture them. As a result, we will manufacture only those aerosols in the U.S. that *do not* contain fluorocarbons. They include:

Pledge furniture polishes
Raid insecticides
J/Wax automotive products
Jubilee kitchen wax
Favor furniture polish
Glade air fresheners
Edge protective shave
Crew bathroom cleaner
OFF! insect repellents
Big Wally foam cleaner
Klean 'n Shine
    multi-surface cleaner
Glory rug cleaner
Shout pre-spotter

Our customers who have welcomed the utility of these products in the convenient aerosol form will continue to be able to depend upon them.

In closing, I want to assure you that we at Johnson Wax will do our best in the tradition of our family to ensure the effectiveness and safety of our products with the best materials available to us.

Sincerely,

Sam Johnson

SAMUEL C. JOHNSON

Jun. 20, 1975

Forecasting through any of the techniques discussed in this chapter provides the means to anticipate and plan for change. Thus, before leaving the subject of forecasting altogether, a few words need to be said about the realities of insuring that forecasts are actually used. The message then in the next section is quite simple: Forecasts must not become ends in themselves; rather they must be made to serve the current and long-range needs of corporate decisionmakers.

THE STATUS OF CORPORATE FORECASTING PROGRAMS

What is the status of corporate forecasting today? What accounts for that status? What can be done to make more effective use of forecasting resources? Steven C. Wheelwright and Darral G. Clarke (1976) conducted an extensive survey concerning the status of forecasting in major corporations in the United States. Their findings are particularly relevant to managers charged with increasing the effectiveness of planning and forecasting and coping with the expanding uncertainties surrounding business decisions.

In virtually all of the 127 companies responding to their survey, the level of commitment to forecasting was significant. But despite substantial commitments to forecasting in terms of budget and manpower, most companies felt that the full promise of that investment was not yet being realized. The feeling was particularly strong, Wheelwright and Clarke report, among management users of forecasts. The following paragraphs describe some of the ways to overcome these feelings and thus provide some of the keys to successful application of forecasts (adapted from Quinn, 1967).

• Managers have some confidence in the validity of data and assumptions about such relatively near futures, but more distant events tend to lack reality unless they actually impinge on current decisions. Forecasters should thus concentrate on problems that require decisions in the time between the present and the date at which a new forecast can reasonably be developed and presented.

• There are an almost infinite number of possible technological threats and opportunities in any period within the reasonable future. Consequently, forecasters should sort out events of highest probability and potential impact and then try to impose an understanding of them on management. In all cases, the person who prepares the forecast must try to make it as meaningful as possible to its recipients, be prepared to "teach" its key elements to those who must use it, and follow up to see that it is accepted. Otherwise the forecast will become just another forgotten report.

• Forecasts should be fitted in with the company's regular cycles of management decision. In some cases top executives are best briefed prior to stockholder or security analyst meetings, when they must make public announcements about the company's future. And normally these executives should also have at least a broad environmental forecast before issuing guidelines for budget preparation. Operating executives generally need more specific analyses at the time they prepare budget proposals in order to help evaluate alternative programs in terms of potential environmental changes. But most of all, top-level staff and executive groups reviewing operating and capital budgets should be familiar with the forecasts. Since some 90 percent of most companies' expenditures are committed during periodic budget reviews, this is the crucial time to make sure that resource allocations reflect the best thinking about future opportunities and threats.

• Although long-term planning is a critical function of top executives, relatively few companies have actually forced developing major executives into close contact with such planning activities. Despite the fact that some oil companies and utilities have claimed excellent results from using planning groups partly as executive training grounds, most companies still follow more traditional, functional training programs. Unfortunately, the very executives who most need exposure to long-term thinking and forecasting are often those least likely to receive it. In a world ever more dominated by competition and change, it is especially important for managers to learn how to include intelligent forecasting in their decision processes. Otherwise, they will be increasingly exposed to the greatest business risk of all: the risk of ignorance.

CHAPTER EIGHT

Implementation

C hapter 6 built upon a single, powerful assumption: The best way for business to cope with its turbulent environment is through the strategic planning process. This means that management must set goals. It means management must consider social impacts. And as we saw in Chapter 7, it means management must have early information on changes in its environment. Now we come to the all-important piston stroke of the strategic planning process: Management must *insure* that the goals are attained. We call this part of the planning cycle *implementation.*

It is useful to think of implementation in two parts. The first part involves the selection by management of programs, products, and projects *consistent with* corporate goals. The second part involves all the adjustments in organizational structure and behavior that are necessary to insure the successful execution of the selected programs, the profitable production and marketing of the selected products, and the timely completion of the selected projects. It is unlikely that much implementation will be possible without some rethinking of the company's organizational chart and incentive structure.

The first half of this chapter focuses on how managers can select programs consistent with company goals. Particular emphasis is placed on how these selections can be brought in line with what we called in Chapter 6 social impact management. If a company is going to have any meaningful goal with respect to social responsibility, it is crucial that this goal somehow influence top management decisions about the activities in which the company will get involved.

Without underplaying its difficulty, this part of the chapter suggests a procedure that eases the way somewhat in relating social responsibility to selection of corporate programs. In brief, this is the way it works. All company activities can be put into one or more of the following categories: traditional activities, social opportunities, indirectly beneficial activities, philanthropic activities, and proactive (i.e., political) activities. The precise meaning of each category will be explained in due course; for now, we only need to note that each must be handled in a special way. In the first section we discuss comprehensive impact assessment and see that it ought to be applied to virtually all traditional business activities. In the second section on social opportunities, we see a different challenge to management: How can these opportunities be recognized? In the third section on indirectly beneficial activities, we tackle the problem of insuring that *all* the costs and benefits have been considered. In the final section of this part of the chapter we examine philanthropic activities, the more popular way in which business has traditionally met its social responsibilities.

The second half of the chapter begins by considering the ways in which a turbulent environment can lead to changes in a company's organizational chart. We shall see, for example, how corporate responses to new social issues tend to occur slowly over several years and to follow a general pattern. First comes only top management involvement; this is followed by staff involvement; finally, the new concern becomes institutionalized among all managers. Institutionalization can take a variety of forms: task forces, permanent management committees, and permanent organization groups. We consider not only general organizational adjustments, but specific examples drawn from the experiences of such organizations as DuPont, Standard Oil (Indiana), Dow Chemical, and General Electric. The chapter ends by reviewing how companies have modified internal procedures and incentives in order to insure that new programs, designed to respond to new external realities, are taken seriously by managers at all levels. ☐

Selecting Programs, Products, and Projects

To see how consistent proposed or ongoing programs are with the goals of a company, we should first group these programs into five broad categories, each of which requires somewhat different handling.

The first category, and by far the largest, consists of all those business activities—finance, marketing, and similar functions—clearly designed to help attain traditional business goals. Social impact management requires that all of these *traditional activities* be subjected to comprehensive impact assessment, a mode of analysis we examine in this chapter.

The second category of business activities consists of *social opportunities*—that is, programs that result from a manager's seeing in the changing macroenvironment not just challenges but also opportunities. These activities benefit both the company and society, and because they can be moneymakers, they have something in common with those in the first category. What makes social opportunities different is this: They are not easy to see; they require an entirely new way of looking at external events. While no one has yet discovered the pedagogy for instilling this kind of vision, we can cite many instances of management's recognizing and grasping opportunities presented by change in the macroenvironment.

The third category consists of *indirectly beneficial activities.* These activities, like those in the second category, benefit both society and business (see Exhibit 8–1). What distinguishes them from social opportunities is this: The benefits to the company are more intangible, which is to say that they are not easily transferred into dollars. Management must assess these activities very carefully and critically. Later in this section we consider how the benefits (tangible and intangible) of these programs can be compared with their costs (tangible and intangible). We shall see that unless the ratio is favorable—that is, unless the benefits exceed the costs—a company should not launch such a program.

The fourth category of business activities consists of *philanthropic activities.* These programs involve making outright gifts, the returns of which are so remote as to defy cost-benefit analysis. A contribution by a corporation to a university is a case in point. While such a contribution is likely to benefit society in a general way, the return to the corporation is hard to trace. Clearly, with so many organizations pursuing companies for donations, management must exercise some discretion. The final category, *proactive activities,* is dealt with separately in Chapter 13. As we shall see, these programs include political action issues—lobbying public officials, influencing public opinion, supporting political candidates, and so forth—that present unique challenges.

EXHIBIT 8–1   An Example of an Indirectly Beneficial Activity

In implementing its strategic plans, a given company will, to varying degrees, engage in five types of activities. As described in the text, these are (1) traditional activities, which are oriented chiefly towards profit; (2) social opportunities, which attempt to capitalize on changes in the environment; (3) indirectly beneficial activities, which probably improve profits—though the amount and way are hard to measure; (4) philanthropic activities, which are charitable contributions that may or may not be beneficial to the company; and (5) proactive activities, which are essentially political actions in defense of the company's interests. When Boston Gas Company commissioned Corita Kent's *Rainbow Design* for its liquified natural gas tanks, it was engaged in the third type of activity. What do you think might be the indirect benefits to Boston Gas, if any?

Source: Photo courtesy of Boston Gas Company, Boston, Massachusetts.

COMPREHENSIVE IMPACT ASSESSMENT*

Business is responsible for its impacts, intended or otherwise. This idea is at the core of the concept of social impact management presented in Chapter 6.

---

* Comprehensive impact assessment is just another term for technology assessment. The latter tends to cause confusion because of people's tendency to construe technology too narrowly. As used in the term *technology assessment*, technology can refer not only to hardware, but also to social technologies, such as the flexible work week or no-fault automobile insurance. Comprehensive impact assessment is also closely related to the environmental impact statement (EIS). While the comprehensive impact assessment searches for all unintended consequences that may follow from the successful fulfillment of a program—so that we can deal with them before they become social issues themselves—EIS focuses almost exclusively on the environmental consequences.

Mark it well: There should be no doubt regarding management's responsibility for the social impacts of its organization. Social impacts are management's business. Drucker writes (1974:327–28):

> Because one is responsible for one's impacts, one minimizes them. The fewer impacts an institution has outside of its own specific purpose and mission, the better does it conduct itself, the more responsibly does it act, and the more acceptable a citizen, neighbor, and contributor it is. Impacts, which are not essential and which are not part of the discharge of one's own specific purpose and mission, should be kept to the absolute minimum. Even if they appear to be beneficial, they are outside the proper boundaries of one's function and will, therefore, sooner or later be resented, be resisted, and be considered impositions . . . .

Methodology

The first step in dealing with impacts is to identify them coldly and realistically. Impact areas are those characteristics of society that will be affected by a company's proposed action or product. (Exhibit 8–2 divides these characteristics into six major categories.) The next step in impact assessment consists of asking the following key questions about the nature of the impacts upon each of the thirty-five subdivisions of Exhibit 8–2:

—Affected group: What social group will be most affected—for example, old or young, rich or poor, workers or managers, the sick or the well?
—How affected: Will the group be affected for better or worse, and in what specific way?
—Likelihood: How likely is the impact to occur—for example, does it have a 50–50 chance?
—Timing: What are the estimated dates for both the initial impact and later widespread effects?
—Magnitude: What will be the cost of impact? (Estimates should be in terms of dollars, percentage increases, or number affected, rather than expressed in adjectives like "large," "small," and so on.)
—Duration: Will the initial impact improve or worsen, and for how long?
—Diffusion: What will be the breadth and depth of impact? (An unfavorable impact concentrated on a few people will cause more social distress than an unfavorable impact of equal total magnitude that is diffused through many people.
—Controllability: Is it likely that some modification could dampen the impact?

Equipped with the findings from the second step of impact assessment, managers might find it useful to pause and ask themselves whether the impacts, if any, are what society is paying the company for.

EXHIBIT 8–2   Identification of Business Impacts

Characteristics of Society

Values
- Personal
- Community
- National
- Other

Environment
- Air
- Water
- Open space
- Noise abatement
- Odor control
- Weather
- Sunlight

Demography
- Total
- Major segments
- Rates [a]

Economy
- Production
- Income
- Employment
- Prices
- Trained manpower
- Natural resources inventory

Social [b]
- National security
- Economic growth
- Opportunity [c]
- Health
- Education
- Safety (e.g., crime control)
- Transportation
- Leisure-recreation
- Other amenities

Institutions
- Political
- Legal
- Administrative
- Organizational
- Traditional
- Religious

[a] Migration, population density, birth and death rates, etc.

[b] Goals and problems

[c] In areas such as improved class relations or eradication of poverty

Source: Adapted from Mitre Corporation, *A Technology Assessment Methodology* (Washington, D.C.: U.S. Government Printing Office, 1971).

Proper impact assessment does not end with the identification of impacts. The manager now needs to consider modifications designed to maximize the favorable impacts and to minimize unfavorable impacts. Modifications may take a variety of forms. If one is assessing the impact of a product, more research, development, or engineering might be in order. Sometimes cooperation of government or education of the public might be more effective. One well-known example of how impact analysis leads to modifications in a project is the special caribou crossings built during the construction of the Alaskan pipeline.

Cycle-Safe: A Case Study in Corporate Impact Assessment. Let us see how the methodology of comprehensive impact assessment works in practice.

In the mid-1970s Coca-Cola Company used a bottle called Cycle-Safe made by the Monsanto Company (Exhibit 8–3). Before launching this new container, Monsanto had subjected the bottle to a thorough impact assessment. They even went so far as to assume some people would find the empty bottles flammable and would cook over them! For four weeks, therefore, Monsanto fed rats hamburger cooked over a Cycle-Safe fire. Tests showed the rats suffered no ill effects.

Finally, Monsanto held a symposium at Hartford, Connecticut, to which it invited over seventy potential critics. The company paraded its suspicions and test results and asked the critics, Have we overlooked anything? The results were flattering. More symposiums were held in Chicago, New York, and Washington. The results remained flattering. The symposiums made the following points (adapted from U.S. Congress, Technology Assessment Board, 1976:31–36):

• The energy required to produce the bottle is comparable to that used in the manufacture of glass and steel containers, and less than that used in the manufacture of aluminum. If the plastic bottles were recycled—that is, recovered, ground into plastic powder, and re-formed into bottles—they would be more frugal energy consumers than their nonrecycled competitors.

• When incinerated under "proper conditions" involving high temperatures and plenty of oxygen, the bottle is "almost completely consumed." Under improper conditions, an increase in smoke is noted. Experimental refuse fires, fueled by 15 percent acrylonitrile-styrene, showed no appreciable increase in harmful gases.

• The bottle is light, resists breakage, and floats. Because it does not decompose naturally, Monsanto claims the bottle will lend "stability" to solid-waste heaps.

• The petroleum energy used to produce the plastic in the bottles is to some extent recoverable, provided the bottles are burned and their heat recovered.

Nevertheless, three years later lawyers for the Natural Resources Defense Council (NRDC) filed suit asking the Food and Drug Administration to withdraw approval of the bottle. According to the NRDC, "serious unresolved questions" about chemicals migrating from the plastic container into the soda pop, and thus into the bodies of the consumers, motivated the suit. Had the NRDC blind-sided Monsanto? Not really. Monsanto had even anticipated this charge in 1973. At that time, it was pointed out that in-depth tests on the possible health effects of chemical migration—ranging from tests for birth defects to tests for cancer—had not been conducted. All the bottle's components were already regulated by the FDA, reasoned Monsanto, so the bottle represented "no new composition of matter."

EXHIBIT 8–3   The Limitations of Corporate Impact Assessment

In one of its most devastating thrusts against a single company, the Federal Drug Administration in 1977 condemned a plastic soft-drink bottle that Monsanto had spent $47 million to bring to market and subject to extensive impact analysis. The bottle in question (shown above) is made of acrylonitrile, which has been shown to cause birth defects in animals. The question that Monsanto and the FDA will be arguing in court—for probably a long time—centers on the likelihood of the acrylonitrile leaching into the soft drinks the bottle would contain.

Source: Photo courtesy of Monsanto Plastics & Resins Co., St. Louis, Missouri.

Acting on the NRDC's complaint, the FDA proposed a ban on Cycle-Safe. The ruling was based on two major considerations. First, no matter how carefully the plastic was made, it would contain stray molecules that would invade the drink if subjected to enough heat for a long period. Second, tests showed that rats fed very large doses of these stray molecules developed an above-normal number of tumors.

Monsanto's lawyers objected on two grounds to the realism of these tests. First, to get the molecules to stray from the container into the drink, the Cycle-

Safe bottle had to be stored at 120°F, the temperature required to disturb the molecules. At this temperature, however, the pressure from the carbon dioxide in the drink would build up and be likely to rupture the container. In other words, there was no way that the bottle, filled with soft drink, could survive a temperature of 120°F for even a month. Second, the cancer-inducing molecules fed to the rats in the experiment noted above were the equivalent of *thousands* of quarts of soft drink consumed daily in the course of a normal human lifetime. Although Monsanto continued to battle the FDA in a federal appeals court, the Coca-Cola Company switched to the polyester bottles of Monsanto's rival, Goodyear Tire and Rubber Company.

Several things about the Cycle-Safe case are worth highlighting. First, the case reveals the limitations of impact assessment. Despite a sophisticated and expensive internal assessment of plastic beverage bottles in the early 1970s, Monsanto was not able to prevent the product from criticism. Second, the case reveals just how tenacious and resourceful some of the challengers of business can be. Third, the case serves to remind us how business can take an issue to court when the decision by an administrative agency proves unsatisfactory. Finally, the case shows how law and science intertwine when attempting to determine just what a "safe" product is.

This is not the last example of impact assessment we shall look at. And, as we shall see, not all cases of comprehensive impact assessment have such an unhappy ending.

FINDING SOCIAL OPPORTUNITIES

Results in business are obtained by exploiting opportunities, not by solving problems. As Peter F. Drucker reminds us (1964:5):

> All one can hope to get by solving a problem is to restore normality. All one can hope, at best, is to eliminate a restriction on the capacity of the business to obtain results. The results themselves must come from the exploitation of opportunities .... "Maximization of opportunities" is a meaningful, indeed a precise, definition of the entrepreneurial job. It implies that effectiveness, rather than efficiency, is essential in business. The pertinent question is not how to do things right, but how to find the right things to do, and to concentrate resources and efforts on them.

In recent years a new source of opportunities for business management has emerged (see Exhibit 8–4 for an example). These opportunities, because they are related to the problems of a changing society, might be termed *social opportunities*. To the extent that a proper aim of business is to satisfy needs in society, the resolution of these problems is not an inappropriate aim, provided that other aims of the business are also served. One of the major tasks of business today is to convert change into opportunity.

EXHIBIT 8–4   Converting Change into Opportunity

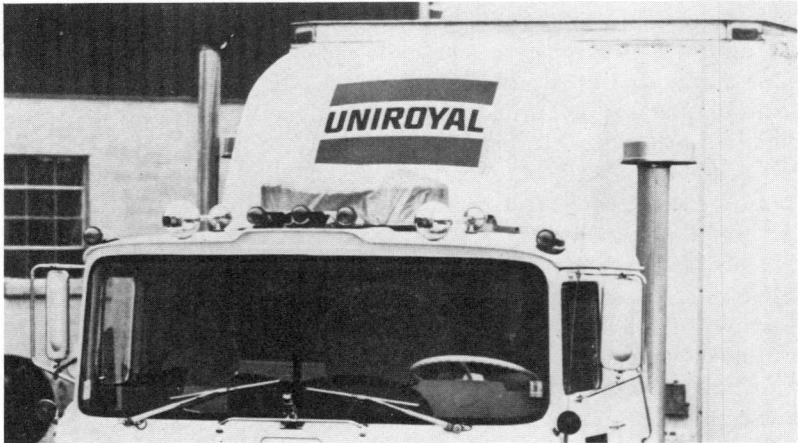

The air deflector is one of the most successful of an array of devices developed since the oil embargo of 1973 to reduce the fuel appetite of U.S. trucks. Despite the initial success of the deflector, many observers have remained skeptical of the claims made about it. Nevertheless, Uniroyal offered a ninety-day guarantee that the device would produce a 10 percent fuel savings.

Source: Photo courtesy of Uniroyal, Inc., New York.

Technological Possibilities: Two Case Studies

In the early 1970s a 3M Chemical Company engineer flew to the company's Cordoba, Illinois, plant to help with the development of an experimental herbicide. On his return flight he discovered that the smell of the herbicide was as effective in repulsing people as its chemical activity was in retarding weeds; passengers avoided sitting anywhere near him. When he got home, he burned his clothes and then wrote a report of the incident for the company. The report prompted 3M to enter a two-year project to reformulate the herbicide and make it virtually odor free. Had it not been for the company's "pollution prevention pays" program—an intensive effort to eliminate pollution at its source rather than to clean up stack gases and effluent—the effort might have stopped there. Instead, 3M went on to develop an entirely new method for producing the herbicide. The result was the elimination not only of the undesirable odor, but also of the need for a $1.1 million waste treatment plant. The herbicide project was one of the first on 3M's list of profitable pollution control efforts.

The list of successes so impressed officials of the Environmental Protection Agency and the Commerce Department that they featured the 3M program at a two-day, interindustry conference in 1976. Explained one EPA spokesman: "3M's is a well-documented philosophy, applied from the top down, and it is the first time pollution prevention has been approved this way or has been applied so widely" (*Business Week,* November 22, 1976).

A second example of an industry seizing a social opportunity involves the nearly 5 billion large trash bags used by American consumers in 1976. Of that number, 15 percent were burned, 5 percent were recycled, and 80 percent went to sanitary landfills or became litter. Environmental groups, concerned about that 80 percent, began proposing legislation to require that disposable plastic products be recyclable or degradable. In 1977 Bes-Pak, an Alabama plastics company, attempted to satisfy the environmentalists and consumers alike with the development of a disappearing trash bag. The plastic bags contain a light-sensitive chemical that causes them to become brittle and begin to decompose after several weeks' or months' exposure to the sun's ultraviolet rays. Ultimately, the bags are reduced to carbon dioxide and water.

Ecological Marketing Strategies

In addition to recognizing technological possibilities, opportunity-minded management must also recognize the existence of an ecological market, both foreign and domestic. Department of Commerce studies estimate that foreign countries will spend billions of dollars a year on pollution control equipment in the 1980s. Though U.S. companies hope to capture many of these dollars, they can expect stiff competition from Japan. That nation, already spending about 2 percent of its GNP on antipollution devices, is in the forefront of creating technology that will keep the environment clean.

Few have given more thought to the subject of ecological marketing than Karl E. Henion II (1976). Henion recommends a particular environmental marketing strategy based on engaging the profit motive of producers of environmentally beneficial products (EN-products). A major company's marketing of aerosols without fluorocarbons and Sears's introduction of its phosphate-free detergent ECOLO-G (which makes the most intimate possible connection between the brand name and the environmental quality of the product) provide dramatic examples of ecological marketing. Ecological marketing strategy plays down the role of government as regulator and stresses its potential role as a more active educator. An important communications challenge for ecological education and advertising, Henion says, is to create visual imagery strong enough to make ecological issues more real to people. He sees the ecologically concerned consumer (ECC) as the principal initial target of ecological marketers—whether producers, government, or nonprofit organizations.

Ecological marketing means greater attention to packaging. Although consumer demand for convenience appears to be well entrenched, according to Henion, there are signs that some consumers are willing "to forfeit a portion of their convenience in exchange for some improvement in environmental quality. Still other consumers, unmindful of environmental consideration but concerned about rising prices, also seem ready to sacrifice some convenience." The following examples (adapted from Henion, 1976:80–84 and 154–56) show the implications of ecological marketing on management strategy.

• The management of Red Owl Stores, Inc., a large supermarket chain in the Midwest, conceived an ecological promotion entitled "Bring 'em Back, Repack, and Save" and designed to stimulate the reuse of various containers. The ecological promotion had three main elements:

1. Cash refunds. The customer received two cents for each paper shopping bag refilled and three cents for each egg carton repacked from a bulk egg display.
2. Advertising to encourage use of refillable glass or plastic milk containers. The usual four-cent refund was given for containers returned.
3. Sale of plastic shopping bags. These reusable bags were sold for twenty-four cents, and customers received two-cent refunds each time the bags were refilled.

The promotion relied on encouragement, not on force; shoppers could decline to participate in the program and still feel comfortable shopping at Red Owl.

• McDonald's practices ecological marketing in many ways. By having its ordertakers ask whether the customer plans to eat the meal in the restaurant, much take-out packaging (paper bags, cup lids, and disposable carrying trays) can be eliminated and replaced with reusable plastic trays, which can mean a substantial reduction in solid waste. With regard to the sandwich boxes McDonald's uses, the company engaged Stanford Research Institute to study the environmental tradeoffs between polystyrene and traditional paperboard. Ordinarily biodegradable paper can be considered environmentally beneficial, but in comparing products with respect to solid-waste generation, weight is an important criterion. According to the Stanford study, Henion reports:

> With respect to weight, polystyrene was found to be better. . . . Besides, its use would eliminate sandwich wraps and collars presently used in connection with the paper sandwich box. In addition to reducing waste at its source, it was found that producing polystyrene requires a great deal less energy than does paper. . . . This material, which is comparable in cost to paper, has a functional advantage of keeping sandwiches warmer while retaining more moisture than paper. Thus, McDonald's ecological marketing practices are quite varied and are made to serve their own economic interests as well as those of the environment by helping to reduce solid waste at its source.

Social Innovation

Buried not too far below the surface of the preceding discussion of technological possibilities and ecological marketing strategies is an important idea: As sources of business opportunity, social change and social innovation have always been at least as important. Drucker reminds us (1974:338):

> The major industries of the nineteenth century were, to a very large extent, the result of converting the new social environment—the industrial city—into a business opportunity and into a business market. This underlay the rise of lighting, first by gas and then by electricity, of the streetcar and the interurban trolley, of telephone, newspaper, and department store—to name only a few. The most significant opportunities for converting social problems into business opportunities may, therefore, not lie in new technologies, new products, and new services. They may lie in solving the social problems, that is, in social innovation which then directly and indirectly benefits and strengthens the company or the industry.

In fact, some of the most successful businesses owe many of their achievements to social innovations, as the following examples illustrate.

● Facing labor unrest in the years prior to World War I, Ford Motor Company announced that it would pay a guaranteed $5-a-day wage to every one of its workers. With the new wage, which was two or three times the current standard, turnover almost disappeared. The resulting savings in production costs were so great that Ford could sell its cars at lower prices and gain market domination (see Drucker, 1974).

● During the years of the Great Depression, IBM, then a very small company, gave its workers employment security by putting them on a salary instead of an hourly wage, in an action, like Ford's, aimed at a major social problem of the time: the fear, insecurity, and loss of dignity that the depression inflicted on workers. By turning a social disease into a business opportunity, IBM created the human potential for the company's subsequent rapid growth (see Drucker, 1974).

● In 1973, responding to new levels of consumer expectations, Volvo began an advertising campaign in the United States that focused on safety. The campaign emphasized the six steps Volvo had taken in regard to auto safety that were in effect before these measures became mandatory in the United States.

● Even earlier than Volvo, the Whirlpool Corporation had begun to look at consumerism as an opportunity to provide customers with better products and services.

● By the late 1970s, inflation had become *the* major problem facing American society. Therefore, a regional chain of food stores centered in Houston, Weingarten's, announced a new marketing concept: the sale of no-name brands of food and other items at a savings to consumers of between 10 and 43 percent on the costs of some items over fancier-packaged items.

In sum, we should not infer from the discussion in this section that converting the problems of society into social opportunities for business is an easy alchemy. For example, by the late 1970s appliance manufacturers were meeting government demands to cut the total energy consumption of their products by 17 percent. But consumers were not buying, apparently because energy-saving appliances cost more initially. Whirlpool, for example, offered two similar models of refrigerators, one of which used 136 kilowatts a month and the other, 99. The more efficient model did not sell as well as the other, which cost about fifty dollars less, even though it would have taken only three years for the buyer to recover the added investment. The lesson here was not lost on Bes-Pak, the maker of the degradable trash bag discussed earlier. The key ingredient in consumer acceptance of that product was the fact that degradable bags cost no more than regular bags.

Furthermore, managers should recognize that some of society's most serious problems tend to defy corporate efforts to convert them into opportunities for performance and contribution. It is doubtful, for instance, whether any business by itself could have done much about the racial problem—at least not until the whole of society had changed its awareness and convictions. Yet, as we shall see in the next section, much remains that business can and should do to increase the health of society. Simply put, a healthy or at least functioning society is a requisite to a healthy business.

IDENTIFYING INDIRECT BENEFITS

In addition to finding social opportunities that are potential moneymakers, managers must consider whether to take actions that are socially responsible but hold little promise for direct tangible returns. Developing a disappearing trash bag and making a Chicano a member of the board represent two different kinds of managerial decisions. This section presents a framework designed to provide some help to those managers considering issues such as the latter.

Before presenting this framework, it is important to be clear on the methodological quicksands into which we are about to step. Ideally, in order for management to make appropriate decisions, the financial implications of socially responsive actions should be integrated into a budgeting and control system. Unfortunately, this has not been feasible, at least so far. The difficulty lies in systematically measuring social costs. While it is easy enough to measure capital spending for pollution control equipment or expenditures for special minority training, determining the effect on operating costs is not so easy. And with actions that affect market position (such as withdrawing offensive advertising or adding safety features), the measurement problems become enormous.

Determining benefits is even more difficult. Robert W. Ackerman asks (1975:55–56):

What is the value to the corporation of, for instance, reducing noxious emissions into the atmosphere below the levels required by current law? There may be some fairly direct benefits in a rosier public image, a better bargaining position with government regulators seeking compliance at other plants, pride among managers that "we're one of the good guys," an attractive posture for recruiting on campus, a jump on meeting future regulations at today's prices; if good fortune abounds, perhaps even a process innovation that will increase yields.

The list could be extended indefinitely. But what are these benefits worth? From the accountant's point of view, they have the unfortunate characteristics of being largely intangible, unassignable to the costs or organizational units creating them and occurring over an undeterminable future time period.

Keeping in mind these difficulties associated with analyzing the indirect benefits of socially responsible activities, let us turn to a simple flow chart that might at least remove some of the subjectivity associated with these kinds of decisions. Exhibit 8–5 presents a series of six steps to be followed before undertaking action of a socially responsible but only indirectly beneficial nature. These steps, as the exhibit suggests, can be viewed as a set of questions that must all be answered affirmatively. In the following sections we look at each of these steps more closely.

Step 1: Establishing the Appropriateness of the Action. The question raised in this step—Is this action appropriate?—guards against a company's undertaking an action that conflicts with its primary role of providing goods and services. Such an action could lead to a serious misallocation of resources, a revolt among the stockholders, and outrage among various segments of society. Consider, for example, the case of the Union Carbide plant in Vienna, West Virginia (see Commentary, "High Responsibility Gone Wrong"). For an even more vivid, though hypothetical example, consider the socially responsible company that decides "to do something" about overpopulation by funding free abortion clinics in a community. Or the socially responsible company that expresses its concern for human life by letting the local right-to-life group hold meetings in the plant conference hall.

As Aldag and Jackson have pointed out, a serious corollary question becomes apparent in thinking through these matters: Does society really want the company to undertake this action? Regardless of whether a right to undertake social action exists, business leaders must ask themselves whether they would be performing net services to society by following such pursuits. At least two factors are involved in answering this question. First, on an economic basis, the public's net gain must be assessed by weighing the benefits of a proposed action against a pair of costs: the direct cost (increased prices to consumers) and the more indirect costs (possible weakening of market mechanisms). Second, on a less tangible level, it must be remembered that when society allows corporations to initiate social action, power is diverted from society at large to those corporations. There are some who would argue that such

EXHIBIT 8–5   Decision Flow Chart for Indirectly Beneficial Programs

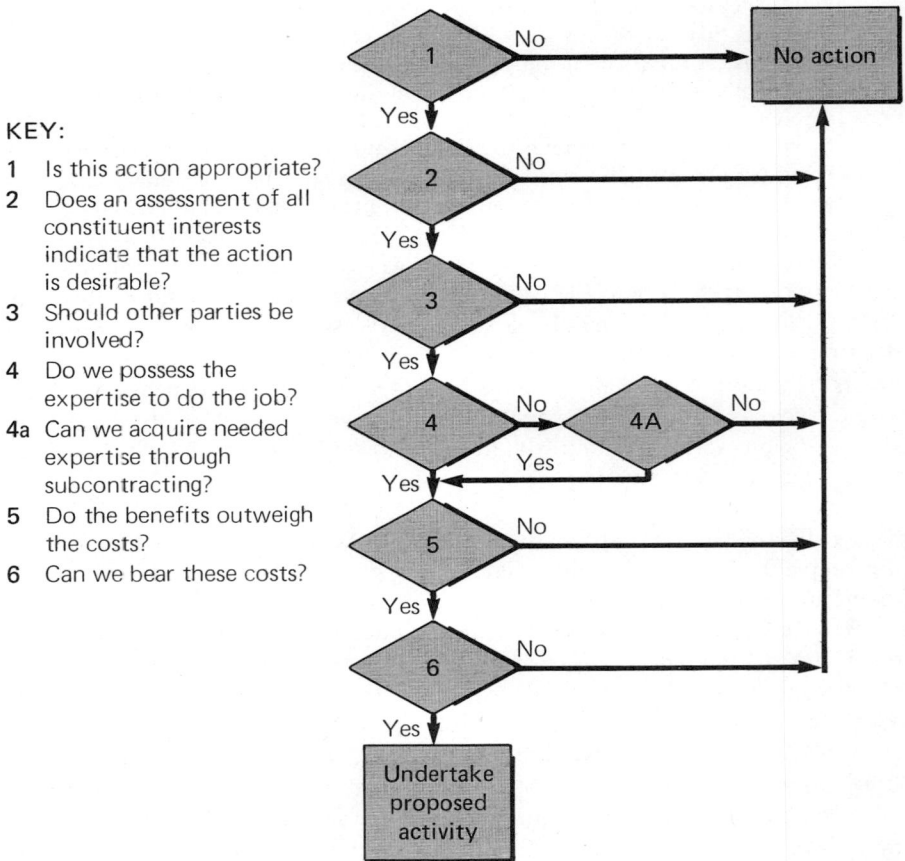

KEY:

1   Is this action appropriate?
2   Does an assessment of all
     constituent interests
     indicate that the action
     is desirable?
3   Should other parties be
     involved?
4   Do we possess the
     expertise to do the job?
4a Can we acquire needed
     expertise through
     subcontracting?
5   Do the benefits outweigh
     the costs?
6   Can we bear these costs?

[Flowchart with decision diamonds numbered 1–6 and 4A. Diamond 1: No → "No action"; Yes ↓. Diamond 2: No →; Yes ↓. Diamond 3: No →; Yes ↓. Diamond 4: No → 4A; Yes ↓. Diamond 4A: No →; Yes →. Diamond 5: No →; Yes ↓. Diamond 6: No →; Yes ↓ to "Undertake proposed activity".]

Source: Modified from Ramon J. Aldag and Donald W. Jackson, Jr. "A Managerial Framework for Social Decision Making," p. 34, *MSU Business Topics,* Spring 1975. Reprinted by permission of the publisher, Division of Research, Graduate School of Business Administration, Michigan State University.

a channeling of power removes many vital questions from the reach of the ballot box and thereby eliminates a major democratic check on the ordering of social priorities. Since business leaders are often faced with conflicting interests and obligations, the forfeiture of such checks is potentially costly to society.

In some areas, such as minority hiring, there is evidence of societal sanction of corporate actions having social impact. In other cases business leaders have been legally constrained from taking "socially responsible" action. For

COMMENTARY: High Responsibility Gone Wrong— A Cautionary Tale

West Virginia, never one of the more prosperous areas of the United States, went into rapid economic decline in the late twenties as the coal industry, long the state's mainstay, began to shrink. . . .

By the late 1940s the leading industrial company in the state became alarmed over the steady economic shrinkage of the region. Union Carbide, one of America's major chemical companies, had its headquarters in New York. But the original plants of the company had been based on West Virginia coal, and the company was still the largest employer in the state, other than a few large coal mines. Accordingly, the company's top management asked a group of young engineers and economists in its employ to prepare a plan for the creation of employment opportunities in West Virginia, and especially for the location of the company's new plant facilities in areas of major unemployment in the state. For the worst afflicted area, however, the westernmost corner of the state on the border of Ohio, the planners could not come up with an attractive project. Yet this area needed jobs the most. In and around the little town of Vienna, West Virginia, there was total unemployment, and no prospects for new industries. The only plant that could possibly be put in the Vienna area was a ferroalloy plant using a process that had already become obsolete and had heavy cost disadvantages compared to more modern processes such as Union Carbide's competitors were already using.

Even for the old process, Vienna was basically an uneconomical location. The process required very large amounts of coal of fair quality. But the only coal available within the area was coal of such high sulfur content that it could not be used without expensive treatment and scrubbing. Even then—that is, after heavy capital investment—the process was inherently noisy and dirty, releasing large amounts of fly ash and of noxious gases.

In addition, the only transportation facilities, both rail and road, were not in West Virginia but across the river, on the Ohio side. Putting the plant there, however, meant that the prevailing westerly winds would blow the soot from the smokestacks and the sulfur released by the power plants directly into the town of Vienna, on the other bank of the river.

Yet the Vienna plant would provide 1,500 jobs in Vienna itself and another 500 to 1,000 jobs in a new coal field not too far distant. In addition, the new coal field would be capable of being strip mined, so the new mining jobs would be free from the accident and health hazards that had become increasingly serious in the old and worked-out coal mines of the area. Union Carbide top management came to the conclusion that social responsibility demanded building the new plant, despite its marginal economics.

The plant was built with the most up-to-date antipollution equipment known at the time. Whereas even big-city power stations were then content to trap half the fly ash escaping their smokestacks, the Vienna plant installed scrubbers to catch 75 percent—though there was little anyone could do about the sulfur dioxide fumes emitted by the high-sulfur coal.

When the plant was opened in 1951, Union Carbide was the hero. Politicians, public figures, educators, all praised the company for its social responsibility. But ten years later the former savior was fast becoming the public enemy. As the nation became pollution-conscious, the citizens of Vienna began to complain more and more bitterly about the ash, the soot, and the fumes that floated across the river into their town and homes. About 1961 a new mayor was elected on the platform "fight pollution," which meant "fight Union Carbide." Ten years later the plant had become a "national scandal." . . .

There is little doubt that Union Carbide's management did not behave very intelligently. They should have realized in the early sixties that they were in trouble, rather than delay and procrastinate, make and then break promises—until the citizens, the state government, the press, the environmentalists, and the federal government all were aiming their biggest guns at the company. It was not very smart to protest for years that there was nothing wrong with the plant and then, when governmental authorities began to get nasty, announce that the plant would have to be closed as it could not be brought up to environmental standards.

Yet this is not the basic lesson of this cautionary tale. Once the decision had been made to employ an obsolescent process and to build an economically marginal plant in order to alleviate unemployment in a bitterly depressed area, the rest followed more or less automatically. This decision meant that the plant did not generate the revenues needed to be rebuilt. There is very little doubt that on economic reasoning alone the plant would never have been built. Public opinion forced Union Carbide to invest substantial sums in that plant to remedy the worst pollution problems—though it is questionable whether the technology exists to do more than a patch-up job. Publicity also forced Union Carbide to keep the plant open. But, once the spotlight shifts elsewhere, most of the jobs in the Vienna, West Virginia, plant are likely to disappear again, if indeed the plant remains open at all.

instance, a firm economically incapable of acting alone on "socially desirable" solutions is often constrained by antitrust laws from acting in concert with competitors. Competitive joint ventures in ghetto areas or joint efforts to combat pollution, for example, have often not been allowed. Thus, in some cases, societal preferences have been codified and present no problem of interpretation to the corporate decisionmaker. But because there is a lag between changes in society's desires and the reflection of those changes in altered legal structures, business leaders must sometimes attempt to gauge societal preferences. Such assessments may prove to be useful leading indicators of future areas in which corporate freedom may be challenged.

Step 2: Assessing of Constituent Interests. This step first attempts an assessment of constituent interests to determine whether the action is desirable on the part of all constituents. This phase obviously requires knowing who a company's constituents are. Shulman and Gale (1972) categorize a company's various constituencies as follows: employees, customers, suppliers, the communities in which it operates, society at large, and competitors. This framework has the advantage of breaking down the rather amorphous concept of society into a set of groups that have identifiable interests in enterprise outputs and that can, at least roughly, be defined operationally. Similarly, Shocker and Sethi (1973) note that the General Electric Company has displayed its political sensitivity by identifying thirteen "constituencies/pressure groups"—including unions, academic critics, and moralists—in order to assess their "influence/effectiveness" regarding corporate activities.

Once the constituents' interests are known, balancing the pros and cons for each group requires considerable management skill. For example, consider the balancing involved in a case like Polaroid's hiring of former Walpole Prison inmates in Massachusetts.

Step 3: Weighing the Involvement of Other Parties. This step entails considering the possibility of joining forces with other institutions, profit and nonprofit. The options available take many forms, as the following examples illustrate.

- One of the most potentially significant efforts by big business to come to grips with the environmental problem was the establishment in 1970 by a group of twenty-five executives from major U.S. corporations of the National Center for Resources, Inc. The center, which is nonprofit, offers information on solid waste technology; research, development, and evaluation programs; public awareness programs; and technical assistance programs. It is also involved in a number of demonstration programs in communities all over the country. Its support comes from industry and labor groups involved primarily in the reproduction, use, and sale of packaging (see Gunn, 1972).
- In September 1976 a group of nine major oil companies with refining and marketing facilities on the New York–New Jersey waterfront formed a mutual aid cooperative after an industry study showed that only through such cooperation would the companies have the capacity to deal with really serious oil spills in the harbor.
- In 1976 the Houston Chamber of Commerce launched its Chemical Recycle Information Program, designed to match waste-chemical producers with possible users through an inventory distributed to subscribers.

Step 4: Evaluating Expertise. Assuming that a proposal has passed the first three steps in the analysis of an indirectly beneficial program, management must then address the question of whether the company has the expertise to be effective in taking the proposed action. The frustration so many business managers experience is often based on a failure to consider this simple and direct question. Ignoring it, these companies charge pell-mell into areas clearly outside their competencies.

For example, consider the efforts of soft-drink companies to develop nutritional beverages for LDCs. Fortifying beverages and foods with protein and vitamins has enormous implications for the underdeveloped world. No one claims that nutritive food and beverages alone can solve the global problem of malnutrition, but many nutritionists think the effort is well worth making. While a few companies have had modest success, including Coca-Cola, the following example (adapted from *New York Times,* April 24, 1978) is more typical: Even with formidable resources of 750 bottlers in 135 foreign countries, Coca-Cola has had problems with vitamin-fortified beverages. In Rio de Janeiro in 1968, the company marketed a 3 percent soymilk protein beverage, a noncarbonated drink in chocolate and caramel flavors fortified with seven vitamins and fat. But the drink had too high a viscosity, and "it tasted something like chalk," according to one former drinker. It was withdrawn after two years.

Lack of in-house expertise, however, should not necessarily lead to the tabling of a proposal. Alternatives should be explored. For example, very little in the training of a manager provides the kind of exposure to the sociological and psychological issues that might help in a minority-hiring program. Nevertheless, several things might be done to compensate for managerial inadequacy in this area. Managerial training programs can be developed, experts can be hired, or the task can be subcontracted. For instance, a minority-hiring program might be set in motion with the help of a firm like EEO Services (a subsidiary of the Bayden International Group), which has offices on Madison Avenue. This company's job specialty is part of the classic role of consulting firms: It tells companies things that are already known to certain levels of management—but it tells them with the impact that only an independent outsider can convey.

COMMENTARY: Responsibility in the Center City— An Encouraging Tale

"We talk a lot about human rights, but I don't know of any human right that is more important than a job." The speaker is William Norris, a Nebraska farmer's son who learned about computers when he was a World War II Navy cryptographer (he helped to break the German code), then sold stock at $1 a share to start Control Data in Minneapolis in 1957. Last year the company had sales of $2.3 billion, and its profits rose by 42 percent. But Chairman Norris . . . is doing much more than adding to his millions. While other people merely fret . . . about hard-core unemployment, this . . . engineer is taking long risks to create jobs for people who had felt left behind and shut out by the system.

So far, 1,000 people—mostly unskilled and black—have found work in plants that Control Data has opened in the ghettos of Minneapolis, St. Paul and Washington, D.C. The number will rise to 1,400 . . . when Norris opens a fourth plant in a renewal area of St. Paul. Other business chiefs have tried to build in the ghetto, only to fail. Norris says he knows why: *"They figured it was just philanthropy. They sent in their money, but not their smarts or their guts."*

When Control Data built its first inner-city plant in Minneapolis in 1968, Norris laid down three rules: *"Make the plant new and modern. Make it profitable. Make us dependent on it, so that we will have to make it work."* The plant accordingly was designed to build intricate components.

Norris also sought out local black leaders and followed their street-smart advice: Build a day-care center for working mothers. Offer to put them on flexible hours, say, 8:30 A.M. to 2:00 P.M., or 1:00 to 5:00 P.M. Don't ask if the applicant has been arrested. Yes, many have been busted, but what difference does that make? Don't ask for personal references. Should the ghetto resident get the corner bookie to vouch that he pays his bills?

At first, absenteeism and quitting were problems. But Norris and his executives held on, training, prodding, sometimes bailing workers out of jail after long weekends. Today, the average worker in the first plant has held his job for five years, building skills and climbing up. The story is much the same at Norris' other inner-city factories. Says he: "Businessmen come to visit those plants, and they ask, 'Jeez, don't you have terrible trouble with people breaking your windows and smearing your walls?' The answer is no—because if somebody gets a notion to do that, they had better watch out. People in the neighborhood protect the plant. It's a source of pride as well as jobs. They feel it is *theirs.*"

Ultimately, Norris figures, America's cities will be rebuilt by big consortiums of private business. The Government will help guarantee bank loans and perhaps kick in some grants; churches and universities will put in investment funds. Construction companies will erect buildings; transport companies will bid for mass transit; energy, environmental control and waste recycling firms will all have roles, and much of the work will be parceled out to small business. The object is not only to raze and remake scabrous neighborhoods, but also to create private jobs, help small entrepreneurs and, not incidentally, to make money.

Control Data is studying cities in which to start, and Norris is talking with some mayors, seeking support. "Dammit," he snorts, "rebuilding the cities will be one of the great growth industries of the future. It will replace the auto as the big provider of jobs—if we Americans can ever get ourselves organized."

Source: Marshall Loeb, "Planting in the Ghettos," *Time,* April 3, 1978 (italics added). Reprinted by permission from *Time, The Weekly Newsmagazine;* Copyright Time Inc. 1978.

Step 5: Assessing Costs and Benefits. This step entails a question that is easy enough to put: Do the benefits outweigh the cost? In trying to answer this question, a decisionmaker is forced to think through just how much a line of action will benefit society. Admittedly, quantifying benefits to society is an activity lacking in mathematical precision. But economics provides us with a variety of tools for dealing with the measurement problem (see Epilogue). More-over, our experience in this area grows richer every year.

In any event, no matter how difficult the measurement problem, the fifth step remains an essential one; it can lead to a more intelligent choice when the decisionmaker is confronted with several alternative lines of action. In situations such as these, the decisionmaker seeks to maximize benefits minus costs or, if resources are limited, the ratio of benefits to costs. Alternatives that show more costs to society than benefits should of course be rejected. Alternatives that show only a marginal impact are mere "window dressing," and managers may as well recognize them candidly as such in order that they can get on with more productive lines of inquiry. Carl Holman, president of the National Urban Coalition, summed it up well for opponents of "window-dressing" measures when he said: "We no longer like the phony deals—a bank staking a black man to a clothing store in a dying neighborhood. They're willing to write off the loss. But why not get that man into a shopping center?" (*Business Week*, June 30, 1973).

Cost-benefit analysis might be used in another way—namely, to insure that the benefits to the company, indirect and often intangible as they might be, exceed the company's outlay of funds. The reason for this type of analysis should be clear enough from the earlier example of the Union Carbide plant in Vienna, West Virginia. Unless a company is convinced that the benefits from a line of action exceed the costs, it is likely that (a) in the short run, managers will fail to take the project seriously and (b) in the long run, the company will abandon the project—often with disastrous consequences.

The following example adapted from Novick (1973) simulates a cost-benefit analysis for a business manager who accepts an array of socially related actions as among the cost options deserving study. Our hypothetical company manufactures fabricated metal products and requires highly skilled machinists. The plant has a total employment of 400, of which 320 are in the high-skill categories. Total annual payroll is about $4 million; annual sales are in excess of $12 million. The city in which the company operates has a population of 200,000. In the last twenty-five years, there has been significant in-migration of lower-income, poorly educated, socially disadvantaged white, black, and Puerto Rican families and individuals. The in-migrants number over 15,000 and create problems in housing, schooling, and welfare. The company in our example already employs 25 people from this group among its 80 low-skill employees.

Because of the size of its sales, payroll, and plant area—more acreage than actually required in its long-range corporate plan—the company has high local visibility. The chief executive officer has decided that his corporate social responsibilities include more than community chest donations and company-paid time off for employees who volunteer for Boy Scout, Red Cross, church, and similar activities. He also has concluded that the town does not know the importance of the role his company plays in its affairs. He has therefore determined to budget $100,000 for the next year to meet the corporation's social responsibilities. The company's planning department has been asked to do a cost-benefit analysis that, in the fixed-budget case, means maximizing benefits for the $100,000 investment.

After several weeks of study, the planning department group identifies five options for the $100,000 social-responsibility budget:

—Alternative A: Invest in a program to increase the number of highly skilled company employees from the socially disadvantaged groups.
—Alternative B: Invest in another local enterprise to enable that organization to increase employment using low-skill workers.
—Alternative C: Develop a new product line within the company that requires medium-grade skills and emphasize the employment of the socially disadvantaged.
—Alternative D: Develop a community recreation center on land surplus to the company's long-range plans and upgrade appearance of plant exterior and grounds.
—Alternative E: Launch a public relations campaign to educate the community on the organization's existing socially oriented programs. [Novick, 1973]

For each of the alternatives, the planning department has developed information indicating the benefits to be anticipated from $100,000 paid out in the next budget year.

—Alternative A: There are no visible gains from recruiting from the socially disadvantaged for skilled until 70 percent of the budget has been spent; moreover, the benefits obtained for the full amount are not promising.
—Alternative B: Investing in [another local enterprise] produces substantial benefits quickly, but shows no growth after reaching its peak level.
—Alternative C: The new product line within the company produces reasonable benefit but does not appear to build onto its early growth.
—Alternative D: The community center and plant appearance program produces fairly high benefits for relatively small outlays and promises increasing benefit when the program is completed.
—Alternative E: The public relations program produces its major benefits with the early dollars, after which additional outlays do not prevent declining benefits. More important, it is very low on the benefit scale. [Novick, 1973]

Before the final decision is made, each alternative must be considered in light of the elements of a cost-benefit analysis:

—Objective: What is to be accomplished;
—Options: Alternative means for achieving the goal;
—Costs: Expenditures to carry out each alternative;
—Effectiveness: Position on the effectiveness scale assigned each alternative according to degree of achievement of goal;
—Criterion: Statement about cost and effectiveness that determines choice. [Novick, 1973]

Let us now apply these elements to our example. Is the objective purely humanitarian—that is, to improve both present status and future opportunity for the socially disadvantaged? Or is the objective based on intelligent self-interest that aims at providing a desirable social service to the community while giving credit to the corporation and not penalizing profits?

Alternatives A and C provide means for improving future economic opportunity for a limited number of the socially disadvantaged group. B offers the maximum benefit in terms of immediate impact on local employment, while D provides a desirable social service, identifies the activity with the corporation, and has potential business impact on those customers that visit the plant. E appears to be a purely self-serving effort that makes no contribution to social needs.

Exhibit 8–6 illustrates the projected costs and benefits for each alternative. Using the area under the curve as the basis of comparison, Alternative B appears to be dominant. However, the promising upturn in the direction of D indicates the desirability of further study of that option. Since we have normalized costs by use of a fixed budget and time period, this oversimplification does not permit an exploration of the full potential of Alternative D, the community center program. At the same time, it makes it clear that further analysis is needed before a commitment is made to what appears to be the obvious choice—Alternative B, investment in a local plant employing low-skill workers.

Step 6: Determining Affordability. Arrival at the final step in the decision flow chart in Exhibit 8–5 presupposes affirmative answers to the preceding five steps. Now the decisionmaker must examine the proposed line of action in light of the current profit position of the firm. Aldag and Jackson write (1975:40):

> If that position is favorable, the corporation may be able to absorb a large portion, or the entirety, of costs incurred in undertaking this action. On the other hand, if the cost structure and competitive conditions are such that absorption is infeasible, increased costs perhaps can be passed on to consumers or covered by governmental subsidy. . . . [a]ntitrust laws may preclude investment and rule out even a desirable action if the competitive structure is such that unilateral action is not possible. On the other hand, governmental sanction of certain actions may be reflected in incentives such as: tax credits on capital investments, accelerated depreciation on investments, construction grants, and training or other grants to help defray costs.

In sum, the purpose of this section has been to present a framework for the systematic examination of the complex sequence of decisions implicit in society-oriented actions whose benefits are at best indirect and often intangible. The purpose, we should bear in mind, was to narrow, or at least clarify,

**EXHIBIT 8–6   Projected Cost and Benefit Measurement of Five
                  Policy Options on a $100,000 Budget**

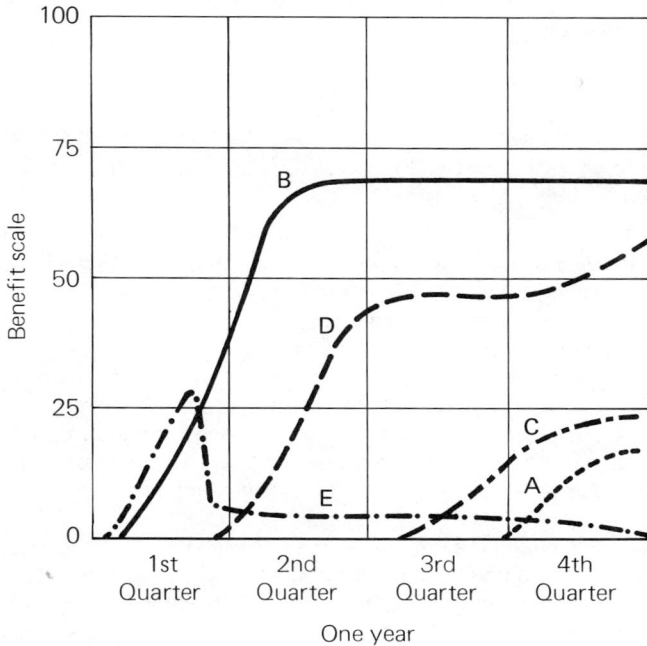

Source: David Novick, "Cost-Benefit Analysis and Social Responsibility," *Business Horizons* (February 1973). Copyright, 1973, by the Foundation for the School of Business at Indiana University. Reprinted by permission.

the bounds of subjectivity, to prevent simplistic answers, and to provide a more solid basis for corporate decision making in meeting its social responsibilities. In the following section we look briefly at the more typical way in which business has gone about meeting its social responsibility.

PHILANTHROPIC ACTIVITIES

Private philanthropy is deeply rooted in American business tradition as corporations have historically met their obligations to society by concentrating on their principal function, which is economic. In recent years corporations and their employees have been major factors in preserving that tradition. Currently, corporations contribute over a billion dollars annually to various charitable organizations. In addition, philanthropic-related business expenses and the time employees at all levels contribute to public service activities are also valued at roughly another billion dollars. Further, company participation in the United Way, including payroll deduction, yields an additional $450 million from individual employees.

COMMENTARY: What Is the United Way?

United Way of America is the United States' largest and most visible charitable institution, an association of over 2,000 chapters, some dues-paying, some not . . . . As a federated campaign organization, United Way got its start in 1887 in Denver, Colorado, raising money on a communitywide basis for ten charitable organizations in a single fund-raising drive. Since 1949, it has narrowed its focus to workplace, so that today the bulk of its funds comes from employees, whether in government or business, under the payroll deduction plan. For both business and labor, the notion of a combined campaign had the virtue of putting an end to countless disruptions in the work schedule that a succession of fund-raising campaigns had previously created. . . .

Because it can call upon the unpaid services of such volunteers—corporation or welfare agency executives no less than the housewives who man the telephones or the solicitors who wander through the plant collecting pledge cards—United Way can keep its costs down. It is these "free" costs that explain why charitable giving is so cost effective. Overall, close to ninety cents on the United Way dollar goes to the purpose for which it was raised, as against seventy-eight cents for the major health agencies.

Of course, in mounting its corporate campaign, United Way usually ends up with exclusive access to the payroll deduction system, and this is what has brought charges from agencies not part of United Way and from competing federated systems—like the Combined Health Agencies Drive (CHAD) in California, or the National Black United Fund—that United Way is attempting to monopolize the payroll deduction process. Several agencies have gone into court in an attempt to break up this dominance. . . .

But when you boil it all down, it seems more than ever that United Way, with its increasing corporate support and payroll deductions scheme, is the wave of the future in charity. You can mount only so many spectacular events; direct mail is becoming prohibitively expensive; bequests, while growing, are not a mass market. Scandals in individual charities further enhance United Way's position because of its tight controls and businesslike supervision.

Source: James Cook, "Is Charity Obsolete?" *Forbes,* February 5, 1979. Reprinted by permission from Forbes Magazine.

Targets of Corporate Giving

The philanthropic organizations with which corporate leaders are personally associated run the gamut of voluntary activity in the United States. When corporate leaders were asked in a survey by Harris and Klepper (1977) to list the three organizations they considered most important (of those with which they had been associated during the past year as a board or committee member, a member of a fund-raising campaign, and so forth), educational institutions dominated (see Exhibit 8–7). The involvement of one out of every two respon-

EXHIBIT 8–7   Organizations Viewed by Corporate Management as Most Important Beneficiaries of Philanthropic Activity

Organizations	Percent of executives involved*
Education:	
Universities and colleges	48%
Educational groups (United Negro College Fund, the Council for Financial Aid to Education, etc.)	18
Secondary and primary schools	5
Total education	71
United Way organizations: United Funds, Community Chests, councils	50
Health:	
Hospitals	18
Health agencies, other medical activities	11
Total health	29
Cultural activities (museums, performing arts, nonacademic libraries)	19
Youth agencies	16
Urban affairs and minority activities	12
Foundations	12
Religious organizations (Catholic Charities, Protestant Council, Jewish Federation) and churches	11
Economic development groups	6
International organizations	5
Other charities (Salvation Army, Goodwill Industries, etc.)	5
Other organizations (public television, environment, community centers, population control, law and justice, etc.)	15

* Based on responses of 334 chairmen and presidents; percentages do not add to 100% because of multiple responses.

Source: James F. Harris and Anne Klepper, "Corporate Philanthropic Public Service Activities," in *Research Papers,* vol. III, sponsored by the Commission on Private Philanthropy and Public Needs (Washington, D.C.: Department of the Treasury, 1977).

dents in United Way activities reflects the fact that business leaders have been instrumental in establishing such federated campaigns in order to bring professionalism and coordination to fund-raising activities. In their support of the arts, top executives may also be taking a leadership role; 19 percent of the respondents rank the arts among their top three philanthropic interests, although only four cents of every contribution dollar went to cultural activities.

Purpose of Corporate Giving

While the size and quality of corporate philanthropy is primarily a reflection of the interest and enthusiasm of top corporate management, these individuals base their philanthropic decisions on company-related considerations. Thus in their survey, Harris and Klepper (1977) asked corporate leaders to check the most important reasons, from a company viewpoint, for undertaking contributions activities in three fields: the United Way, higher education, and the arts (see Exhibit 8-8). Corporate citizenship and improving the business environ-

EXHIBIT 8-8   Corporate Management's Most Important Reasons for Undertaking Philanthropic Activities

Possible reasons for undertaking contribution activities	Specific activities		
	United funds	Higher education	The arts
Corporate citizenship: Practice good corporate citizenship	74%	49%	48%
Business environment: Protect and improve environment in which to live, work and do business	68	46	43
Employee benefits: Realize benefits for company employees (normally in areas where company operates)	47	31	31
Public relations: Realize good public relations value	34	20	32
Pluralism: Preserve a pluralistic society by maintaining choices between government and private-sector alternatives	28	40	10
Commitment: Of directors or senior officers to particular causes, involvement	23	31	28
Pressure: From business peers, or customers and/or suppliers	12	8	17
Altruism: Practice altruism with little or no direct or indirect company self-interest	10	8	15
Manpower supply: Increase the pool of trained manpower or untrained manpower or access to minority recruiting	5	63	2
No contributions or activities in this area	2	2	7

* Based on responses of 417 chairmen and presidents; adds to more than 100% because multiple responses were requested.

Source: James F. Harris and Anne Klepper, "Corporate Philanthropic Public Service Activities," in *Research Papers*, vol. III, sponsored by the Commission on Private Philanthropy and Public Needs (Washington, D.C.: Department of the Treasury, 1977).

ment, two motivations with considerable overlap, understandably ranked particularly high for the United Way. One might argue, however, that the length of time between a gift and an improvement in the business environment has in recent years become rather fuzzy (see Commentary section, "The Smith Test").

In the area of higher education, manpower considerations dominated—a reflection of the long-standing concern of U.S. business with the development of manpower resources. Business and industry are increasingly disappointed with the skill levels of new employees. According to the American Management Association, corporations are spending more than $2 billion on educational training programs, which they would undoubtedly like to see the schools and colleges assume to a greater degree. Complicating the matter is the emergence of (1) a society in which the average skilled workers must be retrained continually to keep up with technological advances and (2) a trend toward mid-career shifts into new occupations. Corporate citizenship and the business environment, along with the preservation of a pluralistic society, were also major reasons for contributing to higher education. Only with respect to the arts was there a lack of consensus. Pure altruism was not a dominant factor in any of these forms of philanthropy, nor was what may be considered its opposite—"pressure" from one source or another.

COMMENTARY: The Smith Test for Philanthropic Activities

Over twenty years ago, the New Jersey Supreme Court handed down a landmark decision in the case of *A.P. Smith Manufacturing Company* v. *Barlow* (1953). In this case, the state supreme court upheld a lower court decision that a corporate gift to Princeton University by A.P. Smith Manufacturing Company, which had been challenged by a stockholder, was legitimate on the grounds that it *strengthened community institutions*. Therefore, it was ultimately beneficial to private business, even though no direct or measurable benefit to the giver could be shown. The lower court, in authorizing the gift, ruled (cited in Buckley, 1977):

> It is the youth of today which also furnishes tomorrow's leaders in economics and government, thereby erecting a strong breastwork against any onslaught from hostile forces which would change our way of life either in respect to private enterprise or democratic self-government. The proofs before me are abundant that Princeton emphasizes by precept and indoctrination the principles which are very vital to the preservation of our democratic system of business and government . . . . I cannot conceive of any greater benefit to corporations in this country than to build, and continue to build, respect for and adherence to a system of free enterprise and democratic government, the serious impairment of either of which may well spell the destruction of all corporate enterprise.

This explanation can serve as a benchmark by which one may see how far corporate giving has drifted from any legal or other rational basis. Today it is hardly unusual for corporate funds to wind up in universities where, for example, the only course in comparative economic systems is taught by an ardent socialist who defends the socialist alternative to the free market system. We must not confuse issues: The right of a professor to teach virtually any doctrine is a constitutional question that was resolved long ago. However, academic freedom is not the issue here; the issue is whether, in the midst of an unprecedented energy squeeze, aggressive international competition, and toughening of federal, state, and local regulations, companies should not expect clear—though not necessarily measurable—benefits from their monetary contributions to the community. American business has been generous with its gifts to community institutions—not too generous but, some observers would argue, too indiscriminate.

Trends in Corporate Giving

Generally speaking, corporate giving today tends to be a fairly low-priority item that is directed by a tired executive or is pushed off to the side of someone's desk. Quick decisions are the rule, and money frequently goes to whomever pleads most loudly. But a few firms are beginning to get fussy. A research associate at the Conference Board, who follows corporate giving activities, maintains that more and more people are being designated as "contributions officers" in big companies. "More companies are drafting guidelines that they are publishing to explain their giving policies. The whole field seems to be growing considerably in professionalism" (Kleinfield, 1978).

The Xerox Corporation, which handed out more than $6.2 million in 1977, is one of the most innovative givers. "We prefer to initiate most of our program, rather than wait to hear from people," says Edward Truschke, the manager of corporate responsibility. "We get about six thousand requests a year, some for oddball things like mountain climbs and comic-book archives. We respond to some worthier ones, but we like to get the ball rolling ourselves" (Kleinfield, 1978). Xerox, for example, was concerned about the aging work force in America. It knew that the University of Southern California had a reputable center of gerontology. A check went off to California for a study on the issues that face people nearing retirement age.

Volunteer Activity: PR in the Best Sense of the Word. According to a survey by the National Center for Voluntary Action, more than three hundred American companies have established volunteer programs, and the number is growing steadily. Further, many companies are allowing employees to do volunteer work on company time. S.V. Roberts (1978) notes that this growth in volunteerism comes at a time when traditional sources of nonpaid labor are dwindling—that is, as more women are entering the work force, the number of housewives who used to spend their afternoons in volunteer work is rapidly dwindling. Corporate programs, like those in Exhibit 8–9, are helping to fill the gap.

Corporations that help their communities through volunteerism also help themselves, sometimes in very direct ways. Clearly, the best way to do business in a community is to have friendly relations with the community, and helping its neighbors is one way that a company can create a desirable business climate. In addition, many corporations encourage volunteer activity as a way of helping their employees to learn new skills, to broaden their outlook, or to ease the pressure of urban living.

Volunteer activity can take several forms (adapted from S.V. Roberts, 1978):

—Lending the services of a company's executives to help a local charity;
—Allowing employees time off from their jobs ("social service leaves")— usually with full pay—to volunteer their services (Xerox, for instance, has a number of employees across the country on service leave. One has worked with a rape-treatment clinic; a deaf physicist has traveled through the country, encouraging deaf children to set higher goals for themselves; and a black manager has helped the United Negro College Fund raise money);
—Allowing employees time off during the day to perform volunteer work (for example, the Hartford Insurance Group gives workers an extra-long lunch hour so they can serve "meals on wheels" to elderly shut-ins; E.B. Industries provides the staff for a volunteer ambulance squad; computer programmers at the United States National Bank of Oregon are released from work for two or three hours a week to help train victims of cerebral palsy to run computers);
—Organizing a company-run volunteer project (this approach has the advantage of earning greater visibility and thus public credit).

Whatever form volunteer programs take, they must be managed. Some companies do so by advertising volunteer openings in their in-house newsletters or on bulletin boards; others designate an employee to coordinate the activities. In the latter cases, organizations seeking volunteers detail their needs, employees indicate their interests, and the coordinator tries to match them up. Xerox, which has an extensive volunteer program, maintains a seven-person board, composed of a cross-section of company workers, to make a final selection of employees who will take social service leaves.

Corporations take different attitudes toward volunteerism. The Shell Oil Company in Houston, for instance, keeps volunteer records in a separate office and does not allow them to be used by personnel officials. Bank of America frankly grades employees on their community involvement.

EXHIBIT 8–9   Volunteerism within the Corporation

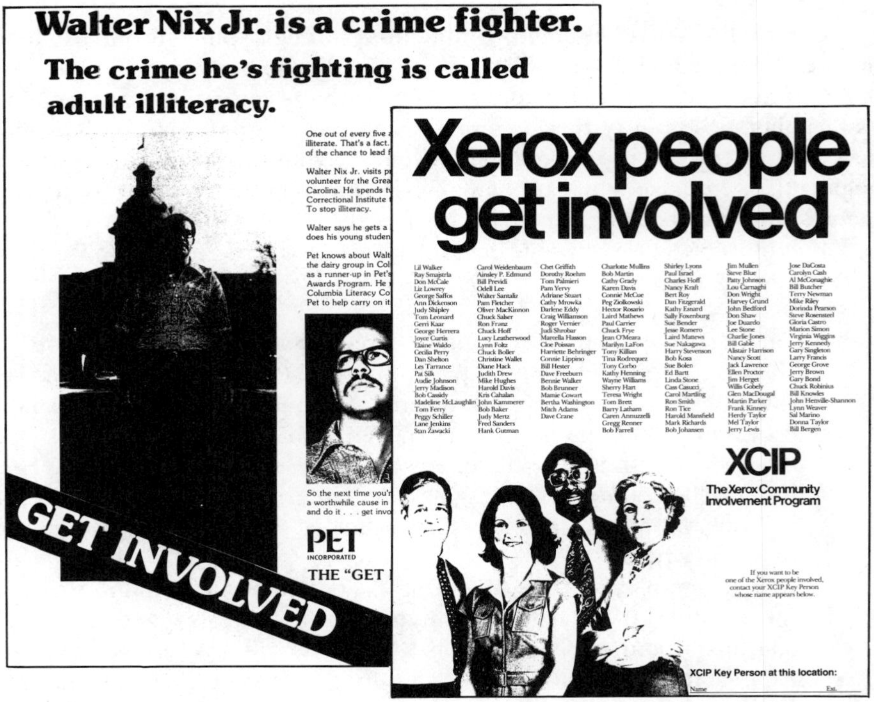

These portions of two posters illustrate the programs established by more than three hundred firms to encourage workers to take part in community volunteer work.

Source: Photos courtesy of Xerox Corporation, Stamford, Connecticut, and Pet, Inc., St. Louis, Missouri.

By now it should be clear that different company activities require different decision-making techniques. For traditional activities, management will probably want to turn to impact analysis. Social opportunities, on the other hand, require management to creatively search for new products and social innovations. For indirectly beneficial activities, management can use cost-benefit analysis. For handling philanthropic activities, management might wish to apply the Smith test (namely, does the gift truly strengthen community institutions?) as well as consider what some more imaginative companies are doing in this area (e.g., encouraging volunteer activity).

Adjusting the Organization

NEW STRUCTURES FOR A TURBULENT ENVIRONMENT

Based on intensive observations in several companies that have been recognized as leaders in managing social impacts, Robert W. Ackerman (1973) found a common pattern of adjustment. The pattern consisted of three phases and spanned a period of at least six to eight years.

In the first phase, which may last for months, or even years, the chief executive recognizes an issue as important. The chief executive's involvement is marked by several activities: speaking out on the issue at meetings of industry associations, stockholders, and civic groups; becoming active in organizations and committees involved in studying the issue or influencing opinion on it; and sometimes committing corporate resources to special projects (e.g., minority businesses, waste-recovery plants, and training centers). Soon the chief executive perceives the need for an up-to-date company policy—a perception he or she takes pains to communicate to all managers in the organization.

However, implementing action on the issue in question does not follow so easily. Ackerman (1973) writes:

> The directives from top management, couched in terms of appeals to long-term benefits and corporate responsibility, fail to provoke acceptable action or achievement. Heads nod in agreement, but the chief executive's wishes are largely ignored. Managers in the operating units lack evidence of the corporation's commitment to the cause; responsibilities are unclear, scorecards are lacking, and rewards for successes or penalties for failures are absent. The managers view as foolhardy any attempt to implement the policy at the risk of sacrificing financial and operating performance.

The key event heralding the beginning of the second phase is the president's appointment of a staff executive who reports to the president or one of the senior staff. This executive's job is to coordinate the corporation's activities in the area of concern, help the chief executive perform his or her public duties, and, in general, "make it happen." The new specialist carries one of a variety of titles that have recently appeared on organization charts: vice president or director of urban affairs, environmental affairs, minority relations, consumer affairs, and so on.

The newly appointed specialist—say, the vice president of urban affairs—may view the problem as essentially a technical one that can be attacked by isolating it and applying specialized skills and knowledge to it. But these efforts, while not without merit, do not have the effect envisaged in the corporate policy. The staff manager's attempts to force action are so alien to the decentralized mode of decision making that he or she becomes overburdened with conflict and crisis-by-crisis involvement. Ackerman explains (1973):

> The only arrows in his quiver, aside from his own powers of persuasion, are the corporate policy and the demands of outsiders. But line managers may consider neither one credible . . . . Consequently, if staff proposals interfere with its operations, middle management stands aside and lets the staff take responsibility (or blame) for the results.

Nevertheless, the job done by the corporate specialist is essential for the eventual implementation of the policy. The issues for top management are crystallizing. A great deal of information that serves to clarify what will be expected of the corporation in the future is being unearthed. The techniques or technologies that will be available to fulfill those expectations are being honed. And, most importantly, according to Ackerman, the chief executive is recognizing that "responsiveness entails a willingness to choose among multiple objectives and uses of resources."

Toward the end of this second phase, the chief executive comes to realize that placing the onus for handling social issues on the specialist is a necessary but inefficient step toward a truly effective response to external challenges. Ultimately, responsiveness is a matter of the organization's willingness to choose among multiple objectives and uses of resources. In this sense, responsiveness must become a *general management responsibility.* The chief executive begins to see that edicts from on high and staff activity do not alone affect change. "Instead, the whole organized apparatus has to become involved. In this third phase, the chief executive attempts to make the achievement of policy a problem for all his managers" (Ackerman, 1973:93). That is accomplished by institutionalizing policy in the operating units.

Institutionalizing Policy

In institutionalizing social responsiveness, most companies have made fairly straightforward adjustments to their organizational charts. We shall consider these types of adjustments first, and then move on to more sweeping redesigns.

Three common ways of institutionalizing social impact management are the task force, the permanent management committee, and the permanent organization group. Terry McAdam (1971:15–16) provides a concise summary of the advantages and disadvantages of each.

> *The task force.* Since it tends to be crisis oriented (as are many corporate responses to social responsibility issues), the task force is not very effective for mid- to long-range planning. Another drawback: It is less able to implement changes in operating practices because few permanent lines of communication exist between it and company operating units. Finally, task force members are nearly always part-time participants in the review and development process; unless they have first-rate staff support, they may not acquire sufficient understand-

ing of specific problems. On the plus side, the task force approach is a good way to get an activity started quickly. If team members are carefully selected, the task force can bring together a group knowledgeable in many key operating elements of the business. Thus, the important factors to make this option effective are good people, a focused effort, and quality staff work.

The permanent management committee. A permanent management committee has many of the attributes of the board committee [see Chapter 5]. It has the same need for good staff work, sufficient time commitment of committee members, and specific background information for decision making. Though a management committee is more familiar with the business than a board committee, it may be hampered somewhat by a lack of objectivity.

The permanent organization group. Having within the organization structure a permanent department or group continuously engaged in analyzing, resolving, and responding to corporate social responsibility issues may be the best option of all. Such a group can, over time, build up stronger communication lines than any of the other approaches. Through regular feedback, it can keep the company alert to issues and ensure continuity of analytic efforts. It also offers continuing evidence of top management's commitment to social responsibility. The only danger is that a permanent organizational unit risks drifting out of the mainstream of activity and becoming too narrowly focused on one pet issue. Although such specialization can be a positive influence on company performance in the chosen area, it prevents management from dealing systematically with the remaining issues.

DuPont: An Example of the Permanent Management Committee. By 1975 DuPont had twenty-four hundred full-time employees engaged in environmental control activities and five corporate committees to direct, coordinate, and implement its environmental policy. These groups are led by the Environmental Quality Committee, which was organized in 1966 as the corporate policy-making committee. A senior vice president is chairman of this committee composed of environmental specialists from several departments. A full-time director of environmental affairs serves as vice chairman. The Manufacturing Environmental Committee, with representatives from all the operating and appropriate staff departments, meets regularly to keep abreast of developing environmental control technology and changing regulations. Their goal is to develop implementation plans for plants within the respective departments. The Product Environmental Committee is similarly organized and deals with customers' safe handling of DuPont products and the impact of these products on the environment as a result of customer use and disposal. The Occupational Safety and Health Committee is concerned with the health and safety of employees in the work environment. The Haskell Liaison Committee coordinates the collection and distribution of information on toxic substances. An environmental forum, held semiannually, brings together plant, engineering, and management personnel throughout the company to exchange information on pollution control technology and to survey and report on companywide environmental activities.

What might committees like these do? First, they can gather data—that is, describe the specific facts and figures necessary for an evaluation of a company's pollution control problems. Such data might include air and water emissions statistics, percent efficiencies of existing pollution control devices, capacity, age, and output of production equipment, raw material and energy-use data, expenditures for pollution control, and legal statutes. Second, they can help decide what to do with the information once it has been acquired. At a minimum, the data should be able to provide answers to such nuts-and-bolts questions as these (Cannon, 1975:112–13):

1. Are the company's air pollution emissions increasing or decreasing?
2. Is the company in compliance with air pollution laws?
3. How do air pollution emissions from the company compare to those of similar plants elsewhere?
4. How effective are company air pollution control systems compared to the best on the market?
5. Are company employees exposed to harmful amounts of air pollution?
6. How much of total city, county, or regional air pollution does the company account for?
7. How does the company's water use compare to the flow of the waterway it discharges into?
8. Is the company discharging harmful levels of water pollution into the waterway?
9. Are the company's water pollution discharges increasing or decreasing?
10. How do company water pollution discharges compare to 1977 and 1983 standards?
11. Is the company in compliance with present water pollution laws?
12. How effective are company water pollution controls compared to the best on the market?
13. What are the company's solid-waste problems and how is it dealing with them?

With answers to questions such as these, committees should be able to evaluate the company pollution record in relation to four yardsticks of performance: legal standards, pollution levels causing adverse effects on the environment, levels of control achievable using the best available (generally known as state-of-the-art) devices, and the performance of other companies in the industry.

The third function of committees should be to develop a set of pollution-control proposals for top management. Of course, the two preceding steps would help clarify the areas in which the company faced its most serious pollution problems. A committee, no doubt, would want to concentrate on encouraging abatement of these problems first. Thus, a committee is often useful to those responsible for capital investments. Once priorities have been set, it is important for a committee to consider the kinds of control that can be used for each pollution source. Five basic control methods are available: installing pollution control equipment, changing fuels or raw materials, changing processes, altering operating and maintenance procedures (including alterations to conserve energy), and shutting down a process.

The final step in preparing a pollution control program is estimating the cost of implementing each control option; without such an estimate, it is impossible to project how and when the company might be able to afford improvements. Trade journals describing other companies' efforts to control pollution by the same strategies are good sources of cost data, as are EPA reports. Environmental consultants and pollution manufacturers of pollution control equipment should also be able to help estimate the capital costs of pollution control devices.

The Department of Social Affairs: An Example of the Permanent Organization Group. Some experts and companies do not think organizational responses of the kind practiced by DuPont go far enough. Michael Mazis and Robert Green state the problem as follows (1971:71):

> After developing an organizational device to respond to one social problem, firms often discover that issues emerge which heretofore were considered insignificant. For instance [a few years ago] beer and soft-drink companies never would have considered their products a controversial social problem; today there are massive advertising campaigns designed to assuage the critics of the disposable aluminum can. To cope with the changing nature of the environment it faces, the corporation needs a new organizational structure, which can anticipate as well as react to a variegated set of societal needs.

A possible answer may lie in the establishment of a "department of social affairs," which Mazis and Green go on to describe (1971:71):

> This department . . . would function on the corporate level and assist operating divisions and departments in the formulation of plans to implement social responsibility programs. . . . The department could perform several functions which the previous single-orientation departments or crisis management techniques could not. First, the department of social affairs could develop a system for processing information concerning the environmental forces which might influence corporate activity. Second, the department could help the firm plan realistic responses which would result in a congruity between long-term profits and benefits to society. The interjection of social concerns into the planning process necessitates recognizing corporate social objectives, setting social goals, and establishing a control mechanism for measuring social performance.

Exhibit 8–10 illustrates how the department of social affairs might accomplish the functions Mazis and Green envision for it. Organizations such as Standard Oil (Indiana) and Equitable Life Assurance Society of the United States have had prototypes of this kind of department in operation since the early 1970s (see Paluszek, 1973).

EXHIBIT 8–10   The Department of Social Affairs Concept

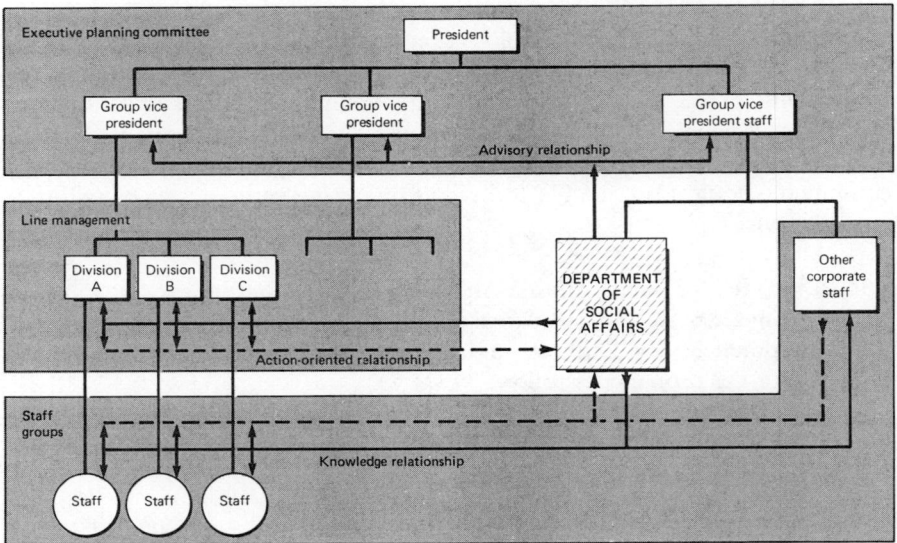

INTERFACES OF DEPARTMENT OF SOCIAL AFFAIRS

Advisory relationship — Top executive committee

Input from department of social affairs:
- — recommendations of social objectives and goals
- — evaluations of social consequences of corporate actions
- — information on social affairs
- — report on firm's social performance

Action-oriented relationship — Line groups (day-to-day working relationship)

Input from department of social affairs:
- — information on social affairs
- — social audit
- — assistance in information to formulate programs to meet social goals
- — aid in design of programs to monitor social aspects of operations (consumer review board, ecological testing, pollution control, community participation)

Output to department of social affairs
- — dissemination of programs to department
- — social performance plans

Knowledge relationship — Staff groups (two-way flow of information)

Input from department of social affairs:
- — information on social affairs
- — advice to staff groups on desirable social actions

Output to department of social affairs:
- — notification of department about staff efforts that could affect social affairs
- — dissemination of information that may have social consequences
- — performance of special projects (market research, financial analysis, and so forth) for department

Source: Robert Green and Michael Mazis, "Implementing Social Responsibility," pp. 68–76, *MSU Business Topics,* Winter 1971. Reprinted by permission of the publisher, Division of Research, Graduate School of Business Administration, Michigan State University.

More Sweeping Redesigns: General Electric's Executive Office and Dow's Matrix Organization. While the department of social affairs concept has already been adopted by a number of companies, it is not the only sophisticated adjustment that a company might make in its organization as it attempts to steer itself through a turbulent, rapidly changing environment. General Electric, the corporation that popularized decentralization in the 1950s and strategic planning in the 1970s, has long been considered the nation's premier management pacesetter. More recently, GE has been pioneering still another organizational concept: adding a new layer of senior management. In December 1977, the company completed the first major top-level reshuffling since Reginald H. Jones became chairman and chief executive in 1972. In the move, GE created a management structure that frees the three-person *executive office* from an ever-increasing internal workload and permits it to focus more attention on external matters, such as government regulation and taxation, that are expected to have an even heavier impact on the corporation in the 1980s.

Traditionally, American business has been built around the organization chart, on which clear-cut hierarchies of power are defined: Orders are handed down, while decisions are passed upward until the buck stops with the chief executive. But as businesses diversify and the macroenvironment grows more complex, top management is discovering that the old functional and product-line hierarchies, despite their straightforwardness, are bogging down. Executives are swamped with data while the company languishes, awaiting orders. In an effort by upper management to get out from under the paper crush and speed up decision making, growing numbers of companies, such as Dow Corning, are trying a still-evolving organizational form, commonly called *matrix management* (see Goggin, 1974:65).

The initiation fee to the matrix organization is very high. Some costs to consider are:

1. Willingness to cope with resistance to change;
2. Top management dedication for years (on the part of, not one, but essentially *all,* top executives);
3. A highly intelligent and motivated middle management anxious to see the whole corporation progress (i.e., no freeloaders);
4. Determination to minimize internal politics (i.e., no empire builders);
5. An abundance of patience on the part of the board of directors, top management, and middle management.

Despite these drawbacks, the idea of the matrix organization is starting to break down barriers to action in traditional hierarchies. In essence, the system pushes decision making down to more people, puts a premium on teamwork, and restores a measure of small-company flexibility to large, complex organizations.

The matrix structure faces up to the fact that two or more lines of authority in a company should sometimes exercise equal influence over the same resources and negotiate for use of those resources. Typically, the functional divisions of a matrix company, such as marketing and manufacturing, form vertical chains of command, while the product-line divisions form horizontal chains that cut across the functional groups. What results is management by compromise (see Exhibit 8–11). For instance, at a certain chemical company, Mr. A is a corporate vice president and manager of the fluids and lubricants business, with profit and loss responsibility for that product line. But Mr. A's manager of manufacturing, Mr. B, is equally responsible to Mr. A and to the director of manufacturing (Mr. C). In effect, Mr. B has two bosses—Mr. A and Mr. C. In every decision he makes, Mr. B is forced to consider marketing and profit goals (Mr. A's chief concerns), as well as the need to fit his manufacturing operations efficiently into the total corporate operation (Mr. C's concerns). And therein lies the real beauty of the matrix: Decisions are handed back down to a manager who is subordinate to both manufacturing and product-line bosses. It is up to him or her to weigh the two viewpoints and develop a plan that most nearly satisfies both bosses. This spreads decision making among more people. But, so the theory goes, it also puts decisions in the hands of the people best qualified to make those decisions. Matrix management gets a lot of work out of people, and it diminishes the pattern of waiting until someone else makes the decision. It was primarily this advantage that interested Dow Corning in the matrix structure ten years ago. By spreading out decision making, Dow Corning executives hoped, the company could handle more information and respond more quickly to changes on all fronts: in technology, economic conditions, or government regulations. At the same time senior management might be relieved of some of the decision-making burden. While these are difficult goals to measure, Dow Corning seems to a large extent to have achieved them.

NEW PROCEDURES AND INCENTIVES
FOR THE 1980s

Shuffling boxes and drawing new ones on a company's organizational chart is a necessary, but not sufficient, condition for generating change in the direction of more responsible behavior among all the company's management. Concern, compassion, and conviction are also necessary. And the larger a company is, the more necessary these qualities become, since top management cannot easily place the mark of its personality on a global operation. Therefore, we must now turn to the problem of how to make social responsibility credible and effective throughout a large organization. Kenneth R. Andrews writes (1973:60):

> The source of difficulty is the nature and impact of our systematic planning processes, forms of control, systems of measurement, and pattern of incentives, and the impersonal way all these are administered....

EXHIBIT 8–11   The Matrix Organization in Action

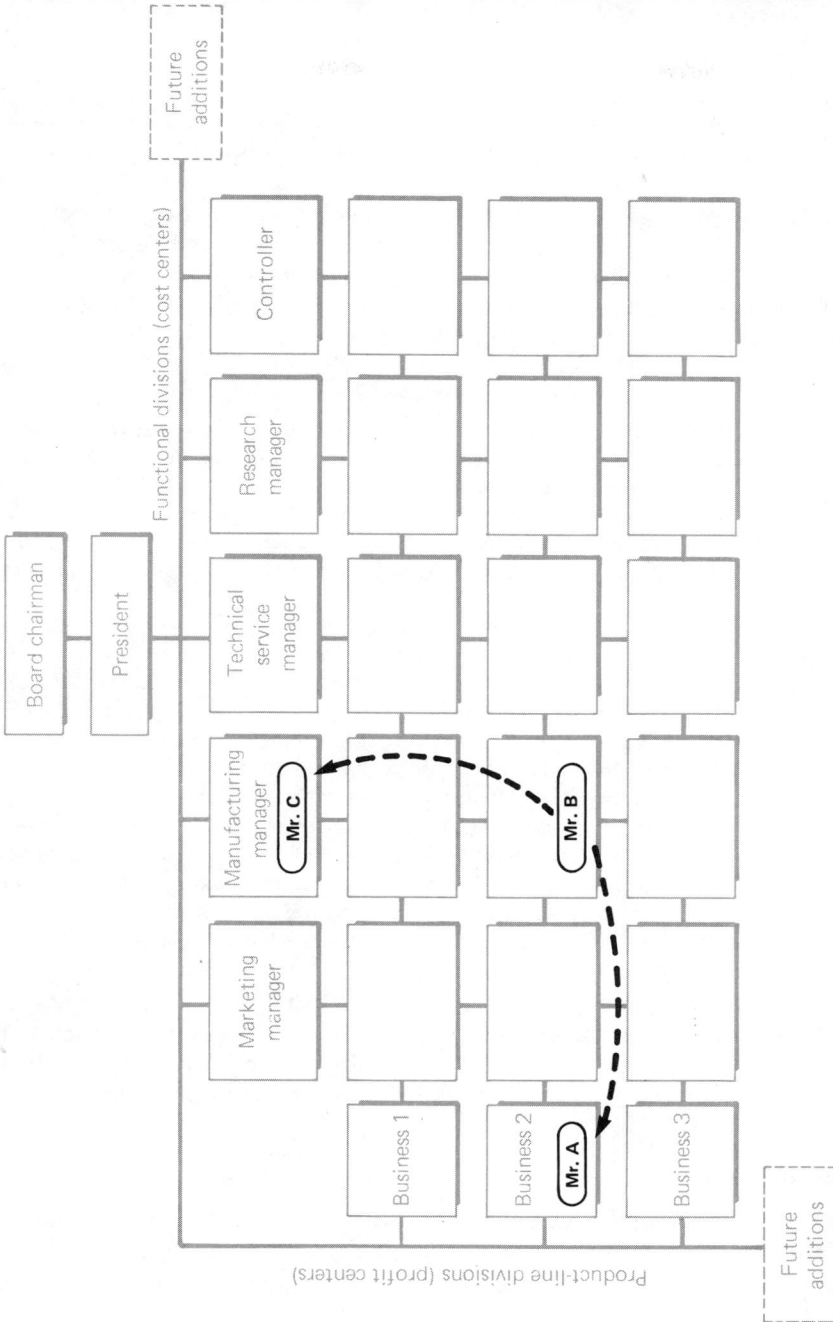

Since progress in career, dependent on favorable judgments of quantifiable performance, is the central motivation in a large organization, general and functional managers at divisional, regional, district, and local levels are motivated to do well what is best and most measured, to do it now, and to focus their attention on the internal problems that affect immediate results.

In short, the more quantification and the more supervision of variance, the less attention there will be to such intangible topics as the social role of Plant X in Community Y or the quality of corporate life in the office at Sioux City.

Actually, a program of action to encourage a companywide sense of social responsibility has already been suggested: the incorporation into strategic and operating plans (of subsidiaries, county organizations, or profit centers) of specific objectives in areas of social concern logically related to the goals and macroenvironment of the company. But how is this accomplished? Andrews explains (1973:61–62):

Once targets and plans have been defined (in the negotiation between organization levels), the measurement system must incorporate in appropriate proportion quantitative and qualitative measures. The bias to short-term results can be corrected by qualitative attention to social and organization programs. The transfer and promotion of managers successful in achieving short-term results is a gamble until their competence in balancing short- and long-term objectives is demonstrated.

Incidentally, rapid rotation virtually guarantees a low level of interest in the particular city through which the manager is following his career; one day it will be seen to be as wasteful as an organization-building and management-development device as it is useful in staffing a growing organization. The alternative—to remain in a given place, to develop fully the company's business in a given city assisted by knowledge and love of the region—needs to become open to executives who do not wish to become president of their companies.

When young middle managers fall short of their targets, inquiry into the reasons and ways to help them achieve assigned goals should precede adverse judgment and penalty. . . . In addition, managers learn that something is important to their superiors other than a single numerical indicator of little significance when detached from the future results to which it relates.

Fortunately, there already are ways in which top management can track—and indeed encourage—the progress of all managers at all levels towards their noneconomic objectives. In this connection, let us consider the use of internal auditing, incentive modification, and training programs.

Internal Auditing

In-house audit groups, necessarily oriented to examining what the public accounting firms must ultimately certify, can be supplemented by adding to their staff personnel who are qualified to counsel managers and to examine and comment on management success and difficulties in the areas of social contribution and organization morale. In the wake of the bribery and kickback scandals of recent years, much of the corporate world has given new emphasis to the value of internal auditing.

General Electric, for example, has a group consisting of 117 auditors who roam the world looking for scandals, possible antitrust violations, and of course loose operations. (The following accounting of GE auditing is adapted from Hartley, 1977.) "The staff is the cement that keeps glued together the concept of financial control and responsibility that GE is known for," says Charles J. Vaughan, who heads the internal auditing team. From top to bottom of GE, managers know that, at least once every three years, auditors will visit each of the company's thirty-five hundred offices and facilities spread among one thousand cities and towns around the world. This includes the office of GE's chairman and president, Reginald H. Jones, who is quizzed by internal auditors on such matters as potential conflict-of-interest situations and expense-account entries.

GE historically has had the reputation of having one of the finest internal auditing operations of any company. For example, the company disclosed about a half-million dollars in questionable payments to foreign government officials by some of the company's overseas operations from 1972 through the first ten months of 1975. But the entire amount had been entered into the books as just that: questionable payments. For instance, a twenty-dollar bribe to get a visa from an Algerian embassy official in Rome was truthfully listed. In 1976 GE circulated a lengthy policy statement conceding that minor political contributions and small gifts to officials to expedite paper work could be tolerated in certain instances in countries where such gifts and contributions were not illegal. However, the company unequivocally banned any and all kickbacks or bribes for the purpose of selling GE goods. GE has been untouched by the bribery and kickback scandals involving other American multinationals in recent years.

GE's auditors maintain that every dollar that comes into the company makes its way through so many records that it would be almost impossible for a secret slush fund to be established without the auditing staff's spotting indications. Furthermore, senior management has no access to company funds. "If Reg Jones ever signed a check, the company would be buzzing about it for days," one executive says. Indeed, top management is a focal point of auditors' interest. The audit staff, for example, makes a point of checking logs of the company's planes to see where executives went and why. And auditors say that they feel no compunction about blowing the whistle on the brass.

The auditing process at GE is always evolving. "Much of the procedure we have is because over sixty-seven years ago someone found something wrong, and a point to check on was added to the list," one auditor says. In recent years, for example, new attention has been paid to energy conservation and to pricing and observance of antitrust laws. Yet another new area of auditing interest is fair employment. "The EEO measurement system developed by General Electric is one of the industry's most comprehensive," Theodore V. Purcell (1974:101–102) writes. Since 1970 the company has conducted annual audits using its six-part EO/MR (equal opportunity and minority relations) measurement format. The format consists of data assembled at corporate headquarters and a questionnaire that every general manager must fill out as part of the annual business review process. From the smallest department to the company as a whole, the performance of every manager (GE has more than twenty-six thousand) and of every plant and component of the corporation is subject to inline review.

Incentive Modification

If measurement of performance is to encompass progress toward social objectives, a company's incentive system must reward and penalize other accomplishments besides those related to economic efficiency. The company must make clear the fact that ". . . persons can be demoted or discharged for failure to behave responsibly toward their subordinates, for example, even if they are successful in economic terms. Career-oriented middle managers must learn, from the response that their organization leadership and community activities receive, how to appreciate the intrinsic worth and how to estimate the value of their own future of demonstrated responsibility" (Andrews, 1973:63). Bendix, for example, has become known in the business world as an avant-garde company in terms of employee relations. At former company president W. Michael Blumenthal's insistence, middle-level managers are judged and paid, in part, according to how well they met preset goals in recruiting and promoting members of minority groups.

Still, measuring accomplishments other than economic ones is a tough problem. Usually, the most important factors—sometimes the only factors—affecting a unit manager's salary or position are the unit's profitability, its market share, its growth rate, and its growth potential. Purcell writes (1974:103–104):

> When EEO considerations are made a factor in the appraisal process, some middle managers put up resistance. The plant manager of a certain large electronics company had the following dialogue with his superior during the manager's annual performance appraisal:
> "Those equal employment people want us to work on those problems of the environment. They want us to hire more blacks, other minorities, and veterans. I've hired those blacks. Often they're late or they don't even show up. The day after payday, I can't find them. Now they want us to hire and promote more women. Why do they hit us so hard? Why don't they leave us alone so we can make some money? Here you want me to do something that, to my way of thinking, is detrimental to our overall business interest right now. I've done well on my budget, I've done well on costs, so forgive me on those EEO targets!"

His boss replied: "You're rationalizing, Bill. Why should I forgive you on those targets? You set them, and you set them within your budget. No, I'll hold you to those targets; I want the whole package. As you know, most of our plants, including yours, are in areas where most of the labor market is minority. If we're going to staff our jobs, we have to tap that market. We've also got a large consumer market in minority areas. It's not just the EEO people. What I'm telling you is that it's now a business problem. It isn't a matter of what you do first or what you do best; the fact is, you've got to do everything very well."

An obvious, but frequently overlooked, fact is that the motivation of employees with regard to social responsibility objectives will almost always be a function of how top management attitudes are perceived. Consider, for example, the situation at General Motors a few years ago. John DeLorean, who was one of GM's rising management stars, quit the company in 1973, complaining that it had "gotten to be totally insulated from the world." And Edward N. Cole retired from the presidency in 1974 with the gloomy remark that "the fun is gone . . . . I wouldn't go into the automobile business again." Today it is hard to find a top executive at GM who is not enthusiastic about what the company is doing. Excitement over the current "challenge" of the automobile business is especially common among engineers. They agree that as Washington sets more and more of the targets, some of the fun may indeed have gone out of the business. But meeting those targets has required a great deal of ingenuity and hard work, so the job has been enormously satisfying. The crux of the change at GM is the company's state of mind: Today it reflects a revivified sense of purpose and a much sharper understanding of the external world. It was difficult for engineers to muster much enthusiasm for their work on safety and emissions controls when the company was publicly condemning the requirements as onerous and ill conceived (see Burck, 1978:96).

Company Training Programs

The message of Chapter 3 was loud and clear: Companies today are operating in a dangerous legal jungle, and defending companies against lawsuits has become expensive, time consuming, and arduous. This is one reason—the best reason—why companies, no matter how small, should educate their employees about new laws. In the area of antitrust compliance, for example, educational programs can be as simple as providing key employees with thumbnail sketches of antitrust laws, landmark cases, and the company's policy toward antitrust. Or they can involve requiring large numbers of employees to attend seminars and detailed presentations on how to avoid anticompetitive dealings.

Large companies seem to recognize better than small and medium-sized ones the need for such educational programs. For example, to facilitate antitrust compliance (we could just as easily select examples of compliance with equal opportunity or dozens of other issues), American Telephone & Telegraph Company has a type of seminar program that reaches more than eighty thousand of its personnel. Texas Instruments Company holds a session every six months with its marketing and sales managers, and corporate attorneys accent their presentations with antitrust-oriented filmstrips prepared by the company's own learning center in Dallas. But, because smaller firms have not concerned themselves with the antitrust-liability problem, they may run greater risks of being sued someday, according to John Shenefield, the federal government's antitrust chief. Justice Department statistics are dramatic indications of the risks. From 1973 to 1977, the department's antitrust division brought price-fixing suits against 263 companies with annual sales of less than $5 million each, but it filed such suits against only 47 of the *Fortune* 500 companies. "Of the companies we indict for antitrust violations, most have no compliance program at all, and those that do tend to have superficial programs," Mr. Shenefield says (*Wall Street Journal,* May 8, 1978).

In sum, the question with which we have wrestled in the last three chapters is worth restating: How can companies respond to their turbulent environment? Part III has attempted to provide a general answer to that question—one that is broadly applicable in a variety of situations. In providing that answer, however, we had to turn to an uncommon vocabulary. In Chapter 6, it will be recalled, the concepts of strategic planning and social responsibility were introduced. In Chapter 7, the concept of decision support system and its relevance to strategic planning were explicated. Finally, in this chapter, we have considered the intricacies of implementation.

What we had to say about implementation may be boiled down to three points. First, management should select all programs, products, and projects in light of company goals. Second, decision-making techniques should vary with the nature of the activity management is considering. Thus for some activities, impact analysis may be most appropriate; other times the task might become one of finding social opportunities or identifying indirect benefits, and the techniques to handle philanthropic and political activities can be very different from those used to launch a new product. The third point about implementation is this. Insuring that new objectives are carried out throughout the company will always require more than a string of stirring memos from top management. This is especially true when employees perceive those objectives to lie in the arena of social responsibility. In such cases, top management should think carefully about establishing new organizational units, setting up new procedures, and providing new incentives (to reward behavior consistent with the new objectives).

In the series of chapters that follow (Chapters 9 through 13), we shall continue trying to wrestle to the ground the question of how companies can respond to the turbulent environment. But our approach will be different than it was here in Part III. Rather than attempt to outline a general answer, we shall be concerned almost exclusively with specific responses to concrete challenges in the major functional areas of business.

THE MACROENVIRONMENT OF U.S. BUSINESS (Chapters 2–4)

Technological
- Effects of technological change
- Process of technological innovation

Economic
- New views of inflation, unemployment, and growth
- Relationship of energy, environment, and economics

Social
- Demographic trends
- Changing social structures
- Changing values
- The "New Class" and adversary culture
- Life cycle of social issues

Political–legal
- Public policies affecting business
- The interest-group state
- Policy administration
- Courts

International
- Changing role of multinationals
- Five worlds of development and the new "Economic Order"
- Technology transfer
- Changes in world trade
- Cultural differences
- Host and home country relations

IMPLICATIONS OF MACROENVIRONMENTAL CHANGE (Chapter 5)
- Government regulation
- Corporate power

STRATEGY FORMULATION (Chapter 6)
- Premises of strategic planning
- Goals and objectives
- The place of social responsibility and ethics

FORECASTING TOOLS (Chapter 7)
- Decision support systems
- Technology forecasting
- Economic models
- Sociopolitical forecasting

STRATEGY IMPLEMENTATION (Chapter 8)
- Programs, projects, products
- Opportunities, costs, benefits

NEW MANAGEMENT OPPORTUNITIES (Chapters 9–13)
- Production
- Research and development
- Finance
- Marketing
- Human resources
- External relations

ALTERNATIVES FOR BUSINESS–SOCIETY RELATIONS (Epilogue)
- Restructuring or market enhancement

SOCIAL IMPACT MANAGEMENT IN MAJOR FUNCTIONAL AREAS

PART **IV**

CHAPTER NINE

Production
and Operations
Decisions

L et us take a moment to review the logic of this book. After the introductory material in Part I, we began in Part II to examine the five environments that constitute the macroenvironment of business, because tomorrow's managers surely will need to be as familiar with technological, economic, social, political, and international change as yesterday's managers were with their immediate environment. Thus, the aim of Part II was to develop a clearer understanding of the macroenvironment. Part III focused on how management can best cope with an increasingly turbulent macroenvironment. Toward that end we examined the concept of strategic planning and how it relates to social responsibility and management values. We also considered the crucial role that timely, accurate, and relevant information plays in strategic planning. In the last chapter of Part III, we faced head-on a most difficult problem—implementing plans.

With Chapter 9, we come to Part IV. In this chapter and the following four, we shall attempt to outline in rather specific terms how management can deal with the challenge of change. Thus, Parts III and IV serve similar purposes but take quite different approaches: Part III provides a general framework for coping; Part IV examines specific solutions to specific problems. Therefore, Part IV is structured around the major functional areas of business—namely, production, finance, marketing, human resources management, and external relations. We begin in this chapter with production and operations decisions. Essentially, what we shall do in the first section is look at the earth as part of a closed system, since the key to understanding such concerns to business managers as pollution and energy shortages is to first understand what an ecosystem is and how it relates to economics. Once that is done, all else falls into place much more smoothly. We shall also see how the second law of thermodynamics sets a limit on what we can do to the environment. The section concludes with a formula for measuring the quality of life in a society. It is worth noting that at least four terms in this formula are things that business can, to a profound degree, help determine: resource availability, pollution, energy consumption, and productivity improvement. The remainder of the chapter explores each of these areas.

In the second section on resource availability, we will try to see just how real the problem of shortages is for industry, as well as what companies can do about it. In the next three sections devoted to exploring the issue of pollution, we shall look at major types of pollution, government laws to control it, and finally, company-level responses to these laws.

Pollution and energy are closely related issues; therefore, the next section begins by reviewing U.S. energy policy. Following that review, we shall consider various methods, such as conservation and cogeneration, that companies have used to survive the energy squeeze. Finally, the last section of this chapter reintroduces a concept first broached in Chapter 2: productivity. The trend in U.S. productivity has not been bright. And, as we shall see, the fault lies neither in the stars nor (entirely) in Washington. Productivity decline is a problem management can, and should, address more aggressively. ☐

ECOSYSTEMS AND ECONOMICS

The recognition that many natural resources are nonrenewable and that no ecological system is indestructible has changed the values of many, if not most, Americans. Quite predictably, these new values have led to the enactment of new, tougher laws. While these laws have affected all business functions, their impact has been particularly severe for production.

Production refers to the process by which a set of inputs (resources) is transformed into some desired output (goods or services); it is a function in which all companies are involved. Exhibit 9–1 presents a sample of input-transformation-output relationships for five types of organizations, where we

EXHIBIT 9–1   Input-Transformation-Output Relationships for Typical Systems

System	Primary inputs	Components	Primary function(s)	Desired output
Hospital	Patients	MDs, nurses, medical supplies, equipment	Health care (physical)	Healthy individual
Restaurant	Hungry customers	Food, chef, waitress, environment	Well-prepared food, well served; agreeable environment (physical and exchange)	Satisfied customer
Automobile factory	Raw materials	Tools, equipment, workers	Fabrication and assembly of cars (physical)	Complete automobile
College or university	High school graduates	Teachers, books, classrooms	Imparting knowledge and skills (informational)	Educated individual
Department store	Shoppers	Displays, stock of goods, sales clerks	Attract shoppers, promote products, fill orders (exchange)	Sale to satisfied customer

Source: Richard Chase and Nicholas Aquilano, *Production and Operations Management* (Homewood, Ill.: Richard D. Irwin, 1973), p. 12. © 1973 by Richard D. Irwin, Inc. Reprinted by permission.

clearly see that production occurs not only in manufacturing companies. To underscore this notion, we shall refer to decisions involving this function as *operating decisions,* rather than as production decisions, the more common term. But whatever the expression, this much is apparent: The macroenvironment of business influences every major aspect of the input-transformation-output relationship. It causes the price of inputs to rise. It causes the methods by which these inputs are transformed into outputs to be altered. And, in many instances, it changes the very nature of the final product or even eliminates that product altogether.

Four factors in the macroenvironment frequently cast long shadows over operations decisions: resource shortages, industrial pollution, energy consumption, and productivity improvement. But before we can begin to analyze these issues, some technical background material is needed to sharpen our understanding of the many problems and perspectives involved in these areas of business decision making. We begin with a discussion of ecology and ecosystems (based on Miller, 1975).

Ecology and Ecosystems

Ecology, a term coined in 1869 by Ernest Haeckel, a German biologist and philosopher, is derived from two Greek words: *oikos* (meaning "house" or "place to live") and *logos* (meaning "study of"). Literally then, *ecology* is the study of organisms in their homes. It is usually defined as the scientific study of the relationships of living organisms with each other and with their environment. It considers how organisms and groups of organisms are structured and how they interact with one another and with their environment. Ecology, unlike other scientific disciplines, takes a broad view. Its message is that of synthesis.

The ecologist is concerned primarily with interactions between five levels of organization of matter: organisms, populations, communities, ecosystems, and the ecosphere. A group of individual organisms (pine trees, sheep, geese) of the same kind is called a *population* (grove, herd, flock). In nature we find a number of populations of different organisms living together in a particular area. This group of plant and animal populations occupying and functioning in a given locality is called a *natural community.* Any organism, population, or community also has an environment, which consists of two major categories: the nonliving, or *abiotic,* components (solar energy, air, water, soil, heat, wind, and various essential chemicals) and the living, or *biotic,* components (plants and animals). If we consider the living and nonliving environment together with the population or community, we have an *ecosystem,* or ecological system. An ecosystem may be a planet, a forest, a pond, a fallen log, a garden, or a petri dish. It is any area with a boundary through which the input and output of energy and materials can be measured and related to some unifying environmental factor. In studying ecosystems, the boundaries drawn around them are arbitrary and selected for convenience.

The large major aquatic ecosystems are lakes, ponds, rivers, springs, swamps, estuaries, coral reefs, seas, and oceans. On land the large major ecosystems—usually called *biomes*—are forests, grasslands, savannas (grasslands with scattered trees or clumps of trees), chaparrals (shrublands), tundra, and deserts. Each of these major types of ecosystems can be divided further. For example, colder regions have coniferous forests, dominated by cold-resisting evergreen trees; temperate regions have deciduous, or leaf-shedding, forests of oaks, maples, and beeches; tropical areas have luxuriant rain forests.

All of the various ecosystems on earth are connected to one another. Thus if we group together all of the various ecosystems on the planet, we have the largest life unit, or planetary ecosystem, the *ecosphere.* The ecosphere can be visualized as a vast gradation of diverse ecosystems, all interconnected in a complex fabric of life. These connections help preserve the overall stability of an ecosystem. Disrupting or stressing an ecosystem in one place can have a complex, often unpredictable, and sometimes undesirable, effect elsewhere. This ecological backlash has been eloquently stated by the English poet Francis Thompson: "Thou canst not stir a flower without troubling a star." The goal of ecology is to find out just how everything in the ecosphere is connected.

Spaceship Earth. In his now classic article, "The Economics of Coming Spaceship Earth" (1966), Kenneth E. Boulding proposed that modern industrial society must move from its "frontier" economy to what we can call a "spaceship" economy. According to Boulding, we have been living by "frontier" rules. Like nineteenth-century pioneers, we have viewed earth as a place of unlimited frontiers and resources, where ever-increasing consumption and production inevitably lead to a better life. If we pollute or destroy one area, we merely move on to another, unspoiled area. Only now the frontiers are gone. The earth, we have discovered, is a closed system, not unlike a spaceship. The chemicals necessary for life must be continuously cycled and recycled throughout the ecosphere. Vital chemicals, such as carbon, oxygen, nitrogen, water, and phosphorus, are recycled by means of the sun's energy, which is used to drive and sustain these *biogeochemical* cycles (*bio* for living; *geo* for water, rocks, and soil; and *chemical* for the processes involved). Although some chemicals are cycled, energy is not; it flows in one direction from the sun through the ecosphere and then back into space. Thus, an ecosystem functions through the two important processes of *chemical cycling* and *energy flow*. These two processes connect the various structural parts of an ecosystem so that life is maintained. A study of ecosystem function involves an analysis of the rates and regulation of energy flow through the system and of chemical cycling within the system.

The major problem with our "frontier" approach is that it is a linear system based on energy flow and matter flow (see Exhibit 9–2). That is, the af-

EXHIBIT 9–2   Flow of Matter and Energy in a "Frontier" Economy

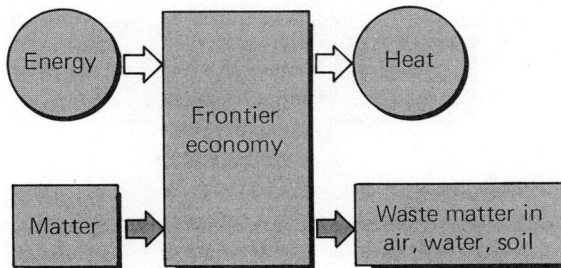

Today's obsolete frontier or linear economy is based on a high rate of energy and matter flow that attempts to maximize the throughput rate of matter and energy.

Source: From *Living in the Environment: Concepts, Problems, and Alternatives* by G. Tyler Miller. © 1975 Wadsworth, Inc., Belmont, CA 94002. Reprinted by permission of the publisher.

fluent nations are attempting to use more and more energy to convert more and more matter into waste material as fast as possible. In other words, we are attempting to maximize the rate of throughput of matter and energy. Boulding contends that we must discard this wasteful and eventually self-defeating system and adopt one that more closely mimics the cyclical systems found in nature that are based on energy flow and matter recycling (see Exhibit 9–3). By recycling many resources and partially reusing some energy before it flows back into the environment, we can reduce the throughput of matter and energy to an optimum rather than maximum rate.

EXHIBIT 9–3   Flow of Matter and Energy in a "Spaceship" Economy

A spaceship economy would be based on energy flow and matter recycling in order to reduce waste and pollution and· to optimize the throughput rate of matter and energy.

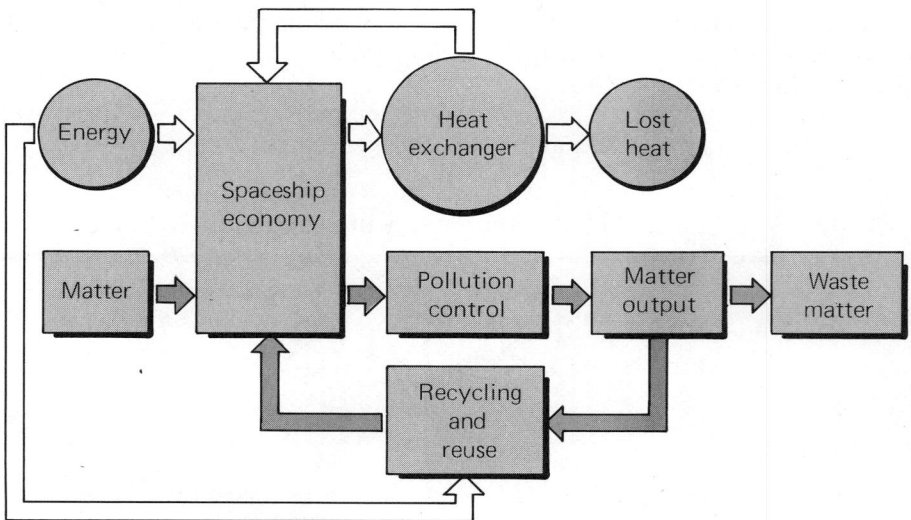

Source: From *Living in the Environment: Concepts, Problems, and Alternatives* by G. Tyler Miller. © 1975 Wadsworth, Inc., Belmont, CA 94002. Reprinted by permission of the publisher.

The Second Law of Thermodynamics. In the United States, until only recently, the overall approach to pollution control has been dilution. In other words, just dump wastes into the air, water, or soil, and they will spontaneously be diluted to harmless amounts or, at least, be dispersed far away from us. But we can see in Exhibit 9–4 what actually happens when we pour a substance like DDT onto the land or spray it into the air on the assumption that it will eventually disperse spontaneously into a more disordered and less harmful state.

Now, some ecologists would argue that the chain of events illustrated in Exhibit 9–4 is an example of the second law of energy or thermodynamics. That law tells us that any system plus its surroundings tend spontaneously toward increasing disorder or randomness. (Scientists frequently use the term *entropy* to refer to a measure of relative disorder.) The human ability to create disorder in the environment while trying to order part of the world is greater than that of any other organism. The production of food; the manufacturing of various chemicals, clothes, shelter, and other supplies; and the burning of fossil fuels to provide heat and to cook foods all greatly increase the disorder in the environment, particularly by the production of heat—that is, the disorderly, chaotic motion of molecules. In a system such as our spaceship, then, some ecologists maintain that the second law determines the ultimate limit of what we can and cannot do. It tells us that maintaining order in the form of life always increases disorder in the surroundings. It also tells us that as we try to support more and more humans at higher and higher levels of energy and resource consumption, the amount of disorder in our life-support system will automatically increase.

While this interpretation of the second law is a useful application of the idea that disorder tends naturally to increase, it is not without flaws.* René Dubos (1978) argues that ecosystems are much more resilient than many ecologists and environmentalists realize. Further, according to Dubos, it is not true that human beings cause damage to the earth whenever they disturb the natural order of things. Nor is it true that natural processes always produce the most viable ecosystems. There are countless examples of ecological recovery that follows human intervention of a benevolent kind—for example, in Jamaica Bay in New York and in rivers like the Thames in Britain and the Willamette in Oregon—pollution was halted and natural forces allowed to work. "What is needed," Dubos writes, "is not esoteric knowledge and technologies, but simply good management and social will."

Sound and fruitful ecosystems of great diversity and stability have been deliberately and artificially created by man. Hawaii, for example, once had few terrestrial vertebrates, no pine trees, oaks, maples, willows, fig trees, or mangroves—only one species of palm and a few orchids. The harmonious profusion that now exists there occurred through the deliberate introduction of foreign species. Or consider the rural areas of France and England: By creating hedgerows, farmers established a varied ecosystem that serves as a reser-

---

* The most powerful mathematical explanation for how certain systems can defy the second law of thermodynamics has been put forward by Ilya Prigogine (1977), a Belgian chemist who won a Nobel Prize in 1977.

EXHIBIT 9–4   Dispelling the Dilution Approach to Pollution Control: The Movement of DDT through the Environment

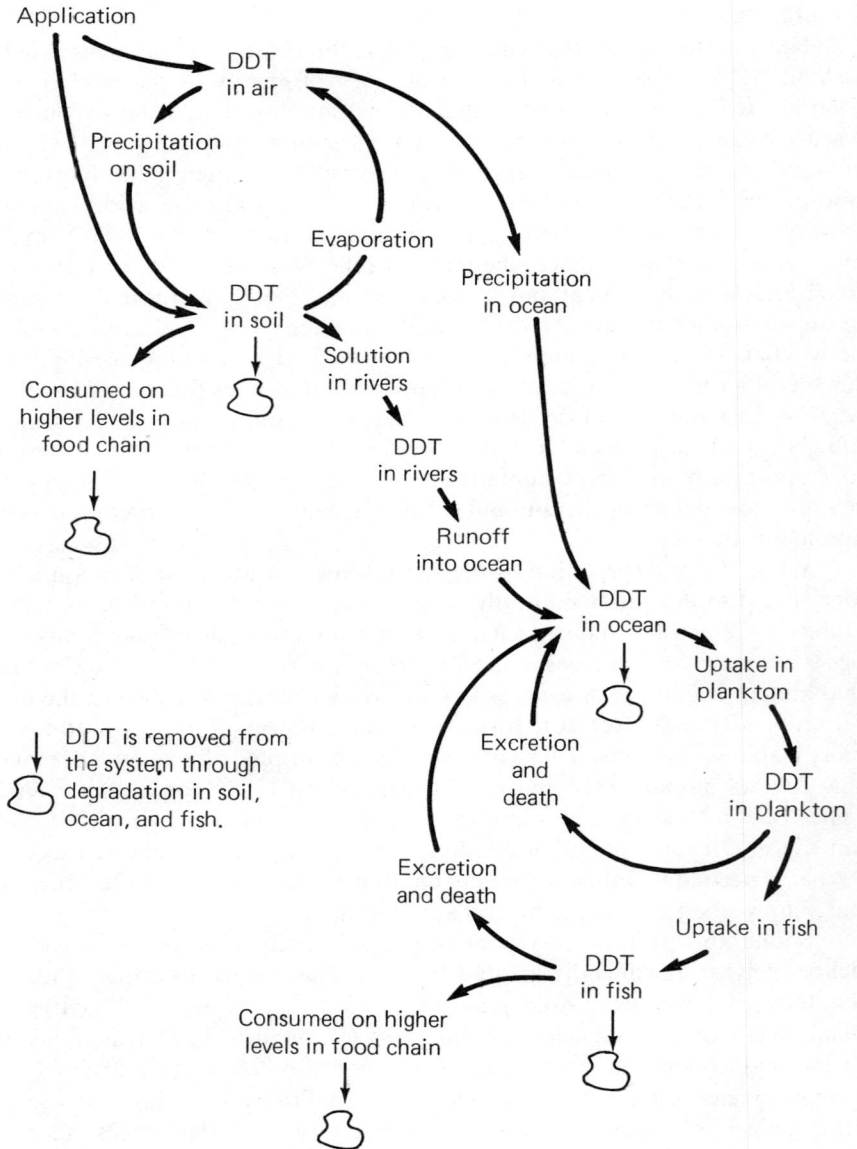

Source: Jørgen Randers, "DDT Movement in the Global Environment." Reprinted from *Toward Global Equilibrium* by Dennis L. Meadows and Donella H. Meadows, eds., by permission of The MIT Press, Cambridge, Massachusetts. © 1973 The MIT Press.

voir for animal and plant species that probably could not survive in either the primeval forest or a completely cleared landscape.

Ecosystems, says Dubos, have continuously evolved in the course of time, first through influence of natural events and now, increasingly, because of human intervention. While conceding that human activities are causing environmental damage, Dubos argues that humans " . . . can use natural resources to create new ecosystems which are ecologically sound, economically productive, and esthetically rewarding."

A corollary of the second law of thermodynamics is that no conversion of energy from one form to another is 100 percent efficient. The efficiency rate of any conversion process may be obtained from the following equation:

$$\text{percent efficiency} = \frac{\text{useful energy output}}{\text{total energy input}} \times 100$$

In other words, if you eat 100 units of energy and you obtain 10 units of useful work, then your efficiency percentage is $10/100 \times 100 = 10\%$. In this case, 90 percent of the input of food, or chemical energy, ends up as wasted heat energy in the environment. Thus, not only can we not get something for nothing, we cannot even break even. As energy is transformed from one form to another, it is degraded into less and less useful forms until it becomes heat energy, the random motion of molecules, which cannot be readily harnessed to perform useful work. A useful form of energy is one that has a high capacity for doing work.

Many of the ways in which we convert energy are particularly inefficient. For example, the efficiency of the internal combustion engine is about 10 to 12 percent. When we deduct friction losses, the automobile is only about 5 percent efficient; 95 percent of the gasoline or chemical energy used to drive a car is wasted and lost as heat to the environment. If we tried to design the most inefficient engine possible, we would be hard pressed to come up with a poorer one than the internal combustion engine. Converting to steam engines could increase engine efficiency to 30 to 40 percent and could decrease most of the harmful chemical pollutants spewing out of the exhausts of automobiles. But, although we can improve efficiency, the second law says we can never reach 100 percent efficiency.

This inescapable inefficiency in the use of energy helps to explain one of the cruelest tradeoffs the dedicated environmentalist faces: At a given level of energy production, the direct cost of supplying energy to the consumer decreases as pollution control is neglected. But, as direct costs decrease, the indirect social and environmental costs (e.g., pollutant-induced diseases and deterioration of buildings) increase in proportion to the degree of environmental degradation (see Exhibit 9–5).

Economic and Business Implications

Spaceship Earth and the second law of thermodynamics are basically physical concepts, but they have important implications for economic well-being and

**EXHIBIT 9–5   Conceptual Environment/Cost Tradeoff Curve at a
Fixed Level of Energy Production**

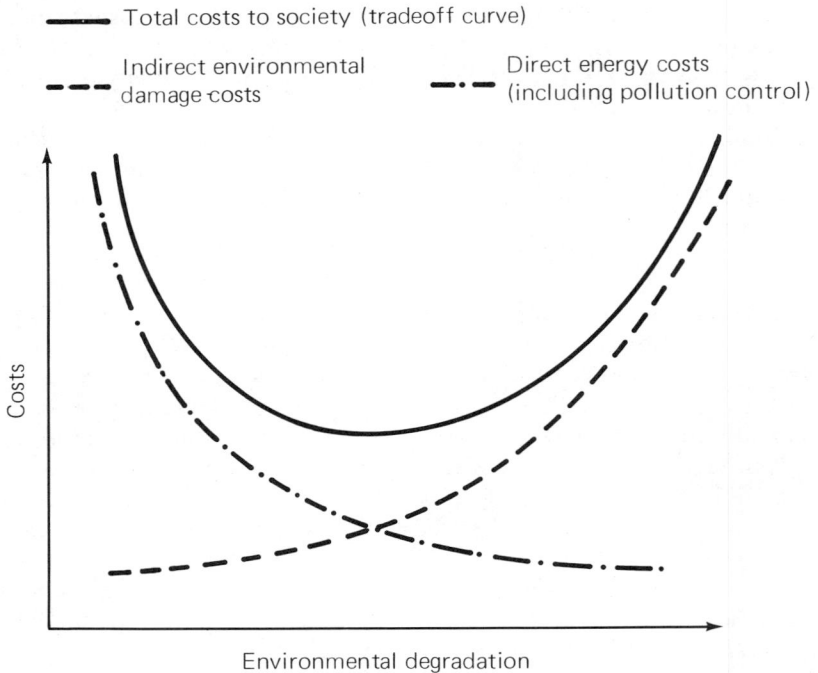

—— Total costs to society (tradeoff curve)

– – – Indirect environmental   –·– Direct energy costs
         damage costs   (including pollution control)

Costs

Environmental degradation

Note: Direct energy cost + Indirect environmental damage
costs = Total costs to society.

Source: U.S. Energy Research and Development Administration, *A Plan for Energy, Research, Development and Demonstration*, vol. I (Washington, D.C.: U.S. Government Printing Office, 1976), p. 32.

business operations. The spaceship economy can be defined as one in which the stock of people and physical wealth is maintained at some desired, predetermined level by carefully controlling the throughput (see Exhibit 9–2), or annual flow of new production (i.e., GNP). In contrast, however, our present economic system attempts to maximize the growth of GNP. Boulding would argue that maximizing GNP for its own sake is absurd. Should not the real aim be to maximize well-being? The basic relationship between natural resources, people, and personal well-being (i.e., a measure of the level of adequacy of living space, shelter, water, air, food, clothing, health, and education) might be expressed in the form of a simple equation:

$$\text{Well-being} = \frac{\text{resources}}{\text{population}}$$

This equation, however, is oversimplified. There are other important factors to consider—some that add to well-being and some that detract from it. On the helpful side, the supply of resources we have is not necessarily fixed. As reserves of a particular resource run down, prices rise, which slows down the rate at which the resources are used and increases the potential and economic feasibility for recycling. More importantly, rising prices as in the case of oil increase the attractiveness for alternatives—like coal and solar energy, which the United States has in abundance (see Exhibit 9–6). Shortages of a particular resource can also stimulate a new wave of exploration that may uncover new deposits, especially in little-explored, underdeveloped countries. For instance, the 1972 launching of the Earth Resources Technology Satellite (ERTS) began a new era of using satellite cameras to scan the entire globe for land, forest, mineral, energy, and water resources. As shortages occur, then, research efforts to find substitutes for the resource and to improve mining efficiency are greatly intensified. For example, aluminum has already replaced steel for many pur-

EXHIBIT 9–6   How Rising Oil Prices Increase the Attractiveness of Alternative Energy Sources

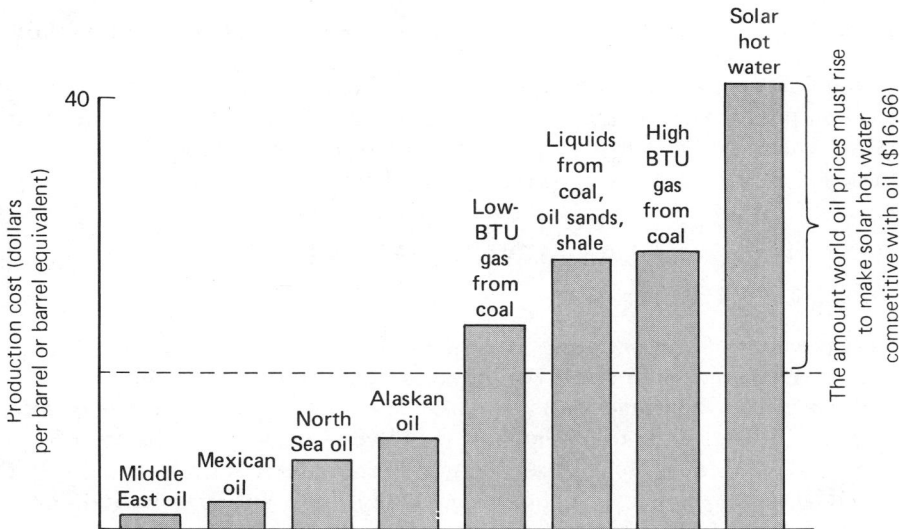

Source: Data based on Shell Briefing Service, 1979. Reprinted by permission of Shell International Petroleum Ltd., London.

poses, and structural plastics reinforced with tiny "whiskers" of other elements are replacing glass, steel, aluminum, and other metals for a number of purposes. Copper provides a dramatic example of improved mining efficiency: The cutoff grade for minable copper has been reduced by a factor of 10 since 1900 and by a factor of 250 over the history of mining. Thus the resources variable in the numerator of our equation is too simplistic. It should be multiplied by at least three additional factors: productivity (e.g., improved mining technology), increased recycling, and the potential for finding a substitute resource.

The denominator of the equation is also oversimplified and needs to include some factors that are not so helpful to our well-being. Besides population increase, increasing per capita rate of consumption and increasing population density tend to detract from our well-being, since industrialization and urbanization produce a much higher usage rate of resources. In addition, some wasteful technologies can accelerate depletion of a resource or introduce substitutes that cause more pollution. Thus the denominator of our original equation should be the product of population size, population density, per capita energy consumption, pollution, and perhaps other factors. Clearly then, the original simple equation disguises many of the realities and complexities of our resource situation. A more realistic but still very crude measure of well-being is:

$$\text{Well-being} = \frac{\text{resources} \times \text{productivity} \times \text{recycling} \times \text{resource substitution}}{\text{population} \times \text{population density} \times \text{per capita energy consumption} \times \text{pollution}}$$

In the following sections we examine four of these factors in more detail: resources, productivity, energy consumption, and pollution. These are the four areas where business can help determine societal well-being—and clearly these are the areas that can affect the well-being of business.

RESOURCE AVAILABILITY: THE PROBLEM OF SHORTAGES

After decades of concentrating on new products, expansion, and marketing, American companies in the 1970s began to face a different problem: a shortage of supplies. By using a projection based on an ever-increasing rate of consumption, it is possible to predict how many years we have left before we exhaust today's known global reserves of nonrenewable natural resources. But experts disagree in their predictions. For example, Edward R. Fried and Philip H. Trezise write (1976:174):

> Natural resources are not in imminent danger of running out. Even finite materials, including mineral fuels, are nowhere near depletion. On the extreme as-

sumption that technology will not be improved, there still would be no basis for predicting a resource constraint on production during the next quarter-century, and probably for a decade or two beyond.

In fact, the capacity to produce nonrenewable as well as renewable commodities continues to expand and the techniques of raw material exploration, development, and production undoubtedly will continue to improve.

The future, of course, may be quite different from such an optimistic forecast. But in any event, managers do face a much more immediate problem than the exhaustion of the earth's last drop of oil: They are likely in the years ahead to be victims of *spot shortages*. In some instances, spot shortages stem from special circumstances, such as strikes, bad weather, or political upheaval abroad. For example, uncertainties in Zaire, which provides the United States with over half of its cobalt, cause concern and fear among users of that metal in advanced industrial nations. Once cherished for the deep blue hues it imparted to ceramics in the Ming dynasty, cobalt is now a vital metal in the production of alloys used in making jet engines, turbines, and other equipment that must function under extreme heat. It is also a component in powerful, lightweight magnets that are used in electrical motors, hi-fi speakers, telephone receivers, and computers.

The sudden development of shortages in key materials forces management to rearrange its priorities. Managers in the 1980s are likely to be as concerned about buying supplies to make a product as they are about selling their finished products. "We were never very concerned about the availability of raw materials," George A. Peterkin, Jr., president of Houston-based Kirby Industries, Inc., recalled wistfully. "After all, there were salesmen walking into our offices" (*Business Week,* September 14, 1974). This new concern over shortages is working subtle changes up and down the organizational ladder. Purchasing managers, unaccustomed to more than perfunctory recognition, find their jobs and their status suddenly enhanced. Product managers, once concerned primarily with selling the product, now worry about getting it made. R&D managers, used to creating new products, must now develop new processes through which the company can make its existing products more efficiently. Shortages of supplies—whether iron ore, oil, or chemicals—affect planning in a number of ways. Take the decision of where to build a plant. As one DuPont executive put it: "In the past we've built plants where markets exist. The question is, will we now build plants where raw materials exist" (*Business Week,* September 14, 1974). Another crucial decision involves whether certain products should continue to be made at all.

Management Responses to Shortages

To assist managers in answering questions about shortages, A.A. Meitz and Breaux B. Castleman (1975) describe a process that helps identify company supply problems and define alternative strategies for dealing with them. The main phases of the approach are: identifying supercritical materials, assessing external supply risks, and devising supply strategies.

In the first phase a task force of purchasing personnel, product managers, production and inventory control managers, and R&D staff assesses the long-term effect supply shortages will have on production. Much of the information required to develop a list of supercritical materials exists in market plans, strategic plans, and various management information systems of the company. Thus the first phase of the approach identifies the inputs that the company cannot do without.

In the second phase the task force is concerned with understanding the supply industries themselves: What political and economic factors affect the company's suppliers? What are the most significant costs in the supplier's operations? What are the market trends in the supplier's industry? How vulnerable are suppliers regarding each critical item identified in the first phase? Vulnerability, as used here, is a function of flexibility in the supplier's production capacity; the effect of energy, fuel, and raw material shortages on its operations; and the importance of the product in its product line. Ideally, for each of the company's suppliers, the task force will develop high and low estimates of the products likely to be available. The task force should also explore possible alternative materials. In other words, if steel became scarce, or too expensive, could aluminum be substituted? Material substitution, however, can be a tricky and exceedingly difficult business.

Having pinpointed the areas in which a company is most vulnerable in the second phase, the job of the task force in the third phase is to provide alternative strategies to minimize the effects of supply shortages on production. For example, the company might offer financial assistance to the suppliers in the form of extend billing, inventory financing, or cooperative advertising. The company might also purchase "insurance" in the form of a small plant that produces some critical supply product. A company might also pursue a strategy of vertical integration. Dow Chemical Company, for example, produces its own natural gas and also buys directly from producers. It pipes the gas to major Dow plants in pipelines it controls. The company also produces its own feedstocks from crude petroleum and has acquired large lignite deposits in Texas to be used for power or feedstocks. Like many other companies, Dow Chemical is also hedging against possible electric power cutoffs at peak load periods. It already generates much of its own power, and it is considering building a new generating plant in Michigan (*Wall Street Journal,* March 31, 1977).

The fact that economic muscle can often demand prompt delivery of supplies suggests a fourth strategy for a company that faces shortages: cutting the ranks of suppliers. When a company spreads its business around too much, it loses purchasing muscle; thus concentrating its orders in the hands of a few large suppliers can increase a company's leverage. The only problem with this strategy is that it also makes the company more vulnerable, since its alternative sources are reduced. Some companies implement still another strategy by trying to plan better and to order supplies further in advance. For example, to be assured of enough of the aluminum and titanium manufactured goods it uses to make aircraft bodies, Lockheed Corporation recently began placing orders one year (rather than ninety days) in advance. For one product, metal fasteners, Lockheed even began placing guaranteed orders two years ahead. Of course, if the airlines' fortunes should nose-dive next year, Lockheed would face the specter of built-up inventories (*Wall Street Journal*, November 16, 1978).

Finally, companies can simply switch to materials that are more plentiful. A number of examples (from *Business Week*, September 19, 1974) are available to illustrate the use of this supply strategy. Refrigerator designers, for instance, work on heat exchangers that use aluminum instead of copper, a metal whose price is both high and erratic; textile mills routinely change their blends as cotton and polyester prices fluctuate; and the food industry uses "meat extenders" (e.g., vegetable protein) as meat prices rise and synthetic flavors as sugar prices do likewise. In other industries, however, opportunities for such radical substitutions are more limited—for example, in such products as farm machinery, steel is needed for strength that is just not available in other materials. Finally, as metal prices continue to rise, DuPont and others have begun to market certain plastics as metal replacement.

In sum, management has a number of alternative strategies available to deal with the increasingly complex issue of supply shortages. As we have seen, the first and most critical step in choosing the best strategy entails identifying the company's most essential resources; the second, assessing the effect shortages—whatever their cause—will have on production.

INDUSTRIAL POLLUTION

Industrial pollution occurs at virtually every stage of business operations (see Exhibit 9–7). Over the next thirty to fifty years, as society tries to change from its linear, frontier economy to more of a closed-loop, Spaceship Earth system, one of management's major tasks will be control of all types of pollution.

Types of Pollution

In this section we consider three types of industrial pollution: air, water, and solid waste. The three other forms of pollution—noise, toxic substances, and radiation—are not included here. Noise (that is, unwanted sound) and toxic substances shall be discussed in a later chapter within the context of industrial working conditions, but manmade radiation, which comes from X rays, radioactive materials, and electronic devices, is not considered at all since 94 percent of this type of pollution comes from medical, rather than industrial, use.

**EXHIBIT 9–7   The Environmental Effects of Resource Use in
                  Business Operations**

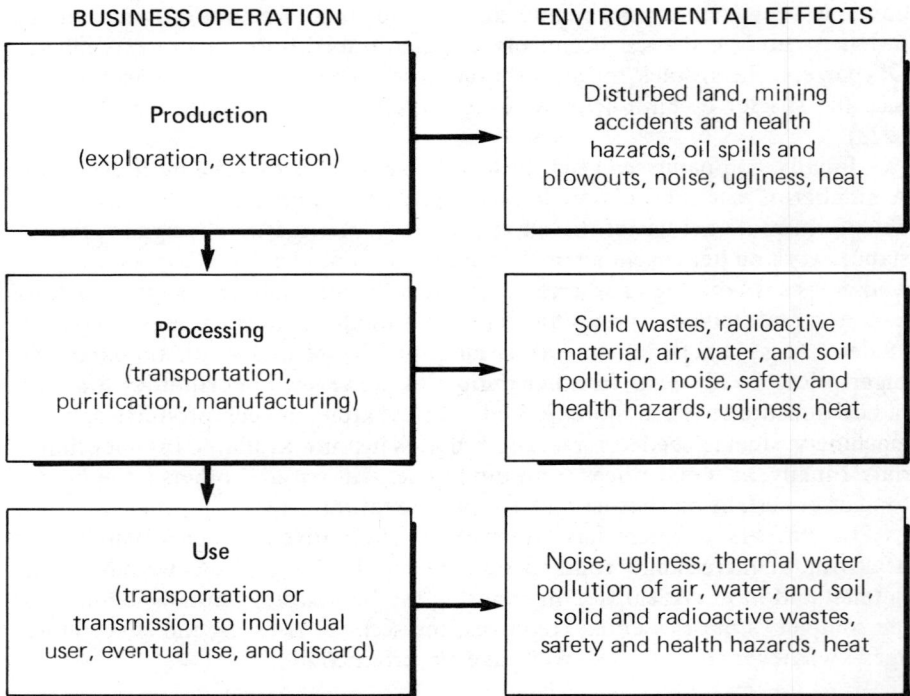

BUSINESS OPERATION	ENVIRONMENTAL EFFECTS
Production (exploration, extraction)	Disturbed land, mining accidents and health hazards, oil spills and blowouts, noise, ugliness, heat
Processing (transportation, purification, manufacturing)	Solid wastes, radioactive material, air, water, and soil pollution, noise, safety and health hazards, ugliness, heat
Use (transportation or transmission to individual user, eventual use, and discard)	Noise, ugliness, thermal water pollution of air, water, and soil, solid and radioactive wastes, safety and health hazards, heat

Source: From *Living in the Environment: Concepts, Problems, and Alternatives* by G. Tyler Miller. © 1975 Wadsworth, Inc., Belmont, CA 94002. Reprinted by permission of the publisher.

Air Pollution. Air pollutants come in five major classes: carbon monoxide, particulates, sulfur oxides, hydrocarbons, and nitrogen oxides. Together they total more than 200 million tons every year in the United States alone. Automobile exhausts make up about 42 percent of this total and provide the largest single source of air pollution. Other major sources include electric power plants, industrial processes, and space heating. Since air pollution affects over six thousand communities, it is unlikely that many of us are unaffected. Exhibit 9–8 shows the principal sources and effects of the major types of air pollutants.

Water Pollution. In the summer of 1969, two railroad bridges over the Cuyahoga River, near Cleveland, were almost destroyed by fire. What made the fire unusual was that it started in the river and then spread to the bridges. The Cuyahoga had become a turbid, chocolate brown mass of diluted industrial wastes, carrying enough oily materials to be inflammable. Not surprisingly, the Cuyahoga had, like a few other rivers in the United States, lost its capacity to support aquatic life, including even the leeches and sludge worms that were the last organisms to survive in the lower reaches of the heavily polluted water.

But the history of water pollution does not begin in 1969. In fact, from the earliest stages of the Industrial Revolution, wastes from industrial processes began to find their way into streams. By the mid-nineteenth century, water pollution was a serious health problem, particularly in densely populated areas. Odors arising from the Thames River in the late 1850s are reported to have made life in London almost intolerable. In cities elsewhere, conditions were not much better; the Chicago Sanitary and Ship Canal, known as Bubbly Creek, was said to have had in places a scum so thick people could walk on it. Further, contaminated water supplies often led to repeated cholera and typhoid epidemics; one of the most famous was London's Broad Street Pump epidemic in 1854, which was caused by direct leakage from privies into the hand-pumped well that provided the neighborhood water supply. Today we divide water pollutants into three broad classes: (1) degradable wastes, (2) nondegradable wastes, and (3) waste heat. Let us take a brief look at each.

Degradable wastes are those, such as organic wastes, that natural processes can reduce. Domestic sewage contains large amounts of organic materials. If these materials do not constitute too heavy a load, bacteria and other organisms in the water can convert them to stable, inorganic materials. The degradation process constitutes natural "self-purification." The rub is that the process of self-purification uses up oxygen in the water—or as the environmental scientists say, it increases the biochemical oxygen demand (BOD) of rivers and lakes. This means less oxygen for other organisms in the water and, in the long run, a "dead" lake or stream. Scientists call this evolutionary process from lake to marsh *eutrophication.* Severely eutrophic water not only kills fish, but also can add to air pollution. For instance, the eutrophic Thames of London in the last century reeked so much that sheets soaked in quicklime were hung in the halls of Parliament to reduce the stench; occasionally, the odors actually forced Parliament to recess.

Nondegradable wastes include salts, soluble gases, and suspended particles. Salts cause corrosion in pipes and industrial machinery. Other nondegradable wastes include metals, such as mercury and lead, that arise from complex manufacturing processes. Generally, the effects of these substances on life are not fully understood, and permissible levels are not properly known. There have been incidents, however, of permanent neurological impairment and death among people who have eaten fish from waters heavily polluted by mercury.

Persistent pollutants are relatively new phenomena: They are termed persistent for the simple reason that the organic material in the water cannot

EXHIBIT 9–8   A Manager's Primer on Industrial Air Pollution

Pollutant	Characteristics	Principal sources	Principal effects
Total suspended particulates (TSP)	Any solid or liquid particles dispersed in the atmosphere, such as dust, pollen, ash, soot, metals, and the various chemicals; the particles are often classified according to size as settlable particles and fine particulates.	Natural events, such as forest fires, wind erosion, volcanic eruptions; stationary combustion, especially of solid fuels; construction activities; industrial processes; atmospheric chemical reactions.	Health: Directly toxic effects; aggravation of asthma or other respiratory or cardiorespiratory symptoms; increased cough and chest discomfort; increased mortality. Other: Soiling and deterioration of building materials and other surfaces; impairment of visibility; cloud formation; interference with plant photosynthesis.
Sulfur dioxide (SO_2)	A colorless gas with a pungent odor; SO_2 can oxidize to form sulfur trioxide (SO_3), which forms sulfuric acid with water.	Combustion of sulfur-containing fossil fuels; smelting of sulfur-bearing metal ores; industrial processes; natural events, such as volcanic eruptions.	Health: Aggravation of respiratory diseases, including asthma, chronic bronchitis, and emphysema; reduced lung function; irritation of eyes and respiratory tract; increased mortality. Other: Corrosion of metals; deterioration of electric contacts, paper, textiles, leather, finishes and coatings, and building stone; formation of acid rain; leaf injury and reduced growth in plants.
Carbon monoxide (CO)	A colorless, odorless gas that is dangerous only to red-blooded animals; it replaces oxygen in the blood.	Incomplete combustion of fuels and other carbon-containing substances, such as in motor vehicle exhaust; natural events, such as forest fires or decomposition of organic matter.	Health: Reduced toleration for exercise; impairment of mental function; impairment of fetal development; aggravation of respiratory and cardiovascular diseases. Other: Unknown.
Nitrogen dioxide (NO_2)	A brownish red gas with a pungent odor, often formed from oxidation of nitric oxide (NO).	Motor vehicle exhausts; high-temperature stationary combustion; atmospheric reactions.	Health: Aggravation of respiratory and cardiovascular illnesses and chronic nephritis. Other: Fading of paints and dyes; impairment of visibility; reduced growth and premature leaf drop in plants.

Pollutant	Characteristics	Principal sources	Principal effects
Hydrocarbons (HC)	All substances containing carbon and hydrogen; gasoline and natural gas are common members of this family; may be gases, liquids or solids; however, it is generally only the gases that pollute the air.	Incomplete combustion of fuels and other carbon-containing substances, such as in motor vehicle exhausts; processing, distribution, and use of petroleum compounds, such as gasoline and organic solvents; natural events, such as forest fires and plant metabolism; atmospheric reactions.	Health: Suspected contribution to cancer. Other: Major precursors in the formation of photochemical oxidants through atmospheric reactions.

Source: U.S. Council on Environmental Quality, *Environmental Quality,* Sixth Annual Report (Washington, D.C.: U.S. Government Printing Office, 1975), pp. 301–03.

effectively dismantle their molecular structures. Pesticides, detergents, and phenols (a compound produced from the distillation of coal and petroleum products) make up the bulk of persistent pollutants. They are extremely toxic to water life; indeed, phenol diluted in an aqueous solution, commonly called carbolic acid, is used as an antiseptic.

Waste heat is a form of water pollution that results when industry uses water in huge amounts for cooling. For example, the water used by steam-generating plants to cool their condensers returns to the stream or lake at an average higher temperature of about 13°F (7°C). Once returned, this warmer water accelerates biological and chemical reactions and reduces the supply of dissolved oxygen. Water temperatures may thus be above the level tolerable for the fish; in any event, higher temperatures promote the growth of undesirable algae. So waste heat, like degradable waste, tends to speed up the eutrophication of lakes. With the growth of the electric power industry almost certain to continue, waste heat will surely become an increasing problem. In addition, nuclear generating plants require almost 50 percent more water for cooling than do equivalent fossil-fuel plants.

Solid Wastes. Although agricultural and mineral solid wastes (principally from mining) make up a large proportion of the total solid wastes in the United States, they constitute a relatively small amount of total solid waste pollutants. The reason is that, fortunately, they are spread over wide areas. Such, however, is not the case with residential and industrial waste. Industry, along with individual householders, generates a vast amount of solid waste—

paper, food, metals, glass, wood, plastic, clothing, rags, rubber, leather, dirt, and so forth—in a relatively concentrated area. Disposal has been largely into open dumps—an approach that has, to understate the case considerably, certain disadvantages. Open dumps burn and contribute to air pollution. Open dumps breed rats and create severe health hazards. Open dumps pollute water sources. And open dumps are an eyesore. In the following chapter we shall examine alternative, even profitable, ways in which industry can dispose of its solid wastes.

Sources of Pollution

Even before people, nature put sources and quantities of polluting materials into the environment: volcanoes, dust storms, hurricanes, pollination, and radiation. Indeed, if we interpret pollution broadly but not incorrectly as any wastes that impair the quality of the environment for living things, then surely we all pollute each time we exhale carbon dioxide. Examples of natural pollution abound (see Beckerman, 1975):

—At a scientific symposium in London in April 1971, Professor Kurti, a professor of physics at Oxford University, reported on work carried out by Professor Elliott Montrol in the United States that showed a car emits only 6 grams of pollutants per mile, whereas a horse, over the same distance, emits about 600 grams of solid pollutants and 300 grams of liquid pollutants.

—U.S. Navy researchers in Washington, D.C., found that trees are a major cause of air pollution—that is, when temperatures top 80°F, hydrocarbons are in effect "boiled" out of trees by the ton and become a component of city smog, and an examination of smog during a six-day period in the nation's capital showed most of the contaminants were from Appalachian vegetation and that auto-related hydrocarbons were a minor contributor.

—Another study has shown that the increase in background radiation experienced by people living next to a nuclear plant is the same increase a person would experience in moving from Brooklyn to Manhattan, since the granite rocks of Manhattan produce more natural radioactivity than the sandy shores of Brooklyn.

Of course, crucial differences do exist between pollution by nature and pollution by industry. The latter tends to be more recurring and concentrated (around cities, for example); thus, it is less likely to be purified by normal ecological processes.

Before we consider the extent of industry's contribution to pollution, one other source should be mentioned: governments. Consider, for example, the city of Baton Rouge. For five years the Environmental Protection Agency

(EPA) pleaded, cajoled, and finally ordered the city to spend $10 million of its funds to upgrade its three sewage treatment plants. Meanwhile, the public works director was admitting that the city had done all that was possible to resist, and only after losing a last, desperate lawsuit against EPA in early 1976 did the tight-fisted community concede the battle and begin construction. Water-quality experts know that the Baton Rouge case is not unique. As Russell Train, former EPA chief, put it, the much-maligned industrial polluters "are far and away ahead of municipalities" in complying with the federal anti-pollution law.

Nevertheless, industry has been responsible for a great deal of pollution. Of about 200 million tons of regulated pollutants going into the air annually as of 1974, more than one-third, in terms of sheer weight, came from industry, including power plants. In terms of noxiousness, industry is responsible for most of the pollution, but half of that 200-million-ton total is carbon monoxide—colorless, odorless, and dangerous in high densities—which comes mainly from automobiles. Industry was also the source of nearly all the particulates and sulfur oxides and half of the oxides of nitrogen, along with 15 percent of the hydrocarbons (see Exhibit 9–9). A standard measure of water pollution is two categories of chemicals: suspended solids and oxygen-consuming substances. By far the biggest producers of these chemicals are "nonspecific sources," such as land runoff. But in terms of specific sources, industry's share of suspended solids almost matches the amount of pollution caused by community sewage, and industry's input of oxygen-absorbing substances is about thirty times that of community sewage.

The results of referendums in a number of states in November 1976 revealed a lot about voters' attitudes toward industrial pollution. On the one hand, measures to limit nuclear power plants were defeated across-the-board: In Colorado and Arizona, the vote was 70 percent against limitation, and in three other states, the no vote exceeded 60 percent. On the other hand, measures to ban the throwaway bottle met with only partial success: Voters in Maine and Michigan passed the measure; Massachusetts narrowly defeated it; and in Colorado it was swamped by a large margin. The conclusion appears to be that while environmental quality is a political consideration, the people are not going to let it interfere excessively with economic growth. Popular insistence that the problem of protecting the environment be met by incremental measures that do not rock the economic boat or take away too many gadgets is broadly based. For example, some minority group spokespersons have maintained that expenditures for clean air and water are expenditures that could, and should, go to improving the quality of their lives. Although pollution affects these groups as much, if not more, than the white middle class, pollution control is surely not quite as high on their list of priorities. Similarly, while a number of national unions have adopted positions favorable to environmental protection, the local union leaders often find the position difficult to maintain when the price becomes unemployment.

EXHIBIT 9—9   Major Ways that Oil Can Pollute Land, Water, and the Atmosphere

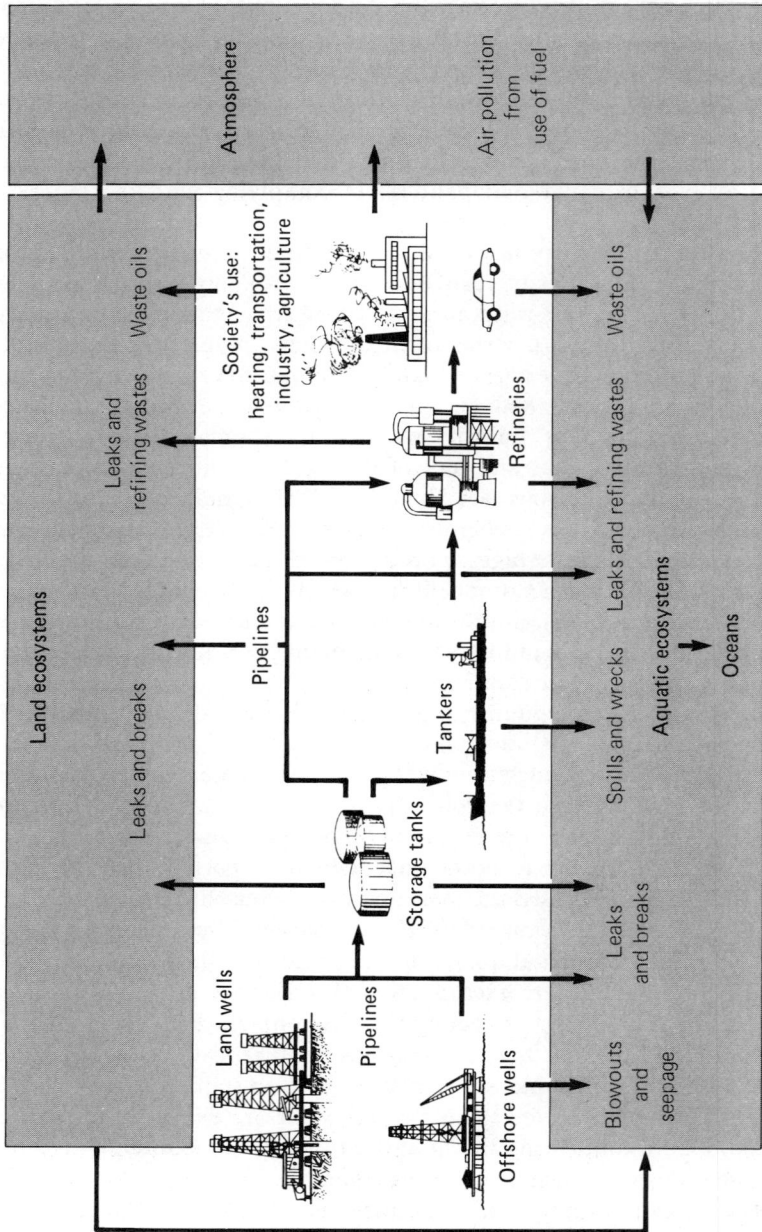

Source: From *Living in the Environment: Concepts, Problems, and Alternatives* by G. Tyler Miller. © 1975 Wadsworth, Inc., Belmont, CA 94002. Reprinted by permission of the publisher.

GOVERNMENT ACTION ON ENVIRONMENTAL QUALITY

In this section we shall review major federal organizations and legislation concerned with the environment. Since the legislation is complex and its administration continuously changing, our best approach is not to dissect each clause of every law, but to emphasize broad goals and institutional settings.

The National Environmental Policy Act of 1969

NEPA makes the condition of the total environment an object of national policy. Section 101 of the act makes explicit the goals of a national environmental policy: to fulfill the responsibilities of each generation as trustee of the environment for succeeding generations; to assure for all Americans safe, healthful, productive, and esthetically and culturally pleasing surroundings; to attain the widest range of beneficial uses of the environment without degradation, risk to health or safety, or other undesirable and unintended consequences; to preserve important historical, cultural, and natural aspects of our national heritage, and maintain, wherever possible, an environment that supports diversity and variety of individual choice; to achieve a balance between population and resource use that will permit high standards of living and a wide sharing of life's amenities; and to enhance the quality of renewable resources and approach the maximum attainable recycling of depletable resources. While these six goals are general guidelines, they specifically require the inclusion of environmental quality among the priorities of federal agencies.

The Council on Environmental Quality. In addition to declaring a national policy for the environment, NEPA established the Council on Environmental Quality (CEQ) to advise the White House on environmental questions. The council reports annually on the state of the environment; projects needs of, and trends in, the environment, including problems created by natural resources depletion and population pressures; reviews federal, state, and local programs in terms of their environmental effects; and formulates programs and recommends legislation to rectify deficiencies in existing environmental policy. While these responsibilities might sound rather impressive, in reality the council has been a little-consulted and fairly powerless agency.

Environmental Impact Statements. The third thing that NEPA does is to require agencies to prepare and submit to CEQ, for all "major federal actions" significantly affecting the quality of the human environment, a detailed statement (EIS) concerning the environmental impact of those acts and a list of alternative courses of action. This "action-forcing" provision has proved to be a major reshaper of governmental planning and decision making. As of April 1976, more than seventy federal departments and agencies had environmental impact statement procedures, and nearly seven thousand impact statements had been filed. As long-established agencies continue to broaden the application of the impact statement requirement and new agencies (such as the Federal Energy Administration) adapt the provision to their decision making, it is expected that the number of statements filed each year will continue to expand.

But the number of statements filed each year does not tell the whole story of the effect EIS's are having on decision making; one must also consider the increasing level of detail the statements involve. For example, when the regents of the University of California recently sat down to discuss building two new dormitories, they had before them an environmental impact statement that ran to 950 pages. Such copious documentation is by no means unusual. An Interior Department environmental impact assessment on the Alaska pipeline stood ten feet high and cost $9 million to compile. Altogether, federal agencies produce over one thousand such statements a year, or four per working day (see Hill, 1976).

The impact statement requirement affects industry as well as government. For example, impact statements have caused long, and sometimes fatal, delays in the construction of nuclear power plants and oil-drilling platforms. Impact statements can also result in the vetoing of plans to build bridges and canals that could obviously help commerce. (Even the Interstate Commerce Commission must consider the environmental impact of different rates charged by interstate freight carriers on the financial feasibility of recycling depletable resources.)

Even if not specifically required to do so by law, many companies will prepare an assessment of the potential environmental impact of a proposed plant for their own internal planning purposes or are willing to work with local concerned citizens to develop such an assessment. Particularly when building a new plant, a company will generally be anxious to get off on the right foot in the community and to work out any environmental problems before construction begins. An internal company assessment will almost certainly cover air and water pollution and pollution control cost factors, and may explore land use, energy, solid waste, construction, and social impacts as well.

Obviously, the wide variety of possible projects and actions have such differing impacts that no one scheme of impact assessment will be universally applicable. But all schemes must at least provide a simple way of summarizing the more important impacts. Exhibit 9–10 shows a fairly straightforward estimate of the impacts of one project. However, the U.S. Geological Survey, located in the Department of Interior, suggests a matrix be used as a checklist or reminder of the full range of actions and impacts. Exhibit 9–11 shows a simplified matrix for a phosphate-mining lease. The matrix provides a format for comprehensive review to remind the investigators of the variety of interactions that might be involved. It helps the planners to identify alternatives that might lessen impact; in fact, the analysis of alternatives is the linchpin of the entire environmental impact statement. For example, in Exhibit 9–11 the number of

EXHIBIT 9–10   Estimated Impact of a 50,000-Barrel-per-Day Surface Shale Oil Facility

Population and services	Construction	Operation
Population		
Direct labor force	1,827.0	1,430.0
Total associated population	13,642.0	10,648.0
Energy consumption (trillions of Btu/year)	1.7	1.3
Land required (acres)	2,700.0	2,100.0
Water consumption (millions of gal/day)	2.0	1.6
Air pollution (ton/year)	510.0	400.0
Water pollution (ton/year)	2,600.0	2,000.0
Public investment costs (millions of dollars)	41.0	16.0
Public annual operating and maintenance costs (millions of dollars)	8.0	6.3

Source: U.S. Council on Environmental Quality, *Environmental Quality*, Sixth Annual Report (Washington, D.C.: U.S. Government Printing Office, 1975), p. 437.

actions listed horizontally is nine and the vertical list of environmental characteristics contains thirteen, which produce a total of 117 possible interactions. Within such a matrix, only a few of the interactions will be likely to involve impacts of enough *magnitude* and *importance* to deserve comprehensive treatment.

A requirement as far-reaching as the impact statement inevitably draws much criticism, particularly from real estate developers unhappy about delayed ventures and from industry chafing against more regulation. One allegation often made is that the process of preparing and filing impact statements is inordinately cumbersome, time consuming, and expensive. Furthermore, there is a widespread notion that environmentalists are constantly going into court and aborting projects they do not like. This notion does not appear to be entirely consistent with the facts; however, many of the suits simply ask that NEPA's impact assessment requirements be followed adequately.

COMMENTARY: The Challenge of the EIS

In 1975 Russell N. Peterson, chairman of the President's Council on Environmental Quality, led off a speech to an august audience with an environmental joke that went something like this:

The Lord was speaking to Moses, with good news and bad.

"The good news is that plagues shall smite your Egyptian oppressors," the Lord said. "The Nile shall be turned to blood. Frogs and locusts shall cover the fields, and gnats and flies shall infest the Pharaoh's people. Their cattle shall die and rot in the pastures, and hail and darkness shall visit punishment upon the land of Egypt. Then I will lead the children of Israel forth, parting the waters of the Red Sea so that they may cross, and thereafter strewing the desert with manna so that they may eat."

And Moses said, "O Lord, that's wonderful; but tell me, what's the bad news?"

And the Lord God replied, "It will be up to you, Moses, to write the environmental impact statement."

The EPA and Enforcement of Other Environmental Laws

Formed in 1970, EPA establishes and enforces most environmental standards in the United States. EPA defines a standard as "the product of fact and theory provided by scientists, and a public value judgment conditioned by the balance of risks against benefits, with a margin of safety on the side of public health and welfare." In short, a standard blends scientific research with political judgments. To enforce its standards, EPA has several tools available. Upon finding a violation, the agency may seek voluntary compliance. Failing that, EPA may order compliance and take court action, which can result in fines (up to $25,000 a day) and jail sentences (up to one year). The laws enforced by EPA also allow citizens to bring suit against violators, and citizens can even bring court action against EPA, should it fail to discharge its duties. Under certain laws, EPA shares enforcement of standards with state and local governments and often goes into action only when the states fail to do so. In all other instances, the federal government has primary enforcement authority. Let us take a look at the four major laws EPA enforces: (1) Clean Air Act of 1970, (2) Water Pollution Control Act of 1972, (3) Resource Conservation and Recovery Act of 1976, and (4) Toxic Substances Control Act of 1976.

Clean Air Act of 1970. To deal with the sources of air pollution noted in Exhibit 9–8, the 1970 Clean Air Act sharply expanded the federal role in setting and enforcing standards for air quality and greatly tightened emission limitations on motor vehicle pollutants. Specifically, Congress directed EPA to use scientific evidence to determine primary and secondary standards for the major air pollutants. Primary standards, which are to be met first, set limits on air pollution that are safe for humans. The more rigorous secondary standards, to be met later, establish levels of pollution that are safe for property, crops, and livestock.

In addition to these general standards, EPA prescribes some specific emission standards. For certain industries, EPA requires that in any plant expansion the best possible pollution control methods and technology must be used.

EXHIBIT 9–11   A Simplified Environmental Impact Matrix for a Phosphate-Mining Lease

Actions that cause environmental impact

Factors and conditions that might be affected	Industrial sites and buildings	Highways and bridges	Transmission lines	Blasting and drilling	Surface excavation	Mineral processing	Trucking	Emplacement of tailings	Spills and leaks
Water quality					2/2	1/1		2/2	1/4
Atmospheric quality						2/3			
Erosion	2/2				1/1			2/2	
Deposition, sedimentation	2/2				2/2			2/2	
Shrubs					1/1				
Grasses					1/1				
Aquatic plants					2/2			2/3	1/4
Fish					2/2			2/2	1/4
Camping and hiking					2/4				
Scenic views and vistas	2/3	2/1	2/3		3/3		2/1	3/3	
Wilderness qualities	4/4	4/4	2/2	1/1	3/3	2/5	3/5	3/5	
Rare and unique species		2/5		5/10	2/4	5/10	5/10		
Health and safety							3/3		

Note: After all the boxes that represent possible impacts have been marked with a diagonal line, the most important ones are evaluated individually. Within each box representing a significant interaction between an action and an environmental factor, place a number from 1 to 10 in the upper lefthand corner to indicate the relative magnitude of impact; 10 represents the greatest magnitude and 1, the smallest. In the lower righthand corner of the box, place a number from 1 to 10 to indicate the relative importance of the impact; again 10 is the greatest.

Source: U.S. Geological Survey, *A Procedure for Evaluating Environmental Impact*, Circular No. 645 (Washington, D.C.: U.S. Government Printing Office, 1971), p. 10.

In industries emitting extremely harmful pollutants, such as asbestos, beryllium, and mercury, all plants—old and new—must observe EPA emission standards. Lastly, EPA can define air pollution levels that pose an immediate and substantial danger to health. When these levels are reached, emergency actions, such as shutting down a plant, can be taken.

Water Pollution Control Act of 1972. The tough 1972 Water Pollution Control Act enabled EPA to concentrate its efforts on some twenty-seven hundred major discharges that account for the vast majority of all industrial wastes discharged into U.S. waterways. In all, about forty thousand industrial water users have been subject to regulation. Under the law, EPA issues national effluent limitation regulations and national performance standards for industries and publicly owned waste treatment plants. No discharge of any pollutant into the water is allowed without a permit. In 1977 deadlines for many requirements of the 1972 act arrived and the act was amended by the Clean Water Act of 1977. Specifically, the new law requires that by 1984 industry must control the discharge of "conventional pollutants" * by using the best conventional pollutant control technology. Discharges of pollutants that are neither "toxic" nor "conventional" are called "nonconventional" pollutants. For these, industry must install the best available control technology by 1984, or within three years after EPA issues effluent limitations guidelines, whichever is later, but no later than 1987. EPA may grant variances from this requirement based on economic hardship. Or, with the concurrence of the state and if an industry can show that the variance will not adversely affect the environment, EPA is authorized to grant variances.

Resource Conservation and Recovery Act of 1976. One of the major legislative achievements of 1976 was the Resource Conservation and Recovery Act. What this measure does in essence is give EPA a real chance at regulating solid waste management and the disposal of hazardous wastes. The act establishes mandatory federal standards for the handling, transportation, and disposal of hazardous materials (such as poisonous chemicals, acids, and explosives); provides for grants to states to make plans for waste disposal and resource recovery (recycling); and funds research, development, and demonstration programs for waste disposal and recycling. Environmentalists were disappointed that amendments spelling out container guidelines and mandatory deposits for beverage containers were defeated as we noted earlier, but for the most part, this measure has met broad acceptance.

Toxic Substances Control Act of 1976. Chemicals are all around us—in our air, our water, our food, and in the things we touch. Many of these chemicals

---

* Conventional pollutants include BOD, suspended solids, fecal coliform, and pH.

have become essential to our lives, and their production contributes significantly to our national economy. But we have little knowledge of the ill effects many chemicals might cause after years of exposure. The Toxic Substances Control Act of 1976 is designed to improve our understanding of these chemicals and to provide controls on those that may threaten health or the environment.

Successes and Failures in Environmental Policy

According to the CEQ (1978), both air and water quality are improving in the United States. As illustrations of progress in cleaning up waterways, the council cited the following facts: Fish now swim in Connecticut's Naugatuck River, long anathema to all sorts of water-borne life; the Detroit River has improved to the extent that it now supports salmon, pike, brown trout, and walleyes; and perch and bass have returned to the Mohawk River in New York State, long thought of as an open sewer. Council chairman Charles Warren also noted "unmistakable and heartening progress" in pollution control for fifty bodies of water surveyed by the CEQ. However the group reported that the goal of "fishable, swimmable" water everywhere in the United States by 1983 is still a long way from attainment, and only a third of the country's municipal waste treatment plants provide secondary treatment.

The good news and bad news are also evident in terms of air quality. While a majority of Americans breathe air that is considered harmful to their health, the evidence is that the nation's air is generally cleaner than in the past. This conclusion is based on a recent study by EPA showing that air in nearly all major metropolitan areas—where most of the U.S. population lives—violates national pollution standards (cited in CEQ, 1978). EPA concluded that the nation's urban areas "must develop new strategies for continuing their progress toward meeting . . . national air pollution standards." According to the EPA administrator, the findings show ". . . we still have many specific areas of the country—especially in our cities—where a significant cleanup task remains." Nevertheless, since 1970, sulfur dioxide air pollution nationally has dropped 27 percent, carbon monoxide levels are down 20 percent, and particulates have decreased 12 percent.

In concluding our discussion of government action in the environmental area, one further point that is often obscured by the many complaints about EPA is worth noting: The EPA frequently bends over backward to minimize the impact of its regulations on industry; not all regulatory agencies are quite as flexible. EPA has granted numerous variances, often to the dismay of environmentalists. When seven steel plants in Ohio's Mahoning Valley, employing twenty-four thousand people, threatened to close rather than install water treatment equipment, EPA immediately excused them from the 1977 rules.

And the agency's controversial "tradeoff" policy—which allows major new sources of pollution into an area with dirty air only if a greater amount of pollution is offset elsewhere in the same region—represents a compromise between air quality and industry's needs for growth.

MANAGEMENT RESPONSES TO INDUSTRIAL POLLUTION

Now that we have identified the types of pollution in our environment and looked at the ways in which the government is attempting to control the quality of the environment, we come to the critical part of our inquiry in this chapter: How can business managers best respond to the challenge of environmental pollution, which occurs at virtually every stage of business operations? How can they cope with the ever-growing body of government regulations designed to control pollution? While Part III outlined a general approach for answering such questions, in this section we consider two concrete, specific approaches that focus on the technical and financial nature of these decisions.

Develop a Pollution Control Program

Although there are numerous and significant gaps in our scientific and technical knowledge of pollution, many, if not most, pollutants currently considered dangerous can be controlled. This task is, of course, a rather technical one, but the following ten steps describe how a pollution control program can be successfully developed and implemented at the plant level (based on Firestone, n.d.).

1. *Determine the ecological background.* Samplings are taken—in other words, the plant is studied through sampling to determine the conditions in and around the plant in terms of air, water, land, and noise.

2. *Analyze results.* The samplings are taken to the laboratory for study and analysis to determine the nature of the samplings and the nature of the pollutant, if any.

3. *Determine the extent of the problem.* All the sampling results are then put into a plant profile and studied as a total problem to determine the nature and extent of the overall problem. Plans are made and priorities set in the light of the total environmental picture.

4. *Bench test.* The problem and proposed solution are then put to a test in small-scale bench tests to determine the feasibility of the remedial plan.

5. *Flow sheet.* If there is a problem, it has been defined, and when the proposed remedy passes the bench test, a master flow chart is prepared, outlining the corrective process or procedure. The process addresses itself to all components of the ecological system.

6. *Pilot plant.* Bench testing merely turns up potential solutions. The most likely result in bench testing is now tried out in pilot plant practice or small-scale prototype system.

7. *Construction.* If pilot plant operations prove the feasibility of the tentative plan, then detailed engineering, procurement, and construction of the full-scale process is started. Design parameters are generated at this step. All pilot plants are sized to generate scale-up parameters.

8. *Startup and operation.* Once the control system is constructed it is put into operation on a trial basis: Any "bugs" in the operation are worked out and full-scale operation begins.

9. *Maintain and operate.* Once in operation, the process must be carefully monitored to determine whether operation is uniform and dependable. Operations soon become full scale and full time. A full-scale program to keep a high level of maintenance and housekeeping is part of the completed package.

10. *Update as required.* Any control system must be kept up-to-date lest the technology fall behind the need. All changes, anywhere in the system, may affect results in pollution control systems. Therefore, constant surveillance is required to insure current adequacy.

Consider Pollution Control as a Sophisticated Investment Decision

Most books on financial management offer no guidance in the area of pollution control investments. Yet, such investments constitute a significant percentage of total plant and equipment investments. In certain areas, such as nonferrous metals, pollution abatement investments become rather awesome; they sometimes approach nearly 30 percent of a firm's total capital investment expenditures. Pollution investments are tricky as well as big. One steel company, for example, converted an open hearth furnace shop into a three-furnace electric shop at a cost of $17.6 million. The cost included $2 million for an air-cleaning system that met the existing air quality standards. Then the state changed the standards. As a result, the company was required to add an entirely new system for air quality control that cost $11 million—that is, five and a half times the original air-cleaning investment, or 63 percent of the entire original investment. In a nutshell, the company that successfully deals with environmental regulations must go beyond the question of how to contract for a piece of hardware and consider other points.

Alternatives to Purchasing Equipment. The company must realize that the most reliable and least costly way to control pollution might not be simply to buy a piece of equipment to stick on the end of a pipe after the pollution is generated, but rather to change the production process. Fri (1974:34) suggests two basic approaches. First, the waste material can be recycled for reuse, or chemicals can be pulled out of a waste stream. The 3M Company, for example, employed one manufacturing process that required a lot of zinc chloride. To meet this material need, the plant produced its own chemical. In the process, however, liquid waste containing quantities of dissolved zinc were discharged into the plant's sewer system. If the operation had continued, zinc would have had to be removed from the wastewater. That would have required removal technology—that is, the removal of the zinc waste through an expensive waste treatment facility. Looking for a better solution, the plant's manager and 3M engineers discovered that another 3M chemical plant had been discarding zinc chloride as a chemical waste in its manufacturing processes. Now all of that zinc chloride "waste" is collected and transported to the first plant, where it becomes a valuable raw material.

An even more fundamental approach is to find and install a more efficient and less polluting process. Regardless of which approach is selected, the company must consider how the unit or plant involved in the pollution problem fits into the company's long-term strategy for markets and growth. The unit may be marginal and due to be phased out shortly, or it may be a chief profitmaker scheduled for expansion. In short, the unit's importance to the company ultimately determines whether the company decides to invest heavily in pollution control, to install just enough controls to keep the unit operating, or to shut the unit down immediately.

The Economics of Pollution Control. A company must understand the basic economics of pollution control before it decides to buy equipment. The first point to be considered concerns the initial capital investment. The company needs to weigh in the benefits of the investment tax credit. Currently this credit provides that up to 10 percent of the cost of new pollution control equipment may be applied against the year's tax liability. For example, if a corporation with a taxable income of $800,000 acquires a piece of equipment costing $1,800,000, 10 percent of that $1,800,000 ($180,000) could be deducted from whatever the tax bite on $800,000 might be. For profitable corporations, then, the effect of this credit is to reduce the true cost of purchasing pollution equipment by 10 percent. However, the company also needs to consider a second point, which is quite simple: Operating and maintenance costs are going to be high. As Exhibit 9–12 shows, operation and maintenance costs will be nearly half of the total cost of control of air pollution and well over half the total cost of control of water and solid waste pollution. Therefore, in deciding upon a particular pollution control system, managers must not focus too much on the initial capital investment and ignore the downstream operating and maintenance costs.

Raising the Money. Where will the money needed for pollution control come from? There are only two sources of funds for corporate capital investments: first, cash earnings less depreciation and dividends paid to stockholders; and

EXHIBIT 9–12   Estimated Incremental Pollution Control Expenditures, 1975–1984

Pollutant	Capital investment	Operation and maintenance cost	Interest and depreciation	Total annual cost
Air pollution	$61.7	$62.2	$74.3	$136.5
Water pollution	65.0	68.8	42.0	110.8
Solid pollution	1.9	6.9	1.0	7.9

Note: Amounts shown are in billions of 1975 dollars.

second, external financing either through debt (borrowing) or equity stock. Government has responded to the problem of scarce funds for the high cost of pollution control investments as it has in a number of areas—housing and energy, for example—by attempting to lower the cost of capital for the specific purpose. Investment tax credits, as we have seen, and accelerated depreciation are two examples.

Other subsidy programs that favor pollution control investments by business include industrial revenue bonds that are issued by state and local governments. The interest from these bonds is exempt from federal taxation; therefore, they can be sold at a lower interest rate than normal bonds. At least $2.5 billion in industrial development bonds was publicly reported to have been issued for pollution abatement in 1975, and the total amount issued may have been much higher. But many analysts consider industrial revenue bonds to be a relatively inefficient form of subsidy. The use of industrial revenue bonds deprives the federal government of tax revenue, and because the bonds compete for funds in tax-free bond markets, they increase the amount of interest that all municipalities pay for all of their new borrowing. Companies, meanwhile, are reluctant to allow debt-to-capital ratios to rise above .30.

A 1976 amendment to the Small Business Act attempts to provide small business better access to tax-exempt financing. Two subsidy programs that tend to favor smaller businesses are the small-business loans program and the municipal treatment grants program. The special small-business loans program is jointly administered by EPA and the Small Business Administration (SBA). EPA verifies that a proposed investment is for abating pollution; if the firm making the investment qualifies under the SBA's economic disaster loan program, the SBA will loan it the necessary funds for up to thirty years at a low interest rate. However, a major problem with these and most subsidy programs should be apparent: Subsidies favor discrete, end-of-pipe investments rather than various types of process changes that may be more efficient and less costly but that do not fall within the guidelines of any of the available subsidy schemes.

Clearly, financing for new pollution control is a complex decision that involves several options: borrowing money, reducing profits, increasing prices, and lowering stockholders' dividends. In addition, financing depends on such factors as the basic cost of engineering, building, and installing a control system; annual operating and maintenance costs; interest rates; and cost savings through tax breaks.

THE DILEMMA OF ENERGY CONSUMPTION

Nowhere is the effect of the international environment on U.S. business more apparent than in the crucial area of energy. Since 1973, when the Organization of Petroleum Exporting Countries (OPEC) grabbed control of the world market and began to exact the wages of monopoly, managers have faced difficult, uncertain times. And the revolution in Iran showed that further bouts of oil price–based inflation and recession are not unlikely.

The U.S. government, without a consistent policy, interjects greater uncertainty into the situation. Industry uses at least one-third of all the energy consumed in the United States. According to the National Petroleum Council, six industries—chemicals, iron and steel, farming and food processing, petroleum refining, paper, and aluminum—account for three-quarters of the total industrial energy use. These few industries offer an easy target for government policies designed to make the United States as self-sufficient in energy as possible.

Although the National Energy Act of 1978 is, at best, only a few watered-down conservation provisions and a new system for regulation of natural gas prices, it is still quite significant. It probably represents the first step in a series of legislative and administrative developments that will have profound effects on industrial and commercial energy users over the next generation. As national energy policy evolves, it will be a major factor in determining the cost and availability of competing fuels. Thus, directly and indirectly, government policy will shape not only short-term usage but also long-term strategies in facilities and process design. Let us look first at the ways in which U.S. energy policy affects business operations. Then we will outline possible management responses to these new realities in the international environment.

National Energy Policy

In one form or another, the federal government has had its hand in energy for decades (see Epilogue). But the shock of the Arab oil embargo, along with the price explosion that followed, vastly expanded that role. Increasingly, the government tells management what fuels it can burn, as well as where, how much, and at what price.

Although generalizations are hazardous, federal energy policy early in the 1980s might be characterized in terms of three key elements. First is a push toward greater reliance on coal. To that end, considerable interest has revolved around the imposition of stiff taxes on the use of oil and gas both by electric utilities and by some large industrial energy users. Such taxes, it is argued, would encourage a switch to coal or perhaps nuclear power.

The second key element of U.S. energy policy is a concern with energy prices. Until recently the government's chief concern has always been that energy prices might be too low. Indeed, federal efforts to prop up energy prices were expanded in the 1950s, after the United States began to import oil. At that time the lush fields of the Middle East were starting to take over as the prime source of world oil, and production costs were so low that even with the added transportation expense, Mideast oil could be landed in the United States at a significantly lower cost than the prevailing U.S. price. Washington therefore established import restrictions. As a result, until 1973, when the quotas were finally abandoned, the sheltered U.S. oil industry enjoyed higher crude oil prices than the rest of the world. But by the end of the 1970s, the prime concern of Washington was that prices might be too high. While there may be little that the government can—or probably should—do to permanently force prices down, at the very least it will have to see that the extraordinary increases are equitably distributed throughout the economy. That takes more intervention, not less.

The high price of oil, since it is set by a foreign cartel, the Organization of Petroleum Exporting Countries, is largely beyond the scope of any national energy policy. Regardless of what the government decides, the events of the late 1970s make it clear that, barring some wholly unexpected technological breakthrough, the future will be marked by substantially higher energy prices than the nation has seen in the past (see Exhibit 9–13). According to some oil experts, the world—at least for the duration of the 1980s—can expect relatively stable oil prices only if Saudi Arabia is willing to gradually increase its oil output to the maximum feasible level. Unfortunately, it is not in Saudi Arabia's self-interest to produce a maximum amount of oil. What happened to the Shah of Iran in 1979 pointed up the inherent instability of absolute monarchies in the face of rapid economic and social change. The lesson has not been lost on the Saudi government. Therefore, what political price future Saudi governments will demand is hard to predict.

Eventually, perhaps, a dramatic technological breakthrough might bring energy self-sufficiency. But meanwhile it will take the most rigorous conservation measures just to prevent the United States from becoming even more dependent on OPEC oil. Private forecasters hold that for the next thirty to fifty years, the United States will be dependent on a strategic import. The problem that policymakers and managers have to address is how to live with this continuing dependence.

One of the most important ways of minimizing dependence, according to former Federal Energy Administrator John C. Sawhill, is by promptly decon-

EXHIBIT 9–13   The Cost of U.S. Energy

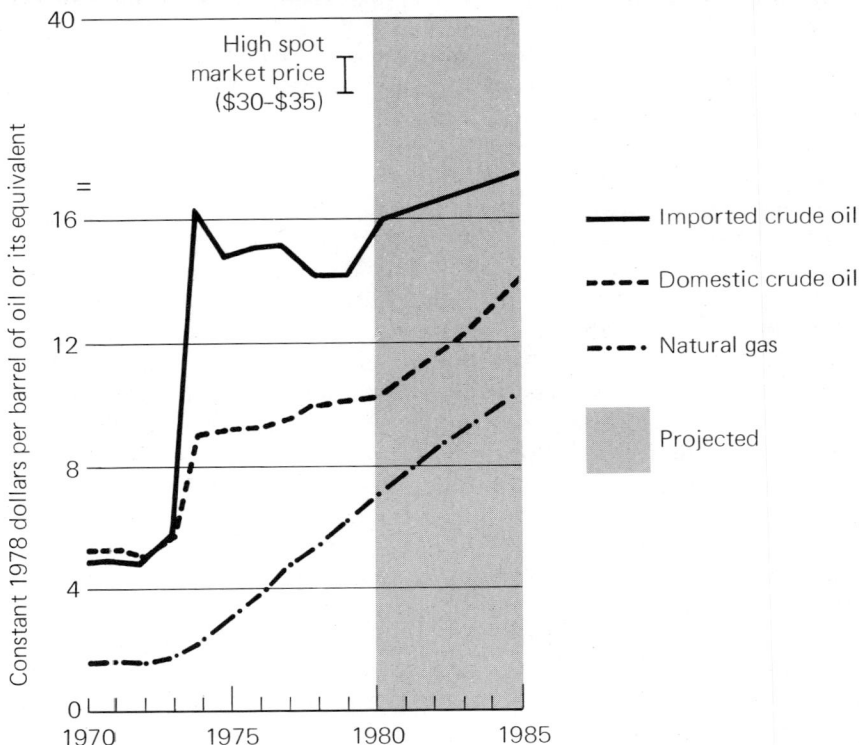

Although the price of oil jumped in 1973–74 with the OPEC increase, the price remained fairly stable until 1978. For this four-year period, oil prices, *adjusted for inflation,* actually dropped 11 percent. The adjusted price of oil produced domestically went up only 18 percent. Natural gas prices, however, jumped 13.9 percent between 1974 and 1978. Total consumer prices at the end of 1978 were less than 1 percent above what they would have been had energy prices simply kept pace with the prices of other goods and services after 1973 (Schurr, 1974:447). What the foregoing analysis fails to recognize, though, are the *social costs* associated with imported oil. These consist mainly of the adverse effects on balance of payments and impact of the ensuing inflation on the fabric of American Society. Robert Stobaugh (1979:47–55) estimates the true costs at about $35 a barrel.

Source: Price data from U.S. Department of Energy, Energy Information Administration, *Monthly Review* (January 1979).

trolling the price of oil. Another way is diversification: The more sources the United States draws from, the more secure are its oil supplies. Oil found anywhere in the world enhances the security of the United States by reducing OPEC's bargaining power. Thus, many oil experts are urging that the United

States go all out to help even the Chinese and Russians find and develop more oil. However, the United States has no formal policy to encourage active development of non-OPEC (e.g., Mexican) oil.

The third key element in energy policy is conservation. Conservation proposals take a variety of forms. For example, the principal conservation proposal in President Carter's energy plan sent to Congress in 1977 was a massive program to install insulation in the nation's existing homes. For the relatively modest cost of $6 billion over five years (relative, that is, to the country's rocketing oil imports bill), officials forecasted dramatic savings in oil and gas consumption. This proposal is related to another: strict federal standards for new construction. Still another conservation proposal calls for putting pressure on Detroit to develop more efficient cars and for imposing a "gas guzzler" tax.

Conservation proposals move the government into a new era of involvement in energy. Historically, the one great area of freedom in energy has been at the consumption end. Although the government has always been involved in pricing and supplies, owners of factories, commercial buildings, and homes have traditionally made their own decisions on what fuel to use and how to use it. That freedom began to give way in the early 1970s, when gas utilities first started running short on supplies. The Federal Power Commission stepped in and told the companies that industrial customers had to be curtailed first and individual consumers last. The idea is rapidly gaining support that conservation may be a cheaper and better—if unfamiliar—way to solve the nation's energy problems than developing new supplies. And there is a deep-rooted feeling in Washington that, if energy conservation is to be as effective as federal planners now believe is essential, it will require demand management on an unprecedented scale.

Management Responses to the Energy Issue

Some experts think that the day will eventually come when the amount of energy needed to make a product will be more important to management than the production costs. Each product will be measured in terms of the economical British thermal unit (Btu) cost for its manufacture. One Btu is equal to the amount of heat required to raise the temperature of water one degree Fahrenheit. A pound of good coal when burned should yield 14,000 to 15,000 Btu; a pound of gasoline, approximately 19,000 Btu. And one cup of creamed cottage cheese when consumed should yield almost one Btu of energy. Obviously, Btu is much too small a unit to talk about energy consumption for the entire United States. For that purpose, the experts speak in terms of quadrillion Btu's per year (1 QBtu = 10^{15} Btu's). U.S. energy consumption in 1977 was about 76 QBtu's. In this section we consider two methods—conservation and cogeneration—that can help U.S. business cope with the energy squeeze in the years ahead.

Energy Conservation. According to corporate financial officers, who keep an eye on high fuel and electricity costs, investment in energy *conservation* is about the most profitable use for capital today. As the director of corporate planning for Dow Chemical Company remarked: "We have tremendous opportunity to invest capital for energy-saving projects. There are over $200 million of good, high-return investment opportunities in our Texas and Louisiana facilities alone. Nearly all of these projects offer over 50 percent pretax return on investment, and there's almost no business risk because output of the plants is already being sold" (Winter, 1978).

Investments in energy conservation help cut the rise in oil imports, which, as we saw in Chapter 4, has played havoc with the U.S. balance of payments and helped drive down the value of the dollar. Since industry consumes about a quarter of the nation's energy, capital programs that cut plant or office energy consumption by 15 percent, 25 percent, or even more can make a real difference. Moreover, investments that cut energy consumption tend to hold down the cost of goods to the consumer. For example, a rubber company's investment of $50,000 in equipment that quickly saves $80,000 in fuel oil helps to restrain tire prices.

Some energy-saving investments involve such exotic things as using solar energy to heat buildings (see Exhibit 9–14) or pasteurize beer, but most are far

EXHIBIT 9–14   Examples of Energy-Saving Investments for an Office Building

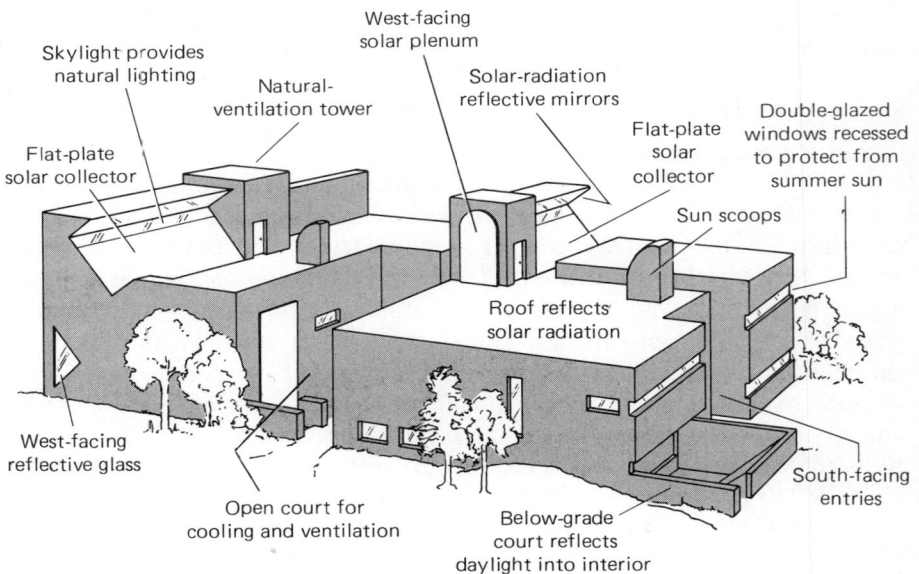

Source: © Richard L. Crowther, Crowther Architects Group, Denver. Redrawn by permission.

more mundane. Common approaches include insulating factory ceilings, over-hauling furnaces to improve efficiency, capturing and recycling heat that for-merly went up the smokestack, and adding furnaces that burn wastes instead of fuel oil. As dull as they may sound, many such investments pay for them-selves in less than a year. The fact that so many energy-saving opportunities exist shows how badly U.S. industry has lagged behind in energy conservation. In many cases, U.S. companies are investing to bring their energy efficiency up to where European companies were a decade or more ago.

Energy Cogeneration. Many experts place hope in the widespread use of *co-generation,* a linkup that combines electricity generation with process heat or steam production. In simple terms, this is the way it works: An ordinary indus-trial boiler that coverts water into steam is replaced by a boiler that produces a hotter, higher-pressure steam. This higher-grade steam can then be sent through a turbine to generate electricity. After it emerges from the turbine, the steam still has the temperature and pressure that an industrial process might require. To be sure, creating the higher-grade steam takes extra energy, but the total fuel savings over separate electrical power and steam production can be as much as 20 percent.

Tom Alexander (1977) describes the merits of cogeneration:

> Cogeneration is nothing new. Industry produces about 29 percent of the total electric power of West Germany, where much of its power is fed into the na-tional grid. . . .
>
> Another form of cogeneration, also far more prevalent in Europe than in the United States, involves a central electric plant that produces and sells steam or hot water to either industry or residential complexes. The general constraint is that everything has to be located close together because of the cost and energy losses associated with piping steam or hot water.
>
> This central-station approach to cogeneration, lately expanded into a more ambitious "energy center" concept . . . generally consist[s] of a power plant plus one or more manufacturing plants sited closely enough together to share steam. More such arrangements would save energy and reduce the amount of waste heat that now winds up polluting lakes and rivers—heat that amounts to about two-thirds of the energy consumed in making electricity. They would also fur-ther a major aim of U.S. energy policy—the switch from oil and gas to coal.

PRODUCTIVITY IMPROVEMENT

In this section we consider productivity, the final factor in the equation stated earlier in this chapter where business can help determine the quality of so-cietal life. As noted in Chapter 2, U.S. output per hour worked rose at an im-pressive rate until the end of the 1960s. In the 1970s, however, the U.S. pro-ductivity rate rose at about the same anemic rate as Britain's and was less than half the more robust rates in France and Germany and only one-quarter of the Japanese rate.

Managers like to blame government regulations and labor leaders (who sometimes equate productivity drives with exploitation) for the declining productivity rate. This blame may not be altogether unfair, but it can tend to obscure an important point: Managers, too, are responsible for the productivity slowdown. Too many are overly concerned with the short-term profits on which their bonuses and stock options are based. With inflation, regulation, and high taxes all biting into today's earnings, managers put off investing in machines that would raise tomorrow's productivity.

It is surprising to see how little companies have done to measure their own productivity, let alone improve it. They pay much more attention to finance, marketing, mergers, and tax manipulation. Few production and operations managers rise to the top in modern business; the accountants reign in the executive ranks. Business schools and their M.B.A. programs sensed the trend and in the past paid scant attention to productivity; few courses were offered in production, efficiency, or industrial engineering.

What can be done? The best answer is probably not to try to "motivate employees more." Any gains that might accrue can have only the slightest effect on the huge gaps that exist now between American and, say, French productivity. Furthermore, this "let's motivate the employees" mentality assumes that people do not want to work—or, more sharply put, that autocratic, bureaucratic organizations have suppressed their desire to work. That is doubtful; people will contribute to the success of an enterprise so long as they feel that they have a part in helping to shape it and are rewarded accordingly.

In general, the most productive companies in the United States do three things. First, they assign responsibility for productivity—that is, they allow initiative to ride high and break up long production lines and impersonal offices into teams of workers who choose their own leaders and decide for themselves how to get the job done. Second, productive companies recognize and reward productivity improvements. Rewards by means of bonuses and time off are essential (and only fair) for high-output workers. Third, productive companies convert as much as possible from electromechanical production processes to electronic ones.

The Greatest Productivity Challenge

It would be redundant to recite once more the growing share of American GNP that the service and information sectors occupy. Unfortunately, management in advanced industrial nations tends to think these sectors are not very susceptible to the employment of mass-production efficiencies. It might be argued that this reluctance to apply efficiency standards to the service and information sectors is behind the rising price levels.

In his seminal article "The Industrialization of Service" (1976), Theodore Levitt argues that as long as managers cling to "preindustrial notions about what service is and does, none of the applied rationality which has produced such magnificent efficiencies in the industrial system will be brought to bear on what remains today a maze of inefficiencies in the service sectors that surround that system." He continues (1976:65):

> Opportunities for service improvement lie all around and yet in the United States, where such improvement has already occurred, these have gone vastly unnoticed. We celebrate the glamorous work of heroic astronauts, accomplishing through science and technology deeds of speculative merit. But we ignore the practical accomplishments of people who produce with lesser tools, simpler methods, and less elaborate organization, a constant stream of productive service results of more mundane though immediate merit.

Levitt then goes on to show exactly how amply we are already benefiting by so much we daily see but do not apprehend and how these benefactions are the result of the "industrialization of service" (see Exhibit 9–15).

EXHIBIT 9–15   "Industrialization of Service" in the Nonindustrial Sector

---

The supermarket represents one industrialization of service. It combines more space and capital in larger but fewer aggregates. Gone, for the most part, are the ancient modes of "service" it displaced with new efficiencies, lower costs, and greater customer satisfaction. Altogether, it is an efficient act of creative destruction.

There are numerous other ways in which service has already been industrialized. While most people regularly see them at work, few are aware of them. Even fewer fully appreciate their revolutionizing importance for our lives and businesses. Thus it is worth a close look at the industrializing modes which already help make service more abundantly productive than it has been in the past. It will help focus effort and energize activity toward the use of these principles in other service activities.

Service can be industrialized in three ways: via hard, soft, and hybrid technologies.

HARD TECHNOLOGIES

These are the most obvious—they substitute machinery, tools, or other tangible artifacts for people-intensive performance of service work. Thus:

1. The electrocardiogram reliably substitutes a lower-paid technician for the higher-paid doctor listening with a stethoscope.
2. The consumer credit card and CRT credit and bank-balance checking machine replace a time-consuming manual credit check for each purchase.
3. Airport X-ray surveillance equipment replaces a lengthy and often embarrassing manual rummage through baggage.
4. The automatic car wash and hot wax coating replace the uneven quality and dignity-destroying work of individuals washing and waxing by hand.
5. The Polaroid Land camera replaces film that must be returned and processed in an essentially people-intensive plant.

6. Automatic coin receptacles at bridges, subway entrances, toll roads, and elsewhere replace human collectors.
7. And the home is full of hard technologies—automatic washers, precooked convenience foods, never-needs-ironing clothing, and chemically treated dirt-resistant clothing, floor covering, and upholstered furniture.

SOFT TECHNOLOGIES

These are essentially the substitution of organized preplanned systems for individual service operatives. Often these involve some modification of the tools (or technologies) employed, but their essential feature is the system itself, where special hardware or routines are specifically designed to produce the desired results. Consider:

1. Supermarkets and other establishments like cafeterias, restaurant salad bars, open tool rooms in factories, and open-stack libraries that enable people to serve themselves quickly and efficiently.
2. Fast-food restaurants, like McDonald's, Burger Chef, Pizza Hut, Dunkin' Donuts, or Kentucky Fried Chicken. At each the same rational system of division of labor and specialization is rigorously followed to produce speed, quality control, cleanliness, and low prices.
3. Prepackaged vacation tours that obviate the need for time-consuming personal selling, extensive tailoring of the product to numerous different kinds of customers, and a great deal of price haggling. . . .
4. Off-the-shelf insurance programs—packaged and unalterable, except via the selection of other packages. Allstate Insurance was the mass-market pioneer, though preceded by the old "industrial" insurance salesman who sold door-to-door and collected weekly, and more recently imitated by off-the-shelf insurance-by-mail.
5. Mutual funds instead of one-at-a-time stock selection, the latter filled with ambiguities, uncertainties, and repetitive reselling and reeducation with each transaction.
6. Christmas Club and payroll-deduction savings systems, both one-time selling and one-time deciding situations, and thereafter automatically, routinely, and inexpensively executed.
7. Fully systematized, production-line, yet personalized income tax preparation service on a walk-in basis—performed at low cost with remarkable accuracy and guarantees. The pioneer and master merchant is, of course, H. & R. Block.

HYBRID TECHNOLOGIES

These combine hard equipment with carefully planned industrial systems to bring efficiency, order and speed to the service process. To illustrate:

1. Computer-based over-the-road truck routing. By careful programming for types and grades of roads, location of stops, congestion of roads, toll-road costs, and mixing-point access, the system optimizes truck utilization and minimizes user cost. Its most extensive and complex incarnation is Cummins Engine's "Power Management Program."

2. Radio controlled ready-mix concrete truck routing, rerouting, and delivery—pioneered early and to an advanced state by Texas Industries of Dallas.
3. Development of unit trains and integral trains that carry, over long distances, only a single commodity (e.g., coal by the Baltimore and Ohio Railroad, grain by the Illinois Central) with few or no intermediate stops. By providing fast long runs at enormous efficiency, the trains can dead-head back and still save money. . . .
4. Preorder shipment of perishables at long distance. The system was pioneered by Sunkist to send trainloads of lemons from California east before orders have been placed, using weather forecasting services for intermediate routing and dropoffs in time to reach cities where expected high temperatures will raise the consumption of lemonade and Tom Collinses. Any lost hot day is a lost day of sales. . . .
5. Limited-service, fast, low-priced repair facilities such as national muffler and transmission shops. Pioneered by Midas, this system features high volume, specialization, and special-purpose tools which combine to produce fast, guaranteed results.

Government recognizes the problems associated with productivity. But recognition is not resolution. Indeed, what can one say about a federal government that is simultaneously trying to control profit margins and studying ways to increase productivity? To say government is working at cross-purposes is perhaps the kindest answer. But at least productivity is on the public agenda—along with inflation, which it affects in a major way. Thomas C. Cochran (1959), the business historian, once pointed out that because production and operations were never a major problem in American business, marketing was the focal point of management attention. Today, however, because of deep and swift currents in the macroenvironment of business, operations management is coming into its own. It is the managers of production and operations who are best placed to help change the variables of resources, pollution, energy consumption, and productivity that, according to our well-being equation on page 376, determine the well-being of society.

CHAPTER TEN

Financial Decisions

———————— **T**he goal of this chapter is to present a clear picture of how changes in the external environment affect the major business function of finance. Consider, for example, how advances in computer technology have been seized upon by a government agency, the Securities and Exchange Commission (SEC), and transformed into a project that will fundamentally alter the stock market. This project, known as the Intermarket Trading System (ITS), links the New York, American, Philadelphia, Pacific, Midwest, and Boston stock exchanges and allows brokers on the floor of one exchange to query and trade on another to get a better price. Before the ITS was hooked up in 1978, brokers on each exchange traded independently of the other five. In this chapter we shall consider several equally dramatic instances of why the finance function cannot be thought of as separate from the external environment.

In the first section we examine the SEC's effort to get companies to disclose more financial data. We consider both the rationale behind this effort and the responses of companies. The second section examines the role of the tax system in shaping the financial management of a company. We first look at the major characteristics of the tax system, modifications that business leaders would like to see in the existing system, and lastly what the 1978 tax law does.

From the perspective of society as a whole, nothing attracts attention quite like business profits. The third section of this chapter, therefore, examines the role that profits play in business operations and whether profits are at an adequate level. The fourth section takes up the often ignored matter of investment in research and development (R&D). Here we shall try to see how a company can construct its R&D program in response to a rapidly changing technological environment.

The last section of the chapter explores the issue of whether inflation has become institutionalized in the U.S. economy. If this is the case—and a number of experts think it is—then serious implications follow for financial management in the 1980s. In the past, for example, operations managers drew up their annual growth plans independent of the financial officers. If the plans were good, they knew they could rely on their financial people to come up with the needed funds. Today, in all but a handful of cash-rich companies, that simple formula—"I'll run the business, you get the money"—no longer works. Companies are now stressing, as perhaps never before, the job of measuring and cutting the costs of doing business. New investments must promise bigger returns than ever before, and old projects that fall below expectations are being lopped off.

As Exhibit 10–1 indicates, experience as a financial executive has become the preferred background for the chief executive officer, while the marketing executive background has lost ground. The reasons for this reversal are fairly clear. In the late 1950s marketing received most of management's attention; advertising and market research flourished. By the late 1960s, with capital plentiful and corporations increasingly diversified, the finance officers, who could make deals and raise new money, had risen to the top. Corporations borrowed to the hilt to keep up their all-important growth rates and make acquisitions. In 1973, however, that bubble burst, and defensive-minded corporations continued to call on the financial people—but this time to get the business back on the track. At the end of the 1970s, with inflation still running at the double-digit level, the financial executive background remained influential in most companies. As we shall see in this chapter, the situation is not likely to change in the years ahead as businesses face increasingly complex decisions in this vital area. □

EXHIBIT 10–1 Changing Professional Backgrounds of Top Corporate Presidents

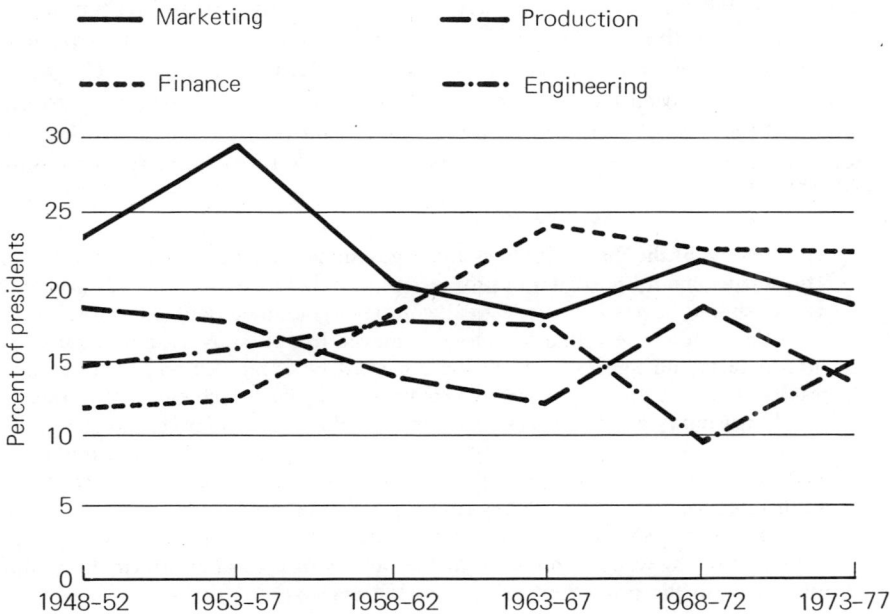

—— Marketing   — — Production

- - - Finance   —·—· Engineering

Source: Data from Golightly International & Company, New York.

FINANCIAL DISCLOSURE

The Securities Act of 1933 requires full and fair disclosure of information about companies selling securities to the general public. The intent of the law is to make it possible for investors to evaluate new issues on an informed, factual, and up-to-date basis. The Securities and Exchange Commission (SEC), an independent agency composed of five commissioners and a chairperson, administers this law. In this section we consider SEC's efforts to improve corporate disclosure of financial data through annual reports, as well as some examples of corporate response.

The Annual Report

Congress has authorized SEC to prescribe the form and content of financial reports to be filed with the commission. Today SEC requires all companies listed on one of the thirteen largest U.S. stock exchanges, or having assets of $1 million or more and a minimum of 500 shareholders, to file detailed 10-K annual reports to the commission. These reports reveal the corporation's income statements, balance sheets (ten-year history), properties, subsidiaries, pending legal proceedings, changes in outstanding securities, research and development expenditures, information on leases, effective tax rate analysis, and much more.

In contrast to the 10-K, the annual reports mailed to shareholders are not always quite as informative. Yet, in the view of Duff & Phelps, a Chicago-based investment research company, two basic considerations—fairness to investors and the cost of capital—should cause all management to strive for excellence in annual shareholders' reports (cited in Arthur Andersen & Company, 1976:3–5):

> The purpose of the disclosure laws and regulations is fairness to all investors. . . . This means that all present and prospective shareholders, and their advisers and agents, should have equal access to all company-generated data and information . . . . We do not believe that fairness is achieved by . . . an overwhelming disclosure of facts and figures. . . . Information must be organized and summarized, results analyzed, and expectations explained in order to achieve real fairness.
>
> Consistently good financial reporting should have a favorable long-run effect on the company's cost of capital. . . . Over a period of time, good reporting leads to informed investors who, because they understand the company, will pay a fair price for its securities. They trust the information received from the company and its management. Minimum or inconsistent reporting often leads to some loss of investors' confidence in the quality of company information and, ultimately, in the price they will pay in the market.

According to Duff & Phelps, management too often simply includes numbers from financial statements in the shareholders' annual reports without explaining the causes or significance of developments. Yet investors need to know, for example, how important a new product is relative to total sales or how much a new plant adds to capacity. Moreover, management does not always discuss corporate objectives and strategies with investors. Annual reports need the addition of "forward-looking information" that includes data on plans (capital expenditures, plant construction, new-product introduction, and financing) and forecasts ("speculation about future outcomes").

In an exhaustive survey of annual reports, Duff & Phelps found that one-third of the companies did not provide key operating statistics—for example, output by major products, selling prices or price indexes, employment, plant capacity, and mineral reserves—which are necessary for comparing the company with the industry, assessing the significance of price changes on sales and margins, or projecting sales growth without additional capacity. Many annual reports were found substandard in four other important areas as well: reporting on pension costs, international ownership and/or activities, identity of major stockholders, and use of replacement cost accounting.

1. Many companies simply do not give adequate data on their pension obligations. Yet investors need to know the funding of accrued liabilities to date, the interest assumption, the actuarial method, and, if there is an unfunded liability, the amount and rate of amortization. From this data they can attempt to determine the impact of future pension expense on profit margins when making earnings projections.

2. SEC requires disclosure of ownership of another corporation if its assets constitute more than 15 percent of total corporate assets. But because foreign operations, as we saw in Chapter 4, can account for as much as 40 to 60 percent of net earnings, Duff & Phelps thinks that all shareholders' annual reports should give special attention to overseas sales, operating expenses, net income, and taxes—data that many simply do not include.

3. Large corporations generally have an extremely wide ownership base, often with no stockholders holding a significant percentage of the stock. While SEC requires listing stockholders owning more than 10 percent of a company's stock, annual reports to shareholders generally tell very little about the identity of major stockholders. But according to a staff study for the House Committee on Banking and Currency (1969), in certain cases even 1 or 2 percent ownership could provide tremendous influence over the management of a company.

4. In 1977 SEC decreed that some one thousand of the nation's largest industrial corporations must account for the effects of inflation on assets and operations. Accordingly, these companies had to disclose the current replacement cost of inventories, plants, and equipment. Under SEC rules, large corporations must calculate what it would cost to replace their productive capacity at current prices and include that information in their 10-K annual reports to the commission. Financial managers have objected to this rule, arguing that they might not replace many of their assets or would replace them with far different kinds of equipment. The resulting "what if" numbers, they complain, are meaningless at best and misleading at worst.

In late 1979, the Financial Accounting Standards Board, a nongovernmental regulatory group, proposed that companies "experiment" with two alternatives in their 1979 reports. Now companies must present key operating, asset, and market data, using *current costs* to determine whether corporate performance had kept pace with the ravages of inflation. Companies must also disclose essentially the same information in *constant dollars* by adjusting its numbers with the official consumer price index to show whether its purchasing power had been maintained. In theory, investors can analyze whether handsome earnings shown in *historical cost* figures were due to good company performance or were simply the result of inflation. The FASB suggests that it may be misleading to tag a company whose sales and earnings have doubled over the past ten years a "growth company" when the general price level in the United States has risen just as rapidly. According to *Business Week* (April

16, 1979), with the new information, balance-sheet inventories would be 35 percent higher on a replacement basis, and it would cost almost twice as much at current prices to replace the average company's productive capacity. Under replacement-cost accounting, annual depreciation charges would be nearly 70 percent greater.

Despite the shortcomings in regard to pension costs, international activities, stockholder identity, and replacement costs, annual reports are considerably better today than they were just a few years ago. For example, since the SEC requires that replacement-cost data appear only in its 10-K filings and since most managers oppose such disclosure, observers thought that only a handful would include the data in shareholder reports. But a survey by *Business Week* (April 16, 1979, p. 118) of annual reports showed that more than 10 percent of the major corporations were sharing replacement-cost data directly with shareholders.

In general, some companies—General Electric, National Distillers & Chemical, W.R. Grace, Koppers, Dow Chemical, Union Carbide, TRW, Champion International, and Textron—have done an excellent job for years both in financial disclosure and in overall readability. The 1977 annual report from the Borg-Warner Corporation, which contains most of the elements that should go into an exemplary shareholders' document, might be singled out for a closer look.

Borg-Warner 1977 Annual Report. Without being overly slick, the excellent graphics in Borg-Warner's forty-page, black-and-white report make it highly attractive and readable. Most important, the key data, including data contained in the footnotes, are extremely easy to find. Furthermore, the report is interesting; its feature section, for example, contains a sophisticated, informative essay on working life from several perspectives ("Why Working Isn't Working, and What To Do About It").

Other carefully planned touches increase the report's usefulness to investors. Product-line sales and earnings data are prominently displayed at the outset. Subsequent pages analyze not only divisional results for 1977 but also discuss in detail the economic outlook for each operating sector for 1978. A question-and-answer section with chairman James F. Bere gives a good feel for top management's style and chief concerns. (Sample questions: What do you see as Borg-Warner's major accomplishments in 1977? What progress can you report on the strategic plan discussed a year ago? You've assigned specific goals to each of your major business groups; has this helped the process along?) Borg-Warner also includes a page of special information for investors: short paragraphs on such things as the annual and regional meetings, stock listings, transfer agents, and how a shareholder can go about reinvesting dividends automatically or can report a change of address.

Unlike most companies, Borg-Warner spells out its key accounting policies before, rather than after, its financial statements. It is one of the 10 percent of companies that give shareholders a look at its replacement-cost numbers, together with an explanation of how the data can be used. Borg-Warner also continues to present an eleven-year summary of major financial items. (Many corporations now only give five-year data.) The report closes with a detailed profile of products and markets.

In sum, the trends in financial disclosure through annual reporting are clearly following three patterns. First, SEC is using the more detailed 10-K report as a benchmark to which the commission would like to see shareholders' annual reports rise. Second, corporate management is expanding the purpose of the annual reports. These reports, bigger and slicker every year, are becoming vehicles to showcase management (especially management's views on government policy) and to advertise products. Third, the annual reports are displaying a new candor. Koppers Company's report, for example, carries line-by-line explanations in the margins beside each of its key financial statements. Shell Oil Company is showing the effect of inflation by applying a price-level index to key financial figures (see Exhibit 10–2). Few companies, however, have yet to match the disarming candor of Berkshire Hathaway's 1978 report. The chairman, Warren E. Buffet, in his letter to shareholders includes this line: "Some of our expansion efforts—largely initiated by your chairman—have been lackluster, others have been expensive failures."

TAX REFORM

The subject of taxes seldom comes up in most discussions of business-society interrelations. Yet few things can infuriate society (read: taxpayers) more than watching business executives live well at public expense. Abuse of corporate expense account deductions—for example, conferences at plush resorts, golf club dues, three-martini lunches, tickets to sports events, and the use of corporate jets—is, not surprisingly, a prime target for tax reformers.

No subject has more of an impact on the financial position of a company than tax reform. Every percentage point the corporate tax rate is cut equals roughly $1.4 billion of revenues. In 1978 the corporate tax rate stood at 48 percent of profits, while Congress held hearings on possible cuts. Whether it eventually approved a 45 or 46 percent rate, or some other rate, was no trivial matter. Nor was the size of the bite on capital gains, since it would have a decided effect on the ability of companies to raise funds. In this section we first look at the characteristics of the tax system, then the reforms business would like to see, and finally the outcome of the 1978 congressional hearings on cuts in the corporate tax rate.

Characteristics of the Tax System

There is a powerful body of theory going back at least to Adam Smith's *Wealth of Nations* (1776) that tells how a tax system ought to be designed to minimize the burden on a free market economy of providing "revenues for the

**EXHIBIT 10–2   An Example of Good Annual Reporting:
Shell's Price-Level Adjusted Financial Information**

Our economy has experienced steadily rising prices primarily as a result of inflation. There is every expectation that price increases will continue. While there are a variety of different opinions on how to reflect and measure the effect of inflation on financial statements, it is generally agreed that traditional concepts and methods of reporting value and income are inadequate for this purpose. Financial statements prepared under generally accepted accounting principles report the actual number of dollars received or expended without regard to changes in the purchasing power of the dollar. Capital investments made over an extended period of time are added together as though the dollars were common units of measurement. Amortization of these prior period costs is deducted from current period revenues in determining net income. Since the purchasing power of the dollar has changed materially from the time these investments were made, this change must be considered for a proper assessment of economic results.

Inflation also affects monetary assets, such as cash and receivables which lose purchasing power during inflationary periods since these assets will purchase fewer goods or services in time. Conversely, holders of liabilities benefit during such periods because less purchasing power will be required to satisfy their obligations.

In the accompanying price level adjusted financial statements historical dollar amounts have been restated to a common unit of measurement, i.e., the dollar as valued at year-end 1978. For example, an asset acquired in 1968 for $1 is restated to $1.90 in terms of 1978 dollars and depreciation is similarly restated. Each year is therefore expressed on a comparable basis which provides a better measure of economic progress.

As the chart below indicates, Shell's profitability ratios are lower when both income and investment are stated in common units of measurement. However, it is also relevant that the Company's return on shareholders' equity, when measured in constant dollars, has shown substantial recovery in recent years from the depressed levels of the late nineteen-sixties and early seventies. This recovery was due to the growth in earnings, which has exceeded the combined effect of inflation and the increase in investment base.

Net Income as a Percent of Shareholders' Equity

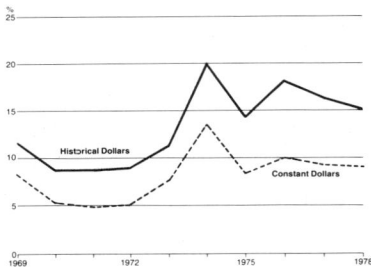

Net Income (Millions of Dollars)

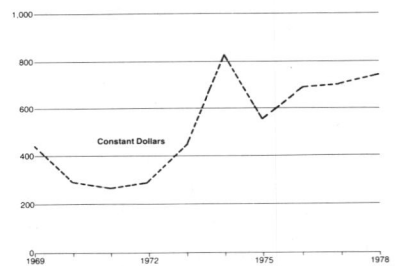

Source: Shell Oil Company, *Annual Report,* 1978, p. 40. Reproduced by permission of Shell Oil Company, Houston, Texas.

sovereign." According to Smith, a tax system must have three salient characteristics: simplicity and certainty; equity; and efficiency.

Businesses, because of the incredible complexity of the tax code, employ legions of lawyers and accountants to tell them not only what their tax bills are, but also how to arrange their business affairs in advance to minimize those bills. Frequently, there is no way of predicting in advance what tax bills will be, partly because of the time lag in writing the regulations that spell out legislation. One consequence of delayed regulations is thousands of cases pending in U.S. tax courts. To Smith, a tax system that was uncertain and overly complex would be inherently arbitrary and would lead to "insolence and corruption of tax gatherers."

Smith explicitly stated that citizens should be taxed according to their ability to pay. Modern tax theory splits Smith's view of equity into two parts: vertical and horizontal. *Vertical equity* has come to mean that the rich should not only pay more taxes than the poor, but also should bear a progressive share of the tax burden—that is, the top rates should rise with incomes. *Horizontal equity* means that people with the same income should pay taxes at the same rate, regardless of the source of the income. The horizontal equity issue pits middle- and upper-income recipients against each other on the basis of how they make their money and how well they can hold on to it and convert it into wealth. For frequently desirable social purposes, Congress over the years has put into the tax code a variety of exemptions, exclusions, and preferences that reduce the taxes payable on income from property—or income that can be realized as capital gains—compared with income from wages and salaries.

To offset this imbalance, the Tax Reform Act of 1969 put a 50 percent tax ceiling on earned income, but it ran the top rate up to 70 percent on the so-called unearned income that is derived from rents, royalties, dividends, and interest. This "reform" merely increased the scramble by high-income recipients to convert income into property forms that were sheltered by the greatest number of preferences, from apartment buildings to oil-drilling ventures. Thus, a company may drill for oil at a cost of $100,000, even though it expects to find only $50,000 in oil. The company drills the hole because the tax advantage of being able to deduct the drilling cost from other income makes it worthwhile to drill. If it weren't for the tax laws, nobody would spend $100,000 to find $50,000 worth of oil. So $50,000 of pure waste is involved in such an undertaking. Financial managers call it buying a tax shelter. A system that would tax income from all sources at the same rates not only would achieve horizontal equity but also would be economically neutral. Companies and individuals would not invest in oil, cattle feeding, timber and real estate simply because these activities are taxed at lower rates. Under a tax system where special preferences were largely eliminated, managers generally would be able to conduct their affairs without worrying about the tax implications.

Relative to other advanced industrialized societies, the U.S. tax system depends heavily on individual and corporate income taxes for revenue. Yet, as most mainstream economists recognize, an income tax system is prone to discriminate against capital because it taxes consumption less heavily than savings and investment, whose future income stream is taxed repeatedly. To offset this bias, Congress and past administrations have larded the tax code with the special preferences that produce wide deviations from both horizontal equity and neutrality. Through the tax system, therefore, the government plays an increasingly large role in deciding where investment is going—for example, into $100,000 notes that will produce $50,000 in oil—instead of leaving the job of allocating capital to the market. According to Gerard M. Brannon, an economist at Georgetown University, the current system is the result of a perennial tug-of-war between people who want to use the tax system to redistribute income and others who think the system should only foster growth. The "compromise" these contenders have fashioned, says Brannon, "starts with a highly progressive tax-rate schedule and an antibusiness tax structure. Then it cuts loopholes to restore business incentives. This is fatuous, both as equity and incentive" (*Business Week,* August 29, 1977, p. 46).

What Business Wants

Whenever Congress begins reconsidering the tax system, leaders of the business community go to Washington and set forth their list of priorities. In 1975 Reginald H. Jones, chairman and chief executive officer of General Electric Company, who certainly qualifies to serve as a spokesperson (see Exhibit 10–3), made several proposals. To get a clearer picture of the "business position" on tax reform, we might take a moment to consider three of Jones's major proposals (adapted from U.S. Department of the Treasury, 1977:68).

1. *Depreciation rates should more nearly recoup replacement costs than historical costs.* One of the most important capital-formation issues for business is the depreciation allowance. Business is concerned about the effect that inflation has had on the replacement cost of capital equipment. Despite the fact that the federal government has speeded up depreciation schedules in recent years, the replacement cost of capital equipment has outrun the original cost claimable for depreciation.

2. *A permanent 12 percent investment tax credit for all industry.* Economists rank a bigger investment tax credit, along with faster writeoffs on capital equipment, as among the most effective ways of increasing capital spending. The investment tax credit, worth $11 billion a year, could be increased from the current 10 percent to, say, 12 percent.

3. *A reduction in the corporate income tax rate.* Reducing corporate income taxes is another way to increase the funds available to companies for reinvestment. One of the drawbacks to the corporate income tax is the perverse effect it has on management decision making: It gives business a powerful incentive to raise capital by borrowing rather than by selling new stock. Interest payments on bonds are counted as a business expense and taxed only as personal income for the recipient. In contrast, regular corporate income is taxed twice—once, when the money is earned by the corporation and again (as personal income) when it is paid out as dividends. Such an arbitrary tax structure favors one class of investors (bondholders) over another (stockholders) and one kind of enterprise (unincorporated partnerships) over another (corporations). More important, the corporate income tax tempts corporations to go deeply into debt to reduce tax liability and thus increases their financial vulnerability in lean times. Numerous schemes for righting the balance have been proposed. Everyone would like to eliminate the bias in favor of debt capital and increase investment without sacrificing government revenue. Perhaps the most straightforward answer is outright abolition of the corporate income

EXHIBIT 10–3   Tax Reform and the Business Community

Reginald H. Jones, chairman of the General Electric Company, is a member of the President's Labor-Management Advisory Committee, the President's Export Council, the Project Independence Advisory Committee, and the Committee on International Monetary Reform. He is also a member of the executive committees of the Business Council and the Business Roundtable. Mr. Jones has written (1975:54–55): "It is obvious to every businessman who has worried over his balance sheet and cut back on his planned investments that corporate tax reform is needed. But it is not obvious to the public and to a Congress that reflects several decades of antiprofits politics . . . . The business community has a selling job to do. The problem of capital formation, and the consequences of inaction, must be set forth in compelling, job-and-pocketbook terms that voters can understand and that politicians will respect." But "Businessmen have not been very good at this sort of political action, and that at least partially accounts for the fix we are in . . . . The old 'soak business' theory of taxation, the old politics of seeking votes by attacking profits, has finally brought this nation to the point of crisis. Congress has to face facts and recognize the proper and necessary function of the producer community in our national life. And the first step is tax reform that will enable business to finance this country's future."

Source: Photo courtesy of General Electric Company, Fairfield, Connecticut.

tax—what is known in tax jargon as *full integration.* After abolition, corporations would continue to transmit funds to the Treasury, but these payments would serve as withholding against the personal income tax liability of individual stockholders. Income, if defined as consumption plus change in net worth, is an attribute of individuals or families, not of business organizations. Corporations do not consume, nor do they have a "standard of living." The term *corporate income* is shorthand for the contribution of the corporate entity to the income of its stockholders.

Clearly, if there is any one theme that runs through this trio of proposals, it is this: The tax system needs to stimulate more investment. (Jones's first two proposals would probably be very effective toward that end. And full integration, while it might not actively promote investment, would have the virtue of ending government influence ovei the way business is financed.) Significantly, by 1978 the Council of Economic Advisers—whose chief concern is to tell the president how best to keep the economy chugging each year at the 5 percent-plus growth rate needed to reach full employment and achieve a balanced budget by 1981—was pushing strongly toward a restructuring of the tax system to stimulate more investment. The CEA argued that 5 percent-plus real growth each year in the gross national product would mean that real spending on new plants and equipment must rise by almost 10 percent a year right through 1981—a rate not seen for such a sustained period since the 11 percent average of 1961–1965.

A New Tax Law

The result of the 1978 congressional hearings on possible tax cuts was a new law that went into effect in 1979. For the first time, business was taxed on a graduated basis rather than according to the time-honored surtax system. What this means for business is shown in Exhibit 10–4. The 2 percent reduction in the maximum rate—from 48 percent to 46 percent—helps all corporations, but clearly, most of the benefits will accrue to the larger companies since profits above $100,000 account for over 90 percent of total corporate profits.

EXHIBIT 10–4   Corporate Income Tax Rates before and after the 1979 Tax Law

Income	Old rate	New rate
$0–$25,000	20%	17%
Next $25,000	22	20
Next $25,000	48	30
Next $25,000	48	40
Any income above $100,000	48	46

To further encourage investment in pollution control equipment and industrial plant improvements, the new law broadens the investment tax credit, while maintaining its 10 percent rate. Obviously, the construction industry and building materials producers also benefit from the extension of the 10 percent investment tax credit to the costs of remodeling and rehabilitation. Other aspects of the new law benefit forest products companies which get a special tax break on the timber they cut and agribusiness, which gets a break on the cost of chicken coops and pigpens.

But even more fundamental issues are involved here—issues that transcend the relative merits of tax cuts for chicken coops. What is the *real* role of profits? Are corporate profits too high? We examine the answers to these questions in the following section.

PROFITS AND INVESTMENTS

At a televised press conference in October 1977, President Carter assailed the U.S. oil companies for seeking "the biggest ripoff in history" and attempting "war profiteering" (see Exhibit 10–5). Not since John Kennedy assailed steel industry leaders in 1962 for abruptly raising prices (see Chapter 3) had an American president so harshly attacked a group of business executives.

But it is one thing to accuse the oil companies of a profits ripoff and quite another to prove it. Critics of the industry have repeatedly denounced oil company profits as everything from exorbitant to obscene. But not even Senator Henry Jackson, the industry's archopponent, has succeeded in making the charge stick. The industry has responded by pointing out that in spite of a nearly fivefold rise in world oil prices since 1972, oil company profits in 1976 (4.7 percent) accounted for a smaller share of gross revenues than they did in 1972 (6.4 percent), before OPEC began jacking up oil prices. After-tax profits were admittedly huge ($14.6 billion), but so was the industry's cost of earning those profits. The industrywide return on investment in 1976 was 9.6 percent, not nearly as good as the automobile companies' 14.6 percent and barely better than the chemical companies' 9.5 percent. Since 1977, domestic oil companies have averaged slightly less than a 9.4 percent return on investment—a rate about on a par with those of the nation's 600 largest manufacturing firms (data from *Time*, October 24, 1977, p. 27).

The Delusion of Profits

If public officials have difficulty getting business profits into perspective, it is hardly surprising to learn that the public as a whole is confused. According to one survey, most of the nation's household heads have no idea of how much profit a manufacturer made (or should make) on every sales dollar. The median estimate was 14 cents, but more than one-fourth of the respondents estimated profits to be 25 cents or more. In answer to how much a company

EXHIBIT 10–5   Public Reaction to Oil Company Profits

Profit is a poorly understood but highly emotional issue. Here an angry President Carter assails potential "war profiteering" by the major oil companies.

Source: Wide World Photos, Inc.

should keep out of every sales dollar it earns, the median estimate was 13 cents (*U.S. News & World Report,* 1976:10). According to Citibank, the actual profit earned in 1975 by the average manufacturer was 4.4 cents.

Therefore, the habitual complaint of many business managers about the economic illiteracy of the public is not entirely unfounded. One might even argue that the greatest threat to the American business system is not the hostility of some of its more strident challengers, but the pervasive ignorance of society with respect to the way the business system functions. But the same managers who complain so loudly about economic illiteracy are themselves contributors to that illiteracy. What they say to each other and their stockholders inhibits both business action and public understanding. In a sense, there is no such thing as profit. As can be seen in Exhibit 10–6, when one follows the cash cycle of a company, one finds only *costs*. What is called *profit,* and reported by financial officers as such, is actually a cost in two respects:

—A genuine cost of a major resource, namely, capital;

—A necessary insurance premium for the real risks and uncertainties of all economic activity.

Thus, once we begin to think in terms of the cash cycle shown in Exhibit 10–6, we see that what we think of as profit is a prerequisite for any economic system.* Rather than being "obscene," profits in the United States may be actually too low to insure continued economic health, which includes, among other things, jobs. In fact, among the top twenty industrialized countries, the United States in recent years has fared badly in terms of new industrial investment per capita; only Luxembourg and Britain rank lower. As a result, the United States may already have become enmeshed in an intolerable economic dilemma in which the nation's private employers no longer create enough new jobs to absorb young workers coming into the labor force. Otto Eckstein, the Harvard economist, has warned that the production capabilities of a number of important basic industries, including the chemicals and paper industries, are so limited that they could create bottlenecks that would impede the unemployment rate from dropping much below 6 percent.

Profits also contribute to economic health by providing a base for retirement security. There is an old myth, which should have been laid to rest decades ago, that dividends flow mainly into the pockets of wealthy individuals. Actually, there has been a historic, if little-heralded, shift in the pattern of share ownership. In terms of dollar value, nearly half of all corporate shares these days are owned by institutions such as pension funds, insurance companies, college endowments, and even churches. Without even realizing it, millions of Americans rely on corporate strength for their own future security. The assurance of a retirement income, the soundness of an insurance policy, or the availability of a college scholarship may well depend heavily on the continued profitability of U.S. corporations.

How Adequate Are Profits?

The adequacy of corporate profits has become the subject of considerable controversy among economists. Some aspects of that controversy include how profits should be measured, which years should serve as standards for comparison, and whether the profits of recent years are part of a secular trend or simply a cyclical symptom. Notwithstanding these issues, the assertion that profits in the United States, rather than being obscene, might be too low to adequately finance the economic health of the nation is obviously a statement that should not be allowed to stand unsupported. Let us, therefore, look at corpo-

---

* Profit is not peculiar to capitalism. The communist economies require a much higher rate of profit because their costs of capital are higher, and central planning adds additional economic uncertainty. Consequently, communist economies operate at a substantially higher rate of profit than any market economy. For ideological reasons, profit in communist countries is called *turnover tax.*

EXHIBIT 10–6   Cash Cycle of a Company

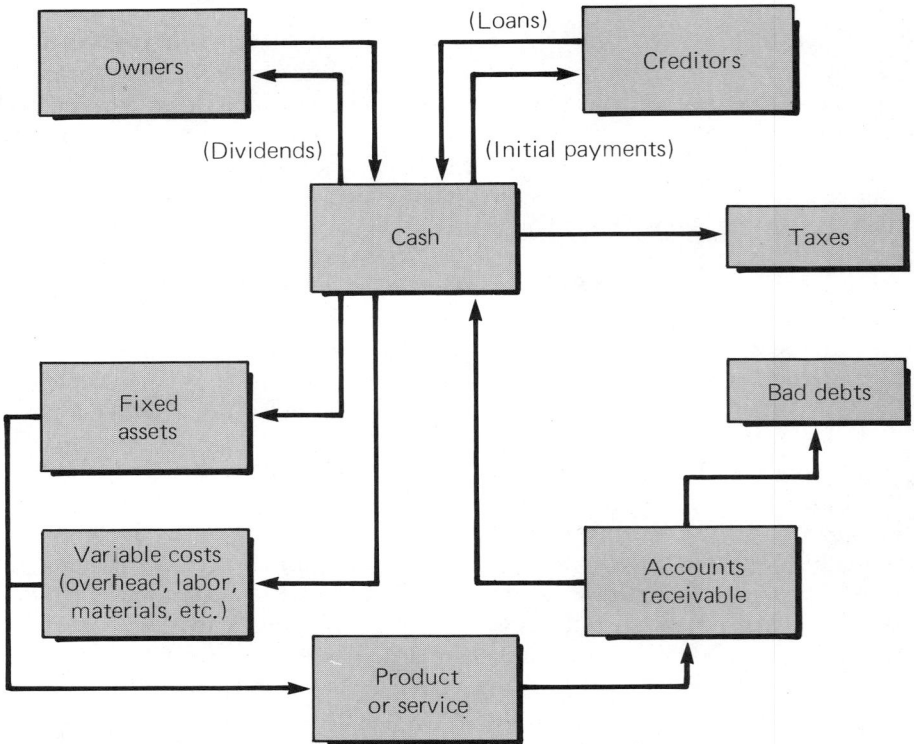

rate profits for a single year, 1978. No fancy analysis is needed to grasp the essence of the problem.

An Analysis of Corporate Profits for 1978. Before taxes, domestic profits by U.S. business in 1978 amounted to about $202 billion. That was more than 16 percent above the previous year and 68 percent more than it earned in 1975. However, the $202 billion figure is inaccurate: By relying on illusionary gains created by inflation and antiquated accounting methods, it overestimates earnings by about one-third. Still, even if appropriate adjustments are made, we are looking at a large amount by the standards of the past.* Before we can ad-

* While it was true that profits tend to climb, over the long run, an ever increasing percentage of national income has been shifting away from profits toward wages and salaries. In 1950, 64.1 percent of corporations' domestic income was used to pay wages, salaries, and fringe benefits, while profits comprised 15.6 percent; by 1975 the share of wages and salaries had risen to 76 percent, while profits had fallen to only 8.3 percent.

just the $202 billion, however, we have to provide for the "senior partner"—the United States Treasury, which levies taxes on the basis of profits as reported, not as adjusted for inflation. After an estimated $84 billion for taxes, only $118 billion will remain. The "junior partners"—the stockholders—now come in for their shares, which will amount to $49 billion. Consequently, the massive $202 billion with which we started has succumbed to two gigantic slices totaling $133 billion. Just $69 billion remains to finance the future growth of these companies. Now if we adjust for inflation and underdepreciation, we have not $69 billion but $27 billion. This adjusted figure is less than companies did in 1977 and no better than they did in the mid-1960s.

The Effect of Profits on Business Investment

It may be true that if corporations want to invest, they have enough funds. But this is not the issue. Corporations will not invest those funds in physical assets unless they believe that such investments will yield an adequate return to the shareholders. Moreover, the apparent increase in the volatility of profit has strengthened the desire of corporations to hold more assets in liquid forms. For example, say a company is considering switching to a new technology that uses more efficient plant equipment than that required by current technology. Specifically, these are the differences:

	Technology A (Current)	Technology B (New)
Selling price	$10/unit	$10/unit
Fixed cost	$1,000/yr.	$2,000/yr.
Variable cost per unit	$8/yr.	$6/yr.

The break-even point for both technologies is the same, namely, 500 units. But the risks involved, due to flux in business conditions, are not. If demand rises to 501 units, the profit from Technology B is $4; if demand goes down to 499, the loss from Technology B is $4. If demand rises to 600, the profit is $400; if it goes down to 400, the loss is $400. In contrast, Technology A minimizes these risks. If demand rises to 600, the profit is $200; but if the demand falls to 400, the loss is only $200. The lesson is clear: To minimize risks, stay with the less efficient Technology A. It appears that the lesson has not been lost on today's corporations (see Commentary section, "Investment and Uncertainty").

COMMENTARY: Investment and Uncertainty

At any given point in time, investment activity and stock market behavior are conditioned . . . by much more than current profit readings. What is ultimately decisive in determining the behavior of investors and businessmen is not the rate of return currently earned on past investments but rather expectations about future earnings. Very often current earnings are an excellent proxy for expectations about future earnings; sometimes they are not. My judgment is that businessmen and investors at present have a sense of doubt and concern about the future that is even greater than would be justified by the low level of true economic profits.

One telling piece of evidence that this is so is the pronounced hesitancy of businessmen in going forward with capital-spending projects that involve the acquisition of long-lived assets. The investment recovery that we have experienced so far in this cyclical expansion has been heavily concentrated in relatively short-lived capital goods that promise quick returns—trucks, office equipment, and light machinery, for example. Major investment projects that cannot be expected to provide payback for many years encounter serious delays in getting management's approval. Indeed, the decline of industrial construction that set in during the recent recession continued through the first quarter of this year—two years after general economic recovery got under way—and has not yet turned around decisively enough to establish a clear trend.

Many businessmen have a deep sense of uncertainty about what the longer future holds and, as a consequence, are discounting expected future earnings more heavily than they ordinarily would in their investment calculations. The special degree of risk that businessmen see overhanging new undertakings means that they often will not proceed with a project unless the prospect exists for a higher-than-normal rate of return. This is not only skewing investment toward short-lived assets; it is also fostering an interest in mergers and acquisitions—something that does not require waiting out new construction undertakings. There has been a noticeable pickup in merger activity recently, but such activity generates neither additional jobs nor additional capacity for our nation's economy.

Source: Arthur Burns, speech delivered at Gonzaga University, Spokane, Washington, October 26, 1977.

R&D INVESTMENT DEFICIENCIES

It would be redundant to take time to again outline the importance of research to a company—and indeed to the nation. Often, untutored management invests in low-level engineering design under the impression it is putting money into applied research. This kind of management keeps wondering why its "new products" are obsolete before they hit the market. For strategic as well as budgetary reasons, top management is getting more and more curious about what to expect from R&D expenditures.

Today cars, cameras, color TV sets, watches, motorcycles, light electronic equipment, many chemicals, outboard motors, tools and equipment of all sorts, steel fasteners, textiles, shoes, and nuclear power plants all bear the stamps "Japan," "Germany," "Korea," "Singapore," "Taiwan," "Italy," "Sweden," and so forth. According to the American Society for Mechanical Engineers, the United States retains leadership in only a handful of major-technology fields, such as computers, aerospace, and heavy electronics. But the

Japanese have already launched a massive, government-backed spending effort to match the United States in computers; the European aerospace industry has gained its first toehold in the United States with the Airebus; and the American edge in heavy electronics has been largely tied to weapons systems and, therefore, not readily transferable to commercial markets.

Reasons for the Decline in U.S. Technology

There are several reasons for the decline in U.S. technological leadership:

—Inadequate levels of federal R&D funding;
—Tax policies that discourage investment in R&D industry;
—Political decisions to have a risk-free society;
—Regulatory agencies whose net effect is to delay or prevent technological change and to increase its cost. (Many regulatory effects are indirect—for example, who is going to develop expensive coal processing when natural gas is selling at half its real market price?)

Two other important reasons for weak technology, however, lie right in the lap of business management. The first is the obsession with "bottom-line results this year." Profits now, despite any future opportunity costs to the firm—that

"Eureka! The E.P.A. willing."
Drawing by Dana Fradon; © 1975 The New Yorker Magazine, Inc.

is, benefits lost by *not* developing a new product—are plainly management decisions. Such decisions are hardly surprising; incentive compensation systems under which managers live tend to deter intelligent risk taking.

The second reason for weak technology is the relative neglect of aggressive management of technology. Missing in many industries are a basic knowledge about the management of innovation and an effort to encourage and feed new technology into business plans and decisions. As a recent issue of M.I.T.'s *Technology Review* told inventors (Roberts, 1977:25):

> If you believe that companies really support the development of new products, you will discover a far different reality. . . . You disturb them. They prefer their immutable picture of the world in which there is a perpetual demand for their existing product lines. . . . It is a fantasy world in which technical obsolescence never occurs and the competition prices products fairly.

Management Responses to R&D Deficiencies

Construct an R&D Program. Management decisions involving a company R&D program consist of three elements: the immediate environment of the business, availability of funds, and availability of R&D projects.

In the context of constructing an R&D program, one of the most important things about the immediate environment that needs to be considered is the position of the company in the market. How formidable is the competition? How formidable is it likely to become in the future? In answering the latter question, technology forecasting, which was discussed in Chapter 7, can be extremely helpful. As might be expected, there is a wide diversity of R&D commitment among various industry groups and within industries themselves. Companies in the fuels group spend about 8 percent of profits on R&D, which is the lowest percentage spent by any group. The semiconductor group topped all industries in commitment to R&D by spending about 117 percent of profits. The automotive group of several vehicle manufacturers spent more than $3.1 billion on R&D in 1977 and led all groups in total dollars spent, while textile and apparel manufacturers combined for only $29 million in expenditures (data from *Business Week*, July 3, 1978). The heaviest spenders in research and development are among the most profitable of U.S. firms. Data from Technical Insights, Inc., on the fifty firms making the largest R&D investments in 1976 show a direct correlation between income and R&D expenditures.* For example, Goodyear, near the bottom of the list in R&D investments, is also low in net income (*Technology Review,* March–April 1978, p. 39). Not without reason, therefore, some shrewd investors have begun to examine price/R&D ratios of prospective companies (see Exhibit 10–7).

In constructing an R&D program, the second element to assess would seem to be funds available. But this factor must be coupled with estimates on the

---

* More accurately, the correlation was between company incomes and their ratios of R&D expenditures to annual sales.

EXHIBIT 10–7   Spending Indicators for R&D

In Minneapolis, stockbroker Ron J. Burger of Dean Witter Reynolds, Inc., has developed a price/R&D ratio. A company with 10 million shares outstanding may spend $125 million on R&D, or $12.50 per share. If the stock is selling at $50 a share, its price/R&D ratio is 4.0, meaning that the investor gets 25 cents worth of R&D each year for every dollar he invests. According to Burger, any company spending above 10 cents per investor dollar is worth considering. "More and more investors are starting to take note of the R&D figures," he says.

profitability of various R&D projects. In theory, one ranks these projects and then, starting at the top of the list, selects as many as one can without exceeding the funds available. Exhibit 10–8 presents a general view of the R&D investment problem. Needless to say, an investment should not be made if it does not return at least the cost of capital—no matter how much funding is available. Given the six alternatives, A through F, which should be selected? Clearly, since the alternative with the highest rate of return should be selected first, a company that has $20 million available to invest should select A, B, and C, in that order. If the company has $30 million, it should select alternatives A through D.

The third element in constructing an R&D program is the hardest, for it involves knowing how to pick the winners in a field where mortality rates are high (see Exhibit 10–9). For example, when the computer came into existence at the end of the 1940s, confounding all the forecasts that said it was a technical impossibility, forecasters estimated a commercial market for not more than twelve machines in the United States. "Only ten or a dozen very large corporations will be able to take profitable advantage of the computer" was a view expressed in 1948. Sometime later IBM made a historic decision not to market the computer because it would never be profitable. The problem was that people failed to see how the machine would be used; they lacked the imagination to think of suitable applications. They thought of the machine as doing only scientific calculations and could only visualize a small number of calculations that were big enough. As the computer industry has grown, forecast after forecast has suffered a similar, if less spectacular, failure of imagination. When disk memory had been available for a few years, some leading computer salespeople said confidently that it was a gimmick that would soon disappear from the marketplace. Similarly, when data transmission first became available, one heard repeatedly that nobody would use it because the mail was cheaper (see Martin, 1977:11).

EXHIBIT 10–8   Selecting among R&D Investment Alternatives

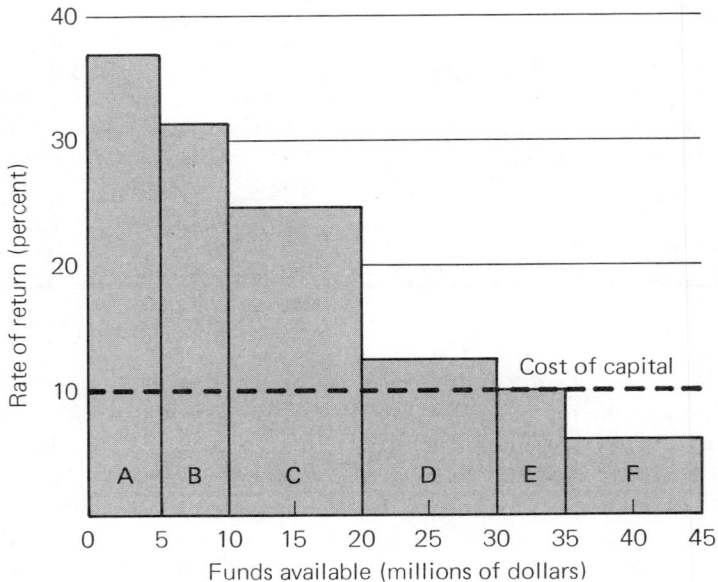

A simplified version of the concept of setting priorities among R&D investment alternatives is depicted here. The horizontal axis measures the dollars of investment during the year ($5 million for Project A, $5 million for Project B, $10 million for Project C, etc.). The vertical axis shows the rate of return on each project. The dashed horizontal line indicates the percentage cost of capital. The strategy is basically this: Invest in projects that promise the highest rate of return (Project A is most attractive, promising a 35 percent return), but avoid those projects that promise less return than the cost of capital (Project F, with only a 5 percent return, should surely be avoided).

The story of the computer is by no means the only example of a situation in which managers with impressive experience have been oblivious to the potential of major new technical opportunities. Technological innovation, therefore, presents a profound challenge. White and Graham write (1978:146–47):

> Businesses that have been slow to react when major innovations have invaded their industry have often relinquished hard-won positions in a very few years, while companies that have successfully exploited the technical and business opportunities such innovations posed have rapidly become industry leaders. Yet

EXHIBIT 10–9   Mortality of New Product Ideas by Stage of Evolution

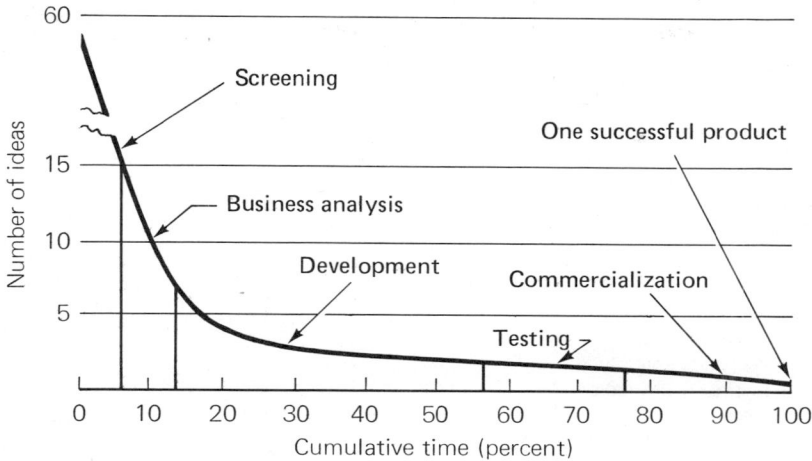

Note: Graph is based on data from fifty-one companies.

even when recognizing the major strategic implications of technology for their companies, general managers have too often evaded the obligation to exercise their management skills. They have let the sophistication of technology and the complexity of converting it to business success convince them that technological innovation is a treacherous area that is best left to experts.

Delegating responsibility to experts is only sensible for products in the midst of their life cycles. With these products, general managers can depend on established systems, and the appropriate question for them to ask during their periodic review is: "Are we doing the job right?" But it is the discontinuous, revolutionary innovation that affects a company's fate. In this situation the question reverses to the tougher "Are we doing the right job?" To answer this question, most companies with an R&D program have instituted charts, indexes, and criteria to profile research proposals. A typical product profile chart is shown in Exhibit 10–10.

Develop an Assessment Plan. In assessing a technical proposal, a streamlined framework based on four major considerations is suggested by White and Graham (1978:147–49):

EXHIBIT 10–10   New Product Profile Chart

	Favorable		Neutral	Unfavorable	
	1	2	3	4	5
R&D					
Development time		✔			
Research know-how			✔		
Development cost	✔				
Personnel	✔				
Patent status	✔				
Equipment				✔	
Marketing					
Present sales capability				✔	
Present service capability		✔			
Effect on present products		✔			
Market trend	✔				
Potential market (estimated sales)		✔			
Promotional requirements					✔
Effect on competitors' products		✔			
Financial					
Capital equipment required				✔	
Effect on cash flow		✔			
Estimated return on investment		✔			
Payback period		✔			
Production					
Familiarity with production processes				✔	
Equipment availability				✔	
Raw material availability		✔			
Environmental impact					
Air			✔		
Water				✔	
Health			✔		

Inventive Merit. A truly significant inventive concept will use its new combination of scientific principles to relieve or avoid major constraints inherent in the previous art. In the case of the transistor, elimination of the heated cathode of a vacuum tube allowed portable radio size and weight to be reduced while offering longer battery life and greater reliability. . . .

Embodiment Merit. Even the most creative invention requires substantial additional engineering to be complete. Approached with imagination, the embodiment of an invention can offer as much scope for improvement as the invention itself. It was such an embodiment opportunity that the Japanese radio manufacturers seized when they made the pocket transistor radio. They reinforced the size and weight advantages that the transistor offered by miniaturizing the ferrite antennae, loudspeakers, and tuning capacitors as well. . . .

Operational Merit. The effect of an innovation on a company's existing business practices is a measure of its operational merit. . . . In the days of tube radio, for example, a franchised dealer network providing maintenance service was a critical element of radio marketing. Not only have transistor portables proved to be much more reliable, but they also are small enough to be mailed to central repair depots. This change in the type of service required allowed Japanese radio manufacturers to use much wider, nonfranchised distribution channels, addressing a whole new market. . . .

Market Merit. When considering market merit, two complicating factors must be borne in mind. First, it is final demand, not intermediate demand, that is the greatest concern. Thus airline passengers' preference for seats in jets rather than in the piston engine planes overcame the reluctance of airline management to retire its undepreciated piston equipment. Second, total revenue opportunity for a given product can be increased in one or both of two ways, either by price reduction if the market is elastic or by an increase in the attractiveness of the product.

The market effect of radical product innovations is best gauged by comparing them with their less radical product competitors. Miniature transistor radios owed their popularity to one attractive feature—mobility. The light weight and small size of the Japanese pocket radio provided play-as-you-go rather than carry-and-set-down portability. Pocket radios needed no substantial price concessions to have major competitive advantage over their bulky U.S. competitors. When in subsequent years Japanese manufacturers reduced their prices to reflect their by-then lower costs, they were able to extend their revenue opportunity still further via market elasticity.

In sum, we have seen that companies construct their R&D programs by first considering three elements—their immediate environment (especially the competition), funds available, and project availability—and then developing a plan for assessing new proposals. To these considerations one other must be added: overall corporate strategy for developing an R&D program. Four alternative strategies that a technology-based business might follow are suggested by Igor Ansoff and John M. Stewart (1967):

> *First-to-Market.* [This strategy] . . . is a somewhat risky strategy, as it demands major expenditures for research before there is any guarantee of a successful product. It also demands heavy development expenditures and perhaps a large marketing effort to introduce an innovative product. The possibilities for rewards from the R&D, however, are tremendous.
>
> *Follow-the-Leader.* This strategy . . . demands strong development engineering: As soon as a competitor is found to have had research successes that could lead to a product, the firm playing follow-the-leader joins the race and tries to introduce a product to the market almost as soon as the innovator.
>
> *Me-Too.* A me-too strategy differs from follow-the-leader in that there is no research or development. In its purest form, this strategy means copying designs

from others, buying or licensing the necessary technology, and then concentrating on being the absolute minimum-cost producer. . . . [Many Japanese firms followed this strategy in the 1960s and 70s.]

Application Engineering. [This strategy] . . . involves taking an established product and producing it in forms particularly well suited to customers' needs. It requires no research and little development, but a good deal of understanding of customers' needs and flexibility in production.

A firm's R&D program should flow from a consideration of all of the elements discussed in this section; otherwise R&D management will be operating under a handicap.

FINANCIAL DECISION MAKING IN A WORLD OF INFLATION

Since the late 1960s, a number of institutional changes have occurred in the U.S. economy that tend to make inflation—the rate of which, at this writing, remains double digit—self-perpetuating. The trend has been towards increased *indexing* not only of labor contracts but of all business contracts. Essentially, indexing is tacking escalator, or cost-of-living, clauses onto all contracts to avoid the painful effects of varying rates of inflation. With indexing, all prices, wages, and interest rates are tied to some measure of price changes. The slow gains and even declines in labor productivity (see Chapters 2 and 9) have also helped to embed inflation deeply into the U.S. economy. The trend toward concentration of market power has made it easier for labor to attempt to obtain increases in excess of productivity gains. While labor maintains real wages, industry raises prices to cover these increasing labor costs and maintain real profits.

In the paragraphs that follow, we shall look at the ways in which inflation has become institutionalized. We shall see how consumers themselves have exacerbated the process. We shall also see how this institutionalization has affected financial decision making in the business system. We shall conclude with a brief prognosis.

The Role of the Consumer

Today consumers tend *not* to react to rising inflation by cutting their spending. The reasons are fairly clear. First, based on recent experience, they assume their incomes will, more or less, keep up. As noted above, many workers, especially those who are union members, have been able to negotiate contracts with automatic cost-of-living adjustments (COLA); since 1975, the Social Security System has been indexed to inflation; and there is the ever-growing trend of households to become two-wage-earner families.

A second major reason why inflation-battered consumers have not cut their spending—and have thus contributed to the continuation of inflation—is that they have ample incentive to buy. Some families deliberately spend everything they earn to buy quickly before the price jumps: Indeed, if one thinks about it, buying, say, a case of tomato sauce is an excellent return-on-investment. Because interest payments are tax deductible, consumers have an incentive to continue spending by using credit, even to the point of getting a bigger mortgage. Consider how an automobile loan helps the consumer "whip" inflation. An auto loan that carries an 11.4 percent interest rate really cost the consumer, if he or she is in the 40 percent marginal tax bracket, only 6.8 percent. The Shakespearean homily, "Neither a borrower, nor a lender be" seems irrelevant in modern America.

Management Responses to an Inflationary Period

Investigate New Product Opportunities. According to a study done by Data Resources, Inc., families will have less money for "nonessentials" in coming years. The reason is that discretionary income for families earning $25,000 or more, measured in 1975 dollars, could decline as much as 30 percent by 1986. Necessities—food, clothing, housing, and transportation—will be claiming a wider share of family budgets (cited in *U.S. News & World Report,* July 25, 1977, p. 45).

This forecast is considered bad news for producers and sellers of such products as toiletries, household goods, and luxury items—things that consumers cut back on in a financial squeeze. Thus companies will be more careful about introducing new products and will spend more time and money on research to be more certain of success. In 1977, for example, many firms hiked research budgets by as much as 30 or 40 percent. "It used to be that you rushed into the market before you were really ready," observed James Affleck, chairman of American Cyanamid, maker of personal-care products and household cleaners. "But now we don't want to bring out a product unless we have a winner" (quoted in *U.S. News & World Report,* July 25, 1977, p. 45).

In a study of small- and medium-sized firms that were able to thrive during the recession of the early 1970s, Donald K. Clifford, Jr., found one of the keys to their success was that they developed their market niches (1977:58):

> Market strategies are born of necessity. . . . [and] the power of the market niche crops up in example after example:
>
> Bandag, Inc., has built a $180 million business in the prosaic field of tire recapping, a business that addresses the economic needs of individual consumers at a time of deteriorating dollar values, yet one that the major tire manufacturers do not want to touch. . . .
>
> Pizza Hut, Inc., has established itself as a dominant performer in its sector of the fast-food market. . . . [and] has succeeded with a concept that the larger restaurant chains neglected and that other smaller chains never learned to exploit effectively.

Whether a company's market niche involves personal-care products, tire re-capping, or fast-food pizzas is immaterial. The real point is that when money is tight, a company researches new product opportunities and then makes every effort to take advantage of them.

Adapt to New Financial Policies. Because the interest rate charged on loans still exceeds the banks' cost of obtaining funds, bankers are encouraging—not restraining—borrowers. As one New York bank economist explained, "If you're a businessman coming in for $1 million, we don't ask if you could get by with $800,000; we're more likely to ask if you couldn't use $1.5 million" (quoted in *Wall Street Journal,* March 6, 1979).

Nowhere has the adaptation to inflation been more pronounced than in U.S. financial markets. The changes include (adapted from *Business Week,* January 29, 1979, p. 93):

—The easing of ceilings on what financial institutions can pay for money.
—The involvement of floating-rate loans (which are not fixed but fluctuate with economic conditions) by financial institutions.
—The rapid growth of those sections of the financial markets that make loans but lie outside the jurisdiction of the Federal Reserve Board.
—New lending techniques—for example, five-year car loans and graduated mortgages with higher payments in later years.
—The proliferation of foreign banks in the U.S. and the Eurodollar market overseas (see Chapter 4).

While corporate borrowing from banks doubled between 1968 and 1978, large companies have been able to quadruple their borrowing from each other through commercial paper notes. Where does all this corporate money come from? With interest rates high, most companies have tried to maintain a positive cash flow. As the Commentary section, "The New Importance of Cash Flow," explains in inflationary periods cash flow becomes a particularly important measure of a company's performance.

COMMENTARY: The New Importance of Cash Flow

While managers and investors look to the bottom line (or reported earnings), the academic community for years has looked to cash flow as a way of gauging a company's future growth. Basically, cash flow is the amount of cash available from operations after adjusting for such noncash expenses as depreciation and deferred taxes. Now it appears that this approach is taking hold in the business and investment community.

How reported earnings show up in annual reports is shown in boldface type in the following example from Kennecott's annual report for 1978.

Consolidated Statement of Changes in Financial Position, Kennecott Copper Corporation and Subsidiaries

	1978 (in thousands of dollars)
Funds provided by:	
Operations:	
Income from continuing operations	**$ 5,014**
Noncash charges to income:	
Depreciation, depletion and amortization	88,659
Amortization of intangible and other assets	4,801
Increase (decrease) in deferred U.S. and foreign taxes on income	8,800
Increase in minority interests	6,718
Funds provided by operations	**113,992**
Proceeds from sale of Chilean notes	30,868
Decrease (increase) in accounts receivable	18,242
Decrease (increase) in inventories	27,005
Disposals of property, plant and equipment	4,568
Increase in accounts payable, accrued expenses and taxes	8,416
Total funds provided	203,091
Funds expended for:	
Property, plant and equipment	161,649
Increase in investments and notes receivable	19,556
Net increase in other accounts	10,769
Total funds expended	191,974
Net funds provided (expended) before items below	11,117
Distributions to stockholders	(19,879)
Sale of Peabody Coal Company and Subsidiaries	—
Acquisition of The Carborundum Company less, cash and marketable securities at acquisition	—
Increase (decrease) in notes payable	(132,697)
Increase (decrease) in long-term debt	70,108
Net increase (decrease) in cash and marketable securities	($ 71,351)

Why have traditionally earnings overshadowed cash flow? The reason appears to have been mainly one of semantics. "I always ask my students, who are executives with major companies, to tell me what a company can do with income," said Thomas E. Huff, an adjunct lecturer of accounting at the Wharton School of the University of Pennsylvania. "They usually give answers like 'pay taxes,' 'pay dividends,' 'pay employees' salaries,' and 'reinvest in the company.' All of these answers are wrong because income is not cash. Cash is the only thing that can pay bills, retire debt, and pay dividends.''

Back in the 1960s and early 1970s, earnings per share was a fairly useful investment tool. It provided an indication of a company's dividend growth rate, but only because a variety of accounting and financial policies kept corporate financial reporting fairly close to the ''cash-received'' basis of accounting. In the last few years, companies have been moving away from the cash basis. As we have seen in this chapter, because of high inflation, companies increasingly reflect unrealized income on an income statement; the depreciation cost of goods sold and the cost of replacing productive assets are understated. The result, David J. Hawkins writes in a 1978 article appearing in the *Financial Analyst Journal,* is that earnings-per-share figures are no longer reliable approximations of the cash available to finance future growth.

Source: Text adapted from ''Cash Flow as a Guide to Growth,'' by Deborah Rankin, *New York Times,* May 23, 1978. © 1978 by The New York Times Company. Reprinted by permission. Example financial data reprinted courtesy of Kennecott Corporation, New York.

Companies have also adjusted to inflation by becoming rather adroit in passing on rises in the costs of materials and labor. Having considerable discretion in setting prices, firms in relatively concentrated industries are likely to raise prices more quickly than might otherwise be the case and more than is needed to cover costs in order to protect profit margins against anticipated further inflation. Thus a kind of inflationary psychology sets in. These prices increase, of course, then become costs to other sectors with the result that the initial expectations become self-fulfilling prophecies as the increases work their way through the economy.

We can conclude this chapter by noting that in the long run, inflation rates will probably unwind, though slowly. The assumption for this forecast, Farb and Jones (1976:79) write, is that "the experience of the 1970s was the result of the coincidence, unlikely to be repeated, of a series of events—OPEC, crop failures, devaluation, simultaneous boom in all industrial countries." These two economists add a strong word of caution, however: "While another bunching-up of shocks like those of the 1970s is not likely, the chances of one or more shocks are not so low, and a disastrous crop failure or similar event could add new fuel to the inflationary pressures" in an increasingly interdependent world economy.

CHAPTER ELEVEN

Marketing Decisions

Marketing involves, essentially, the determination of consumer wants and the movement of goods and services from the producer to the consumer. This chapter considers how the new consumerism affects marketing decisions and what management responses are available.

Crossing this Gobi Desert of a subject will require several stops. In the first section we shall try to sharpen our idea of what is meant by consumerism. We shall see that consumerism is not really new; we shall examine what exactly the consumers are asking; and we shall see why consumerism is here to stay.

The second and third sections deal with a wide range of issues involving product promotion and product use. Among the former we shall consider issues such as advertising, packaging and labeling, selling practices, and warranties; among the latter, the safety and reliability of products. The fourth section examines four major ways in which management can respond to the consumer challenge. First is to develop a consumer-oriented program; second is to organize for consumerism; third is to monitor promotional practices; and fourth is to prepare a product recall strategy.

The final section of the chapter takes a more critical look at consumerism—or, more specifically, at what some of the consumer advocates are saying. In particular, we shall consider the charges that (a) too much is spent on advertising and (b) no price is too high to insure safety. □

WHAT CONSUMERISM MEANS

Laws to protect consumers did not arise on the coattails of Ralph Nader. Legislation concerning standardization of weights and measures, public health and safety, transportation, communication, licensing, and zoning is all designed to protect the consumer from exploitation. Such legislation has a long tradition in the United States, as a few early milestones in consumer legislation quickly illustrate. In 1872 the federal government prohibited the use of mails to defraud. In 1906 Congress passed the Pure Food and Drug Law, which prohibited the misbranding of drugs. In 1907 it passed the Meat Inspection Act, which authorized the Department of Agriculture to inspect slaughtering, packing, and canning plants. And in 1914 it set up the Federal Trade Commission.

The 1907 move by Congress toward control over sanitation in the meat-packing industry provides a classic example of the life cycle of a social issue (see Chapter 2). Following a number of structural changes (such as the industrialization of meat packing), problems of sanitation in the industry began to become increasingly visible. Yet nothing much was done until a dramatic precipitating event occurred: In 1906 Upton Sinclair, a forerunner of Rachel Carson and Ralph Nader, published *The Jungle*. Describing the sanitation problem in lurid detail (see the Commentary section for an excerpt from this work), Sinclair was able to propel the issue on to the policy agenda.

COMMENTARY: The Jungle

With one member trimming beef in a cannery and another working in a sausage factory, the family had a first-hand knowledge of the great majority of Packingtown swindles. For it was the custom, as they found, whenever meat was so spoiled that it could not be used for anything else, either to can it or else to chop it up into sausage. With what had been told them by Jonas, who had worked in the pickle rooms, they could now study the whole of the spoiled-meat industry on the inside, and read a new and grim meaning into that old Packingtown jest—that they use everything of the pig except the squeal.

Jonas had told them how the meat that was taken out of pickle would often be found sour, and how they would rub it up with soda to take away the smell and sell it to be eaten on free-lunch counters; also of all the miracles of chemistry which they performed, giving to any sort of meat, fresh or salted, whole or chopped, any color and any flavor and any odor they chose.

In the pickling of hams they had an ingenious apparatus, by which they saved time and increased the capacity of the plant—a machine consisting of a hollow needle attached to a pump; by plunging this needle into the meat and working with his foot, a man could fill a ham with pickle in a few seconds. And yet, in spite of this, there would be hams found spoiled, some of them with an odor so bad that a man could hardly bear to be in the room with them. To pump into these the packers had a second and much stronger pickle which destroyed the odor—a process known to the workers as "giving them thirty percent."

Also, after the hams had been smoked, there would be found some that had gone to the bad. Formerly these had been sold as "Number Three Grade," but later on some ingenious person had hit upon a new device, and now they would extract the bone, about which the bad part generally lay, and insert in the hole a white-hot iron. After this invention there was no longer Number One, Two, and Three Grade— there was only Number One Grade. The packers were always originating such schemes—they had what they called "boneless hams," which were all the odds and ends of pork stuffed into casings; and "California hams," which were the shoulders, with big knuckle joints, and nearly all the meat cut out; and fancy "skinned hams," which were made of the oldest hogs, whose skins were so heavy and coarse that no one would buy them—that is, until they had been cooked and chopped fine and labeled "headcheese!"

It was only when the whole ham was spoiled that it came into the department of Elzbieta. Cut up by the two-thousand-revolutions-a-minute flyers, and mixed with half a ton of other meat, no odor that ever was in a ham could make any difference. There was never the least attention paid to what was cut up for sausage; there would come all the way back from Europe old sausage that had been rejected, and that was moldy and white—it would be dosed with borax and glycerine, and dumped into the hoppers, and made over again for home consumption. There would be meat that had tumbled out on the floor, in the dirt and sawdust, where the workers had tramped and spit uncounted billions of consumption germs. There would be meat stored in great piles in rooms; and the water from leaky roofs would drip over it, and thousands of rats would race about on it.

It was too dark in these storage places to see well, but a man could run his hand over these piles of meat and sweep off handfuls of the dried dung of rats. These rats were nuisances, and the packers would put poisoned bread out for them; they would die, and then rats, bread, and meat would go into the hoppers together. This is no fairy story and no joke; the meat would be shoveled into carts, and the man who did the shoveling would not trouble to lift out a rat even when he saw one—there were things that went into the sausage in comparison with which a poisoned rat was a tidbit.

There was no place for the men to wash their hands before they ate their dinner, and so they made a practice of washing them in the water that was to be ladled into the sausage. There were the butt ends of smoked meat, and the scraps of corned beef, and all the odds and ends of the waste of the plants that would be dumped into old barrels in the cellar and left there.

Under the system of rigid economy which the packers enforced, there were some jobs that it only paid to do once in a long time, and among these was the cleaning out of the waste barrels. Every spring they did it; and in the barrels would be dirt and rust and old nails and stale water—and cartload after cartload of it would be taken up and dumped into the hoppers with fresh meat and sent out to the public's breakfast. Some of it they would make into "smoked" sausage—but as the smoking took time, and was therefore expensive, they would call upon their chemistry department and preserve it with borax and color it with gelatine to make it brown. All of their sausage came out of the same bowl, but when they came to wrap it, they would stamp some of it "special," and for this they would charge two cents more a pound.

Source: Upton Sinclair, *The Jungle* (Cambridge, Mass.: Bentley, 1973).

What Consumers Want

Despite the fact that consumerism is not a new phenomenon, today's movement differs from yesterday's in intensity and breadth. Philip Kotler (1972) captures the essence of the new version nicely: "Consumerism is a social movement seeking to augment the rights and powers of buyers in relation to sellers." The seller's argument that the customers have all the powers they need because they can refuse to buy the product is no longer acceptable. Consumer advocates say that the buyers are not getting the information they need about products because advertising is deceptive—either crudely or subtly. Often, for example, the sellers fail to deliver the warranty, the safety, and the performance they promise. Furthermore, much of the buying public is not equipped to understand the tricky phrasing or technical language in advertising and on packages.

Basically, consumer advocates seek four rights. First is the right of consumers to products and services that will increase the "quality of life"—that is, in addition to being convenient to the consumer and profitable to the company, products, packaging, and market practices must be "life enhancing." The more notable manifestations of this right have been the regulation of product ingredients (e.g., in detergent and gasoline), the promotion of packaging (e.g., biodegradable containers), and the establishment of consumer representation within the policy-making councils of the company (e.g., a consumer advocate on the board of directors).

Second is the right of consumers to be informed. Specific shortcomings frequently mentioned include failure to disclose the true interest cost of a loan, the true cost per standard unit of competing brands, true product ingredients, nutritional quality, and product freshness. To correct these problems, consumer advocates support regulations requiring truth in lending, unit pricing, ingredient labeling, nutritional labeling, and open dating, respectively.

Third is the right of consumers to protection against questionable products and marketing practices—a reaction to the let-the-buyer-beware philosophy of the past. Consumer advocates say that customers have neither the ability nor the time to understand complex information about a product; therefore, some group or government agency should help them. The expansion of government agencies and the issuance of new powers to existing agencies are reflections of this right. Finally, consumer advocates demand a fourth right—a reasonable relationship between price and quality.

Why Consumerism Is Here To Stay

Clearly, the consumer movement has made its mark: Government has expanded its power in the area of consumer protection enormously, and the "four rights" outlined above have become deeply imbedded in the public consciousness. In 1978, when Congress defeated a proposal that would have established a consumer agency, some members of the business community concluded that the consumer movement was about to disappear over the horizon of business worries. But business had to take a closer look. After the proposal's defeat, Esther Peterson, White House consumer adviser, was given by executive order many of the powers that would have been vested in the consumer agency. Perhaps an even more significant development for the 1980s is the new emphasis by consumer leaders on state and local politics, accompanied by a growth in local consumer action groups. Consumerism has special appeal, too, for the new breed of younger, more active state legislators and attorneys general, who find the movement both fun and good politics. (Who loses votes attacking, say, high public utility rates?)

Despite these new realities, recent surveys have indicated that business response to consumerism has continued to be spotty. The surveys imply that in many cases, business is continuing to operate in the dark and is failing to see the deep resentment behind the consumer movement. For example, according to one survey of twenty-four-hundred metropolitan households (Arthur Best and Alan R. Andreasen, 1977), one out of five purchases made by members of those households resulted in consumer dissatisfaction with some factor other than price. Less than half of the dissatisfied consumers complained; of those who did, one out of three was unhappy about the way the complaint was resolved. It appears that because complaints handling can be costly and because the problem is not always clear-cut, many companies exhibit a kind of consumer inertia.

Another major survey of consumer attitudes was released jointly in 1977 by Louis Harris Associates and the Marketing Sciences Institute associated with Harvard Business School. More than two thousand interviews had been conducted, including four hundred with consumer activists, consumer affairs regulators, or other consumer specialists. Significantly, the survey showed that consumers believed they had sharpened their shopping skills and that they were currently receiving more product information and better labeling. Consumers also perceived an improvement in product safety in recent years. But about half of the respondents believed that they "get a worse deal" in the marketplace than they did ten years ago. In addition, 61 percent thought that the quality of goods and services had worsened, 73 percent said that products did not last as long as they did a decade ago, and 64 percent asserted that they had more difficulty in getting products repaired. Finally, a large number insisted that most of the products they used regularly did not live up to advertising claims. The survey concluded that "the business community is sharply out of step with the American people on consumerism issues."

In light of these survey results, we can clearly see that consumerism is bound to affect business. In order to appreciate exactly how, we shall begin in the next section by looking at issues involving product promotion and in the following section, at those involving product use. Once that is done, we can then consider what business managers might do in response to consumerism.

PRODUCT PROMOTION

Many consumer complaints relate not to the product itself—that is, its safety, its quality, and so on—but to the fashion in which it is marketed and serviced. A simple way of categorizing these complaints is to relate them to the typical sequence of consumer experiences in the purchase of goods and services. First, prior to making a purchase, the consumer encounters advertising and packaging. Second, at the time of the transaction, the consumer comes in contact with the selling practices of the vendor. At this point, too, credit terms may be arranged. Then, having made the purchase, the consumer may seek service or performance against warranties stipulated in the sales agreement. Business behavior at each step in the purchasing sequence has been the subject of menacing public criticism and governmental surveillance and regulation.

Advertising

How big is the modern advertising business? If we include everybody who advertised in 1976—manufacturing companies, service operations, retailers, wholesalers, distributors, associations, labor unions, schools, churches, governments, politicians, individuals placing want ads—Americans spent over $33 billion on advertising in 1976 (*Historical Statistics,* series T444–446). By its very nature, advertising is open to abuse and misinterpretation. Except for want ads, advertising of simple products (the claims for which consumers can, and do, check), advertising directed to professional buyers, and advertising by some mail-order houses, much advertising is misleading at best and fraudulent at worst.

What is the public reaction to advertising in general? A widely cited survey by Raymond A. Baner and Stephen A. Greyser (1968) revealed that 41 percent of the public surveyed were favorable and 14 percent were unfavorable toward advertising. The other 42 percent were either indifferent or ambiguous. Some experts, however, believe that public attitudes may have changed since 1968. The growth of the consumer movement appears to have raised doubts about the usefulness, truthfulness, and costs of advertising. Unfortunately, we have no comprehensive statistical data since the 1968 survey, though the following assessment was made in a 1977 survey by Louis Harris Associates (1977):

> Mistrust of advertising, and the claims made by business in its advertising, runs through many of the findings in this survey. The public questions the honesty and accuracy of advertising. Almost everyone believes that some advertising is misleading, 46 percent of the public think that most or all of television is seriously misleading, and 28 percent hold similar views about print-media advertising.

Some advertising is indeed what people in the field call *puffery.* To them, the term stands for a kind of legitimate artistic license—which, they claim, is accepted by the public as such. Nobody really believes, for example, that United flies "the friendly skies" while other airlines are daily strafed by Zeros, Messerschmitts, MIG-15s, and unfriendly UFOs. Nor could any half-educated adult really believe this Fiat advertisement: "Among the wonderful Italian things America has discovered, nothing is more so than Fiat's 1100D sedan. That includes the wine, women, the music, the art—even great historic Roma . . . ." But a case like the "Pepsi generation," another example of puffery, may be more uncertain. Are there buyers who might think that Pepsi drinkers are inherently more active, more charming, more "together" than those who imbibe Mr. Pibbs? And puffery in the advertisement of children's toys and sugar-coated cereal probably *is* viewed by a five-year-old as truth.

Some advertising manipulates the language. Recent research by Richard Harris of Kansas State University confirms, for example, that people do not discriminate between what is directly stated and what is implied. He gives these examples of ways in which consumers are misled by linguistic manipulation:

—The use of hedge words that weaken the statement—"Knock-out capsules *may* relieve tension";
—The use of comparative adjectives that give no comparison—"Chore gives you whiter wash" (which is undeniably true because it could be completed with any phrase, such as ". . . than washing with coal dust");
—The use of inadequate or incomplete survey or test results;
—The use of a negative question that implies an affirmative answer—"Isn't quality the most important thing to consider in buying aspirin?" (the answer to which might very well be no, but the assumption is yes);

—The use of expressions such as "hospital-tested" or "doctor-tested" that give little information but lend an air of scientific respectability.

Some advertising is truly false either intentionally or mistakenly. For example, the FTC found that a national baking company was falsely advertising its product: "Our bread will help you lose weight." In this case, the Federal Trade Commission not only ordered the company to stop making this claim but also to spend 25 percent of its advertising budget for six months on advertising that states: "Our bread is not effective in weight reduction, contrary to possible interpretations of prior advertising."

Thus far we have not mentioned what are probably the two most significant aspects of modern advertising. The first concerns the sheer innocuousness of much television advertising—for example, those hundreds of hours of adults squeezing toilet paper and cats singing or dancing for their dinners. The second aspect concerns the ability of advertising people, using the latest behavioral research, to manipulate the buyer. These aspects are somewhat different in kind from the advertising issues previously noted. The FTC can and has stopped false claims, but stopping a crass commercial or subtle manipulation is not so easy—nor is it necessarily desirable in terms of civil liberties. Perhaps the best way to clarify these issues surrounding modern advertising is to take a close look at advertising in a specific industry.

The Pet Food Industry: A Case Study in the Power of Advertising. In the summer of 1978, Morris the Cat died. His passing touched off a great debate among the management of the H.J. Heinz Company: Should they announce his passing or just quietly switch to a stand-in? But what if the news leaked out? Would they be accused of a cover-up? Eventually, the sad announcement was made. That well-paid executives had to spend time on such a decision illustrates how big advertising has become in the pet food industry. In the early 1960s pet food could be purchased in a supermarket, but one had to look for it. By 1965, however, Americans were spending $700 million a year on pet food. By 1978, they were spending over $3.1 billion (data from Ingrassia and Garino, 1979). That is an increase of almost 450 percent in fourteen years. Today consumers no longer have to search for pet food; indeed, they must select from among a perplexing variety of brands and special diets.

It could be argued that this rapid rise in the popularity of pet foods is largely the result of clever advertising strategy by the pet food manufacturers. Their television ads "with their shots of dogs, puppies, cats, and kittens in adorable action" not only have helped persuade pet owners to buy their products, but also, according to Thomas Whiteside (1976:53–54), "may even have influenced many people to go out and buy pets so they could dish out for them the pet food being advertised." Before analyzing current promotional strategies, let us take a moment to recall the origins of today's fierce competition for the pet food market.

In 1969, when the big tobacco company, Liggett & Myers, began to diversify, one of its first moves was to acquire the company that made the canned dog food Alpo. At the time, a keystone of their advertising strategy was, in a word, "meat." But, by the late 1960s, Ralston Purina and other Alpo competitors were counter attacking the "all-meat" strategy and citing studies showing that puppies fed all-meat diets suffered digestive upsets and bone changes and that animal protein was really not essential to a dog's diet at all. Moreover, some experts said that it might even be better to feed dogs something they do not like as well as meat (such as ordinary dry, hard dog food) since obesity was a major health problem among dogs. Anticipating FTC action, the "Alpo 1969 Plan" declared: "We want to hammer home the Alpo 100 percent meat story as strongly as possible before that (FTC regulation) happens." In 1969 the FTC did, in fact, issue a set of guidelines that obliged the Alpo people to make a change in the phrase "Your dog needs meat." Alpo, undaunted, changed the slogan to "Your dog loves meat" (Whiteside, 1976:69).

The meat war is now history. Today the keystone of many advertising strategies of pet food companies is, in a word, "price." A higher price, according to the unceasing advertising barrages, means a higher quality of product. While this pitch, having been perfected by perfumers decades ago, is hardly new, the pet food manufacturers have given it a subtle twist: A higher price means a more sensitive, caring pet owner. The point was captured neatly in a 1979 *New Yorker* cartoon where a small dog glares up from his bowl at a man holding a can. In the middle of the picture stands his disapproving wife, who says: "He's looking right at you, too. I hope you're proud of yourself for saving eight cents on that brand."

The pet food companies did not arrive fortuitously at the strategy of linking price with the worth of the owner; motivational research pointed the way. As one study said about consumer free will (cited in Whiteside, 1976:76):

> Advertising is usually downgraded by people as an effective element in their product and brand selections. They prefer to believe in the myths of their own autonomy in decision making. . . . Advertising implies to an individual that peers value the same brand of product as he or she does. Therein, the individual is assured of the rightness of his choice. But such forms of advertising influence are not in the realm of the admissible.

Much of the pet food advertising also takes advantage of anthropomorphism—that is, the tendency of owners to see human traits in their animals. Cats and dogs may or may not prefer blends of tuna and egg flavors or of beef and cheese essences; but the dishes do appeal to the owners and that, after all, is what is important. Otherwise, why dye meat red when dogs are color blind?

Anthropomorphism, however, goes beyond mundane matters of what should or should not taste good. Studies done on the behavior of owners for manufacturers of pet food found an increasingly indulgent attitude. One study puts the situation this way (cited in Whiteside, 1976:79):

> Many of the women [interviewed in the study] indulge their dog's behavior. He is allowed to behave in "human ways" in getting on furniture, in insisting that he "go with the family" and in his desires to go out on demand. Many are proud of their pet's idiosyncrasies. . . . The attitude is parallel seen in families with "permissive" atmospheres for children and [where] opportunities for "self expression" are many and are encouraged.

Thus, if the family dog turns up its nose at the food in front of it, the reaction of the owner is not to simply wait and let the dog get hungry. As the study explains: "Few of these owners have tried to discipline the dog to eat recommended foods simply because they are supposed to be 'good for the pet.' Those foods that the dog rejects or even eats reluctantly will not be repurchased." When instances of stubbornness occur, "the owners seem to be secretly proud that their pets could not be coerced into eating something against [the pets'] wishes."

Another motivational research study cited by Whiteside suggests a possible source of the dog owner's secret pride: ego projection. "By ego projection, owners unconsciously want to teach their dogs to be and act like themselves. In effect, such owners condition a dog to be a fussy eater, which in turn reinforces a belief that their dog is special, unusually discerning, and, in a general sense, superior." This type of research explains, to a degree, why paunchy pets are no longer fed table scraps. But to be accurate, *social change* has also played a part in the move away from table scraps for pets since Americans eat out more now and meals at home tend more and more to be convenience dishes. A further consideration is that young adults are having children later and less often and a dog or cat, they believe, makes a nice "baby substitute" (Ingrassia and Garino, 1979).

In sum, clever advertising (some would use harsher words) does seem to help explain why it is now so confusing to walk down the aisles of a supermarket and see the dozens of brands of pet food. Over the next several years it is unlikely that spending levels for advertising pet food will diminish. Manufacturers must now convince the owners that dry dog foods really do look, feel, and taste better than meat. The situation is not unlike the detergent and toothpaste business a couple of decades ago when blue dots, green specks, and exotic-sounding formulas seemed to pop in and out of a product every month.

Packaging and Labeling

Like advertising, the package and label on a product provide the producer an opportunity to communicate with potential customers. Consumer advocates point out that they also provide an opportunity for deception. Daniel Boorstin (1973) argues that packaging arrived essentially unnoticed in the late nineteenth century, but has literally come to dominate the American consciousness. By the early twentieth century, the language had even acquired a new verb, *to package.*

In tracing the evolution of packing into packaging, Boorstin notes that packing has always been around; people, especially manufacturers, have always needed to put things into containers to store them or to move them. But progress in packing was held up until the invention of paper-making machines and the successful use of wood pulp as a raw material. By 1900, practically all paper was being made out of wood pulp. "The cheap paper bag," one economist in 1889 boasted, "had been the most effective innovation during the preceding decade in speeding up American retail sales. . . ." As Boorstin (1973: 437) observes: "A salesman could be making a second sale in the time it took to wrap a parcel in paper and twine."

As early as the 1870s, some stores were putting their names on shopping bags as a form of advertisement. Packing was slowly becoming packaging. By 1925 the American Sugar Refining Company was using the following argument—often forgotten by today's environmentalists—to encourage the use of packaging (Boorstin, 1973:440):

> Do you know that it takes a man about an hour and three-quarters to weigh out a 350-pound barrel of granulated sugar in 5-pound paper bags; that a man averages only about sixty-nine 5-pound bags when he weighs out a 350-pound barrel; that the 5 pounds lost by spillage and down-weight represent 1.4 percent of the cost price of the sugar; that, in addition to sugar wasted, bags, twine, and labor amount to about forty cents added to the cost per cwt. of the sugar; and that 350 pounds of Domino Package Sugars mean 350 pounds sold with a profit on every pound; that no time is lost and no material or sugar wasted; that, therefore, a retailer makes more money per pound when he sells Domino Package Sugars . . . .

Boorstin's account of the evolution of packaging is loaded with remarkable insights: "Packaging created new uses, and opened wider markets, with the result that products themselves were transformed." For example, by 1920 the tea bag had made tea available without the tea pot. And as early as 1909, ice cream had been transferred from a dish into an edible package, the ice cream cone, which from an environmental standpoint, is probably the ideal type of package. Modern packaging has also been instrumental in democratizing objects—that is, equalizing their appearance. It is often hard for a consumer looking at a machine-made package to guess the quality of the product inside.

From a marketing standpoint, fancy packaging can have its limits, as the Procter & Gamble people responsible for Pringle's Potato Chips have learned. In 1976, *Snack Food,* a trade publication, estimated that Pringle's had garnered 10 to 15 percent of the $1 billion potato chip market. But by 1977 the market share of Pringle's was only 6 or 7 percent. Some industry sources believed the slip was due to the fact that the product's costly package, a tube resembling a tennis ball container, had forced the retail price of the product 10 percent above that charged by competing chips. A *Snack Food* article also suggested that at a time when "natural" foods were becoming increasingly popular, many consumers viewed Pringle's as a "make-believe" product. As one executive put it, Procter & Gamble "got so hung up on making something that didn't break, they forgot to make it taste good" (*Wall Street Journal,* June 24, 1979).

In addition to the marketing concerns of fancy coverings, there is another issue involved in packaging: the federal government's requirements that packaging and labeling contain relevant information on a product's nutritional contents, safety, efficiency, or usage. One court has held that the standard of clarity applicable to a package label is not what it says to "the reasonable consumer," but rather what it communicates to "the ignorant, the unthinking and credulous" (*Business Week,* May 18, 1974, p. 78). State and local governments are also becoming more active in the area of product labeling. As a greater number of states and localities pass labeling legislation, the likelihood decreases that a nationally marketed product can have a single label that will meet the requirements of all the jurisdictions in which the company hopes to sell it. Exhibit 11–1 provides an interesting example of efforts to promote such legislation in New York State.

Selling Practices

Selling practices, once epitomized by the methods of W.C. Fields' snake-oil salesman and other fly-by-night operators, have long been sources of consumer complaints. Today sophisticated techniques are used to foist products on a gullible public. Surely the modern supermarket would impress even Fields. In the aisles of the country's 183,700 grocery stores and supermarkets, where consumers finally decide what and how much to buy, they get plenty of help. Milk, always a big draw, is often placed at the rear of the store; shoppers must pass high-profit "impulse" items, such as snack foods, to get to it. And nonnutritious products are often positioned near nutritious items so that people will associate the two. For example, orange drinks, which are only 10 percent juice and 90 percent water, are often positioned near fresh oranges.

In any event, consumers apparently are *not* impressed by dubious selling techniques. Such practices as bait-switch, lo-balling (advertising a price lower than that which will actually be charged), fear selling, and free gimmicks are increasingly being brought under control via strengthened state laws and city ordinances. Most of these practices are not subject to federal control because the perpetrators do not engage in interstate commerce. But there are ample exceptions. For example, in 1976 the FTC ordered Sears, Roebuck & Company to stop its "bait-and-switch" tactics to sell major home appliances. The technique is simple: A company advertises a widget-warmer at a remarkably low price. But at the store, the salesperson tells the customer that the advertised model has a tendency to curl the widgets while it warms them. Thus, the

EXHIBIT 11–1   Codebreaker for the Consumer in New York

In 1977, the New York State Consumer Protection Board began to distribute keys to many of the complex food manufacturers' codes that prevent consumers from determining how long food items have been on the shelf. By surveying 84 food manufacturers and getting inside information from supermarket sources in cases in which the manufacturers had refused to cooperate, the board was able to crack the "freshness" codes used on many foods to conceal the dates on which they were packed. The keys to the codes, together with information on how long the products can be expected to remain fresh after being packed, were combined in pocket-sized booklets and distributed free to consumers and posted in supermarkets that had agreed to help.

Many food manufacturers use elaborate coding systems. The Keebler Company, which makes cookies and crackers, uses a letter and number code, such as "A003." The letter refers to the Keebler bakery where the product was made, while the three digits stand for the month and day of the year it was made. But which numbers stand for what dates are revealed only to a person who has access to a number chart that fills two pages in the booklet. Other companies, such as the Beech-Nut Corporation, use simpler codes. The first digit of the code "7115" on one of their baby foods refers to the year, 1977; the second two digits refer to the week, the eleventh (March 13 through 19), and the last digit gives the day of the week, the fifth day (Friday). Beech-Nut told the board that its products last for at least two years after the coded date.

Companies use codes, instead of open dates, because some consumers might not believe that two-year-old baby food is still good to eat. In a recent letter to an official in Massachusetts, which is considering an open-dating law, George Koch, president of the Grocery Manufacturers of America, noted that "one of the primary goals and, indeed, accomplishments, of food processing technology is to retard spoilage of foods which would otherwise be very perishable. Thus, date labeling of such products would create false and misleading conceptions of product difference in the mind of consumers."

According to the New York State board, twenty-one states have open-dating laws, but most cover only easily perishable items, such as milk and bread. (FDA regulation requires that dates and batch numbers be attached to food products in case recalls are necessary.) The board takes issue with the contention that there is no freshness problem with products whose shelf life is longer than sixty days; according to Rosemary Pooler, executive director: "Everything is perishable—it's just a question of degree." The board's survey showed that there was also disagreement among food manufacturers themselves as to what needed to be open-dated. General Foods open-dates its Post breakfast cereals, but General Mills, which makes Cheerios and Wheaties, does not.

Source: Adapted from *Consumer Protection in New York State* (Albany: New York State Consumer Protection Board, 1978); and Francis Cerra, "New York State Consumer Unit Deciphers Codes on Food Dieting," *New York Times,* August 21, 1977.

customer often winds up walking out with the higher-priced, unadvertised widget-warmer. If practiced blatantly and as a general rule, the bait-and-switch technique can diminish the value of all advertising, because consumers simply learn to disregard the advertisements.

The Case of Consumer Credit. An issue closely related to selling practices is consumer credit. Extending consumer credit makes money for business, and there is certainly nothing wrong with that. The problem is that many consumers do not know the true costs of credit, or even the existence of alternatives. *True costs* of credit consider the difference between what one would pay by pursuing another alternative and the cost of pursuing the present alternative. For instance, there are several legitimate methods for computation of service charges. Each will show the same annual percentage rate but will mean different costs to the consumer. Variables include the addition of extra service charges, the date from which interest is computed, and whether the last payment is deducted before computation is made. In recent years the FTC has attempted to educate the public in regard to consumer credit. The emphasis has been on "shopping" for credit the same way one shops for everything else—that is, at more than one place. By seeking the lowest annual percentage rate (APR), the FTC points out, one can save up to $557 in financing $2,000 for two years.

In 1968 Congress devised a law called the Truth in Lending Act, which forced creditors to state plainly—in a supposedly simple document provided with a loan agreement or sales contract—the actual cost of credit. By 1977 Congress was beginning to realize that its solution had created new problems and had prompted semantic warfare of magnificent proportions. The law and its complex accompanying regulations has been engendering waves of lawsuits—more than two thousand in 1976—against merchants and other creditors (see *Wall Street Journal,* August 5, 1977).

Originally, Congress intended for the truth-in-lending disclosure form to be simple. As the bill progressed toward enactment, however, additional disclosure requirements were attached, and after the law took effect, the FTC added still more. In its final form, the bill required that besides stating the finance charge (the total cost of credit) and the true annual percentage rate (the interest rate on the amount of the loan that the consumer has at his or her disposal), the lender must disclose a variety of other data, including statements of any extra charges that will be incurred if the borrower defaults or falls behind in payments, the details of how various items being disclosed were computed, and the nature of any ownership right that the seller retains until the property is fully paid for.

Most of the suits brought under the Truth in Lending Act have nothing to do with disclosure of the cost of credit, the original point of the law. Lawyers have hit on the act as a nearly ideal mechanism for suing lenders on a variety of issues. A typical suit seeks, for example, to force a merchant to pay for repairs to a washing machine because *it was purchased on credit.* Thus, truth in lending has become the preferred vehicle for a great number of cases that used to be brought, if at all, under state laws. The increase is encouraged by one of the provisions in the law, which specifies that a creditor who loses a suit under the Truth in Lending Act must pay the fees of the plaintiff's attorney (see *Wall Street Journal,* August 5, 1977).

Meanwhile, there is little evidence that the law is having the side effect for which congressional sponsors had hoped. It was assumed in 1968 that clear statements of the cost of credit would prompt consumers to shop for the lowest price and would thus help to lower interest rates. Some credit experts say that lower interest rates have not resulted because the disclosures required under the act have become so complex that they are nearly unintelligible.

Warranties

The Magnuson-Moss Warranty–Federal Trade Commission Improvement Act, which took effect in 1975, for the first time set standards for what must be incorporated in a product warranty and for how the warranty must be worded. Under the Warranty Act, all warranties must be easy to read and understand. They must be written in ordinary language, not "legalese." Fine print is not allowed. Every term and condition of the warranty must be spelled out in writing. If a condition is not there, it is not part of the warranty. The FTC enforces the Warranty Act, though it does not handle private cases. As it does with the Truth in Lending Act, the commission conducts a limited consumer education effort with the Warranty Act (see Exhibit 11–2).

A distinction must be made between warranties and service contracts. The latter are not warranties at all. Warranties come with a product at no additional charge. Service contracts give extra protection for an extra fee. In the case of product warranties, there is no difference between *warranty* and *guarantee.* Both terms mean the same thing—namely, a promise by a manufacturer or seller to stand behind a product. But there is a big difference in the kinds of promises made. There are two types of written warranties: *full* and *limited.* These words have been given special meanings by the Warranty Act.

The label *full* on a warranty includes the following conditions:

—A defective product will be fixed (or replaced) free, and removal and reinstallation will be included if necessary;

—A defective product will be fixed within a reasonable time after a customer complains;

—A customer will not have to do anything unreasonable (e.g., ship a piano to the factory) to get warranty service;

—The warranty is good for anyone who owns the product during the warranty period;

—If the product cannot be fixed (or has not, after a reasonable number of tries), the customer has the choice of getting a new product or having the purchase price refunded.

EXHIBIT 11–2   How the FTC Educates the Consumer about Warranties

IF THE PROBLEM ISN'T SOLVED

Your warranty rights don't run out at the end of the warranty for problems you complained about during the warranty period. The company must still take care of those problems, no matter how long it takes.

Here's what to do if you have trouble.

ONE Make sure you have contacted the right person in the company. If the manufacturer gives a warranty, don't stop with the seller. Write (or call) the manufacturer at the address given in the warranty. Explain exactly what you think it owes you under the warranty—repair, replacement, refund, consequential damages.

TWO Contact a local consumer protection office or complaint center. It may be able to help you and tell you more about your rights. Check your phone book under the name of your city, county, or state government.

THREE In some cases there will be an organization which hears and decides disagreements informally, if both sides are willing. The company or a local consumer protection office can tell you who to contact. Check your warranty—this may be a required first step in solving the problem.

FOUR If the amount of money involved is small, you can go to a small claims court. There costs are low, procedures are simple, and a lawyer is usually not needed. The clerk of the small claims court can tell you how to bring your lawsuit.

FIVE If your product was manufactured after July 4, 1975, you can sue the company under the Warranty Act. If you win you can get money damages or any other type of relief the court decides to give you. This includes the cost of bringing the lawsuit and your attorney's fees.

If the product was manufactured before July 4, 1975, you can still sue the company under state law. You should contact a lawyer or consumer protection office for information.

SIX Report violations of the law to the Federal Trade Commission. The FTC *cannot* help you directly with a warranty problem. But it needs to know if companies are obeying the warranty rules. Write the FTC if a company does not make warranty information available.

HOW YOU CAN USE WARRANTIES

Read warranties before you buy to get the best deal. It may be worth it to pay more for a product with a better warranty. The extra money is like insurance—it protects you against the chance of a big repair bill. Comparing warranties now can save you money and headaches later.

Read the warranty when a problem comes up. The warranty is a contract that spells out your rights. Show the warranty to the company if it doesn't do what it promised.

KEEP YOUR SALES SLIP WITH YOUR WARRANTY. You may need it to prove the date you bought the product, or that you were the original purchaser.

Source: Federal Trade Commission, consumer handout, Washington, D.C., n.d.

One important thing the word *full* does not promise: A full warranty does not have to cover the whole product. It may cover only part of the product, like the picture tube of a TV, or it may leave out some parts, like tires on a car. Thus, if the warranty covers only the picture tube, and the sound goes bad, the consumer pays for repairs to the sound system.

A warranty is *limited* if it gives anything less than a full warranty. *Limited* means, "Be careful, something is missing." For example, a limited warranty may:

—Cover only parts, not labor;
—Allow only a pro rata refund or credit (i.e., the longer the customer had the product, the smaller the refund or credit);
—Require the customer to return a heavy product to the store for service;
—Cover only the first purchaser;
—Charge for handling.

A product can carry more than one written warranty. For example, it can have a full warranty on part of the product and a limited warranty on the rest.

In contrast to written warranties, *implied warranties* are rights created by state law, not by the company. All states have them. The most common implied warranty is the *warranty of merchantability*. This means the seller promises that a product is fit for the ordinary uses of the product. For example, a reclining chair must recline; a toaster must toast. If a product is unfit for ordinary use, buyers have the legal right to get their money back. Another implied warranty is the *warranty of fitness for a particular purpose*. If a customer buys a product on the seller's advice that it can be used for a special purpose, then this advice may create a warranty. For example, a seller who suggests a certain sleeping bag for zero-degree weather warrants that the sleeping bag will be suitable for zero degrees. Implied warranties come automatically with every sale, even though they are not written out. If a seller says nothing about warranties, the customer still gets the implied warranties. A seller can usually be exempted from implied warranties by stating—in writing—that a certain product comes with no warranty at all ("as is"). But a seller cannot, by giving a written warranty, become exempt from the implied warranties. Thus if a consumer gets a written warranty, he or she gets the implied warranties too. Spoken promises and advertising claims can also be warranties, and the consumer has a legal right to get what the company promises. These kinds of warranties are covered only by state law, not federal law.

Normally, warranty rights under all these warranties include the right to *consequential damages*—that is, the company must not only fix the defective product, but also pay for any damage the product caused. If, for example, a freezer breaks down and the food inside spoils, the company must pay for the food lost. Consequential damages can have important effects that reach far beyond the product itself. If the buyer is physically injured by a defective product, he or she usually has a right to get money damages from the company. A company can usually exempt itself from extra responsibility by saying in the warranty that it does not cover consequential damages. This type of disclaimer can be included in both full and limited warranties.

PRODUCT USE

Consumer concerns about product use may be grouped into two categories: safety and reliability. A rough measure of the strength of consumer concern about these issues might be the rise in court cases involving product liability. In 1960 there were fewer than 50,000 product liability cases; by 1975 there were 1.5 million. Among the reasons for the increase are these (adapted from Berenson, 1972):

—Packaging prevents proper inspection of the merchandise.
—The complexity and number of today's products precludes proper buyer appraisal—How does one judge safety, quality, price, suitability, and other characteristics of a video tape recorder?
—The explosion of advertising makes rational purchase choice difficult— How does one choose intelligently from among the 7,000 to 9,000 product appeals in the average supermarket?
—Most transactions between seller and buyer—not to mention those between the manufacturer and buyer—are impersonal.
—Rapid product innovations may cause honest errors in safety and design.
—The monetary success of some products liability lawyers has encouraged more court cases.

Product Safety

The board chairman of a lawn mower manufacturing company claims he saw two men trying to cut a hedge with a power mower. "It's impossible to invent an idiot-proof machine," he says. A leading vacuum cleaner company that has had its share of liability had trouble in putting together, in writing, all of its product safety standards and making them a part of top management policy. "In the past," its president says, "We would wonder who in their right mind would pick up puddles of water with the vacuum cleaner. Now we say, 'Don't pick up puddles of water with the vacuum cleaner' " (*Business Week*, July 4, 1970). Cynics speak of the day when hammers will be sold with tags saying, "Don't place thumb under head when in use."

In reality product safety is not a joking matter. According to the National Commission on Product Safety, an estimated 20 million people injure themselves in the home each year with consumer products—that is, four times as many people as are hurt in highway accidents. In fact, consumer concern with home safety is surpassing consumer concern with automobile safety. Thirty thousand Americans are killed, 110,000 are permanently disabled, and 585,000 are hospitalized annually as a result of incidents involving consumer products. Despite these sobering statistics on product safety, the ratio of injuries to appliances has actually gone down. If the home accident rate experienced in the 1930s had prevailed in 1970, there would have been a 57 percent increase in fatal home accidents. That there was not was due in part to greater emphasis on safety in manufacturing requirements.

In 1972 Congress passed the Consumer Product Safety Act and created the Consumer Product Safety Commission (CPSC) to remove "unreasonable risk" from almost every consumer product. (Exhibit 11–3 lists the products considered "most dangerous" by CPSC; note that lawn mowers are only a meager number 17.) What constitutes "unreasonable risk" depends on a variety of factors. Is the risk obvious—that is, can we assume that if people buy a particular product they know what they are letting themselves in for? Is the

EXHIBIT 11–3　The Most Hazardous Products: CPSC's Top Twenty

The twenty goods that the Consumer Product Safety Commission rates most hazardous, based on frequency and severity of accidents involving them:

1. Bicycles and equipment
2. Stairs, steps, ramps, landings
3. Football equipment, apparel
4. Baseball equipment, apparel
5. Swings, slides, seesaws, other playground equipment
6. Nonglass tables
7. Swimming pools, related equipment
8. Beds
9. Liquid fuels
10. Nails, carpet tacks, screws, thumbtacks
11. Basketball equipment, apparel
12. Chairs, sofas, sofa beds
13. Bleaches, dyes, cleaning agents, caustic compounds
14. Architectural glass, including glass doors
15. Floors and flooring materials
16. Cooking ranges, ovens, related equipment
17. Lawn mowers
18. Skates, skateboards, scooters
19. Furnaces
20. Bathtubs and nonglass shower enclosures

Source: Consumer Product Safety Commission, "Hazard Index, FY 1977," Washington, D.C.

risk one that can be removed without defeating the whole purpose of the product? Does the product involve special risks for children or elderly people?

As with most laws regulating business, it is an agency—in this case, the Consumer Product Safety Commission—that supplies the law's meaning. Once CPSC decides that a product is too risky, it can apply a number of remedies. It can use information programs to educate people about the risks of, say, using a power mower and how to avoid injuries. It can seek the cooperation of the industry in drawing up corrective standards. As a last resort, if it detects an imminent hazard that should be removed from the marketplace immediately, the commission can go into court and stop production.

Moreover, the commission can actually tell manufacturers how to make their products safe. For instance, in 1977, citing the fact that 0.008 percent of the population are injured every year in matchbook-related accidents, CPSC issued comprehensive matchbook regulations requiring that the striking surface be on the back, that the staple be placed so that it cannot be nicked by the match, and that the match not protrude from the closed matchbook, not crumble, not break, not delay igniting for more than two seconds, not afterglow for more than five seconds, and not reignite. Here, it should be noted, the commission begins to tread a thin line between setting *performance* standards and imposing *design* standards.

One further point about the Consumer Product Safety Act: Manufacturers and distributors are required to report to the commission any time they have a product they believe could present a substantial hazard. CPSC must rely on industry for a great deal of this information because there are hundreds of thousands of products on the market and the commission has only enough staff to look into a few high-priority items. Many companies are willing to come forward with information on hazardous products, but a large number are not reporting because they are unclear on what CPSC expects them to report.

Of much greater concern than the Consumer Product Safety Act to manufacturers are product liability laws. In 1978 alone, manufacturers and retailers paid an estimated $2.75 billion for product liability insurance, compared with an estimated $1.13 billion in 1975. Some experts speculate that the United States is becoming a "no-fault" economy—at least as far as the consumers are concerned—where producers and sellers will be held responsible for all product-related injuries no matter what the consumer does with products. State supreme courts are spearheading this legal revolution. The judges have tossed out the old rule that manufacturers and sellers are liable only when they are *negligent or unreasonably careless in what they made or how they made it.* In place of the old standard, they have adopted a much tougher one: strict liability. Now the product itself, rather than the way in which it is used, is put on trial; a time-honored legal concept—that a defendant is responsible for injuries only when his or her wrongful conduct has caused them—is vanishing.

By easing the plaintiff's burden in proving a case, the courts have allowed injured people to win, or settle on favorable terms, suits that might never even have been filed before. Consider, for example, cases like the following (adapted from *Business Week,* February 12, 1979).

- To scent a candle, a teenager poured perfume made by Fabergé, Inc., over a lit wick. The perfume ignited and burned a friend's neck. Claiming that Fabergé had failed to warn consumers of the perfume's flammability, the friend won a $27,000 judgment. Despite its argument that there was no way to foresee that someone would pour perfume onto an open flame, Fabergé lost its appeal.
- A construction worker was riding a forklift truck, which was not equipped with a roll bar, on steep terrain when the truck capsized and injured him. In a unanimous decision, the California Supreme Court in 1978 ruled that the burden was on the manufacturer to demonstrate that the forklift's benefits outweighed its risks. Otherwise, the court said, the operator's injuries showed that the forklift was defectively designed.
- In 1975 a paralyzed high school football player won a $5.3 million judgment against Riddell, Inc., a maker of football helmets. A Miami jury came in with the verdict, even though the helmet was never introduced at the trial. Today, 14 percent of a Riddell helmet's cost is due to insurance, litigation, and settlements; before the Florida case, these factors cost 1 percent.

Where will the preoccupation with consumer safety end? "It is possible to argue," says Richard A. Epstein, professor of law at the University of Chicago, "that any product which can be made safer, regardless of cost, is a product which the jury can find unsafe." In 1979 the Department of Commerce unveiled a "model uniform product liability law" that would, if adopted, change the ground rules for product litigation throughout the United States. Regardless of whether Congress enacts some version of it, the model is certain to influence state legislatures because it is comprehensive and evenly balanced between producers and consumers. Meanwhile, companies—especially those in "high-risk" industries (e.g., chemicals)—have been increasingly forming self-insurance trusts to protect themselves against the apparently arbitrary rate-setting procedures of insurance companies.

Product Reliability

Safety is not the only issue of product use that concerns the consumerists. As Willy Loman laments in Arthur Miller's *Death of a Salesman,* "Once in my life I would like to own something outright before it's broken! I'm always in a race with the junkyard! I just finish paying for the car and it's on its last legs. The refrigerator consumes belts like a goddamn maniac. They time those things.

They time them so when you've finally paid for them, they're used up." Loman's outburst captures a sense of the exasperation that we have all felt more than once. And if Miller ever chooses to write *Death of a Salesman, 1980,* he might wish to add to Loman's lament a few words about the connection between product obsolescence and natural resource depletion and waste pollution.

The issue of product obsolescence and what to do about it is, however, much more complex than many imagine. Playwrights aside, few people have bothered to look very deeply into it. For example, as Lund (1977:50) points out: "Appliance manufacturers have generally not conducted product-life studies. If they have, they have not published the results. They are concerned, and probably rightly so, that consumers would misconstrue life expectancy figures to mean that they are assured at least that many years of life from their appliances." In 1973, when the Center for Policy Alternatives at M.I.T. began studies of the life spans of appliances, the center found that only four studies had been done on the subject in the past twenty years. Reviews of these studies indicate that there was little change in service lives of new products over the twenty-five-year period bracketed by the four studies. In the time span between the two most nearly comparable studies—1967 and 1972 Department of Agriculture surveys—the trend seems to have been in the direction of shorter product life.

As Lund (1977) notes, there is no question that from a technical standpoint, longer-lasting appliances could be made. Longer product life could be achieved in either of two ways. First, each component of an appliance could be designed for maximum durability. Materials could be selected for wear and corrosion resistance; gear trains could replace rubber belts and pulleys; sensitive parts could be sealed from the atmosphere; circuits could be made more tolerant of ambient variations in humidity, altitude, line voltage, and human error. Second, appliances could be built in which everything could be easily and economically repaired.

But, according to Lund, even though appliances could be made more durable through improved product design, indications are that product durability does not govern the life of consumer durables (1977):

> In fact, there is evidence that today's appliances may be more durable than their predecessors, even though they are not longer-lived. The M.I.T. study showed that the reliability of both refrigerators and color television receivers had improved significantly in the recent past. First-year service incidence (frequency of need for repair service) for refrigerators declined 50 percent in the fourteen-year period from 1958 to 1972; the service incidence rate for television sets declined over 50 percent in the eight years between 1965 and 1972.

Despite these statistics, the fact that products that still function or that could be repaired are being discarded is a clear indication that factors other than durability are affecting consumer decisions to discard appliances. Lund suggests a number of factors: service costs relative to new appliance prices, the effects of consumer affluence, a weak used-appliance market (in contrast, say, to the used-car market), population mobility, appearance (a scratch or out-of-style exterior can be the cause of death), and unavailability of replacement parts. So we see that Willy Loman's lament was somewhat beside the point. The factors cited above are, in effect, the real obstacles that must be overcome if increased product life is to be possible.

COMMENTARY: On Product Durability

Any product could be made more durable, but only for a higher price. Because consumer tastes are incredibly diverse, there is no single level of product durability that is optimal for all consumers. One dimension of competition among business firms involves experimentation with various degrees of product durability. Consequently, consumers are offered a wide range of durability and prices for products. No one has ever documented a case in which firms refused to produce goods of greater durability when customers were willing to pay the costs of added durability. If an error is made, competition among firms forces the mistaken firm to correct its error or go out of business.

Source: Daniel K. Benjamin, "Is Planned Obsolescence a Serious Problem?" in M. Bruce Johnson, *The Attack on Corporate America* (New York: McGraw-Hill, 1978).

MANAGEMENT RESPONSES TO CONSUMERISM

Having examined the various consumer issues involved in product promotion and product use, we can now turn to the major objective of this chapter: how business can respond to the challenge of consumerism. Specifically, in this section we consider four strategies that can enhance marketing decisions.

Develop a Consumer-Oriented Program

A survey of top management by *Business Week* (September 12, 1977) bears this conclusion: By making a consumer orientation a basic part of the company's goals and managerial philosophy, the company can gain a competitive advantage for its product or service. As the survey found, top managers stressed the value of consumer programs not in terms of corporate virtue but in terms of profit. A comment by Joseph B. Danzansky, president of Giant Food, Inc., was not atypical: "A can of beans is a can of beans. But whether customers buy from us or from the competition can often depend on how they perceive our treating them." Big companies must take the initiative in dealing

EXHIBIT 11–4   Most Constructive Consumer Programs

Consumer program	All respondents	Respondents' industry Consumer durable products manufacturers	Consumer nondurable products manufacturers
Upgrading product quality and performance standards	51%	55%	54%
Establishing industry product standards	26	29	29
Increasing research commitments to better identify consumer wants and needs	24	13	30
Modifying products for greater safety, ease of use, and repair	23	36	21
Making postsale follow-up calls on consumers	22	13	10
Supporting industry self-regulation efforts (e.g., Better Business Bureau)	20	14	21
Making advertisements more informative	19	10	16
Developing owners' manuals on product use, care, and safety	16	27	8
Creating new organizational positions to deal with consumer affairs	15	12	16
Providing more informative product labeling	14	16	36

Note: These figures are derived from aggregate responses to the question: *Considering your own industry,* please check the three programs you consider most constructive in responding to consumerist pressures. Ratings are included for only the ten most frequently mentioned programs among the sixteen listed in the questionnaire.

with today's more vociferous customer or risk losing repeat sales. For that reason, Danzansky authorized Giant Food's consumer adviser to sponsor an ad campaign urging customers to stop buying meat because of skyrocketing prices in 1972.

In the last several years a wide variety of consumer-oriented programs have been undertaken by large companies in different industries. Some programs focus on improved service (e.g., Whirlpool's Cool-Line), some on increased communication between customers and executives (e.g., Stop and Shop's consumer boards), and some on better problem solving for consumers

Industrial products manufacturers	Advertising-media-publishing	Banking-investment-insurance	Government	Personal consumer services	Retail or wholesale trade
60%	32%	36%	45%	61%	42%
33	11	13	28	22	23
11	13	17	22	14	35
35	14	7	31	9	20
29	19	24	8	22	16
12	30	29	17	31	20
9	48	38	11	23	24
29	9	2	15	4	17
8	8	21	22	16	15
10	16	8	8	5	25

(e.g., the consumer affairs/action offices of several companies). Greyser and Diamond (1974) asked executives to review a list of sixteen consumer-oriented programs instituted in the wake of consumerism and to select the three they personally considered the most constructive. As shown in Exhibit 11–4, upgrading product quality and performance standards was by far the dominant choice.

Although managers have probably realized for a long time that their markets were somehow intertwined with society, only with the rise of the consumer movement has much hard thinking been devoted to social impact management through consumer-oriented programs. Reconciling marketing decisions with what happens to society is becoming an essential management task. This new outlook adds to the traditional marketing concern (customer satisfaction) a new goal—namely, *long-run consumer welfare.* In other words, a product should serve not only the consumer's desires but also the consumer's interests. When the consumer's immediate desires and long-run interests conflict, the successful company will resolve the dilemma in favor of the long-run interests. In practice, what this means is that the company can help insure its own long-run survival and profitability through the adoption of a company-wide consumer-oriented program designed to reduce all impacts that adversely affect the consumer.

Organize for Consumerism

As a result of the product use consumer issues and legislation outlined in this chapter, almost all manufacturing companies have added new responsibilities to their quality control departments and set up product safety review boards. These departments and boards monitor and correct, as necessary, all phases of product development. The review boards are composed of representatives of the quality control, engineering, manufacturing, marketing, and legal departments and may also include the company insurer.

Further, some companies are turning to outside experts to help them in making product safety audits. Later, if necessary, these auditors can act as expert witnesses before regulatory bodies or in court cases. The rise of consumerism has also prompted many companies to set up consumer affairs departments. Initially, consumer advocates tended to regard such departments as public relations ploys. By the late 1970s, however, the corporate consumer affairs professionals appeared to be developing some real muscle within their organizations. In a growing number of companies, they have exerted influence on functions ranging from product development to marketing campaigns.

For a consumer affairs department to be effective, it must, like any other unit, have a clearly defined set of responsibilities and corresponding authority. While the specific functions of consumer affairs departments will vary, Aaker and Day (1972) maintain that they should incorporate at least four related activities:

1. Consumer affairs departments should not only receive customer complaints and problems but have sufficient authority to resolve them—by overriding the desires of the operating departments, if necessary.
2. Consumer affairs departments should develop and operate an information system with the dual function of (a) monitoring the extent of consumer satisfaction and (b) detecting areas of basic consumer discontent that may have a negative impact on the company or to which the company may be uniquely qualified to respond.

3. Consumer affairs departments should participate in corporate planning and policy-making sessions in order to provide an appraisal of the company's products and marketing programs based on consumer interests as gained through the monitoring process.

4. Consumer affairs departments should contribute to the development of corporate social objectives, programs to implement those objectives, and operational measures by which the programs can be evaluated.

Monitor Promotional Techniques

In a dramatic reversal of its advertising, the ski industry recently began to say that gliding down the slopes can be hazardous to your health. The shift from heralding skiing as a glittering, romantic, and safe way to spend a day outdoors to stressing the inherent risks has appeared in almost everything from reports of ski conditions to signs on the slopes. What prompted this change was a Vermont Supreme Court decision that upheld a jury award of $1.5 million to a twenty-one-year-old man who had been paralyzed below the neck as the result of a skiing accident. The court's judgment, in effect, shifted the responsibility for injury from skier to ski area. As one official of Colorado's Aspen Ski Corporation explained, "We've got no choice but to try it. There are ambulance chasers all over the place, and if by taking the fluff out of our ads we can protect ourselves from phony suits, then it's worth the effort." Sign-covered slopes can now be found in ski areas all over the country. "We've got more signs than people," explained the manager of Maine's Pleasant Mountain ski area. "We warn them about the potential dangers of everything but breathing." The suit-motivated changes also extend to the way ski conditions are reported. The days of describing conditions as "good" or "excellent" are gone; ski areas have killed all the adjectives and now are just reporting the facts. Another change can be seen in promotional literature. Brochures no longer say, "Our ski school can teach you how to ski quickly and safely." Now they just say you can learn quickly (example based on an Associated Press story, *Houston Post,* December 3, 1978).

Obviously, no industry today can take a freewheeling approach to advertising. Management must monitor its advertising, look for deception, and make necessary changes—preferably before million-dollar lawsuits are filed. These are the crucial questions management must ask: Does the advertising inform the customer? Does the product perform as advertised? Is the sales force engaged in hard sell to the extent of misrepresentation? Do the sales people promise too much for the product or service? Is the company promoting the product to a market segment that can neither afford the product nor benefit from it?

Increasingly, companies are able to turn to outside groups for guidance in developing policies and procedures in the areas of advertising, selling, and packaging. Indicative of the help available is the National Advertising Review

Board, an industry self-regulatory organization. The board has developed the following checklist for reviewing company advertising to minimize the likelihood of a company's violating federal product-safety requirements (1974:5):

—Is anything shown, described, or claimed in the advertisement that raises questions of consumer safety?

—Is everything known that should be known about the product's performance under both normal and misuse circumstances?

—Is there anything in the advertisement that might prove harmful to children who cannot comprehend the most familiar hazards in consumer products and tend to imitate what they see?

—Is allowance made in advertising situations for the susceptibility to suggestions of the elderly or the consumer predisposed toward risk taking?

Prepare a Product Recall Strategy

As noted earlier, when Congress passed the Consumer Product Safety Act of 1972, it gave the CPSC power to prescribe mandatory safety standards for products for which specific safety legislation did not already exist. Still, hazardous products do reach consumers. Hence, hazardous products have to be recalled from the marketplace in the shortest possible time. Section 15 of the Consumer Product Safety Act requires manufacturers to notify the CPSC within twenty-four hours of discovering that a product they have produced and sold is defective and possibly dangerous. The commission can order a manufacturer, wholesaler, distributor, or retailer to notify the public and recall for repair, replacement, refund, or destruction any product it deems hazardous. Failure to comply with such an order can lead to civil penalties; willful violation can lead to further fines and, possibly, imprisonment. Clearly, companies must develop effective product recall strategies, not only to comply with CPSC requirements, but also to avoid costly legal battles and to keep the product line viable. Product recall might even be viewed as an opportunity, for reasons cited by Fisk and Chandran (1975:91):

> First, the ability to show that a product safety problem is being handled professionally can be proof that quality control systems work to protect the customer even after the product is sold. Service after sale offers many unexploited opportunities for extending customer loyalty. An excellent example is American Motors "Buyer Protection Plan": the company recalls and repairs manufacturing defects at company expense—even providing the customer, in some cases, with a replacement car and lodging expenses for the duration of the repairs. These services, highlighted in creative advertisement, have not only helped AMC's image but have enlarged its market share as well.
>
> Second, a product traceability and recall system, along with good quality-control procedures, can provide a good-faith legal defense in many product liability cases. . . .
>
> [Third] . . . a system can enable the manufacturer to keep in touch with the consumer. Companies expend great effort and skill to determine what customers

will buy, but they rarely find out whether customers are harmed by the product after purchase.

Despite these benefits, product recall can be very expensive for a company. While the cost varies from product to product, it can in fact far exceed the price of the product itself. Jacob and Mundel (1975:16–17) report that one company estimated that it cost on the average five dollars to recall each defective nineteen-cent item. The costs included notifying each user by return receipt letter or personal telephone call; locating, inventorying, removing, and disposing of suspect items; redesigning the item; overtime manufacturing of new items; printing labels and instructions; packing, shipping, installing, and testing new items; recording and reporting the actions taken; and possibly paying medical and legal fees in connection with consumer complaints—all in addition to lost sales.

Thus, companies need to plan carefully for product recalls. The Grocery Manufacturers of America (1974:57–58) suggest that a coded identification number for each product or batch of products can expedite product recalls. Computers keep track of the numbers throughout the distribution chain. The minimum identification should include the labeling of each shipping package and container with a code indicating item, batch or period (day, month, year), and plant. In most companies, the normal distribution system can be reversed for return and pickup of the recalled products. Of course, inventory and accounting systems must also make adjustments for product recalls, and wholesalers must be reimbursed. Postage-paid, detailed warranty cards are a good method of providing the manufacturer with the names and addresses of purchasers of certain types of products. Some companies have even conducted "dry runs" of recall procedures. Often, a single executive is assigned recall responsibilities and given the authority to halt production and to begin notification of dealers and customers. An example of an action plan for a situation that may require a product recall is shown in Exhibit 11–5.

In sum, we have in this section considered a number of strategies that can help business respond to a variety of issues involved in the consumer movement. As with any approach to social impact management, successful implementation of these strategies is predicated on an understanding not only of specific problems but of larger issues. Thus, before we conclude this chapter, let us return to the topic of consumerism and focus for a moment on two areas of business: advertising and product safety. Because these two areas have a significant impact on society, they have become the consumer concerns that have, and will continue to have, a significant impact on business.

REFLECTIONS ON CONSUMERISM

The Pros and Cons of Advertising

Would the elimination or restriction of advertising lower the costs consumers must pay for a product? One of the chief consumer complaints about advertis-

EXHIBIT 11–5   A Product Recall Plan

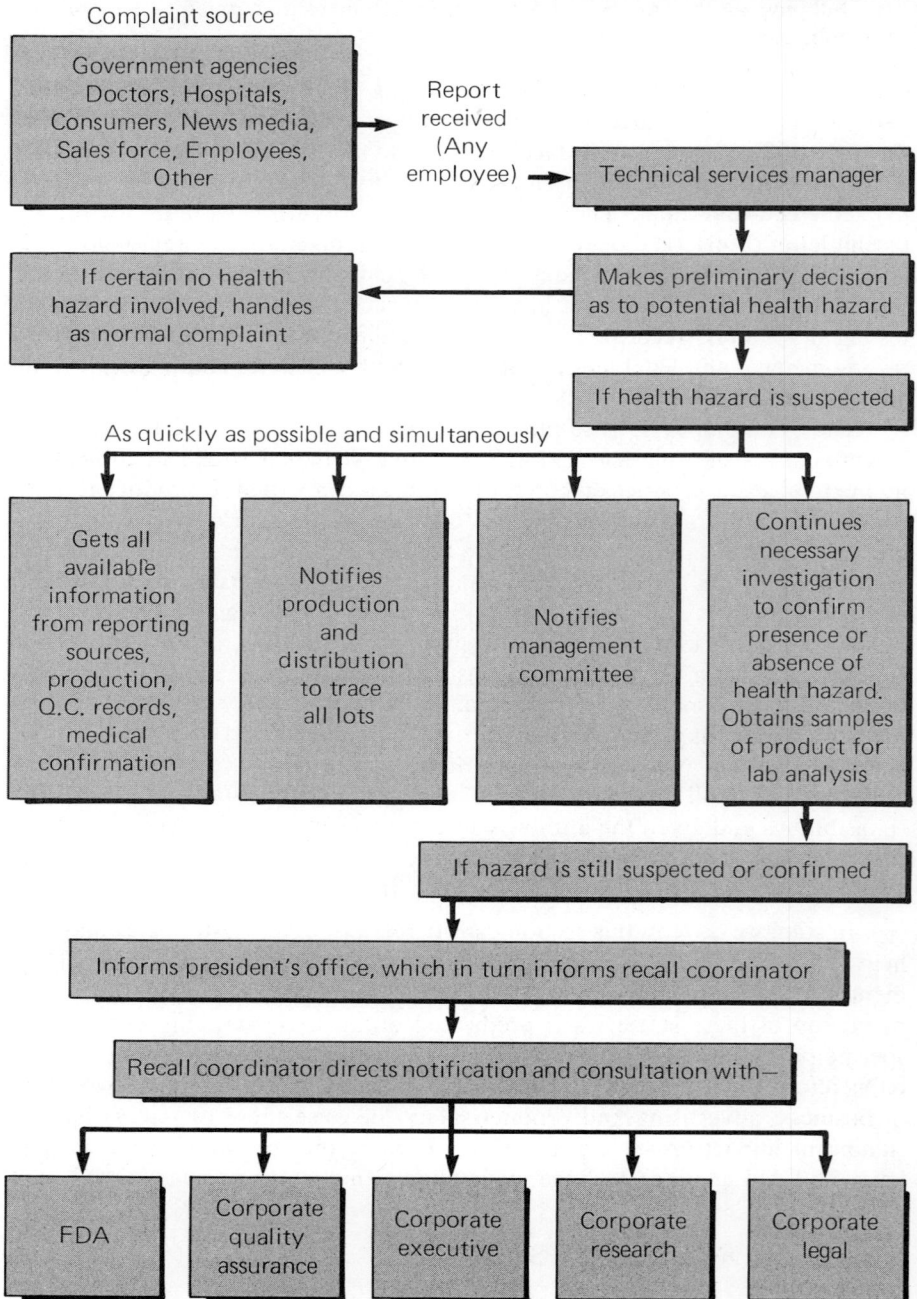

Complaint source

Government agencies Doctors, Hospitals, Consumers, News media, Sales force, Employees, Other

Report received (Any employee) →

Technical services manager

↓

Makes preliminary decision as to potential health hazard

←

If certain no health hazard involved, handles as normal complaint

↓

If health hazard is suspected

As quickly as possible and simultaneously

Gets all available information from reporting sources, production, Q.C. records, medical confirmation	Notifies production and distribution to trace all lots	Notifies management committee	Continues necessary investigation to confirm presence or absence of health hazard. Obtains samples of product for lab analysis

↓

If hazard is still suspected or confirmed

↓

Informs president's office, which in turn informs recall coordinator

↓

Recall coordinator directs notification and consultation with—

FDA	Corporate quality assurance	Corporate executive	Corporate research	Corporate legal

Source: *Guidelines for Product Recall* (Washington, D.C.: Grocery Manufacturers of America, Inc., 1974), pp. 28–29. Reprinted by permission.

ing is that it adds to the cost of the products and services. On the average, about three cents of every dollar that business collects from consumers goes to advertising, but this cut varies from product to product. For hair-care products, advertising might cost as much as thirty-four cents on the dollar; for some drugs and soft drinks, almost twenty cents.

Consumer advocates suggest that, if advertising expenditures were reduced, companies could afford to sell at lower prices. They also contend that expensive, nationwide advertising campaigns, when successful, can develop such brand loyalty for a few brands that it becomes impossible for newcomers—especially smaller companies—to enter the field. As a result, a few large companies can continue to dominate the market and charge higher prices than they could in a more competitive situation. Critics further contend that a good bit of advertising confuses and misleads the public more than it gives solid information about products.

In 1972 the FTC used these arguments against advertising when it told Congress that the price of cereal could be cut by 25 percent. The cereal industry, however, maintained that advertising allowed retailers to sell cereals at lower prices than would otherwise be possible. For example, cornflakes used to have marked seasonal swings in consumption; sales increased during the summer months by as much as 100 percent over winter sales. After the cereal manufacturers started advertising on television in the early 1950s, winter sales picked up relative to summer sales. Manufacturers asserted that the smoothing of the consumption pattern, brought about by increased advertising, lowered costs to consumers.

Further, manufacturers claimed that prices would be even higher if they were not allowed to advertise. The increased consumer demand generated by advertising motivated retailers to carry more complete lines of cereals and to make sure the shelves were always stocked. Thus, the manufacturer did not have to provide personnel or equipment for servicing stores. The data furnished by cereal companies seemed to support their contention: Prior to 1940, distribution and selling costs accounted for 35 percent of sales revenues; in the 1960s, for only 25 percent.

The more conventional argument for how advertising reduces costs is based on reduction in unit costs. In other words, advertising stimulates demand so that higher levels of production are possible. Consider, for example, pocket calculators. Without advertisements informing potential customers of the availability and advantages of pocket calculators, demand would have remained very limited. Manufacturers would have been unable to set up the large-scale, efficient production methods that have allowed them to cut the original cost of the calculators in half.

In sum, the pro-advertising argument holds that even though spending for advertising may increase the prices in the short run, it has the opposite effect in the long run because of its impact on production costs. Further, the economy would grow more slowly as sales fell and new products went unnoticed. There would be fewer jobs, and living standards would rise much less rapidly. Access to entertainment and information would be much more re-stricted, since industry's multibillion-dollar-a-year advertising budget pays for most television programs and covers a major part of the cost of publishing newspapers and magazines.

The Price of Safety

Clearly, a major thrust of the consumer movement is, as we have seen in this chapter, toward the reduction of injury and illness associated with product use. Similarly, unions, the Occupational Safety and Health Administration (OSHA), and other groups have been equally concerned with reducing injury and illness associated with product manufacturing. Although we shall have more to say in the next chapter about safety in the workplace (where the product is actually made), let us consider here for a moment the costs of both kinds of safety concerns to the consumers and manufacturers of risk-associated products.

   The consumer movement has not been able to repeal that hoary law of economics: There is no free lunch. For example, if a soft-drink company spends X number of dollars to reduce the chance of a fly's being found in one of its bottles to one in five million, can it afford to double its investment to increase the odds to one in ten million? At what point will the consumer, the public, and the government be unwilling to pay the extra price for the reduction of risks involved? In the workplace, the cost of removing hazards can be extremely high. For example, clearing the air of dangerous emissions in coke plants would cost $250 million or more a year. Thus, we need only to remember the simple law of economics—there is no free lunch—to see that business must respond to consumer pressures and adjust to government controls by passing on the extra costs to consumers.

   In any event, the basic question we might ask is how much are American consumers willing to pay to save lives. How many millions or billions of dollars would we pay in higher prices to keep disease-carrying insects out of our soft drinks or to keep a dozen coke-oven workers alive? Victor Fuch, an economist at Stanford University, attempts to put this emotion-charged issue in perspective (1974:19):

> But surely health is more important than anything else! Is it? Those who take this position are fond of contrasting our unmet health needs with the money that is "wasted" on cosmetics, cigarettes, pet foods, and the like. "Surely," it is argued, "we can afford better health if we can afford colored telephones." But putting the question in this form is misleading. For one thing, there are other goals, such as justice, beauty, and knowledge, which also clearly remain unfulfilled because of resource limitations. In theory, our society is committed to providing a speedy and fair trial to all persons accused of crimes. "Justice delayed is justice denied." In practice, we know that our judicial system is rife with delays and with pretrial settlements that produce convictions of innocent people and let guilty ones escape with minor punishment. We also know that part of the answer

to getting a fairer and more effective judicial system is to devote more resources to it.

What about beauty, natural or manmade? How often do we read that a beautiful stand of trees could be saved if a proposed road were rerouted or some other (expensive) change made? How frequently do we learn that a beautiful new building design has been rejected in favor of a conventional one because of the cost factor? Knowledge also suffers. Anyone who has ever had to meet a budget for an educational or research enterprise knows how resource limitations constrain the pursuit of knowledge.

What about more mundane creature comforts? We may give lip service to the idea that health comes first, but a casual inspection of our everyday behavior with respect to diet, drink, and exercise belies this claim. Most of us could be healthier than we are, but at some cost, either psychic or monetary. Not only is there competition for resources as conventionally measured (i.e., in terms of money), but we are also constantly confronted with choices involving the allocation of our time, energy, and attention. If we are honest with ourselves, there can be little doubt that other goals often take precedence over health. If better health is our goal, we can achieve it, but only at some cost.

The message that Fuchs is conveying is simple: Within limits set by genetic factors, climate, and other natural forces, every nation *chooses* its own death rate by the value it places on health in comparison to other goals. For example, meeting U.S. energy needs in the year 2000 will entail producing enough radioactive emissions from proposed nuclear power plants to increase cancer deaths by nine per year in the United States. According to some estimates, the risk for the average citizen is comparable to being a fraction of an ounce overweight, smoking 0.03 cigarettes a year, or driving one mile in a car. On the other hand, members of the Union of Concerned Scientists could command headlines by proclaiming that these estimates are too low and the real risks of producing the needed nuclear energy are comparable to the risk of smoking 3 cigarettes a year or driving one hundred miles in a car.

Obviously, some risk is a part of living. If public policymakers who set speed limits and license nuclear power plants have to make decisions that statistically affect how many people will live, so must the individual make decisions about personal levels of risk. "One will be safer in a one-story house where there are no stairs, safer having someone else shovel your snow, and safer riding trains and buses than driving. By a suitable choice of activities and goods, a person can achieve any level of risk that he desires" (Oi, 1977:17).

It is not difficult to explain why individuals engage in risky activities: to achieve the benefits associated with the activities. In economic terms, individuals will pursue risky activities to the point where the benefit of the activity is just about equal to the expected accident cost generated by the activity. Expected accident costs depend on the chances of being injured in pursuing the activity as well as the actual costs of the injury, such as medical bills and losses in wages or salary, and the anticipated costs of pain, suffering, or possible impairment.

Accordingly, a society should view as unacceptable any risk-associated products and activities wherein the costs of avoidable accidents and the costs of accident prevention exceed the benefits. The consumer movement, so it would seem, seldom follows this rule in determining whether a given situation calls for government regulation. Reliance on mandatory safety standards in the workplace and in consumer products would hardly seem in the public interest—at least, if the public interest rests on minimizing the sum of accident costs and accident prevention costs. As Walter Oi writes (1977:32): "Do we want safety at any price? No—but when the price is less than the benefits we derive from more safety, we will pay that price."

CHAPTER TWELVE

Human Resources

Decisions

Freud was once asked by someone attending one of his lectures what the normal person should do. Freud gave a wonderful reply: *Lieben und arbeiten* (love and work). This chapter is about *arbeiten*.

A major function for any company is the management of its work force. In the past, the general practice was to refer to this function simply as personnel management. But today, for reasons that will soon be clear enough, the preferred term is rapidly becoming *human resources management*. We need to recognize how certain changes in the macroenvironment are creating new challenges and raising new issues in the area of work-force management. For example, consider these impacts:

—New technology (such as voice analyzers, computer data banks, and television surveillance) has infringed on employee privacy in some companies.

—Post–World War II economic trends have drastically reduced the percentage of the work force that labor unions have traditionally looked to for membership.

—New economic trends, by increasing the number of technical people in the work force, have necessitated certain changes in the leadership style of managers.

—New values and attitudes (such as suspicion of authority and desire for rewarding work) have placed new pressures on managers in general and human resources directors in particular.

—New laws (such as the Civil Rights Act of 1964 and the Occupational Safety and Health Act of 1970) have established new regulators to look over the manager's shoulder.

—Stiffer competition from overseas has, in several industries, resulted in the formation of new management-labor alliances in the United States.

—Demographic change and federal legislation have forced employers to reconsider retirement policies.

—Because so many married women are now working, both they and their husbands often find themselves with more money and less time to spend it than ever before. As a result, many two-income couples have begun to pressure employers for new benefits (such as more flexible working hours or less work time).

—During the 1980s, with the ranks of new entrants into the labor market ket severely thinned by the passing of the "baby-boom years," employers will have to adjust to a relative shortage of labor for the entry positions in business.

While this list of particulars could be expanded, a more useful exercise would be to distill from this welter of impacts a few broad themes. External change has affected (and will probably continue to affect) decision making in the area of human resources in at least three ways. First, external changes have reshaped society's concept of work. Second, they have profoundly influenced employment practices. And third, they have made managers more accountable for the health and safety of the workers. In this chapter we shall build around these three themes.

In the first section, we shall try to make a balanced assessment of how extensive work dissatisfaction is. This assessment is followed in the second section by a discussion of possible management responses to some of the troubles in the workplace. Specifically, we shall see why companies need to look upon human resources as an investment decision; to organize responsibility for jobs (i.e., to exercise less control over the details of a worker's job); to plan for human resources; and to protect the privacy of employees. In the third section on this topic, we pause to reflect on the conflict between the individual and the organization.

The fourth section of this chapter deals with the often confusing issue of equal employment opportunity. After a quick review of existing laws and their current interpretation, we consider how to implement an affirmative action program. We also take a look at the thorny issue of reverse discrimination.

The fifth section of this chapter traces the development of the industrial safety movement up to and including the Occupational Safety and Health Act. In this section we shall note some of the steps a company can take to insure the health and safety of its employees.

In the final section we take a look at labor unions in the United States today. Despite the sluggish growth of unions in recent years, it would be a serious mistake to write them off. Declines in membership have occurred in the past, and each time the unions have staged strong comebacks. Thus, there is no good reason to assume unions will not find a way to prosper in a future economy based on services and information. In this section we also consider the outlook for labor-management relations in the future as well as the role that negotiated employee benefits have played in the workplace. We conclude the chapter with a review of the ways human resources management—with or without unions—can maximize the attractiveness of their employee benefits. ☐

TROUBLES IN THE WORKPLACE:
THE ISSUE OF WORKER SATISFACTION

Changing Conceptions of Work

"In the sweat of thy face shall thou eat bread, till thou return unto the ground." Beginning with that famous passage in Genesis, in which Adam was expelled from Eden, attitudes toward labor have undergone almost constant change. While the Greek and Roman cultures did not view work as a punishment for sin, they did associate it with degradation and slavery. During the Middle Ages, and certainly through the early stages of capitalism (see Chapter 1), a great deal of religious significance was attached to work. But by the mid-1800s contradictory views began to appear. On the one hand was the gospel of Horatio Alger: Know thy work and do it. A latter-day prophet of the American work ethic was Elbert Hubbard, whose essay "A Message to Garcia" (1899), sold over 40 million copies—mostly to industrial firms for circulation to their employees (see Commentary section, "A Message to Garcia"). This parable of perseverance in the job, no matter how difficult, was based on an actual incident in the Spanish-American War, when President McKinley sent Lieutenant Andrew Rowan to meet General Calixto Garcia Iñiguez, leader of the Cuban forces fighting against Spain.

In opposition to the traditional American work ethic was the view that something was fundamentally wrong with the mindless pursuit of work. For example, Alexis de Tocqueville wrote in 1835 (Tocqueville, 1956:217):

> When a workman is unceasingly and exclusively engaged in the fabrication of one thing, he ultimately does his work with singular dexterity; but at the same time he loses the general faculty of applying his mind to the direction of the work. He every day becomes more adroit and less industrious; so that it may be said of him that in proportion as the workman improves, the man is degraded. What can be expected of a man who has spent twenty years of his life in making heads for pins?

COMMENTARY: A Message to Garcia

When war broke out between Spain and the United States, it was very necessary to communicate quickly with the leader of the insurgents. Garcia was somewhere in the mountain fastnesses of Cuba—no one knew where. No mail nor telegraph message could reach him. The President must secure his cooperation, and quickly.

What to do!

Someone said to the President, "There's a fellow by the name of Rowan who will find Garcia for you, if anybody can."

Rowan was sent for and given a letter to be delivered to Garcia. How "the fellow by the name of Rowan" took the letter, sealed it up in an oilskin pouch, strapped it over his heart, in four days landed by night off the coast of Cuba from an open boat, disappeared into the jungle, and in three weeks came out on the other side of the island, having traversed a hostile country on foot and delivered his letter to Garcia, are things I have no special desire now to tell in detail.

The point I wish to make is this: McKinley gave Rowan a letter to be delivered to Garcia. Rowan took the letter and did not ask, "Where is he at?" By the Eternal! there is a man whose form should be cast in deathless bronze and the statue placed in every college of the land. It is not book learning young men need, nor instruction about this and that, but a stiffening of the vertebrae which will cause them to be loyal to a trust, to act promptly, concentrate their energies, do the thing—"Carry a message to Garcia!"

General Garcia is dead now, but there are other Garcias. . . .

You, reader, put this matter to a test: You are sitting now in your office—six clerks are within call. Summon any one and make this request: "Please look in the encyclopedia and make a brief memorandum for me concerning the life of Correggio."

Will the clerk quietly say, "Yes, sir," and go do the task?

On your life, he will not. He will look at you out of a fishy eye and ask one or more of the following questions:

Who was he?

Which encyclopedia?

Where is the encyclopedia?
Was I hired for that?
Don't you mean Bismarck?
What's the matter with Charlie doing it?
Is he dead?
Is there any hurry?
Shan't I bring you the book and let you look it up yourself?
What do you want to know for?
And I will lay you ten to one that after you have answered the questions, and explained how to find the information, and why you want it, the clerk will go off and get one of the other clerks to help him try to find Garcia—and then come back and tell you there is no such man. Of course I may lose my bet, but according to the law of average, I will not.

Source: Excerpted from Elbert Hubbard's unpublished essay, "A Message to Garcia" (1899).

Tocqueville was not the only writer to develop this view of the dehumanized worker, nor was he the most famous. Marx, especially in his earlier writing, drove home a similar point, which we shall consider more closely in Chapter 14. (For an incisive treatment of what work has meant through history, see Hannah Arendt's *The Human Condition,* Chapter 4.)

Work in America

Today, when we want to understand the nature of work, we no longer turn to pseudo-bohemians like Hubbard or brilliant philosophers like Tocqueville; we appoint a task force. Thus, in late 1971 an official task force was appointed by the secretary of Health, Education and Welfare to study the issue of work in America. The final report, released one year later, was entitled *Work in America.* Its major conclusions serve as a good summary of the prevailing wisdom about work:

—American workers at all levels are becoming more and more dissatisfied with the quality of their working lives. This dissatisfaction saps the economic and social strength of the nation.

—In addition to such widely acknowledged problems as boredom and absenteeism, other work-related problems are a decline in physical and mental health, decreased family and community stability, increased drug and alcohol abuse, less "balanced" political ideas, and certain forms of adult delinquency.

—The two main causes of work-related problems are (1) the diminishing opportunity to become one's own boss (as more and more corporations organize work to minimize the independence of individuals) and (2) outmoded faith in the application of scientific management.

This landmark study, whose recommendations are often referred to as the "humanization of work," quickly became a hot item—"must reading" for employers, congressional representatives, and labor leaders. It prompted continuing, and mostly favorable, press and scholarly comment and became an official handbook on work. The report offered the following possible remedies for the problems it diagnosed:

—*Job enlargement:* Increase the number of tasks and responsibilities a worker is given, so that jobs can "grow" and thus become more satisfying.

—*Job enrichment:* Redesign jobs and tasks for the purpose of adding greater challenge, responsibility, variety, or independence.

—*Job rotation:* Training all members of a work group to be capable of freely replacing each other or doing each others' work.

—*Participative management:* Make a systematic effort to get more people, particularly lower-level people, involved in planning and decision-making activities that concern them and their work. (According to a 1977 poll by Daniel Yankelovich, 54 percent of Americans believe they have a "right" to share in decisions that affect their jobs.)

The report was ammunition in the hands of the reform-minded, a persuasive influence for those on the fence, and a challenge to the established order that it criticized. Its message to management was direct: Unless work is "humanized" quickly, something "increasingly intolerable" may happen to our society (Dickson, 1975:23–24).

Other Views of the World of Work

Surprisingly little statistical evidence supports *Work in America*'s findings of boredom, tedium, and impersonalized and dehumanized work. One of the most eminent scholars in the field has noted that the report's conclusions "are in the eye of the beholder and in phrasemakers of 'blue-collar blues' and 'lunch-pail lassitude' rather than in the workplace or work force" (Dunlop, 1978:86). Evidence from a study by Flanagan, Strauss, and Ulman (1974), indicates that changes in behavioral measures such as workers' productivity, quit rates, absenteeism, accidents and strikes are explained by conventional economic determinants and that there is no basis for ascribing any role to changes in worker attitudes and motivation.

Indeed, the results of survey after survey seem to contradict the plethora of think pieces coming out of universities on the worker dissatisfaction. As Exhibit 12–1 shows, worker satisfaction is at a high level and is on the increase. The largest blemish in this generally rosy picture appears among the youngest workers; in 1976, only 51 percent of those under twenty-one years of age ex-

EXHIBIT 12–1   Satisfied Workers as a Percentage of Total Workers, 1958–1976

Worker characteristics	Survey research center surveys			National opinion research center surveys				
	1958	1969	1973	1962	1964	1972	1975	1978
Male	81	88	91	84	92	85	90	87
Female	—	81	89	81	—	86	87	90
White	—	86	90	84	92	87	89	88
Black and other	—	77	85	76	88	78	85	85
Under 21 years	—	75	77	59	88	55	85	83
21–29 years	74	76	84	74	87	76	82	88
30–39 years	79	88	92	82	93	88	88	86
40–49 years	85	87	94	84	92	89	92	95
50 years and over	90	91	96	88	94	92	93	88
Education								
Grade school	88	88	93	83	94	86	88	88
High school	77	86	89	81	90	85	90	88
Some college		81	88	86	89	83	90	86
College degree	81	85	91	90	94	88	85	88
Graduate work		91	96	84	93	87	84	92

Note: Survey questions asked were variants of "How satisfied are you with your job (or your work)?" Figures for "satisfied" combined responses such as "very satisfied," "somewhat satisfied," and "fairly satisfied."

Source: Data from the *Statistical Abstract of the United States,* various years (Washington, D.C.: U.S. Government Printing Office).

pressed satisfaction with their work. Still, the finding is not altogether surprising. Relative dissatisfaction among these younger groups has appeared in every survey since 1958. The evidence also indicates that women are less satisfied than men with the financial rewards and challenges of their jobs, but their overall satisfaction scores do not differ significantly from those of men. Racial differences in worker satisfaction appear greater than male-female differences but less than differences found across age levels.

Dunlop (1978) has concluded that changes in the workplace over time generally seem to have been favorable. Unskilled work has undergone a relative decline, and professional, technical, and clerical positions have increased substantially. Higher wages, fringe benefits, and legislation provide increased protection against risks, not only of the workplace, but of modern life in general. An emphasis on education and retirement, changes in schedules of working hours, and increased opportunity for part-time work have tended to mitigate job dissatisfaction. Company policies in large enterprises have generally focused concern on people in the workplace, partially as a consequence of professional personnel functions and partially as a result of the effects of labor organizations on management. Moreover, these changes are not frozen; they continue to be made in response to the aspirations, pressures, and opportunities of economic growth. Indeed, the problem the modern workplace presents to management is perhaps best stated as a question of how to keep adapting company policies to changing conditions.

Robert Schrank (1978a), who holds a doctor's degree in the sociology of work, faults the prevailing wisdom about work, not because it seems so blind to statistical evidence, but because it lacks a sense of "the humanity, the poetry, and the community of people that is created by workers at their work places." His book, *Ten Thousand Working Days*, is quite different from *Work in America;* it is written from experience. Schrank, unlike many recent writers on the "quality of work," acquired his academic title forty years after he first went to work in a furniture factory in New York City. He also worked as a plumber's helper, a farm laborer, an auto mechanic, a machinist, and a union organizer. In writing about these jobs, Schrank contributes some major insights about the real nature of work and workers. For example, he believes that even unpleasant jobs can give satisfaction to workers if the "schmooze" factor is present. *Schmooze* is a Yiddish term meaning "to gab" or "chew the rag." According to Schrank, it is a form of socializing "that probably keeps many people interested in crummy jobs." Although many behavioral scientists ignore the value of "schmoozing" in their theoretical models for motivating workers, the theoretical basis of Schrank's book makes good common sense. As he says: "I dwell on the amenities of the job—the freedom to work at one's own pace, to break when you wish, to come in late, to go home early or late, shop in the middle of the day, take a long lunch hour, get paid by the week or month—because I believe this may be the stuff of which high levels of job satisfaction are made." The desire of blue-collar workers to control their own work pace is very human and not really much different from the desire of managers to gain freedom and autonomy in their jobs. But Schrank thinks the comparison of blue-collar workers to managers is often pushed too far. Unlike the men and women in corporate management and the professional world, many workers do not want more power, responsibility, or challenge in their jobs. As Schrank observes, "Blue-collar workers prefer to make bowling the center of their lives." And that, he adds, "may be a greater demonstration of autonomy and creativity than building a better high-speed gear box." While Schrank is very much in favor of increasing job satisfaction—particularly by giving workers more say in decisions that affect their working lives—he is not optimistic about making the radical changes in the organization that would be necessary to achieve real worker participation (see Commentary section, "How to Relieve Worker Boredom").

COMMENTARY: How to Relieve Worker Boredom

Forty years of work in factories and offices have convinced me that many of the problems that industrial psychologists are now trying to alleviate are simply inherent in mass production. I am skeptical of people who tell factory workers their jobs can become creative, autonomous, challenging, and self-actualizing. . . .

The schemes proposed by management psychologists usually tend to diversify or rearrange the tasks carried out by each worker. But the tasks themselves remain basically just as dull and repetitive as before. Clearly, if workers prefer multiple tasks, and find the new arrangement better than the old ones, they should be given such options. But rearrangement should not be sold as autonomy, creativity, and self-actualization, because that creates new expectations that cannot be fulfilled, and results in just another feeling of letdown, leading to more frustration and discouragement. For the same reason psychologists should not claim that the worker will necessarily be happier, healthier, or better adjusted as a result. I know of one instance in which women assembling steam irons in a General Electric plant, each putting on a small part, had their jobs "enriched." As a result, each had to assemble the whole iron, to test it, and so forth. The result—they could no longer talk about TV, movies, sports, lovers, gossip; in a word, "schmooze." They were so unhappy they filed a grievance complaint asking the company if they could go back to the old assembly line.

Industrial psychologists use terms like "autonomy," "satisfaction," "creativity," and "quality-of-work-life" so commonly these days that I'm not sure the words have a distinct meaning anymore. One must always ask, "Compared with what?"

Most factory work—and much office work as well—is repetitious and dull. As long as it is, job satisfaction for workers will depend to a great extent on the freedom they have on the job to do things unrelated to their assigned work. I think such freedom offers far more potential for increased autonomy than any rearrangement of the work itself.

Source: Excerpted from Robert Schrank, "How to Relieve Worker Boredom." Reprinted from *Psychology Today* (July 1978), pp. 79–80. Copyright © 1978 Ziff-Davis Publishing Company.

MANAGEMENT RESPONSES TO TROUBLES IN THE WORKPLACE

In the preceding discussion, our purpose was not to discount problems in the workplace brought to light in *Work in America,* but to try to bring them into sharper focus. Indeed, making work, especially hard work, more rewarding becomes a greater management challenge every year. In this section we consider four human resources management strategies that can be applied to a number of problems associated with worker satisfaction and motivation.

Invest in Human Resources

The authors of *Work in America* maintain that human resources demand attention because worker dissatisfaction, unabated, can lead to catastrophe. An important factor to be considered within this framework is that the development of human resources by management provides a high potential rate of return on a relatively low-cost, low-risk investment. Ted Mills (1975) refers to the advocates of this view as the "ROI" (return on investment) school of human resources. According to Mills, top management in the United States is increasingly turning to human resources development (HRD) as a means for better management of a conspicuously underdeveloped business resource: its people. American managers have begun to perceive important results from HRD activities—for example, significantly diminished accident, absenteeism, and error rates and significantly increased morale, quality of product or service, and productivity. Another reason for management's growing interest in HRD is the rising cost of labor. Developing ways to cut labor costs by fuller development of the work force already employed is sound management.

To illustrate the potential returns involved in HRD, Mills cites the case of one large service company, with hundreds of thousands of employees, that had never gotten around to accurate measurement of the cost of turnover—a major symptom of motivational problems. Upon the formation of its new HRD department in 1972, the company decided to measure turnover costs by analyzing a group of forty-five thousand skilled operatives with an abnormally high (but, it was believed, inevitable) turnover rate. The company had assumed that turnover costs were "around $1,550 per new employee." The analysis, which carefully computed recruiting, training, breakin, and other noncharged costs, found the true cost for each new employee was $12,865— that is, a multimillion-dollar annual operating cost not represented in any existing divisional or corporate accounting.

Not surprisingly, the reassessment of the importance of human resources has led to an increase in the importance of company personnel directors. Not long ago, the personnel department was represented on many corporate organization charts as an orphaned box that did not seem to fit anywhere. To many executives, the mission of the people who worked in "personnel" appeared to be recruiting secretaries who could not type and planning company picnics. Today, as Meyer (1976:85) finds, many personnel directors are doing much more than picnic planning.

● Companies eager to increase their workers' productivity have discovered that an alert personnel director is in a unique position to contribute to the company's return on investment (ROI). One vice president of industrial relations wondered why productivity rates in Japanese factories were so high. He flew to Japan, visited some factories, and concluded that part of the answer lay in the use of committees, made up of both workers and supervisors, that met regularly to hear suggestions for meeting production goals. On his return to the United States, he got clearance to form Japanese-style committees of workers and supervisors at the company's plant. One modification of the Japanese plan involved the offer of a cash bonus to both workers and managers if productivity really did increase beyond the goal set by the company. What the vice president did, essentially, was to install the Scanlon Plan. (Originally conceived by the late industrial-relations specialist Joseph Scanlon, the incentive plan invites both workers and management to come up with labor-saving ideas and then calls for paying everyone in the plant a bonus if the ideas submitted increase production while keeping payroll costs below a certain base.) One year and 400 suggestions later, productivity at the plant was up 15 percent. The company was able to cancel plans to invest $250,000 in added manufacturing capacity, because output increased without it.

• An idea developed by IBM's vice president for personnel illustrates how a personnel executive can help both a company and its employees through a difficult economic period. He developed a policy allowing IBM's employees to defer vacation time for as long as they wanted. Postponement of vacations was actively urged during years of booming business activity, which thus helped keep the lid on the number of employees at work during peak periods. The payoff for both IBM and its employees came when recession took a bite out of IBM's production. Rather than being dropped from the payroll, employees were urged to take their saved up weeks or even months of vacation time.

Organize Responsibility for the Job

One source of trouble in the workplace stems from the fact that management generally exercises too much control over how employees perform their jobs. Prescribing procedures for every aspect of workers' jobs is not unlike degrading the natural environment by evading pollution control standards. In both instances, management is affecting the fabric of a society in ways that are neither justifiable nor profitable. In the long run, a strong management hand in the workplace is ineffective because (a) it requires too much of the manager's time (which could be better used in setting goals, raising funds, entering new markets, and the like) and (b) it leads to reduced worker motivation and, in some cases, strikes.

A strike is precisely what happened in 1972 at the General Motors plant in Lordtown, Ohio. The common explanation for this highly publicized wildcat strike was that the workers, partially because they were relatively young (average age, twenty-four), simply rebelled against the boredom, monotony, and strict rules of the assembly line. But there was more involved; the workers felt that they could have done a better job than GM's industrial engineers in designing their own work. For example, the workers objected to a rule by management that forbade two workers temporarily doubling-up on a single job—even though this practice improved product quality and offset assembly-line boredom.

By establishing labor-management committees, many companies have successfully promoted worker participation in decision making on a wide range of issues. At Amsco Equipment Company, for instance, when the opportunity arose for in-house manufacture of a product that had previously been purchased, the company's labor-management committee suggested using production workers to develop a cost estimate. A team of four workers and an engineer was formed, and by conferring with the workers most concerned, the team developed realistic estimates of the time required to make and assemble the components in question. The team came in with an estimate significantly lower than either the purchase price of the existing product or the previous estimate by the company's industrial engineering department (example adapted from Batt and Weinberg, 1978:98–101).

The main point here should not be misinterpreted: The need for technical advice, such as that provided by industrial engineers, has not disappeared, nor should management abrogate its responsibilities. Rather, by giving workers responsibility for selected organizational tasks, companies can make the most effective use of the workers' knowledge and experience in the areas where workers *are* the experts and at the same time increase the workers' levels of job satisfaction and motivation through their participation in the decision making process. Of course, how far a company can go in this direction depends on the kind of work to be done, on the education and skill level of the work force, and on the culture and tradition of the organization.

Plan for Human Resources

A casual approach to human resources planning will no longer suffice for two important reasons. In the first place, the flow of management personnel is uneven. In the years 1985 to 1990, managers aged 45 to 65—a group that has traditionally held 60 to 70 percent of senior management jobs—will number only between 11 and 18 percent of the total management population. The ranks of management will contain 88 percent more managers aged 20 to 34 than aged 45 to 59 (data from *Business Week,* February 20, 1978, p. 68). The upshot of these data is that by 1990 companies will be faced with a cadre of managers who are far less experienced than managers of the past. The solution of retiring senior managers early so that junior managers can move up more quickly (and thus be less green by 1990) is not a viable one for human resource planners. In 1978 Congress raised the mandatory retirement age to seventy, and there is no way of predicting how many of today's managers will opt to retire early or wait until age seventy. Nevertheless, there are ways of creating competent managers for 1990. For example, training programs for junior managers can be intensified to help them cope with a future environment of even more sophisticated technology, government regulation, shortages, and consumerism. Similarly, fast tracks for the most promising younger managers can be established.

The second reason why companies need to pay attention to human resources planning is to make sure that the technical and professional personnel, which are the fastest-growing segment of the work force, continue to perform throughout their careers. In the past, the tendency was to reward, say, promising, highly talented engineers by promoting them to managerial positions even though they might not have shown any particular aptitude for or interest in management. Promotion into management positions seemed the best way to reward talented professional and technical people. However, aside from the fact that this policy was not always beneficial insofar as an employee's real expertise lie in developing new patents rather than writing memos, it is a policy that companies of the future will find more and more difficult to follow. As a higher percentage of personnel fall into the professional and technical category, the economics of the situation will make promotion to management impossible; there simply will not be enough management positions to go around. Technology-based organizations, therefore, will have to rethink the way in which they develop, maintain, and reward their work forces. Paul H. Thompson and Gene W. Dalton (1976) suggest three broad steps by which managers of human resources can make improvements in the way the technical employees' careers develop: reward technical contribution, reduce barriers to lateral transfers, and focus on careers (with semiannual reviews). More specifically, Thompson and Dalton suggest that companies reward technical workers by paying for performance not position, seeking their input in company decision making, and increasing their visibility and image.

Develop a Privacy Protection Policy

Although individuals' ability to protect themselves from record-keeping abuses has improved somewhat in recent years, most record-keeping relationships between business and individual employees are often dangerously one-sided.

When an individual applies for work today, it is not unusual for the employer to ask him or her to divulge a considerable amount of personal information and to allow the employer to verify and supplement it. In addition, the individual may be examined by the company physician, given a battery of psychological tests, interviewed extensively, and subjected to a background investigation. Consider, for example, the following questions a prospective employee might be asked: Do you cry frequently? How many abortions have you had? Do you have any sexual difficulties? Do you bite your nails? These questions come from forms used in numerous corporate medical examination programs. While the answers are no doubt important for a thorough physical examination, they can become part of the records that are kept for the employee's entire career. After the individual is hired, the records expand to accommodate attendance and payroll data, information on various types of benefits, performance evaluations, and much other information. Justifiably, all of this data creates a broad base of recorded information about an employee that raises a number of concerns about the employee's right to privacy within the employee-employer relationship.

In 1978 the National Privacy Protection Study Commission concluded that a privacy protection policy should have three objectives. While these objectives are applicable to a variety of business operations (e.g., granting consumer credit), they are particularly pertinent to the issues of creation, maintenance, use, and disclosure of employee records. First, a proper balance should be created between what an individual is expected to divulge and what he or she seeks in return; in short, intrusiveness should be minimized. Second, record-keeping operations should minimize the extent to which recorded information about an individual is a source of unfairness in any decision about him or her; in short, fairness should be maximized. Third, the organization's obligations with respect to uses and disclosures of information about an individual should be clearly defined; in short, legitimate, enforceable expectations of confidentiality should be created.

Although divulging information about oneself may have little significance for an individual who needs a job, an employer's adherence to these objectives in record-keeping operations can alleviate employees' sense of uncontrolled exposure to intrusion on personal privacy. For example, the preliminary health questionnaire used by IBM includes a detailed explanation of its purpose. The Cummins Engine Company's employee profile form, a copy of which is routinely sent to all employees, lists all possible users within the corporation, tells which information on the form goes to which users, and invites employees to address questions to the record-system manager or the personnel office. Other companies are allowing employees to see what were once-secret personnel records (excluding outside letters of recommendation). "You have to worry about the fantasies of workers about what is in the record; employee access to records is the only way to hold down wild rumors and misconceptions," Alan F. Weston, an authority on the privacy issue and author of the thorough study, *Privacy and Freedom,* contends (quoted in the *Wall Street Journal,* April 24, 1978). According to Weston, safeguarding an employee's privacy and staying out of his or her personal affairs as much as possible may improve the working environment and help morale.

REFLECTIONS ON THE CONFLICTS BETWEEN THE INDIVIDUAL AND THE ORGANIZATION

Let us consider for a moment the place of the individual in an organization, especially a large corporation. In recent years a great deal of discussion has been generated over managerial styles. The subject was probably best crystallized in Douglas McGregor's *The Human Side of Enterprise* (1960). What McGregor did in this important book was to offer managers two basic approaches to managing the worker. On the one hand, there was the traditional somewhat authoritarian approach (Theory X) founded on the notion that workers are lazy, dislike work, and require both carrot and stick. They cannot take responsibility for themselves and, therefore, require close supervision. Advocates of McGregor's Theory Y, on the other hand, make strikingly different assumptions about the nature of workers: People have a psychological need to work and even want responsibility. The implication is that managers should approach their task in a more open, more democratic way that enables individuals to achieve their own goals by directing their efforts toward the goals of the company. Today many, probably most, major corporations try to follow this prescription, though in a variety of modified forms. This widespread effort to adhere to Theory Y would seem to suggest that all is well for the individual within the large organization—or at least that things are headed in the right direction. Without denying that this trend from authoritarian to democratic manager has been both necessary and proper, we should note that in their drive to reduce conflict between individual employees and the company, some managers and many academics have set what some experts term unrealistic goals both for the company and for the employee.

Take the goal of making workers happier and happier at their jobs. Eli Ginzberg has reservations (1978):

> I go along with Adam Smith, who argued that there's no prospect of trying to make everybody happy in his work; it can't be done. That's my own view. I don't think you have to have people who curse every day they show up for work and are so unhappy they can't stand it. But I'd also argue that it isn't feasible to make the job arena a source of major happiness. What you can do is take some of the worst dimensions out of unpleasant tasks, make the workplace cleaner, safer, more healthful.
>
> The basic question a person must ask is not just whether he likes his job, but whether he's happy with his total role in life, whether his work and his leisure combined give him reasonable satisfaction.

Or take the goal of eliminating authority and constraints. How far can this goal be pushed? What will the results be? The fact is that authority and constraints are *inherent* in any work situation. Well over half of the agricultural workers are self-employed, but how much personal autonomy do they have? Anyone remotely familiar with the operations of a farm or ranch knows that they have very, very little. One does not plant crops, milk the cows, and repair a broken fence when one feels moved to do so. These constraints—nay, encroachments—on the lives of the self-employed farmer are just as sure and inflexible as the demands of the most authoritarian supervisor. Likewise, the "freedom" of a self-employed person in the business world is a strange sort of freedom. Such a person is, in the words of Galbraith (1973:73), "almost wholly free, as the (larger) organization is not, to exploit his labor force since his labor force consists of himself."

Let us put these reservations about Theory Y into the context of a rapidly changing business environment. It is far from clear that a company grappling with high energy bills and burdensome federal regulations, when faced with fierce competition from a foreign corporation or with capture by another company, will feel that its chances of survival will be enhanced because workers are represented in the decision-making process. As Sennett observes (1979:46):

> It is ironic that our society should just now be struggling with the question of the quality of the experience of work. Some of the competition we face in the world economy comes from countries like Korea, which are able to make use of both high technology and cheap labor—that is, laborers whose struggle for existence is so precarious that the sheer fact of holding a job is all-important to them and any thought about the quality of the work experience an unimaginable luxury. Or we compete with countries like Japan, which have a strict, paternalistic set of values that give work and the relations between employers and employees a meaning. Is discontent about working the ultimate luxury of late capitalism? Many employers believe the money, time, and effort put into responding to this discontent are a diversion of resources when the main task is surviving in an increasingly tough international economy.

The simple answer to these problems would be an authoritarian, back-to-Theory-X response. But, as H.L. Mencken said, to every knotty problem there is a solution—neat, simple, and wrong. The answer, obviously, must be found elsewhere—in more technological innovations, more reasonable government policy, more leadership by example, and better human resources management.

EQUAL EMPLOYMENT OPPORTUNITY

Around the turn of the century, the Supreme Court was deciding the Insular Cases, which involved the question of whether goods shipped in from the Philippines were taxable as imports. After the justices discoursed at length on whether the Constitution followed the flag, and offered opinions concurring in part and dissenting in part, a little old man rose at the rear of the courtroom and addressed the bench. "Please, your Honors," he asked plaintively, "do I get me lemons back?"

The story, no doubt apocryphal, illustrates well the frustration experienced by many companies as they try to develop programs to hire and promote the disadvantaged. Some people blame this frustration on the ambiguity and contradictions in federal policy. Whatever the cause, it is well worth the trouble for managers to give heavy attention to the subject. As we shall see in this section, failure to do so can result in multimillion dollar fines, government control of certain internal operations of a company, loss of lucrative government contracts, and a tarnished image for the company. For example, probably the most far-reaching civil rights agreement ever negotiated was the 1973 AT&T case. Under heavy federal pressure, AT&T agreed, among other things, to give 26,000 women and racial minority employees immediate wage increases that amounted to $36 million in the first twelve months alone. Another $15 million was handed out to satisfy past claims of job discrimination. And the huge company's hiring and promotion practices were almost completely brought under the scrutiny of the government. The purpose of what follows, then, is to develop an understanding of the requirements of equal employment opportunity laws and the operating procedures of governmental enforcement agencies. We also want to see the importance of good human resources management to the success of affirmative action programs.

Overview of Equal Opportunity Laws and Regulations

Several major federal laws have been enacted to deal with the problems of discrimination in employment. The provisions of these laws are many and complex, but their goal is simply to increase the participation of minorities and women in all levels of an employer's work force. The Civil Rights Act of 1964 is the keystone so far as basic compliance is concerned. Commonly referred to as "Title VII," it bans discrimination by employers of fifteen or more people on the basis of race, color, religion, sex, or national origin. It covers all terms and conditions of employment and holds the employer responsible for any discrimination within the organization. Charges may be brought by an individual employee or by the Equal Employment Opportunity Commission (EEOC), the administering federal agency. Should the suit be lost, the employer is usually required to pay dollar damages, stop the discriminatory practices, and make specific changes in its personnel practices. In short, Title VII requires a company to assure equal employment opportunities to all individuals.

No sooner had the law seemed to fulfill old promises at last, than President Johnson was observing in a historic commencement address at Howard University in June 1965:

> But freedom is not enough. You do not take a person who, for years, has been hobbled by chains and liberate him, bring him up to the starting line of a race and then say, "You are free to compete with all the others" and still justly believe that you have been completely fair.
>
> Thus it is not enough just to open the gates of opportunity. All our citizens must have the ability to walk through those gates.
>
> This is the next and the more profound stage of the battle for civil rights. We seek not just freedom but opportunity. We seek not just legal equality but human ability, not just as a right and a theory but equality as a fact and equality as a result.

The years that followed President Johnson's promise for positive approaches to equal opportunity saw the clarification of existing legislation and the passage of new acts.

By the Equal Pay Act of 1963, women could no longer be paid less than men for doing substantially the same work. The 1963 act covered most private and public employees subject to the Fair Labor Standards Act, including executive, administrative, professional and outside sales employees who are otherwise exempt from its minimum wage and overtime provisions. In 1974 amendments to the Fair Labor Standards Act extended coverage to large numbers of employees, including most federal, state and local government employees (employees of state and local schools and hospitals were previously covered) as well as employees of certain small chain stores, telegraph agency employees, and employees of large motion picture theaters, among others. The Wage and Hour Division of the Department of Labor enforces the act.

Men and women performing work in the same establishment under similar conditions must receive the same pay if their jobs required: equal skill, equal effort, and equal responsibility. "Equal skill" includes such factors as experience, training, education, and ability. Skill applies to the performance requirements of the jobs under consideration, and not to the skills that employees may possess but do not need to perform the job. "Equal effort" is the measurement of the physical or mental exertion needed for the performance of a job. Two jobs may require equal effort, even though the effort may be exerted in different ways. For example, men and women working in a bottle factory may be doing essentially equal work; however, the men occasionally may have to lift boxes. Intermittent extra physical exertion does not warrant extra pay. (Of course, if substantial differences exist in the amount or degree of effort required in the performance of two given jobs, the equal pay standard would not apply even though the jobs might be equal in all other respects.) "Equal responsibility" means that if jobs are otherwise equal, a minor or insignificant difference in the degree of responsibility does not qualify the job for extra pay. For instance, the equal pay standard usually would apply to men and women tellers in a bank even though there might be a variation in the types of accounts handled by each employee.

The Age Discrimination in Employment Act of 1967 provides that it is unlawful to fail to hire or to discourage any individual, or to treat employees differently in any way because of their age. The act, as amended in 1978, protects employees between the ages of forty and seventy. With the passage of the Federal Rehabilitation Act of 1973, the protection afforded women and minorities was extended to the disabled. Government contractors and subcontractors must now take affirmative action to employ and advance in employment qualified disabled individuals at all levels in the organization, including the executive level. State enactments, 1976 amendments to the Rehabilitation Act, and HEW rulings have further strengthened the legal protection afforded the handicapped. Finally, the Vietnam Era Veterans Readjustment Assistance

Act of 1974 requires government contractors to exercise affirmative action to hire and promote veterans.

Also included among the outgrowths of President Johnson's promise for positive approaches to equal opportunity were affirmative action efforts at all levels of government. For instance, President Johnson issued Executive Orders 11246 and 11375 that required companies with federal contracts to have affirmative action programs to recruit workers on a nondiscriminatory basis and that those with contracts over $50,000 and fifty or more employees develop and put into effect written affirmative action programs. Department of Labor guidelines issued in 1970 emphasized that affirmative action programs should be "result oriented":

—An acceptable affirmative action program must include an analysis of areas within which the contractor is deficient in the utilization of minority groups and women, and further, goals and timetables to which the contractor's good faith efforts must be directed to correct the deficiencies and, thus to increase materially the utilization of minorities and women, at all levels and in all segments of the work force where deficiencies exist.

—Affirmative action programs must contain an analysis of all major classifications at the facility, with explanation if minorities are currently being underutilized in any one or more job classifications.*

Although the guidelines applied only to federal contractors, the EEOC and the courts interpreted the Civil Rights Act as having similar provisions.

Affirmative Action and
Human Resources Management

Affirmative action, as interpreted under the Civil Rights Act, does not mean that a company must simply eliminate discriminatory practices; it means that it must take very positive steps to assure that minorities and women are hired, developed, promoted, and appropriately meshed into all levels and parts of the organization. The primary means for a company to develop a positive program for aggressively solving equal opportunity problems is the affirmative action plan (AAP). The AAP must include the following specified information:

—A policy statement of the company's EEO philosophy and intentions;
—A plan for disseminating the policy to employees and to the outside people with whom the company deals;

* Job "classification" refers to one or a group of jobs having similar content, wage rates, and opportunities. "Underutilization" means having fewer minorities or women in a particular job classification than would reasonably be expected by their availability.

—An assignment of EEO responsibilities;
—An analysis of deficiencies, including the number of minority and women employees versus availability, the mix of minorities and women in the work force versus availability, the distribution of minorities and women by job level, and anticipated obstacles to progress;
—Specific goals for women and minorities for the coming year;
—Specific plans for meeting the goals;
—An internal audit of the company's activity in the above areas.

While the primary responsibility for maintaining compliance with the laws and regulations rests with a company's management, the day-to-day responsibility for getting the job done rests largely with each supervisor, who must take an active part if violations are to be avoided. Ultimately, every employee plays a part in helping to get the job done. The essential thing to remember is that the thrust of affirmative action is twofold. First, discriminatory practices must be ended, and second, positive steps must be taken to assure that minorities and women are hired, developed, and promoted.

Hiring. The core question to be considered if the company's hiring procedures are to be in compliance with the intent of the EEO laws is this: Does the individual applying for the job have the capabilities to perform up to required standards? During interviews and preemployment inquiries, questions asked must be the same for any applicant and should be limited to areas having a direct bearing on an applicant's ability to perform the work. All information requested must apply directly to the individual's ability to handle the position. Ability or aptitude tests are proper, but they must have a valid relation to the jobs involved, must predict success on the job, and must be given and used in a manner that is fair to every applicant.

Hiring on the basis of ability presumes that management is able to draw distinctions among the qualifications of competing candidates fairly and objectively. Recent court decisions have made it clear that all selection tools must be valid and job related. For example, on March 8, 1971, the Supreme Court ruled in *Griggs* v. *Duke Power Company* that psychological tests given to job applicants had to be job related. Prior to the date the Civil Rights Act of 1964 went into effect, Duke Power Company had openly discriminated against blacks. After July 2, 1965, any black employee who had a high school diploma and who passed the Wonderlic Personnel Test and the Bennett Mechanical Comprehension Test could become a coal handler. Not surprisingly, the company's lawyers were hard pressed to prove what these two tests or a high school diploma had to do with measuring how well a person could shovel coal. By an 8-to-0 vote, the Court decided that the screening devices were illegal. "What Congress had commanded," ruled Chief Justice Warren Burger, in what many lawyers consider his finest opinion, "is that any tests used must measure the person for the job and not the person in the abstract."

Employers have numerous methods available to evaluate candidates for employment: performance tests, panel interviews, ratings of relevant training and experience, or any combination of these factors with written tests. For most jobs, a combination of job-related testing devices, rather than any single test, provides a better measure of the knowledge, skills, and abilities needed for successful job performance. The essential point here is that a company should not try to find coal shovelers who can scan Virgil correctly, but coal shovelers who are properly qualified for shoveling.

In hiring, the line between quotas and goals (less rigid requirements than quotas) is exceedingly thin. An effective affirmative action plan does not necessarily require quotas, but follows a recommendation that can do much to help break down artificial barriers to minority-group employment: Offer preferential treatment to disadvantaged persons and minority-group members. This recommendation means that affirmative action attempts to remedy the results of past discrimination and increase its employment of minorities. Specifically, preferential treatment includes selective certification for certain positions, training programs to allow the disadvantaged to become fit for merit system jobs, and aggressive recruiting for minorities (see Exhibit 12–2).

Accordingly, employment examinations should not be culturally biased—for example, an overly sophisticated English vocabulary on a written test for a Chicano. Individuals who have spent the majority of their lives in a low-income urban setting should not find that the examination favors a middle-class suburban background. If the tasks to be performed can be recorded through careful job analysis, any one of three selection methods can be used to determine relative ability: (1) competitive performance tests of a sample of the job to be done (e.g., typing or driving); (2) bio-data forms to determine and rate relevant experience and training and to obtain accurate appraisals of the candidate's qualifications from past employers, trainers, and associates; and (3) structured oral interviews by selection boards containing minority and female representatives. Oral interviews are particularly important in jobs such as telephone switchboard and receptionist positions, where public speaking is a job requirement. If determining relative ability to perform the job is not feasible, other methods are available in cases where minorities and women are underrepresented. For example, if management recognizes that all tests are subject to a statistical margin of error (even if the test is valid) and that there is no sanctity to "passing marks" or relative rankings, the pass-fail test might be used. In this system, only the minimum essential requirements for the job are established, and priority in appointment from among all those with "pass" grades goes to those individuals whose group (race, sex, or nationality) is most underrepresented in the particular position (Kranz, 1974:438).

Compensation. Any jobs requiring equal levels of skill, effort, and responsibility must equally compensate the employees doing those jobs. To establish two jobs as being unequal, the differences in skill, effort, and responsibility

EXHIBIT 12–2   Minority Recruiting

Harold Taylor, a GE manager, talks to eighth graders at Kirk Junior High School in Cleveland.

"I'm going back to junior high. But not to get an education."

Harold A. Taylor   Harold Taylor, GE manager

Harold Taylor wants to turn your teen-agers on to what turns him on: engineering. And he'd like you to help.

His junior-high visits are part of a nationwide program to encourage minority careers in engineering. It's a program that GE has joined other companies in supporting for the last 7 years.

Students with a knack for math and science ought to think about engineering as a career. So people like Harold Taylor go out to schools and help students set up their own science clubs. They show them around GE plants so they can see what an engineer actually does. They talk to students about what it really takes to become an engineer.

Here's how you can help. If your children have natural ability in math and science, encourage them to think about careers in engineering. Get them to talk to their teachers and guidance counselors about the training they'll need to become engineers.

The national program is working. Last year it helped literally hundreds of minority-group members get ready to enter U.S. engineering schools. And that's good. Engineering is important work. It pays well, offers plenty of opportunity. It's a field in which minorities ought to be well represented.

This year the program should do even more. With an assist from people like Harold Taylor. And a lot of other GE people who want to keep a good thing going.

Progress for People

GENERAL ⬤ ELECTRIC

General Electric encourages minority youths, in such ads as this, to enter engineering.

Source: Poster courtesy of General Electric Company, Fairfield, Connecticut.

must be substantial, not slight. Compensation is considered to include all types and methods of remunerating employees. For example, salary, clothing, and overtime pay are considered compensation if a company contributes to them. Thus, a company's affirmative action program should see that any differences in these forms of compensation are not applied in a discriminatory manner.

Promotion. Title VII guarantees that all employees will receive the same consideration so far as advancement is concerned. Whether promotions are made by regular progression, seniority, testing, recommendations by supervisors, or some other method, they must be made without bias. When supervisors make recommendations for advancement, extreme care must be taken that no discrimination—conscious or unconscious—plays any part in the decision. The rules covering transfers have the same general intent as rules for promotion. The opportunity to transfer from one job, one plant, or one classification to another must be open to all employees on an equal basis. While any such moves are, of course, subject to availability of openings, every employee who applies must be given equal consideration, as long as the individual has the capabilities to meet the requirements of the new position. Where seniority is a factor, it is essential that all employees have an equal opportunity to accrue the needed time to qualify for promotion or transfer. Further, the law, as extended by executive order, requires that very positive efforts be made to develop the potential of minorities and women so that they will get a fair share of the promotions.

Affirmative Action and Reverse Discrimination

For a long time, a particularly troublesome question has been this: Is it fair to favor minorities over whites for purposes of affirmative action? In 1979, the U.S. Supreme Court ruled in the landmark case of *United Steelworkers of America* v. *Weber* that employers can choose to give special job preference to blacks. This ruling was a strong endorsement of affirmative action programs. Brian Weber, a white, laboratory analyst at a chemical plant in Gramercy, Louisiana, had sued both his employer, the Kaiser Aluminum & Chemical Corporation, and his union, the Steelworkers Union, in 1974. He charged that he had been illegally excluded from a training program for higher-paying skilled jobs. The company, which had never been found guilty of past discrimination, had, with the union, set up the special training program for high-paying jobs, in which 50 percent of the places were reserved for minorities. When blacks with less seniority than Weber were admitted, he claimed racial discrimination.

Although Weber was upheld in two lower courts, he lost in the Supreme Court by a 5-to-2 vote. The justices ruled that employers can indeed give blacks special preference for jobs that were traditionally all white. Whether or not the company itself has had discriminatory job practices in the past, a company can use affirmative action programs to remedy "manifest racial imbalance" in employment. The majority opinion felt that the lower courts' rulings had followed the letter of the Civil Rights Act of 1964 but had ignored its spirit. The primary concern of Congress was with "the plight of the Negro in our economy." Therefore, the majority argued:

> It would be ironic indeed if a law triggered by the nation's concern over centuries of racial injustice and intended to improve the lot of those who had been 'excluded from the American dream for so long' constituted the first legislative prohibition of all voluntary, private, race-conscious efforts to abolish traditional patterns of racial segregation and hierarchy.

What is the potential impact of the *Weber* decision? For managers, it means that they can establish AAPs on their own or with unions to correct an imbalance in the work force without fear of being harassed by reverse discrimination suits brought by other employees. For minorities and women, it establishes a legal basis for an accelerated campaign to win preferential treatment in hiring and promotion. For government, it gives more reason to press companies that have been lagging in their affirmative action programs. Although the decision stressed the importance of employers voluntarily developing AAPs, it is possible that the government will begin pushing for outright quotas for minorities. Certainly, it has given federal affirmative action enforcement officials more confidence when they ask a court to order an affirmative action hiring remedy. Finally, while the ruling means greater opportunity for blacks at last, for white males, such as Weber, it also means the possibility of losing a long-sought job or promotion to less qualified minority applicants.

In sum, we have seen in this section that numerous federal laws have been enacted to deal with the problems of discrimination in employment. The mechanics of complying with the EEO laws depend on the particular law involved. As we have seen, the courts have issued rulings in many areas that deal with discrimination in specific employment practices. In all cases, the approach of the courts has been clear: No delays will be permitted a company in moving toward full compliance with EEO laws. The prescribed remedy against discrimination in employment is twofold: stop the practice and institute reforms. To accomplish the goals of EEO laws, administering agencies, working with the courts, may require payment of back wages, reinstatement of employees, promotions, and affirmative action programs. Agencies may also order specific reforms and obtain injunctions.

The picture is not altogether one-sided, however. A company has every right to defend its employment practices in every situation where it feels that discrimination does not exist. But it is important to remember that the burden of proof is always on the company. In job testing, for example, it must be shown beyond doubt that a test's only purpose is to determine whether an individual can perform a job safely and efficiently. The test must predict a candidate's potential success on the job and not just be a convenient method of choosing people. A company's decisions about overtime, job assignment, disciplinary actions, promotions, and discharges can be defended, provided all individuals have been treated in a completely fair and equal manner. Thus, management of human resources increasingly depends on honest, creative efforts to comply with EEO requirements. The most successful companies will be able to substantiate that they are doing all possible to comply with— even surpass—the regulations with aggressive, on-going affirmative action programs.

OCCUPATIONAL SAFETY AND HEALTH

A coal miner in West Virginia cannot breathe. A pesticide-plant worker in Texas can no longer walk. A hospital anesthesiologist in Chicago suffers a miscarriage. These workers, along with hundreds of thousands of others across the nation, have something in common: All are victims of occupational diseases. The safety and hazards associated with the workplace have been a major source of government concern. Consider this fact: during World War II, while 292,000 U.S. servicemen were killed in battle, 300,000 U.S. workers were killed in industrial accidents. Furthermore, the extent of job-induced illness is unknown; health officials fear that it may be far greater than was thought a few years ago. In 1972 the federal government calculated that roughly 100,000 Americans die and 390,000 are disabled yearly because of occupational diseases. More recently, government scientists have estimated that at least 20 percent of all cancer cases are linked to the workplace.

Development of the Industrial
Safety Movement

Occupational disease itself is not a new story. Bernardino Ramazzini, the Italian doctor who is considered the grandfather of occupational medicine, wrote the first systematic exposition of occupational disease *(De Morbis Artificium)* in 1700. Ramazzini recognized that paints were a factor in the poisoning of painters and various metals were a factor in the poisoning of artisans who worked with them. He also made studies of diseases in other occupations (e.g., lung diseases of miners). He was probably the first physician to add the query "What is your occupation?" to the preparation of medical case histories. Before Ramazzini there were scattered reports on industrial health—for example, a pamphlet by Ulrich Ellenbog in 1473 "on the poisonous wicked fumes and smoke" that afflicted goldsmiths and a treatise on the diseases of miners by Georgius Agricola in 1556. Later European literature dealing with the development of power-driven machinery and the resulting growth of industry contains many references to the unsafe and unhealthful working conditions that accompanied the changeover from the home workshop to the industrial plant (see Exhibit 12–3). A comprehensive study of industrial disease was made by Charles Turner Thackrah in 1831, and by the middle of the nineteenth century, efforts to improve industrial working conditions were being made by governments and trade guilds.

In the United States, until the mid-nineteenth century, common-law principles placed the cost of industrial accidents on the injured worker in the vast number of cases. To recover in a lawsuit against the employer, the employee

EXHIBIT 12–3   Occupational Disease: Why the Mad Hatter Was Really Mad

The damages of certain occupational disease have long been recognized, though the exact cause have not always been clear; hence, problems like "painters' colic" were attributed to lead poisoning and "grinders' consumption" to inhaling dust. Even the Mad Hatter in *Alice in Wonderland* exhibited symptoms of an occupational disease common to hatmakers of the time who used mercury in curing beaver furs. Although much knowledge about industrial disease has been gained since Lewis Carroll wrote *Alice in Wonderland,* the hazardous effects of many substances found in the workplace remain unknown. Because the effects of exposure to toxic and carcinogenic substances often do not appear until years after initial exposure, diagnosing worker-related illness remains difficult.

Source: Drawing reproduced courtesy of Random House from *Alice in Wonderland* by Lewis Carroll.

had to prove that the employer either was personally at fault or had violated a clearly defined responsibility. Furthermore, the injured worker had to overcome the defense of contributory negligence—that is, the legal presumption that the worker knew and had assumed the risks of the work. Although the courts recognized that certain duties were assumed by the employer—such as providing a reasonably safe place to work and reasonably safe machines, tools, and appliances kept in a reasonably good state of repair, as well as issuing safety rules and warnings of dangerous conditions—a violation of such duties would not result in employer liability if one of the common-law defenses was applicable.

The proponents of reform of the employers' liability laws turned to a type of legislation that had been adopted in Germany under Bismarck in 1884 and that had spread rapidly to most European countries and to England. The intent of this compulsory "workmen's compensation" legislation was to provide compensation, regardless of fault, for all work-connected injuries. Costs would be paid by the employer as part of the expense of production. The first workmen's compensation laws in the United States (with very limited application) were enacted in Maryland in 1902 and Montana in 1909. New York passed a comparable bill in 1910. But all three acts were declared unconstitutional by the highest courts of the respective states.

Then something happened. (Recall that in our discussion in Chapter 2 of the life cycle of social issues, the point was made that frequently a precipitating event is necessary in order for an issue to be translated into an effective public policy.) In March 1911, a fire at the Triangle Shirtwaist Company in New York City claimed the lives of 154 employees, most of them young women. As flames spread throughout the eighth floor, some workers jumped to their deaths, and later, scores of charred bodies were found piled against closed doors. The doors had been kept bolted, a newspaper reported, "to safeguard employers from the loss of goods by the departure of workers" (Schnapper, 1972:358). From the ashes of this disaster sprang a flurry of workmen's compensation legislation and tough new factory inspection laws.

Most employers had recognized some degree of moral responsibility in protecting their workers from industrial accidents prior to the enactment of compensation laws, but it was not until after passage of the laws that industry began to realize that accidents could be expensive as well as unfortunate. The cost factor provided the first real stimulus for industrial accident prevention and is still the chief driving force behind the interest in industrial safety among insurance companies and employers.

Many large industries, realizing the seriousness of accident costs, have aggressively sought means of preventing them. Among the early formal plant safety programs were those organized by the steel corporations and by the General Electric Company. Organizations such as the National Safety Council, which had its beginning in 1915, assisted tremendously with the organized safety movement. State and federal agencies also became extremely active in safety and accident prevention. The U.S. Bureau of Mines, created in 1910, was one of the first agencies to seek means of accident prevention in the mining industry.

The Occupational Safety and Health Administration

Because efforts to make the workplace safer were fragmented, and because serious safety problems remained, Congress in 1970 passed the Occupational Safety and Health Act. It remains one of the most sweeping efforts by government to regulate business for social ends. The stated purpose of the law was to assure "so far as possible, every working man and woman in the nation safe and healthful working conditions." To this end, the law created a new federal agency, the Occupational Safety and Health Administration (OSHA) and gave that agency a complicated, twenty-two-step process to follow in setting standards. The enabling legislation gave OSHA a Hobson's choice: It could either follow the twenty-two-step procedure to develop "consensus" standards of its own, or it could use the myriad of existing industrial guidelines that were sprinkled through various other laws and codes. In a rush to meet its mandate, OSHA adopted many of the existing safety and health rules for companies with government contracts and made laws of the voluntary guidelines issued by the American National Standards Institute (ANSI).

Once OSHA made voluntary standards mandatory, charges of over-regulation came quickly, and the agency is still carrying the ANSI standards as an albatross around its neck. For example, some of the standards, such as rules specifying the height at which fire extinguishers should be hung on walls, have more to do with property protection than with safety. Others are simply antiquated—ANSI's test method for determining the strength of safety shoes, for instance, has not been changed since it was adopted in 1944. Not surprisingly, managers have spotted the anachronisms and the outright irrelevancy of some of the tests and standards and have extrapolated these deficiencies to the agency as a whole. In addition to being unrealistic, the standards have been criticized for being voluminous. The steel industry, for one, is staggering under a load of fifty-six hundred regulations from twenty-seven different agencies— and OSHA alone accounts for four thousand of those rules. Further, a study by the Diebold Group, Inc., a management consulting firm, has pointed out that OSHA levied only $124 million in fines over a twelve-month period ending in early 1977. Since the agency is responsible for policing so many companies, simple division demonstrates that the average fine must be extremely small. But the costs of *complying* with OSHA standards far outweigh the costs of violating them. For example, one study indicates that meeting OSHA's ninety-decibel factory noise standard—one of the agency's most disputed rules—could cost industry as a whole *$13 billion* (cited in *Business Week,* April 4, 1979).

Accordingly, through its first six years, OSHA was attacked on numerous grounds. First and foremost was the issue of rules (see Exhibit 12–4). Another issue was the agency's "misplaced priority." These criticisms stemmed from the fact that in 1976, for example, OSHA ran 101,819 safety inspections in U.S. business but only 6,977 health inspections, and critics maintained that

**EXHIBIT 12–4   The Importance of Business
                 and OSHA's Safety Regulations**

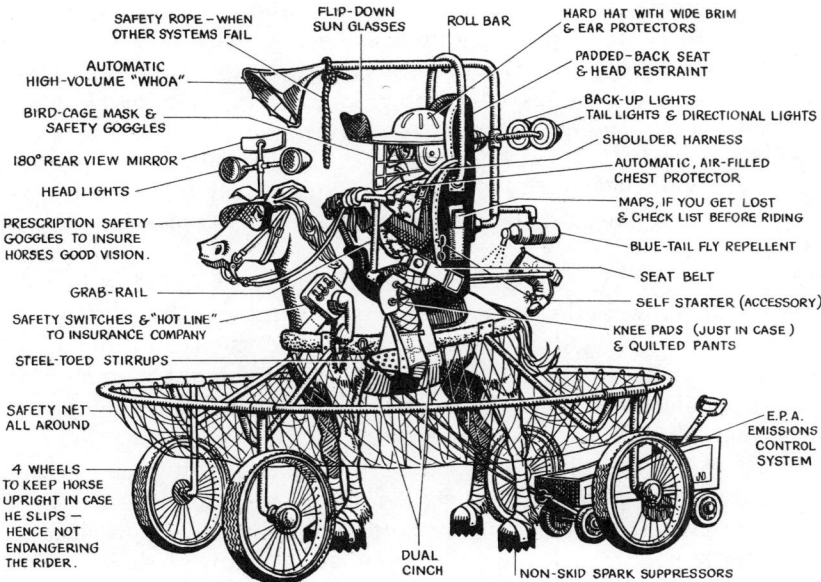

SAFETY ROPE – WHEN OTHER SYSTEMS FAIL
FLIP-DOWN SUN GLASSES
ROLL BAR
HARD HAT WITH WIDE BRIM & EAR PROTECTORS
AUTOMATIC HIGH-VOLUME "WHOA"
PADDED–BACK SEAT & HEAD RESTRAINT
BIRD-CAGE MASK & SAFETY GOGGLES
BACK-UP LIGHTS
TAIL LIGHTS & DIRECTIONAL LIGHTS
180° REAR VIEW MIRROR
SHOULDER HARNESS
AUTOMATIC, AIR-FILLED CHEST PROTECTOR
HEAD LIGHTS
PRESCRIPTION SAFETY GOGGLES TO INSURE HORSES GOOD VISION.
MAPS, IF YOU GET LOST & CHECK LIST BEFORE RIDING
BLUE-TAIL FLY REPELLENT
GRAB-RAIL
SEAT BELT
SAFETY SWITCHES &"HOT LINE" TO INSURANCE COMPANY
SELF STARTER (ACCESSORY)
STEEL-TOED STIRRUPS
KNEE PADS (JUST IN CASE) & QUILTED PANTS
SAFETY NET ALL AROUND
E.P.A. EMISSIONS CONTROL SYSTEM
4 WHEELS TO KEEP HORSE UPRIGHT IN CASE HE SLIPS – HENCE NOT ENDANGERING THE RIDER.
DUAL CINCH
NON-SKID SPARK SUPPRESSORS

Cowboy after O.S.H.A.

"Cowboy after OSHA" reflects the impatience of business with the detailed safety rules that OSHA has promulgated. In 1978, and no doubt partially in response to this criticism, OSHA proposed the revocation of some 1,100 safety requirements, including, for example, a rule that required a fire extinguisher be a certain number of inches from the floor. (The new rule simply requires that fire extinguishers be readily accessible.) Also eliminated was a prohibition against ice in drinking water, a rule that dated back to the days when ice came from ponds.

Source: Drawing by James Devin. Reprinted by permission of artist James M. Devin, Independence, Mo., copyright 1972; and by permission of *National Safety News Magazine*, July 1972.

more emphasis should have gone toward reducing the risks created by the toxic and cancer-causing chemicals to which workers are sometimes exposed. Other issues concerned OSHA's efficiency and effectiveness. When the language of OSHA's enabling legislation instructed OSHA not to minimize risk, but to seek absolute safety, it in effect encouraged the new agency to impose its judgment on employers instead of leaving them any choice in the matter of the most efficient approaches to safety precautions. Thus, like old-fashioned building codes, OSHA rules were seen as prescribing details rather than regulating performance. For example, when the agency specified that so-called engineering controls—machine enclosures, for example—are the only acceptable way to meet the industrial noise standard, business managers argued that for many plants, the installation of such controls is economically prohibitive and that their judgment should be paramount as to when hearing protection for workers is sufficient (e.g., when earmuffs are being used). How effective was OSHA during its first six years—that is, what impact did it have on work-related accidents and illnesses? According to the U.S. National Center for Health Statistics the number of work-related deaths per 100,000 people was 2.9 in 1970, 2.8 in 1973, 2.6 in 1974, and 2.6 in 1975. A slide in the injury rate did occur between 1973 and 1976, but it stemmed chiefly from a reduction in minor injuries and illness; there was little, if any, evidence of a decline in serious accidents.

In 1977 President Carter appointed an administrator, Eula Bingham, who had a new view on what the agency's priorities should be. "We're going to get tough on the health hazards in the workplace that cause irreversible injury—cancer, nerve damage, leukemia, lung disease and all the rest." Other parts of Bingham's plan included canceling regulations that have little or nothing to do with safety and health (such as one requiring coat hooks on toilet doors), improving OSHA's relationship with small businesses, and limiting safety inspections almost entirely to industries where accident rates are highest—that is, construction, manufacturing, and transportation. Exhibit 12–5 provides a list of the ten most widespread safety violations that occur in these industries.

Management Responses to Worker Safety

Since the turn of the century, companies and industries have made a complete turnaround on the issue of worker health and safety. During the 1970s, for example, Johns-Manville, the leading asbestos company, spent several millions of dollars on medical research into occupational hazards; numerous corporations have expanded their medical staffs; industry has also established its own toxicological-testing center in Research Triangle Park, North Carolina; and scientific data pointing to occupational dangers are increasingly being heard in top management meetings.

Indeed, management that does not weigh the health and safety implications of its operational decisions had better learn to do so quickly. As they say

**EXHIBIT 12–5   The Most Common Industrial Safety Violators:
OSHA's Top Ten**

1. National electrical code requirements (from loose wires to underground equipment)
2. Safety of abrasive wheel machinery
3. Construction and placement of compressed gas containers
4. Marking of exits
5. Safety of pulleys in mechanical power-transmission gear
6. Maintaining portable fire extinguishers
7. Safety of drives in mechanical power-transmission gear
8. Guarding floor and wall openings, platforms, and runways
9. General housekeeping requirements (from unmopped puddles to flammable rubbish piles)
10. Effectiveness of machinery guards

Source: OSHA, Office of Data Systems, "Violation and Penalty Data from SIC Code, FY 1975," Washington, D.C.

in safety circles, "It costs more to have accidents than to prevent them." What are the costs of an accident? Obviously, there are the direct costs of medical expenses and possibly legal compensation. But management must also recognize the indirect costs of an accident like the time lost by executive or staff personnel in assisting the injured employee, in investigating the accident, in arranging for replacement of the injured employee, in training a new employee, in preparing a report and handling related correspondence, and in conducting safety meetings to prevent similar accidents. Indirect costs also include lost production and possibly the cost of repairing damage to machinery, equipment, or materials. More difficult to measure, perhaps, but no less critical among the indirect costs of an accident is the effect an accident can have on employee morale and on public attitude toward the company. Experience has shown that throughout industry, these indirect costs of accidents are four times greater than direct costs.

The heart of a successful response to the issue of worker health and safety is not found in sophisticated laboratories or boardrooms, nor at the bottom line of cost analyses, though these factors are vital to a company's safety effort. Rather, the real push for worker safety must stem from the development of a safety program that is intrinsically based on human resources management.

Perhaps the most obvious requirement of such a program is *safety education and training*. Since few workers will, on their own initiative, undertake to educate themselves, an organized course of instruction is necessary. Then safety training should be instituted to extend the education program to specific occupations, processes, jobs, or activities within the company.

The safety program should also include *inspection*—not only by OSHA inspectors but by top management (usually on a quarterly basis) and safety engineers or by safety committees that include managers, engineers, as well as workers who must do the jobs involved. Company participants in safety inspections need not undertake and master job analysis techniques like a production engineer. However, they must be familiar with what job analysis involves and be able to analyze specific jobs or operations sufficiently to discover hazards and suggest appropriate means of correction. Thus the safety inspection should detect motions, positions, or actions that are likely to yield injuries:

—Reaching across moving equipment;
—Incorrect posture in lifting or handling materials or equipment;
—Hazardous positions in relation to equipment;
—Hazardous positions of workers in relation to one another;
—Off-balance positions;
—Restricted vision while operating equipment.

The safety inspection should also yield information about the amount and type of equipment and tools, including personal protective equipment, needed to carry out particular jobs safely.

The next phase in the development of a safety program calls for assessing the company's overall safety record. To appraise safety performance and to help spot trends, some yardstick must be used that compares the company's accident experience with that of other companies in the industry. The number of disabling injuries per million hours worked is one such yardstick (DeReamer, 1967):

$$\text{Disabling injury frequency rate} = \frac{\text{Number of disability injuries} \times 1,000,000}{\text{Employee-hours of exposure}}.$$

According to this formula, a plant that had, say, 750 employees would work about 1,500,000 hours each year. If six disabling injuries occur in a given year, then the disabling injury rate would be 4 (6 × 1,000,000 ÷ 1,500,000).

Once the safety appraisal is completed, the safety program enters its final, and perhaps most difficult, phase: *arousing and maintaining interest in safety*. To see the importance of this phase, let us consider how one large wholesale bakery approached its safety problem (example taken from Komaki, Barwick, and Scott, 1978). For three years, the injury frequency rate in the bakery had averaged about 35 disabling injuries per million hours worked. Then the rate jumped to 53.8—more than double that of the bakery industry generally and substantially higher than rates in such hazardous occupations as meat packing and mining. An initial investigation by three industrial psychologists revealed that safe practices were not being maintained because workers received little, if any, positive reinforcement for performing safely—nor were workers being trained to avoid unsafe practices. In response to these findings, the bakery tried a behavioral approach in which a system of reinforcement was used. The first step was to produce an observational code wherein specific work practices were identified as safe, unsafe, or not observed. The code was then reviewed with the workers, and they received instruction and training in avoiding unsafe practices. Next, workers were encouraged to improve their safety performance in order to improve the company's safety ranking, and a departmental goal of 90 percent safe performance was agreed to by the employees. Finally, workers were told their safety performance would be observed and recorded on a graph for all to see. (Workers responded favorably to this aspect of the program, even to the point of clapping and cheering when the first results were posted.) Supervisors were also asked to recognize individual workers when they performed selected activities safely and to make specific comments on their performance.

After the program had been in effect for eleven weeks in one department and three weeks in another, the observers stopped observing and providing reinforcing feedback. Then, to assess the effect of this reversal phase, observations and reinforcements were reinstituted five weeks later for a period of four weeks. The results clearly demonstrate the importance of arousing and maintaining interest in safety. During the reversal phase, safety performance in the two departments dropped back near the original baseline rates (71 and 72 percent) in contrast to the substantially improved rates of 96 and 99 percent the employees achieved when reinforcing feedback was provided.

ORGANIZED LABOR AND EMPLOYEE BENEFITS

In this section, we first take a brief look at labor unions—their characteristics and trends within labor in the United States today. We then consider the outlook for labor-management relations with emphasis on the role that negotiations for employee benefits have had and will continue to have in the workplace. In the final section we review actions human resources management should include in its operations to maximize the attractiveness of employee benefits.

Characteristics of American
Labor Organizations

Structural Features. American unions have over 19 million members, or approximately 30 percent of nonagricultural employees. (The percentage of nonagricultural employees in unions is over 50 percent in Great Britain, 35 percent in Japan and Germany, and from 60 to 80 percent in Scandinavian countries.) While the percentage of labor organization membership in the

United States has remained relatively stable over the past decade, membership has slipped about ten points below the level of the first decade after World War II (see Exhibit 12–6). This decline has been greatly influenced by the growth of the service- and information-based economy. In addition to declining slightly, over a twenty-year period union membership changed somewhat in character. The percentage of white-collar members grew from 13.6 percent in 1955 to over 18 percent in 1976. The percentage of women union members also increased, 16.6 percent to almost 22 percent in the same period.

Labor organization membership is unequally distributed among sectors and regions of the United States. Transportation, communications, public utilities, some parts of the construction industry, and some manufacturing industries (e.g., basic steel and automobiles) are highly organized. But finance, real estate, most retail trade, and service industries are very lightly organized. Government employees, who were relatively poorly organized (with some notable exceptions) prior to 1960, have since experienced a significant surge of union membership. The five most highly organized states are New York (45.5 percent of nonagricultural employees are members of unions or similar associations), Michigan, West Virginia, Pennsylvania, and Washington. The five

EXHIBIT 12–6   U.S. Union Membership as a Percentage of Total Labor Force, 1900–1976

	Union members (in millions)	Total labor force (in thousands)	Union membership as percentage of all employees outside of agriculture
1900	.791		6.1
1920	2.116		19.5
1930	3.401	50.080	11.7
1934	3.088	52.490	12.0
1937	7.001	54.320	22.8
1945	14.322	65.290	35.8
1951	15.946	65.982	33.7
1954	17.022	67.818	35.1
1961	16.303	73.031	30.2
1969	19.036	84.230	27.0
1974	20.199	93.240	25.8
1975	19.473	94.793	25.3
1976	19.432	96.917	24.5

Note: U.S. Bureau of Labor Statistics estimates combined union and association membership to have been 22,809,000 in 1974 and 22,463,000 in 1976.

Source: U.S. Bureau of Labor Statistics, *Directory of National and International Labor Unions in the United States, 1977* (Washington, D.C.: U.S. Government Printing Office, 1978).

least organized states are Florida, Texas, Mississippi, South Carolina, and North Carolina, with only 9.8 percent (Dunlop, 1978).

The American labor movement is decentralized: over 175 national unions with 71,000 affiliated local unions. More than 60 percent of the national unions are affiliated with the AFL-CIO; and 85 percent of the local unions are in these national unions. The twelve largest national unions, with a half-million members or more, account for approximately half of all union members. Each local or intermediate labor organization conducts its internal affairs and makes its decisions under its constitution and procedures, subject to the Labor-Management Reporting and Disclosure Act of 1959. As a consequence of this decentralization—which means more officers—American labor organizations must assess their members dues that are relatively high compared to those applied in other countries. Dunlop (1978) cites one study that suggests that American unions have one paid officer for every 300 members; Great Britain, meanwhile, has one paid officer for every 3,000 members.

Collective Bargaining. Although the fact is not widely recognized, labor organizations have helped increase productivity by their effects on training, morale, methods and forms of compensation, safety, support of orderly procedures, and discipline in the workplace. Recognition of this function of labor unions comes through quite clearly in George Meany's perceptive definition of collective bargaining (cited in Dunlop, 1978:82–83):

> On its philosophical side, collective bargaining is a means of assuring justice and fair treatment. In the economic realm it is a means of prodding management to increase efficiency and output, and of placing upon trade unions great responsibilities to limit their demands to practical realities. A failure to recognize the unique role of collective bargaining is a failure to understand the distinctive new nature of American private enterprise as it has evolved over the past seventy-five years.

As commonly used in the United States, collective bargaining refers to at least three separate forms of labor-management activity. First are the periodic negotiations for a new collective agreement that sets the terms of employment. The second activity encompasses the day-to-day administration of the provisions of the agreements, including the steps in grievance procedures and arbitration provisions. Each agreement typically specifies a grievance procedure— that is, a series of steps in which representatives of the two sides seek to resolve disputes over the meaning or the application of the agreement. Agreements also tend to specify an arbitration process, including the selection of arbitrators or umpires. (In the next chapter we shall see how the importance of arbitration has grown in recent years.) The third labor-management activity involved in collective bargaining includes informal joint consultations and conferences that explore common problems concerning improved productivity, affirmative action, and community affairs.

Trends Within Labor. Although the basic characteristics of U.S. labor organizations have remained largely unchanged in the past several decades, a few developments are significant. We have already noted the relative decline in union membership as a percentage of the labor force. Another trend is a significant increase during the past decade in the annual number of *decertification elections*—that is, secret ballot elections conducted by the National Labor Relations Board (NLRB) in which workers vote to oust a union. In fiscal 1977 unions lost 628 of 811 such contests, compared with 157 losses in 221 decertification elections in 1966. Decertification elections occurred mainly in small units, often with the implicit encouragement of the employer. But aggressive management is not the only explanation for the rise in decertification votes. Many studies point to the fact that younger workers do not see the advantages of having a union. If they lose their jobs, they know others are available. They come from greater affluence, are better educated, and do easier work for shorter periods than earlier generations of workers. Rather than the traditional struggles with management, they seek recognition, independence, and individuality.

The Outlook for Labor-Management Relations

Union Actions. Given the relative decline in blue-collar workers and the rise in the number of younger workers, how bleak is the future for unions? Only a poor student of history would write off American unions entirely. For example, in the early depression years, organized labor's membership had slipped to a fifteen-year low of 3 million, and the outlook was indeed bleak. Yet, within a year, the unions were surging ahead on the crest of New Deal legislation. By 1938 the membership had doubled. Of course, history does not tell us what will happen to labor trends in the decade of the 1980s, although it does suggest that embattled unions can stage strong comebacks. Indeed, there are already a number of straws in the wind that suggest unions are going to fight to make a strong comeback.

- The UAW and other big unions, such as the Steelworkers, the Teamsters, and some building-trade unions, are investing more money and labor on campaigns against specific issues.
- Many unions are introducing new techniques, such as the use of financial pressure that the unions, their members, and allies can bring to bear as investors by threatening to withdraw business from banks and insurance companies. Further, many unions have begun to claim that while most pension plans are administered solely by employers, union member employees actually own the funds and, therefore, should have a voice in investing them (e.g., to prohibit investments in antiunion companies).
- Unions are beginning to concentrate more on organizing service industries, though the high turnover rate of workers in retail sales, banks, and hospitals continues to present a problem.

• For some time, unions have been expanding the scope of collective bargaining. For example, successful efforts to expand such employee benefits as health insurance and related benefits has been going on for some time to cover both more people and more situations (see Exhibit 12–7). Negotiations have also improved the retirement benefits of those already retired, provided supplemental unemployment benefits, and enhanced job security in numerous ways. Special training provisions and some modifications of the units in which seniority rights and other perquisites are exercised have been negotiated to agree with the requirements of Equal Employment Opportunity laws. A legal services benefit, analogous to medical benefits, has been negotiated in a few situations. And as we saw at the end of Chapter 10, the number of successful negotiations for cost of living allowances has been on the rise.

Management Resistance to Unionization. As unions begin to struggle against declining membership and adopt more aggressive strategies, management in nonunion companies will be spending more time resisting unionization. The reason for management's resistance appears to be twofold. First is the traditional desire to avoid restrictions on managerial authority and decision making. The second is the cost. One profit-conscious personnel director at a western bank with five thousand employees estimates that living with a union would mean a 20 percent cost increase. The point is not the validity of the figure, but the fact that the management of the bank believes the figure to be accurate. (Many directors of human resources now realize that negotiations over benefits—particularly pensions, which are regulated by federal law—are becoming increasingly critical. A rule of thumb is that employee-benefit costs are going twice as high as wages today.)

The success of major companies that operate without unions, such as IBM, Eastman Kodak, and Texas Instruments, is encouraging other firms to stiffen their resistance. Many managers, however, knowingly or otherwise, have gone too far in trying to maintain nonunion status and have taken such actions as illegally discharging employees, threatening to close a plant or withhold benefits from prounion workers, or refusing to bargain in good faith with a union. Roughly one-third of the allegations of these activities have been found worthy of NLRB hearings and have ultimately been resolved through NLRB procedures. The managers who have been successful in resisting unionization in recent years have adopted enlightened approaches to dealing with the needs of workers. The key to their success has been to eliminate sources of complaints that can attract employees to unions. Such complaints usually involve pay, benefits, or grievance procedures. Some nonunion companies are willing to spend as much on salaries and benefits as any union company. As B.F. Goodrich's employee relations vice president explains, "We don't save on wages at nonunion plants, but we save on flexibility" (*Business Week,* December 4, 1978). Another thing that most nonunion businesses have in common is a resistance to firing people. As a vice president of a large aerospace company put it, "You practically have to assault a vice president to get fired here."

EXHIBIT 12–7   Wage and Salary Workers Covered under Negotiated Employee-Benefit Plans, 1960–1973

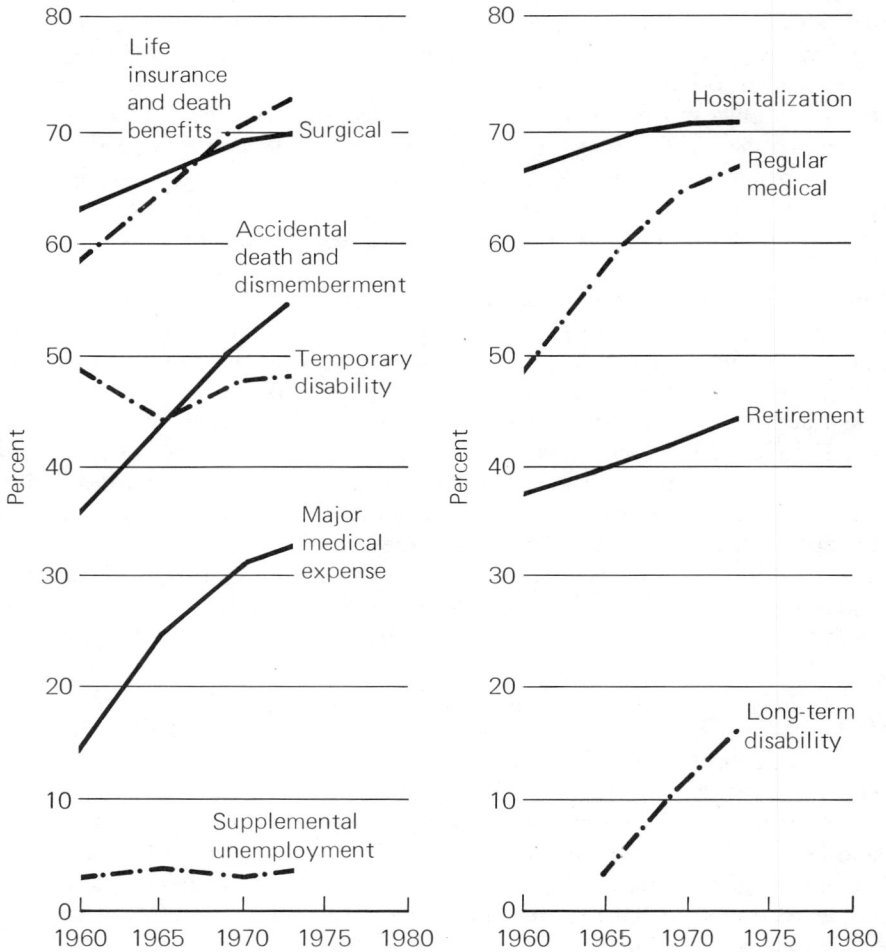

Source: U.S. Department of Commerce, *Social Indicators, 1976* (Washington, D.C.: U.S. Government Printing Office, 1977), p. 121.

In addition to stepping up company programs to avoid employee complaints in regard to pay, benefits, and grievance procedures, some companies have also taken steps to counter union propaganda and to discourage workers from signing union recognition cards, which state a worker's desire to be represented by a particular union. (If enough cards are signed, they lead either to company acceptance of a union, or, more likely, to a union-representation election. To show how willingly some people sign things, a consultant once handed out cards to 125 managers at a meeting; all of them unwittingly signed what turned out to be a fake union authorization card "for a little thing called the International Chicken Flickers, making me their authorized union representative.") Aggressive efforts to counter union propaganda have included publicizing union problems—with newspaper clippings describing union scandals, for example, or with pictures showing strikers shivering in cold weather or on a picket line. Some experts on resisting unionization have pointed out the merits of publicizing for employees the union's "economic motive for organizing"—that is, the dues money they stand to gain. Accordingly, employees should be encouraged to consider the hypothetical example of a plant with 600 employees, each of whom pays $10 a month in union dues. The union in question collects $72,000 a year and $1.4 million over twenty years (Hyatt, 1977).

The Potential for Cooperation. Where resistance is not an issue in labor-management relations—that is, in companies where management has learned to live with unions—the pattern of closer union-management cooperation, which has come to characterize a few industries in recent years, may become more widespread. A good example of this pattern is the experimental negotiating agreement between the steel union and the steel companies—an agreement with strong limits on strikes. If unions and employers in at least a few industries begin to come under structural pressure because of the inroads made by foreign competition in U.S. markets, the future might see this pattern of cooperation repeated elsewhere. While closer union-management cooperation involves no direct public policy consequences, it could raise questions about price and wage policies. For example, if labor and management succeed in obtaining some government assistance in the form of higher tariffs, the government would, in a sense, find itself helping to underwrite price and wage policies in the industry in question. On the more positive side, the development of closer labor-management relationships could lead to wider experimentation with joint management-union efforts to raise productivity. Federal legislative programs designed to encourage such union-management cooperative efforts have been suggested in recent years and could take on an even greater importance in the future.

Maximizing Employee Benefits

With or without unions, the primary mission of human resources operations is to satisfy the human resources needs of the company as efficiently as possible by recruiting, selecting, placing, orienting, evaluating, training, developing, and retaining effective personnel—all within the bounds of company goals, needs, and budget; EEO laws; worker safety regulations; and in many cases, union contracts. One of the ways human resources management can attract, retain, and develop the most effective employees is by maximizing the attractiveness of employment for the types of employees sought.

Clark Abt (1977:77–80) suggests that a study of the total current and potential benefits—employee benefits, social benefits, and job opportunity benefits—generated by the company for its employees to identify the steps that would maximize the company's attractiveness. Such an audit would include the following (modified from Abt):

—Inventory of all current benefits by the company to employees;
—Formulation of an employee-benefits preference inventory, in which employees note relative perceived worth associated with each item;
—Formulation of a questionnaire survey of employees' perceptions of the relative worth of social benefits and job opportunities, as well as the degree of disadvantages, associated with company employment (see the example questionnaire in Exhibit 12–8);
—Follow-up interview to clarify any ambiguities in responses;
—Comparison of employee preference inventories with current benefits inventory and identification of "low-preference, high-cost" components to be eliminated and "high-preference," "presently unavailable," or "underavailable" components for possible addition;
—Redesign of company benefits programs to respond maximally to employee preferences within the budget and associated reallocation of subbudgets;
—Review and analysis of additional, highly valued benefits requiring additional budget to determine whether potential return on additional investment is justified;
—Consistency check, using a survey of employee responses to the new benefits plan, and determination of whether significant improvement in perceived worth has been achieved without significant budget expansion;
—Communication of the resulting changes to employees and stockholders and demonstration of the improved benefits gained with no diminution of return on investment.

A number of other approaches to manage as well as maximize employee benefits have been tried. For example, under recent tax laws, some companies now offer flexible benefit plans—known as *cafeteria plans*—in which employees choose their own individual fringe benefits. Under these plans, employers provide minimal "core" coverage in life and health insurance, vacations, and pensions. The employee buys additional benefits to suit his or her own needs, using credits based on salary, service, and age. A few companies offer "well pay," the opposite of sick pay. These companies give workers who, say, have been neither absent nor late for a full month an extra eight hours of wages.

EXHIBIT 12–8　Maximizing Benefits: An Employee Questionnaire on Job Opportunities

Listed below are different kinds of opportunities which a job might afford. If you were to seek a job, (A) How much importance would you personally attach to each of these opportunities, and (B) To what extent does your present job actually provide such opportunities?

(Please check one answer for each line in (A) and (B)).

	(A) Importance to You Personally					(B) Extent Provided by Your Present Job				
	Not Important	Moderately Important	Important	Very Important	Extremely Important	Not Provided	Minimally Provided	Adequately Provided	Well Provided	Completely Provided
1. To make full use of my present knowledge and skills	1	2	3	4	5	1	2	3	4	5
2. To grow and learn new knowledge and skills	1	2	3	4	5	1	2	3	4	5
3. To earn a good salary	1	2	3	4	5	1	2	3	4	5
4. To advance in administrative authority and status	1	2	3	4	5	1	2	3	4	5
5. To build my professional reputation	1	2	3	4	5	1	2	3	4	5
6. To work on difficult and challenging problems	1	2	3	4	5	1	2	3	4	5
7. To have freedom to carry out my own ideas	1	2	3	4	5	1	2	3	4	5
8. To contribute to broad technical knowledge in my field	1	2	3	4	5	1	2	3	4	5
9. To reject working on anything that I consider unethical	1	2	3	4	5	1	2	3	4	5
10. To work with colleagues that share my goals and beliefs	1	2	3	4	5	1	2	3	4	5
11. To depend on my work for my preferred rewards	1	2	3	4	5	1	2	3	4	5
12. To expect that I can predict the results of my work	1	2	3	4	5	1	2	3	4	5

Thank you for your cooperation. If you have any comments you feel are relevant to this Questionnaire or the Social Audit, please feel free to note them in the space provided below. ___

Source: Reprinted by permission of the publisher from *The Social Audit for Management,* Clark Abt, © 1971 by AMACOM, a division of American Management Associations, p. 79. All rights reserved.

This type of positive reinforcement could also be used to encourage safety by offering a bonus based on any reduction in company-paid premiums on industrial accident insurance. And finally, a growing list of large companies is adopting an employee stock ownership plan (ESOP) that provides free stock to all employees. In 1977, for example, the American Telephone & Telegraph Company, the nation's largest corporation in terms of stockholders and profits, disclosed a move to give 1.6 percent of its total stock to its 927,000 employees, provided the IRS approved. (ESOPs are not to be confused with ordinary employee stock-purchase plans like those many corporations have for salaried employees.)

To conclude this chapter, we might for a moment consider the workplace in the year 2001. It seems safe enough to predict that at the start of the twenty-first century, human resources operations will be at the core of businesses that succeed in an economy characterized by service and knowledge, competition and shortages. In such an economy, the attitudes of workers will be more crucial than ever. As James O'Toole writes (1979:11 and 12):

> The success or failure of the national enterprise rests on the willingness of individual workers to take responsibility for the quality and quantity of their work, to take initiative in those increasingly frequent situations that cannot be routinely handled, to show a real interest in the welfare of customers, suppliers, and fellow workers . . . .
>
> Because of increasing balance-of-payments deficits and the declining dollar, American managers may no longer be able to afford to play golf on company time, and American workers may no longer be able to afford to goof off or sabotage cars on the assembly line. The nation can only afford such behavior if it doesn't want oil, bauxite, coffee, French wines, and Japanese radios.

CHAPTER THIRTEEN

External Relations

Decisions

T his chapter treats the decisions that involve what we defined in Chapter 8 as proactive political activities. Although management's approach to production, finance, and marketing decisions borders on reverence, managers do not generally accord decision making in the area of external relations the same degree of attention. But management needs to cross the threshold and begin the systematic integration of external relations decisions into the formulation and implementation of company objectives at all levels of organization. Reginald H. Jones, chairman of General Electric, has observed that managers ". . . will have to become activists rather than adaptive. There will be no room for Neanderthals."

In the first section of this chapter we shall see why companies get involved—indeed, cannot help but get involved—in the political process. Four major reasons will be suggested: interest group actions; economic conflicts (usually with other companies); union actions; and, most important, governmental action. The remainder of the chapter explores the various ways in which companies participate in essentially political activities. One way is by trying to shape public opinion. In the second section, therefore, we take a look at information activities—particularly advocacy advertising—that can help business influence public opinion, as well as the ways in which managers can be more effective in dealing with the media when trying to influence public opinion. An obvious way in which companies get involved in politics is by participating in electoral activities. The third section of this chapter discusses three ways: voluntary political activity, contributions to political campaigns, and political action committees. The fourth section deals with attempts to influence legislators and bureaucrats. Here we briefly review such means as coalition building and letter writing and then consider lobbying in greater detail. These means for influencing public opinion, political campaigns, legislators, and bureaucrats do not exhaust the ways in which companies can enter the political arena; there is also litigation and, in more recent times, arbitration, which are the subjects of the next section. Once all the routes for entering the political arena have been explored, in the final section we reflect on the role the external relations function should play in accomplishing the company's goals in the political arena. □

WHY BUSINESS GETS INVOLVED IN THE POLITICAL PROCESS

Exhibit 13–1 provides us with a diagram of why and how a company enters the political arena. The four boxes on the left represent the major reasons for a company's becoming involved in the political process. The boxes on the right side of the figure represent an attempt to give some order to the many options available once a company decides to enter the political arena. Before turning to these ways in which firms participate in the political process, we first need to be clear about *why* they do so.

In Response to Government Action

Chief executives today would be almost unanimous in saying that the biggest problem they face is the impact of government on the corporation. As we have seen throughout this book, it is not enough anymore to run a company well and provide the products and services the public wants. Top managers must now be as concerned about public policy as they are about anything else they do. In Chapter 6 we saw that the elimination or at least reduction of social impacts is a responsibility of business. Ideally, managers will convert impact management into business opportunities, but this is not always possible. Fre-

**EXHIBIT 13–1   A Model of Why and How a Firm
Enters the Political Arena**

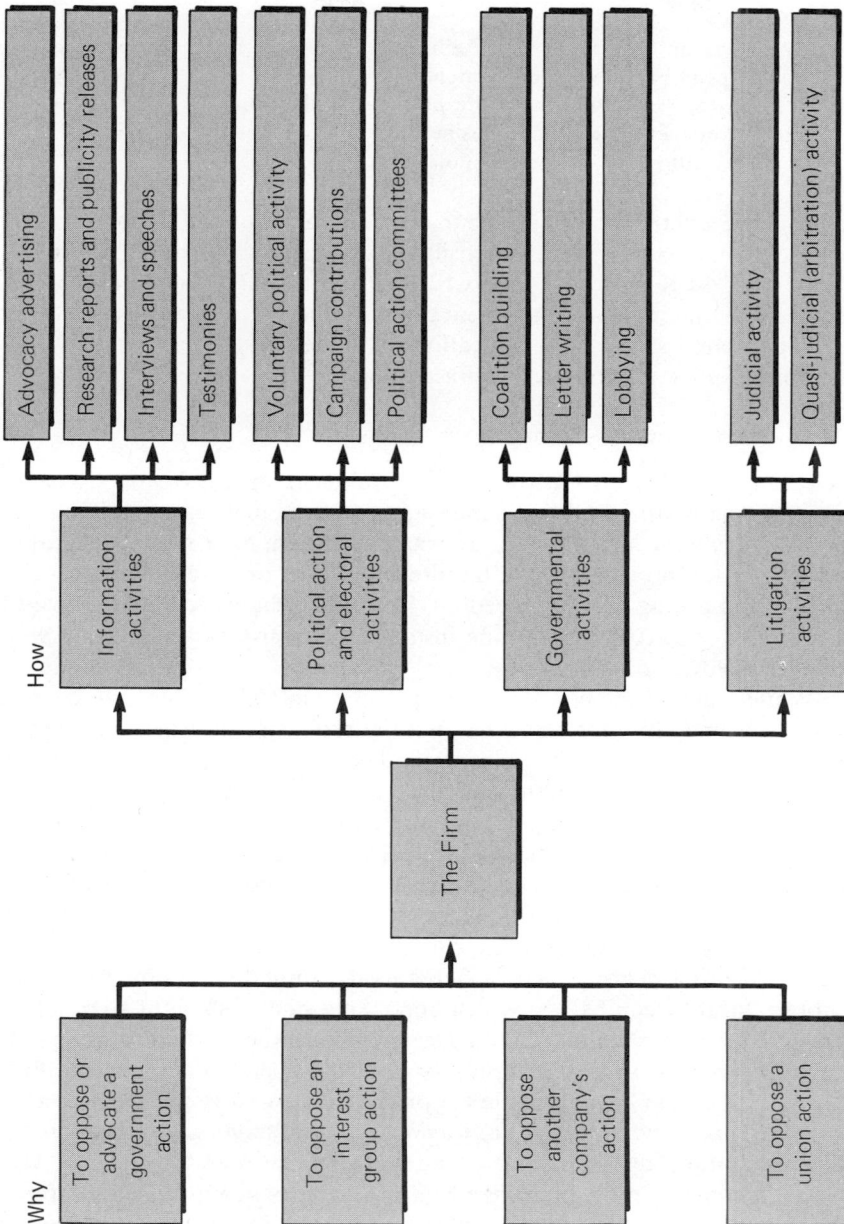

How

Information activities
- Advocacy advertising
- Research reports and publicity releases
- Interviews and speeches
- Testimonies

Political action and electoral activities
- Voluntary political activity
- Campaign contributions
- Political action committees

Governmental activities
- Coalition building
- Letter writing
- Lobbying

Litigation activities
- Judicial activity
- Quasi-judicial (arbitration) activity

The Firm

Why
- To oppose or advocate a government action
- To oppose an interest group action
- To oppose another company's action
- To oppose a union action

quently, eliminating an impact means increasing production costs and is, therefore, a competitive disadvantage unless everybody in the industry accepts the same rule. And industrywide acceptance can be achieved only by legislation and regulation. Drucker has written (1974:334–35; 337):

> Whenever an impact cannot be eliminated without an increase in costs, it becomes incumbent upon management to think ahead and work out the regulation which is most likely to solve the problem at the minimum cost and with the greatest benefit to public and business alike. And it is then management's job to work at getting the right regulation enacted.

Accordingly, whether to oppose or to advocate government action on an impact problem, business has a responsibility to become involved in the political process. And as Robert A. Leone writes (1977:65): "Rather than responding piecemeal to one regulatory problem after another, a company ought to have a sell-articulated strategy for allocating its limited resources to satisfy its responsibilities in ways consistent with corporate goals."

In Response to Interest Groups

For seven years Myron Cherry did everything he could to stop Consumers Power Company from building a nuclear generating plant in a small industrial town in Michigan. This Chicago attorney, representing a group of local citizens, fought the project through hundreds of hours of government regulatory hearings and a long court proceeding. He bullied, badgered, and outraged a small legion of adversaries; in one instance, he nearly came to blows with a Consumers Power official.

While Cherry was not able to stop the project altogether, the company president blamed him for helping to put the project eight years behind schedule and nearly five times above its original cost estimate. Thus, as Cherry was losing battle after battle, he was slowly winning the war.

Similar actions are being taken more and more these days by various interest groups. In relentlessly opposing certain corporate projects, such groups have focused public attention on various problems and dangers of business activities. More importantly, perhaps, they have learned to take advantage of the intricacies of government regulation—for one example, licensing procedures. Thus, a licensing hearing, once a bureaucratic formality, is now likely to resemble a "trial by combat" in which opponents vigorously fight a corporation at every turn (Emshwiller, 1978). Organizations such as the National Resources Defense Council, the Center for Law and Social Policy, and the Public Citizens Litigation Group provide the public-interest movement a legal arm to flex in the courts and administrative agencies. Legal advocacy is structured not only by organizational capabilities, but also by the *rules of standing*, which govern the rights of individuals like Myron Cherry or groups like the three just mentioned, to bring suit in court or participate in administrative proceedings.

Most importantly, courts have broadened the concept of "interest" to include noneconomic concerns; hence, the opponents have more angles from which to launch their courtroom attacks.

In Response to Economic Conflicts

In Chapter 5 we discussed the concepts of pluralism and countervailing power. That discussion should have made clear the fact that for economic reasons, a company might wish to oppose in the political arena an action of another company. The reasons can take several forms. The most common stems from the type of economic conflict that can occur between two companies in the same industry. For example, competing chains of grocery stores may attempt to differentiate themselves in terms of cleanliness, price, and convenience. Then one chain may decide to neutralize competition by launching a game; for example, it might offer customers disks to be used in a cash bingo game. Thus, it would not be surprising if competing chains pressed the Federal Trade Commission to investigate the legitimacy of the game-playing operation. The competitors might even back legislation prohibiting such practices.

Companies who are in different industries but who seek the same market can also have reason to turn to the political arena. For example, if a city held a referendum on whether subscription (pay) television would be legal, the local theater owners would probably campaign against it ("Subscription TV means the end of free television!"). Finally, another reason why a firm might enter the political arena results from the economic conflict that can arise between companies on different levels within a channel of distribution—for example, between a drug manufacturer and a drug wholesaler. The former might be pressing the state legislature for repeal of a law that prohibits the pharmacist from substituting another brand of the drug selected by the physician without first telling the physician. Since the same drugs vary greatly in price, depending on the brand, wholesalers might view such repeal as a threat to profit; hence, they would oppose repeal.

In Response to Union Actions

The scene is so familiar that it takes on the ritual of a Japanese tea ceremony. Union and management representatives march in front of television cameras on the opening day of negotiations for a new contract. The union people lay down a pile of "demands." The management people view these with alarm and mention a few "objectives" of their own. Nobody smiles. Then both sides disappear behind closed doors and reemerge in public a few days before the contract deadline. Usually they have an agreement, and everyone is smiling. So goes the process of collective bargaining—most of the time.

What happens when both sides fail to emerge smiling? It becomes largely a matter of politics for both labor and management. The *strike* is organized labor's most powerful weapon, and it is usually supplemented with picketing.

Another powerful weapon is the *boycott.* Union members and their sympathizers constitute an enormous bloc of purchasing power than can bring pressure on management. But management has its political arsenal, too. For example, it can go to court to obtain an *injunction*—that is, a court order directing someone to do something or refrain from doing it. Although seldom used, another method that the U.S. Supreme Court has upheld is the *lockout,* which prevents workers from entering a struck business. The lockout enables management to operate a plant on its own or shut it down. Of course, when labor and management are at an impasse and unable to reach an accord, a less dramatic means of resolving differences is available: A third party can be consulted to help settle differences before (or even after) a strike is in progress. The third party may be a *conciliator,* who merely brings labor and management together for a discussion of differences, or a *mediator,* who offers specific settlement suggestions but has no power to enforce them. The federal government maintains the Federal Mediation and Conciliation Service, and many states have a similar service. The mediators or conciliators are full-time, expert neutrals whose sole function is to assist in resolving labor-management disputes. An *arbitrator,* on the other hand, is a neutral third party who has the power to settle disputes. Both sides abide by the result, which is thus known as *binding.* If both parties agree to resort to arbitration, it is known as *voluntary* arbitration. If they are forced to arbitrate, usually by the government, it is known as *compulsory* arbitration. As we shall see later in this chapter, the trend toward arbitration in labor disputes—and indeed in a variety of other areas of management concern—has been quite remarkable in recent years.

Political conflict between labor and management involves more than collective bargaining. Unions help elect—and defeat—politicians. Labor representatives can be found in the lobbies of Congress and every state legislature. Presidents and governors rely on union leaders for advice and support. Interest groups of every sort—civil rights, environmental, and women's rights, to name a few—court the unions, too. In short, unions take an active role in politics. Accordingly, since labor and business do not always see eye to eye on many, though not all, major issues of public policy, business must be as active as organized labor in the political arena.

INFORMATION ACTIVITIES

Many of the challenges imposed on management by the macroenvironment are produced by public opinion—that is, the collective beliefs of many people on some societal issue, such as pollution or the workplace. To our definition only this need be added: Collective beliefs *matter*—that is, they can become guides to action and to public decision making, even though, as we noted in Chapter 2, there is often a time lag between the crystallization of public opinion and the enactment of laws to give it expression.

Thus, business can never really afford to ignore public opinion, and the dangers of doing so are becoming even greater. In the last decade, as we have seen throughout the preceding chapters, public opinion has taken on new force. Many more organized groups, devoted to promoting changes in business practice, exist. These groups, to the extent that they are effectively organized and led, can rapidly mobilize public opinion on issues that are not in the best interests of business by holding public meetings, boycotts, and pickets or by capturing media time. Clearly, then, participation in the political process means that business must play a more active role in the shaping of public opinion (see Exhibit 13–2).

As can be seen in Exhibit 13–1, there are a variety of ways in which business can conduct information activities that help sway public opinion: advocacy advertising, research reports and publicity releases, interviews and speeches, and hearing testimonies. In this section we take a closer look at the first of these—advocacy advertising—and at a topic closely related to all—the news media. We want to see where the news media stand in relation to business and how business managers can most effectively deal with the media.

Advocacy Advertising

In the early 1970s many businesses decided that public affairs and corporate image advertising would be stepped up. For example, IBM and IT&T began waging extensive campaigns to better explain themselves to the public. And, with the energy crunch, most oil companies began replacing product promotion with some sort of image advertising. A few firms even began to advocate, through advertising, issues of public policy. Today, many companies are aggressive practitioners of what S. Prakash Sethi (1977) calls "advocacy advertising." The leader among these firms is Mobil Corporation, which spends roughly one-quarter of its public relations budget on magazine and newspaper ads that argue for mass transit and a national energy policy, champion higher-quality TV fare, debunk congressional proposals to break up the oil companies, and debate vigorously in print with the media whenever the company disagrees with media's coverage of oil industry matters.

How well does advocacy advertising work? Yankelovich, Skelly, and White, Inc., conducted a survey for twenty-six corporate clients on the question of where public policy issues were headed. In the course of the poll, the firm examined the reactions of both the American public and its leaders to public issue ads. The pollsters referred specifically to Mobil's ads on energy deregulation and to the ads of the American Forest Institute on forest conservation.

The poll showed that the Mobil ads have, indeed, had a high visibility. Among administration, congressional, and other government leaders, for example, 90 percent had read them. "That would indicate that you get pretty good penetration with these ads," Vice President Grady Means, of Yankelo-

Exhibit 13–2   Speaking Out on Public Issues

William M. Agee, who became chairman and chief operating officer of Bendix Corporation after W. Michael Blumenthal was appointed secretary of the Treasury Department, made at least fifteen speeches in 1978 on topics ranging from social security and industrial innovation to the Bakke decision and pension funding. "Companies like ours are a public institution with several publics to account to, not just the shareholders. This requires a different type of informational approach. Part of my job is to be a public figure and to take positions on public issues, not just company activities."

Source: Quotation from *Business Week*, January 22, 1979. Photo courtesy of Bendix Corporation, Southfield, Michigan.

vich, concluded. On the other hand, though the ads were found useful by 33 percent of government leaders polled, 66 percent said that the ads were of little or no use to them in understanding energy deregulation issues and indicated that the ads did not influence their opinion on any policy matter. According to Means, many of those surveyed were irritated not so much by the content as the tone of the ads; they described the ads as "abrasive." Mobil executives, however, were pleased with the 33 percent favorable rating. And the charge of abrasiveness came as no surprise; the ads were intended to stimulate.

The News Media

Advocacy advertising may be viewed as a response to the alleged bias of the news media against business. It would be hard to conceive of an issue more central to a discussion of how business can influence public opinion than this allegation. In examining this issue, it is important to make a distinction between true antibusiness bias and a probing, cynical attitude. Similarly, there is the disturbing question to be kept in mind of whether the Western news media, by giving disproportionate attention to whatever issue is "in fashion," exercise a kind of de facto censorship.

To illustrate this issue, let us consider the example of the *Argo Merchant* affair. When the tanker ran aground in 1976 off the coast of Massachusetts and began to disgorge its cargo of oil, the media covered the event around the clock; called it "an ecological disaster to marine life," and predicted that the black muck would spread across the ocean floor and wipe out such bottom-dwelling species as lobsters, crabs, flounders, and scallops. So convincing were these predictions of disaster that a group of Cape Cod fishermen brought a $60 million suit against the owners and the captain of the *Argo Merchant* for destroying their livelihood. Although the oil spill was one of the most widely publicized events in American history, it cannot be characterized as having the most comprehensive coverage. For example, the Coast Guard kept trying to tell anyone who would listen, that the *Argo Merchant* carried no. 6 fuel oil, which is significantly lighter than seawater and that there was thus no way the oil could blanket the ocean floor. (Eventually, according to the Coast Guard, floating no. 6 fuel oil can coagulate into tar balls that will sink to the bottom, but these balls have hard outer surfaces and are inert and nontoxic.) Further, three months after the grounding of the *Argo Merchant,* after careful study, the government issued a report concluding that the spill had caused "minimal" biological and aesthetic damage. This finding was carried by United Press International (March 31, 1977), but it did not make headlines and certainly not network news—perhaps because such a conclusion was just not "in fashion."

Dealing with the Media. Consider the following situation: A company has a small explosion and fire. A door blows off and injures a worker, who is treated and released from the hospital. The company has no one on the scene trained in media relations. The anxious personnel manager talks to the home office and then faces a waiting television reporter who wants to know what happened. "It's none of your business," he tells the reporter. Because of that remark, the incident escalates from a one-newscast story; it appears a number of times on television, with a commentary by the reporter, who ends with the statement, "But it *is* my business." Of course, the reporter is right.

How might a manager trained to cope with such a situation have responded? His answer might have been: "We had an explosion in a small room.

A fire resulted from it. The door flew off and struck a workman on the arm. The workman, John Doe, was taken to a local hospital and released. We do not know the cause of the explosion. As soon as we do, you will be notified. I cannot answer any other questions at this time" (*Houston Post,* May 15, 1977).

The average business manager is usually not prepared either psychologically or professionally to deal with news reporters; nevertheless, today's managers do have to meet the news media. Accordingly, Chester Burger (1975) has offered a couple of general rules that managers can use in dealing with the news media—even in the face of hostility, criticism, and attack. First, managers must recognize that reporters are skilled in the art of asking provocative questions. Second, managers should never walk into a planned meeting with the news media planning to "wing it." They must learn to anticipate likely questions and attempt to research the facts before the meeting. Burger then goes on to offer the following specific suggestions:

1. Talk from the viewpoint of the public's interest, not the company's. As AFL-CIO President George Meany once said, "The trouble with you business guys is that you talk about 'capital formation.' What you should be talking about is 'job formation' . . ." (cited in Loeb, 1978b).
2. Speak in personal terms (rather than the hypothetical "we" or the impersonal "the company") whenever possible.
3. Do not make statements that can't be quoted. Experienced company spokespersons quickly learn that there is no such thing as "off the record."
4. State the most important fact at the beginning of every statement or response.
5. Do not become angry or argue with reporters. A company spokesperson cannot win an argument with a reporter in whose power the published version of the story lies.
6. Do not repeat undesirable or misleading words a reporter might use in a "loaded" question. The question will not be quoted, only the answer.
7. Provide a direct answer to a direct question.
8. Do not attempt to evade issues when the answer is really unknown or confidential. The best course of action is a straightforward answer: "I don't know, but I'll find out for you" or "I'm sorry, I can't give you that information."
9. Tell the truth even if it hurts. For example, in the early 1960s one large steelmaker, trying to make an unpopular price boost more palatable, expressed the amount of increase in pennies per pound rather than dollars per ton, the traditional pricing method. This action only served to antagonize reporters saddled with the tedious chore of converting the data back to dollars per ton.

In concluding this discussion of the importance of a manager's being able to deal with the media in order to carry out the company's information activities, we should note that many companies are establishing special training programs for key managers. For example, in an effort to better equip its managers for coping with an oil spill, the Gulf Oil Company sponsors a tense nine-hour seminar called "Bad Day at Bunker Point." Using a variety of audiovisual dramatizations and simulated confrontations, the seminar conveys vividly the public outcry that accompanies the grounding of a giant tanker. As oil continues to spurt out and the weather becomes worse, tourist interests, fishermen, reporters, environmentalists, local politicians, the Coast Guard, and the EPA all clamor for immediate answers. The audience of Gulf managers must deal with each of these groups and, at the same time, solve the technical problem of the spill. As in any real emergency, information dribbles in—incomplete and often erroneous. Spill-scene interviews with the news media are videotaped and later critiqued. Similarly, the technical decisions are criticized by a panel of experts in marine operations, insurance, law, and government. The lessons of the seminars are valuable to virtually any manager facing a crisis: Expect the possibility of a pungent confrontation from the local community. Plan carefully and rehearse regularly for emergencies. And, deal swiftly and frankly with the public.

POLITICAL ACTION AND ELECTORAL ACTIVITIES

In today's turbulent environment, it is becoming increasingly clear that business must not only establish more honest and forceful information activities, but must also become actively involved in politics. If ours is a political system of competing interests, then it is imperative that business develop strategies to protect its interests in the political arena. In this section we return to Exhibit 13–1 to take a brief look at how the business community can influence that most fundamental of our political institutions—elections. As in any discussion of electoral politics, we want to focus on two basic issues: the organization of people as a politicized constituency and the all-important aspect of financial contributions to political campaigns. We consider the strategies of encouraging voluntary political activity and organizing political action committees.

Voluntary Political Activity

One example of companies that have effectively encouraged their employees to become involved in politics is Budd Company, a diversified supplier to the transportation industry, located in Troy, Michigan. Ignatius (1976b) notes that in 1976 Budd introduced a "discretionary bonus" plan for about 30 percent of its high-level managers. Monetary incentives averaging several thousand dollars each are granted for eleven categories of activity, one of which is "involvement in government affairs." In grading performance in this category, the company reviews participation of personnel in local political campaigns, the number of letters written to congressional representatives and other government officials on issues affecting the company, and managers' ability to organize in-plant political education committees.

Individual employees can be encouraged to get involved in politics in numerous ways. The following are some of the more obvious methods of political involvement that can be suggested to employees:

—Work through a party organization (which is one of the best ways to get to know elected officials and thus build personal influence and credibility).

—Work through a political organization (which is a good way to help influence policymaking that deals with issues of interest to the company).

—Run for office in the local community, such as for school board, alderman/alderwoman, park board, legislature, county commissioner, coroner, judge, library board, board of taxation, and so on.

—Get appointed to a committee, board, commission, or advisory group.

—Attend public hearings.

In addition to the proven effectiveness of labor's political activities mentioned earlier, what makes the need for volunteer work by members of the business community particularly important is the tactics used by many of the public-interest groups that are challenging business. Exhibit 13–3 shows the tactics members of public-interest groups consider most effective. Another important tactic, the manipulation of various formulas to apportion delegate votes, involves electoral politics. These formulas, Lebedoff (1978) explains,

EXHIBIT 13–3　Political Activities Considered Most Effective by Members of Public-Interest Groups

	Very effective or effective (Percent)
Personal presentation	53
Testifying at congressional hearing	20
Litigation	29
Letter writing	47
Contact by influential member or constituent	34
Political demonstrations	8
Contributing money to candidates	6
Publishing voting records	18
Releasing research	30
Public relations activities	24

Source: From Jeffrey M. Berry, *Lobbying for the People: The Political Behavior of Public Interest Groups* (copyright © 1977 by Princeton University Press), Table VIII–1, p. 214. Reprinted by permission of Princeton University Press.

were originally meant to avoid the old practice of winner-take-all and to give each candidate his or her fair share of delegates. But, in the hands of the new interest groups, the formulas serve another purpose. Rules have been introduced that are so complicated and difficult that only students of politics can understand them; democracy is no longer comprehensible to the average person, and hundreds of thousands of people have been driven out of the political process by labyrinthine rules and tiresome procedures. Thus, if members of the business community are too concerned with day-to-day operations, then individuals who perhaps place less value on political integrity will mold tomorrow's macroenvironment for the business manager. Clearly, business must do more than encourage voluntary activity.

Campaign Contributions and Political Action Committees

The basic method by which businesses enter the political fray remains direct financial contributions. Although according to federal laws such contributions must be entirely personal, they do tend to increase the importance of individual companies and the entire business system when the contributions are pooled on a corporate or industrywide basis.* Many corporations and industries, therefore, have formed political action committees (PACs), which serve as vehicles for collecting and channeling funds to sympathetic candidates and favored causes. Examples of industrywide PACs include the Business-Industry Political Action Committee sponsored by the National Association of Manufacturers, the Banking Profession Political Action Committee (BANKPAC) sponsored by bankers, the Bread Political Action Committee (BREADPAC) sponsored by the American Bakers Association, and the American Medical Political Action Committee (AMPAC) set up by doctors and drug firms.

Between 1974 and 1975 the number of corporate PACs grew from 89 to 508 partially in response to new regulations established in 1975. In that year the Federal Election Committee, which was set up in the wake of the Watergate scandals, ruled that companies could pay the expenses of political action committees and decide on the recipients of the collected money. Companies are barred from giving corporate funds to candidates, but company-sponsored committees are allowed to contribute up to $5,000 to a federal candidate before a nominating convention and another $5,000 afterward. For companies that have more than one committee—Dow Chemical Company, for example, has seven—the permissible contribution is multiplied accordingly. A com-

---

* Executives are remarkably reluctant to contribute, however. Epstein (1972:61) found that in 1968 only about one out of five officers and directors of the very largest industrial firms, including government contractors, contributed to political parties. Since large manufacturing firms, particularly those strongly influenced by governmental decisions, have generally had higher rates of political contributions by their officials than other businesses, the 20 percent figure is probably a generous indicator of the financial participation of business executives as a whole.

pany's political clout is further enhanced because its political action committee may contribute unlimited amounts to other committees, such as those maintained by associations that serve the company's industry. In effect, the 1975 ruling by the Federal Election Commission signified the extension to business of the right long enjoyed by organized labor to solicit political funds and decide upon the recipients. At the same time, however, the ruling has set off a sometimes bitter debate on the wisdom of allowing an activity that could lead to coercion on the part of employers or that could weigh the contributory balance toward conservative candidates.

Differences in the Political Efforts of Business and Labor. In the 1976 elections labor contributed $17.5 million to candidates, while business contributed $12.6 million. The money on both sides was collected and spent by political action committees. Yet the difference between the political efforts of labor and business goes beyond the few extra millions of dollars that labor spends on direct contributions to candidates. In the first place, labor has been much more effective in determining the outcome of elections through nondirect contributions. For example, during the 1976 campaigns affiliated union groups were said to have fielded at least 600 full-time organizers, 10,000 telephone callers, 70 million pieces of literature, and thousands of volunteers. Their get-out-the-vote effort alone was estimated to cost over $2.5 million.

Another sharp contrast between the political activities of labor and business lies in the direction that contributions are channeled. Labor targets for contributions candidates who, once elected, can help labor in specific ways. Business, however, tends to spread its contributions around—that is, to touch all bases by helping friends as well as foes. An analysis of the 1976 elections by the Republican National Committee shows that the labor PACs gave almost all their money (97.5 percent) to Democrats, including a very large number who were challenging incumbent Republicans. In contrast, the business PACs gave less than one-fifth of their funds to business-oriented challengers trying to unseat liberal Democrats; instead, they gave most of their money to incumbent Democrats and Republicans or to Democratic and Republican candidates likely to win vacant seats. Clearly, business used much of its money to "buy" access to incumbents or expected winners, even if the candidates were not particularly probusiness, rather than taking a chance on trying to elect men and women who might be sympathetic to business but who had tougher battles to win. Often, business committees contributed equally to both the Democratic and Republican candidates in a race. In other words, they tried to "play it safe," no matter who won.

GOVERNMENTAL ACTIVITIES

Public policies are the decisions made by elected and appointed government officials, and as we have seen throughout this book, these decisions are of crucial concern to business. As Exhibit 13–1 points out, there are three major ways in which business can have an impact on government public policy decisions: coalition building, letter writing, and lobbying. In this section we briefly review the first two of these activities and then look at lobbying in detail.

Building Coalitions and Letter Writing

The saying that "congressmen first learn how to count and then to think" is a succinct statement of the rationale behind the closely related strategies of coalition building and letter writing that many businesses are beginning to employ to influence public policy. For example, for the first time in fourteen years, General Motors in 1975 solicited the support of its stockholders, dealers, and suppliers to secure a five-year postponement of tougher emissions and safety standards. In a mailing to this massive coalition, GM enclosed the names and addresses of senators and representatives from appropriate states. Similarly, in the fall of 1975 Marathon Oil Corporation mailed to its one million credit-card holders a series of leaflets designed to expand the ownership base of American business. As William S. Mitchell, president of Safeway Stores, observed in calling for the development of a business activist movement, "31 million communications from 31 million stockholders would cause a groundswell that could not be ignored" (*Nation's Business,* August 1975, p. 51). Thus, companies are looking to their shareholders as an important but heretofore neglected constituency. But stockholders do not constitute the only group through which companies can form coalitions. Toward the end of the 1970s, business began to recognize the benefits of alliances with other groups—such as the NAACP, the National Urban League, and some labor unions—in the political debate on a number of policy issues. The most elemental action that members of such coalitions and constituency groups can take to make their numbers and influence visible is writing to members of Congress. Representative Morris K. Udall has provided his constituents with some solid advice on how to go about expressing their views to their elected representatives (see Commentary section, "On Writing Congressional Representatives").

COMMENTARY: On Writing Congressional Representatives

Surprisingly few people ever write their Congressman. Perhaps 90 percent of our citizens live and die without ever taking pen in hand and expressing a single opinion to the man or woman who represents them in Congress—a person whose vote may decide what price they will pay for the acts of Government, either in dollars or in human lives.

This reluctance to communicate results from the typical and understandable feelings that Congressmen have no time or inclination to read their mail, that a letter probably will not be answered or answered satisfactorily, that one letter will not make any difference anyway. Based on my own 16 years' experience, and speaking for myself, I can state flatly that most of these notions are wrong. On several occasions a single, thoughtful, factually persuasive letter did change my mind or cause me to initiate a review of a previous judgment.

Some Fundamentals
Here are some suggestions that apply to all congressional mail:

- Address it properly: "Hon. _____ , House Office Building, Washington, D.C. 20515." Or "Senator _____ , Senate Office Building, Washington, D.C. 20510." This may seem fundamental, but I once received a letter addressed like this: "Mr. Morris K. Udall, U.S. Senator, Capitol Building Phoenix, Arizona. Dear Congressman Rhodes . . . ."
- Identify the bill or issue: About 20,000 bills are introduced in each Congress; it's important to be specific. If you write about a bill, try to give the bill number or describe it by popular title ("clean air," "minimum wage," etc.). The letter should be timely: Sometimes a bill is out of committee, or has passed the House, before a helpful letter arrives. Inform your Congressman while there is still time to take effective action.
- Concentrate on your own delegation: The representative of your district and the senators of your State cast your votes in the Congress and want to know your views.
- Be reasonably brief: Your opinions and arguments stand a better chance of being read if they are stated as concisely as the subject matter will permit.

Do's
- Write your own views—not someone else's: A personal letter is far better than a form letter or signature on a petition.
- Give your reasons for taking a stand: Statements like "Vote against H.R. 100; I'm bitterly opposed" don't help me much. But a letter which says "I'm a small hardware dealer, and H.R. 100 will put me out of business for the following reasons . . . " tells me a lot more.
- Be constructive: If a bill deals with a problem you admit exists, but you believe the bill is the wrong approach, tell what the right approach is. If you have expert knowledge, share it with your Congressman: Of all the letters pouring into a Congressman's office every morning, perhaps one in a hundred comes from a constituent who is a real expert in that subject. The opinions expressed in the others are important, and will be heeded, but this one is a real gold mine for the conscientious member.
- Say "well done" when it's deserved: Congressmen are human, too, and they appreciate an occasional "well done" from people who believe they have done the right thing.

Don'ts

- Don't make threats or promises: Congressmen usually want to do the popular thing, but this is not their only motivation; nearly all the Members I know want, most of all, to do what is best for the country. Occasionally a letter will conclude by saying, "If you vote for this monstrous bill, I'll do everything in my power to defeat you in the next election." A writer has the privilege of making such assertions, of course, but they rarely intimidate a conscientious Member, and they may generate an adverse reaction. He would rather know why you felt so strongly. The reasons may change his mind; the threat probably won't.

- Don't berate your Congressman: You can't hope to persuade him of your position by calling him names. If you disagree with him, give reasons for your disagreement. Try to keep the dialogue open.

- Don't pretend to wield vast political influence: Write your Congressman as an individual—not as a self-appointed spokesman for your neighborhood, community, or industry. Unsupported claims to political influence will only cast doubt upon the views you express.

- Do not demand a commitment before the facts are in. If you have written a personal letter and stated your reasons for a particular stand, you have a right to know my present thinking on the question. But writers who "demand to know how you will vote on H.R. 100" should bear certain legislative realities in mind: (1) On major bills there usually are two sides to be considered, and you may have heard only one; (2) The bill may be 100 pages long with 20 provisions in addition to the one you wrote about, and I may be forced to vote on the bill as a whole, weighing the good with the bad; (3) It makes little sense to adopt a firm and unyielding position before a single witness has been heard or study made of the bill in question; and (4) A bill rarely becomes law in the same form as introduced. It is possible that the bill you write me about you would oppose when it reached the floor.

Source: Excerpted from "The Right to Write," address by the Honorable Morris K. Udall of Arizona in the House of Representatives, Wednesday, November 2, 1977. *Congressional Record,* November 3, 1977, p. E6822.

Lobbying

Lobbying is the practice of trying to influence governmental decisions, particularly legislative votes, by agents who serve interest groups. The term originated in the 1830s, when representatives of interest groups wanting to influence legislative decisions tended to congregate in the lobbies of Congress and state legislatures. As a means by which interest groups and individuals can tell government decisionmakers how much they care about particular political decisions, lobbying is a legitimate and valuable element in the governmental process. Indeed, the right to "petition the Government for a redress of grievances" is a part of the First Amendment. Because of the unsavory connotation the term has acquired, there is a tendency to forget the useful and legitimate nature of lobbying, and many attempts have been made to regulate the practice of lobbying on both state and national levels. The basic federal law is the Regulation of Lobbying Act of 1946, which requires registration of, and regular financial reports from, all individuals and agents seeking to influence legislation.

As the pressures on business have increased, business has poured money and resources into lobbying on an unprecedented scale. In 1968 Washington had more than five hundred lobbyists. Virtually every major corporation employs a lobbying firm, if not a full-time representative. Not without reason, Walter Guzzardi, Jr. (1978b:54) has called lobbying "the country's great growth industry." While no one knows the current number of lobbyists in Washington, one recent directory suggests about five thousand.

Understanding the Committee System of Congress. Congress is an intricate, complex institution. Both the House and the Senate have their own set of leaders. Each body also has its own set of formal rules and procedures. Exhibit 13–4 shows in broadest outline how a bill winds its way through this byzantine institution to emerge as a law.

As intricate and complex as the congressional structure is, a few generalizations are possible; they are also relevant to state legislatures and, with certain exceptions, to city councils. Because Congress is a highly decentralized institution in which power is widely dispersed, decision making generally involves coordination among autonomous units. Members tend to accept the work and expertise of other members on various committees; in return, they expect little interference in their own work. This fragmentation of political power and relative autonomy are of decisive importance to lobbyists. Under such conditions, it is seldom necessary to influence all 535 members of Congress; it suffices to win the battle in committee, or even subcommittee, and then all is clear sailing.

Exhibit 13–5 lists the standing congressional committees with which business managers should be familiar. At any given time, it is quite unlikely that only one committee would be of interest to business. To understand this point, let us consider the example of managers in the garment-manufacturing business. Since the price of cloth will certainly affect business, managers must be interested in the Agriculture Committee, which considers cotton subsidies and wool imports. Since transportation costs affect the business, they also must be interested in the Interstate and Foreign Commerce Committee. Since labor legislation affects the business, managers must be interested in the activities of still another committee. And since labeling packaging, and copyrights also affect the garment industry, the managers might as well become familiar with the total committee system.

In deciding which senators and representatives within congressional committees to approach on legislative matters, business managers, like professional lobbyists, need to keep in mind the tendency of committee members to develop close personal identifications with particular issues. Most members of Congress attempt to stake out certain issues as "their" issues; this is the way political careers are made. Lobbyists, recognizing this phenomenon, must thus

EXHIBIT 13–4   How a Bill Becomes Law

Most bills begin as similar proposals in both houses...

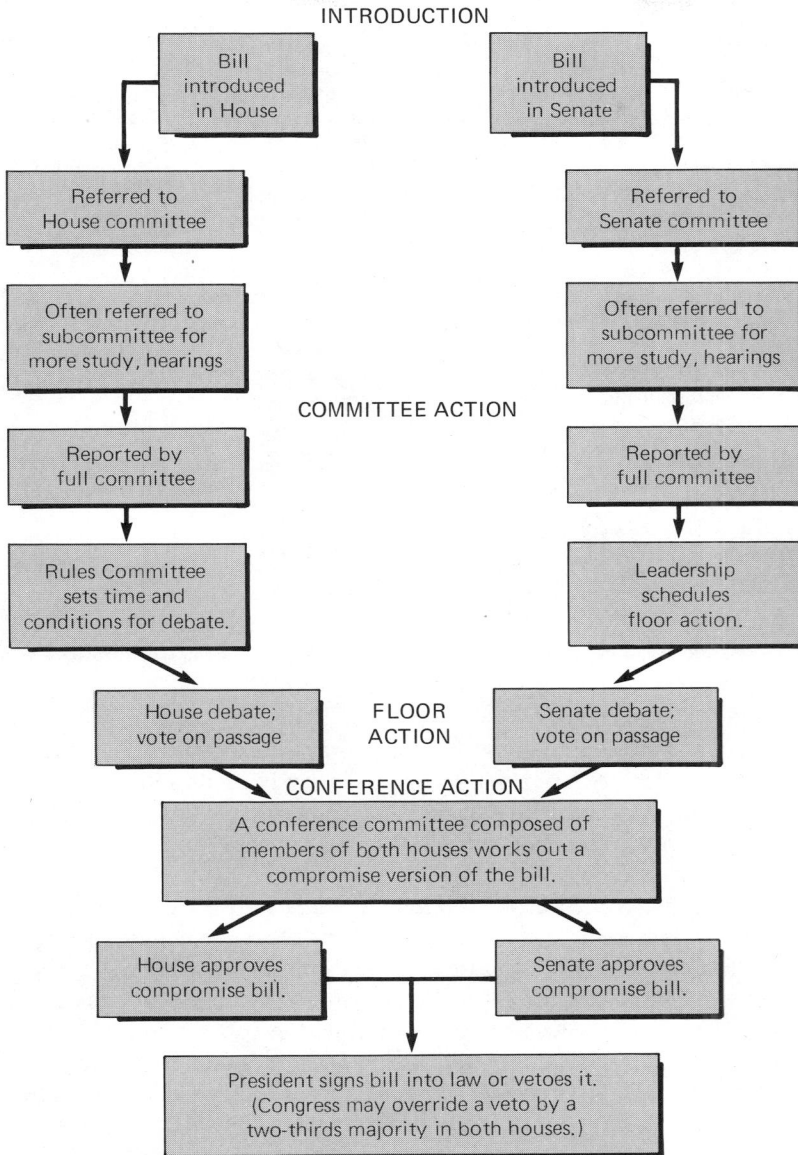

INTRODUCTION

| Bill introduced in House | | Bill introduced in Senate |

| Referred to House committee | | Referred to Senate committee |

| Often referred to subcommittee for more study, hearings | | Often referred to subcommittee for more study, hearings |

COMMITTEE ACTION

| Reported by full committee | | Reported by full committee |

| Rules Committee sets time and conditions for debate. | | Leadership schedules floor action. |

| House debate; vote on passage | FLOOR ACTION | Senate debate; vote on passage |

CONFERENCE ACTION

A conference committee composed of members of both houses works out a compromise version of the bill.

| House approves compromise bill. | | Senate approves compromise bill. |

President signs bill into law or vetoes it. (Congress may override a veto by a two-thirds majority in both houses.)

Source: Leonard Freedman, *Power and Politics in America,* 3rd ed. (No. Scituate, Mass: Duxbury Press, 1978), p. 244. Copyright by Wadsworth Publishing Company, Inc. Reprinted by permission.

EXHIBIT 13–5   Standing Committees of Congress

House committees	Senate committees
Agriculture	Agriculture, Nutrition, and Forestry
Appropriations	Appropriations
Armed Services	Armed Services
Banking, Finance, and Urban Affairs	Banking, Housing, and Urban Affairs
Budget	Budget
District of Columbia	Commerce, Science, and Transportation
Education and Labor	Energy and Natural Resources
Government Operations	Environment and Public Works
House Administration	Finance
Interior and Insular Affairs	Foreign Relations
International Relations	Governmental Affairs
Interstate and Foreign Commerce	Human Resources
Judiciary	Judiciary
Merchant Marine and Fisheries	Rules and Administration
Post Office and Civil Service	Veterans' Affairs
Public Works and Transportation	
Rules	
Science and Technology	
Small Business	
Standards of Official Conduct	
Veterans' Affairs	
Ways and Means	

seek out committee members with whom they share areas of interest. One committee member, for example, may be especially identified with the pharmaceutical field; another, with safeguarding the rights of small business; while a third may have expert knowledge on nuclear energy.

The Theory of the Iron Triangle. Political scientists are fond of describing the operations of congressional committees in terms of *iron triangles* or *subsystems politics.* These terms refer to a pattern of relationships that involve some committees or subcommittees, an agency or two, and the interest groups concerned with the policy area in question. For example, the subsystem focused on the management of public grazing lands in the western states is composed of the House and Senate Interior committees and appropriations subcommittees, the Bureau of Land Management, and groups representing western ranches. Such subsystems develop because everyone cannot possibly be interested in every area of public policy. Thus, the business manager who is keenly interested in policy affecting the garment industry may have little or no interest in public land policies and consequently will leave them to others who, in turn, largely ignore policy related to the garment industry.

One distinguished political scientist has argued that the formulation of public policy comes to be a kind of closed game, played by interest-group spokespersons, members of the House and Senate committees, and officials of administrative departments, which takes something of the "form that it would take if there were not elections or no concern about the nature of public opinion; that is, those immediately concerned make themselves heard in the process of decision" (Key, 1961:526–27). But this view of policymaking can be overemphasized. For example, for forty years a subsystem involving the House Agriculture Committee, the Sugar Division of the Department of Agriculture, and representatives of the sugar industry was primarily responsible for the formation of policy on sugar prices. But in 1974 the authorizing legislation for sugar price supports came up for renewal in a time of sharp inflation. Consumer groups and industrial users, concerned about high prices, opposed the renewal of the legislation and caused its defeat. Thus, a qualification of the iron triangle theory is in order: When new legislation or the renewal of existing legislation is needed, approval from the larger political system is needed. Often that approval will be forthcoming (as it was for decades in the case of sugar), since, as we said, Congress tends to delegate authority to the experts in any given area. In many cases, however, some sort of disruptive event may expand interest in an area and produce (a) defeat for a subsystem or (b) control of the subsystem by the larger political system.

Decision Points in Policymaking. Another aspect of the congressional structure that is of interest to business managers and lobbyists is that it is serial—that is, it involves a number of different approvals. Because many things can happen to a bill along the way, proposed legislation must be constantly watched. Also, because the decision-making process is serial, opportunities for delay abound (see Exhibit 13–6). Taking advantage of these opportunities may be useful when lobbyists oppose a bill. For example, the Consumer Protection Agency Bill has more than once been thwarted by business lobbyists.

Congressional Staffs. Congressional office staffs can be very helpful both to lobbyists trying to influence some legislative outcome and to managers seeking specific help on a particular problem a firm might face. The help provided by congressional staffs is referred to as *casework*. Staff caseworkers generally have up-to-the-minute knowledge of activities within the federal bureaucracy; they can tell a manager where to get help and whom to see, as well as how to get maximum effect from his or her efforts.

While staff size, organization, and operations vary widely from office to office, a typical House member will have a staff of about five; a senator will have a dozen or more. House office staffs, tend, therefore, to be made up of generalists. Accordingly, managers and lobbyists need not be too concerned

EXHIBIT 13–6   Points at which Delay or Defeat of a Bill May Occur in the House

Delay	Defeat
Committee inaction in referring to a subcommittee	Committee inaction
Subcommittee inaction (prolonged hearings; refusal to report)	Negative vote in committee
	Subcommittee inaction
Committee inaction (prolonged hearings; refusal to report)	Negative vote in subcommittee
	Rules Committee inaction
Rules Committee inaction (refusal to schedule hearings; prolonged hearings; refusal to report)	Negative vote in Rules Committee
	Defeat of rule on the floor
Slowness in scheduling the bill	Motion to strike enacting clause
Floor action (demanding full requirements of the rules)	Motion to recommit
	Final passage
Reading of the journal	
Repeated quorum calls	
Refusing unanimous consent to dispense with further proceedings under the call of the roll	
Prolonging debate	
Various points of order	

Source: From Lewis A. Froman, Jr., *The Congressional Process: Strategies Rules, and Procedures.* Copyright © by Little, Brown and Company (Inc.). Reprinted by permission.

with whom he or she deals. But senators, with their larger staffs, give individuals more specialized responsibilities. Typically, heading a senator's staff is the administrative assistant, a kind of alter ego for the senator who decides whether a problem or case should go directly to the senator and who will see that it does, if necessary. In addition to an administrative assistant, a senator has legislative assistants. These staff members, who are almost always lawyers with considerable government experience, keep the senator informed on legislative matters affecting the senator's committee assignments and on the status of bills in which the senator has an interest.

Also playing a pivotal role in the formation of public policy are the staffs of each committee. Although members of Congress must eventually make the final decisions, committee staffs help write legislation, perform studies on the effect of proposed legislation, and feed legislators questions to ask during congressional hearings.

State House Lobbying. For at least three good reasons, it is folly for a company to assume that lobbying in Washington alone suffices. First, the scope of government at the state and local levels has expanded in recent years even more rapidly than at the national level. Local government expansion has been encouraged by the national government's policy of *revenue sharing*—that is, the massive redistribution of tax dollars to the states with few, if any, strings attached. Second, activities at the state level have tended to follow the pattern of the national level; accordingly, state legislatures are moving in a variety of areas of concern to business. For example, in addition to traditional concern with taxes and labor, state legislatures are now deeply involved in job safety, environmental control, land use, and consumer protection. Third, the old tradition of personal relations between business and state legislatures is changing as a new breed of legislators begins to appear. Many of these legislators entered politics at the height of the consumer and environmental movements. Their support of an issue will be won, not by banquets and small favors, but only by sound research and professional expertise. The problems of the state-level lobbyist for business are compounded by the fact that many of the new legislators have little business experience; consequently, their empathy for the problems of business is somewhat less than that of earlier generations of legislators.

Given these three factors, many companies are expanding their state government lobbying efforts. The aim of such efforts is essentially the same as in Washington: to keep informed about upcoming policy that may affect business operations and to attempt to shape policy by presenting the company's position. In addition to contributing to the development of a legislative program, the well-prepared state lobbyist, with established access to the state bureaus is able to offer advice on appointments to advisory commissions; to exercise influence over the use (or threat) of a veto on a given piece of legislation;* and by developing rapport and respect, to contribute to a favorable political/business climate.

Lobbying in the Bureaucratic Maze. In lobbying the executive branch, whether in Washington or in state capitals, lobbyists must deal with elected and appointed officials (e.g., the governor, the White House staff, or department and bureau heads and their assistants). Within the departments of the executive branch are increasing numbers of professional career administrators whose everyday actions can have a significant effect on business. The goal of lobbying at this level is to foster an understanding of the day-to-day problems of a particular industry. "Iron triangles" to the contrary, lobbying the professional career administrator (or regulatory commissioner or board member) is in many cases the most challenging aspect of the lobbyist's job. One business executive expressed the problem succinctly: "Regulators in general are far tougher [than legislators] to lobby because they rarely have an elective constituency on whose good will they are dependent" (Public Affairs Council, 1973:14).

---

* Forty-three states give the governor an item veto on appropriation bills; revenue sharing and
  bloc grant programs from Washington give added discretionary authority to the governor.

The structure of the typical federal department is a pyramid. At the top is a secretary, appointed by the president with the advice and consent of the Senate. Under the secretary is a deputy secretary or undersecretary and, often, additional undersecretaries for especially important functions that fall within the department. In addition, each department has three or more assistant secretaries with specific areas of responsibility, some in substantive fields and others in such areas as administration, which involves budgeting, personnel, internal management, and so on. Specific operational responsibility in a department usually falls to a bureau or office headed by a chief or a director, who may or may not be a presidential appointee.

By and large, it is more effective to deal at the lowest possible level in the executive branch. If a manager has a problem involving hog bristles, the best approach is try to go, not to the president, but to the person most concerned with hog bristles in the Department of Agriculture. If, however, a manager does not know the right person to see, he or she can write directly to the appropriate cabinet officer. The department's correspondence-control operation will automatically route the manager's letter to the person most concerned. In many cases, the federal department or agency with which a company is concerned has field offices located in designated federal regions across the country (see Exhibit 13–7). It is less tedious, less expensive, and possibly more effective to initiate an inquiry through a local field office. A manager can usually visit or talk directly with the key person in the office. In some cases, the field person will come to the company office to visit. Thus, the company can have an expert in the utilization of government services working to get the answers to its questions. In the event a problem is not within the scope of the field office, a manager might need to go to the seat of responsibility—most often in Washington.

In sum, because many government policies can have a sizable effect on company profits, the business manager who neglects the lobbying function is every bit as irresponsible as one who ignores the company's capital structure or level of employee motivation. For example, the need for effective lobbying by the chemical industry was immediately apparent when in implementing the Toxic Substances Control Act of 1976, the EPA drafted a proposal outlining the procedures manufacturers should follow in reporting chemicals they had produced or processed during the past three years. One problem was the EPA's definition of small business; it was so restrictive that few chemical manufacturers were exempt from the complex rules and extensive reporting requirements. Therefore, many small businesses would suffer undue hardship. Also, because the EPA feared that an inadequate definition of intermediate chemicals (byproducts or intermediate states of a chemical as it progresses toward final form) might exclude some substances from the notification requirement, it defined as intermediate any chemical that "could be isolated." But, though a large number of intermediates can be isolated in a chemical reaction, only a few actually are isolated. Thus, the original EPA definition could have led to a flood of costly and useless information. Clearly, the way in which is-

**EXHIBIT 13–7 Standard Federal Regions, Including Sites of
Government Field Offices**

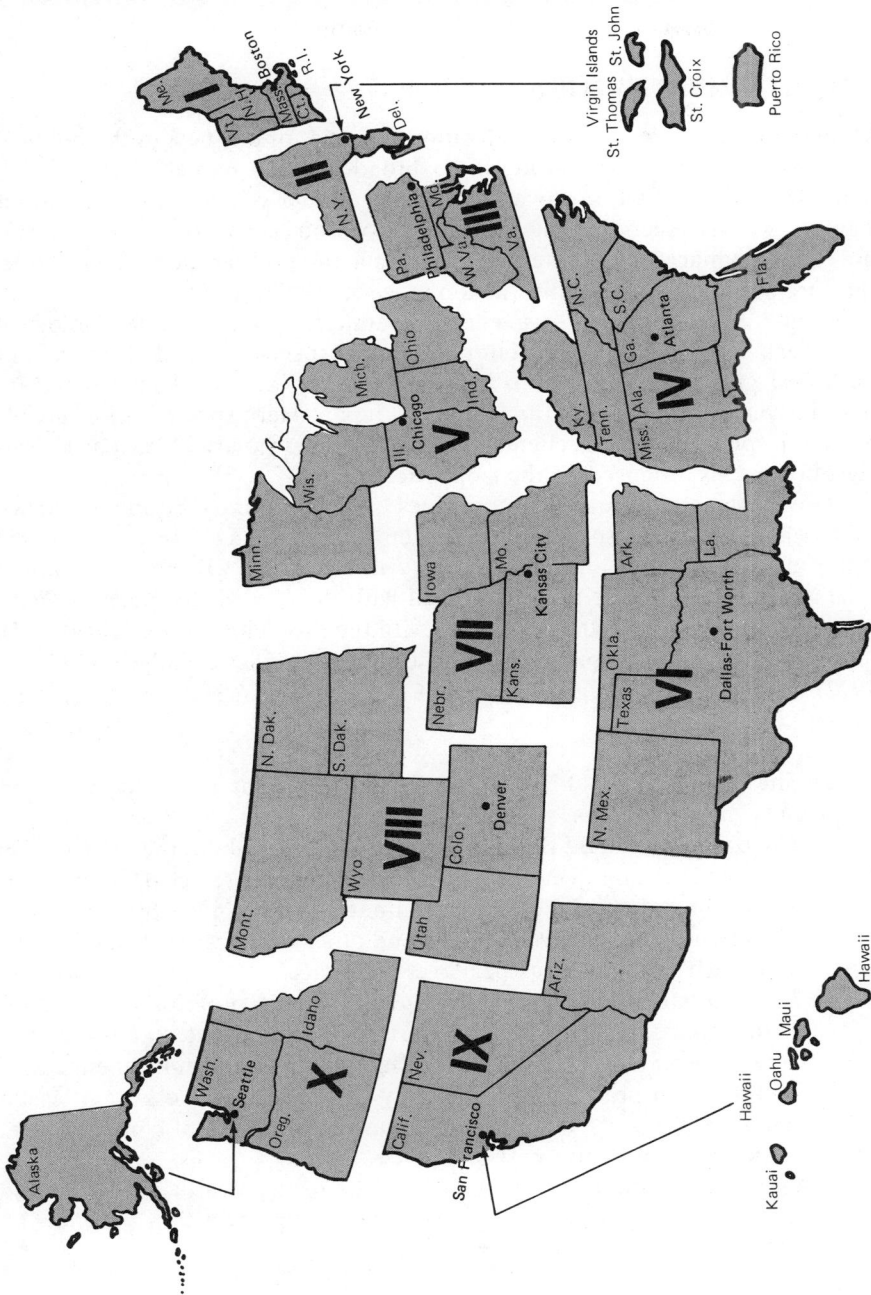

sues such as these are resolved can have a profound effect on the competitiveness of a firm. For this reason, more and more firms are expanding their activities that can influence public policy.

LITIGATION ACTIVITIES

While the focus of this section is litigation activities of business in the political arena, we shall begin by considering a broader issue—namely, how general managers can cope with an ever-increasing number of specialists. In earlier chapters, we have seen that one of the most obvious consequences of the rapidly changing macroenvironment of business is the proliferation of specialists. They are ubiquitous: affirmative action officers, regulatory affairs analysts, international relations specialists, energy planners, economists, technological forecasters, safety officers, air pollution control specialists, and so forth. But the fastest growing of all groups of specialists are lawyers. Today there are more lawyers in Ohio alone than in all of Japan. Here specialization breeds ever more specialization, as clients demand lawyers who are at least as knowledgeable and experienced as their opponents.

One of the great unrecognized ironies of contemporary business practice is that when it comes to specialists, managers do not manage. Accordingly, one of the major tasks of management theory in the 1980s will be to formulate some systematic guidance on how to deal with the specialist problem in general (see Commentary section, "Dealing with the Problems of Specialization"). For the more specific problems of specialized legal services, Nader and Green (1977) have proposed six guidelines that can help businesses deal effectively with outside law firms:

1. The company should speak to several law firms before deciding on one; in other words, shop around.
2. The company should not be shy when inquiring about the rates. While it is true that final fees and expenses cannot be predicted exactly, it is worth remembering that if cost estimates can be made by contractors on billion-dollar projects, lawyers and other consultants should be able to at least estimate costs per level of service.
3. The company should regularly inquire about progress and ask for status reports. It should not let quarterly bills with statements like "For Services Rendered . . . $20,000" go unexplained and unchallenged.
4. To the extent practical, the company should give its work to at least a couple of firms. That way the company has a basis of comparison to judge the quality and cost of services.
6. Companies should convey to the consultants the idea that "they should spend the company's money as if it were their own firm's money."

COMMENTARY: Dealing with the Problems
of Specialization

Let us consider the case of a general manager in the restaurant industry. What kinds of specialized knowledge would he or she need to be effective? The list is much longer than one would at first think. Our manager would need to know about real-estate leases for restaurant purposes; about regulation of health, food, and liquor at the federal, state, and local levels of government; about any applicable sales taxes and the income taxation of people much of whose income comes in tips; about innovations in the food preparation technology; about unemployment and compensation insurance in the restaurant trade; about how downturns in the economy will affect expansion; about liability insurance to protect people who find crawling things in their tossed salad; about the growth pattern of the city; about labor relations with the unions of the waiters, chefs, and dishwashers; about the collection of delinquent charge accounts; about the warranties given by food suppliers; and about the bankruptcy and reorganization of restaurants. Next, to begin dealing with the problems created by the need for specialized knowledge in these areas, our hypothetical restauranteur might want to reflect on the following questions (suggested by Gruber and Niles, 1976:103): "In what areas of knowledge are you your own source of specialized information? How do you keep current in these areas? In what areas of needed specialization does the company have an in-house capability? Is it weak or strong? How effectively is your specialized knowledge used?"

A couple of things should emerge from this line of analysis. First, the manager will begin to see gaps in his or her specialized knowledge. This recognition raises, in turn, the question of whether it is better to establish an in-house source or to hire an outside firm. In deciding, our general manager will have to make tradeoffs among cost (in-house is usually cheaper), quality (outsiders are usually better), and objectivity (outsiders are probably less biased in their advice). Going through the exercise of developing the list and asking the series of questions can have another payoff. It helps clarify the considerable problems of communication that can result when general managers meet specialists. Can the former adequately explain to the latter what exactly is needed? Does the latter understand the limits of their knowledge when advising, in what is perhaps (for the specialist) a new industry? Does the specialist tell the general manager *everything* he or she needs to know or just what they ask for? Does the specialist reveal the relative accuracy of the advice or information (such as, "95 percent confident," "give or take a hundred," and "I don't know"). In short, as Gruber and Niles (1976:103) ask, "Is there a real dialogue between user and the specialists?"

Coping with "The Litigious Society"

At the heart of the legal specialization problem is the fact that besides struggling before regulatory agencies, companies today find themselves frequently engaged in courtroom warfare with other companies, with representatives of interest groups, as well as with consumers and stockholders. More and more individuals are realizing how easy it is to file a suit—to the extent that the growing spirit of contentiousness is earning America the title "the litigious society." In 1977 the total bill for all legal services to corporations was $24 billion (*Wall Street Journal,* April 13, 1978), a good part of which was spent on lawsuits. In many cases the costs of lawsuits are driven up to the benefit of lawyers (in excess of what the number of suits filed would indicate) by the flagrant use of delaying tactics (see Commentary section, "The Delaying Game").

COMMENTARY: The Delaying Game

Corporate lawyers have become masters at using special procedures and strategies to slow down a case. With huge assets at stake, corporations are willing to pay the resulting high legal fees. Their ultimate aim: to get the plaintiff to settle for much less or drop the suit altogether. Among the delaying procedures are discovery, inundation, and counterattack. First, the "discovery process" helps a lawyer find out what evidence an opponent has, which in theory means requesting documents, taking out-of-court testimony, and submitting written questions (called "interrogatories") that contribute to a quicker trial since lawyers are able to narrow the dispute beforehand. In practice, however, lawyers demand too much and respond with too little, and the haggling often brings cases to a standstill. Second, once the material has been turned over, lawyers often switch to a strategy of inundation—that is, producing tons of documents. As one SEC attorney puts it, "Business lawyers will paper a little guy to death"—more literally, they delay the case proportionate to the amount of documents they introduce. Finally, corporate lawyers are delaying cases by counterattacking. For example, a regulatory agency might be charged with misconduct in bringing a lawsuit. This strategy has the advantage of broadening the scope of the case and hence protracting it.

Corporate clients are no longer watching helplessly as the costs of legal services rise. In addition to taking the kinds of cost-conscious actions recommended by Nader and Green, companies are beginning to "think settlement."

Managers are coming to realize that an out-of-court agreement can be an *opportunity* as well as a big moneysaver. For example, Ryan (1978) reports that in 1977 Congoleum Corporation and Universal Leaf Tobacco Company were battling in court over Universal's opposition to an acquisition bid from Congoleum. Then the combatants agreed to bury the hatchet. Congoleum gave up and was reimbursed by Universal for some of its costs. The companies said they acted because "the proceedings in the courts are uncertain of resolution and will not be resolved for an extended period of time and will involve extensive expenses to both parties." The settlement freed Congoleum executives from filing time-consuming depositions, and the company was able to proceed with its successful acquisition of Curtis Noll Corporation of Cleveland shortly after the settlement.

When businesses cannot agree on their own, they may still avoid litigation through the process of arbitration. The American Arbitration Association, started in 1926 by a group of New York business leaders looking for a way of settling disputes in textiles, commodities, and securities without going through the courts, has twenty-four regional offices and a list of fifty thousand individuals available for arbitration panels. The A.A.A. supplies arbitrators without cost for one or two days, and for $200 to $300 a day thereafter. Often, the case is settled in the first two days; rarely does a case take as long as thirty days. The decisions are usually final, without appeal, and there is a fine if one side delays the proceedings. Besides being relatively fast and cheap, arbitration has two other important advantages. First, unlike ordinary lawyers or judges, arbitrators understand the issues. Generally, business people (e.g., bankers, accountants, architects, engineers, and lawyers) do the arbitrating. A second advantage of arbitration is its confidentiality. For example, dissolution of a partnership can be achieved without the inner workings of the firm becoming public property, as would happen in a court proceeding.

In 1977 the number of commercial cases handled by the association rose to 4,550 from 4,093 the year before and from only 1,499 a decade earlier. One recent case arbitrated by the A.A.A. involved a $360 million coal-supply contract. The A.A.A. is also the arbitrator for the construction industry, where it handled disputes involving $134 million in claims in 1977, and for textile and clothing groups, where the association handed down $13 million in settlements in the same year.

Today millions of contracts, insurance policies, and other types of agreements include arbitration clauses. Arbitration of labor grievances has become so routine that, for all practical purposes, they are outside the formal legal system. This increased use of arbitration procedures thus means that specialists in general and lawyers in particular are no longer worth whatever they cost. In the next decade, effective managers will treat them as just another operating expense. Specialists may not become less important, but business's use of specialists will be more subject to rational analysis.

POLITICS IS EVERY MANAGER'S CONCERN

It would be wrong to conclude this chapter without noting that participation in the political process is not for chief executive officers alone to worry about. Few companies that are effective in the external relations function ignore the political potential that lies within the employee ranks. There is, in fact, a definite trend toward more involvement of managers at the plant and regional levels in politics and government, especially when state and local issues are concerned. In the words of one external relations officer: "We have to recognize that the name of the game is grass-roots involvement. A plant manager acquainted with his legislator, or assisting in his campaign, or writing him a personal letter on a particular issue—these things may count more than whatever I can do. After all, he's a constituent" (Public Affairs Council, 1973:19). Some companies have systematized what has been called a "man-to-man defense," whereby executives and managers are assigned to cultivate personal relationships with designated legislators or administrators. Other companies conduct periodic inventories of middle management to discover "who knows who" in state government. A large number of companies occasionally request that managers, on a voluntary basis, communicate the company position on a pending issue to elected officials or administrators.

Although most experienced external relations officers recognize the importance of grass-roots involvement, there are problems. According to the Public Affairs Council (1973:20), more than one company has been embarrassed by a manager's letter that overstated a problem, threatened a legislator, or was otherwise impolitic. If managers are to play an effective role in the company's external relations program, they will benefit from some help with the subtleties of politics and government, some form of communication and information to keep them up to date and motivated, and some overall assistance and guidance from the company's external relations department. The fact is that the vast majority of managers find themselves poorly equipped to handle political activities.

Suppose a company lost $700 million or suffered an eight-year delay in completing a project. If the reason was lack of skill in a particular functional area—that is, if management was behind the times in marketing techniques or careless in its financial analysis—the board of directors and top management would not simply shrug their shoulders and say, "That's the way it goes." Yet this is almost exactly what happens in thousands of companies when any gross failure of management performance occurs in the area of external relations. But the days of this kind of toleration are numbered. In the turbulent macro-environment of business, to paraphrase Reginald H. Jones, "there is no room for Neanderthals."

THE MACROENVIRONMENT OF U.S. BUSINESS (Chapters 2–4)

Technological
- Effects of technological change
- Process of technological innovation

Economic
- New views of inflation, unemployment, and growth
- Relationship of energy, environment, and economics

Social
- Demographic trends
- Changing social structures
- Changing values
- The "New Class" and adversary culture
- Life cycle of social issues

Political–legal
- Public policies affecting business
- The interest-group state
- Policy administration
- Courts

International
- Changing role of multinationals
- Five worlds of development and the new "Economic Order"
- Technology transfer
- Changes in world trade
- Cultural differences
- Host and home country relations

IMPLICATIONS OF MACROENVIRONMENTAL CHANGE (Chapter 5)
- Government regulation
- Corporate power

STRATEGY FORMULATION (Chapter 6)
- Premises of strategic planning
- Goals and objectives
- The place of social responsibility and ethics

FORECASTING TOOLS (Chapter 7)
- Decision support systems
- Technology forecasting
- Economic models
- Sociopolitical forecasting

STRATEGY IMPLEMENTATION (Chapter 8)
- Programs, projects, products
- Opportunities, costs, benefits

NEW MANAGEMENT OPPORTUNITIES (Chapters 9-13)
- Production
- Research and development
- Finance
- Marketing
- Human resources
- External relations

ALTERNATIVES FOR BUSINESS-SOCIETY RELATIONS (Epilogue)
- Restructuring or market enhancement

EPILOGUE

In the Preface, I noted four central concepts that provide the bedrock for the study of business and society: the macroenvironment of business, strategic planning and forecasting, the management of social impacts, and scenarios of the future. By the end of Chapter 13, we had examined the first three concepts in some detail but had said very little about the fourth. The purpose of this Epilogue is to remedy this deficiency by answering the question: Where does the American business system go from here?

A good place to begin to look for answers to that question is on the continuum of economies that appeared in the first chapter (see Exhibit 1–4). The important parts of that continuum, along with three alternative futures for the United States, are reproduced below:

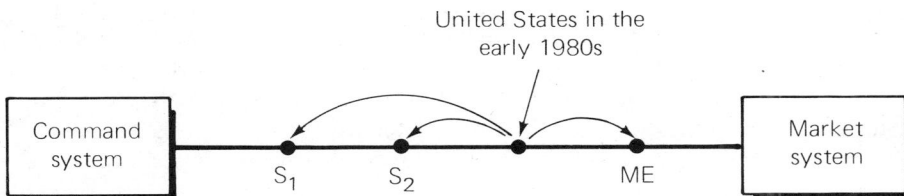

Points S_1 and S_2 represent two different versions of socialism for the United States. Since defining socialism is a little like trying to nail jelly to the wall, we had better take a moment to examine what is meant here by socialism and how the S_1 and S_2 versions differ.

Every economy must have some arrangement for producing goods and services and for distributing those goods and services. To the degree that a society places the task of production in public (rather than private) hands, the economy tends to be socialistic. Likewise, to the degree that it places the task of distribution in some central body (rather than the market), the economy also tends to be socialistic. Because we are talking about degrees, the brands of socialism that can exist are mathematically infinite. Let us, therefore, agree to consider only the two generalized points on the continuum. The first, S_1, we shall call "pure socialism." In such systems, private ownership of the means of production has been virtually eliminated and distribution of goods and services has been virtually taken over by some central agency (more than likely, the state bureaucracy). The second point, S_2, we shall call "modified socialism." In such a system, we see a selective takeover by government of certain industries, the establishment of various public agencies to compete directly with private enterprise (e.g., a National Energy Corporation to serve as a "yardstick" to assess the performance of major oil companies), an ever-increasing involvement by government officials in internal operations of private companies, and an attempt to make both employers and employees less subject to free market forces. The main features of the third point on the continuum, market enhancement (ME), are easily summarized: less regulation of business, a limit on the size of government, and a greater effort by government to achieve national goals through (rather than outside) the market system.

Warning. Much to the consternation of business executives, the Federal Trade Commission has grown quite fond of posting large labels on packages telling the consumer what to expect inside the cellophane. The approach recommends itself here. Accordingly, I want to warn the reader that this Epilogue contains material that is speculative and value laden. Clearly, we can never *know* the future in the sense that we can know the chemical formula for rayon or the date for ratification of the U.S. Constitution. Consequently, what follows is speculation.

   Still, there are different kinds of speculation. Some speculation is the "blue-skies" variety, which seldom proves correct. The speculation we shall be engaged in, however, is best described as scenario writing based on clearly established trends. All that means is that we shall be looking at three internally consistent pictures of the future of business-society relations in the United States that are based on trends as visible as the front page of the local newspaper. Pure socialism in the United States? Listen to what some of America's best known economists and foremost labor leaders are saying.* Modified socialism in the United States? Listen to what some leading members of Congress—not to mention presidential aspirants—are saying.* Market enhancement in the United States? Look at the recent turnabouts in the French and British economies, the deregulation of the airline and other industries in the United States, the tax revolt in California, and the market-oriented approaches to pollution control by the EPA.†

   Since this Epilogue is concerned not only with the probability of the three scenarios but also with their desirability, what follows also involves questions

---

* Although, to be sure, they do not use the word "socialism" when giving their solutions to current economic problems. What we really hear is a kind of "pidgin" socialism, but the substance of what they say ought not to be ignored—namely, more public ownership and less reliance on market forces.

† A recent example of such "market-oriented" approaches might be helpful. The EPA, whose regulations cost business $15.4 billion in 1978, announced in January 1979 the "bubble" concept, which encourages factory owners themselves to devise the least expensive way to meet a standard for their plants' total emissions. In the past, the EPA simply ordered the owners to install expensive pollution control devices for each specific pollutant.

of value. Let me be quite clear on this point. Every economic system, every mix between a command and market system, represents either conscious or unconscious choices with respect to certain tradeoffs. How much inequality is acceptable in order to obtain greater economic efficiency? How much individual liberty is acceptable to secure more social welfare? What are the real needs and purposes of human life? These are economic questions, yes; but they are also profoundly value-laden questions—for that reason, I have chosen to treat them here rather than in the preceding thirteen chapters of text.

Joan Robinson (1970:122) the distinguished British economist, has wisely written: "Every human being has ideological, moral, and political views. To pretend to have none and to be *purely objective* must necessarily be either self-deception or a device to deceive others. A candid writer will make his preconceptions clear and allow the reader to discount these if he does not accept them." Therefore, let me state clearly and concisely my preference. When I look at the possible futures for the U.S. economy, I must confess that I would take my chances with the ME scenario rather than S_1 or S_2.

One final introductory remark: The long survival of the American business system, in my opinion, will be determined not in the marketplace, not in the courts, not in political elections, but in the arena of ideas. Yet it is here that business managers are singularly ill-equipped to do battle. A major neglect in business school curricula in general, and in business and society courses in particular, is in coming to grips with this fundamental truth: Ideas *do* matter. Ideas shape the pictures in our heads and these, in turn, influence our actions. Business managers should stop allowing their critics to consider this arena of ideas uncontested terrain. ☐

Alternative Futures for American Business

SCENARIO NUMBER ONE: PURE SOCIALISM

What It Might Look Like. In the classical vision of socialism, such as presented in the early writings of socialist thinkers, the workers (or proletariat) become the ruling class.* One of their first acts is "to centralize all instruments

---

* As the Industrial Revolution spread, countless critics and socialist theories emerged. For example, Saint Simon, Fourier, Cabet, Blanqui, and Robert Owen attacked capitalism and proposed various ways of achieving socialism: state ownership, national workshops, communes, and revolution. These critics and theories deeply influenced Karl Marx, the great synthesizer of socialist thought.

of production in the hands of the state" and to increase productive forces at a rapid rate. Once the middle class (or the bourgeoisie) had been defeated, there would be no more class divisions, since the means of production would not be owned by any group. The coercive state, formerly a weapon of class oppression, would be replaced by a rational structure of economic and social cooperation and integration. Such bourgeois institutions as the family and religion, which had served to perpetuate bourgeois dominance, would vanish, and each individual would find true fulfillment. Thus social and economic utopia would be achieved, although its exact form could not be predicted.

While the classical vision of socialism is sketchy, it is at least a single, coherent vision. The same cannot be said for the views of socialist thinkers today. While the modern view retains all the sketchiness of the older vision, modern socialist thinkers show little agreement on what the socialist future would be like. What follows is a not untypical formulation by Paul Baran (1968:xvii): "A society can be developed in which the individual would be formed, influenced, and educated . . . by a system of rationally-planned production for use by a universe of human relations determined by and oriented toward solidarity, cooperation, and freedom." The optimal use of resources in such a planned economy would ". . . represent a considered judgment of a socialist community guided by reason and science." Others have commented simply that production should be directed toward the "true" needs of the individual and not toward the wants expressed in the marketplace. Still others advocate "participatory socialism"—for example:

> Most fundamentally, socialism means democratic, decentralized, and participatory control for the individual: It means having a say in the decisions that affect one's life. Such a participatory form of socialism certainly requires equal access for all to material and cultural resources, which in turn requires the abolition of private ownership of capital and the redistribution of wealth. But it also calls for socialist men and women to eliminate alienating, destructive forms of production, consumption, education, and social relations. Participatory socialism requires the elimination of bureaucracies and all hierarchical forms and their replacement, not by new state or party bureaucracies, but by a self-governing and self-managing people with directly chosen representatives subject to recall and replacement. Participatory socialism entails a sense of egalitarian cooperation, of solidarity of people with one another, but at the same time it respects individual and group differences and guarantees individual rights. It affords to all individuals the freedom to exercise human rights and civil liberties that are not mere abstractions but have concrete, day-to-day meaning. [Lindbeck, 1971]

For a more nuts-and-bolts picture of what socialism might be like in the United States, the Socialist Labor party's explanation (see Exhibit E–1) might be more satisfying than the preceding statement.

The New Philosophers' Critique. Since Marx and other nineteenth-century socialist theorists wrote, the world has seen at least eighty regimes come and go

EXHIBIT E–1   The Socialist Labor Party's View

The SLP's Goal – A Socialist America

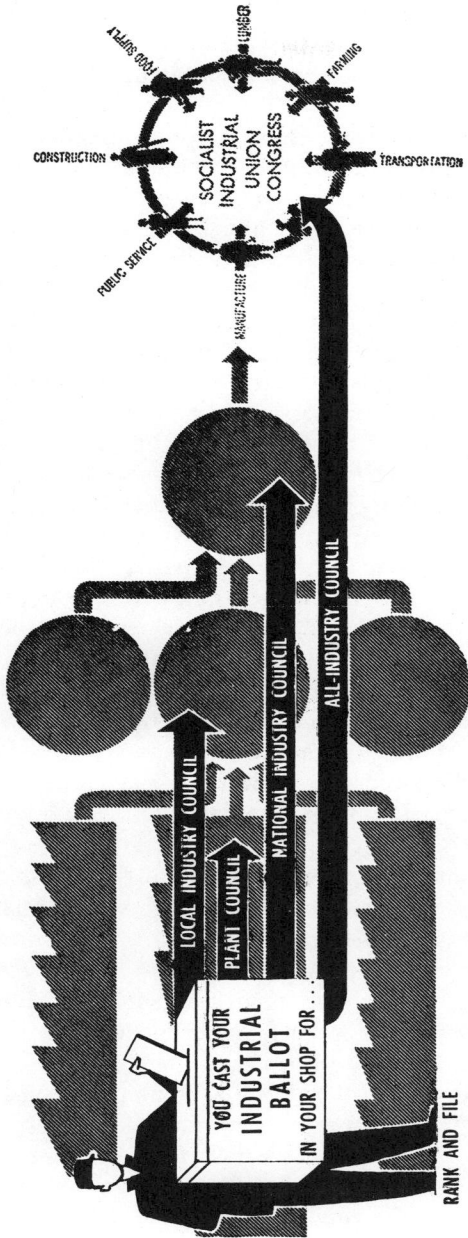

Socialism is the collective ownership by all the people of the factories, mills, mines, railroads, land and all other instruments of production. Socialism means production to satisfy human needs, not as under capitalism, for sale and profit. Socialism means direct control and management of the industries and social services by the workers through a democratic government based on their nationwide economic organization.

Under socialism, all authority will originate from the workers, integrally united in socialist industrial unions. In each workplace, the rank and file will elect whatever committees and representatives are needed to facilitate production. Within each shop or office division of a plant, the rank and file will participate directly in formulating and implementing all plans necessary for efficient operations.

Besides electing all necessary shop officers, the workers will also elect representatives to a local and national council of their industry or service—and to a central congress representing all the industries and services. This all-industrial congress will plan and coordinate production in all areas of the economy.

All persons elected to any post in the socialist government, from the lowest to the highest level, will be directly accountable to the rank and file. They will be subject to removal at any time that a majority of those who elected them decide it is necessary.

Such a system would make possible the fullest democracy and freedom. It would be a society based on the most primary freedom—economic freedom.

calling themselves socialists. As Michael Novak writes (1978): "Socialism has quit the ethereal world of books and theory, and assumed the weight of historical embodiment. In discussing socialism today, we are no longer talking merely about hopeful visions, but about actual experiments, whose successes and failures may be observed. Socialism has been incarnated." And, he adds, its "flesh sags upon its bones."

Perhaps no group of observers has been more vigorous or trenchant in its analysis of how far short of the dream the reality of twentieth-century socialism has fallen than a group of young French writers. This group, composed of many former radicals, began to be heard in the mid-1970s, shortly after the works of Alexander Solzhenitsyn began to appear in the West. What were they saying? Their first message was that socialism is a grossly inefficient system. Their second message, however, was their primary one: Socialism is inherently destructive of individual liberties. Let us consider both points.

Inefficiency under socialism.   Socialist writing says very little about the capacity of capitalism to produce goods and services in abundance. The omission is not happenstance. As Marx and Engels conceded in the *Communist Manifesto,* capitalism ". . . has created more massive and more colossal production forces than have all the preceding generations together." Further, they continue: "Capitalism has accomplished wonders far surpassing Egyptian pyramids, Roman aqueducts, and Gothic cathedrals . . . " And, we might add, despite predictions to the contrary, capitalist economies have experienced long-term increases in both overall production and average per capita income. Between 1925 and 1975, the standard of living roughly doubled and, in some countries tripled—despite two depressions, a world war, and loss of colonies.

Modern economic history tells us that wherever countries of comparable resources have run the production race together, the economy with a significant private sector has clearly done more in fulfilling the aspirations of its people than its socialist counterpart. Compare Austria to Czechoslovakia, West Germany to East Germany, Greece or Spain to Bulgaria, South Korea to North Korea. Apparently less comparable would be Japan and India; after all, Japan, which was devastated in a world war, must import most raw material, like iron ore, while India has considerable raw materials, including iron ore. Yet, in the year of India's independence (1947), the socialist-leaning country produced 1.2 million tons of steel, slightly more than Japan. In 1973, however, Japan poured 119 million tons of steel—more than seventeen times India's production.

Comparison of the United States and the USSR is, in many respects, even more astonishing. As Revel (1977:150), a French journalist loosely associated with the New Philosophers, has pointed out, the whole policy of détente with the West, which Brezhnev has promoted since 1970, has as its main objective what amounts to contracting out to the capitalist world the development of what is perhaps the planet's greatest reservoir of energy and raw materials. (And the same is true for the People's Republic of China.)

Nevertheless, one fact remains: In the past, the growth rates of some communist countries (especially the USSR) have been comparatively strong. But for the most part, this high growth has been achieved not through high levels of technological proficiency (as in the West) but through a rapid shift of labor from agriculture to industry and an extraordinary mobilization of capital through forced savings. For the USSR, the problem now is that these methods have been played out. Lindblom writes (1977:297):

> No further great shift of manpower or mobilization of capital is possible. Leadership is also concerned because the productivity of capital and labor in the Soviet and European communist systems has been declining. Technological advance does not offset diminishing returns from investment, as it does in other industrialized systems. Growth of man-hour labor productivity, once higher in the Soviet Union than in any of the most industrialized market-oriented systems, has (since 1958) fallen behind, as Kosygin lamented at the 1966 Party Congress. The European communist systems have identified the same problem.

Why the relatively poor performance of socialist economies vis-à-vis market economies? The answers lie at the very heart of socialist theory. First, in socialist countries, the prices of goods and services are set arbitrarily with little regard to the relative scarcity or true costs of inputs or to the unsatisfied demand for particular outputs. Second, the system provides too little reward to those who take the risks inherent in innovations that are designed either to save scarce resources or to give consumers what they want. Even if prices are made more rational, the reformers have found that the incentive to entrepreneurship—that is, the taking of business risks—fails to work without the creation of independent profit centers.

Nor does worker self-management, such as is found in Yugoslavia and advocated by some American socialists, offer a solution to the problem of inefficiency. Obviously, there is the possibility of managerial incompetence, when workers choose indulgent rather than competent managers. And, in some cases, electoral politics within the enterprise permit a director to use his or her position to build up a following. Loyalty to the party may generally count for more than managerial skill. Another problem is that the employee's short time horizon may turn out to be more troublesome than managerial incompetence. "Any worker or other group managing an enterprise can deprive the enterprise of growth capital by making excessive wage payments or other distributions in the form of dividends or bonuses. In the same way, it can diminish its working capital. Excessive distributions do appear in fact to pose a frequent, though not disabling, problem in Yugoslavia, for the Yugoslav formula grants the employee no share either to hold or to sell on leaving the firm. All he can take from the enterprise, he must take while he is an employee" (Lindblom, 1977:336). Moreover, based on the positions taken in the past by unions in this country—issues such as plant location, discrimination, technological innovation, and pollution—it seems unworldly to suppose that once control of an enterprise was in their hands that the public interest would suddenly be served any more nobly.

Repression of individual liberties.   Now let us consider the second thrust in the New Philosophers' critique of socialism—that socialism is inherently destructive of individual liberties. Bernard-Henri Levy (quoted in Safire, 1977) recounts how he and some friends were sitting in a Paris bar planning to take out an ad that said, "The Soviet Union is not truly a socialist country." But Levy said "No, we should take an ad that says—'The Soviet Union *is* a socialist country. The brutality is not on the way to the system, the brutality is a part of the system'." Clearly, what Levy and the other "new philosophers" were saying is that the empirical evidence is too overwhelming to ignore any longer: Socialism carries in its genes repressive tendencies. The question of why there is this tendency toward repression can be answered at several levels.

First, a latent threat of coercion undoubtedly exists when the state owns certain kinds of industries. The one that comes most readily to mind is the media—radio, television, publishing, and cinema. These industries, if state controlled, could quite easily be used to "educate" citizens into "proper behavior" and "right thinking." Alternatively, they could be used to deny a public voice to those with views inconsistent with state bureaucrats. While these actions are not inevitable, the temptation to take them can prove irresistible. A striking example of this repression of opinion—from the land that brought us the Magna Carta—is the experience of Winston Churchill. "From 1933 to the outbreak of World War II, he was not permitted to talk over British radio, which, of course, is a government monopoly administered by the British Broadcasting Corporation. Here was a leading citizen of his country, a man who was desperately trying by every device possible to persuade his countrymen to take steps to ward off the menace of Hitler's Germany. He was not permitted to talk over the radio to the British people because the BBC was a government monopoly and his position was too 'controversial' " (Friedman, 1963:19). More recently, a Labor Party commission recommended that radio, television, and newspapers be entirely nationalized to take them out of the hands of "special interests."

A second, less obvious explanation of why a socialist government tends to repress certain actions flows from such a government's efforts to achieve a "just" distribution of income. For example, I would bet that the Rolling Stones in one night can earn more money than Mozart did in a lifetime. Thousands of people cheerfully spend their wages to hear the Rolling Stones play; consequently, after giving performances for a year, the group members wind up with millions of dollars more than the rest of the people. We can carry this example a step further by assuming that some of the people in a socialist economy decide to forego Rolling Stones performances and records for several years, and with the money they manage to save, they decide to produce a new kind of baby toy. The item sells well and more people drop out of the socialist economy to help produce this highly sought after novelty item. Is this likely to lead to an unjust situation? The point illustrated by both parts of this example is that a socialist government would probably need to forbid people to use the resources that they labored for and earned in a socialized industry in a manner that they choose. A "just" distribution requires continuous interference in people's lives. Robert Nozick (1975:164) puts the dilemma neatly: "The socialist society would have to forbid capitalist acts between consenting adults."

A third and final source of repression of individual liberties in socialism is, paradoxically, its commitments to virtue and its belief in the perfectibility of humankind. The view, which runs like a steel thread through most socialist writing, is this: Once economic conditions have been restructured, the dawn of a new age for human beings can commence. But the rub is this: Under such conditions, it is difficult for government to tolerate dissent. While capitalist societies regard disagreements over public policies as mere choices among expedients, *morally committed* socialist societies do not: Choices become matters of good versus evil, and aberrant belief becomes tantamount to dangerous moral subversion. The reason for this fundamental difference between a capitalist society and a socialist one is that life in the former begins with a secular, rather than sacred, view of political actions. Politics in capitalist countries, as Robert L. Heilbroner (1978a:47) points out, is "dedicated to pragmaticism rather than principle, to expediency and compromise rather than to moral absolutism. It therefore regards political or intellectual dissent as a nuisance, perhaps even a danger to be combated, *but not as an apostasy.*" In contrast to capitalism, Heilbroner continues: "To the extent that socialism means a morally committed and spiritually dedicated society, it is likely to view as impieties the actions or beliefs that a less religious society would accept as mere disagreements."

In sum, we have arrived at what is perhaps the most important distinction that can be made among political systems; those that recognize that government is of secondary significance and those that do not. "Render unto Caesar what is Caesar's—not because every Caesar deserves it," Solzhenitsyn (1976a:24–25) writes, "but because Caesar's concern is not the most important thing in our lives."

SCENARIO NUMBER TWO: MODIFIED SOCIALISM

What It Might Look Like. Most Americans recognize fairly well the limitations of socialism in its pure form, but what about socialism in the subtler shade of gray such as we spoke about in the introduction to this Epilogue? In a political democracy, the pressures to move towards position S_2 can be quite strong. As we saw in Chapter 5, under certain conditions markets do indeed fail. Today, more than ever, when that happens, few voters expect government to "do nothing." Faced with mounting inflation, instituting wage and price controls is a popular course of action. Faced with mounting government deficits, raising corporate income taxes is an easy solution. Dissatisfied with the performance of an industry, letting the government run it—or, at least, more tightly control it—is a quick answer. This type of modified socialism works two ways, for in addition to satisfying the concerned public, it can also mean protection for faltering companies and industries. Often acting in concert with their unions, enterprises are able to get their special interests taken care of at the expense of the public. Who in Wyoming, for example, is going to cry very loud if he or she must pay a few extra cents for clothes because the lobbies of the New England textile industry make cheaper imports hard to come by? Who in New England is going to lobby Congress if he or she must pay a little more for tomatoes because the Southern California farm workers successfully thwart mechanization?

The common denominator in all of the above examples is that government tries more and more to be "responsive" to demands from the polity and, as a consequence, relies less and less on market forces. For every blemish in society, there is a governmental remedy. This mindset is not thoroughgoing socialism and hardly requires that politicians be steeped in socialist theory, but then it is hardly capitalism either.

The Chicago School's Critique. To develop a clearer understanding of just what can happen when government intervenes in the market, an obvious place to begin is with the views of those economists who are the strongest advocates of the free market. In a sense, this group really represents two separate but similar schools*—the Austrian School and the Chicago School—but, for our purposes, it is inappropriate to consider them together. We are interested in the Chicago School, which summarily disposes of much of the faith in the efficacy of government action that forms the theoretical underpinnings of the S_2 position.

First, government bureaucracy defies control by elected public officials better than even the largest, most obdurate private company. For example, estimates by OSHA officials put the total costs of federal worker sickness and injury at $5 billion in 1977. These estimates indicate not only a broad lack of compliance with the provisions of the Occupational Health and Safety Act by federal agencies, but also a pattern of resistance to OSHA's efforts to see that the rules are followed. Clearly, the constraints that inhibit the control of one government agency by another are much less in evidence in dealing with private business, universities, and hospitals. As Wilson and Rachal (1977:9) put it: "A federal agency can terminate a contract with or deny grant money to a firm, though it cannot affect the budget of another agency. A private organiza-

---

* After all, two of the leading figures of the Austrian school, Ludwig von Mises and Friedrick A. Hayek, taught at various times at the University of Chicago. In 1974 Hayek won the Nobel Prize in economics and in 1976 Milton Friedman, who has been the most influential member of the Chicago school for the past generation, duplicated the effort.

tion can be sued or enjoined in court by a government agency; it is rare in the extreme for one agency to sue another. A GS-13 government official must be taken seriously by a corporate president earning ten times his salary; a GS-15 official will ordinarily ignore a lowly GS-13." In addition, the three levels of government (federal, state, and local) in themselves inhibit control, and I doubt that any top administrator in EEO or EPA would deny that it is easier to get the compliance of Dow Chemical than Baton Rouge.

Second, government bureaucracy defies the biological concept of death.* Government bureaucracies, like the Federal Energy Administration, defy death through public relations gimmicks that help maintain their visibility and perceived need. The other route to bureaucratic immortality is by cultivating the support of special interest groups. Of the two methods to achieve immortality, the second is the greater.

Third, government bureaucracy vitiates the ideal of socially responsible business. "To be accountable for performance," Peter Drucker (1974) has written, "economic institutions and their managers have to have autonomy. One cannot be accountable for what one has no authority over and cannot control." In many ways, regulations emanating from Washington are creating a subtle bureaucratization of industry. Managers take fewer initiatives; they think like bureaucrats. One executive has likened running a pension fund today under the 1974 ERISA law to driving an automobile with the Labor Department's foot on the gas pedal, the Treasury's hand on the emergency brake, and so forth. To carry that metaphor forward, if the executive's car hits a pedestrian, who is liable? In such an atmosphere, social responsibility perishes.

Fourth, government bureaucracy stifles innovation in society. Anyone who has dealt with the U.S. Postal Service within the last five years might be inclined to say, "So, what else is new?" If the Chicago School tells us that government bureaucracies tend to resist innovation, they are making no revelations. But the general capacity of government at the highest policy-making levels to develop creative responses to societal problems is even lower than many might expect. In fact, in an investigation of major domestic legislation that became law during the period 1949–1972, I was able to find only forty-two instances of truly inventive public policies.* The really decisive point for our purpose, however, is not government's incapacity to innovate, but its chilling effect on innovation in industry. The long-term costs to the United States of retarded innovation due to uncontrolled inflation, insufficient investment credits, and excessive regulations are, I think, immeasurable.

Fifth, government bureaucracy, when intervening to correct market failures, may generate unanticipated side effects. A number of examples of un-

---

* I know of only two federal programs that have even been flatly abolished: The U.S. government no longer makes rum in the Virgin Islands and no longer breeds horses for the cavalry.

* Of course, the key to this line of research depends on how one defines and then operationalizes the concept "inventive." For details on the author's research, see Starling (1979:211–22).

foreseen consequences of government action were cited in Chapter 5. To repeat just one: Since profits allowed utilities are typically calculated on the
basis of return of capital, the industry responds by inefficient substitution of
capital for labor. Of course, as we saw in Chapter 8, it is not always possible
for private firms to recognize all possible consequences of their actions, but
something else is operating when we turn to the case of government bureaucracies. The likelihood of unforeseen externalities is increased by the buildup of
strong political pressures for action before there has been adequate knowledge
or adequate time to consider potential side effects.

Sixth, government bureaucracy, by placing new authority in the hands of
some to be exercised over others, may generate distributional inequities. We
have already noted how the market tends to generate distributional inequalities of wealth and income. But bureaucracies tend to generate inequalities of
power. Wolf writes (1979:129):

> Public policy measures place authority in the hands of some to be exercised over
> others. Whether the authority is exercised by the social worker, the welfare case
> administrator, the tariff commissioner, the utilities regulator, the securities ex-
> aminer, or the bank investigator, power is intentionally and inescapably lodged
> with some and denied to others.
>
> The power may be exercised with scruples, compassion, and competence. It
> may be subject to checks and balances, depending on the law, on administrative
> procedures, on the information media, and on other political and social institu-
> tions. Nevertheless, such redistribution of power provides opportunities for in-
> equity and abuse.

Examples of the opportunity for abuse abound: government contracts obtained through bribery; granting import licenses and preferential exchange
rates to relatives, friends, and associates of politicians; and so forth.

To make the foregoing criticisms of modified socialism more concrete, we
might consider how government bureaucracy has coped with one problem—
energy shortages. The Carter administration's *National Energy Plan* (April
1977), which in a modified form became the law of the land in October 1978,
had this to say: "National policy toward oil and gas has been erratic, complex,
and ineffective. Continuing uncertainties, particularly as to price, have retarded both production and conservation investment." In order to understand
this assessment, let us begin with a historical review (based largely on McDonald, 1978, and Melloan and Melloan, 1978). The logical starting point is the
Supreme Court's *Phillips* decision of 1954, which gave the Federal Power
Commission control over natural gas prices at the wellhead. As predicted at
the time by many economists, government imposition of rigid, artificially low
prices for natural gas—unrelated to the law of supply and demand in a competitive market and not reflecting the rising prices of all other goods and services—discouraged domestic exploration for new sources of gas and oil. Domes-

tic production held up well for a few years after government price fixing began—and consumer prices actually declined in relationship to the costs of other goods and services—because the industry was producing from pools discovered, proven, and developed years before. In the 1960s, however, oil companies found it increasingly attractive to seek crude oil abroad. Production costs in places like Saudi Arabia, Kuwait, and Libya were only pennies a barrel. The international oil companies soon were awash in cheap crude oil, and they rapidly expanded refining and marketing operations abroad to make use of it. They also managed to get U.S. import quotas raised (quotas were finally removed altogether in the early 1970s). Thus, exploratory drilling in the United States declined sharply during the 1960s. By the end of the decade, U.S. surplus productive capacity had dropped to the point where control of the world price of crude oil had moved abroad, to the members of the Organization of Petroleum Exporting Countries (OPEC).

At the same time that the OPEC cartel was gaining strength, Congress and the president were embarking on legislative programs that seemed designed to curtail domestic production of oil and gas while increasing consumption:

—The Tax Reform Act of 1969, which reduced by 5.5 percent the industry's oil-depletion allowance, cost the oil industry an estimated $700 million a year, which was immediately reflected in a drastic reduction in domestic exploration.

—The National Environmental Policy Act of 1969 was immediately seized upon by environmentalist groups as a legal weapon to stop the building of nuclear power plants, to prevent oil exploration and drilling on the outer continental shelf, to curtail oil production in offshore fields already explored and tapped, to prohibit the leasing of oil shale lands, and to reduce the production of coal. (Perhaps the most significant result of all the environmentalist moves was the six-year delay in construction of the Alaska pipeline.)

—The Federal Coal Mine Health and Safety Act of 1969 imposed upon mine operators compliance costs of more than a billion dollars and drastically reduced the already low worker productivity in the mines.

—The Clean Air Act of 1970 forced electric utilities to convert from coal to cleaner fuels, which had the effect of increasing demand for gas and oil at the same time the above factors were suppressing domestic production.

In the early 1970s, with domestic prices controlled and inflation raging, there was even less incentive to drill for oil and gas in the United States than there had been in the 1960s. By 1974, price controls (see Chapter 3) had largely collapsed due to the combination of a weak dollar and the inability of a single nation, even one as powerful as the United States, to control world prices. One alternative for the United States at this point would have been to free energy controls to encourage a resumption of domestic exploration and development under the high OPEC price umbrella. Lifting controls would also have made the development of alternative energy sources more attractive (see Exhibit 9–6). Oil would never be cheap again, but freed of controls, oil would begin to reflect its true market price. Considering the fact that the 1974 dollar was worth only 62.5 percent of its 1967 value, inflationary pressures alone dictated higher prices. Instead of lifting controls, however, Congress passed the Emergency Petroleum Allocation Act of 1973. It put oil under the control of the new Federal Energy Office (FEO), later to become the Federal Energy Administration, which, in turn, became the core of a new Department of Energy. The FEO, setting out to "allocate" supplies made scarce by price controls, tangled the oil industry in massive bureaucratic red tape. As former Treasury Secretary William E. Simon recalls (1978:53):

> As for the centralized allocation process itself, the kindest thing I can say about it is that it was a disaster. Even with a stack of sensible-sounding plans for even-handed allocation all over the country, the system kept falling apart, and chunks of the populace suddenly found themselves without gas. There was no logic to the pattern of failures. In Palm Beach suddenly there was no gas, while ten miles away gas was plentiful. Parts of New Jersey suddenly went dry, while other parts of New Jersey were well supplied. Every day, in different parts of the country, people waited in line for gasoline for two, three, and four hours. The normal market distribution system is so complex, yet so smooth that no government mechanism could simulate it. All we were actually doing with our so-called bureaucratic efficiency was damaging the existent distribution system.

In 1977 the Carter administration revealed a sweeping, interventionist program based on the assumption that the United States had nearly exhausted its fossil fuel supplies.* The plan featured some $70 to $80 billion in taxes designed to discourage energy consumption, called for federal takeover of electricity rate setting from the states, and sought expansion of natural gas price controls to the intrastate market. In 1979, Carter revealed an even more sweeping plan, which proposed a new, government "Energy Security Corporation" to siphon $140 billion in "windfall profits" from the oil companies over the next ten years and to loan this money to companies to develop synthetic fuels. President Carter also proposed an "Energy Mobilization Board" to knock down barriers to energy production erected by government itself. The economic case for the multibillion-dollar loan program is not strong. The evi-

---

* According to Carter's own director of the U.S. Geological Service, domestic natural gas reserves are "about ten times the energy value of all (previous) oil, gas, and coal reserves of the United States combined" (*Congressional Record,* 18 June 1979, p. H4688). According to The Brookings Institution, the United States has 400 years of coal left (Owen and Schultze, 1976:430–39). In 1970, the known world reserves were six times as large as they had been in 1950.

dence indicates rather clearly that synthetic fuels will not be competitively priced if their commercial development is started today. In fact, the very companies that would receive DOE contracts for synthetic fuels projects have explicitly made the judgment that synthetic fuel technology is not commercially feasible at the present time. The U.S. General Accounting Office (1976) supports this view: "Government financial assistance for commercial development of synthetic fuels should not be provided at this time." Academics tend to line up with industry and the GAO. A six-year study by the Energy Project at the Harvard Business School concluded that conservation supplemented by solar power would be twice as cost-effective as a crash program on synthetic fuels (Stobaugh and Yergin, 1979). In short, if synthetic fuels were an attractive alternative, private industry would have already moved in this direction. The proponents of the loan program maintain that the real reason companies have not so moved is lack of capital. These objections, however, do not wash. Surely, any expenditures for synthetic fuels development must be paltry when stacked against the huge sums spent on the Alaskan pipeline. Moreover, unlike fusion and certain kinds of solar energy, the technology for synthetic fuels has been around at least thirty years; thus the research and development expenses are relatively modest.

Why then is government so anxious to press billions of dollars into the hands of oil companies as a subsidized inducement to build synthetic fuels plants? Some members of Congress have suggested that the program is, in effect, a government subsidy to pay for government regulation. A more likely explanation, however, is that it is a pork barrel—that is, it provides many a member of Congress with an opportunity to get a synfuel plant built in his or her district. Politically speaking, this is irresistible stuff.

The budget for the Department of Energy is already equal to half the after-tax profits of all the major oil companies combined; its annual budget amounts to around nine cents per gallon of gasoline. Why do we still have an energy crisis and repeated gasoline shortages? The answer is found in Economics 101: If you want a shortage, have the government legislate a price. The main reason Europeans are not stalled in gasoline lines (like the Americans) is that fuel prices have long been allowed to rise. The main reason European automobile manufacturers produce fuel-saving vehicles is that the gradually rising prices there—not government mandates—dictated it.

SCENARIO NUMBER THREE: MARKET ENHANCEMENT

What It Might Look Like. Now we want to consider the possibility that the American economy moves in a quite different direction than suggested in the preceding two scenarios—that is, toward a system of market enhancement (ME). Exhibit E–2 provides an overview of business-government relations that

EXHIBIT E–2   A Functional Diagram of Business-Government
                 Relations in a Market Enhancement System:
                 A Crude Model

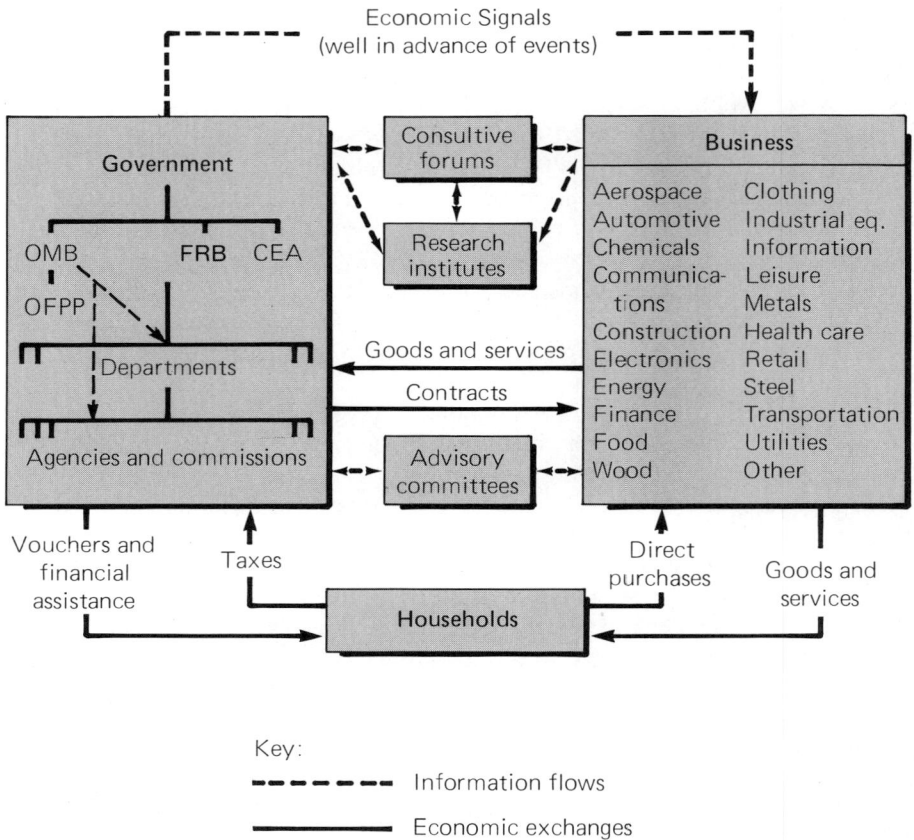

Economic Signals
(well in advance of events)

Government	Consultive forums	Business

Government

OMB   FRB   CEA

OFPP

Departments

Agencies and commissions

Consultive forums

Research institutes

Advisory committees

Business

Aerospace   Clothing
Automotive   Industrial eq.
Chemicals   Information
Communica-   Leisure
tions   Metals
Construction Health care
Electronics Retail
Energy   Steel
Finance   Transportation
Food   Utilities
Wood   Other

Goods and services

Contracts

Vouchers and
financial
assistance   Taxes

Households

Direct
purchases   Goods and
                 services

Key:

– – – – – – Information flows

—————— Economic exchanges

could emerge in the late-1980s or 1990s. Note that there are no new governmental agencies, though some existing ones will have new responsibilities or will find that their old responsibilities have become more crucial. For example, the Office of Management and Budget (OMB) would aggressively monitor the costs and benefits of proposed agency actions; in the Congress (not shown), the Congressional Budget Office (CBO) could fulfill a similar function. The

Office of Federal Procurement Policy (OFPP) would find its responsibilities especially important in this new system as government contracted to private industry the implementation of most social objectives. Any further expansion in the size of the government would be keyed to growth in national income.

Perhaps the central ideas in this scenario are a new division of labor and increased communication between government and industry. Government bureaucrats would be less involved in the "doing" part of public policy. But could industry pick up the slack? Charles Lindblom thinks so (1977:88–89):

> The private sector can build and operate a highway, for example, as is illustrated by privately maintained toll roads. It can build and operate educational and research institutions that survive by selling services for a fee. It can provide the services of a judiciary through organizations like the American Arbitration Association that offer adjudication at a price. It can provide military and police services, as illustrated by mercenaries in Angola in the 1970s and by Pinkerton and other private police forces on hire. It can provide postal services, as illustrated by growing private postal services in the United States. It can also build, maintain, and govern an entire city on the proceeds of sales of land and houses to occupants.

This new division of labor, however, hardly means that government officials would be superfluous. Rather than becoming involved in the nuts and bolts of program management, they could focus increasing amounts of time on looking ahead, on defining and promoting necessary industrial change, and on anticipating new social problems. When problems are detected, government's main aim would be, as far as possible, to resolve them through the market system.

The center of Exhibit E–2 shows how consultation between the public and private sectors would play a vital role in the system. One of the most striking differences between business-government relations in the United States and those in Western Europe and Japan is the relative lack of meaningful communication between the government and business, especially before government makes a major move. What follows from this comparative lack of consultation is, in a word, uncertainty. Therefore, in the third scenario, existing consultative forms of business (e.g., the Business Roundtable and the hundreds of advisory committees) would grow in influence, as would government-labor forums. Effective consultation would minimize abrupt shifts in policy (especially economic policy) and, when changes are absolutely required, telegraph the anticipated changes well in advance of execution.

What would the representatives of business and government consult about? A number of items were suggested in Chapters 9 through 13 and here we need only list a sample agenda: capital formation; procurement practices; national urban, water, and material policies; inflation and unemployment; and increasing productivity. These consultations would be no "Star Chamber" in which two elites decide what is "best" for society; that is not the idea at all. To use a rather shopworn term, the aim might be described as one of dialogue.

Through dialogue, business might begin to see more clearly its own responsibilities and government might begin to see more accurately the problems business management faces.

The American business system itself would continue to be a mix of large MNCs, medium-sized firms, and small business. At least two powerful forces in a ME system would help to preserve the future of big corporations. First is increased competition from foreign giants and regional trading blocks. According to research by Stobaugh (1977:39), the largest non–U.S. firms are still growing faster than their U.S. rivals even though these foreign firms have passed their U.S. rivals in size. Second are certain technological and marketing imperatives. There is some evidence that these imperatives—which, as Alfred D. Chandler suggested in Chapter 1, accounted for the wave of industrial growth that swept the U.S. economy in the early years of the twentieth century—are still operative. Today, many observers of the steel and petrochemical industries argue that mergers are badly needed to "rationalize" these industries.

Meanwhile, small business should also have a vital role to play in the ME scenario. Often they can do a better job in satisfying consumer needs (repair service is a good example) than the giants. They can also serve as a kind of back-up system when giants falter. Research indicates that by a number of measures, the smaller technological firms are at least as innovative (if not more so) than the giants in their industry; at a minimum, they can force their big brothers to innovate. Finally, small business tends to be much more job intensive. To maintain the health of a ME system, therefore, government through tax policy, equitable regulation and procurement policies, and antitrust action would want to keep small business alive—regardless of how big the MNCs grow.

It would be erroneous to interpret the scenario I have just sketched as some sneaky welfare scheme for business. Crucial to its effective operation is one principle in particular—namely, that market forces be allowed to operate as freely as possible. When John Kenneth Galbraith and other critics speak of "corporate socialism," they are not just being snide; more than a trace of truth resides in that term. Among other things, in a ME system, companies would have to be allowed to belly-up, and physicians and lawyers would have to be allowed to advertise and prevented from controlling entry into their professions. In short, the ME prescription list of bitter pills would, I believe, be rather long.

Radical Critique. To see some possible shortcomings in the third scenario, the most obvious approach is to review what radical thinkers have been saying about capitalism. This approach is quite appropriate, since the ME scenario would represent to the radicals an even more virulent form of capitalism than they have been suffering from in recent years. I shall use "radical" much as I did "Chicago School" in the last critique—that is, as a kind of convenient blanket term to cover a wide range of thinking. Into this category I would lump communists (Eastern and Western), socialists (Eastern and Western), America's radical economists, and a variety of political splinter groups in the United States who call for a sweeping restructuring of the American political economy. Before I attempt to present the radical criticisms, however, I think it absolutely essential that we review three basic ideas of Karl Marx: (1) historical materialism, (2) the labor theory of value, and (3) alienation. Unless one understands these three ideas, much of what contemporary radicals are saying can sound like gibberish.

Historical materialism. Marx was very much a child of the nineteenth century. He shared with his contemporaries a deep concern for change, growth, and evolution. So, to solve the riddle of change, Marx developed a materialist conception of history. This theory purports to explain why feudalism gave way to capitalism and why capitalism must eventually give way to socialism. (Whether Marx thought this evolutionary process would come to an end with the achievement of the classless communist society is one of many interesting questions we must leave unanswered here.) According to Marx, people in every society have a certain set of productive forces: skills, technology, and natural resources. These productive forces determine not only the way people make their living, but also the way they relate to one another in producing goods and services. Marx called these productive forces and these relationships the "economic structure of society" and everything else that makes up society—that is, all the noneconomic attributes such as religion, politics, law, modes of thought, and views of life—"the superstructure."

Marx then took a huge step beyond mere classification: He asserted that the economic structure of society *determines* the superstructure—that is, the economic or material lives of people decisively shaped their ideas. (What this implies, if true, about the objectivity of Marx's own ideas is another interesting, but not central, question we must let pass.) For example, Laplanders, living in the tundra, eat, raise families, obey laws and customs, and practice religion in their particular ways, and these ways are inevitable developments from the means of production of a nomadic Arctic society. Similarly, the means of production of a self-sufficient manorial economy in the Middle Ages determined the makeup of feudal society where a class of serfs supported a class of nobles. The connection between the economic structure and the superstructure of society became the guiding principle of Marx's studies.

According to Marx, the stage of development of a society's means of production thus determined the class structure: Over time, people develop new ways of extracting a living from their environment; these new forces of production inevitably become incompatible with the older class structure. The growing contradiction between the rising class, associated with the new means of production, and the old ruling class, based on its control of older production forces, becomes a class struggle. The struggle intensifies until, as a result of revolution, the new class, associated with the new and superior means of production, prevails. Thus did the rising middle class replace, after long struggle, the class of feudal nobles. And in turn, the middle class (or bourgeoisie) faces a struggle with a new rising class, the workers (or proletariat). Marx viewed this new struggle as the result of change in the mode of production—namely, the introduction of the factory system.

This theory of history of course proved to be wrong: Countries least likely to become communist—those where industrialization was least advanced— were the first to do so; those most likely—the United States and Great Britain—never did. However, we are not concerned with Marx as a forecaster of history; the important point for our purposes is that Marx's views on historical materialism allow modern radical critics of capitalism to freely ascribe, with theoretical if not empirical or scientific justification, virtually any social ill or blemish to the underlying mode of production.

The labor theory of value. The second core idea in Marxism that we want to review is the labor theory of value. Marx maintained that the true value of a commodity is determined by the amount of labor required to make it and that commodities that can be produced in the same amount of time have equal value. Marx did not hold, however, that the value of an object is proportional to the number of simple, undifferentiated labor hours that went into its production; rather, he held that these hours must all be socially necessary. In other words, the object must be useful; if a thing is useless (e.g., a big knot), the labor that went into making it does not count as labor. If, on the other hand, someone works 1,000 hours on something of even *slight* utility, the necessary condition for value has been met. But, can we say that it is worth 1,000 hours? "No," according to Marx (*Das Kapital*), "the labor spent on [objects] counts effectively only insofar as it is spent in a form that is useful for others." Further, Marx adds, "Whether that labor is useful for others . . . can be proved only by the act of exchange."

To explain capitalism's exploitation of workers, Marx applied his concept of value to human labor as a commodity: The value of human labor is equivalent to what is necessary to keep the workers alive. Thus, the capitalist pays wages that are determined by the exchange value of the workers' labor for what they need for subsistence—that is, to feed, clothe, and educate themselves. The value of the commodities they produce, however, is greater than the value of the commodities they can purchase with their wages. Marx called this difference in value, which represents the profit of the capitalist, *surplus value (s)*. Marx called the amount of capital required to pay the wages the *variable (v)*, which is the bare minimum the capitalist pays to get the workers' use value. According to Marxian theory, then, the capitalist flourishes through exploitation of workers—that is, by appropriating the surplus value of their labor. As was said earlier, Marx was very much a child of his times, and while he was preoccupied with change, so too was he preoccupied with production. That he tended to view a capitalist economy as one enormous factory is no where more apparent than in the formulation of his labor theory of value.

Alienation.   In light of some rather significant shortcomings in the two basic Marxian ideas of historical materialism and the labor theory of value, Marxist scholars since World War II have begun to emphasize a new core idea: alienation. These scholars have discovered in Marx's work the view that workers in a capitalist system are indifferent to, or estranged from, their work because of the very nature of the system. Despite the fact that the word "alienation" does not occur even once in Sidney Hook's pioneer account (*From Hegel to Marx,* 1936) of Marx's intellectual development, or that Daniel Bell (1960) has cogently argued that Marx repudiated the idea of alienation relative to his central theme, we need to look at the idea because the current crop of Marxist intellectuals put considerable emphasis on it in their critiques of capitalism.

To Marx, human beings seek to satisfy certain primary needs: drink, food, clothing, and the development of their powers and their intellectual and artistic abilities. In this undertaking, people discover that they are productive beings who humanize themselves by their labor. By their creative abilities and by their labor, they realize their identity. But in a capitalist society, people become alienated beings, strangers in a strange land. As Marx explains (*Economic and Philosophic Manuscripts,* 1844), "The worker becomes poorer the more wealth he produces, the more his production increases in power and in extent. The worker becomes a cheaper commodity, the more commodities he produces. The increase in value of the world of things is directly proportional to the decrease in value of the human world . . . ." Marx adds that ". . . the object which labor produces, its product, stands opposed to it as an alien thing, as a power independent of the producer." Consequently, workers are related to the product of their labor as to an *alien* object. The more they exert themselves, the more powerful becomes this alien world of objects and the poorer becomes the workers' inner world. Manufacturing complicates the issue, for as Marx said, the worker is "deformed into a detail worker; he becomes an appendage to the machine"—a machine that actually produces the objects.

In concluding this brief review of alienation, we must remember the unavoidable fact that Marxist thought and practice simply did not develop along this line; rather, it followed the narrow road of his economic conceptions of property and exploitation. Humanistic concepts of work and labor were left unexplored. Indeed, these root insights—that alienation is a consequence of the organization of work and that giving workers a sense of meaning in their daily lives requires examination of the work process—were both lost until the neo-Marxists artfully rediscovered them in an effort to make Marx more palatable to modern Western tastes.

Having described the three core ideas in Marx, we are now in a position to attempt a brief summary statement of what, according to the radicals, is wrong with capitalism. Exhibit E–3 is only a skeletal picture of their case against capitalism, but to the extent that the exhibit reveals the major radical objections to a more unbridled market system, it suffices for our purposes.

A Rejoinder to the Radical Critique. What can be said in response to the melange of radical criticisms shown in Exhibit E–3? Let us proceed slowly, point by point.

   Pollution.   To attribute pollution to capitalism alone is naive, dishonest, or a little of both. As we know from the excellent research of Marshall Gold-

EXHIBIT E–3   The Radical Critique of Capitalism: A Skeletal View

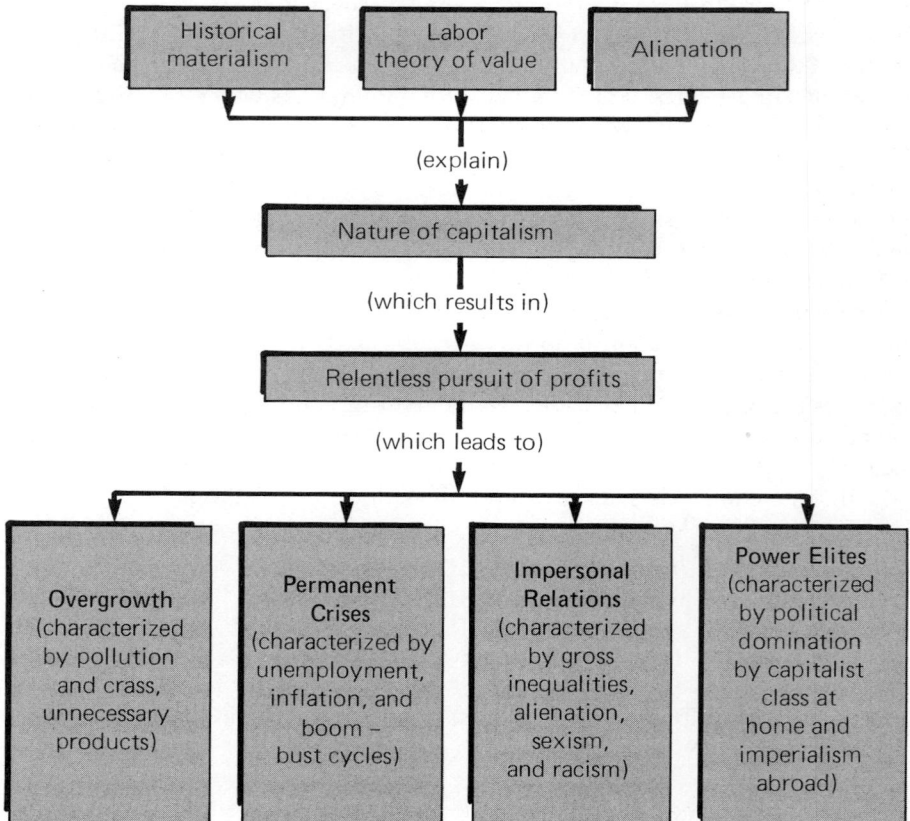

man (1972), the Soviet Union's record on environmental matters is quite poor. (We do not know just how poor, since there is no Moscow branch of the Sierra Club to trumpet failures abroad.) Not only is pollution a serious problem in socialist countries, but the destruction of the environment predates capitalism by several thousand years. The massacre of the forest, the transformation of vast stretches of land into dust bowls, and the erosion of land were the works of people who had as little knowledge of capitalism as they had of ecological systems.

Unnecessary products. Let us consider the criticism that consumer preferences for unnecessary products are "fabricated" by companies through production, advertising, and sales operations. For example, Robert L. Heilbroner (1978b) speaks disparagingly of "the plastic wealth . . . that industrialism generates." The term *plastic wealth* refers to goods that people spend money for and, generally speaking, would like to have more of. The refusal to accept people's preferences as expressed in the market is basic to the radical critique of capitalism, but to call the objects of consumer wants "plastic" is less an authentic judgment and more a matter of personal dislike.

Inflation and unemployment. Regarding what I consider to be the most serious economic charge—namely, that inflation and unemployment are "capitalism as usual"—two responses might be made. First, these economic afflictions are not necessarily inherent in the capitalist system. They arise out of the intrusion of politics and political values into economic processes and decision making. Wages and prices are not entirely determined by the capitalist market; rather wages and prices are managed—that is, "formed deliberately by political considerations stemming from power and values, not from the intersection of market forces of supply and demand" (Etzioni, 1978). The more obvious examples of how this comes about are described by Etzioni (1978):

> Within a few months late in 1977, the legal minimum wage was increased substantially for the next three years, from $2.30 per hour to $3.25 by January 1, 1981. This will increase unemployment in the sector in which youth is most concentrated. The decision was not made between employers and employees. Indeed, the youth—who is the one most often drawing the minimum wage—is hardly in the position to bargain for it. Nor was it made by unions pressuring management. Unions put pressure on the Democratic President and Congress, which, having just turned down several of their other requests, found it politically necessary to respond to this one.
>
> Similarly, the payroll taxes that finance Social Security were substantially increased, adding to the costs of labor, and hence of products, not as a result of new fringe benefits awarded by employers to employees but through government action.

As a second point to be made to counter the charge that inflation and unemployment are "capitalism as usual," we might say that long lines and assigned jobs are "socialism as usual." In socialist countries, inflation caused by demand appears not as increased prices (prices are controlled), but as long lines in the stores. If a product is scarce and its price fixed, a black market inevitably appears. For example, the results of rent control have been privileges for those who happen to have a contract for a rent-controlled apartment (or have influence with the housing authority) and a housing shortage and black markets for the general public. As a Swedish economist writes (Lindbeck, 1971:39):

> It does not seem that New Left students in various parts of the world have shown much understanding of these aspects of price control, for they have made control of rents one of their main, concrete short-run proposals. After seeing how low-income families in the rent-controlled city of Stockholm have waited in the official queue for apartments for five to eight years, while high-income families always get apartments through good "contacts" or the black market, it is difficult to see the virtues of rent control . . . .

Inequality. The importance radicals place on equality is puzzling. If growth and additional consumption are so unimportant to the radicals—if not a downright evil—how then can equality in income and consumption be so important? Why do radical critics like Richard Parker (1975:6) decry the inequality in distribution of *two* cars among families: "Automobiles show the same pattern of maldistributed wealth. While 29 percent of working-class families reported owning two or more cars, 46 percent of upper middle-class families did." And Parker cites a further instance of the maldistribution: While two-thirds of working-class families primarily bought low-priced used vehicles, three-quarters of upper middle-class families bought new cars. This inconsistency between the desire for no growth, on the one hand, and the desire for second (preferably new) cars for working-class families, on the other, is a problem more for logicians and philosophers than for us. More to the point is how the radicals could answer the following counterarguments.

First, the problem of inequality is ultimately insolvable. In reaching greater degrees of economic equality, how does a society accommodate the increasing sensitivity to inequalities? Then, once that magic point of absolute equality is attained, how does a society dampen inequalities along other dimensions: looks, intelligence, popularity, aesthetic sensitivity, physical grace, political power, empathy, sexuality, the ability to sink 40-foot jump shots, and so forth?

Second, the statistics belie the charge of great inequalities in the United States. For example, the poorest 5 percent of income recipients in capitalist America received 13.3 percent of the national income, while the same group in "classless" Yugoslavia receive 15 percent.

Third, carrying out the necessary redistribution would probably result in a bloody (literally) revolution. On the other hand, if property owners were paid full market value, the results would be shockingly small. Using 1973 data illustratively, Arthur Okun (1975:52–54) has worked through the arithmetic of a very ambitious redistribution program that nationalized the entire corporate sector and at the same time provided full compensation to the owners; the resulting net transfer of after-tax income away from property owners is about $13 billion—or just a percent of GNP.

To my mind, the crucial issue is whether or not the level of inequality in society is a proper one. The crucial issue is not statistical measures of equality, but rather the extent to which a market economy, based on the profit motive, achieves production and allocation of resources in accordance with the preferences of the individuals in that society. Workers are most exploited in those societies that have the lowest productivity.

Alienation. To the radical, work is a person's main activity and should be "truly human." It should be satisfying. It should be freely chosen. It should develop the person's talents. The view in the U.S. industry, at least in the past, has been somewhat different. One chooses work, not for its intrinsic value or interest, but because it provides income for other goals. Because it tells us what people *ought* to do—namely, meaningful work—the concept of alienation is normative. But why should work be the central activity of one's life? What is intrinsically more important about a job than a family, a religion, or an avocation? Does not the relative importance of work vary from individual to individual, from culture to culture? One thinks of the reply of Alfred North Whitehead when informed that young men in Denmark with Ph.D.s were being forced to sell shoestrings because of economic conditions. Good, replied the great man, "they can also meditate on philosophical problems" all day. How true is it that being subordinate in a work scheme adversely affects self-esteem? Does being ordered about make one feel inferior, whereas self-esteem is heightened if one plays some role in democratically selecting and advising one's authorities? Nozick thinks not (1974:246):

> Members of a symphony orchestra constantly are ordered about by their conductor (often capriciously and arbitrarily and with temper flare-ups) and are not consulted about the overall interpretation of their works. Yet they retain high self-esteem and do not feel that they are inferior beings. Draftees in armies are constantly ordered about, told how to dress, what to keep in their lockers, and so on, yet they do not come to feel they are inferior beings. Socialist organizers in factories received the same orders and were subject to the same authority as others, yet they did not lose their self-esteem. Persons on the way up organizational ladders spend much time taking orders without coming to feel inferior.

Even accepting the premise that, in order to avoid alienation, work should be made more meaningful and democratic, one is left with the problem of what to do about it. If a foundation offered researchers a $10-million grant to find out, their recommendations would probably include practices like job enrichment and job rotation, which, as we noted in Chapter 12, were pioneered in the Western capitalist societies. Perhaps even more significant than such techniques in the campaign against worker alienation is the enormous rise in the percentage of skilled (as opposed to manual) jobs. Whatever alienation might mean, most of us would prefer running lab tests to picking cotton. And it is capitalism, far more than socialism, that has produced the rise in skill levels. Could alienation be any better controlled under socialism? For the answer, we can look to Michael Polanyi, the Hungarian-British scientist and philosopher, who once observed workers in England no more feel that they own British Railways than that they own the British Navy.

Sexism and racism. Of all the radicals' charges, sexism and racism can perhaps be most easily dismissed. It would be shortsighted to view the traditional forms of discrimination as having essentially disappeared in the United States, but progress is evident—for example, according to U.S. Bureau of Census data, between 1955 and 1975, black male workers increased their pay from 63.5 percent to 76.9 percent of the average pay for white males, and between black and white women the wage gap disappeared entirely. Problems of discrimination do remain, but accepting the premise that a socialist country like the Soviet Union, where they still warn of a "yellow peril" and where anti-Semitism runs high, is somehow less racist than, say, Denmark, Norway, or New Zealand, requires a high toleration for distortion.

Class domination. A less wrongheaded radical charge shown in Exhibit E–3 is that the capitalist class—or, let us say, the very rich—controls government. We saw in Chapter 5 that a number of political scientists do not agree with the findings of radical social studies concerning the existence of a cohesive economic (especially a corporate) power elite that dominates political decisions. The more persuasive interpretation builds on the notion of plural elites. Even when it can be shown that business leaders have disproportionate influence on certain policy decisions (not a hard thing to demonstrate), it can also be shown that many other interests—for example, labor unions, feminist groups, and even governmental bureaucracies—have carved out their own niches of power and privilege. And to make what should be a painfully obvious point by now: Over the last several years, business has been forced to accept a vast number of quite costly regulatory impositions in the areas of health and safety practices, environmental protection, and the disclosure of consumer information. Business interests consistently fought these impositions and almost as consistently lost. If business interests are all-powerful, as the radicals claim, why was the capital gains tax first instituted in the United States? Why was the United States the last industrialized country to establish a cabinet-level office to represent business in government?

Imperialism. Radical criticism also includes the charge that imperialism characterizes the political relationships of a capitalist system. Efforts to understand the actual behavior of businesses in the lesser-developed countries have been generally handicapped by the voluminous and confusing nature of the evidence. Partly as a result, relatively simple ideas, such as those found in Lenin's *Imperialism: The Highest Stage of Capitalism* (1917) and Barnet and Muller's *Global Reach* (1974), have had enormous appeal. Yet any sober study of history or close-up view of the complex relations between multinational corporations and host countries suggests that radical theories on the nature of relations between capitalist states and lesser-developed countries are excessively simple. Current trends in international business relations run directly counter to the imperialism thesis. By the mid-1970s a wave of disenchantment with investment in the LDCs had begun to spread to the boardrooms of multinational corporations and led to cutbacks in investment. The U.S. attitude might be summed up as follows: If the investment climate is not attractive in LDCs, then money will go where the weather is fairer—for example, to the equally developed and equally capitalistic countries of Western Europe.

As a result of the radical critique, we might be led to the conclusion that the version of capitalism under which we live is not merely vulnerable, it is practically defenseless. The real weakness is not hard to spot: The American business system does not possess a clear theoretical (i.e., ideological) legitimacy within the framework of a liberal democratic society. Executives continue to study their balance sheet, to decide whether the dancing bears on the cereal box should be going clockwise or counterclockwise around the bowl, and to read the latest self-help paperbacks. Meanwhile, a gradual usurpation of managerial authority by a "new class"—mainly through the transfer of this authority to the new breed of regulatory officials (who Irving Kristol calls the prototype of the "new class")—is almost irresistible.

Yet it is not really hard to make a decent case, on a pragmatic level, for capitalism. First, as even the radical critics admit, markets do have an enormous capacity to provide a milieu of comfortable living. Second, markets neglect the future no less than the most sophisticated planning systems. To the skeptic, Milton Friedman (1971) puts this question: "How did we make the transition from using wood to using oil, from using oil to using natural gas? How in God's name did we make that transition without a Federal Energy Agency?" In a market system, one can always buy a piece of the future, as Lindblom (1977:87) explains:

> If, in a market system, an owner of a natural resource comes to believe that the resource will become scarcer in the future, he will be motivated to withhold some of it from the current market in order to take advantage of the higher price in the future. If he is not yet an owner, he will be motivated to buy the resource and hold it for the future. This both enriches him and conserves the resource.

Third, markets greatly facilitate economic choice. In a market system, no DOE needs to allocate energy or come to any judgement about what is important to produce. Consumers, suppliers, and managers simply decide whether to buy more or less of any given type of energy. And the decision is always one of marginal choice. The process of choice is described by Wassily Leontief (1971:20):

The price of any particular product reflects in a concentrated manner—as the round curved mirror hanging over the mantelpiece in an old-fashioned parlor reflects in miniature the entire room—the structural, that is, technological, characteristics of the entire economy of which that product is but a small component part. The market price of a ton of steel or of a kilowatt-hour of electric energy communicates to the buyer of these products how the available supply of various primary resources and the production methods used in all the different branches of the particular economy affect the physical availability of one ton of steel or, respectively, of one kilowatt-hour of electric energy. In order to make possible the computation of the "correct" accounting prices of steel and electric energy in an ideal, centrally planned economy, the central technological data bank would have to provide the central planning office with tapes carrying a detailed quantitative description of the technical "cooking recipe" of each and every sector of the national economy that contributes directly or indirectly to the production of these goods.

In choosing between two or more possible methods of production, one, for example, requiring more steel and the other more electric power, the planner must take into account the prices of these as well as those of all the other inputs. In insisting on this we really are saying that the acceptance or rejection of a technological innovation in one particular industry cannot be rationally decided upon without knowledge of the technologies, that is of the methods of production, that are or could be used in all the other industries.

Fourth, market systems tend to avoid the infringements on individual freedom that we saw so plainly in socialist systems.

In the following section, we shall examine these and other merits of capitalism. What we shall find is that efficiency and freedom provide a necessary but insufficient basis for a defense of capitalism. What else might be required will be revealed in due course.

CAN CAPITALISM SURVIVE?

Efficiency and Freedom under Capitalism. As though the script were written by a Greek tragedian, the great productive capacity of capitalism carries the seeds for the system's destruction. Among the first to make this startling observation from a non-Marxist perspective was Joseph Schumpter (1942) in his *Capitalism, Socialism, and Democracy.* The Schumpter thesis may be summed up as follows: Since capitalist enterprise, by its very achievements, tends to automatize progress, it tends eventually to make itself superfluous. The important social function of entrepreneurship loses its importance. Innovation itself is reduced to routine. Technological progress increasingly becomes the work of teams of trained specialists. The romance of earlier commercial adventure wears away, "because so many more things can be strictly calculated that had of old to be visualized in a flash of genius" (Schumpter, 1942:132).

Meanwhile, other ominous things are occurring according to Schumpter: The capitalist process is undermining its own institutional framework. Today few corporations are owned by a single individual or family; the figure of the proprietor—with his or her specific proprietary interest—has vanished. Today there are only salaried executives, big stockholders, and small stockholders. None of these groups, it is fair to say, has the attitude of an owner. Nor do they take the attitude of an owner. Nor do they take the attitude characteristic of that curious phenomenon—so full of meaning and so rapidly passing— that is covered by the term "property." Further, the term *freedom of contract* once meant, according to Schumpter (1942:142), ". . . individual contracting regulated by individual choice between an indefinite number of possibilities. The stereotyped, unindividual, impersonal and bureaucratized contract of to-day . . . which presents but restricted freedom of choice has none of the old features, the most important of which become impossible with giant concerns or impersonal masses of workmen or consumers." Thus, the capitalist process pushes into the background all those institutions—the institutions of property and free contracting in particular—that express the needs and ways of the truly "private" economic activity.

Even more important to the future of capitalism is the disintegrating effect the capitalist process has on the family. Schumpter observes that, "to men and women in modern capitalist societies, family life and parenthood mean less than they meant before and hence are less powerful molders of behavior . . . ." Schumpter suggests that the increasing proportion of marriages that produce no children or only one child ". . . is wholly attributable to the rationalization of everything in life, which . . . is one of the effects of capitalist evolution. As soon as men and women . . . acquire the habit of weighing the individual advantages and disadvantages of any prospective course of action . . . they cannot fail to become aware of the heavy personal sacrifices that family ties and especially parenthood entail under modern conditions." Deborah Baldwin, an editor of *Environmental Action,* might be seen as the kind of modern member of capitalist society Schumpter is describing. In an article entitled "Motherhood and the Liberated Woman," she explains why many twenty-eight-year-old women do not have children and do not know if they want them (Baldwin, 1978:52–53):

> I am twenty-eight years old and work in a white-collar professional job. I am childless, as are practically all the other women I know of my generation and class. We are today's women—perseveringly independent, mobile, our own best friends. Many of us have taken great pains to free ourselves from the sticky bindings of family, but the bindings of a career are ones we have eagerly assumed. . . .
>
> Now everybody has a career and a lot of personal freedom. As a result, America has evolved from the child-centered society I grew up in to a society that's at best indifferent and at worst outright hostile to children. In California, 70 percent of the rental housing is for adults only; in forty-six of the fifty states, tenants with children can be discriminated against. Among couples, there's a reluctance on both husband's and wife's part to give up anything in order to have children.

Capitalism diminishes the values of family life at the same time that it implements new tastes. The suburban home, for example, is no longer an indispensable requirement of comfortable middle-class living. Townhouses, high-rise apartments, and condominiums now represent a rationalized style of life that provides all the essentials of comfort and refinement. Baldwin describes this new style of middle-class life: "Today, like many of my friends, I live in an apartment in downtown Washington. Every morning my husband and I walk together to our jobs. We feel smug about not having to fight traffic commuting into the city, and we like it here—we feel as if we have the best of all worlds."

While the new style of life holds obvious advantages for the middle class, it bodes ill for the capitalist system. Because the outlay on the most durable elements of home life—especially the house itself and furniture—used to be financed from previous earnings, capital had to be accumulated. Now the need for accumulation of capital is drastically reduced. Freedom from this need, plus the rise in income levels, means that for the upper middle class, the desirability of having incomes beyond a certain level is reduced. For example, successful men, women, and couples who can pay for the best available accommodations and for the best available quality in objects of personal consumption and use (which are increasingly being turned out by capitalist production), will likely have all they need for themselves. Further, Fred Hirsch (1976) argues in his *Social Limits to Growth* that once the basic material needs are satisfied, individuals pursue "positional goods"—that is, goods, such as having servants (as opposed to appliances) or a job with authority (as opposed to a good salary), whose possession by some implies nonpossession by others.

What does Schumpter's thesis mean for the efficiency of the capitalist engine of production? First, the family is no longer the mainspring of the typically middle-class kind of profit motive that led to self-interested productivity or even entrepreneurship. Further, as Schumpter (1942:160) points out, "the bourgeois worked primarily in order to invest, and it was not so much a standard of consumption as a standard of accumulation that the bourgeois struggled for .... With the decline of the driving power supplied by the family motive, ... he drifts into an antisaving frame of mind and accepts with readiness antisaving theories ...." Finally, we might add that a general sense of disappointment inevitably occurs when productivity, having satisfied material needs, fails to provide everyone with the increase they expect in positional goods. Because the American system of capitalism stands or falls on how well it meets the expectations of individuals, this sense of disappointment has grave political consequences for the system. The individual begins to acquire a different view of the values and standards of the capitalist order of things. The upper middle class, which includes society's most potent shapers of public opinion and public policy, begins to "... absorb the slogans of current radicalism and seems quite willing to undergo a process of conversion to a creed hostile to its very existence.... This would be most astonishing and indeed very hard to explain were it not for the fact that the typical bourgeois is rapidly losing faith in his own creed" (Schumpter, 1942:161). Recent history is full of examples of the kind of thing Schumpter is talking about, and the only explanation is that the capitalist order of things no longer makes any sense to the upper middle class; it does not really care.

Many of the points in Schumpter's thesis have been refined and carried forward by contemporary thinkers. For example, Daniel Bell argues in his *The Cultural Contradictions of Capitalism* (1976) that the free market has seduced the once prudent middle class with promises of new pleasures. From working and achieving, which are the driving forces of capitalism's success, the middle class has "swung" to spending and enjoying. The "impulse quest" is its only program. Today's middle class, Bell says, has neither a sense of loyalty to its society nor a significant philosophy. This drive for hedonism, as Morris Janowitz (1978) points out in his *Social Control of the Welfare State,* is not merely a function of the state but rests on increased affluence in general: "Systematic obsolescence and the social definition of consumption stimulated by mass advertising contribute to the inability of increased material well-being to create, for important segments of the population, personal satisfaction and effective indulgence. This is what is meant by 'consumerism,' the social arrangements under which increased material consumption creates only demands for more indulgence, with resulting personal dissatisfaction."

In sum, I believe that Schumpter, Bell, and Janowitz are getting pretty close to a genuine problem of present-day capitalist society. Clearly, productive efficiency is insufficient to assure its survival, and unfortunately there are other problems. Many defenders of capitalism, recognizing the hollowness of the capitalism-is-efficient argument (though perhaps not for the complex reasons given by Schumpter), have tried to seize the high ground by touting the close connection between a free market system and a free political system. Modern democracy was indeed born in conjunction with capitalism. And today, among the 144 nations of the world, the connection is still holding fast. If we define democracy as a system that displays, to a greater or lesser extent, some mechanisms of popular control and some guarantees of individual liberties, trouble begins when political freedom converges with the hedonism we saw flowing from the productive efficiency of capitalism. Individuals are free to press government for wants and satisfactions not fulfilled in the market. This chain of events can be shown schematically as follows:

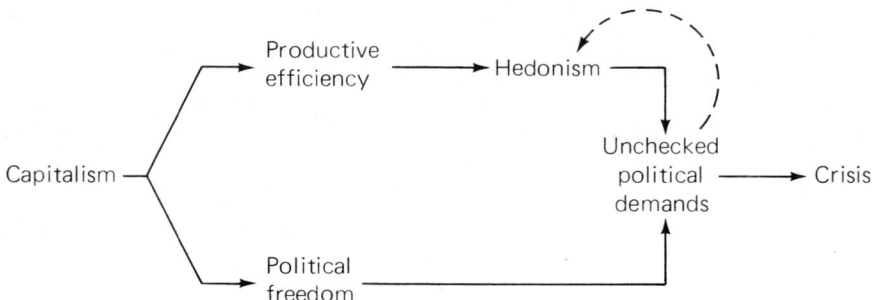

The feedback loop running from unchecked "political demands" to "hedonism" represents an axiom, to which there are no known exceptions: *l'appétit vient en mangeant* ("appetite comes with eating"), or in other words, as human needs are satisfied, expectations rise. An important political corollary, to which I know no exceptions, is that what the public wants, electioneering politicians will promise. However, while there is a limit to the amount of food an individual can absorb, there is no definable limit to the amount of material and positional goods or improved health, education, and protection services any individual can consume (see Stassinopovlos, 1978:50–74). Sooner or later, demand outstrips the capacity of the economy to deliver; the result, as indicated in the schematic, is crisis.

We must not overlook the linkage in the bottom portion of the diagram; it represents in the simplest of terms the potential for use and abuse of political freedom by all segments of the system. Of crucial importance to our concern with the future of capitalism is how this linkage applies to business managers. Despite their incantations about nonintervention by government, about "free enterprise" in its truest sense, a large number of business people do not hesitate to use their political freedom—their right to petition government—the moment they run into trouble. Witness for just one example the demand of many U.S. industries for import protection. Indeed, throughout this book we have seen many examples of this kind of use and abuse of political freedom.

The pernicious cycle of use and abuse can be broken in only one of two quite different ways: coercive control by government or a commitment to social responsibility by business. Coercive control is not a very pretty alternative. The other way to break the cycle—a commitment to social responsibility by business—has been frequently mentioned throughout this book. But now I want to expand its application beyond managers to *all* citizens. In this broader view, social responsibility refers to society's capacity for *self*-regulation in pursuit of a set of higher moral values. When social responsibility is missing, when individuals express less personal responsibility to institutions and less willingness to sublimate personal needs or desires to those of a larger group, then government cannot set priorities decisively. The system is strained. Under such conditions, capitalism is practically defenseless.

Social Responsibility and the Continuation of Capitalism. The key element in the defense of capitalism, the one which will bring all of the criticisms and counterarguments into balance, is social responsibility. The concept is a venerable one. The proudest boast of Pericles (Thucydides, Bk II, 35–46) was that Athens had found the secret of enabling its citizens to continue the care of private interests without losing regard for the society as a whole: "An Athenian citizen does not neglect the state because he takes care of his own household; and even those of us who are engaged in business have a very fair idea of politics. We alone regard a man who takes no interest in public affairs, not as a harmless, but as a useless, character . . . ."

Modern states, large, remote, and impersonal, cannot fill the place in modern life that the city filled in the life of a Greek. Nevertheless, the idea that a harmonious society requires some self-imposed restraint carried forward in history. For example, few passages in Thomas Jefferson's memorable first inaugural address deserve better remembrance than this: "All . . . will bear in mind this sacred principle, that though the will of the majority is in all cases to prevail, that will to be rightful must be reasonable. . . . Let us, then, fellow citizens, unite with one heart and one mind. Let us restore to social intercourse that harmony and affection without which liberty and even life itself are but dreary things." And perhaps the most intellectual of all American presidents, Woodrow Wilson, spoke these words: "Oh, how I wish I could warn all my countrymen against deification of mere intellectual acuteness, wholly unaccompanied by moral responsibility."

By the mid-1950s, Walter Lippmann was writing that the United States had abandoned concepts of social responsibility, or what he termed "the public philosophy." The survival of the public philosophy, Lippmann (1954:161) believed, depended on whether its principles and precepts ". . . can be reworked for the modern age. If this cannot be done, then the free and democratic nations face the totalitarian challenge without a public philosophy which free men believe in and cherish, with no public faith beyond a mere official agnosticism, neutrality, and indifference. There is not much doubt how the struggle is likely to end if it lies between those who, believing, care very much—and those who, lacking belief, cannot care very much."

The problem of communicating the public philosophy to a modern democracy, Lippmann recognized correctly, is particularly severe. The public philosophy is in deep contradiction with the popular doctrine of the mass democracies: "The public philosophy is addressed to the government of our appetites and passions by the reasons of a second, civilized, and therefore acquired nature. Therefore the public philosophy cannot be popular. For it aims to resist and to regulate those very desires and opinions which are most popular" (Lippmann, 1954:162).

Until the concept of social responsibility is revived, an adequate defense of capitalism will remain an elusive goal. But whether social responsibility can be revived remains, at this writing, highly problematic. Any serious effort at revival would require at least three things: institutional reform, leadership, and a commitment to individual growth.

Institutional reform. Institutional reform is the first and probably least difficult road back to social responsibility. For example, stronger political parties could act to counterbalance interest-group politics. By playing a more decisive role in elections of congressional representatives, political parties might expect that individual members would be more beholden to their congressional leaders than to special-interest groups. While it would be fatuous to argue that congressional leaders (e.g., the Senate minority leader and the Speaker of the House) always serve the public interest, it is reasonable to expect that over the long haul (say, one session of Congress), those leaders' positions will approximate the public interest far better than will the positions of individual members, who now depend almost exclusively on the favor of special interests in their states and districts. Freed from the constraints of interest-group politics, government policymakers could generate greater social responsibility in the private sector by following a market enhancement scenario. Heavy regulation and centralization could be minimized, since they tend to undermine the concept of corporate social responsibility, which implies a certain degree of autonomy. Efforts to promote small business would be particularly efficacious. Businesses of all sizes would, in turn, include social responsibility in their planning process. Corporations would set up new units to implement new goals that result from a consideration of social responsibility and would look outside their own industries for a certain percentage of board members.

Leadership. The second road back to responsibility requires a rethinking of managerial style. The current literature on managerial behavior focuses almost exclusively on processes and techniques to motivate underlings. But somewhere in this voluminous literature a niche must again be found for that musty old notion of "leadership"—that is, the quality that fills men and women with a desire to do what is right and gives them the will to carry out what is right. Developing this sort of leader is not likely to be easy, because right decisions are often hard decisions that are likely to be unpopular with stockholders, employees, or even other managers. As Herman Hesse (1976:61) wrote, "A normal ape never thought of abandoning his tree and walking upright on the ground. The one who first did that, who first tried it, who had first dreamt about it, was a visionary and eccentric among apes, a poet, an innovator, and no normal ape. The normal ones, as I saw it, were there to maintain and defend an established way of life. . . ." Today the need is for leaders who, through their own example, will raise business and other managers to new possibilities and who have the ability and will to take positions that clearly embody the public interest. To find the richest examples of this sort of leader, we have to look to other times and places. Consider, for example, Cecil B. De Mille, who gave up a million-dollar contract because he refused to pay the sum of one dollar to a labor union with a closed shop. Or consider the time de Gaulle was split from the majority of postwar leaders because of his Algerian policy. A politician who had just returned from a visit to Algeria remarked that all his friends there were bitterly opposed to the general's policy. *"Changez vos amis"* (Change your friends), de Gaulle replied (quoted in Stassinopoulos, 1978:125). We might agree or disagree with De Mille's attitude toward unions or de Gaulle's policy for Algeria, but the crucial point is that both leaders acted out of deeply felt values. The management development model has yet to be drawn that will capture and explain this kind of leadership.

Individual growth. We come at last to the third road back to responsibility: a commitment to individual growth. Modern capitalist society seems to have forgotten the chief lesson of human experience, which is the insight of great religions and philosophies that individuals either grow (in character, in spirit, in civic duty, and so forth) or muddle "from distraction to distraction," as T.S. Eliot put it. The absence of this commitment is, if not the prime reason, certainly one of the main reasons why hedonism and freedom go relatively unchecked in contemporary society. Ironically, the enemies of freedom have recognized that humankind is not driven exclusively by material self-interest but also has a need, as Lenin was shrewd enough to see, "for a transcendent ideology." But political and business leaders in the United States continue to talk in terms of the narrowest kind of middle-class self-advancement and choose to ignore the spiritual or transcendent dimension. It is hardly surprising, then, that the leaders in capitalist societies are unable to compete rhetorically with the idealism of the socialist leaders. And the defenders of capitalism will remain mute unless they begin to think in terms of the following simple linkage:

Capitalism ⟶ Freedom ⟶ Individual growth

The defense of capitalism will remain half-hearted unless it places *ultimate value on the individuality of each human being*. A human being is not to be valued as a productive unit in some econometric model for the building of some utopian tomorrow, nor as a freely spending and freely consuming member of the middle class. The true aim of human progress must be a turning inward to become ourselves and to exceed ourselves.

Systems with utopian aims seek to achieve the transformation of society by restricting freedom and substituting suppression. Capitalism, while it can exist in an authoritarian state, offers societies the chance to develop into liberal democracies where individuals have an opportunity to grow in self-knowledge and to freely overcome their limitations. Advocates of capitalism respect—or, at least, protect—the individual because capitalism lays no claim to sweeping plans to change society. Capitalism simply does not purport to possess detailed sociological knowledge. Advocates of capitalism, therefore, do not talk in the utopian way about means and ends; such talk is illogical. What the utopian sees as "the means," the capitalist sees as one set of events close in time, followed by another, more distant set of events (the utopian's "ends"). But since the more distant set of events will be followed by another, even more distant set of events, the ends are not really *the* ends. How, then, can one claim privileges or justify extraordinary sacrifices for what is merely the next set of events in an endless series? If all individuals have equal moral claims and moral worth, it cannot be right to sacrifice one generation to the next.

People obviously differ about the kind of society they want; both reactionaries and radicals do so, even among themselves. Therefore, whenever a group gets into power with the aim of putting its blueprint into production, it will have to render the opposition ineffective, if not coerce opponents into serving an end they disagree with. A capitalist society, however, cannot impose common social purposes. A government with utopian aims *has to*; it is bound to become authoritarian. Thus, it will view individuals who oppose sweeping changes as, in Karl Popper's (1966) apt phrase, "enemies of society." Popper goes on: "For ideal goals . . . are a long time coming, and the period over which criticism and opposition have to be stifled is prolonged more and more; so intolerance and authoritarianism will intensify, albeit with the best of intentions." Inevitably, then, opponents will become victims in what follows.

The linchpin, then, in the argument for capitalism is that it provides the conditions—unintentionally, to be sure—for the growth and protection of the individual human being. Here our argument converges with the pluralist, anti-dogmatic ideas on liberty held by Aleksandr Herzen the nineteenth-century Russian revolutionary (quoted in Berlin, 1978):

> All that is ultimately valuable are the particular purposes of particular persons; and to trample on these is always a crime because there is, and can be, no principle or value higher than the ends of the individual, and therefore no principle in the name of which one could be permitted to do violence to or degrade or destroy individuals—the sole authors of all principles and all values.

ENRICHMENT EXERCISES AND CASE STUDIES

Exercises

EXERCISE 1: BUSINESS DECISION MAKING
AND ETHICAL REASONING

Although the problems in this exercise are drawn from a wide variety of business situations, they have at least one thing in common: They raise questions of values. In other words, managers of equal competence will reach different solutions to the extent that they have different values. The idea in this exercise is not to find the "right" decision but to practice ethical reasoning. For each problem, you should consider three questions. First, can you explain aloud to someone else exactly how you arrived at your final decision? Otherwise, you have made your decision on intuition. While this approach might lead you to some pretty good answers, it is not ethical reasoning; nor is it very serviceable over the long haul. Ethics, as we said in Chapter 6, is the study of values. To think ethically, therefore, requires you at some point to confront a second question: What values are important to you? Then, after going through a few of the problems, you need to ask yourself a third question: Is there any consistency in your reasoning? Do you tackle the ethical issues in each problem the same way, or do you jerry-build an approach from scratch for each problem?

If you have an opportunity to discuss your decisions with others, and to hear their decisions as well, it is especially important to focus on the three above questions. Otherwise, discussion can quickly degenerate into heated but muddled arguments for this or that decision or for the superiority of a particular value (e.g., truth over beauty, individual over society). While such arguments are entirely appropriate in their place, the purpose of this exercise is not to generate that kind of discussion. A good way to avoid falling into such arguments is to prepare a written statement based on your final decision. Think of the statement as something you will have to read before a legislative committee, an administrative hearing, a management review committee, a board of directors, a public gathering, or a television camera.

1. As the advertising manager for a medium-sized newspaper in New York City, you have just received an ad from the Chamber of Commerce in a growing Southern city in which the Statue of Liberty is portrayed hitchhiking south under a heading reading, "Everyone's leaving for the sun belt." Do you print it?

2. As vice president of marketing for a large food company, you have just received the final recommendations of two separate committees you appointed to study the issue of children's advertising. Committee A recommended three actions:

1. Ban all television advertising aimed at young children (under the age of eight);
2. Ban television advertising of high-sugar products most likely to cause tooth decay in advertising aimed at older children (eight to twelve years of age);
3. Require that television advertising of all sugared products aimed at older children be offset by messages on nutrition and dental care paid for by the advertisers of the sugared products.

Committee B recommended four actions:

1. Include affirmative disclosures in advertisements for products most likely to cause tooth decay;
2. Air separate ads containing affirmative disclosures and nutritional information, funded by advertisers of high-sugar products;
3. Limit the use of certain advertising techniques or messages for either high-sugar products or for all products aimed at very young children;
4. Limit the number and frequency of high-sugar product ads aimed at all children and all ads aimed at very young children.

Which set of recommendations, if either, do you prefer?

3. After five years of research that cost $13 million, your medium-sized firm develops a paper copier. This product is not only cheaper to produce and sell, but also more reliable than that offered by the dominant firm in the field. (Your copier uses a liquid toner rather than the powder peddled by the competition.) The head of the project is naturally enthusiastic about the test results that demonstrate your product's superior performance. He recommends to the company's marketing vice president that she create a showstopping ad campaign—one that states the superiority of your firm's product over the competition's models. The product chief wants to name names and to knock the competition. The marketing vice president is opposed. As she puts it: "Comparative advertising makes a mockery of pretensions to culture and refinement and decent corporate behavior. Furthermore, hostile claims and counterclaims can mislead and confuse the consumer." As company president, are you persuaded by your marketing vice president?

4. Several months ago the United Furniture Workers took an interest in the small factory where you are director of personnel. After a few weeks, union organizers began to feel that a National Labor Relations Board (NLRB) election could be won. Meanwhile, the company management did nothing. Now the union has become confident enough to send nineteen of its supporters to work wearing union buttons and "tee" shirts. Sixteen of these supporters work in the company's cabinet shop. Management responds by calling in a labor consultant who meets with you and the plant manager. The consultant asks whether present economic considerations dictate any reduction in the labor force. The plant manager says yes, particularly in the cabinet shop. You knew that not only is this true, but also that thirteen of the union supporters in the cabinet shop have the least seniority. While it is illegal to fire a worker for belonging to a union, firings carried out strictly on the basis of seniority and for reasons of economy are legal. It certainly seems as though the breaks are all in the company's favor, but the plant manager asks whether you have any reservations about firing the infamous thirteen. What is your response?

5. You are being considered for promotion in your firm, and during a conversation with the company president, he asks whether you think it would be desirable for the employees to be able to express their preferences, by some suitable voting means, on issues of company policy like the following:

—Hiring new supervisors;
—Plant and office relocation;
—Mandatory retirement age;
—Bidding for controversial defense contracts (for example, chemical and biological warfare);
—Doing business with repressive regimes;
—Purchases of new plant and office equipment;
—Scheduling of breaks.

Knowing that your answers will be considered in the decision on your promotion, how would you respond?

6. Accountants at your electronics firm uncovered $1.1 million in fictitious sales at a subsidiary. The head of the subsidiary denied responsibility for the erroneous entries. As vice chairman of the parent firm, you took the case to the police but came away dissatisfied. When the police discovered no one had been hurt, the attitude they adopted was, "We'll get around to it eventually." You thus consider filing suit against the head of the subsidiary. You reason that it is important to disclose the problem and demonstrate to the stockholders that management is trying to protect their interests. The company's chief counsel advises otherwise as follows: "There's a definite danger in trying to hang a company's wrongdoings on one individual. For one thing, just consider the publicity and implications of sloppy management the case could produce! It seems to me it is far easier to fire this guy than to put together a tight legal case against him. Remember: Courts of law require the defendant be guilty beyond a reasonable doubt. But it's your decision . . . ." Do you think you should follow the advice of counsel or proceed with the suit?

7. Your fifty-eight-year-old friend, a magazine advertising salesman, has confided that because of a merger, he is now out of a job. You know that in spite of a good record, his chances of getting a job elsewhere in a business where youth is favored in hiring are not good. He is a vigorous, healthy man, with only a considerable amount of gray in his hair to suggest his age. He and his wife have decided that if he touches up his hair with black dye, he could easily pass for forty-five, which is the age he plans to state on the resumé he is preparing. He tells you that he knows that the truth about his age might well come out in time, but he calculates that he can deal with that situation when it arises. Meanwhile, he asks to include your name on his resumé as a character reference. Do you agree with your friend's proposed actions, and would you be willing to recommend him to a prospective employer? (Example based on Carr, 1968.)

8. As company president, you find that an aging executive, within a few years of retirement and his pension, is not as productive as he used to be. This executive has tended to delegate more and more of his responsibilities to two young and capable MBAs; in fact, it seems unlikely that he could manage his department without them. Further, the two younger executives have made it known to you that they will leave unless brighter opportunities open. Should you keep the aging executive on?

9. You are the program manager for a small but rapidly growing FM radio station. For the past several weeks you have been playing a record close to the top of the charts and frequently requested by listeners. You have just been notified by a spokesman for the black community that the record is degrading to all women and, in particular, to black women. He requests that you stop playing it. Do you ignore the request, draft a polite mind-your-own-business letter, or comply?

10. Suppose you are the manager of a division of a large organization based in New York. A management opening occurs in your Denver office for which one of the women in your New York office is the best qualified candidate. It would be a very good career opportunity for her, but she is married to a rising young executive in a local company. Moreover, they have a three-year-old child and a newly purchased home in the suburbs. Also, you play poker with her husband every other week. Should you offer her the job? (Example based on Boyle, 1973.)

11. A well-known science reporter has offered your publishing firm a sizzling manuscript about a reclusive millionaire who bears a strong resemblance to a noted real person. In the story, the millionaire hires an unscrupulous biologist, a jungle laboratory, and a nubile virgin and then has himself cloned. It's all true, the author says, but she cannot provide proof because of a vow to protect the millionaire's privacy. Would you make the decision to publish what could be your next best seller, or would you reject the manuscript without proof that the cloning actually happened?

12. The dean of a local business school has asked you, as manager of a public accounting firm, to take a small number of foreign students as accounting apprentices for a few months. Based on previous experience with accounting students who lack any contact with practical business conditions in the United States, you fear that honoring the request could prove very time consuming and costly to the firm. How should you respond to the dean's request?

13. You are considering two people for promotion in your firm. The first seems the most qualified, but the second happens to be the nephew of the president of your firm's biggest customer. It seems to you that promoting the latter will help the company's standing with its biggest customer. Who would you promote?

14. As the president of a clothing company, you have the opportunity to hire a competitor's plant supervisor. This supervisor is thoroughly familiar with the new fall styles of the competitor, and, according to rumor, the style is going to sweep the market. It is understood that, if hired, the supervisor is prepared to tell you all about the new style. What should you do?

15. As manager of the Chicago division of your large firm, you know that one of the employees moved to Chicago in the first place because his wife has a serious disease that can be treated only by a certain specialist here. An excellent opening comes up in San Francisco for which the employee would be ideal. Should you offer him that position even though his wife is now undergoing treatment with the specialist. If your answer to this question is different from your answer to question 10, how do you explain the difference? (Example based on Boyle, 1973:94.)

16. You are sales manager at a mid-sized electronics firm and have just found out that one of the salesmen whose salary (including commissions) comes to about $28,000 per year usually supplements his income by about $1,500 per year by charging certain unauthorized personal expenses against his expense account. He tells you he feels guilty from time to time, but he does it because he believes it is pretty much common practice in the company. What should you do?

17. You are district manager of a grocery store chain. One of the stores in your district is in a very poor, black section of a large city. Since the store's opening two decades ago, the neighborhood has changed, and sales volume has dropped. Five years ago the chain opened another, much larger, store in a nearby suburb. In the last two years, because of low volume and high pilferage, the small store has become a costly operation. To counter costs, markups have been higher than in the other stores in your district. This fact has not gone unnoticed by a local black group, which has just begun a boycott. Their demand is simple: Charge here what you charge in the white suburbs.

The chain's regional operations office is disturbed by the adverse publicity the boycott has generated. They leave it up to you: Should this store be closed down?

18. In a high-powered management consulting firm, a young executive who reports to you returns from an extended vacation with a beard, long sideburns, and hair like Felix Mendelssohn. He also stops wearing a coat and tie and begins appearing in T shirts with such inscriptions as "Save the Whales" on the front. Although the company has no policy on employees' attire, some company personnel seem irritated by his appearance. The young executive, however, still seems to perform his work with the same high-level of dedication and professional competence he demonstrated before his vacation. Further, you have no idea what the reaction of the firm's clients will be. What if anything should you do?

19. You run a young, rapidly expanding advertising agency. Some of your best employees have become increasingly active in consumer affairs. At first, they only attended meetings, signed petitions, and participated in other innocuous activities. Later, they began making statements to the press and were interviewed on television. Finally, last weekend two of them were arrested while demonstrating at the construction of a nearby nuclear power plant. A few colleagues have suggested to you that such behavior is doing the firm more harm than good since these individuals are frequently identified with your agency. But one of your best customers has said that he finds such involvement gratifying ("it shows they care"). As you contemplate how to handle this situation, you are told by a trusted friend that two of your staff workers are members of the Klu Klux Klan. How would you react to the activities of the executive and staff workers? Should the nature of the activism make any difference?

20. As special assistant to the manager of a large paper-products plant, you have become concerned about the tendency of certain shifts in some departments to effectively become segregated—that is, all black or all white. Assuming this arrangement is not contrary to any existing EEO regulation, should you listen to the advice of one of the white foremen and let "nature run its course" or should you heed the request of the black foreman who urges you to take corrective action?

21. Your aerospace firm has been awarded a large government contract, and as part of that contract, you must award a certain percentage of your subcontracts to minority companies. A friend tells you about several companies in which security and 51 percent of the stock is owned by minority persons, but whites with experience still control the management. Essentially, the white entrepreneur simply took one of the foremen, put "president" on his hard hat, and gave him a station wagon and some stock. According to the Small Business Administration, there is nothing wrong with this procedure from a legal standpoint. Would you recommend these companies to your firm to help meet its government contract requirements?

22. At a managers' meeting of your large toy and sporting goods retail chain, the company president has suggested the possibility of requiring all employees to submit to polygraph, or lie detector, testing to cut down on theft. One of the managers states: "I don't like it, but it's the only tool left. At our store, from 50 to 70 percent of our loss goes to employees; shoplifters don't take us for nearly as much." Assuming these figures are roughly correct for your branch store, would you request polygraph testing for your employees?

23. According to the *Wall Street Journal* (November 8, 1978), John L. Ebeling quit a $15,000-a-year job as product public relations manager for Winnebago Industries, Inc., because he could not in good conscience continue promoting recreational vehicles made without what he thought was sufficient regard for quality and safety. He explained this in a two-page letter to more than five hundred reporters, editors, and acquaintances around the country. Do you think this act was justifiable? How might the company have avoided it?

24. Assume that a key manufacturer is selling master automobile keys through the mail. Obviously, if car thieves wanted a set, there is no perfect method for the manufacturer to prevent them from getting one. The attitude of the manufacturer is not unlike that of mail-order handgun manufacturers: "No law requires me to cross-examine my customers." Do you think either manufacturer is correct? Can you think of any compromise between doing nothing and "cross-examining" customers? Does public policy need to be changed?

25. A number of American breweries are making domestic imitations of German beer and selling it in bottles that are virtually identical to the ones that used to contain the imported beer. Industry spokespersons have denied that this packaging technique and misleading television commercials are being used in order to trick buyers into thinking they were buying a German-made product. What do you think?

26. According to government health officials, someone dies every five minutes from cancer caused by smoking. Although cigarette advertising has become less objectionable in recent years, with more emphasis on low tar and nicotine and on rational choice, a few companies continue to try to lure the young into taking up an addictive habit through advertising that makes smoking seem glamorous and attractive. Should there be some special "Dishonor Roll" for the tobacco companies and advertising agencies responsible for such ads, and for the newspapers and magazines that publish them?

27. Should a U.S. drug company adhere to U.S. labeling standards in the sale of its products abroad? Or would such adherence be tantamount to administering an implied rebuke to the local government for failing to protect its consumers adequately or to imperiling all sellers in the local market in a way that powerful MNCs can afford but fledgling LDC firms cannot?

28. Should a U.S. MNC operating in an LDC keep wages as high as it can economically afford to, even though it risks being accused of trying to monopolize the best of the local talent?

29. A common characteristic of many multinational firms is their dependence for sales on the decisions of government officials or purchasing agents, who are in a position to demand an improper payment. A classic example is the request for a sizable "fee" by a minister of a country negotiating with an American company for a communications system. The minister said he would need the money for additional security forces to control anti-American agitation that might develop as a result of the sale. Moreover, multinational industries are often involved in sales of such magnitude that kickbacks are easy to disguise in the purchase prices. How do you think such situations should be handled?

30. A type of misconduct that has received much public attention lately is the tendency for employees of federal regulatory agencies to eventually take jobs with industries they once investigated. Many people have questioned how diligent a watchdog a federal employee can be if he or she has a $60,000 executive position in mind after retirement from "public service." Do you think public employees should be prohibited from later working in industries they once helped to regulate?

EXERCISE 2: INDUSTRYWIDE FUTURES RESEARCH*

This exercise is designed to show how attempts at forecasting and monitoring future trends can operate on an industrywide basis. Clearly, the exercise is not a job for one person. The first step is to select an industry for which the re-

---

* This exercise is based on the Trend Analysis Program of the American Council of Life Insurance in Washington, D.C. Further details are available in the Council's publication *How TAP Works.*

search will be performed—for example, the insurance, automobile, or banking industry. Next, each participant chooses one of the following seven categories of research:

1. Communications,
2. Health and biomedicine,
3. Science,
4. Social developments,
5. Business and economics,
6. Politics and government,
7. Technology.

The next step is to assign each participant one or more of the following publications to monitor over a specified period of time:

Advertising Age
American Journal of Sociology
American Scholar
American Review of Political
   Science
Architectural Record
Atlantic Monthly
Atlas

Behavior Today
Business Economics
Business Quarterly
Business and Society Review
Business Horizons
Business Week

Center Magazine
Challenge
Columbia Journalism Review
Conference Board Record

Daedalus
Datamation

Ebony
The Economist
Electronic News
Esquire

Financial Times of Canada
Forbes

Foreign Affairs
Fortune
Futures
The Futurist

Harper's
Harvard Business Review
IEEE Spectrum
Ladies Home Journal
House Beautiful
The Humanist

Industry Week
Inforsystems
Intellect

Journal of Consumer Affairs

Local newspapers

MBA
Money

National Journal
National Review
New Republic
New Scientists
Newsweek
The New York Review of Books
The New York Times

Popular Science

Progressive
Psychology Today
Public Interest

Ramparts
Rolling Stone

Saturday Review
Science (American Association
   for the Advancement of
   Science)
Science News
The Sciences (New York
   Academy of Sciences)
Scientific American

Skeptic
Social Policy
State-level business magazines

Technology Forecasting and
   Social Change
Technology Review

Village Voice
Vital Speeches of the Day
Vogue

Wall Street Journal
Washington Monthly
Wharton Magazine
Woman's Wear Daily

Each monitor then reviews each issue of his or her assigned publication for articles that relate to the chosen category of research. If an article meets the following criteria, the monitor abstracts the article and submits it to an "abstract analysis committee" for further review and analysis:

1. The article should involve an idea or event that is indicative of either a trend or shift in the macroenvironment;
2. The implications to be drawn from the article should have some relation to the long-range concerns of both U.S. society and the selected industry.

The analysis committee periodically goes over the abstracts and decides which of them appear of greatest significance to the industry under study. As the final step in the exercise, the analysis committee prepares a summary of the most significant abstracts and submits it to all the participants.

The following examples demonstrate how articles on particular topics within the seven categories of research can be effectively abstracted (Institute of Life Insurance, 1976):

Communications

Interactive TV
Television technology that enables viewers to interact with programs via home-based terminal linkups. Such interactions could involve personalized requests for information, registering of opinions or votes, purchases of merchandise being shown, or open conversation with the instructor or entertainer on the screen and others watching the program.
   Some implications of use: Local and regional decisionmaking can be made available for instantaneous feed-in and feedback by community members;

educational programming can be more responsive to individual viewers; access to information and shopping made faster and more convenient; opportunity for face-to-face personal interactions with others in the community, at shopping centers, and at schools may be diminished.

Health and Biomedicine

Amniocentesis

A simple, but not yet routine, prenatal procedure involving the insertion of a needle through the abdominal wall of the mother and into the amniotic sac surrounding the fetus. Amniotic fluid is withdrawn and fetal cells cultured from it are examined for disorders which result from extra, broken, or missing chromosomes. For example, if the cells exhibit 47 chromosomes rather than the normal 46, the fetus is suffering from mongolism and the child will be severely retarded. This procedure also enables the doctor to determine the sex of the fetus, which helps predict the chances of sex-linked hereditary defects like hemophilia. This is not "genetic engineering" in that no tampering is done with the genes themselves. The entire field of birth and genetic engineering is interesting in and of itself, involving such things as in vitro fertilization, cloning, and sperm and ova banks.

Some implications of use: Diminished incidence of genetically defective births; heightened debate regarding abortion; re-evaluation of health care and insurance procedures; possible tradeoff of individual freedom of decision (e.g., abort or risk having a defective child) for social goals.

Social Developments

Credentialism and Underemployment

Credentialism refers to the growth of the value placed on the accumulation of degrees and diplomas as opposed to inherent individual qualities, such as intelligence, and to work-related experience. The spreading of credentialism fueled the widescale belief on the part of the public, and especially employers and prospective employees, that advanced education is the most important prerequisite for good employment and upward social mobility. This led to minority interest group pressures on the higher educational system, and the decision to rearrange social status via universal access to that system. In turn, people were asked for academic credentials in jobs which previously did not require them, leading to a situation where many people are "underemployed" that is, working below or outside their level of educational attainment.

Some implications of this development: Already there are more college graduates than jobs needing that much education; the picture is likely to get worse as government spending gets cut back; less-educated persons will be hardest hit, with higher educated personnel filling more of the clerical and support positions, and technology continuing to eliminate many menial jobs.

Science

Hydroponics

The growing of plants in cultures rather than soil. Using this technique, plants may be grown in water, sand, or gravel that has been supplied with the necessary nutrients and aeration system for plant growth. The main advantage of hydroponics is that high crop yields can be obtained in places where soils are infertile or otherwise toxic to plant growth. While this method of plant growth has been around for years, it is gaining increasing attention because of the expense of fertilizers and the near-saturation of arable land on a worldwide basis. While it is most economical on a large scale, hydroponics has been applied successfully by enthusiastic amateurs in private greenhouses.

Some implications of further development and use: Reduced fertilizer use and greater reliance on solar energy could lessen the cost of large crop yields in food-poor nations, as well as expand crop capacity in soil-poor nations and regions.

EXERCISE 3: IN–OUT BASKET

In the various memos, letters, and conversations in this exercise you will find some nitty-gritty problems business managers encounter every day. As many managers realize, a problematic situation stated directly or indirectly in writing is often just the tip of the iceberg. Take a close look at the items in this exercise and try to find out the underlying problem in each. Assume you are the person to whom the communication is addressed and think about what decisions should be made in order to respond or maybe even what decisions should be postponed. Then, draft a concise response. In sharing your responses with others, be prepared to back up your line of thinking on both financial and ethical grounds.

> **1.** Interoffice Memo to: Director of Human Resources
>   From: Production Supervisor

I know company policy about employee records has tightened up a lot in the last year. But I've got a simple request. Could you please tell me if the two workers whose names and social security numbers are listed below have had any criminal convictions? Several of our female employees have been accosted late at night on the company parking lot. Although no one has been raped as yet, it seems only a matter of time before a rape is committed—unless we can pin down who is doing this. I have not arbitrarily selected these two people. They have been at the plant the shortest period of time, so I know less about them than my other employees. Furthermore, one has already been involved in making some suggestive remarks to one of our secretaries.

> **2.** Letter to: Company President
>   From: Ad Hoc Group for a Company-Sponsored Day Care Center

We, the undersigned, have been with this company for a cumulative total of 275 years. But we are frustrated! Why can't we have a company-sponsored day care center for our children? Many of us feel that we shall have to seek employment elsewhere if this matter can't be resolved. By the way, this is our third letter to you.

3. Interoffice Memo to: All Plant Managers
   From: Company Vice President for Human Resources

Please forgive this impersonal form letter, but I'm trying to get immediate feedback from as many sources as possible. Here at corporate headquarters, we've been kicking around the possibility of instituting a "new philosophy" of labor-management relations. Under the new arrangement, blue-collar workers would be treated essentially like white-collar employees. They would receive weekly salaries instead of hourly wages, participate in the corporate pension program, and get paid for sick absences. Any thoughts you might have on the arrangement would be greatly appreciated.

4. Letter to: Plant Manager
   From: Former Operations Supervisor

As you know, because of my auto accident last year, it looks like I'll need the use of a walking cane the rest of my life. Since my accident, I have been reassigned from my old job as supervisor to a desk job of shuffling papers. I would like you to reassign me to my old job of supervising plant operations. Maybe I can't navigate those catwalks so well anymore, but I still know what's going on up there. And that's really what "supervision" is all about. Nobody mentions "handicapped" where I can hear it, but I know what they're thinking. What they *don't* know is that I can spot a problem faster from ground level than they can when they're right next to it up there. Many people made it big without all of their "equipment" in perfect running order. FDR, for instance. And the guy who built the Brooklyn Bridge—he finished the job while he was in a wheelchair. Or Toulouse-Lautrec and Steinmetz; one was a dwarf and the other a cripple, and they certainly made their marks! Their minds were in perfect health, and so is mine. I still understand every step in this process and I've kept up on the new developments. I know my job. If all that's needed to handle this job is a pair of good legs, they'd better write "distance runner" or "dancer" into the job description! I wish I could get people to stop worrying so much about what I can't do, and think about what I *can* do—and how well I do it. I enjoy working and hope that you will rule favorably on this request.

5. Interoffice Memo to: Vice President of Human Resources
   From: Company President

Please note the attached letter from the ad hoc group for a company-sponsored day care center. What do you think? More specifically, I'd like you to do a six-month analysis of the possibility of implementing day care centers at all our major offices and plants. Meanwhile, for my own protection, please outline for me the major steps or points you intend to cover in your analysis.

6. This problem involves not a letter or memo in your basket but a real person sitting in your office. Assume that you are the director of human resources and she has come to complain, though in a very level-headed way. You listen carefully and know that when she has finished you will need to have some pretty good answers.

"The first day I walked into my office I was on cloud nine! But it didn't take long to come down to earth. Not when I accidentally found out the man I'd replaced had been paid more than they were paying me! Something else made me wonder about this new job, too. I noticed the people I worked with didn't treat me as they had my predecessor. They didn't seem to want to take me into their confidence. Actually, it was almost as if they resented me. Also, why was I not exempt?* The man I succeeded had been. If I'm doing his job, why shouldn't I have the same classification? I don't want any special consideration, I just want to be treated like everyone else. After all, I am qualified for the job! I'm not heavily into this women's lib thing, though I do think about it sometimes. The men in this section are polite enough, but they don't make me feel I'm part of the team. I don't want to think it's just because I'm a woman, but what else could it be?"

7. Again, the problem involves dealing with a live person, not cold paper. But this time you will have the luxury of listening in rather than being on the firing line. This exercise attempts to show how a boss ought to deal with a difficult employee (reprinted from Sennett, 1979*):

> Dr. Richard Dodds, a physics research worker, entered the office and showed his superior, Dr. Blackman, a letter. This letter was from another research institution, offering Dodds a position.
>
> Dodds: What do you think of that?
>
> Blackman: I knew it was coming. He asked me if it would be all right if he sent it. I told him to go ahead, if he wanted to.
>
> Dodds: I'm really quite happy here. I don't want you to get the idea that I'm thinking of leaving, unless, of course, he offers me something extraordinary.
>
> Blackman: Why are you telling me all this?
>
> Dodds: Because I didn't want you hearing from somebody else that I was thinking of leaving . . . .
>
> Blackman: It's up to you . . . A good man always gets offers. You get a good offer and you move, and as soon as you have moved, you get other good offers. It would throw you into confusion to consider all the good offers you will receive. Isn't there a factor of how stable you want to be?
>
> The discussion continued on how it would look if Dodds changed jobs at this point, and finally Dodds said:

---

* Most executives are exempt from the Fair Labor Standards Act.

* "The Boss's New Clothes," *New York Review of Books,* February 22, 1979, p. 45, as abridged from Abraham Zaleznik, "The Dynamics of Subordinacy," *Harvard Business Review,* May–June 1965.

Look, I came in here, and I want to be honest with you, but you go and make me feel guilty, and I don't like that.

Blackman: You are being as honest as can be.

Dodds: I didn't come in here to fight. I don't want to disturb you.

Blackman: I'm not disturbed. If you think it is best for you to go somewhere else, that is OK with me.

Finally Dodds blurts out:

I don't understand you. All I wanted was to show you this letter, and let you know what I was going to do. What should I have told you?

Blackman: That you had read the letter . . . but that you were happy here and wanted to stay, at least until you had a job of work done.

Dodds: I can't get over it. You think there isn't a place in the world I'd rather be than here in this lab . . . .

How do you interpret what is going on here? Do you approve of the way in which Blackman handled Dodds?

8. Interoffice Memo to: President
         From: Chairman of the Board

As you are aware, seasonal agricultural workers are still enmeshed in a tragic cycle of poverty. We need to make a much stronger effort in our organization to break this cycle in our own citrus groves, and I am asking you to develop a project in a frontier, uncharted area—to establish a program to correct the problems of seasonal workers and commit whatever funds and talent are necessary to do the job. To get things rolling, I want to ask a couple of things. First, what four or five principles do you think should guide a new agricultural labor program? Second, what specific actions might we take in the following areas:

—Employment and income,
—Housing,
—Health, education, and social services,
—Organizational development and support,
—Community relations and support.

9. Interoffice Memo to: Vice President for Public Affairs
         From: President

Well, I think I've hit on a way to show our corporate benevolence that none—not even our sharpest critics—can quarrel with. I propose that we establish three $100,000 prizes to be awarded annually for achievement in cancer research. Please give me your reaction promptly, since I want to take the proposal before the board this Thursday.

10. Interoffice Memo to: Manager, Design Engineering
        From: Manager, Engineering Department

The executive vice president has informed me that based on review of incoming orders and projected expense levels, we are going to have to trim expenses throughout the group. In order to meet that cutback, I am asking you to let two of your twenty-nine engineers go. I think that you will agree with me that the place to cut is the bubble-memory development program, since it can be slowed down without hurting any systems now in production or on the market. As I recall, we have only three people on that project. One is Jack Martin, who is an outstanding engineer. Since he is the center of the program, we will need to keep him on board for the time when we can revive the bubble-memory development program. The other two are Tom Rawlins, the first black engineer we hired, and Longworth Smith, who is white. Neither of them are going to become really great engineers, though both have a good attitude and some potential for growth. Still, I think you'll agree, they are both well below the rest of your engineers in qualifications. This is a tough decision, I know. If you can think of any way out, *please let me know.* Clearly, Smith must go. But Rawlins is another matter. You might want to consider letting one of your other twenty-seven engineers go, though Rawlins could never really replace them. Coming in on a new project this late is difficult for even hotshot engineers! Moreover, such an action would be preferential treatment, wouldn't it? (Exercise based on Purcell, 1971.)

11. Interdepartment Memo to: President
        From: Vice President for Marketing

As you know, our sales executives spend a lot of time wining and dining our customers. I have lately become rather concerned about the wining part of the task of entertaining our customers. Based on personal observation, as well as the opinions of the sales executives themselves, alcoholism is clearly a growing problem in our company. And it is not limited solely to the sales force. We need some sort of policy on how to handle it. Should we fire them outright? Give them a second chance? Have their supervisors work with their doctors, ministers, and families? Or should we go even further by providing counseling and treatment? Please let me know your thoughts on how to handle our alcoholic personnel.

12. Interoffice Memo to: Coordinator of Company Combined
                                 Community Fund Drive
        From: Chief Counsel

Well, I see it is that time of year again. Don't you know the Combined Community Fund drive has serious weaknesses? One is that it seems to be part of the dehumanizing process that afflicts modern life. As an "employee," I rebel at being *told* how much I should contribute as a "fair share." Because who got together? If I'm tired of having other people tell me everything in my life, how must our assembly-line workers feel?

13. Interoffice Memo to: Coordinator of Company Combined
                                             Community Fund Drive
             From: Company Sales Representative

Thanks but no thanks. The Combined Community Fund is not getting my "fair share." Here's why: The Fund has been too slow to recognize the emergence of minority groups or to recognize anything new that has come along. It tends to be service oriented. But what the black, Hispanic and Indian communities need is social activism!

14. Workers at the Eaton Corporation summarized their composite critique of employee relations in a report to the Battle Creek manager that took the form of a letter written by one factory employee explaining why he brings so little of himself to his workplace. Clearly, this letter makes quick, glib answers impossible (Scobel, 1975:133–35):

Dear Sir:

What you are asking me, as I see it, is why am I not giving you my best in exchange for the reasonable wages and benefits you provide me and my family.

First, I'm not trying to blame anybody for why you don't see the "whole" me. Some of the problem is company policy, some is in union thinking, some is just me. Let me tell you why, and I'll leave it to bigger minds than mine to figure out blames and remedies.

I'll begin with my first day on the job eleven years ago—my first factory job, by the way. I was just nineteen then. Incidentally, my cousin started work in your office as a clerk typist on the same day. We used to drive to work together. She still works for you, too.

The first thing I was told that day by the personnel manager and my foreman was that I was on ninety days' probation. They were going to measure my ability to start out stealing or coming to work drunk or getting into fights or horseplay. What made it even worse was when I later found out that no one told my cousin she was on probation. I asked her if she had seen the rules, and here it is eleven years later and she still doesn't know there are about thirty-five rules for those of us working in the factory.

What it boils down to is that your policies—yes, and the provisions of our union contract—simply presume the factory man untrustworthy, while my cousin in the office is held in much higher regard. It's almost like we work for different companies.

After I had been here about eight months, a car hit my car broadside on the way to work. My cousin and I were both taken to the hospital right away and released several hours later. As soon as I was released by the hospital, I called the plant to tell them what happened. I couldn't get through to my foreman, so I told my tale to a recording machine. When my cousin didn't show up by nine o'clock, her boss got worried and called the house and then the hospital. When he found out my cousin had a broken arm and some cuts, but was basically okay, he sent for a taxi to take her home.

Both my cousin and I ended up missing four days' work. On each of the next three days, I called and told the tape recorder I would not be in. I never heard from anybody in the company and when I got back to work later that week, my supervisor said, "Sure glad to see you're okay . . . it's a shame you spoiled your perfect attendance record . . . ."

Sir, I don't come to work to be worried about by someone. But I have some difficulty understanding why, when I'm absent, nobody really cares. It seems as if the company's just waiting for me to do something wrong. When I got back to work from that car accident, you started getting another little chunk less from me. Does that sound crazy? Or does it seem selfish?

Sir, why must I punch a time clock? Do you think I'd lie about my starting and quitting times? Why must I have buzzers to tell me when I take a break, relieve myself, eat lunch, start working, go home? Do you really think I can't tell time or would otherwise rob you of valuable minutes? Why doesn't the rest room I must use provide any privacy? Why do I have to drive my car over chuck holes while you enjoy reserved, paved parking? Why must I work the day before and after a holiday to get holiday pay? Are you convinced I will extend the holiday into the weekend—while, by the way, my cousin is thought to have more sense than that?

I guess I'm saying that when you design your policies for the very few who need them, how do you think the rest of us feel?

Sir, do you really think I don't care or don't know what you think of me? If you are convinced of that, then you will never understand why I bring less than all of myself to my workbench.

You know, sir, in my eleven years, I've run all kinds of machinery for you, but your company has never even let me look at what the maintenance man does when he has to repair one of my machines. No one has ever really asked me how quality might be better or how my equipment or methods might be improved. In fact, your policies drum it into me good and proper that you really want me to stay in my place. And now, you want to know why I don't pour it on? Wow! Don't you realize that I may want to contribute more than you let me? I know the union may be responsible for some of this—but again, I'm trying to explain why, not whose fault it is.

You know, sir, I would like a more challenging job, but that isn't the heart of the matter, not for me at least. If there were a sense of dignity around here, I could not hold back the effort and ideas within me, even if my particular job was less than thrilling. Many of my buddies do not want a greater job challenge, but they do want their modest contributions respected.

You know, my neighbor is a real quiet, sweet old man who just retired from here last month. When I ask him how he sums up his life's work, he says—and I can almost quote him exactly—"A pretty good place to work—only thing that really bothered me was that warning I got twenty-six years ago for lining up at the clock two and one-half minutes early."

Well, sir, I suspect twenty-six years ago you may have corrected this quiet, nice guy for lining up early at your clock. But the price you paid was making him a "clock watcher" for twenty-six years. I wonder—was that warning all that necessary? Why couldn't you have just told him why lining up early isn't a good idea and then relied on him to discipline himself? I wonder.

It has been said, sir, that factory people look upon profit as a dirty word. I don't feel that way, but you know, it's almost as if love is the dirty word here.

Why don't I give my best? Well, I guess I have a kind of thermostat inside me that responds to your warmth. Do you have a thermostat inside you?

15. Interoffice Memo to: Assistant Plant Manager
        From: Company President

Please be advised that a joint meeting of the OSHA Committee and the Accident Investigation Committee is scheduled for tomorrow at the Brookville plant, which has the worst safety record of any of our plants. Before Harry got sick, he was chairperson of the joint committee and was highly valuable in directing the meetings toward achieving our overall safety goals. Since you're filling in for him, you will want to attend the meeting tomorrow fully prepared. I will be available in the morning to go over a list of questions or points you think need to be raised at the meeting.

Case Studies

If you get the feeling that questions of right and wrong do not present themselves readily to managers and that decision making in the increasingly turbulent environment will become ever more complicated, then this book will have served its intended purpose. The case studies in this section all involve in one way or another many of the topics we have discussed throughout the text. They are included here to offer you an opportunity to apply your knowledge, sensitivity, and judgment to some realistic business and environmental situations. Your responses to the issues and situations suggested in each case should be based on your answers to four basic questions: (1) What is the problem? (2) What are the alternatives? (3) What is the social responsibility of the firm? (4) What course of action should be recommended? As in the real world of business, knowing what questions to ask and the ability to take a sound approach to a problem are often the crucial steps toward seeking a solution that is at once profitable and ethical. Remember how we opened this book and when considering these cases do not merely tend to the sails and rigging of your vessel, but be constantly alert to the real forces behind your journey—the winds.

CASE STUDY 1:
WALT DISNEY PRODUCTIONS*

The Legacy

The creative talents of Walt Disney were exceptional by any standard of business performance. He pioneered new motion picture concepts. That he put Mickey Mouse on the screen is known throughout the world. But consider his skillful blending of symphonic orchestration and animation in *Fantasia*. That film was so far ahead of its time that it lost money when it was released in 1941, yet in the last decade it has netted Disney Productions over $1 million a year.

Walt Disney engineered the transition into television when other producers were being thrown into depression. Always creative and ever daring, he seized the opportunity—a decade before anyone else—to revive a moribund amusement park business with the new concept of the theme park. Even his fundamental business strategy had the stamp of creativity; each operation—movies, television, and amusement parks—supported the others.

---

* This case study was developed by the author from publicly available information in the Walt Disney Productions annual report of 1978 and other sources as cited in the text. The case is designed to serve as a basis for classroom discussion rather than to illustrate effective or ineffective business practices.

Since its founder's death in 1966, Walt Disney Productions has remained a highly profitable enterprise. Since 1966, in fact, its profits have grown at a compounded annual rate of 22.6 percent, to the $82 million that the company earned in 1977 on sales of $629.8 million. About two-thirds of that revenue (compared with slightly less than half of its revenues in 1970) comes from its two amusement parks, Disneyland and Disneyworld. It is one of Wall Street's premier growth stocks.

But there is a growing suspicion among some outside observers that all is not well. Specifically, they are asking whether the company is too wedded to the original ideas of its founder. Was not Walt Disney's real legacy creativity and daring? If he were alive today, would he still be exploiting ideas he had developed in the 1950s and 1960s? Or, just possibly, would he be thinking of ways to seize new opportunities in the technological and social changes of the 1980s?

Coping with Change

Consider how Disney himself might have reacted to the commercial appearance of the video tape recorder (VTR). Would he have sued Sony Corporation—as did Disney management in 1976 (see *Business Week*, July 31, 1978)—to block the marketing of Sony's Betamax on the grounds that it infringed on Disney's copyrights? Or would he have cashed in on the impending video recorder bonanza (as other motion picture companies tried to do) by distributing tapes of the movies that are stored in Disney's vast library?

Perhaps an even bigger challenge than technological change for Disney management will be social change. The reasons for impending social change are clear: The number of American children aged five through nine is expected to drop 5 percent in the next eight years; the number of ten-to-fourteen-year-olds, 14 percent. The prime U.S. market for Disney products is the five-to-eight-year-old. It would be hard, if not impossible, for the Disney management to capture much more of that shrinking market.

At the same time that the market is shrinking, the mores of American society are changing. Some of these changes put strains on the family unit; others, new demands on the creative artist; and still others, limitations on corporate strategies. For example, as the Disney company moved into the Sierras to build its $80 million ski village, it suddenly found itself facing what so many other industries have had to face: the environmentalists. But Disney management was unaccustomed to this kind of challenge. Building a ski village in the face of environmental opposition was not quite like moving into the mountains with a film crew to photograph lizards and cactus flowers. After a Sierra Club suit and other complications forced Disney management to abandon the original site, they focused on a site at Independence Lake (see Gottschalk, 1978). But this time management became impatient with an ever-increasing number of permits and suggestions from state officials. Finally, they angrily suspended all work on the project, after having spent $2 million.

New Ventures

In fairness to management, the aim of getting into the ski business does represent at least an effort to cope with demographic shifts. But the idea of a ski resort had originated, not with current management, but with Walt Disney himself some years ago. The same might be said of the centerpiece of the new venture Disney management is engaged in—the Experimental Prototype Community of Tomorrow. Dubbed Epcot, the community will be designed for adults instead of children. When it opens in 1982 in Orlando, Florida, Epcot will present many new forms of technology in its "Future World" and the history, arts, and crafts of thirteen countries in its "World Showcase."

The stress will be on sophistication. In "Future World," the visitor will go through pavilions describing the latest technologies involving the sea, land, space, energy, transportation, and health. For example, in the land pavilion, sponsored by Kraft, Inc., the visitor will see a variety of shows and attractions dramatizing the challenges in the important areas of nutrition, food production, and harvesting. Proceeding to "World Showcase," the visitor can tour pavilions sponsored by various countries. In West Germany's pavilion, for example, one can take a simulated trip along the Rhine, the Tauber, and the Ruhr. Detailed miniatures of famous landmarks, including the Cologne Cathedral, can be seen. After all this, the visitor can relax in a beer garden.

The stakes in this new venture are huge; Epcot's cost will exceed $500 million. But construction will be aided by lease payments from an expected six or seven corporate sponsors and thirteen countries. Moreover, the company has been accumulating cash to build Epcot (about $300 million thus far) and will probably not even have to go to the bank.

But Epcot, like ski resorts in the Sierras, has its critics. As Earl C. Gottschalk, Jr., reports (1979):

> There are other naysayers in the intellectual community and among the media. Michael Harrington, a socialist and social critic writing in *Harper's* magazine, condemns Epcot for its "technological gimmickry" and for presenting American multinational corporations as the only solvers of man's problems. In *New West* magazine, architectural critic John Pastier calls Epcot "an incomplete, simplified, and possibly distorted view" of the world's future and of other nations.
>
> Martin Sklar, a vice president at Disney WED Enterprises, says, "We admit to being optimistic over man's future. You can call Epcot our answer to the gloomy future predictions of the Club of Rome." (The Club of Rome, a group of intellectuals, said in 1972 that technology couldn't solve man's problems and that present economic growth couldn't be sustained.) But Mr. Sklar adds, "We don't have the answers. We're just communicators. We expect Future World to be a series of turnons to new ideas in many fields and that it'll stimulate people to study these problems on their own."

Assume that you are the new top management of Walt Disney Productions and that the financial means for new ventures are available. The only thing lacking is a winning strategy. How would you go about thinking through what the alternatives might be? A word of caution: Do not ignore people problems. In effecting change, how are you going to keep the old guard from getting too upset? And how are you going to bring in—and keep—young, creative people?

CASE STUDY 2:
NOVA MINERAL CORPORATION*

The ocean floor, lying beyond the submerged margins of the continents, is one of the most inhospitable environments on the planet. It is a region of continuous darkness, crushing pressure, and sparse but marvelously adapted life. The deep seabeds also contain deposits of important minerals. Large areas are carpeted with manganese nodules—the size of a potato, on the average—that contain over twenty different metals. It is thought that the nodules are formed by a natural chemical process whereby particles of metal attach themselves to solid objects like shells, stones, sharks' teeth, and whale bones. Although the nodules were first discovered a century ago by the historic oceanographic expedition of the H.M.S. *Challenger,* their abundance and importance were not fully appreciated until the 1960s, when technological advances began to make deepsea mining look not only feasible but also commercially attractive. Current interest centers on the nodules' nickel, copper, cobalt, and manganese content. These metals are crucial to industry. The seabed areas of prime interest to industry are so extensive that planned commercial ventures are likely to use only a small percentage of the nodule deposits. Nodule mining promises a nearly inexhaustible supply of important minerals, access to which could contribute significantly to future global economic growth.

How valuable are the minerals on the ocean floor? It is estimated that a single deepsea mining operation that collects 3 million dry tons of nodules per year could produce somewhere between 35,000 and 40,000 tons of nickel per year. By the year 2000, twenty mining operations would be producing roughly the equivalent of today's total world consumption of nickel (700,000 tons). The technology of mining nodules at depths of three miles or more is considered proved; only the engineering task of scaling up from test-sized to full-sized vessels and equipment remains to be completed. The preferred mining tool appears to be a kind of vacuum cleaner head that sucks the nodules into a

* The Nova Mineral Corporation in this case study is fictitious; the background data and events are actual and based on information gathered by the author from the following sources: Lawrence B. Krause and Hugh Patrick, eds., *Mineral Resources in the Pacific Area,* Papers and Proceedings of the 9th Pacific Trade and Development Conference (San Francisco: Federal Reserve Bank of San Francisco, 1978); *U.S. News & World Report,* August 28, 1978; William Wertenbaker, "Mining the Wealth of the Ocean Deep," *New York Times Magazine,* July 17, 1977, pp. 14*ff.*; *Wall Street Journal,* April 6, 1978, and July 31, 1978; Kennecott Corporation, *Annual Report,* New York 1978; *AEI Journal on Government and Society* (October 1978):8–11; and U.S. Department of State, *Constitution for the Sea,* International Organizations and Conferences Series 123 (Washington, D.C.: U.S. Government Printing Office, 1976).

pipe trailed by the mining ship, which is equipped with ultrasensitive stabilizing and navigational gear. Once raised from the depths, the nodules will be hauled by barge to processing sites on land. An alternative mining method, a continuous line of buckets revolving to the ocean floor and back to the ship, may be used in more rugged terrain.

Economic and Political Uncertainties

In recent years, a new pessimism has overtaken the deepsea mining industry. Managers in some manganese mining ventures have begun to reexamine their projects. The first reason for the pessimism is economic. Prices of nickel and copper, the key metals contained in the trillions of tons of nodules estimated to lie on the ocean floor, are sharply depressed by worldwide overproduction from land mines. There is little hope for any quick price recovery and thus little appetite for the huge capital outlays required to tap the ocean ores. Some experts estimate that nickel prices will have to rise 50 percent and copper prices will have to double to make seabed mining economically feasible.

Still, the United States has considerable interest in seabed mining. It now imports nearly all its manganese and cobalt, 90 percent of its raw nickel, and about 20 percent of its copper. Seabed mining easily could make the nation self-sufficient in each of these metals. Aside from national-security benefits, the impact on the U.S. balance of payments could be profound. J.G. Wenzel, chairman and president of Ocean Minerals Company, the operating arm of a consortium that includes Lockheed, Royal Dutch/Shell, and Standard Oil of Indiana, calculates that the United States could save $40 billion in foreign payments by the year 2000 if seabed mining starts by 1985 (*Wall Street Journal,* July 31, 1978).

Another reason for the pessimism is that, even if the economic uncertainties could be overcome, a number of political hurdles remain. Will it be legal for U.S. firms to mine the sea floor? If so, under what national or international restraints and forms of taxation? The 158-nation UN Conference on the Law of the Sea has been wrestling since 1973 with a treaty that would govern access to the oceans. Many lesser-developed countries are insisting that the treaty set up an international agency empowered to rigidly control all aspects of deepsea mining, including licensing, production limits, and tax output. LDCs, fearing that the major industrial nations will be the only ones with the capital and technology to harvest the oceans' riches, insist that ocean minerals belong to every nation equally. Also, emerging nations that now depend heavily on land-based mining for export earnings fear that their markets may be disrupted by large-scale sea mining; thus, they want a hand in controlling it.

In 1979 the conference met for the third time, but prospects for completing its work seemed remote. The conferees have agreed in principle on the creation of an International Seabed Authority to oversee mining operations and the division of the proceeds. They have also agreed to the establishment of an entity called the Enterprise, which would mine the Third World's share of nodules. The industrial and developing nations disagree, however, on how much power the international authority should have and how the mining operation should be apportioned between the Enterprise and private mining companies.

Elliot Richardson, head of the U.S. delegation to the conference, has voiced the United States' adamant opposition to proposals that would give the Third World control over marine resources through the seabed authority. He warned that miners from the United States and other industrial nations must have sufficient incentive to accept the risks of mining ventures. Otherwise, no one—including the poorer countries—will benefit from this common heritage. Furthermore, Richardson said, the United States will not delay congressional enactment of a seabed mining law. Although the prospect of a separate U.S. seabed mining law has angered some Third World delegates, Richardson believes it may prod the conference toward a final agreement, which makes the risks worth taking (see *U.S. News & World Report,* August 28, 1978).

The conference has spent six years writing a new international law of the sea. It has agreed upon 90 percent of the 300 proposed articles in a draft treaty covering such tough, wide-ranging issues as navigation, territorial waters, economic development of continental-shelf marine resources, fisheries, pollution control in the oceans, and marine research. The seabed mining issue has proven the toughest nut to crack. But Richardson notes that Third World delegates should be aware that, with or without a treaty, the United States and other industrial nations will mine undersea nodules. As he put it in an interview: "If it were to become clear at any point that the Law of the Sea Conference had failed to create an international system for mining, it would then become desirable to consider the possibility of a multilateral treaty. Initially, this would embrace industrial countries represented in the consortia that are now preparing to engage in deep-seabed mining. Other countries, including developing countries, could be invited to participate" (*U.S. News & World Report,* August 28, 1978).

Nova Mineral Corporation's Decision

Among the U.S. firms betting heavily that the first commercial production of deepsea minerals will begin by 1985 is Nova Mineral Corporation. This corporation, which had a net income of $200 million in 1978, tends to suffer greatly from depressions in the worldwide copper market; in 1975, for example, the company had a negative cash flow. These extremely adverse business conditions have, in the view of the company president, Fred Milliken, made diversification into other metals almost imperative. Milliken believes that nickel is the key to Nova Corporation's prosperity.

The most pressing question that Milliken faces is how fast Nova should proceed with its ocean mining program. A drastic cutback was also a real possibility. Nova and the other members of its consortium have already invested nearly $50 million in exploration and research. Milliken estimated that a plant and related ships costing over $500 million would require about $235 million yearly to operate. At current metal prices, he calculates that the operation would just about break even, and he expected such an operation to come on line soon after 1985.

To see where the company should try to be in 1985, Milliken called a meeting of senior corporate executives, top managers, and staff personnel assigned to the ocean mining program, and a few outside consultants. What follows are some random notes Milliken jotted down during the three-hour meeting:

—The state of Hawaii, buoyed by the development of its first geothermal well, which opens the possibility of cheap and plentiful electric power for processing, is now actively courting prospective ocean mining companies.

—While failures are to be expected in any new venture, ocean mining is more than normally unpredictable because complicated machinery tends to break down at sea.

—Many economists anticipate a very large increase in nickel and copper prices; other experts indicate that the price of manganese will go very much higher ten to twelve years from now and that high-grade land sources of manganese will be exhausted within twenty-five years.

—One company already has a 560-foot vessel that can take a thousand tons of nodules a day from the ocean bottom, which is a fairly close approximation of commercial mining.

—We really don't know the environmental impact of deepsea mining (e.g., the animals in the path of the dredge will probably be killed; others may be suffocated by stirred-up sediment).

—Compared to mining ashore, mining the floor of the sea has advantages: A deposit of manganese nodules can be found without drilling or blasting; every nodule to be mined during a project can be counted before a single piece of mining machinery is ordered; and no shafts need be bored or mountains bulldozed to reach the ore.

—The profits of nodule mining are a big uncertainty: Although the Ocean Mining Administration has concluded that nodule mining could turn an annual profit of 12 to 22 percent, this figure might mean just breaking even.

After the meeting Milliken added the following comments to his notes. Treaty proponents maintain that domestic legislation and outright mining by American-led consortia might make it difficult to consummate the law of the sea negotiations. For the United States to begin mining the alleged "common heritage" before the international mining enterprise is launched could so anger the countries in the majority that an opportunity to negotiate a comprehensive treaty would be gone forever. But support of the bill in Congress might provide better resource allocation than the most likely law of the sea treaty. The bill's enactment could strengthen the hand of the U.S. delegation at the United Nations. And the absence of a treaty per se would have the ultimate benefit of preventing the creation of an inherently inefficient system of regulation—the kind of system that would stem from acknowledging an international organization as the sole authority in the exploitation of deepsea minerals.

Assume you are Milliken and must begin mapping corporate strategy on a number of fronts. How would you proceed? Would you begin by putting corporate support behind the seabed law in Congress or the UN treaty negotiations?

CASE STUDY 3:
CON EDISON*

Consolidated Edison Company of New York, Inc., supplies electric service in almost all of New York City and in most of Westchester County. In 1978, earnings per share declined but not below the 1976 earnings so that the company's cash position appeared satisfactory. It financed $314 million of construction in 1978 and retired $40 million of securities without external financing. In January 1978, the Board of Trustees increased the quarterly common dividend to 55 cents per share, and in January 1979, to 61 cents. Standard & Poor upgraded its rating of Con Edison's mortgage bonds to "A" from "A–".

Regardless of its financial picture, Con Edison continually finds itself immersed in tough political and legal battles. In 1979, for the sixth time in the same number of years, Con Ed petitioned the state and county environmental authorities for special permission to burn cheaper but dirtier high-sulfur oil in place of the increasingly expensive imported low-sulfur oil required by law in conjunction with its energy strategy for the 1980s.

Con Ed's Strategy for the 1980s

Short-range planning for Con Edison is designed mainly to reduce dependence on imported oil by substituting coal and nuclear fuels, and to reduce discriminatory taxes levied on electric and steam consumption. The company, in

---

* The Con Edison information contained in this case study was obtained from *Con Edison Annual Report, 1978*, pp. 2–3 and 5–7, and from Con Edison Stockholders' Report, "An Energy Strategy for the 1980s for New York City and Westchester County," March 1979.

cooperation with the state power authority, has the technical and financial capability to substitute domestic coal and uranium for a major portion of its boiler fuel requirements. It would thereby save customers hundreds of millions of dollars and reduce the some $600 million or more per year that the company pays for oil, most of which is imported from foreign countries. What Con Edison lacks, but is trying to get, are governmental approvals to let them "do what needs to be done."

More than 60 percent of the electricity supplied in Con Edison's service area is generated by burning oil. If the short-range planning steps the company recommends are taken, oil would account for about 25 percent of the fuel used to supply electricity. Consumers in Con Ed's service territory could save billions of dollars over the rest of this century, and the company could achieve substantial independence from the OPEC oil cartel. Specifically, Con Ed's energy strategy calls for steps to:

> 1. Permit the state power authority to construct its proposed coal- and refuse-burning plant at an in-city site, and a nuclear plant upstate. Con Edison would purchase the output of these units as a substitute for electricity generated by imported oil.
> 2. Permit Con Edison to burn coal at three generating units that can burn coal. Con Edison would install 99.5 percent efficient electrostatic precipitators and a capacity to switch to low-sulfur oil when warranted by air quality conditions. With coal burned at these plants and at the power authority's in-city plant, total sulfur dioxide and particulate emissions from power plants in New York City would still be far below their 1966 levels.
> 3. Repeal discriminatory taxes . . . on the fuel used to generate electricity. For fuel burned in the City, the sales tax on fuel is compounded by gross receipts taxes and additional sales taxes on the electricity produced from the fuel, so that New York City customers pay more than $1.18 for every dollar Con Edison pays for oil.
> 4. Intensify energy conservation efforts, . . . [even though] on a per capita basis, the service area is already the most energy efficient in the United States.

The longer range planning, for 1990 and beyond, centers around an ambitious research and development program. If successful it could enable the company to burn clean "liquefied coal" in New York City plants and to add small, efficient fuel cell generators at substations throughout the system as the load grows. Among the other Con Edison R&D programs that seek, in cooperation with industry, better ways to produce and deliver electricity economically are: a fuel cell power plant project under construction at a company site on the East Side of Manhattan (a fuel cell generates electricity by converting fuel chemically in a process similar to a battery rather than by burning fuel); a compact high-voltage, direct current (HVDC) transmission project; and a solar-assisted hot water systems project.

The Opponents' View of Sulfur Dioxide Pollution

A number of environmental groups oppose Con Ed's strategy of trying to reduce the low-sulfur requirement (e.g., Sierra Club and Natural Resources Defense Council). Many public officials with the city's Air Resources Board, Brookhaven National Laboratory, and the state's Consumer Protection Board and Environmental Conservation Department are also skeptical. As they point out, if sulfate concentrations produce only small increases in the mortality rate (say, a fraction of a percent), this can still mean a lot of deaths when multiplied by millions of people in the region. Moreover, they point out that the public is hardly clamoring to lower air quality to save money (*New York Times,* April 10, 1979).

While sulfur dioxide is not an especially toxic gas, it can convert, in a humid atmosphere, into sulfates and sulfuric acid. Scientists have managed to link sulfates to bronchitis, asthma, lower respiratory system disease, susceptibility to virus disease, and heart-lung disease. The following two paragraphs, excerpted from the *Seventh Annual Report of the Council on Environmental Quality,* give the federal government's position on sulfur dioxide pollution (1976:216–17 and 221–22):

> The primary air quality standards for sulfur dioxide (SO_2) and total suspended particulates (TSPs) were derived from population studies involving both pollutants. Therefore, SO_2 and TSP air quality data should be examined together. More recent evaluations confirm that the two pollutants in association are related to health effects. However, their presence may only indicate the existence of other pollutants such as sulfates. Evidence now shows that these compounds may be primarily responsible for the health effects originally attributed to SO_2 and TSP.
>
> SO_2 and TSP levels have shown marked decreases over the past five years in almost all regions analyzed, giving evidence of the effectiveness of national and local regulatory programs. All cities except St. Louis show a clear and significant improvement.... [The analysis provides] the SO_2 trend history for New York City. Where the downward trends in TSP are temporarily reversed, the reason is attributable to differences in weather from one year to the next. An exceptionally cold winter increases TSP and SO_2 levels, as more fuel is burned, while a very mild winter does the reverse.

The Outlook

As Con Edison moves into the 1980s, it continues to navigate rough political waters, and the opposition is formidable. The state appears willing to allow the company to prove its case. If it can successfully do that, then Con Edison will need federal approval. Meanwhile, the environmentalists will no doubt be laying mines along the regulatory route. The overriding question to be answered is what should Con Ed's strategy be.

CASE STUDY 4:
RILEY CORPORATION*

The Riley Corporation is a large company that, through seven operating companies, produces and services industrial heaters, boilers, filters, pumps, deep-well pumping equipment, and water-cooling towers. In 1980, its profits were well over $36 million from total revenue of $245 million. At its June 1982 annual meeting, President R.J. Powell promised stockholders, who had raised grave concerns about the faltering nuclear construction market upon which a significant proportion of sales were based, that "Riley will remain competitive in the energy field. For example, our company has begun to explore the possibility of alternative energy resources, such as geothermal energy."

The basic idea behind geothermal energy is quite simple: Harness energy from steam, hot water, or magma (molten rock) under the earth's crust and then use it to spin turbines on the surface. According to the U.S. Geological Survey (Circular #726, 1975), the United States has a total energy content of steam and hot water in excess of 400,000 quads; the energy content of magma is, in theory, almost limitless. In 1974, the Geothermal Energy Act committed the federal government to helping industry develop this abundant resource.

The immediate decision facing Powell was this: Whether to lease 9,000 acres of geothermal land in New Mexico and to begin drilling, using techniques borrowed from the oil industry along with some equipment already produced by the Riley Corporation. To help arrive at a decision, he called a meeting with several staff departments that had been studying the proposal for several weeks.

The research director, who spoke first, noted that the technologies for utilizing each of the three types of geothermal resources are in varying stages of development. Geopressured hot water and steam appear nearest to commercialization, but the ability of geopressured resources to sustain flow over extended periods is untested. Union Oil Company, the largest producer of geothermal energy in the world, operates the only commercial projects in the United States and sells the steam to a public utility. Currently, Union has several additional plants under construction. The research director stressed the likelihood that the company's laboratory could contribute to Riley's leadership in the development and production of geothermal energy, since the technology is not all that different from the kind the lab staff has already been working on.

---

* This fictitious case study was developed by the author to serve as the basis for classroom discussion.

The deputy director of research was less optimistic. There would be the danger of rapid obsolescence in this emerging field. The company would be a latecomer to the R&D sweepstakes. And the company would have to develop an exploration team. "You just don't stomp around the countryside with bare feet and drill wherever you find a patch of warm ground. And once you tap a reservoir of steam, there's no way to know how long it will last." The research director tried to smile when the deputy mumbled something about teaming up with other companies seeking to advance geothermal energy.

Powell turned next to the marketing vice president. She began by noting the obvious fact that utilities were anxious to find alternatives to oil. Glancing at the research director, she added that in her opinion, the utilities might even be likely sources of cash to expand the field. Why not devise a plan to sell the steam to them under a formula that pegs the price to the cost of oil? But the marketing vice president had some less favorable views as well. Foremost was the question of how Riley would develop the new market channels to peddle steam. Even assuming effective distribution channels could be developed, she thought that the chances of high sales were dim—at least in the near future. (Union Oil, the undisputed leader, was making little more than $20 million a year.) Another area of concern centered on what government might do. For example, what if it drastically increased solar energy incentives?

The vice president of production agreed that possible government actions were not to be discounted. For example, he pointed out to Powell that the possibility of environmental regulation was not unlikely. He suspected that geothermal energy might involve such problems as noxious gas emission ("a smell just like rotten eggs"), land subsidence, stimulation of seismicity, groundwater contamination, waste brine disposal, surface water contamination, and cooling water discharge. Nevertheless, the production vice president concluded on an upbeat note; he had visited several geothermal pilot plants and had little doubt that Riley could establish its own.

The last individual to speak at the meeting was the vice president for finance: The initial investment at the New Mexico site would be on the order of $30 million and about $5 million per year thereafter. He saw "no problem" in raising that kind of money. However, the decision was fraught with uncertainty. What happens to the inflation rate, interest rates, and oil prices would be of profound importance to the company.

Assume that you are the corporate planning director and that on the day after the project meeting, Powell tells you that there are far too many uncertainties for the company to come to a decision at the present time. He asks you to prepare a set of assumptions about the relevant future that would reduce the range of uncertainty surrounding the proposed project.

CASE STUDY 5:
THOR TIRE & RUBBER COMPANY*

For the last several years, Expansion, Inc., a New York based conglomerate, had been making noises that it wanted to shut down its Thor Tire & Rubber Company plant in Columbus, Ohio. These rumblings had become so frequent and lasted so long, that most workers ignored them. The 120-day strike last year seemed proof enough that workers simply did not believe a shutdown possible.

But one brisk October morning company president Jim Young got the word from New York: The decision had been made. He was to announce that the $15-million plant would close in one week. The following month, existing equipment would be dismantled and shipped to various buyers. Columbus was Young's hometown; an announcement was not easy. He began to write out the announcement: "With great reluctance and deep regret . . . ."

Young went on to outline the reasons why the parent company in New York had decided as they had:

1. High labor costs: Studies showed unit labor costs were 250 percent higher at Columbus than at the company's most efficient plant (in Little Rock).
2. Technological change: Consumers were demanding tougher, longer-lasting radials, while the Columbus plant was geared to produce only conventional tires. The one-million-square-foot, four-story building was simply not suited for the new production process that would have to be installed.
3. Pollution regulations: The Ohio Environmental Protection Agency continued to tighten pollution standards over those in effect in other areas of the country, and the cost of meeting these standards would be high.

After a brief hesitation, Jim Young penned the last line of his announcement: "Let us not forget that in the final analysis that it is up to the cities to save themselves."

Despite Young's sincere concern and care in preparing the announcement, it was not well received. Aside from the fact that the workers' viewed Young's tears as crocodile tears, financially, they felt, it would have been possible to keep the plant open. Indeed, while profits were never high, no loss had been recorded in seventeen years. Sweeping aside Young's carefully reasoned

---

* This fictitious case study was developed by the author to serve as the basis for classroom discussion.

three points, the union spokespersons argued that the rubber industry had entered a period of sluggish growth and that the owners simply wanted to concentrate corporate resources on aerospace and chemicals. The union also noted that it had never failed to meet management requests when a real need had arisen. For example, two years ago union officials had asked Young point blank how much money it would take to keep the plant open. On the basis of the information he provided, they were willing to sign a productivity contract. In fact, even though he had not released the actual figures, they had agreed to increase daily work hours (from six to eight), to forego union meetings on company time and paid lunch hours, and to allow for increases in management authority. (They had, however, rejected any requests for reductions in pay.)

The effect of the shutdown on the community was hard to measure with any accuracy. Thor Tire & Rubber Company had employed 1,200 people who had poured a good part of the $16-million annual payroll into the local economy. The human impact, however, was almost impossible to assess, but is perhaps best captured by considering the plight of a fifty-six-year-old plant foreman sitting in front of a short stack of form-letter rejections from other local companies. Clearly, no one seemed willing to hire a man seven years from retirement—age discrimination laws or no age discrimination laws.

Obviously, a plant shutdown—the result of a conscious decision by managers—raises important general questions: How does the concept of social responsibility apply in such circumstances? What options might the company have explored but did not? How should employees be compensated? If the company is relocating, what conditions should it look for in its new home? How can it analyze these? Further, this issue might be an interesting one to examine from perspectives other than management's: What course of action should the union leaders take? What course of action should the mayor take?

CASE STUDY 6: DREAMS, INC.

This case study illustrates how science fiction—good science fiction—can anticipate the future. (Some corporations even hire science fiction writers to help in their corporate planning.) While this story raises quite a variety of mind-stretching questions, you might want to focus on three: How does a company go about pricing and marketing something like creativity? Should creativity be marketed? And, most crucially, what should public policy be toward the technological innovation that is the subject of the story? Today the Federal Communications Commission seems to have its hands full in trying to decide what to do about sex and violence on television. How would it cope with Dreams, Inc.?

Dreaming Is a Private Thing*

Isaac Asimov

Jesse Weill looked up from his desk. His old spare body, his sharp high-bridge nose, deep-set shadowy eyes, and amazing shock of white hair had trade-marked his appearance during the years that Dreams, Inc. had become world-famous.

He said, "Is the boy here already, Joe?"

Joe Dooley was short and heavyset. A cigar caressed his moist lower lip. He took it away for a moment and nodded. "His folks are with him. They're all scared."

"You're sure this is not a false alarm, Joe? I haven't got much time." He looked at his watch. "Government business at two."

"This is a sure thing, Mr. Weill." Dooley's face was a study in earnestness. His jowls quivered with persuasive intensity. "Like I told you, I picked him up playing some kind of basketball game in the schoolyard. You should've seen the kid. He stunk. When he had his hands on the ball, his own team had to take it away, and fast, but just the same he had all the stance of a star player. Know what I mean? To me it was a giveaway."

"Did you talk to him?"

"Well, sure. I stopped him at lunch. You know me." Dooley gestured ex-pansively with his cigar and caught the severed ash with his other hand. " 'Kid,' I said—"

"And he's dream material?"

"I said, 'Kid, I just came from Africa and—' "

"All right." Weill held up the palm of his hand. "Your word I'll always take. How you do it I don't know, but when you say a boy is a potential dreamer, I'll gamble. Bring him in."

The youngster came in between his parents. Dooley pushed chairs for-ward, and Weill rose to shake hands. He smiled at the youngster in a way that turned the wrinkles of his face into benevolent creases.

"You're Tommy Slutsky?"

Tommy nodded wordlessly. He was about ten and a little small for that. His dark hair was plastered down unconvincingly, and his face was unreal-istically clean.

Weill said, "You're a good boy?"

The boy's mother smiled at once and patted Tommy's head maternally (a gesture which did not soften the anxious expression on the youngster's face). She said, "He's always a very good boy."

Weill let this dubious statement pass. "Tell me, Tommy," he said, and held out a lollipop which was first hesitantly considered, then accepted. "Do you ever listen to dreamies?"

"Sometimes," said Tommy in an uncertain treble.

Mr. Slutsky cleared his throat. He was broad-shouldered and thick-fingered, the type of laboring man that, every once in a while, to the confusion of eugenics, sired a dreamer. "We rented one or two for the boy. Real old ones."

Weill nodded. He said, "Did you like them, Tommy?"

"They were sort of silly."

"You think up better ones for yourself, do you?"

The grin that spread over the ten-year-old features had the effect of taking away some of the unreality of the slicked hair and washed face.

Weill went on, gently: "Would you like to make up a dream for me?"

Tommy was instantly embarrassed. "I guess not."

"It won't be hard. It's very easy. . . . Joe."

Dooley moved a screen out of the way and rolled forward a dream recorder.

The youngster looked owlishly at it.

Weill lifted the helmet and brought it close to the boy. "Do you know what this is?"

Tommy shrank away. "No."

"It's a thinker. That's what we call it because people think into it. You put it on your head and think anything you want."

"Then what happens?"

"Nothing at all. It feels nice."

"No," said Tommy, "I guess I'd rather not."

His mother bent hurriedly toward him. "It won't hurt, Tommy. You do what the man says." There was an unmistakable edge to her voice.

Tommy stiffened and looked as though he might cry, but he didn't. Weill put the thinker on him.

He did it gently and slowly and let it remain there for some thirty seconds before speaking again, to let the boy assure himself it would do no harm, to let him get used to the insinuating touch of the fibrils against the sutures of his skull (penetrating the skin so finely as to be almost insensible), and finally to let him get used to the faint hum of the alternating field vortices.

Then he said, "Now would you think for us?"

"About what?" Only the boy's nose and mouth showed.

"About anything you want. What's the best thing you would like to do when school is out?"

The boy thought a moment and said, with rising inflection, "Go on a stratojet?"

"Why not? Sure thing. You go on a jet. It's taking off right now." He gestured lightly to Dooley, who threw the freezer into circuit.

Weill kept the boy only five minutes and then let him and his mother be escorted from the office by Dooley. Tommy looked bewildered but undamaged by the ordeal.

Weill said to the father, "Now, Mr. Slutsky, if your boy does well on this test, we'll be glad to pay you five hundred dollars each year until he finishes high school. In that time all we'll ask is that he spend an hour a week some afternoon at our special school."

"Do I have to sign a paper?" Slutsky's voice was a bit hoarse.

"Certainly. This is business, Mr. Slutsky."

"Well, I don't know. Dreamers are hard to come by, I hear."

"They are. They are. But your son, Mr. Slutsky, is not a dreamer yet. He might never be. Five hundred dollars a year is a gamble for us. It's not a gamble for you. When he's finished high school, it may turn out he's not a dreamer, yet you've lost nothing. You've gained maybe four thousand dollars altogether. If he *is* a dreamer, he'll make a nice living and you certainly haven't lost then."

"He'll need special training, won't he?"

"Oh, yes, most intensive. But we don't have to worry about that till after he's finished high school. Then, after two years with us, he'll be developed. Rely on me, Mr. Slutsky."

"Will you guarantee that special training?"

Weill, who had been shoving a paper across the desk at Slutsky and punching a pen wrong side to at him, put the pen down and chuckled. "Guarantee? No. How can we when we don't know for sure yet if he's a real talent? Still, the five hundred a year will stay yours."

Slutsky pondered and shook his head. "I tell you straight out, Mr. Weill— after your man arranged to have us come here, I called Luster-Think. They said they'll guarantee training."

Weill sighed. "Mr. Slutsky, I don't like to talk against a competitor. If they say they'll guarantee training, they'll do as they say, but they can't make a boy a dreamer if he hasn't got it in him, training or not. If they take a plain boy without the proper talent and put him through a development course, they'll ruin him. A dreamer he won't be, that I guarantee you. And a normal human being he won't be, either. Don't take the chance of doing it to your son.

"Now Dreams, Inc. will be perfectly honest with you. If he can be a dreamer, we'll make him one. If not, we'll give him back to you without having tampered with him and say, 'Let him learn a trade.' He'll be better and healthier that way. I tell you, Mr. Slutsky—I have sons and daughters and grandchildren so I know what I say—I would not allow a child of mine to be pushed into dreaming if he's not ready for it. Not for a million dollars."

Slutsky wiped his mouth with the back of his hand and reached for the pen. "What does this say?"

"This is just an option. We pay you a hundred dollars in cash right now. No strings attached. We'll study the boy's reverie. If we feel it's worth following up, we'll call you in again and make the five-hundred-dollars-a-year deal. Leave yourself in my hands, Mr. Slutsky, and don't worry. You won't be sorry."

Slutsky signed.

Weill passed the document through the file slot and handed an envelope to Slutsky.

Five minutes later, alone in the office, he placed the unfreezer over his own head and absorbed the boy's reverie intently. It was a typically childish daydream. First Person was at the controls of the plane, which looked like a compound of illustrations out of the filmed thrillers that still circulated among those who lacked the time, desire, or money for dream cylinders.

When he removed the unfreezer, he found Dooley looking at him.

"Well, Mr. Weill, what do you think?" said Dooley with an eager and proprietary air.

"Could be, Joe. Could be. He has the overtones, and for a ten-year-old boy without a scrap of training it's hopeful. When the plane went through a cloud, there was a distinct sensation of pillows. Also the smell of clean sheets, which was an amusing touch. We can go with him a ways, Joe."

"Good." Joe beamed happily at Weill's approval.

"But I tell you, Joe, what we really need is to catch them still sooner. And why not? Someday, Joe, every child will be tested at birth. A difference in the brain there positively must be, and it should be found. Then we could separate the dreamers at the very beginning."

"Hell, Mr. Weill," said Dooley, looking hurt. "What would happen to my job then?"

Weill laughed. "No cause to worry yet, Joe. It won't happen in our life-times. In mine, certainly not. We'll be depending on good talent scouts like you for many years. You just watch the playgrounds and the streets"—Weill's gnarled hand dropped to Dooley's shoulder with a gentle approving pressure—"and find us a few more Hillarys and Janows, and Luster-Think won't ever catch us. . . . Now get out. I want lunch, and then I'll be ready for my two o'clock appointment. The government, Joe, the government." And he winked portentously.

Jesse Weill's two o'clock appointment was with a young man, apple-cheeked, spectacled, sandy-haired, and glowing with the intensity of a man with a mission. He presented his credentials across Weill's desk and revealed himself to be John J. Byrne, an agent of the Department of Arts and Sciences.

"Good afternoon, Mr. Byrne," said Weill. "In what way can I be of service?"

"Are we private here?" asked the agent. He had an unexpected baritone.

"Quite private."

"Then, if you don't mind, I'll ask you to absorb this." Byrne produced a small and battered cylinder and held it out between thumb and forefinger.

Weill took it, hefted it, turned it this way and that, and said with a denture-revealing smile, "Not the produce of Dreams, Inc., Mr. Byrne."

"I didn't think it was," said the agent. "I'd still like you to absorb it. I'd set the automatic cutoff for about a minute, though."

"That's all that can be endured?" Weill pulled the receiver to his desk and placed the cylinder in the unfreeze compartment. He removed it, polished either end of the cylinder with his handkerchief, and tried again. "It doesn't make good contact," he said. "An amateurish job."

He placed the cushioned unfreeze helmet over his skull and adjusted the temple contacts, then set the automatic cutoff. He leaned back and clasped his hands over his chest and began absorbing.

His fingers grew rigid and clutched at his jacket. After the cutoff had brought absorption to an end, he removed the unfreezer and looked faintly angry. "A raw piece," he said. "It's lucky I'm an old man so that such things no longer bother me."

Byrne said stiffly, "It's not the worst we've found. And the fad is increasing."

Weill shrugged. "Pornographic dreamies. It's a logical development, I suppose."

The government man said, "Logical or not, it represents a deadly danger for the moral fiber of the nation."

"The moral fiber," said Weill, "can take a lot of beating. Erotica of one form or another has been circulated all through history."

"Not like this, sir. A direct mind-to-mind stimulation is much more effective than smoking-room stories or filthy pictures. Those must be filtered through the senses and lose some of their effect in that way."

Weill could scarcely argue that point. He said, "What would you have me do?"

"Can you suggest a possible source for this cylinder?"

"Mr. Byrne, I'm not a policeman."

"No, no, I'm not asking you to do our work for us. The Department is quite capable of conducting its own investigations. Can you help us, I mean, from your own specialized knowledge? You say your company did not put out that filth. Who did?"

"No reputable dream-distributor. I'm sure of that. It's too cheaply made."

"That could have been done on purpose."

"And no professional dreamer originated it."

"Are you sure, Mr. Weill? Couldn't dreamers do this sort of thing for some small, illegitimate concern for money—or for fun?"

"They could, but not this particular one. No overtones. It's two-dimensional. Of course, a thing like this doesn't need overtones."

"What do you mean—overtones?"

Weill laughed gently. "You are not a dreamie fan?"

Byrne tried not to look virtuous and did not entirely succeed. "I prefer music."

"Well, that's all right, too," said Weill tolerantly, "but it makes it a little harder to explain overtones. Even people who absorb dreamies might not be able to explain if you asked them. Still, they'd know a dreamie was no good if the overtones were missing, even if they couldn't tell you why. Look, when an experienced dreamer goes into reverie, he doesn't think a story like in the old-fashioned television or book-films. It's a series of little visions. Each one has several meanings. If you studied them carefully, you'd find maybe five or six.

While absorbing them in the ordinary way, you would never notice, but careful study shows it. Believe me, my psychological staff puts in long hours on just that point. All the overtones, the different meanings, blend together into a mass of guided emotion. Without them, everything would be flat, tasteless.

"Now, this morning I tested a young boy. A ten-year-old with possibilities. A cloud to him isn't just a cloud; it's a pillow, too. Having the sensations of both, it was more than either. Of course, the boy's very primitive. But when he's through with his schooling, he'll be trained and disciplined. He'll be subjected to all sorts of sensations. He'll store up experience. He'll study and analyze classic dreamies of the past. He'll learn how to control and direct his thoughts, though, mind you, I have always said that when a good dreamer improvises—"

Weill halted abruptly, then proceeded in less impassioned tones, "I shouldn't get excited. All I'm trying to bring out now is that every professional dreamer has his own type of overtones which he can't mask. To an expert it's like signing his name on the dreamie. And I, Mr. Byrne, know all the signatures. Now that piece of dirt you brought me has no overtones at all. It was done by an ordinary person. A little talent, maybe, but like you and me, he can't think."

Byrne reddened a trifle. "Not everyone can't think, Mr. Weill, even if they don't make dreamies."

"Oh, tush," and Weill wagged his hand in the air. "Don't be angry with what an old man says. I don't mean *think* as in *reason,* I mean *think* as in *dream.* We all can dream after a fashion, just like we all can run. But can you and I run a mile in under four minutes? You and I can talk, but are we Daniel Websters? Now when I think of a steak, I think of the word. Maybe I have a quick picture of a brown steak on a platter. Maybe you have a better pictorialization of it, and you can see the crisp fat and the onions and the baked potato. I don't know. But a *dreamer* . . . he sees it and smells it and tastes it and everything about it, with the charcoal and the satisfied feeling in the stomach and the way the knife cuts through it, and a hundred other things all at once. Very sensual. Very sensual. You and I can't do it."

"Well, then," said Byrne, "no professional dreamer has done this. That's something, anyway." He put the cylinder in his inner jacket pocket. "I hope we'll have your full cooperation in squelching this sort of thing."

"Positively, Mr. Byrne. With a whole heart."

"I hope so." Byrne spoke with a consciousness of power. "It's not up to me, Mr. Weill, to say what will be done and what won't be done, but this sort of thing"—he tapped the cylinder he had brought—"will make it awfully tempting to impose a really strict censorship on dreamies."

He rose. "Good day, Mr. Weill."

"Good day, Mr. Byrne. I'll hope always for the best."

Francis Belanger burst into Jesse Weill's office in his usual steaming tizzy, his reddish hair disordered and his face aglow with worry and a mild perspiration. He was brought up sharply by the sight of Weill's head cradled in the crook of his elbow and bent on the desk until only the glimmer of white hair was visible.

Belanger swallowed. "Boss?"

Weill's head lifted. "It's you, Frank?"

"What's the matter, boss? Are you sick?"

"I'm old enough to be sick, but I'm on my feet. Staggering, but on my feet. A government man was here."

"What did he want?"

"He threatens censorship. He brought a sample of what's going around. Cheap dreamies for bottle parties."

"God damn!" said Belanger feelingly.

"The only trouble is that morality makes for good campaign fodder. They'll be hitting out everywhere. And to tell the truth, we're vulnerable, Frank."

"*We* are? Our stuff is clean. We play up adventure and romance."

Weill thrust out his lower lip and wrinkled his forehead.

"Between us, Frank, we don't have to make believe. Clean? It depends on how you look at it. It's not for publication, maybe, but you know and I know that every dreamie has its Freudian connotations. You can't deny it."

"Sure, if you *look* for it. If you're a psychiatrist—"

"If you're an ordinary person, too. The ordinary observer doesn't know it's there, and maybe he couldn't tell a phallic symbol from a mother image even if you pointed them out. Still, his subconscious knows. And it's the connotations that make many a dreamie click."

"All right, what's the government going to do? Clean up the subconscious?"

"It's a problem. I don't know what they're going to do. What we have on our side, and what I'm mainly depending on, is the fact that the public loves its dreamies, and won't give them up.... Meanwhile, what did you come in for? You want to see me about something, I suppose?"

Belanger tossed an object onto Weill's desk and shoved his shirttail deeper into his trousers.

Weill broke open the glistening plastic cover and took out the enclosed cylinder. At one end was engraved in a too-fancy script in pastel blue: *Along the Himalayan Trail.* It bore the mark of Luster-Think.

"The Competitor's Product." Weill said it with capitals, and his lips twitched. "It hasn't been published yet. Where did you get it, Frank?"

"Never mind. I just want you to absorb it."

Weill sighed. "Today everyone wants me to absorb dreams. Frank, it's not dirty?"

Belanger said testily, "It has your Freudian symbols. Narrow crevasses between the mountain peaks. I hope that won't bother you."

"I'm an old man. It stopped bothering me years ago, but that other thing was so poorly done it hurt.... All right, let's see what you've got here."

Again the recorder. Again the unfreezer over his skull and at the temples. This time Weill rested back in his chair for fifteen minutes or more, while Francis Belanger went hurriedly through two cigarettes.

When Weill removed the headpiece and blinked dream out of his eyes, Belanger said, "Well, what's your reaction, boss?"

Weill corrugated his forehead. "It's not for me. It was repetitious. With competition like this, Dreams, Inc. doesn't have to worry yet."

"That's your mistake, boss. Luster-Think's going to win with stuff like this. We've got to do something."

"Now, Frank—"

"No, you listen. This is the coming thing."

"This?" Weill stared with half-humorous dubiety at the cylinder. "It's amateurish. It's repetitious. Its overtones are very unsubtle. The snow had a distinct lemon sherbet taste. Who tastes lemon sherbet in snow these days, Frank? In the old days, yes. Twenty years ago, maybe. When Lyman Harrison first made his Snow Symphonies for sale down South, it was a big thing. Sherbet and candy-striped mountaintops and sliding down chocolate-covered cliffs. It's slapstick, Frank. These days it doesn't go."

"Because," said Belanger, "you're not up with the times, boss. I've got to talk to you straight. When you started the dreamie business, when you bought up the basic patents and began putting them out, dreamies were luxury stuff. The market was small and individual. You could afford to turn out specialized dreamies and sell them to people at high prices."

"I know," said Weill, "and we've kept that up. But also we've opened a rental business for the masses."

"Yes, we have, and it's not enough. Our dreamies have subtlety, yes. They can be used over and over again. The tenth time you're still finding new things, still getting new enjoyment. But how many people are connoisseurs? And another thing. Our stuff is strongly individualized. They're First Person."

"Well?"

"Well, Luster-Think is opening dream palaces. They've opened one with three hundred booths in Nashville. You walk in, take your seat, put on your unfreezer, and get your dream. Everyone in the audience gets the same one."

"I've heard of it, Frank, and it's been done before. It didn't work the first time, and it won't work now. You want to know why it won't work? Because in the first place, dreaming is a private thing. Do you like your neighbor to know what you're dreaming? In the second place, in a dream palace the dreams have to start on schedule, don't they? So the dreamer has to dream not when he wants to but when some palace manager says he should. Finally, a dream one person likes, another person doesn't like. In those three hundred booths, I guarantee you, a hundred and fifty people are dissatisfied. And if they're dissatisfied, they won't come back."

Slowly Belanger rolled up his sleeves and opened his collar. "Boss," he said, "you're talking through your hat. What's the use of proving they won't work? They *are* working. The word came through today that Luster-Think is breaking ground for a thousand-booth palace in St. Louis. People can get used to public dreaming if everyone else in the same room is having the same dream. And they can adjust themselves to having it at a given time, as long as it's cheap and convenient.

"Damn it, boss, it's a social affair. A boy and a girl go to a dream palace and absorb some cheap romantic thing with stereotyped overtones and commonplace situations, but still they come out with stars sprinkling their hair. They've had the same dream together. They've gone through identical sloppy emotions. They're *in tune,* boss. You bet they go back to the dream palace, and all their friends go, too."

"And if they don't like the dream?"

"That's the point. That's the nub of the whole thing. They're bound to like it. If you prepare Hillary specials with wheels within wheels within wheels, with surprise twists on the third-level undertones, with clever shifts of significance, and all the other things we're so proud of, why, naturally, it won't appeal to everyone. Specialized dreamies are for specialized tastes. But Luster-Think is turning out simple jobs in Third Person so both sexes can be hit at once. Like what you've just absorbed. Simple, repetitious, commonplace. They're aiming at the lowest common denominator. No one will love it, maybe, but no one will hate it."

Weill sat silent for a long time, and Belanger watched him. Then Weill said, "Frank, I started on quality, and I'm staying there. Maybe you're right. Maybe dream palaces are the coming thing. If so, we'll open them, but we'll use good stuff. Maybe Luster-Think underestimates ordinary people. Let's go slowly and not panic. I have based all my policies on the theory that there's always a market for quality. Sometimes, my boy, it would surprise you how big a market."

"Boss—"

The sounding of the intercom interrupted Belanger.

"What is it, Ruth?" said Weill.

The voice of his secretary said, "It's Mr. Hillary, sir. He wants to see you right away. He says it's important."

"Hillary?" Weill's voice registered shock. Then, "Wait five minutes, Ruth, then send him in."

Weill turned to Belanger. "Today, Frank, is definitely not one of my good days. A dreamer should be at home with his thinker. And Hillary's our best dreamer, so he especially should be at home. What do you suppose is wrong with him?"

Belanger, still brooding over Luster-Think and dream palaces, said shortly, "Call him in and find out."

"In one minute. Tell me, how was his last dream? I haven't absorbed the one that came in last week."

Belanger came down to earth. He wrinkled his nose. "Not so good."

"Why not?"

"It was ragged. Too jumpy. I don't mind sharp transitions for the liveliness, you know, but there's got to be some connection, even if only on a deep level."

"Is it a total loss?"

"No Hillary dream is a *total* loss. It took a lot of editing, though. We cut it down quite a bit and spliced in some odd pieces he'd sent us now and then. You know, detached scenes. It's still not Grade A, but it will pass."

"You told him about this, Frank?"

"Think I'm crazy, boss? Think I'm going to say a harsh word to a dreamer?"

And at that point the door opened and Weill's comely young secretary smiled Sherman Hillary into the office.

Sherman Hillary, at the age of thirty-one, could have been recognized as a dreamer by anyone. His eyes, though unspectacled, had nevertheless the misty look of one who either needs glasses or who rarely focuses on anything mundane. He was of average height but underweight, with black hair that needed cutting, a narrow chin, a pale skin, and a troubled look.

He muttered, "Hello, Mr. Weill," and half-nodded in hangdog fashion in the direction of Belanger.

Weill said heartily, "Sherman, my boy, you look fine. What's the matter? A dream is cooking only so-so at home? You're worried about it? Sit down, sit down."

The dreamer did, sitting at the edge of the chair and holding his thighs stiffly together as though to be ready for instant obedience to a possible order to stand up once more.

He said, "I've come to tell you, Mr. Weill, I'm quitting."

"Quitting?"

"I don't want to dream anymore, Mr. Weill."

Weill's old face looked older now than at any other time during the day. "Why, Sherman?"

The dreamer's lips twisted. He blurted out, "Because I'm not *living*, Mr. Weill. Everything passes me by. It wasn't so bad at first. It was even relaxing. I'd dream evenings, weekends when I felt like it, or any other time. And when I didn't feel like it, I wouldn't. But now, Mr. Weill, I'm an old pro. You tell me I'm one of the best in the business and the industry looks to me to think up new subleties and new changes on the old reliables like the flying reveries and the worm-turning skits."

Weill said, "And is anyone better than you, Sherman? Your little sequence on leading an orchestra is selling steadily after ten years."

"All right, Mr. Weill, I've done my part. It's gotten so I don't go out anymore. I neglect my wife. My little girl doesn't know me. Last week we went to a dinner party—Sarah made me—and I don't remember a bit of it. Sarah says

I was sitting on the couch all evening just staring at nothing and humming. She said everyone kept looking at me. She cried all night. I'm tired of things like that, Mr. Weill. I want to be a normal person and live in this world. I promised her I'd quit, and I will, so it's good-bye, Mr. Weill." Hillary stood up and held out his hand awkwardly.

Weill waved it gently away. "If you want to quit, Sherman, it's all right. But do an old man a favor and let me explain something to you."

"I'm not going to change my mind," said Hillary.

"I'm not going to try to make you. I just want to explain something. I'm an old man, and even before you were born I was in this business, so I like to talk about it. Humor me, Sherman? Please?"

Hillary sat down. His teeth clamped down on his lower lip, and he stared sullenly at his fingernails.

Weill said, "Do you know what a dreamer is, Sherman? Do you know what he means to ordinary people? Do you know what it is to be like me, like Frank Belanger, like your wife Sarah? To have crippled minds that can't imagine, that can't build up thoughts? People like myself, ordinary people, would like to escape just once in a while this life of ours. We can't. We need help.

"In olden times it was books, plays, movies, radio, television. They gave us make-believe, but that wasn't important. What *was* important was that for a little while our own imaginations were stimulated. We could think of handsome lovers and beautiful princesses. We could be attractive, witty, strong, capable—everything we weren't.

"But always the passing of the dream from dreamer to absorber was not perfect. It had to be translated into words in one way or another. The best dreamer in the world might not be able to get any of it into words. And the best writer in the world could put only the smallest part of his dream into words. You understand?

"But now, with dream-recording, any man can dream. You, Sherman, and a handful of men like you supply those dreams directly and exactly. It's straight from your head into ours, full strength. You dream for a hundred million people every time you dream. You dream a hundred million dreams at once. This is a great thing, my boy. You give all those people a glimpse of something they could not have by themselves."

Hillary mumbled, "I've done my share." He rose desperately to his feet. "I'm through. I don't care what you say. And if you want to sue me for breaking our contract, go ahead and sue. I don't care."

Weill stood up, too. "Would I sue you? . . . Ruth"—he spoke into the intercom—"bring in our copy of Mr. Hillary's contract."

He waited. So did Hillary and Belanger. Weill smiled faintly, and his yellowed fingers drummed softly on his desk.

His secretary brought in the contract. Weill took it, showed its face to Hillary, and said, "Sherman, my boy, unless you *want* to be with me, it's not right you should stay."

Then before Belanger could make more than the beginning of a horrified gesture to stop him, he tore the contract into four pieces and tossed them down the waste chute. "That's all."

Hillary's hand shot out to seize Weill's. "Thanks, Mr. Weill," he said earnestly, his voice husky. "You've always treated me very well, and I'm grateful. I'm sorry it had to be like this."

"It's all right, my boy. It's all right."

Half in tears, still muttering thanks, Sherman Hillary left.

"For the love of Pete, boss, why did you let him go?" demanded Belanger. "Don't you see the game? He'll be going straight to Luster-Think. They've bought him off."

Weill raised his hand. "You're wrong. You're quite wrong. I know the boy, and this would not be his style. Besides," he added dryly, "Ruth is a good secretary, and she knows what to bring me when I ask for a dreamer's contract. The real contract is still in the safe, believe me.

"Meanwhile, a fine day I've had. I had to argue with a father to give me a chance at new talent, with a government man to avoid censorship, with you to keep from adopting fatal policies, and now with my best dreamer to keep him from leaving. The father I probably won out over. The government man and you, I don't know. Maybe yes, maybe no. But about Sherman Hillary, at least, there is no question. The dreamer will be back."

"How do you know?"

Weill smiled at Belanger and crinkled his cheeks into a network of fine lines. "Frank, my boy, you know how to edit dreamies so you think you know all the tools and machines of the trade. But let me tell you something. The most important tool in the dreamie business is the dreamer himself. He is the one you have to understand most of all, and I understand them.

"Listen. When I was a youngster—there were no dreamies then—I knew a fellow who wrote television scripts. He would complain to me bitterly that when someone met him for the first time and found out who he was, they would say: 'Where do you get those crazy ideas?'

"They honestly didn't know. To them it was an impossibility to even think of one of them. So what could my friend say? He used to talk to me about it and tell me: 'Could I say, "I don't know"? When I go to bed, I can't sleep for ideas dancing in my head. When I shave, I cut myself; when I talk, I lose track of what I'm saying; when I drive, I take my life in my hands. And always because ideas, situations, dialogues are spinning and twisting in my mind. I can't tell you where I get my ideas. Can you tell me, maybe, your trick of *not* getting ideas, so I, too, can have a little peace?'

"You see, Frank, how it is. *You* can stop work here anytime. So can I. This is our job, not our life. But not Sherman Hillary. Wherever he goes, whatever he does, he'll dream. While he lives, he must think; while he thinks, he must dream. We don't hold him prisoner; our contract isn't an iron wall for him. His own skull is his prisoner. He'll be back. What can he do?"

Belanger shrugged. "If what you say is right, I'm sort of sorry for the guy."

Weill nodded sadly. "I'm sorry for all of them. Through the years I've found out one thing. It's their business: making people happy. Other people."

APPENDIXES

AND

REFERENCES

Appendix A
Public Policies Affecting Business

These public policies . . .	Charge this agency . . .	With these responsibilities . . .	Which affect these business functions . . .
Army Organization Act of 1920 and laws pertaining to the preservation of navigable waters	Corps of Engineers (est. 1824)	Supervising construction along waterways and marshlands, dredging operations, and mine dumping	Production and operations management
The National Bank Act of 1863	Comptroller of the Currency (est. 1863)	Chartering and regulating national banks	Financial management
Interstate Commerce Act of 1887 Hepburn Act Panama Canal Act Transportation Acts of 1920, 1940, 1958 Motor Carrier Act of 1935 Regional Rail Reorganization Act of 1973 Railroad Revitalization and Regulatory Reform Act of 1976	Interstate Commerce Commission (est. 1887)	Regulating rates and routes of railroads, most truckers, and carriers	Competition and trade
Sherman Act of 1890 Clayton Act of 1914	Antitrust Division (est. 1890)	Regulating all activities that could affect interstate commerce, from trade restraints and illegal agreements to mergers	Competition and trade
Federal Reserve Act of 1913, as amended Defense Production Act of 1950 Bank Holding Company Act of 1956 Truth in Lending Act of 1969	Federal Reserve Board (est. 1913)	Regulating state-chartered banks that are members of the Federal Reserve System and setting money and credit policy	Financial management
Federal Trade Commission Act of 1914, as amended	Federal Trade Commission (est. 1914)	Curbing unfair trade practices, protecting consumers, and maintaining competition	Competition and trade

These public policies . . .	Charge this agency . . .	With these responsibilities . . .	Which affect these business functions . . .
Agriculture Appropriation Act of 1931 Food and Drug Act of 1906 Food, Drug, and Cosmetic Act of 1938 Food Additives Amendment of 1958 Color Additive Amendments of 1960 Drugs Amendments of 1962 Fair Packaging and Labeling Act of 1966 Radiation Control for Health and Safety Act of 1968	Food and Drug Administration (est. 1931)	Regulating the safety and efficacy of drugs and medical devices, the safety and purity of food, and labeling	Safety and health
Federal Home Bank Act of 1932	Federal Home Loan Bank Board (est. 1932)	Chartering and regulating federal savings and loan institutions	Financial management
Federal Reserve Act of 1933 Federal Deposit Insurance Act approved September 21, 1950	Federal Deposit Insurance Corporation (est. 1933)	Regulating state-chartered banks not in the Federal Reserve System, as well as mutual savings banks, in conjunction with states	Financial management
Communications Act of 1934 Communications Satellite Act of 1962	Federal Communications Commission (est. 1934)	Regulating broadcasting and other communications (through licensing and frequency allocation), as well as interstate telephone and telegraph rates and levels of service	Competition and trade
Securities Act of 1933 Bretton Woods Agreements Act of 1945 Internal Revenue Code of 1954	Securities and Exchange Commission (est. 1934)	Regulating all publicly traded securities and the markets on which they are traded, administering public disclosure laws, and policing securities fraud	Financial management
National Labor Relations Act of 1935 Taft–Hartley Act of 1947 Landrum-Griffin Act of 1971 Health Care Institutions Act of 1974	National Labor Relations Board (est. 1935)	Regulating labor practices of unions and companies and conducting representation elections	Safety and health

These public policies . . .	Charge this agency . . .	With these responsibilities . . .	Which affect these business functions . . .
Reorganization Plan of 1961 Shipping Act of 1916 Merchant Marine Acts of 1920, 1928, 1936, and 1941 Intercoastal Shipping Act of 1933 Federal Water Pollution Control Act Amendments of 1972, Section 311	Federal Maritime Commission (est. 1936)	Regulating foreign and domestic ocean commerce, mainly by overseeing agreements reached by a variety of rate-making conferences of ship carriers	Competition and trade
Civil Aeronautics Act of 1938 Federal Aviation Act of 1958	Civil Aeronautics Board (est. 1938)	Regulating airline fares and routes	Competition and trade
Department of Transportation Act of 1966 Airport and Airway Development Act Amendments of 1976	Federal Aviation Administration (est. 1958)	Regulating aircraft manufacturing through certification of airplane airworthiness	Safety and health
Public Contracts Act of 1962 Civil Rights Act of 1965 Vietnam Era Veterans Readjustment Act of 1974	Office of Federal Contract Compliance Programs (est. 1962)	Administering prohibitions against discrimination by race or sex on the part of employers holding federal contracts	Safety and health
Title VII of the Civil Rights Act of 1964, as amended by the Equal Employment Opportunity Act of 1972	Equal Employment Opportunity Commission (est. 1964)	Investigating and conciliating complaints of employment discrimination based on race, religion, and sex	Human resources management
Reorganization Plan No. 3 of 1970, effective December 2, 1970	Environmental Protection Agency (est. 1970)	Developing and enforcing standards for clean air and water, controlling pollution from pesticides, toxic substances, and noise, approving state pollution abatement plans, and ruling on environmental impact statements	Productions and operations management

(continued)

These public policies . . .	Charge this agency . . .	With these responsibilities . . .	Which affect these business functions . . .
Highway Safety Act of 1970 National Traffic and Motor Vehicle Safety Act of 1966, as amended Highway Safety Act of 1966, as amended Clean Air Amendments of 1970 Energy Policy and Conservation Act of 1975	National Highway Traffic Safety Administration (est. 1970)	Regulating manufacturers of autos, trucks, buses, motorcycles, trailers, and tires in an effort to reduce the number and severity of traffic accidents	Safety and health
Occupational Safety and Health Act of 1970	Occupational Safety and Health Administration (est. 1971)	Regulating safety and health conditions in all workplaces—except those run by government	Safety and health
Consumer Product Safety Act of 1972 Flammable Fabrics Act of 1954 Refrigerator Safety Act of 1956 Hazardous Substances Act of 1960 Poison Prevention Packaging Act of 1970	Consumer Product Safety Commission (est. 1972)	Reducing product-related injuries to consumers by mandating better design, labeling, and instruction sheets	Safety and health
Energy Reorganization Act of 1974 Atomic Energy Act of 1946 Atomic Energy Act of 1954 as amended	Nuclear Regulatory Commission (est. 1973)	Regulating civilian nuclear safety, which basically involves licensing atomic power plants	Production and operations management
Federal Energy Administration Act of 1974 Energy Policy and Conservation Act of 1975 National Energy Act of 1978	Federal Energy Administration (est. 1973)	Controlling the price of most domestic crude oil and some refined products, principally gasoline	Production and operations management
Commodity Futures Trading Commission Act of 1974	Commodity Futures Trading Commission (est. 1974)	Regulating futures trading on ten commodity exchanges	Financial management
Employment Retirement Income Security Act of 1974	Pension Benefit Guarantee Corporation (est. 1974)	Overseeing pension plans	Human resources management

These public policies . . .	Charge this agency . . .	With these responsibilities . . .	Which affect these business functions . . .
Department of Energy Organization Act of 1977 National Energy Act of 1978	Federal Energy Regulatory Commission (est. 1977)	Regulating interstate transmission and wholesale price of electric power, rates and routes of natural gas pipelines, and under a court ruling in the 1950s, the wellhead price of gas for interstate shipment	Production and operations management
Federal Mine Safety and Health Amendments Act of 1977 Mine Safety Act of 1910 Federal Coal Mine Health and Safety Act of 1969	Mine Safety and Health Administration (est. 1977)	Enforcing all mine safety regulations, including air quality and equipment standards	Safety and health

Source: Adapted and updated from *U.S. Government Manual, 1979* (Washington, D.C.: U.S. Government Printing Office) and *Business Week,* April 4, 1977, pp. 52, 53, and 56.

Appendix B
Business Information Sources

The purpose of this appendix is to list a selected number of useful government publications, research institute services, and important periodicals and newspapers. All the publications that follow are basic and comprehensive rather than specialized and are relevant to the major themes of this book.

GOVERNMENT PUBLICATIONS

The following publications form the backbone of any governmental statistical reference collection. Unless otherwise indicated, they can all be obtained from the U.S. Government Printing Office, Washington, D.C., 20402.

Statistical Abstract of the United States. U.S. Bureau of the Census.
    Published annually; serves as the prime source for U.S. industrial, social, political, and economic statistics and as a bibliographical guide; contains tables of national statistics and a short section of tables devoted to regional, state, and metropolitan statistics, with sources listed at the foot of each table; includes a "Guide to Sources of Statistics," which lists important statistical publications arranged by subject, as well as a descriptive list of recent Bureau of the Census publications.

U.S. Fact Book. New York: Grosset & Dunlap.
    Paperback version of *Statistical Abstract;* published annually; contains summary statistics as well as graphs.

Catalog. U.S. Bureau of the Census.
    Published annually; contains list of all Census Bureau publications.

Survey of Current Business. U.S. Department of Commerce.
    Published monthly; contains about twenty-five hundred statistical series.

Business Statistics. U.S. Department of Commerce.
    Published biennially as a supplement to *Survey of Current Business;* provides a historical record of the statistical series that appear in the *Survey;* includes tables of annual averages, beginning with the year 1947, and monthly figures for the most recent years; contains an appendix of monthly and quarterly statistics for over 400 series dating back to 1947.

U.S. Industrial Outlook. Bureau of Domestic Commerce, U.S. Department of Commerce.
    Published annually; contains five-year projections on several hundred indicators in particular industry sectors (e.g., chemicals, paper, steel), arranged according to the Standard Industrial Classification (SIC) code (the methods used to derive forecasts are not explained); includes an attempt to assess the impact of potential

social, technological, demographic, and political developments on the future course of the indicators.

Federal Reserve Bulletin. U.S. Board of Governors of the Federal Reserve System, Washington, D.C. 20551.
   Published monthly; includes some international financial statistics and basic business statistics on construction, employment, prices, national income, and the well-known Federal Reserve Board's index of industrial production.

Business Conditions Digest. U.S. Bureau of Economic Analysis, Department of Commerce.
   Published monthly; contains charts and back-up statistical tables for the leading economic time series of most use to business analysts and forecasters; includes four sections: national income and GNP, cyclical indicators, analytical measures, and international comparisons.

Monthly Labor Review. U.S. Bureau of Labor Statistics.
   Contains current statistics covering employment, unemployment, hours, earnings, consumer and wholesale prices, productivity, and labor-management data.

Survey of Current Business. U.S. Department of Commerce.
   Published monthly; covers general business indicators, commodity prices, construction and real estate, domestic trade, labor force, employment and earnings, finance, foreign trade of the United States, transportation and communication, chemicals and allied products, lumber and products, metals and manufactures, petroleum and coal products, pulp and paper products, rubber and rubber products, stone and glass products, textile products, and transportation equipment; includes special reports appearing at regular intervals—for example, "National Income Issue" (July); "Aspects of International Investment" (August); "Balance of Payments" (usually quarterly); "Corporate Profits" and "Local Area Personal Income" (April); "Plant and Equipment Expenditures" (about 3 times yearly); "State and Regional Income" (twice yearly).

Economic Indicators. U.S. Council of Economic Advisers.
   Published monthly; contains statistical tables and charts for the basic U.S. economic indicators, usually quoted annually for about six years and monthly for the past year; includes total output, income, spending, employment, unemployment, wages, production and business activity, prices, money, credit, security markets, and federal finance.

Social Indicators. U.S. Office of Management and Budget.
   Published biennially; similar in concept to *Economic Indicators;* provides selected statistics and charts on U.S. social conditions and trends, with sources of data listed; examines major social areas: population, the family, housing, social security and welfare, health and nutrition, public safety, education and training, work, income, wealth, expenditures, culture, leisure and use of time, social mobility, and participation.

Commerce Business Daily. U.S. Department of Commerce.
   Provides information on contract awards and subcontract opportunities, Defense Department awards, and surplus sales.

U.S. Government Manual.
    Published annually; describes the organization, purpose, and programs of most agencies and lists top personnel.

Federal Register.
    Published daily; provides indispensable information on federal agency regulations and other legal documents (see Exhibit B–1).

Government Information Services and Publications

National Technical Information Service, U.S. Department of Commerce, 5285 Port Royal Road, Springfield, Va. 22161.
    Central source for public sale of U.S. and foreign government-sponsored research, development, and engineering reports and other analyses prepared by national and local government agencies, their contractors or grantees, or by special technology groups; has an on-line computer research service (NTISearch) and more than 1,000 published searches in stock; makes available summaries of 500,000 federally sponsored research reports published from 1964 to date; adds about 70,000 new summaries and reports annually; sells copies of whole research reports, on which summaries are based, in paper or microfilm.

Weekly Government Abstracts. National Technical Information Service.
    Contains series of twenty-six weekly newsletters, summaries of new research reports, and other specialized information.

NONGOVERNMENT PUBLICATIONS

Standard Corporation Records. Standard & Poor Corporation, subsidiary of McGraw-Hill, 345 Hudson St., New York, N.Y. 10014.
    Multivolume annual publication updated weekly; serves as one of the best sources of financial information on publicly held corporations.

Moody's Manual. Moody Industrial Services, Inc., subsidiary of Dun & Bradstreet, 99 Church St., New York, N.Y. 10017.
    Multivolume work published annually and updated semiweekly; contains information on publicly held corporations.

Nongovernment Information Services and Publications

Predicasts, Inc., Cleveland, Ohio.
    Publishes reports and technology and business outlook in particular industries or product groups (such as *Predicasts* quarterly, which contains 10,000 forecasts); performs original studies on a proprietary basis for individual clients; offers special library services (such as custom bibliographies); issues several abstract journals (e.g., *Chemical Market Abstracts* and *Electronics and Equipment Market Abstracts*); issues a series *(Predi-Briefs)* containing a separate bulletin in each of thirty-five areas, from agricultural chemicals to transportation electronics.

EXHIBIT B-1   Finding Information on Federal Rules and Regulations

PARALLEL CODIFICATION OF LEGISLATION AND REGULATION

LEGISLATION

is published first as   is compiled annually in the   is codified in the

Slip Law   **U.S. Statutes at Large**   **U.S. Code**
(Public Law 94-409)   **(90 Stat. 1241)**   **(5 U.S.C. 552b)**

LEGISLATION IS IMPLEMENTED BY FEDERAL AGENCIES AS RULES AND REGULATIONS

which are published daily in the   and codified annually in the

Code of Federal Regulations
(17 CFR 200.400—200.410)

Federal Register
(42 FR 14691)

Source: Reproduced from Office of the *Federal Register,* National Archives and Records Service, General Services Administration, *How to Use the Federal Register* (Washington, D.C.: Government Printing Office, 1976).

Worldcasts. Predicasts, Inc.
> Published quarterly; covers forecasts on economic issues outside the United States.

Bureau of National Affairs, Inc., 1231 25th Street, N.W., Washington, D.C. 20037.
> Provides a daily series of reports on government activities that affect business operations; publishes the following weekly reports: *Energy Users Report, Environment Reporter, Occupational Safety and Health Reporter, Product Safety and Liability Reporter, Affirmative Action Compliance Manual,* and *EEOC Compliance Manual.*

PERIODICALS AND NEWSPAPERS

While managers cannot expect to monitor all of the publications relevant to their particular industry, any manager serious about staying on top of changes in the macroenvironment would do well to monitor as many of the following as possible:

Baron's
Business Week
Economist
Financial Executive
Forbes
Fortune
Harvard Business Review
Industry Week
Journal of Marketing
New Scientist
New York Times
Public Interest
Public Opinion
Regulation
Sloan Management Review
Technology Review
U.S. News & World Report
Wall Street Journal
Wharton Magazine

INDEXES

Business Periodicals Index. H.W. Wilson Company, 550 University Avenue, Bronx, N.Y.
> Includes a wide variety of articles appearing in periodicals, trade presses, and financial services dealing with corporations, industry, and finance.

New York Times Index. New York Times Company, 229 West 43 Street, New York, N.Y. 10036.
> Major newspaper index published semimonthly; cumulates annually.

Wall Street Journal Index. Dow Jones & Company, Inc., 22 Cortland Street, New York, N.Y. 10007.
   Major newspaper index published monthly.

INFORMATION SOURCES FOR
FOREIGN BUSINESS

U.S. Department of Commerce, Domestic and International Business Administration, Washington, D.C. 20230.

United Nations. Sales Section, UN Publications, New York, N.Y. 10017.

Organisation for Economic Cooperation and Development (OECD), 2 Rue André Pascal, Paris, France.

References

Aaker, David A., and George A. Day. 1972. "Corporate Responses to Consumer Pressures." *Harvard Business Review,* November, pp. 144*ff.*

Abernathy, William J., and Balaji A. Chakravarthy. 1978. "Government Intervention and Innovation in Industry." Harvard Business School Working Paper. Cambridge, Mass.: Harvard Business School, pp. 78–84.

Abt, Clark. 1974. "The Social Audit Technique for Measuring Socially Responsible Performance." In Melvin Anshen, *Managing the Socially Responsible Corporation.* New York: Macmillan.

_____. 1977. *The Social Audit for Management.* New York: AMACOM.

Ackerman, Robert W. 1973. "How Companies Respond to Social Demands." *Harvard Business Review,* July–August, pp. 88–98.

_____. 1974. "Public Responsibility and the Businessman." In B. Taylor and K. Macmillan, *Top Management.* London: Longman.

_____. 1975. *The Social Challenge of Business.* Cambridge, Mass.: Harvard University Press.

_____, and Raymond A. Bauer. 1976. *Corporate Social Responsiveness.* Reston, Va.: Reston.

Ackoff, Russell L. 1967. "Management Misinformation Systems." *Management Science* 14, no. 4 (December).

_____. 1970. *A Concept of Corporate Planning.* New York: Wiley.

Aguilar, Frank J. 1967. *Scanning the Business Environment.* New York: Macmillan.

Aldag, Ramon J., and Donald W. Jackson, Jr. 1975. "A Managerial Framework for Social Decision Making." *MSU Business Topics,* Spring, pp. 33–40.

Alexander, Tom. 1976. "Industry Can Save Energy Without Stunting Its Growth." *Fortune,* May, pp. 186*ff.*

_____. 1977. "The Deceptive Allure of National Planning." *Fortune,* March, pp. 148*ff.*

_____. 1978. "New Fears Surround the Shift to Coal." *Fortune,* November, pp. 50*ff.*

Alter, Steven. 1977. "A Taxonomy of Decision Support Systems." *Sloan Management Review* 19, no. 1 (Fall):39–56.

Andreasen, Alan R., and Arthur Best. 1977. "Consumers Complain—Does Business Respond?" *Harvard Business Review,* July–August, pp. 93–101.

Andrews, Kenneth R. 1971. *The Concept of Corporate Strategy.* Homewood, Ill.: Dow Jones–Irwin.

_____. 1973. "Can the Best Corporations Be Made Moral?" *Harvard Business Review,* May–June, pp. 57–64.

Anshen, Melvin, and Francis D. Wormuth. 1954. *Private Enterprise and Public Policy.* New York: Macmillan.

Ansoff, H. Igor. 1973. "Management in Transition." *Challenge to Leadership.* New York: Free Press.

_____, and John M. Stewart. 1967. Strategies for a Technology-Based Business." *Harvard Business Review,* November–December, pp. 71–83.

Arendt, Hannah. 1959. *The Human Condition.* New York: Doubleday Anchor Books.

_____. 1978. *Thinking.* The Life of the Mind, vol. 1. New York: Harcourt Brace Jovanovich.

Armstrong, J. Scott. "Social Irresponsibility in Management." *Journal of Business Research* 5 (September):185–213.

Arthur Andersen & Co. 1976. *A Management Guide to Better Financial Reporting.* Philadelphia: Duff and Phelps, Inc.

Arthur D. Little, Inc. 1975. *The Consequences of Electronic Funds Transfer.* Study prepared for the National Science Foundation under contract NSF-C844. Cambridge, Mass.: Arthur D. Little, Inc.

Ayres, Robert U. 1969. *Technologies Forecasting and Long Range Planning.* New York: McGraw-Hill.

Bailey, Anthony. 1978. *Rembrandt's House.* Boston: Houghton Mifflin.

Baker, Henry G. 1973. "Identity and Social Responsibility Policies." *Business Horizons,* April, pp. 23–28.

Baldwin, Deborah. 1978. "Motherhood and the Liberated Woman." *Washington Monthly,* July–August, pp. 50–56.

Ball, George W. 1967. "Cosmocorp: The Importance of Being Stateless." *Columbia Journal of World Business* (November–December).

———. 1976. *Diplomacy for a Crowded World.* Boston: Little, Brown.

Ball, Robert. 1976. "The Hard Hats in Europe's Boardrooms." *Fortune,* June, pp. 180*ff.*

Banfield, Edward C. 1974. *The Unheavenly City Revisited.* Boston: Little, Brown.

Baran, Paul. 1968. *The Political Economy of Growth.* New York: Monthly Review Press.

Barnes, Harry Elmer. 1937. *An Intellectual and Cultural History of the Western World.* New York: Cardon.

Barnet, R.J., and R.E. Muller. 1975. *Global Reach: The Power of the Multinational Corporations.* New York: Simon and Schuster.

Bartos, Rena. 1978. "What Every Marketer Should Know About Women." *Harvard Business Review,* May–June, pp. 73–85.

Batt, William L., Jr., and Edgar Weinberg. 1978. "Labor Management Cooperation Today." *Harvard Business Review,* January–February, pp. 96–104.

Battelle Memorial Institute. 1978. "Probable Levels of R&D Expenditures in 1978: Forecast and Analysis," (GCS 2-78) C-1. Covina, Calif.: Procurement Associates.

Bauer, P.T., and B.S. Yamey. 1977. "Against the New Economic Order." *Commentary,* April, pp. 25–31.

Bauer, Raymond, Ithiel de Sola Pool, and Lewis Anthony Dexter. 1972. *American Business and Public Policy,* 2nd ed. Chicago: Aldine-Atherton.

Baughman, James P., George C. Lodge, and Howard W. Pifer, III. 1974. *Environmental Analysis for Management: Instructor's Guide.* Homewood, Ill.: Irwin.

Beckerman, Wilfred. 1975. *Two Cheers for the Affluent Society.* New York: St. Martin's Press.

Beer, Samuel H. 1978. "Federalism, Nationalism and Democracy in America." *American Political Science Review* 72, no. 1 (March):9–21.

Bell, Carolyn Shaw. 1978. "The Benefits of Regulation." *New York Times,* July 25.

Bell, Daniel. 1960. "In Search of Marxist Humanism." *Soviet Survey* 32 (April):21–31.

———. 1973. *The Coming of Post-Industrial Society.* New York: Basic Books.

———. 1976. *The Cultural Contradictions of Capitalism.* New York: Basic Books.

Benjamin, Daniel K. 1978. "Is Planned Obsolescence a Serious Problem?" In M. Bruce Johnson, *The Attack on Corporate America.* New York: McGraw-Hill.

Bennett, William J. 1978. "When Values Are Substituted for Truth." *Wall Street Journal*, July 25.

Bennigson, Lawrence A., and Arnold I. Bennigson. 1974. "Product Liability: Manufacturers Beware!" *Harvard Business Review*, May–June, pp. 122*ff.*

Bennis, Warren, and Philip Slater. 1973. "Organizational Democracy." In Fred Best, *The Future of Work*. Englewood Cliffs, N.J.: Prentice-Hall.

Berenson, Conrad. 1972. "The Product Liability Revolution." *Business Horizons* 15, no. 5 (October):71–80.

Bergsten, C. Fred. 1973. "The Threat from the Third World." *Foreign Policy*, Summer, pp. 102–24.

Berle, A.A., Jr., and G.C. Means. 1932. *The Modern Corporation and Private Property*. New York: Macmillan.

Berlin, Isaiah. 1978. *Russian Thinkers*. London: Penguin.

Berry, Jeffrey M. 1977. *Lobbying for the People*. Princeton, N.J.: Princeton University Press.

Berstein, Peter W. 1978. "Psychographics Is Still an Issue on Madison Avenue." *Fortune*, January, pp. 78*ff.*

Berul, L.H. 1977. "Data Based Defense Against Product Liability." *Management Review* 66 (November):18–20.

Bethell, Tom. 1978. "Class War." *New York Times*, May 31.

Bidney, David. 1940. *The Psychology and Ethics of Spinoza*. New Haven, Conn.: Yale University Press.

Blake, George B. 1978. "Graphic Shorthand as an Aid to Managers." *Harvard Business Review*, March–April, pp. 7*ff.*

Blair, John M. 1976. *The Control of Oil*. New York: Pantheon.

Blockhurst, Richard, and Jan Tumlir. 1977. *Adjustment, Trade, and Growth in Developed and Developing Countries*. New York: Unipub.

Blumberg, Philip I. 1975. *The Megacorporation in American Society*. Englewood Cliffs, N.J.: Prentice-Hall.

Bock, Betty. 1969. *Mergers and Markets:7*. Studies in Business Economics, no. 105. New York: Conference Board.

————. 1972. *Dialogue on Concentration, Oligopoly and Profits*. Report no. 556. New York: Conference Board.

Bok, Sissela. 1978. *Lying: Moral Choice in Public and Private Life*. New York: Pantheon.

Boorstin, Daniel J. 1973. *The Americans: The Democratic Experience*. New York: Random House.

Bork, Robert H. 1978. *The Antitrust Paradox*. New York: Basic Books.

Boulding, K.E. 1966a. *Economic Analysis*. New York: Harper & Row.

————. 1966b. "The Economics of Coming Space Ship Earth." In Henry Jarrett, *Environmental Quality in a Growing Economy*. Baltimore, Md.: Johns Hopkins University Press.

Bower, Joseph L. 1978. "The Business of Business Is Serving Markets." *American Economic Review* 68 (May):322–27.

Boyer, William W. 1964. *Bureaucracy on Trial*. New York: Bobbs-Merrill.

Boyle, M. Barbara. 1973. "Equal Opportunity for Women in Small Business." *Harvard Business Review*, May–June, pp. 85–94.

Bradley, David G. 1977. "Managing Against Expropriation." *Harvard Business Review*,

July–August, pp. 75–83.

Bradshaw, Thornton. 1977. "My Case for National Planning." *Fortune,* February.

Breckenridge, John B. 1978a. "Small Business and Job Creation—Part II." *Congressional Record,* November 9, pp. E5985–86.

_____. 1978b. "The Future of Small Business in America." *Congressional Record,* November 9, pp. E5983–85.

Brehm, Howard E. 1975. "How to Establish a Product Safety Program." *Quality Progress* 8 (February):28–29.

Brenner, Steven N., and Earl A. Molander. 1977. "Is the Ethics of Business Changing?" *Harvard Business Review,* January–February, pp. 57–71.

Bright, James R. 1963. "Opportunity and Threat in Technological Change." *Harvard Business Review,* November–December, pp. 76–86.

_____. 1968. *Technological Forecasting for Industry and Government.* Englewood Cliffs, N.J.: Prentice-Hall.

_____. 1972. *A Brief Introduction to Technology Forecasting.* Austin, Tex.: Pemaquid Press.

_____. 1973. *A Guide to Practical Technological Forecasting.* Englewood Cliffs, N.J.: Prentice-Hall.

Brody, Jane E. 1978. "Food Additives: Do They Hurt?" *New York Times,* July 12.

Browning, Edgar K. 1976. "Inequality, Income, and Opportunity." *Public Interest,* no. 43 (Spring):90–110.

Brozen, Yale. 1969. "Competition, Efficiency and Antitrust." *Journal of World Trade Law* 3.

_____. 1978. "Antitrust Witch Hunt." *National Review,* November 24, pp. 1470*ff.*

Buckley, William F., Jr. 1977. "Giving Yale to Connecticut." *Harper's,* November.

Burck, Charles G. 1978. "How GM Turned Itself Around." *Fortune,* January, pp. 96*ff.*

Burger, Chester. 1975. "How to Meet the Press." *Harvard Business Review,* July–August, pp. 62–70.

Burnham, James. 1941. *The Managerial Revolution.* Bloomington: Indiana University Press.

Burns, Arthur. 1977. Speech delivered at Gonzaga University. Spokane, Washington, October 26.

Byington, S. John. 1976. Interview. *U.S. News & World Report,* August 23, pp. 33–35.

Bylinsky, Gene. 1978. "The Japanese Spies in Silicon Valley." *Fortune,* February.

_____. 1979. "Industry's New Frontier in Space." *Fortune,* January, pp. 77*ff.*

Cannon, James. 1975. *A Clear View: A Guide to Industrial Pollution.* Emmaus, Pa.: Rodale Press.

Capron, W.M., and R.G. Noll. 1971. "Summary and Conclusion." In W.M. Capron, *Technological Change in Regulated Industries.* Washington, D.C.: Brookings.

Carmichael, Stokely, and Charles V. Hamilton. 1967. *Black Power.* New York: Random House.

Carr, Albert Z. 1968. "Is Business Bluffing Ethical?" *Harvard Business Review,* January–February.

Carruth, Eleanore. 1973. "The Legal Explosion Has Left Business Shell-Shocked." *Fortune,* April.

Carson, Deane. 1977. "Companies as Heroes? Bah! Humbug!!" *New York Times,* December 25.

Cary, William L. 1974. "Federalism and Corporate Law: Reflection upon Delaware."

Yale Law Journal 8, no. 4 (March):663*ff.*

Center for Futures Research. 1978. *Emerging Social and Worker Entitlements.* Los Angeles: Graduate School of Business, University of California.

Cerra, Frances. 1977. "New York State Consumer Unit Deciphers Codes on Food Dieting." *New York Times,* August 21.

Cetron, M.J., and Audrey Clayton. 1974. "Social Forecasting: A Practical Approach." In Andrew A. Spekke, *The Next 25 Years.* Washington, D.C.: World Future Society.

Chamberlain, Neil W. 1973. *The Limits of Corporate Responsibility.* New York: Basic Books.

Chambers, John C., Sartinder K. Mullick, and Donald D. Smith. 1971. "How to Choose the Right Forecasting Technique." *Harvard Business Review,* July–August, pp. 57–86.

Chambre, Henri. 1974. "Marxism." *Encyclopedia Britannica, Macropaedia,* vol. 11, pp. 553–60.

Chandler, Alfred D., Jr. 1962. *Strategy and Structure.* Cambridge, Mass.: MIT Press.

———. 1977. *The Visible Hand: The Managerial Revolution in American Business.* Cambridge, Mass.: Harvard University Press.

Chen, Gordon, and Edward A. Zanc. 1969. "The Business Core Curricula Eight Years after Gordon-Howell and Pierson Reports." *Collegiate News and Reviews,* October.

Chinitz, Benjamin. 1974. "Regional Development." In McKie, *Social Responsibility and the Business Predicament.* Washington, D.C.: Brookings.

Christopher, Robert C. 1978. "They Try Harder." *New York Times Magazine,* January 22.

Clark, Peter B., and James A. Wilson. 1961. "Incentive Systems: A Theory of Organization." *Administrative Science Quarterly* 6 (September):129–66.

Clarke, Arthur C. 1962. *Profiles of the Future.* London: Victor Gollancz.

Clifford, Donald K., Jr. 1977. "Thriving in a Recession." *Harvard Business Review,* July–August, pp. 57–65.

Cobb, Roger W., and Charles D. Elder. 1971. "The Politics of Agenda-Building." *Journal of Politics* 33, no. 4 (November):892–915.

Cochran, Thomas C. 1959. *Basic History of American Business.* New York: Van Nostrand.

Cole, Barry, and Mal Oettinger. 1978. *The Reluctant Regulators.* Reading, Mass.: Addison-Wesley.

Committee for Economic Development. 1978. *Jobs for the Hard-to-Employ: New Directions for a Public Private Partnership.* New York: CED.

Commoner, Barry. 1972. *The Closing Circle.* New York: Knopf.

Congressional Research Service. 1976. *An Approach to Tax Reform Issues.* Washington, D.C.: U.S. Government Printing Office.

Congressional Budget Office. 1976. *The Number of Federal Employees Engaged in Regulatory Activities.* Print of the Subcommittee on Oversight and Investigation of the Committee on Interstate and Foreign Commerce, U.S. House of Representatives. Washington, D.C.: U.S. Government Printing Office.

Conrady, W.N. 1972. "Accounting Education: For What Purpose?" *Journal of Contemporary Business* (Winter).

Cony, Ed, and Peter Kann. 1977. "In China, Equality Is Elusive." *Wall Street Journal,*

December 1.

Cook, James. 1979. "Is Charity Obsolete?" *Forbes*, February 5, pp. 45–51.

Corneulle, Richard. 1975. *De-Managing America.* New York: Vintage Books.

Council of Economic Advisers. 1977. *Economic Report of the President.* Washington, D.C.: U.S. Government Printing Office.

Council of Economic Advisers. 1979. *Economic Report of the President.* Washington, D.C.: U.S. Government Printing Office.

Council on Environmental Quality. 1978. *Annual Report.* Washington, D.C.: U.S. Government Printing Office.

Cravens, Gwyneth. 1977. "How Ma Bell Is Training Women for Management." *New York Times Magazine*, May 29, pp. 12*ff.*

Crittenden, Ann. 1977a. "In the Corporate World More Talk Than Progress." *New York Times*, May 1.

––––––. 1977b. "The Case of the Black Entrepreneur." *New York Times*, July 31.

Crouch, Robert L. 1978. "Are Corporate Pricing Policies a Primary Cause of Inflation?" In M. Bruce Johnson, *The Attack on Corporate America.* New York: McGraw-Hill.

Dahl, Robert A. 1970. *After the Revolution?* New Haven, Conn.: Yale University Press.

––––––, and Charles E. Lindblom. 1953. *Politics, Economics, and Welfare.* New York: Harper & Row.

Darnacy, Arsen, and Gary Nuss. 1976. "Environmental Impacts of Coca-Cola Beverage Containers." Appendix C in U.S. Congress, Technology Assessment Board, *Technological Assessment Activities.* Washington, D.C.: U.S. Government Printing Office, pp. 299–305.

Davis, K., and R. Blomstrom. 1975. *Business and Society: Environment and Responsibility*, 2nd ed. New York: McGraw-Hill.

Davis, Ruth M. 1977. "Evolution of Computers and Computing." *Science* 18 (March):1096–1102.

Deal, Emit B. 1977. "Business Core Curricula Revisited." *Collegiate News and Views* (Spring).

De Muth, Christopher C. 1977. "Tubthumping in the Political Marketplace." *Wall Street Journal*, November 30.

De Reamer, Russell. 1967. "Accident Prevention and Safety." In H.B. Maynard, *Handbook of Business Administration.* New York: McGraw-Hill.

Deutsch, Karl. 1963. *Nerves of Government.* Glencoe, Ill.: Free Press.

Dewey, Donald J. 1974. "The New Learning: One Man's View." In Harvey J. Goldschmid et al., *Industrial Concentration: The New Learning.* Boston: Little, Brown.

De Witt, Karen. 1979. "Business Wins Friends and Influences Washington." *New York Times*, January 7.

Dickson, Paul. 1975. *The Future of the Workplace.* New York: Weybright and Talley.

Domhoff, G. William. 1967. *Who Rules America?* Englewood Cliffs, N.J.: Prentice-Hall.

––––––. 1974. "State and Ruling Class in Corporate America." *Insurgent Sociologist* 4, no. 3.

Dow Chemical, U.S.A. 1975. *EEO . . . The Legal Side.* Supervisors' Handbook, Form no. 225-17-75. Midland, Michigan.

Dowling, William. 1978. *Effective Management and the Behavioral Sciences.* New York: AMACOM.

Drotning, Phillip T. 1974. "Organizing the Company for Social Action." In S. Prakash Sethi, *The Unstable Ground.* Los Angeles: Melville.

Drucker, Peter F. 1964. *Managing for Results.* New York: Harper & Row.

_____. 1974. *Management: Tasks, Responsibilities, Practices.* New York: Harper & Row.

_____. 1975. "The Delusion of Profits." *Wall Street Journal,* February 5.

_____. 1976. *The Unseen Revolution.* New York: Harper & Row.

_____. 1977. "Helping Small Business Cope." *Wall Street Journal,* April 21.

Dubos, René. 1978. *The Resilience of Ecosystems.* Boulder: Colorado Associated University Press.

Dunlop, John T. 1978. "Past and Future Tendencies in American Labor Organization." *Daedalus,* Winter, pp. 79–96.

Dunn, Frederica Hoge. 1978. "The 'Best Man' Theory and Why It Fails." *New York Times,* July 16.

Easterlin, Richard A. 1978. "What Will 1984 Be Like?" Presidential Address before the Population Association of America, April.

Easton, David. 1965. *A Systems Analysis of Political Life.* New York: Wiley.

Emshwiller, John R. 1978. "Using the Law's Delay, Myron Cherry Attacks Atomic-Power Projects." *Wall Street Journal,* March 10.

Engler, Robert. 1978. *The Brotherhood of Oil: Energy Policy and the Public Interest.* Chicago: University of Chicago Press.

Epstein, Edwin M. 1969. *The Corporation in American Politics.* Englewood Cliffs, N.J.: Prentice-Hall.

_____. 1972. "Corporations and the Political Imperative." *Business and Society Review,* Summer, pp. 54–67.

Erdman, Paul E. 1976. *The Crash of '79.* New York: Simon and Schuster.

Estes, Ralph. 1976. *Corporate Social Accounting.* New York: Wiley.

Etzioni, Amitai. 1978. "Why We Chose to Have Stagflation." *Business Week,* February 27, p. 18.

Ewing, David W. 1958. *Long-Range Planning for Management.* New York: Harper and Brothers.

_____. 1977. "What Business Thinks About Employee Rights." *Harvard Business Review,* September–October, pp. 81–94.

Fairlie, Henry. 1973. *The Kennedy Promise.* New York: Doubleday.

Farb, Warren E., and Douglas N. Jones. 1976. *Dealing with Inflation and Unemployment.* Congressional Research Service, pp. 76–78. Washington, D.C.: Government Printing Office.

Farnsworth, Clyde H. 1978a. "Import Battle." *New York Times,* February 19.

_____. 1978b. "Complying with Government Regulation." *New York Times.* April 13.

Fedo, Michael W. 1978. "Rehabilitation Is Good Business." *New York Times,* August 6.

Fenn, Dan H., Jr. 1967. "The Case of the Latent Lobby." *Harvard Business Review,* January–February.

Firestone. n.d. *Excellence in Environmental Engineering.* Employee Communications Department, Firestone Corporation. Akron, Ohio.

Fisher, J.C., and R.H. Pry. 1971. "A Simple Substitution Model of Technological Change." *Technological Forecasting and Social Change* 3, no. 1:75–88.

Fisk, George, and Rajan Chandran. 1975. "How to Trace and Recall Products." *Harvard Business Review,* November–December, pp. 90–96.

Fiske, Edward B. 1978. "Growth of Ethics Courses Shows Major Change on U.S. Campuses." *New York Times,* February 20.

Flanagan, Robert J., George Strauss, and Lloyd Ulman. 1974. "Worker Discontent and Work Place Behavior." *Industrial Relations,* May, pp. 101–23.

Foster, Le Baron R. 1964. *Telling a Company's Financial Story.* New York: Financial Executives Research Foundation, Inc.

Fourquin, Guy. 1977. *Lordship and Feudalism in the Middle Ages.* London: Allen & Unwin.

Fowler, Elizabeth H. 1977. "The Obsolescence of Professionals." *New York Times,* June 24.

French, Benjamin U., Jr. 1976. "Product Complaints and the Corporation Today." Paper presented at the American Management Association's Handling Product Complaints Seminar, October 13.

Freund, Ernst. 1928. *Administrative Powers over Persons and Property.* Chicago: University of Chicago Press.

Fri, Robert W. 1974. "Facing Up to Pollution Controls." *Harvard Business Review,* March–April, pp. 38–44.

Fried, Edward R., and Philip H. Trezise. 1976. "The United States in the World Economy." In Henry Owen and Charles L. Schultze, *Setting National Priorities.* Washington, D.C.: Brookings.

Friedlaender, Ann F. 1969. *The Dilemma of Freight Transport Regulation.* Washington, D.C.: Brookings.

Friedman, Joel I. 1978. "An Overview of Spinoza's Ethics." *Synthese* 37:67–106.

Friedman, Milton. 1953. *Essays in Positive Economics.* Chicago: University of Chicago Press.

——. 1962. *Capitalism and Freedom.* Chicago: University of Chicago Press.

——. 1971. "Does Business Have a Social Responsibility?" *Bank Administration,* April, pp. 13–14.

——. 1976. "Adam Smith's Relevance for 1976." International Institute for Economic Research, Original Paper 5. Ottawa, Illinois: Green Hill.

Froman, Lewis A. 1967. *The Congressional Process: Strategies, Rules, and Procedures.* Boston: Little, Brown.

Fuchs, Victor R. 1974. *Who Shall Live? Health, Economics, and Social Choice.* New York: Basic Books.

Galbraith, John K. 1955. *The Great Crash of 1929.* Boston: Houghton Mifflin.

——. 1962. *American Capitalism,* 2nd ed. Boston: Houghton Mifflin.

——. 1967. *The New Industrial State.* Boston: Houghton Mifflin.

——. 1973. *Economics and Public Purpose.* Boston: Houghton Mifflin.

——. 1977. *The Age of Uncertainty.* Boston: Houghton Mifflin.

——. 1979. "The Thinking Man's Trip Around the World." *Esquire,* February 27, pp. 66*ff.*

Gallese, Liz Roman. 1975. "The Soothsayers: 'Futurists' to Discern What Is Lying Ahead." *Wall Street Journal,* March 31.

Gatts, Robert R., Robert G. Massey, and John C. Robertson. 1974. *Energy Conservation Program Guide for Industry and Commerce.* National Bureau of Standards Handbook 115. Washington, D.C.: U.S. Government Printing Office.

Gellman, A.J. 1971. "Surface Freight Transport." In W.M. Capron, *Technological Change in Regulated Industries.* Washington, D.C.: Brookings.

Gertsner, Louis V., and M. Helen Anderson. 1976. "The Chief Financial Officer as Activist." *Harvard Business Review,* September–October, pp. 100–06.

Gerzon, Mark. 1977. "Counterculture Capitalists." *New York Times,* June 5.

Gilder, George. 1978. "Prometheus Bound." *Harper's* 257 (September):35–42.

Gillette, Dean. 1977. "How Regulations Encourage and Discourage Innovation." *Research Management* 20, no. 2 (March):18–21.

Gimpel, Jean. 1976. *The Medieval Machine: The Industrial Revolution of the Middle Ages.* New York: Holt, Rinehart and Winston.

Ginzberg, Eli. 1976. "The Pluralistic Economy of the U.S." *Scientific American* 235, no. 6 (December):25–29.

_____. 1978. "Hard Work on the Way Out?" Interview in *U.S. News & World Report,* January 23, 47–49.

Givens, William L., and William V. Rapp. 1979. "What It Takes to Meet the Japanese Challenge." *Fortune,* June, pp. 104*ff.*

Glazer, Nathan. 1976. *Affirmative Discrimination.* New York: Basic Books.

Gluck, Frederick W., and Richard N. Foster. 1975. "Managing Technological Change." *Harvard Business Review,* September–October, pp. 139–50.

Goggin, William C. 1974. "How the Multidimensional Structure Works at Dow Corning." *Harvard Business Review,* January–February, pp. 54–65.

Goldman, Marshall I. 1972. *The Spoils of Progress: Environmental Pollution in the Soviet Union.* Cambridge, Mass.: MIT Press.

Goodman, Stephen H. 1978. "We Should Restrain U.S. Financing of Export Programs." *Wall Street Journal,* July 12.

Gordon, David M. 1975. "Recession in Capitalism as Usual." *New York Times Magazine,* April, pp. 18*ff.*

Gottschalk, Earl C., Jr. 1979. "Disney to Shift Target of Some Parks." *Wall Street Journal,* January 26.

Green, Wayne E. 1976. "The Delaying Game." *Wall Street Journal,* May 26.

Greyser, Stephen A., and Steven L. Diamond. 1974. "Business Is Adapting to Consumerism." *Harvard Business Review,* September–October, pp. 38 *ff.*

Griffith, Thomas. 1977. "Weyerhauser Gets Set for the 21st Century." *Fortune,* April, pp. 75 *ff.*

Griskey, Richard G. 1977. "Whatever Happened to American Technology?" *World Future Society Bulletin,* November–December, pp. 7–13.

Grocery Manufacturers of America. 1974. *Guidelines for Product Recall.*

Gross, Bertram M. 1968. *Organizations and Their Managing.* New York: Free Press.

Gruber, William H., and John S. Niles. 1976. *The New Management.* New York: McGraw-Hill.

Guth, William D., and Renato Tagiuri. 1965. "Personal Values and Corporate Strategy." *Harvard Business Review,* May–June.

Guzzardi, Walter, Jr. 1975. "What We Should Have Learned About Controls." *Fortune,* March, pp. 102 *ff.*

_____. 1978a. "A Search for Sanity in Antitrust." *Fortune,* January, pp. 72 *ff.*

_____ 1978b. "Business Is Learning How to Win in Washington." *Fortune,* March, pp. 52 *ff.*

Gyllenhammar, Pehr G. 1977. "How Volvo Adapts Work to People." *Harvard Business Review,* July–August, pp. 102 *ff.*

Hacker, Andrew. 1974. "Business Corporation." *Encyclopedia Britannica, Macropaedia,* vol. 5.

Haley, Martin Ryan, and James M. Kiss. 1974. "Large Stakes in Statehouse Lobbying." *Harvard Business Review,* January–February, pp. 125–35.

Hall, Edward T. 1973. *The Silent Language.* Garden City, N.Y.: Anchor Press.

Harrington, Michael. 1976. *The Twilight of Capitalism.* New York: Simon and Schuster.

Harris, James F., and Anne Klepper. 1977. "Corporate Philanthropic Public Service Activities." In *Research Papers,* vol. III. Sponsored by the Commission on Private Philanthropy and Public Needs. Washington, D.C.: Department of Treasury.

Hartley, William D. 1977. "More Firms Now Stress In-House Auditing." *Wall Street Journal,* August 22.

Hartz, Louis. 1948. *Economic Policy and Democratic Thought.* Cambridge, Mass.: Harvard University Press.

Hatch, Orrin G. 1978. Speech delivered to the Senate on the Humphrey-Hawkins Bill, October 12. *Congressional Record,* October 13, 1978, pp. S18952–56.

Hawkins, David J. 1977. *Financial Analysts Journal,* November–December, pp. 48–53.

Hayek, Friedrich A. 1960. *Constitution of Liberty.* Chicago: University of Chicago Press.

Hayes, Samuel L., III. 1977. "Capital Commitments and the High Cost of Money." *Harvard Business Review,* May–June, pp. 155–61.

Hill, Gladwin. 1976. "Environmental Impact Statements." *New York Times,* July 3.

Hilsman, Roger. 1975. *The Crouching Future.* Garden City, N.Y.: Doubleday.

Hirsch, Fred. 1976. *Social Limits to Growth.* Cambridge, Mass.: Harvard University Press.

Hirschman, Albert O. 1977. *The Passions and the Interests: Political Arguments for Capitalism Before Its Triumph.* Princeton, N.J.: Princeton University Press.

Hecht, James L. 1970. *Because It Is Right: Integration in Housing.* Boston: Little, Brown.

Heckert, Richard E. 1976. "The Changing Environment for Industrial Research and Development." Speech given at University of Illinois, May 1, Urbana.

Heilbroner, Robert L. 1975. *Corporate Social Policy.* Reading, Mass.: Addison-Wesley.

———. 1962. *The Making of Economic Society.* Englewood Cliffs, N.J.: Prentice-Hall.

———. 1977. "Trying to Make Sense of It." *New York Times,* October 10.

———. 1978a. "Capitalism, Socialism, and Democracy: A Symposium." *Commentary* 64 (April):46–48.

———. 1978b. "Boom and Crash." *New Yorker,* August 28, pp. 52 *ff.*

Henderson, Hazel. 1971. "Toward Managing Social Conflict." *Harvard Business Review,* May–June, pp. 82–90.

Henion, Karl E., II. 1976. *Ecological Marketing.* Columbus, Ohio: Grid.

Henry, Harold W. 1973. "Policy and Planning Impacts of Environmental Protection in Major Corporations." Paper presented at national meeting of Academy of Management. Boston.

Hershey, Robert. 1975. "Planning for the Unthinkable." *Harvard Business Review,* July–August, pp. 20 *ff.*

———. 1978. "The Quintessential Multinational." *New York Times International Economic Survey,* February 5, pp. 22–23.

Hesse, Hermann. 1976. *My Belief.* London: Jonathan Cape.

Hollie, Pamela G. 1978. "The Energy Strategy of the Heaviest Energy User." *New*

York Times, February 5.

Hollomon, J. Herbert. 1976. "What It All Means." Proceedings of a symposium on technological innovation. Sponsored by Energy Research and Development Administration, April 19–20. Washington, D.C.

Holsendolph, Ernest. 1973. "The Management Doctors." *New York Times,* November 11.

Hruska, Roman. 1974. Commentary in Harvey J. Goldschmid et al. *Industrial Concentration: The New Learning.* Boston: Little, Brown.

Hunt, Morton M. 1954. "Bell Labs' 230 Long-Range Planners." *Fortune,* May, pp. 120 *ff.*

Hurst, J.W. 1956. *Law and the Conditions of Freedom.* Madison: University of Wisconsin Press.

Hutchinson, John. 1976. "Evolving Organizational Forms." *Columbia Journal of World Business,* Summer, pp. 48–58.

Hyatt, James C. 1977. "Firms Learn Art of Keeping Unions Out." *Wall Street Journal,* April 19.

Ignatius, David. 1976a. "Stages of Nader." *New York Times Magazine,* January 18, pp. 8*ff.*

———. 1976b. "Bashful Business—Despite Liberal Laws Most Companies Shun Partisan Politicking." *Wall Street Journal,* October 27.

Ingrassia, Paul, and David P. Garino. 1979. "Producers of Pet Food Fight Fiercely for Piece of Tempting Market." *Wall Street Journal,* February 22.

Institute for the Future. 1973. *Project Aware.* Menlo Park, Calif.: IFF.

Jacob, Richard M., and August B. Mundel. 1975. "Quality Tasks in Product Recall." *Quality Progress* (June).

Jacoby, Neil H. 1970. "The Multinational Corporation." *The Center Magazine,* May.

———. 1971. "Capitalism and Contemporary Social Problems." *Sloan Management Review* 12, no. 2 (Winter):33–43.

———. 1973. *Corporate Power and Social Responsibility.* New York: Macmillan.

———. 1977. "The Corporate State: Myth or Reality?" *Wharton Magazine* 1, no. 4 (Summer):21–26.

———, et al. 1977. *Bribery and Extortion in World Business.* New York: Free Press.

Janowitz, Morris. 1978. *Social Control of the Welfare State.* Chicago: University of Chicago Press.

Janssen, Richard F., Mike Tharp, Norman Pearlstine, and Anthony Patrick. 1978. "Surge in Protectionism." *Wall Street Journal,* April 14.

Jaroslovsky, Richard. 1978. "A Washington Lawyer Thrives by Negotiating the Bureaucratic Maze." *Wall Street Journal,* August 14.

Jensen, Michael C. 1978. "Inflation Effects on Business Mixed." *New York Times,* June 6.

Joachim, Harold H. 1964. *A Study of the Ethics of Spinoza.* New York: Russell & Russell.

Johnson, Paul. 1977. *Enemies of Society.* New York: Atheneum.

Johnson, Sheila K. 1975. "It's Action, but Is It Affirmative?" *New York Times Magazine,* May 11, pp. 18 *ff.*

Jones, Reginald H. 1975. "Why Business Must Seek Tax Reform." *Harvard Business Review,* September–October, 49–55.

Jones, Robert T. 1976. "Executive's Guide to Antitrust in Europe." *Harvard Business*

Review, May–June, pp. 106–18.

Joskow, Paul L., and Robert S. Pindyck. 1979. "Should the Government Subsidize Non-Conventional Energy Supplies?" MIT-EL 79-003WP. Cambridge, Mass.: Center for Energy Policy Research.

Kahn, Alfred E. 1971. *The Economics of Regulation,* vol. II. New York: Wiley.

Kahn, Herman, William Brown, and Leon Martel. 1976. *The Next 200 Years.* New York: Morrow.

Kain, John F. 1974. "Urban Problems." In James W. McKie, *Social Responsibility and the Business Predicament.* Washington, D.C.: Brookings.

Kalecki, Michael. 1971. *Selected Essays on the Dynamics of the Capitalist Economy, 1933–1970.* Cambridge, Mass.: Cambridge University Press.

Kassalow, Everett M. 1978. *Some Labor Futures in the United States.* CRS-78-21-5. Washington, D.C.: Congressional Research Service.

Katona, George, and Burkhard Strumpel. 1978. "A New Economic Era." *Public Opinion,* March–April, pp. 9–11.

Keller, Walter. 1962. *East Minus West.* New York: G.P. Putnam.

Key, Vladimer O., Jr. 1961. *Public Opinion and American Democracy.* New York: Alfred A. Knopf.

———. 1964. *Politics, Parties and Pressure Groups.* New York: Harper & Row.

Keynes, John M. 1936. *The General Theory of Employment, Interest and Money.* New York: Harcourt Brace.

King, William R. 1978. "Developing Useful Management Decision Support Systems." *Management Decision* 16, no. 4:262–73.

Kissinger, Henry. 1977. "The Future of Business and the International Environment." Address given at the first meeting of the Future of Business Project for Strategic and International Studies at Georgetown University, Washington, D.C., June 28.

Klein, Thomas A. 1977. *Social Costs and Benefits of Business.* Englewood Cliffs, N.J.: Prentice-Hall.

Kleinfield, N.R. 1978. "Corporate Charity: Running the Alms Race." *New York Times,* January 1.

Kneese, Allen W., and Charles L. Schultze. 1975. *Pollution, Prices, and Public Policy.* Washington, D.C.: Brookings.

Knight, Frank H. 1921. *Risk, Uncertainty, and Profit.* Chicago: University of Chicago Press.

Komaki, Judy, Kenneth D. Barwick, and Lawrence R. Scott. 1978. "Behavioral Approach to Occupational Safety." *Journal of Applied Psychology* 63, no. 4 (August):434–45.

Kotler, Philip. 1972. "What Consumerism Means for Marketers." *Harvard Business Review,* May–June, pp. 48*ff.*

Kraas, Louis. 1978. "Boeing Takes a Bold Plunge to Keep Flying High." *Fortune,* September, pp. 42–50.

Kranz, H. 1974. "Are Merit and Equity Compatible?" *Public Administration Review,* September–October.

Krasnow, Erwin G., and Lawrence D. Longley. 1978. *The Politics of Broadcast Regulation.* New York: St. Martin's Press.

Kristol, Irving. 1975. "Corporate Capitalism in America." *Public Interest,* no. 41 (Fall):124–41.

———. 1978. *Two Cheers for Capitalism.* New York: Basic Books.

_____, et al. 1975. *America's Continuing Revolution: An Act of Conservation.* Washington, D.C.: American Enterprise.

Kronholz, June. 1977. "A Living Alone Trend Affects Housing, Cars, and Other Industries." *Wall Street Journal,* November 16.

_____. 1978. "Management Practices Change to Reflect Role of Women Employees." *Wall Street Journal,* September 15.

Landes, David S. 1974. "Economic History Since 1500," *Encyclopedia Britannica, Macropaedia,* vol. 6.

Large, Arlen J. 1978. "Government Is Backing a Vast Array of Research on New Energy Sources at $3 Billion Annual Cost." *Wall Street Journal,* January 24.

Lasch, Christopher. 1977. *Haven in a Heartless World: The Family Besieged.* New York: Basic Books.

Lave, Lester B., and Eugene P. Seskin. 1977. *Air Pollution and Human Health.* Washington, D.C.: Resources for the Future.

Lawson, Herbert G. 1978. "Timetable Is Slipping in Programs to Mine Metals under the Sea." *Wall Street Journal,* July 31.

Lebedoff, David. 1978. "The Dangerous Arrogance of the New Elite." *Esquire,* August 29, pp. 20 *ff.*

Leff, Nathaniel H. 1978. "Multinationals in a Hostile World." *Wharton Magazine,* Spring, pp. 21–29.

Lenz, R.G., Jr. 1975. "Development of Attributes and Parameters for Trend Extrapolation." Paper presented at 26th Technology Forecasting Course. Industrial Management Center, Hilton Head Island, South Carolina, January.

Leonard, John. 1977. "What Have American Writers Got Against Businessmen?" *Forbes,* May 15.

Leone, Robert A. 1977. "The Real Costs of Regulation." *Harvard Business Review,* November–December, pp. 57–66.

_____. 1978. Author's Reply to Letter to the Editor. In *Harvard Business Review,* January–February, pp. 51–52.

Leontief, Wassily. 1971. "The Trouble with Cuban Socialism." *New York Review of Books,* January 7, pp. 19 *ff.*

Lerner, Abba P. 1946. *The Economics of Control.* New York: Macmillan.

Levitt, Theodore. 1970. "The Morality (?) of Advertising." *Harvard Business Review,* July–August, pp. 84–92.

_____. 1976. "The Industrialization of Service." *Harvard Business Review,* September–October, pp. 63–74.

_____. 1977a. "Corporate Responsibility: Taking Care of Business." *The American Spectator,* November, pp. 21–26.

_____. 1977b. "Marketing and Corporate Purpose." Paper delivered as part of the Key Issues Lecture Series. New York University, March 2.

Lewis, Paul. 1978. "European Businessmen Don't Take Their Morality So Seriously." *New York Times,* March 5.

Libenstein, Harvey. 1976. *Beyond Economic Man.* Cambridge, Mass.: Harvard University Press.

Lilley, William, III, and James C. Miller III. 1977. "The New 'Social Regulation.'" *Public Interest,* no. 47 (Spring):49–61.

Lindbeck, Assar. 1971. *The Political Economy of the New Left.* New York: Harper & Row.

Lindblom, Charles E. 1977. *Politics and Markets.* New York: Basic Books.

Linneman, Robert E., and John D. Kennell. 1977. "Shirt-Sleeve Approach to Long Range Plans." *Harvard Business Review,* March–April, pp. 141–50.

Lippmann, Walter. 1954. *The Public Philosophy,* Boston: Little, Brown.

Lipset, S.M. 1978. "Marx, Engels, and America's Political Parties." *Wilson Quarterly,* Winter, pp. 92 *ff.*

Livingston, J. Sterling. 1971. "Myth of the Well-Educated Manager." *Harvard Business Review,* January–February, pp. 78–89.

Lodge, George C. 1975. *The New American Ideology.* New York: Knopf.

Loeb, Marshall. 1978a. "Planting in the Ghettos." *Time,* April 3.

––––––. 1978b. "Telling Jimmy About Jobs." *Time,* June 12.

Lorange, Peter, and Richard F. Vancil. 1976. "How to Design a Strategic Planning System." *Harvard Business Review,* September–October, pp. 75–81.

––––––. 1977. *Strategic Planning Systems.* Englewood Cliffs, N.J.: Prentice-Hall.

Louis, Arthur M. 1978. "Lessons from the Firestone Fracas." *Fortune,* August, pp. 44 *ff.*

Louis Harris Associates. 1977. *Consumerism at the Crossroads.* Study commissioned by Sentry Insurance Company. New York: Louis Harris Associates.

Lovdal, Michael L., Raymond A. Bauer, and Nancy H. Treverton. 1977. "Public Responsibility Committees of the Board." *Harvard Business Review,* May–June, pp. 40 *ff.*

Lund, Robert T. 1977. "Making Products Live Longer." *Technological Review.* January, pp. 49–55.

Lynch, Mitchell C. 1977. "Many Concerns Stress Product Development and Reduce Research." *Wall Street Journal,* October 18.

McAdam, Terry W. 1971. "How to Put Corporate Responsibility into Practice." *MSU Business Topics,* Winter, pp. 68–76.

McCarry, Charles. 1972. *Citizen Nader.* New York: Saturday Review Press.

McCarthy, Daniel J., Robert J. Minichiello, and John R. Curran. 1975. *Business Policy and Strategy.* Homewood, Ill.: Irwin.

McCarthy, E. Jerome. 1971. *Basic Marketing,* 4th ed. Homewood, Ill.: Irwin.

McClelland, David C. 1961. *The Achieving Society.* Princeton, N.J.: Van Nostrand.

Maccoby, Michael. 1976a. *The Gamesman.* New York: Simon and Schuster.

––––––. 1976b. "The Corporate Climber." *Fortune,* December, pp. 98 *ff.*

––––––. 1978. "Trust Is Also the Business of Business." *New York Times,* March 31.

McColough, C. Peter. 1975. "The Corporation and Its Obligations." *Harvard Business Review,* May–June, pp. 127–38.

McConnell, Grant. 1966. *Private Power and American Democracy.* New York: Knopf.

McCracken, Paul W. 1978. "Inflation Must Be Fought." *Wall Street Journal,* March 13.

McDonald, Larry. 1978. "Production Not Restriction: A Response to President Carter's National Energy Plan." Extensions of remarks in the U.S. House of Representatives. *Congressional Record,* October 14, pp. E5849–61.

Mace, Myles L. 1976. "Designing a Plan for the Ideal Board." *Harvard Business Review,* November–December, pp. 20 *ff.*

McElheny, Victor L. 1977. "Plastic Bottles: Where the Battle Stands." *New York Times,* November 9.

McFarland, Andrew A. 1976. *Public Interest Lobbies.* Washington, D.C.: American Enterprise Institute.

McGregor, D. 1960. *Human Side of Enterprise.* New York: McGraw-Hill.

McKean, Roland W. 1974. "Collective Choice." In James W. McKie, *Social Responsibility and the Business Predicament.* Washington, D.C.: Brookings.

McKie, James W. 1974. *Social Responsibility and the Business Predicament.* Washington, D.C.: Brookings.

McNair, Malcolm P. 1957. "What Price Human Relations?" *Harvard Business Review,* March–April, pp. 15–23.

Macrae, Norman. 1976. "The Coming Entrepreneurial Revolution." *The Economist,* December 25.

———. 1972. "The Brisk Recessional," *The Economist,* December 23, pp. 45–62.

Maddox, Norman. 1972. Domesday Syndrome. New York: McGraw-Hill.

Magee, Bryan. 1973. *Karl Popper.* New York: Viking.

Malabre, Alfred L., Jr. 1976. *Understanding the Economy.* New York: Dodd, Mead.

———. 1978. "More and More People Seek and Find Jobs." *Wall Street Journal,* January 18.

Malley, Deborah DeWitt. 1975. "Lawrence Klein and His Forecasting Machine." *Fortune,* March, pp. 152 *ff.*

Mandell, Mel. 1978. " 'A Natural Electronic Marriage' of Information Tools." *New York Times,* July 9.

Mansfield, Edwin. 1961. "Diffusion of Technological Change." In National Science Foundation, *Reviews of Data on Research and Development,* October.

———, et al. 1971. *Research and Innovation in the Modern Corporation.* New York: Norton.

Marcus, Edmond, and Richard L. Heaton. 1977. "Bad Day at Bunker Point." *Harvard Business Review,* January–February, pp. 10*ff.*

Marcus, Sumner, and Kenneth D. Walters. 1978. "Assault on Managerial Autonomy." *Harvard Business Review,* January–February, pp. 57–66.

Marris, Robin. 1977. "The Present State of Capitalism." *New Republic,* May 21, pp. 39–41.

Martin, James. 1977. *Future Development in Telecommunications.* Englewood Cliffs, N.J.: Prentice-Hall.

Martin, William F., and George Cabot Lodge. 1975. "Our Society in 1985—Business May Not Like It." *Harvard Business Review,* November–December, pp. 143–52.

Maslow, Abraham. 1965. *Eupsychian Management.* Homewood, Ill.: Irwin.

Mast, Gerald. 1976. *A Short History of the Movies.* Indianapolis, Ind.: Bobbs-Merrill, 1976.

Mayer, Caroline E. 1977. "America's Mystery Profession." *U.S. News & World Report,* December 19, pp. 39–42.

Mayer, Martin. 1967. *The Lawyers.* New York: Harper & Row.

———. 1974. *The Bankers.* New York: Ballantine Books.

———. 1976. *Today and Tomorrow in America.* New York: Harper & Row.

Mazis, Michael, and Robert Green. 1971. "Implementing Social Responsibility." *MSU Business Topics* 19, no. 1:68–76.

Meadows, Donella H. 1972. "Reckoning with Recklessness." *Ecology Today,* January, pp. 11–47.

Meadows, Edward. 1978. "Tracking the Ever-Elusive Gross National Product." *Fortune,* May, pp. 100 *ff.*

Meitz, A.A., and Breaux B. Castleman. 1975. "How to Cope with Supply Shortages." *Harvard Business Review,* January–February, pp. 91–96.

Melloan, George, and Joan Melloan. 1978. *The Carter Economy.* New York: Wiley.

Meltzer, Allan. 1977. "It Takes Long-Range Planning to Lick Inflation." *Fortune,* December, pp. 96 *ff.*

Menzies, Hugh D. 1978. "Union Carbide Raises Its Voice." *Fortune,* September, pp. 86–89.

Meyer, Herbert E. 1976. "Personnel Directors Are the New Corporate Heroes." *Fortune,* February, pp. 84 *ff.*

———. 1978. "Those Worrisome Technology Exports." *Fortune,* May, pp. 106 *ff.*

Miller, G. Tyler, Jr. 1975. *Living in the Environment: Concepts, Problems, and Alternatives.* Belmont, Calif.: Wadsworth.

Miller, Henry E. 1978. "A Manufacturer Tries to Neutralize the Energy Uncertainties." *Harvard Business Review,* May–June, pp. 6 *ff.*

Miller, Roger. 1973. *Economics Today.* San Francisco: Canfield Press.

Mills, C.W. 1956. *Power Elite.* New York: Oxford University Press.

Mills, Ted. 1975. "Human Resources—Why the New Concern?" *Harvard Business Review,* March–April, pp. 120–34.

Mitchell, Edward. 1974. "Research on Energy Policy-Making." In Hans H. Landsberg et al., *Energy and the Social Sciences.* Washington, D.C.: Resources for the Future.

Mitre Corporation. 1971. *A Technology Assessment Methodology.* Washington, D.C.: U.S. Government Printing Office.

Molitor, Graham T.T. 1975. "Schema for Forecasting Public Policy Change." In Andrew A. Spekke, ed. *The Next 25 Years.* Washington, D.C.: World Future Society.

———. 1977. "How to Anticipate Law-Making Action." Paper delivered to Public Affairs Council Conference. Mayflower Hotel, Washington, D.C., June 23.

Morse, R.S. 1967. *The Automobile and Air Pollution.* Washington, D.C.: U.S. Department of Commerce.

Moss, Robert. 1977. "Let's Look Out for No. 1!" *New York Times Magazine,* May, pp. 31 *ff.*

Mossberg, Walter S. 1977. "Postal Service Is Losing Out on R & D." *Wall Street Journal,* May 10.

Myers, Sumner, and Eldon E. Sweezy. 1978. "Why Innovations Fail." *Technology Review,* March–April, pp. 40–46.

Nader, Ralph. 1971. "A Citizen's Guide to the American Economy." *New York Review of Books,* September, pp. 14 *ff.*

———, and Mark Green. 1977. "Don't Pay Those High Legal Bills." *New York Times Magazine,* November 20, pp. 53 *ff.*

———, Mark Green, and Joel Seligman. 1976. *Taming the Giant Corporation.* New York: Norton.

Nathanson, Robert B. 1977. "The Disabled Employee: Separating Myth from Fact." *Harvard Business Review,* May–June, pp. 6–8.

National Advertising Review Board. 1974. *Product Advertising and Consumer Safety.* New York: National Advertising Review Board.

National Business Council for Consumer Affairs. 1972a. *Corporate Policies and Procedures on Advertising and Promotion.* Washington, D.C.: U.S. Government Printing Office.

———. 1972b. *Guiding Principles for Responsible Packaging and Labeling.* Washington, D.C.: U.S. Government Printing Office.

National Commission on Technology, Automation and Economic Progress. 1966. *Technology and the American Economy.* Washington, D.C.: U.S. Government Printing Office.

National Privacy Protection Study Commission. 1978. *Personal Privacy in an Information Society.* Washington, D.C.: U.S. Government Printing Office.

National Science Board. 1977. *Science Indicators.* Washington, D.C.: U.S. Government Printing Office.

National Science Foundation. 1975. *The Consequences of Electronic Fund Transfer,* NSF/RA/X-75-015. Washington, D.C.: U.S. Government Printing Office.

———. 1977. *Assessment of Future National and International Problem Areas,* vol 1. Washington, D.C.: U.S. Government Printing Office.

Newman, Robert A. 1974. "Internal Decision Making." In *Selected Proceedings, Workshops on Implementing Social Responsibility.* Sponsored by the Public Affairs Council. Washington, D.C., June 12–13.

New York State Consumer Protection Board. 1978. *Consumer Protection in New York State.* Albany, N.Y.

Nietzsche, Friedrich. 1967. *The Will to Power.* Edited by Walter Kaufmann. New York: Vintage Books.

Nisbet, Robert A. 1973. Interview in *Psychology Today,* December, pp. 43–64.

Noll, Roger G., Merton J. Peck, and John J. McGowan. 1973. *Economic Aspects of Television Regulation.* Washington, D.C.: Brookings.

Nordhaus, William, and James Tobin. 1972. "Is Growth Obsolete?" *Fiftieth Anniversary Colloquium V,* National Bureau of Economic Research. New York: Columbia University Press.

North, Harper Q., and Donald L. Pyke. 1969. "Probes of the Technological Future." *Harvard Business Review.* May–June.

Novick, David. 1973. "Cost-Benefit Analysis and Social Responsibility." *Business Horizons,* February.

Nozick, Robert. 1974. *Anarchy, State, and Utopia.* New York: Basic Books.

Oi, Walter. 1977. "Safety at Any Price?" *Regulation,* December, pp. 16–23.

Okun, Arthur M. 1975. *Equality and Efficiency.* Washington, D.C.: Brookings.

Olson, Mancur, Jr. 1971. *The Logic of Collective Action.* Cambridge, Mass.: Harvard University Press.

Oreffice, Paul F. 1978. "Let's Stop Dumping U.S. Jobs." Speech to Common-Wealth Club of California, January 27.

Organization for Economic Co-operation and Development. 1972. *The Industrial Policy of Japan.* Paris: OECD.

Orren, Karen. 1974. *Corporate Power and Social Change.* Baltimore: Johns Hopkins.

O'Toole, James. 1979. Draft of a paper prepared for the Conference on Working in the 21st Century. Richmond, Virginia, April 6.

Owen, Bruce M., and Ronald Braeutigam. 1978. *The Regulation Game: Strategic Use of the Administration Process.* Cambridge, Mass.: Ballinger.

Owen, Henry, and Charles L. Schultze. 1976. *Setting National Priorities.* Washington, D.C.: Brookings.

Packard, Vance. 1957. *The Hidden Persuaders.* New York: McKay.

———. 1960. *The Waste Makers.* New York: McKay.

———. 1977. *The People Shapers.* Boston: Little, Brown.

Paluszek, John L. 1973. "How Three Companies Organize for Social Responsibility." *Business and Society Review/Innovation,* Summer, pp. 16–20.

Parker, Richard. 1975. "Fact and Fancy About America's Classless Society." In R.L. Heilbroner and P. London, *Corporate Social Policy*. Reading, Mass.: Addison-Wesley.

Parsons, Talcott. 1951. *The Social System*. Glencoe, Ill.: Free Press.

Peacock, Leslie G. 1978. "International Financial Issues—The View of a Banker." *National Journal*. Reprinted in *Congressional Record*, August 2, pp. E4286–89.

Peltzman, Sam. 1973. "An Evaluation of Consumer Protection Legislation." *Journal of Political Economy* 81, no. 5 (September–October):1049–91.

Perry, George. 1976. "Stabilization Policy and Inflation." In Henry Owen and Charles L. Schultze, *Setting National Priorities: The Next Ten Years*. Washington, D.C.: Brookings.

Persons, Robert H., Jr., Sue N. Atkinson, and Robert L. Rouse. 1978. *Economics for the Citizen*. North Scituate, Mass.: Duxbury Press.

Pertschuk, Michael. 1976. "The Lawyer-Lobbyist." In Ralph Nader and Mark Green, *Verdicts on Lawyers*. New York: Crowell.

Platt, Robert B. 1974. "Input-Output Forecasting." In William Butler et al. *Methods and Techniques of Business Forecasting*. Englewood Cliffs, N.J.: Prentice-Hall.

Polsby, Nelson W. 1963. *Community Power and Political Theory*. New Haven, Conn.: Yale University Press.

Popper, Karl. 1966. *The Open Society and Its Enemies*. Princeton, N.J.: Princeton University Press.

Press, Frank. 1978. Speech before annual meeting of the American Association for the Advancement of Science. Washington, D.C., February.

Preston, Lee E., and James E. Post. 1975. *Private Management and Public Policy*. Englewood Cliffs, N.J.: Prentice-Hall.

Prigogine, Ilya. 1977. *Self-Organization in Non-Equilibrium Systems*. New York: Wiley.

Privacy Protection Study Commission. 1977. *Personal Privacy in an Information Society*. Washington, D.C.: U.S. Government Printing Office.

Proxmire, William. 1978. "The Foreign Payoff Law Is a Necessity." *New York Times*, February 5.

Public Affairs Council, 1973. *The Third House: An Informal Survey of Corporate Lobbying at the State Level*. Washington, D.C.: Public Affairs Council.

————. 1974. *Checklist for the Washington Office*. Washington, D.C.: Public Affairs Council.

Pugh, George Edgin. 1977. *The Biological Origin of Human Values*. New York: Basic Books.

Purcell, Theodore V. 1971. "The Case of the Borderline Black." *Harvard Business Review*, November–December.

————. 1974. "How GE Measures Managers in Fair Employment." *Harvard Business Review*, November–December, pp. 99–104.

Quinn, James Brian. 1969. "Technology Transfer by Multinational Companies." *Harvard Business Review*, November–December, pp. 147–61.

————. 1977. "Strategic Goals." *Sloan Management Review*, Fall, pp. 22–37.

Quirt, John. 1978. "Why the Future No Longer Looks So Golden in California." *Fortune*, March, pp. 13 *ff*.

Raiffa, Howard. 1968. *Decision Analysis*. Reading, Mass.: Addison-Wesley.

Rankin, Deborah. 1978. "Cash Flow as a Guide to Growth." *New York Times*, May 23.

Ratner, Joseph. 1954. *The Philosophy of Spinoza.* New York: Modern Library.

Redford, Emmette S. 1965. *American Government and the Economy.* New York: Macmillan.

———. 1968. *Democracy and the Administrative State.* New York: Oxford University Press.

Reinhold, Robert. 1977. "New Population Trends Transforming U.S." *New York Times,* February 6.

Reischauer, Edwin O. 1977. *The Japanese.* Cambridge, Mass.: Harvard University Press.

Reisman, David, Nathan Glazer, and Revel Denny. 1961. *The Lonely Crowd.* New Haven, Conn.: Yale University Press.

Revel, Jean-François. 1977. *The Totalitarian Temptation.* Translated by David Hapgood. Garden City, N.Y.: Doubleday.

Reynolds, Alan. 1977. "Questions about Corporate Profits." *Chicago World Report.* Reprinted in *Congressional Record,* October 27, pp. S17949–50.

Ricklefs, Roger. 1978. "For the Businessman Headed Abroad, Some Basic Training." *Wall Street Journal,* January 16.

Ricks, David A., Marilyn Y.C. Fu, and Jeffrey S. Arpan. 1974. *International Business Blunders.* Columbus, Ohio: Grid.

Rienow, Robert, and Leona T. Rienow. 1969. *Moment in the Sun.* New York: Ballantine Books.

Roberts, Edward B. 1977. "Generating Effective Corporate Innovation." *Technology Review,* October–November, pp. 25–33.

———, and Alan L. Frohman. 1978. "Strategies for Improving Research Utilization." *Technology Review,* March–April, pp. 32–39.

Roberts, Paul Craig. 1978. "The Breakdown of the Keynesian Model." *Public Interest,* no. 52 (Summer):20–33.

Roberts, Steven V. 1978. "The Employee as Volunteer." *New York Times,* November 19.

Robinson, Dwight E. 1975. "Style Changes: Cyclical, Inexorable, and Foreseeable." *Harvard Business Review,* November–December, pp. 121–31.

Robinson, Joan. 1970. *Freedom and Necessity.* New York: Pantheon.

Robinson, Marshall A., Herbert C. Morton, and James D. Calderwood. 1967. *An Introduction to Economic Reasoning.* Garden City, N.Y.: Anchor Books.

Robinson, Romney. 1974. "International Trade." *Encyclopedia Britannica, Macropaedia,* vol. 18.

Robock, Stefan H., Kenneth Simmonds, and Jack Zwick. 1977. *International Business and Multinational Enterprises.* Homewood, Ill.: Irwin.

Rogers, Michael. 1977. "The Selling of the Counterculture." *Rolling Stone,* May 19.

Rogge, Benjamin A. 1976. *The Wisdom of Adam Smith.* Indianapolis, Ind.: Liberty Press.

Roosa, R.V. 1976. "Economic Planning: A Middle Way." *New York Times,* February 8.

Rose, Stanford. 1978. "The Secret of Japan's Export Prowess." *Fortune,* January, pp. 56 *ff.*

Rosten, Leo. 1977. "New Multinational Corporations." *Saturday Review,* January.

Rostow, W.W. 1978. Interview in *New York Times,* May 21.

Rowan, Roy. 1977. "A Peaceful Asia Beckons Investors." *Fortune,* October, pp. 188 *ff.*

Ruder, William, and Raymond Nathan. 1975. *The Businessman's Guide to Washington.* New York: Macmillan.

Rumelt, Richard P. 1974. *Strategy, Structure, and Economic Performance in Large Industrial Corporations.* Boston, Mass.: Harvard Business School, Division of Research.

Rummel, R.J., and David Heeman. 1978. "How Multinationals Analyze Political Risk." *Harvard Business Review,* January–February, pp. 67–76.

Russell, Bertrand. 1945. *A History of Western Philosophy.* New York: Simon and Schuster.

Rust, Edward B. 1973. "What Nader Really Wants." Address to Public Service Award luncheon. Palmer House, Chicago, Illinois, September 18.

Ryan, John. 1978. "Regulation and Fees Boost Legal Expenses." *Wall Street Journal,* April 13.

Sabatier, Paul A. 1977. "Regulatory Policy-Making." *Natural Resources Journal* (July):415–60.

Safire, W. 1977. *Full Disclosure.* New York: Doubleday.

Salamon, Lester M., and John J. Segfried. 1977. "Economic Power and Political Influence." *American Political Science Review* 71, no. 3 (September):1026–43.

Salveson, Melvin E. 1959. "Planning Business Progress." *Management Science* 5, no. 3 (April):217–37.

Sampson, Anthony. 1973. *Sovereign State of ITT.* New York: Stein & Day.

Samuelson, Paul A. 1976. *Economics.* New York: McGraw-Hill.

Sanford, David. 1976. *Me and Ralph.* Washington, D.C.: New Republic.

Schein, Edgar H. 1977. "Increasing Organizational Effectiveness Through Better Human Resources Planning and Development." *Sloan Management Review,* Fall, pp. 1–20.

Schelling, Thomas C. 1974. "Command and Control." In James W. McKie, *Social Responsibility and the Business Predicament.* Washington, D.C.: Brookings.

Schenfield, John H. 1978. "Antitrust Policy—Populist Philosophy or Economic Necessity?" Speech before Los Angeles County Bar Association. Los Angeles, California, January 30.

Schlesinger, Arthur, Jr. 1945. *The Age of Jackson.* Boston: Little, Brown.

———. 1959. *The Age of Roosevelt.* New Haven, Conn.: Yale University Press.

Schnapper, M.B. 1972. *American Labor.* Washington, D.C.: Public Affairs Press.

Schon, Donald A. 1971. *Beyond the Stable State.* New York: Random House.

Schrank, Robert. 1978a. *Ten Thousand Working Days.* Cambridge, Mass.: MIT Press.

———. 1978b. "How to Relieve Worker Boredom." *Psychology Today,* July, pp. 79–80.

Schumpter, Joseph. 1942. *Capitalism, Socialism, and Democracy.* New York: Harper and Brothers.

Schurmann, Franz. 1974. *The Logic of World Order.* New York: Pantheon.

Schurr, Sam H. 1979. *Energy in America's Future.* Baltimore, Md.: Johns Hopkins University Press.

Schwartz, Anna J. 1973. "Secular Price Change in Historical Perspective." *Journal of Money, Credit & Banking,* February 5.

Schweitzer, Glenn E. 1977. "Regulation, Technological Progress, and Societal Interests." *Research Management* 20, no. 2 (March):13–17.

Scobel, Donald N. 1975. "Doing Away with Factory Blues." *Harvard Business Review,* November–December, pp. 132–42.

Scott, Bruce R. 1973. "The Industrial State: Old Myths and New Realities." *Harvard Business Review,* March–April, pp. 133 *ff.*

Seidman, Harold. 1970. *Politics, Position, and Power.* New York: Oxford University Press.

Sennett, Richard. 1979. "The Boss's New Clothes." *New York Review of Books,* February 22, pp. 42–46.

Sethi, S. Prakash. 1977. *Advocacy Advertising and Large Corporations.* Lexington, Mass.: Lexington Books.

Shapiro, Irving S. 1978. "Today's Executive: Private Steward and Public Servant." *Harvard Business Review,* March–April, pp. 94–101.

Shapley, Willis H. 1976. *Research and Development in the Federal Budget: FY 1977.* Washington, D.C.: American Association for the Advancement of Science.

———. 1978. *Research and Development in the Federal Budget: FY 1979.* Washington, D.C.: American Association for the Advancement of Science.

Shaw, Gaylord. 1973. "Government as Promoter, Sustainer, and Subsidizer of 'Private Enterprise.'" In Robert H. Haveman and Robert D. Hamrin, *The Political Economy of Federal Policy.* New York: Harper & Row.

Shepard, William G. 1971. "The Competitive Margin in Communications." In William M. Capron, *Technological Change in Regulated Industries.* Washington, D.C.: Brookings.

Sheppard, Harold L., and Neal Q. Herrick. 1972. *Where Have All the Robots Gone?* New York: Free Press.

Shiskin, Julius. 1976. "Employment and Unemployment: The Doughnut or the Hole?" In Department of Labor, *Monthly Labor Review* 99, no. 2 (February):3–10.

Shocker, Allan D., and S. Prakash Sethi. 1973. "An Approach to Incorporating Societal Preferences in Developing Corporate Action Strategies." *California Management Review* 15, no. 5 (Summer):74–105.

Shonfield, Andrew. 1965. *Modern Capitalism.* London: Oxford.

Shoup, Carl S. 1974. "Taxation of Multinational Corporations." In *The Impact of Multinational Corporations on Development and on International Relations.* New York: Department of Economic and Social Affairs, United Nations.

Shulman, James S., and Jeffrey Gale. 1972. "Laying the Groundwork for Social Auditing." *Financial Executive* 40, no. 3 (March):38–42.

Shultz, George P., and Kenneth Dam. 1977. *Economic Policy Beyond the Headlines.* New York: Norton.

Silk, Leonard S. 1963. *Forecasting Business Trends.* New York: McGraw-Hill.

———. 1975. "Economics for the Perplexed." *New York Times Magazine,* March 2, pp. 8*ff.*

———, and David Vogel. 1976a. *Ethics and Profits.* New York: Simon and Schuster.

———. 1976b. *The Economists.* New York: Basic Books.

———. 1978. "How Carter Can Stop Inflation." *New York Times Magazine,* June 18, pp. 12 *ff.*

Simon, William E. 1978. *A Time for Truth.* New York: McGraw-Hill.

Sinai, Allen, and Terry Glomski. 1978. "The Carter Tax Proposal: Impact on Business Spending." *Data Resources Review* 7 (January):1.11–1.16.

Sinclair, Upton. 1906. *The Jungle.* New York: New American Library.

Skinner, Richard W., and William L. Shanklin. 1978. "The Changing Role of Public Relations in Business Firms." *Public Relations Review,* Summer, pp. 40–45.

Slichter, Sumner H. 1961. "The American System of Industrial Relations." In John T. Dunlop, *Potentials of the American Economy: Selected Essays of Sumner H. Slichter.* Cambridge, Mass.: Harvard University Press.

Smelser, Neil J. 1963. *Theory of Collective Behavior.* New York: Free Press.

Smith, Bruce R. 1978. "How Practical Is National Economic Planning?" *Harvard Business Review,* March–April, pp. 131 *ff.*

Smith, E. Paul. 1978. "Measuring Professional Obsolescence." *Academy of Management Review,* October, pp. 914–17.

Smith, Hedrick. 1976. *The Russians.* New York: Ballantine Books.

Smith, Lee. 1978. "The Boardroom Is Becoming a Different Scene." *Fortune,* May, pp. 150 *ff.*

Smith, Paula. 1977. "More Clout for Corporate Economists." *Dun's Review,* January, pp. 61–64.

Smith, Robert S. 1976. *The Occupational Safety and Health Act.* Washington, D.C.: American Enterprise Institute.

Sobek, Robert S. 1973. "A Manager's Primer on Forecasting." *Harvard Business Review,* May–June, pp. 6 *ff.*

Solzhenitsyn, Alexander. 1976a. "As Breathing and Consciousness Return." In *From under the Rubble.* London: Fontana.

———. 1976b. Speech in accepting the American Friendship Award of the Freedoms Foundation at the Hoover Institution, Stanford, California. Reprinted in part in *Wall Street Journal,* June 15.

———. 1978. "A World Split Apart." Commencement address delivered at Harvard University, June 8.

Stanford Oil Company of California. 1975. *Safety Training Manual.* Personnel Department, Safety Division. San Francisco, Calif.

Starling, Grover. 1977. *Managing the Public Sector.* Homewood, Ill.: Dorsey Press.

———. 1979. *Politics and Economics of Public Policy.* Homewood, Ill.: Dorsey Press.

Stassinopoulos, Ariana. 1978. *After Reason.* New York: Stein & Day.

Stein, Herbert. 1978. "Is Government Our Partner?" *Wall Street Journal,* January 30.

Steiner, George A. 1969. *Top Management Planning.* New York: Macmillan.

———. 1972. "Should Business Adopt the Social Audit?" *The Conference Board Review,* May, pp. 7–10.

Stigler, George J. 1966. *The Theory of Price.* New York: Macmillan.

———. 1975. *The Citizen and the State: Essays on Regulation.* Chicago: University of Chicago Press.

Stobaugh, Robert B. 1975. "U.S. Taxation of United States Manufacturing Abroad." Statement before U.S. House of Representatives, Committee on Ways and Means, July 24.

———. 1977. "Competition Encountered by U.S. Companies that Manufacture Abroad." *Journal of International Business,* Spring–Summer.

———. 1979. "After the Peak." In Robert B. Stobaugh and Daniel Yergin, *Energy Future.* New York: Random House.

———, and Daniel Yergin. 1979. *Energy Future.* Cambridge, Mass.: Harvard University Press.

Stone, Christopher D. 1975. *Where the Law Ends.* New York: Harper & Row.

Stoppard, Tom. 1972. *Jumpers.* New York: Grove Press.

Taylor, Bernard. 1976. "New Dimension in Corporate Planning." *Long Range Planning,* December, pp. 80–106.

Thomas, Dan R.E. 1978. "Strategy Is Different in Service Businesses." *Harvard Business Review,* July–August, pp. 158–65.

Thomas, Lewis. 1974. *Lives of a Cell.* New York: Viking.

Thompson, Paul H., and Gene W. Dalton. 1976. "Are R & D Organizations Obsolete?" *Harvard Business Review,* November–December, pp. 105–16.

Thucydides. 1900. *History of Peloponnesian Wars.* Translated by Benjamin Jowett. London: Oxford.

Thurston, Philip H. 1971. "Make TF Serve Corporate Planning." *Harvard Business Review,* September–October, pp. 98 *ff.*

Toan, Arthur B. 1972. "Social Information and Social Measurement." Paper presented to the Committee on Social Measurement, American Institute of Certified Public Accountants. Denver, Colorado, September.

Tocqueville, Alexis de. 1956. *Democracy in America.* Edited and abridged by Richard D. Heffner. New York: Mentor Books.

Tolchin, Martin. 1977. "Lobbying in the 'Public Interest' Is More Effective." *New York Times,* November 20.

Tucker, William. 1977. "Environmentalism and the Leisure Class." *Harper's,* December, pp. 49–80.

Tumlir, Jan, and Richard Blockhurst. 1977. *Adjustment, Trade, and Growth in Developed and Developing Countries.* New York: Unipub.

Turner, Louis. 1973. *Multinational Companies and the Third World.* New York: Hill and Wang.

———. 1978. *Oil Companies in the International System.* London: Royal Institute of International Affairs.

Uhal, Bro. 1977. "IBM Reaches for a Golden Future in the Heavens." *Fortune,* June, pp. 173 *ff.*

U.S. Agency for International Development. 1978. *AID's Challenge in an Interdependent World.* DN-RIA-199. Washington, D.C.: U.S. Government Printing Office.

U.S. Congress, House Committee on Banking and Currency. 1969. *Commercial Banks and Their Trust Activities.* Washington, D.C.: U.S. Government Printing Office.

U.S. Congress, House Committee on Interstate and Foreign Commerce. 1976. *Federal Regulation and Regulatory Reform.* Washington, D.C.: U.S. Government Printing Office.

U.S. Congress, Joint Economic Committee. 1975. *Notes from the JEC* 1, no. 19, July 1. Washington, D.C.: U.S. Government Printing Office.

———. 1977. *Survey of Business Leaders' Opinions on National Economic Planning.* Washington, D.C.: U.S. Government Printing Office.

———. 1978. *Special Study on Economic Change.* Washington, D.C.: U.S. Government Printing Office.

U.S. Congress, Senate Committee on Government Affairs. 1977. *Study of Federal Regulation,* vol. III. Washington, D.C.: U.S. Government Printing Office.

U.S. Congress, Senate Committee on Government Operations. 1974. *Disclosure of Corporate Ownership.* Washington, D.C.: U.S. Government Printing Office.

U.S. Congress, Senate Committee on Labor and Public Welfare. 1974. *Regulation of New Drug R & D by FDA.* Washington, D.C.: U.S. Government Printing Office.

U.S. Congress, Technology Assessment Board. 1976. *Technology Assessment Activities in the Industrial, Academic, and Governmental Communities.* Washington, D.C.: U.S. Government Printing Office.

U.S. Council on Environmental Quality. 1975. *Environmental Quality.* Washington, D.C.: U.S. Government Printing Office.

U.S. Council on International Economic Policy. 1977. *International Economic Report of the President.* Washington, D.C.: U.S. Government Printing Office.

U.S. Department of Commerce. 1972a. *Japan: The Government-Business Relationship.* Washington, D.C.: U.S. Government Printing Office.

———. 1972b. *The Multinational Corporation: Studies on U.S. Foreign Investment,* vol. 1. Washington, D.C.: U.S. Government Printing Office.

———. 1976a. *Handbook of Cyclical Indicators.* Washington, D.C.: U.S. Government Printing Office.

———. 1976b. *Energy Management Guide,* NBS Handbook 120. Washington, D.C.: U.S. Government Printing Office.

———. 1977. *Social Indicators 1976.* Washington, D.C.: U.S. Government Printing Office.

U.S. Department of Treasury. 1973. *Statistics of Income: Individual Income Tax Returns.* Washington, D.C.: U.S. Government Printing Office.

———. 1977. *Blueprints for Basic Tax Reform.* Washington, D.C.: U.S. Government Printing Office.

U.S. Equal Employment Opportunity Commission. 1974. *Affirmative Action and Equal Employment: A Guidebook for Employers.* Washington, D.C.: U.S. Government Printing Office.

U.S. Federal Trade Commission. 1977. *Your FTC: What It Is and What It Does.* Washington, D.C.: U.S. Government Printing Office.

U.S. General Accounting Office. 1976. *Status and Obstacles to Commercialization of Coal Liquefaction and Gasification,* RED-76-81. Washington, D.C.: U.S. Government Printing Office.

———. 1977a. *An Organized Approach to Improving Federal Procurement and Acquisition Practices,* PASD-77-128. Washington, D.C.: U.S. Government Printing Office.

———. 1977b. *Government Regulatory Activity,* PAD-77-34. Washington, D.C.: U.S. Government Printing Office.

U.S. News & World Report. 1976. *1976 Study of American Opinion: Summary Report.*

U.S. Office of Management and Budget. 1977a. *Budget in Brief—FY 1978.* Washington, D.C.: U.S. Government Printing Office.

———. 1977b. *Issues '78: Perspectives on Fiscal Year 1978 Budget.* Washington, D.C.: U.S. Government Printing Office.

U.S. President. 1965. Public Papers of the Presidents of the United States. Washington, D.C.: Office of the *Federal Register.*

Utterback, James M. 1976. "The Dynamics of Technological Innovation." In *Proceedings of a Symposium on Technological Innovation.* Washington, D.C.: U.S. Government Printing Office.

Uyterhoven, Hugo E.R., Robert W. Ackerman, and John W. Rosenblum. 1977. *Strategy and Organization.* Homewood, Ill.: Irwin.

Vanston, John H. 1975. "Technology Forecasting: A Management Overview." Paper presented to the World Future Society Conference. Washington, D.C., June.

Vernon, Raymond. 1974. "Foreign Operations." In James W. McKie, *Social Responsi-*

bility and the Business Predicament, Washington, D.C.: Brookings.

———. 1977. *Storm Over the Multinationals.* Cambridge, Mass.: Harvard University Press.

Voegelin, Eric. 1975. *From Enlightenment to Revolution.* Durham, N.C.: Duke University Press.

Wallich, Henry C. 1978. "Stabilization Goals: Balancing Inflation and Unemployment." *American Economic Review,* May, pp. 159–69.

Walzer, Michael. 1978. "Teaching Morality." *New Republic.* July 10, pp. 10–12.

Warner, Rawleigh, Jr. 1974. "Energy Resources—And the Public." Speech at the 42nd annual convention of the Edison Electric Institute. New York, June 3.

Wattenburg, Ben J. 1976. *In Search of the Real America.* New York: Doubleday.

Waverman, Leonard. 1975. "The Regulation of Intercity Telecommunications." In A. Philip, *Promoting Competition in Regulated Markets.* Washington, D.C.: Brookings.

Ways, Max. 1976. "The American Kind of Worker Participation." *Fortune,* October, pp. 168 *ff.*

Weaver, Paul H. 1978. "Regulation, Social Policy, and Class Conflict." *Public Interest* no. 50 (Winter):45–63.

Webber, James B., and Rebecca A. Ojala. 1976. "Introducing Futures to the Business World." *World Future Society Bulletin,* September–October.

Weidenbaum, Murray L. 1975. *Government-Mandated Price Increases.* Washington, D.C.: American Enterprise Institute.

———. 1977. *Business, Government, and the Public.* Englewood Cliffs, N.J.: Prentice-Hall.

———, and Reno Harnish. 1969. *Government Credit Subsidies for Energy Development.* Washington, D.C.: American Enterprise Institute.

Weisskopf, Thomas E. 1972. "Capitalism and Inequality." In Richard Edwards et al., *The Capitalist System.* Englewood Cliffs, N.J.: Prentice-Hall.

———. 1978. "Sources of Cyclical Downturns and Inflation." In Richard Edwards et al., *The Capitalist System.* Englewood Cliffs, N.J.: Prentice-Hall.

Wessel, Milton R. 1976. *The Rule of Reason.* Reading, Mass.: Addison-Wesley.

Weston, J. Fred. 1972. "Implications of Recent Research for the Structural Approach to Oligopoly." *Antitrust Law Journal* 41.

Wheelwright, Steven C., and Darral G. Clarke. 1976. "Corporate Forecasting." *Harvard Business Review,* November–December, pp. 40 *ff.*

White, George R., and Margaret B.W. Graham. 1978. "How to Spot a Technological Winner." *Harvard Business Review,* March–April, pp. 146–52.

Whiteside, Thomas. 1976. "Onward and Upward with the Arts." *New Yorker,* November 1, pp. 51 *ff.*

Wilcox, Clair, et al. 1976. *Economies of the World Today.* New York: Harcourt Brace Jovanovich.

———, and William G. Shepherd. 1975. *Public Policies Toward Business.* Homewood, Ill.: Irwin.

Wilkins, Mira. 1974. *The Maturing of the Multinational Enterprise.* Cambridge, Mass.: Harvard University Press.

Will, George F. 1978. "Deregulation 'Impudence.'" Reprinted in *Congressional Record,* October 6, pp. E5457–58.

Wilson, Edward O. 1978. *On Human Nature.* Cambridge, Mass.: Harvard University Press.

Wilson, Ian H. 1974. "Socio-Political Forecasting: A New Dimension to Strategic Planning." *Michigan Business Review,* July.

Wilson, James Q., and Patricia Rachal. 1977. "Can Government Regulate Itself?" *Public Interest* no. 46 (Winter):3–14.

Winter, Ralph E. 1978. "Firms Spend Millions to Cut Use of Energy." *Wall Street Journal,* February 9.

Wolf, Charles, Jr. 1979. "A Theory of Non-Market Failures." *Public Interest,* no. 55 (Spring):114–33.

Wolfe, Tom. 1976. *Mauve Gloves & Madmen, Clutter & Vine.* New York: Farrar, Straus and Giroux.

Work in America: Report of a Special Task Force to the Secretary of Health, Education and Welfare. 1973. Cambridge, Mass.: MIT Press.

World Bank. 1976. *World Tables, 1976.* Baltimore: Johns Hopkins University Press.

Wren, Christopher S. 1978. "Russia in Entropy." *Harper's,* June, pp. 31–38.

Yankelovich, D. 1974. *The New Morality: A Profile of American Youth in the Seventies.* New York: McGraw-Hill.

Zalesnik, Abraham, and M.F.R. Kets de Vries. 1975. *Power and the Corporate Mind.* Boston: Houghton Mifflin.

Zentner, René. 1976. "The Shell Oil Company—Planning with Multiple Scenarios." *World Future Society Bulletin,* September–October.

INDEX